The Federal I
of Base Ball (

ALSO BY ROBERT PEYTON WIGGINS
AND FROM McFARLAND

*The Deacon and the Schoolmaster: Phillippe and Leever,
Pittsburgh's Great Turn-of-the-Century Pitchers* (2011)

*Jungle Combat with the 112th Cavalry:
Three Texans in the Pacific in World War II* (2011)

Chief Bender: A Baseball Biography (2010)

The Federal League of Base Ball Clubs

The History of an Outlaw Major League, 1914–1915

ROBERT PEYTON WIGGINS

McFarland & Company, Inc., Publishers
Jefferson, North Carolina, and London

The present work is a reprint of the illustrated case bound edition of The Federal League of Base Ball Clubs: The History of an Outlaw Major League, 1914–1915, *first published in 2009 by McFarland.*

LIBRARY OF CONGRESS CATALOGUING-IN-PUBLICATION DATA

Wiggins, Robert Peyton.
The Federal League of Base Ball Clubs : the history of an outlaw major league, 1914–1915 / Robert Peyton Wiggins.
  p.   cm.

Includes bibliographical references and index.

ISBN 978-0-7864-6939-0
softcover : 50# alkaline paper ∞

1. Federal League of Base Ball Clubs — History.
2. Baseball — United States — History.
3. Baseball players — United States — Statistics.
I. Title.
GV875.F43W54   2012
796.357′640973 — dc22   2008037037

British Library cataloguing data are available

© 2009 Robert Peyton Wiggins. All rights reserved

No part of this book may be reproduced or transmitted in any form or by any means, electronic or mechanical, including photocopying or recording, or by any information storage and retrieval system, without permission in writing from the publisher.

On the cover: Brooklyn manager Lee Magee and Buffalo manager Larry Schlafly, 1915 (George Grantham Bain Collection, Library of Congress)

Manufactured in the United States of America

McFarland & Company, Inc., Publishers
Box 611, Jefferson, North Carolina 28640
www.mcfarlandpub.com

Table of Contents

Preface 1
Introduction 3

1. Federal League Beginnings	9
2. A Challenge to Organized Baseball	21
3. Lucky Charley	28
4. "A Fifty Per Cent Raise Looked Too Good to Turn Down"	35
5. The Baseball Players' Fraternity	45
6. The Federal League Survives a Crisis	51
7. Ad Brennan and Tom Seaton	58
8. The World Tourists	62
9. Opening Day	66
10. "The Nerviest Proposition I Ever Saw"	72
11. Three Finger Brown	78
12. Weeghman's "Edifice of Beauty"	84
13. The Emery Ball Specialist	93
14. The Terrapins Set the Pace	99
15. Rowdyism and Umpire Woes	105
16. Washington Park	110
17. Pittsburgh's Rebels	117
18. "I Will Pitch for the One That Gives Me the Most Money!"	123
19. Prince Hal	128
20. Ty Cobb of the Feds	135
21. Tinker's Invalids	142
22. Fielder Jones	147
23. The Stretch Run	152
24. A Gloomy State of Affairs	160

Table of Contents

25. The Big Train Almost Becomes the Federal Express	168
26. The Federal League vs. Organized Baseball	173
27. Jumpers and Flip-Floppers	178
28. "An Embarrassing Situation"	186
29. Opening Day 2	193
30. Benny Kauff Goes Astray	201
31. Rebels Resurgent	207
32. The Top Whale Goes Down	214
33. Buffalo's Got the Blues	218
34. "This Season You Are Playing for Me"	222
35. The Colonial League	228
36. Lee Magee Style	232
37. "My Resignation Was Wired to Mr. Ball This Afternoon"	240
38. "The Belgium of Baseball"	245
39. The Deacon Takes the Pulpit	249
40. The Tribune's Amateurs	256
41. Davenport and Plank	264
42. The Pivotal Series	269
43. The Big Bluff	276
44. Peace!	284
45. The Big Auction	291
46. The Aftershock	298
47. The Browns/Terriers	305
48. The Cubs/Whales	311
49. The Outcasts	318
50. The Benny Kauff Story	322
51. Back into Good Society	329

Epilogue 336
Chapter Notes 341
Bibliography 353
Index 355

Preface

Any fan of the deadball era knows of the Federal League. My interest in baseball's most well-known outlaw league began years ago when Marc Okkonen's illustrated work *The Federal League of 1914–1915* (1989) piqued my interest. There was little information on the defunct league among recent sources, an occasional chapter or a few pages in a handful of books. As I surveyed available newspaper files from that era on microfilm at my local library an interesting story began to take shape. And as research continued, I became convinced that the Federal League was important not only as one of a small handful of serious rivals to the National and American Leagues — but as an organization that brought both immediate and long-term changes to Organized Baseball.

Electronic resources such as SABR's BioProject, the LA84 Foundation Web site, and databases including Paper of Record, Newspaper Archives and ProQuest provided access to valuable information that further contributed to the narrative. Recent books such as Martin Kohout's *Hal Chase*, Stuart Shea's *Wrigley Field* and Susan Dellinger's biography of Edd Roush provided significant insight into the Federal League and the Deadball Era.

I chose not to editorialize on the merits or failures of the Federal League and have left it to readers to make their own judgment as to the legitimacy and legacy of that outlaw league and the handful of wealthy men who acted on a dream to become baseball magnates.

I would like to thank the staff of the National Baseball Library in Cooperstown for their assistance in the final stages of my research. I also would like to thank numerous employees from a number of libraries and historical societies that I visited or contacted. Finally, I want to thank my wife for helping me with my limited computer skills and her indulgence during my travels to research this volume.

Introduction

The Federal League of Base Ball Clubs is remembered, if remembered at all, as the outlaw circuit that made a short-lived attempt in 1914 to form a third major league. Accounts of the league usually include observations that the Federals signed minor leaguers and washed-up major leaguers for players; the newcomers produced only one notable player of their own in Hall of Famer Edd Roush; the Chicago owner built a ballpark that would become known as Wrigley Field; and the 1922 U.S. Supreme Court ruling that gave baseball its antitrust exemption came from the famous case *Federal Baseball Club of Baltimore vs. National League of Professional Baseball Clubs.* However, the outlaw league was far more relevant than that.

The impact of the Federal League on major league baseball was significant. The Federal League affected the stability of Organized Baseball both during its time and for years afterward. In 1914 and 1915 professional baseball salaries skyrocketed due to competition with the Federals for major league caliber players. Lower minor leagues folded by the dozen, partly due to the Federal League's presence, and even several upper-level minor league clubs had to relocate or seek financial support from the traditional major leagues. Organized Baseball's settlement with the "outlaws" was hardly a total capitulation by the Feds as it is often portrayed. The financial obligations owed to the Federals by major league baseball hung over the operations of some of the poorer clubs for years.

The war between Organized Baseball and the Federal League accentuated the inequity of the owner/player relationship in professional baseball. The temporary bargaining option the Federal League offered to the players gave them a taste of freedom from the indentured servitude which the oppressive reserve rule perpetuated. And the Federal League's opposition to the National Agreement gave the fledging players' union the leverage it needed to achieve some concessions from owners on playing conditions and player contracts. For the first time players discovered what could be achieved in salaries through the threat of free agency. Once the Federal League folded, salaries and players' rights were rolled back to pre–1914 standards and the Players' Fraternity (union) was crushed after an abortive call for a strike in late 1916. The seeds of the baseball scandals at the end of the decade may have been sown in the rollback of players' rights and salaries following Organized Baseball's settlement with the Federals.

When the Federal League came on the scene in 1913, baseball was *the* American spectator sport. At that time, there was no National Football League, no National Basketball Association, and collegiate football was usually only of local or regional interest. While major league clubs supplemented their incomes by playing numerous exhibition games on off days during the season, the players organized barnstorming teams and played all across the nation during the off season. Thus hundreds of thousands of devout baseball fans had never seen an official major league baseball game.

In the days before radio and television, the main, and often the only, sources for major league baseball results were the nation's daily newspapers. In the second decade of the twentieth century, newspapers played a pivotal role in the life of a baseball fan. The day's scores and game reports were published in late afternoon and early evening editions. At a time when most people had never seen a major league baseball game, the newspapers' sports columnists shaped the perception of the game. A reporter's prose could make the difference between a player becoming a hero or a villain, a league becoming successful or going down as a footnote in history.

By 1913, the Associated Press had wires strung across the United States with extensions into every major league ballpark. A.P. reporters at the games transmitted batteries, the score by innings, descriptions of key plays and lineup changes to newspaper offices throughout the country. Thus, a sports desk at a place like Amarillo, Texas, could have access to current game information as quickly as big city newspapers.

Both sides in the war between Organized Baseball and the Federal League used the newspapers and tabloids to further their own interests. Most major league cities featured several daily newspapers and, in many cases, sports editors chose sides in the leagues' disputes.

Baseball reporters often distinguished the Federal League clubs from their counterparts in Organized Baseball by referring to the newcomers as "Federals" or "Outlaws." Instead of the Pittsburgh Rebels, Brooklyn Tip Tops, Kansas City Packers, and St. Louis Terriers, the press developed abridged sobriquets for their game reports: Pittsfeds, Brookfeds, Kawfeds, and S'loufeds.

In addition to daily newspapers, baseball fans could get news about their favorite teams and players from two weekly publications, each costing a nickel. Founded in 1883 by the noted baseball journalist Francis C. Richter, *Sporting Life* was published in Philadelphia. Still edited by Richter in 1914, *Sporting Life* supported the Federal League's stance that it was a legitimate major league.

In the early days of *Sporting Life*, Richter warned that the restrictive measures of the reserve clause threatened the prosperity of the National League and American Association. He supported John Montgomery Ward's attempt to unionize players in the Brotherhood Association to the point that he allowed Ward to publish articles critical of the reserve clause in *Sporting Life*. Richter gained considerable clout from his membership in the rules committee and he was even offered the presidency of the National League in 1907.[1]

Richter opposed the National League's monopoly following the demise of the American Association in 1891 and became an independent alternative to *The Sporting News*' unquestioned support of Organized Baseball during the time of the war with the Federals. It was no surprise that *Sporting Life* supported the Federal League's right to challenge the existing major leagues' monopoly.

Richter made his publication's position clear in its editorial page: "'Sporting Life' has no interest whatever in the Federal League, and no support therefore, except as the third major league.... We are strongly of the opinion that there is both demand and room for a third major league, despite the contrary claims of the old-line leaders — claims which are based wholly on the total attendance of a very young league, and conveniently ignore the tremendous recession of patronage in their long-established leagues, and which began several years before the new major league was even dreamed of."[2]

Initially, *The Sporting News*' editor and owner, Charles C. Spink, embraced the idea of a third major league. However, the fifty-one-year-old Spink died on April 22, 1914, after attending a Federal League game between St. Louis and Chicago. His son and successor as editor of the baseball tabloid, J.G. Taylor Spink, was an acknowledged admirer of Ban Johnson and a self-professed "friend and champion of organized baseball."[3] After young Spink's ascension to editor, *The Sporting News* served as the unofficial mouthpiece for the two established major leagues.

"My policy was to print the Federal League box scores and their news, but editorially we were hostile," Spink stated in 1974. "Joe Villa, our New York correspondent, and a particular friend of Ban Johnson, fired our heaviest barrages against them. Joe always referred to them as the 'Lunchroom League,' or the 'Flap Jack Circuit.'"[4]

Villa specialized in the exposé and served as Organized Baseball's leading propagandist during the baseball war. Week after week, he penned contemptuous and sometimes scandalous attacks on the Federal Leaguers in his front-page column in *The Sporting News*. Ironically, Spink's tabloid devoted hundreds of thousands of words in attacks on a circuit it maintained did not deserve coverage as a major league.

Earlier attempts to organize an alternative major league by the Union Association (1884) and the Players' League (1890) were essentially efforts to break major league baseball's restrictive salary structure. The American Association (1882–90) was somewhat more successful, but it collapsed after the war with the Players' Association led to the defection of some of its clubs to the National League. The only lasting effort to form a new league after the inauguration of the National League of Baseball Clubs in 1876 was the American League. While the Players' League was organized principally because of player reform, the American and National Leagues entered professional baseball strictly as capital ventures.

At the instigation of Charles Comiskey in 1893, Ban Johnson, a former Cincinnati newspaper reporter, gained the presidency of the Western Association. When the National League dropped four of its twelve clubs following the 1899 season, Ban seized the opportunity. In 1900 he renamed his circuit the American League and a year later expanded into three Eastern cities. He then declared his circuit a "major league." The American League upstarts annulled their participation in the National Agreement and declared open warfare with the Nationals over player contracts. Two years of raids on National League rosters and escalating player salaries convinced the older league to file for peace with Johnson.

The American and National Leagues operated without interference for the next ten years, cooperating to restrict player salaries and the scope of contracts. Each league was made up of eight clubs and these sixteen major league baseball franchises in eleven cities operated with no relocations or changes in structure from 1903 to 1953. The major leagues operated within a rigid structure known as the "National Agreement," whereby the players were employed and paid at the discretion of the club owners. The governing body of the two leagues was a three-man National Commission that interpreted and implemented the National Agreement.

The term "Organized Baseball" was understood to stand for the National and American Leagues and minor leagues operating under the National Agreement. Any leagues or teams not a signatory of the National Agreement were considered "outlaws."

After the formation of the American League in 1901, major league baseball attendance rose yearly until 1910. During that period, baseball became an urban game as its success mirrored the rapid growth of cities in the early part of the century. Prospective baseball investors saw the Chicago Cubs earn $1.2 million between 1906 and 1915. The 1912 "Half million dollar World Series" netted each of the participating teams almost $150,000. From 1909 to 1914, ten new larger steel ballparks were built for major league clubs. Fans flocked to games, taking advantage of cheap transportation on new trolley lines that took them to modern baseball parks built along the rail routes. When Brooklyn's Ebbets Field opened in 1913, it was located at the junction of nine trolley lines.[5]

Professional baseball's economic boom only marginally affected players' income during the five years prior to 1914. Major league salaries ranged between $1500 to $2500 for rookies and substitutes, although the Players' Fraternity said some first year major leaguers were paid as little as $900 for the 1912 season. On the opposite end of the spectrum was Ty Cobb, the best player in the game, whose salary for 1913 was $12,000 after batting .420 and .410 the two prior seasons. Baseball's magnates didn't seem to be concerned that attendance figures remained constant at a little over six million from 1910 to 1913 and did not come close to matching the record attendance of 7,236,000 in 1909.[6]

While the average major league player's salary in 1913 was around $3200 (it grew to $7300 by 1915), the average baseball fan earned far less. A blue-collar worker earned approximately $700 a year, while a skilled craftsman took in about $1200 annually. In 1914, ticket prices to major league games were still reasonable: $1 to $1.25 for covered grandstand, though bleacher seats were upped to fifty cents in 1913. In major league parks, the bleachers were dominated by the working class, second and third generation immigrants, and even a few African Americans. Patrons of the grandstand tended to be the well-dressed professionals or businessmen who had gone straight from work to the afternoon ball game. Stylishly dressed women began appearing in the grandstands in increasing numbers, particularly on the specially designated "ladies' days."

In the early part of the twentieth century, minor league baseball thrived as an inexpensive, and often the only, entertainment in smaller cities. The American Association, an upper minor league, reported more than 1,400,000 paid admissions for the 1911 season. By 1913 there were thirty-nine minor leagues within the membership of the National Association of Professional Baseball Leagues.

Two years before the Federal League declared itself a challenger to the existing majors, John T. Powers, head of the Wisconsin-Illinois League he had organized in 1905, acted on his dream of establishing a third major league. In February of 1912, he announced the formation of a new circuit he dubbed the Columbian League. Powers' Columbian League didn't get off the ground because one of his main investors, Otto F. Stifel, a wealthy St. Louis brewer, withdrew in March and doomed the effort.[7] However, Powers was determined to make his league a reality and would try again a year later.

At about the same time, a group of investors from eight Eastern cities (six in existing major league markets) formed a professional league outside Organized Baseball using players unaffiliated with other professional clubs. This effort, which was called the United States League, was made up of clubs in Chicago, Cincinnati, Cleveland, New York, Pittsburgh, Reading, Pennsylvania, Richmond, Virginia, and Washington.

The United States League began play on May 1, 1912, but bad weather, failure to meet payrolls, and low attendance, especially in New York, plagued its clubs. After winning only two of its first seventeen games, the New York club, which played its games at a semi-pro park called Bronx Oval, was the first to fold, dropping out when it could not provide enough players to field a team for a game on May 27.[8] On June 1, league President William Wittman's own club in Reading filed for bankruptcy. Pittsburgh's Marshall Henderson assumed the league's presidency, and the remaining club owners decided to continue, but without an official schedule. The final game of the U.S.L. was in Richmond on June 26, 1912, when the Rebels played against the independent "Newman's" with the proceeds going to the players for back salaries.

A baseball tabloid, *The Sporting Life,* eulogized the infant United States League in its

May 11, 1912, issue: "...if the league fails it will put to a finish for a time, thoughts of battling the big fellows" (the American and National Leagues). That conclusion did not last for long.

Better organized and financed than the United States League, John T. Powers's Federal League began modestly and quietly in 1913 as an organization outside of Organized Baseball. The Federals put clubs in Chicago, Cleveland, Pittsburgh, Indianapolis, St. Louis, and Covington, Kentucky.

The Federal League was an "outlaw" organization because it did not subscribe to the National Agreement. Considered merely a nuisance at first, within a year the Federal League became a threat to the actual foundation of the traditional two major leagues. The Federals put teams in major league cities, provided major league stadiums for their games, and paid salaries in excess of those in the current major leagues. According to baseball historian Harold Seymour, the Feds employed 221 players; of that number, "18 players jumped major-league contracts; 25 broke minor-league contracts; 63 disregarded reserve claims of major league clubs; and 115 ignored the minor-league reserve."[9]

Although the Federals signed only a few of the major leagues' current big-name stars (Joe Tinker, Hal Chase, Eddie Plank, Chief Bender), they did employ several former baseball stars who were well known to the average fan. The most famous of that number were "Three Finger" Brown, George Mullin, and Danny Murphy.

Professor Seymour observed, "Someone once said that history is the propaganda of the victors. This epigram fits Organized Baseball. The American League, for example, was once an outlaw itself. After a hard two-year fight, it succeeded in elbowing its way into major-league standing and the respectability; the league took on a glow of legitimacy that belied its freebooting origins."[10]

While Organized Baseball decried the outlaws as "pretenders," most of the nation's newspapers printed the Federals' scores and standings on an even footing with the two traditional major leagues. Ironically, the organized major leagues' voracious campaign against the Federal League both in the press and in the courts gave credibility to the newcomers, though Organized Baseball never publicly acknowledged the outlaws.

1

Federal League Beginnings

In February 1913, long-time minor league executive John Powers announced the formation of a new independent baseball league in the Midwest. Despite the losses suffered by the United States League, a few of that circuit's investors and some new moneyed men joined together in Grand Rapids, Michigan, to plan their strategy. The new league vowed to respect the National Agreement and said it would find players among "free agents, semi-pros and unsigned youngsters."[1] A second meeting in Indianapolis on March 8 unveiled a revised list of franchises and a new name: The Federal League of Base Ball Clubs.

In the Federal League's fold of investors was Otto Stifel, who had bailed out of Powers's Columbian League a year earlier. The Chicago franchise was backed by a large number of investors including club president Charles L. Sherlock and Edward C. Racey, vice president and treasurer. Also on board were Indianapolis hotel magnate J. Edward Krause and the principal backers of the Pittsburgh U.S.L. franchise, Marshall Henderson and William McCullough.[2]

Manager Deacon Phillippe's Pittsburgh club of the United States League had done fairly well in 1912. When the U.S.L. ceased operation in late June, the "Filipinos" were in first place with 19 victories. The team's success convinced its owners, principally William Tice McCullough, that Pittsburgh could be a two-baseball-team town.

A month after the failure of the U.S.L., McCullough contacted Edward Barrow, president of the International League, about the possibility of transferring either the Reading or Jersey City team to Pittsburgh. They took up the matter with Pirates' owner Barney Dreyfuss, who flatly refused to sanction the idea of another baseball club in his territory.[3]

When the Federal League tentatively organized in the winter of 1912–13, it was expected to field teams in St. Louis, Detroit, Indianapolis, Pittsburgh, Chicago, Grand Rapids, Cincinnati, and Cleveland. Powers felt he needed a franchise in Cleveland, sixth largest city in the United States, for the Midwest circuit to survive.

Cleveland had been a member of the United States League with a hotel manager named William Murphy the chief backer. Murphy and his associates lost $10,000 in the U.S.L. venture and quit the game. However, Fred Bramley, who owned an amusement park and an adjoining baseball park, wanted into professional baseball. Since Luna Park was a corporation, he had to convince the other stockholders to join him.[4]

At the League meeting of magnates on March 8, Powers was elected president; Bramley vice-president; James A. Ross, Indianapolis, secretary; and John A. George, Indianapolis, treasurer. Edward E. Gates of the Indianapolis law firm of Matson, Gates and Ross, Attorneys, was general counsel for the League. Each club was required to post a $5,000 guarantee before the season began and $50,000 in bonds were to be provided by each club to go toward salaries and upgrading playing facilities for the league's first season.[5]

The prospective Kansas City and Detroit entries did not work out so the Federal League would open its inaugural season with six clubs, with plans to eventually expand to eight teams. The six cities represented were Chicago, Pittsburgh, Cleveland, St. Louis, Indianapolis, and Cincinnati. This put the Feds in competition with the major leagues in five cities and in one American Association city. The one minor league market, Indianapolis, had been a member of the National League as recently as 1889. In Chicago the Federals had to compete against the White Sox and Cubs, and St. Louis had the Feds' Terriers along with the Cardinals and Browns. The League opted for a 120-game schedule; its season would open on May 6 and end September 14.

Among the Federals' top executives, only in St. Louis was there previous big league experience. Stockholder Edward A. Steininger had served as president of the St. Louis Cardinals until Helen Britton inherited the club in 1911. Lloyd Rickart, a former Browns executive, became the Terriers' secretary. The St. Louis club had no ballpark and no players, so Otto Stifel, as the largest stockholder, went about to remedy that, and the investors lost $75,000 on the 1913 season.[6]

In the beginning, the Federals made no attempt to sign established major league players. The Federal League's most recognizable baseball names were not among the players it employed, but among its managers. In early April the league announced that former Pirates pitching star Charles "Deacon" Phillippe would manage the club in Pittsburgh. A few days later, Burt Keeley, a pitcher with Washington in 1908 and manager of Chicago's U.S.L. club in 1912, was hired in the same position for the Windy City's Federal League entry. Cleveland was attempting to hire Cy Young as manager and had former Cleveland Naps third baseman Bill Bradley as a fallback choice.[7]

Playing facilities in the infant Federal League would range from the former home of the Pittsburgh Pirates that seated 16,000, to the tiny park in Covington, Kentucky. When the plan to place the Cincinnati team in that city's Hippodrome Park fell through, a club was hastily organized across the Ohio River in Covington.

William Reiden, president of the Bavarian Brewery, and R.C. Stewart, president of Stewart Iron Works, raised $12,000 in capital stock for the baseball park in Covington. Less than a month before the season was scheduled to open, ground was broken at a Covington downtown park known as "Shinkle Playgrounds" for a field and bleachers designed to hold 4200 spectators. The playing field was small: only 194 feet down the right-field line, 267 feet to dead center and 218 feet down the left-field line.[8] On April 17, the Covington franchise announced that long-time Pittsburgh Pirates pitcher Sam Leever would pilot the Blue Sox.

The Pittsburgh Federal League team would play its games at Exposition Park, originally constructed in 1890 for use in an "outlaw" league — the Players' (Brotherhood) League. The city's National League club moved in a year later and played there until Exposition Park was abandoned by the Pirates when Forbes Field opened in 1909. The Federals took over the stadium after the previous tenants from the United States League folded after less than two months of operation in 1912. The Federals' home at the confluence of Allegheny and Ohio Rivers had major league credentials and a good central location. The main drawback was its susceptibility to flooding.

Opening day games in Pittsburgh and Covington were threatened when the Federal League grounds in those two cities on the Ohio River were flooded following a heavy rainfall on March 31. However, both clubs had their parks in shape for their respective opening dates.

Cy Young, baseball's most famous pitcher, agreed to manage the Cleveland club less than two weeks before the Federal League season began. Like most of the new league's clubs in 1913, the local Federals employed few players who had previous major league experience and the play was hardly above semi-pro quality. Young's team of youngsters did have a veteran presence behind the plate in John Kleinow, an eight-year major league veteran, mostly with the New York Americans.

The first official game ever in the Federal League was the 1913 season opener matching Young's Cleveland club and the Blue Sox of Covington on May 3. More than 1,000 of the curious came to Cleveland's Luna Park, home field of the Green Sox, a nickname derived from the youthfulness of the team. "Cy Young, manager of the Cleveland team, got a big hand when he appeared on the field," noted the local papers. The two teams battled to a 6-to-6 tie in a game called after the tenth inning due to darkness.[9]

As in the other Federal League openers, the game in Pittsburgh on May 6 was preceded by a parade through downtown. A big crowd, announced at 7,225, assembled at Exposition Park, but Indianapolis ruined the festivities with a 9-to-5 win over Phillippe's club. Likewise, Chicago spoiled the St. Louis club's opener the same day before 3,500 fans at St. Louis University's baseball grounds. Tom McGuire pitched the Brownies to a 7–4 win and the Chicago Federals went on to take four straight from Stifel's club.

A former major league star who was employed by the Federal League in its inaugural season was long-time National League first baseman Jake Beckley, who became an umpire in the rookie circuit. Nicknamed "Eagle Eye," the powerful slugger batted .300 or better thirteen times, accumulated 2930 major league hits, and hit 244 triples to rank fourth on the all-time list. A powerful man at 5'10", 200 pounds, Jake rattled opposing players when on a hot streak with the blood-curdling cry of "Chickazoola."[10] Beckley retired from professional baseball in 1911, but kept in shape by playing with amateur teams around his hometown of Hannibal, Missouri.

The *Chicago Daily Tribune* commented on Beckley's prowess as a Federal League arbiter in a game between Chicago and Pittsburgh. "Old 'Eagle Eye' Jake Beckley, who was in the National League for more years than he can remember, officiated as umpire and kept the players on the jump every minute, with the result the game was decided in less than an hour and a half, despite the severe heat. Jake is almost as good an umpire as he was a player, and the swatsmiths had little chance to 'kick' on his decisions."[11] Jake's career as an umpire lasted that one season.

There was considerable excitement for the official opening game in Covington on Friday, May 9. Box seats at "Shinkle Playgrounds" were $1, seats in the first eight rows of the grandstand were 75 cents, the remaining grandstand seats were 50 cents, and bleacher tickets were a mere 25 cents. The event led a local newspaper to run the banner headline "Covington Goes Crazy, Baseball Crazy."

"On Opening Day in Covington, there were lines with thousands of people throughout downtown Covington," it was reported. "A parade commenced at Scott and 12th street making its way to the ballpark via Madison and Fifth. In the ballpark bands were playing and bombs containing tiny American flags were bursting overhead. The crowd was too big for the stands so fans lined all the way around the edge of the playing field. Any balls hit into the spectators were ground rule singles."[12] Covington pitcher Walter Justus shut out the St. Louis Terriers 4 to 0.

A day later, Indianapolis became the fifth Federal League club to hold its home opener. The city declared a half-day holiday and the 6,000 fans in attendance at the hastily constructed ballpark at Riverside Beach were forced to wait for Governor Ralston, who was late in arriving to throw out the first pitch. The home crowd reserved their loudest cheers for center fielder and lead-off batter Al Kaiser, who was noted for being one of the fastest players in the American Association when he played for Indianapolis in 1912. The game was not particularly well played, but the fans got their money's worth when the Hoosiers scored the winning run in the bottom of the eleventh inning to beat Chicago, 6–5. The game was punctuated by a successful hidden ball trick, Indianapolis right fielder Tiemeyer being the victim. The Keeleys had their own embarrassing moment when left fielder Lynch was hit in the face by a ball as he fell in the outfield's loose sand.[13]

On May 10, 1913, a reorganized United States League opened its season with clubs in eight cities: Baltimore, Brooklyn, Lynchburg, Va., Newark, New York, Philadelphia, Reading and Washington. After the New York team would not play in Newark the next day because the players had not been paid the guarantee for the opening game, Washington and New York were dropped. Only three days into the U.S.L.'s second season, President William Wittman announced the project would be abandoned.

On May 14, a day after he jumped the Indianapolis American Association club to play for the Pittsburgh Federals, Ray Ashenfelter took the mound at Exposition Park before about 1,400 bugs in a game against St. Louis. Ashenfelter not only won the game, 5–0, he came within one scratch hit of pitching a no-hitter. That hit was made by St. Louis second baseman Barton leading off the first inning and witnesses said that either second baseman Menosky or first baseman Sabrie should have fielded the roller.[14]

However, the Federal League did not have to wait long for its first no-hitter as a Terriers pitcher named Reymer threw a no-run, no-hit game against Pittsburgh only two games later. St. Louis left fielder Miller saved the no-hitter with a "circus catch when he raced to the fence and pulled down a smash with his ungloved hand."[15]

After playing their first fourteen games on the road, the Chicago Federals opened at home against the Filipinos of Pittsburgh on May 23. Of the handful of ex-major leaguers on the Keeleys' roster, the most recognizable to Chicago fans was thirty-two-year-old pitcher Fred Olmsted, who went 21–20 with the White Sox from 1908 through 1911. The right-handed spitballer led the American Association in wins with Minneapolis in 1912 when he finished with a 28–10 record, but he didn't fare well with the Keeleys and was released on June 5.

The Chicago "Keeleys," or "Browns" as they were also called, played their games on the North Side at the DePaul University baseball field. On a day when both the White Sox and Cubs had open dates, the city put on a gala opening for the Federals. There was an automobile parade, a brass band played and a plethora of floral arrangements gave home plate the appearance of a "small conservatory." The Chicago sheriff threw out the first pitch and local photographers and moving-picture men recorded the festivities. Though advance notices claimed that 7,000 persons could be accommodated in the DePaul facility, the day's crowd was estimated at 2,000.

After the opening ceremonies, the main excitement of the day was the arrival of Chicago White Sox President Charles Comiskey, who was accompanied by a party that included legendary pitcher Ed Walsh. Comiskey's presence caused so much excitement that the right field spectators swarmed onto the field to get a better view of the magnate, delaying the game until the American League group found their seats.[16]

The game itself was a disappointment for the locals. Pittsburgh started Ray Ashenfelter who had already won the first two games he pitched in the Federal League, including one over the Keeleys a few days earlier in the Smoky City. Though he was touched for eight hits and allowed four walks, the Filipinos' left-hander pitched his way out of several jams and beat the Chicagoans, 7 to 1.[17]

As the season progressed, the upstart Federals began to attract the attention of Organized Baseball. After the Independent League signed Ashenfelter and Fred Link of the Indianapolis Indians and offered inducements to other Indianapolis players, President Johnson of the American League and President Tom Chivington of the American Association scheduled a meeting with Association owners to discuss means to combat the Federal League's encroachment.

In the first decade of the century, there were a number of rough characters in the major leagues. Some were well known to the average baseball fan: John "Mugsy" McGraw, Ty Cobb and Frank Chance. Another of this type of player was the St. Louis Federal League Club's manager, John "Rowdy Jack" O'Connor.

O'Connor played or managed in the major leagues for twenty-two years between 1887 and 1911. In his obituary of O'Connor in 1937, John E. Wray of the *St. Louis Post Dispatch* summarized Rowdy Jack's baseball career with the phrase, "O'Connor saw three baseball wars and profited by them."[18]

When Ban Johnson's American League decided to raid the Pittsburgh National League champions in 1902, O'Connor, a catcher on that club, completed a deal by which several Pirates, including Jack Chesbro and Tommy Leach, agreed to defect to the New York Americans. Jack was paid $40,000 for the coup, four times the amount he was ever paid in salary. He was paid $10,000 to manage the St. Louis Browns in 1910.

O'Connor was manager of the Browns until he was dismissed by Ban Johnson in 1911. It was charged that the St. Louis manager purposely stationed third baseman Red Corriden too far back in a season-ending game with Cleveland so that Nap Lajoie could get enough bunt base hits to beat out Ty Cobb for the batting title and the Chalmers Automobile award.[19] Following his release by the Browns, O'Connor went to court and received a verdict of $5,000 from the St. Louis club. Jack then accepted $5,000 to manage the St. Louis Federal League Club for 1913.[20]

All the while he was manager of the St. Louis Federals, O'Connor did not forget his grudge against Ban Johnson and periodically threatened Organized Baseball with lawsuits ranging from obstructing his activities as manager to stealing his players. That June, he retained attorneys to file suit in federal district court naming each of the American League clubs as defendants. He charged that the national baseball agreement was a violation of the Sherman antitrust law and asked for $25,000 in damages.[21]

Just before the start of a game in St. Louis with the Indianapolis club on June 28, 1913, O'Connor got into an argument with umpire Jack McNulty. President Powers had hired McNulty only a few days earlier and the game that day was to be the umpire's first for the Federal League.

"The trouble arose when O'Connor wanted McNulty to show his authority for being on the grounds to umpire the game," reported the *Kansas City Star*. "A dispute followed and all of a sudden O'Connor's fist shot out and landed flush on the umpire's jaw. Nearby spectators jumped over the fence and surrounded the belligerents."[22]

After several blows were struck, Michael Kinney, a state senator as well as director of the St. Louis club, and Nathan Hall, a member of the municipal assembly, separated the combatants.[23] A day later, President Powers suspended O'Connor indefinitely and accessed him a fine of $200. As for Umpire McNulty, who suffered a broken jaw, he retired from baseball. Following the end of the season, Jack lost his job as manager of the St. Louis club and became a defendant in a lawsuit filed by McNulty. The ex-umpire sued O'Connor and the St. Louis Federal League Club for $35,000 in damages. Eventually, a judge ruled that the club owners were not responsible for O'Connor's actions and the jury returned the verdict solely against Rowdy Jack. The former Terriers manager was ordered to pay $1,500 in damages to McNulty.[24]

One of O'Connor's most important contributions to the St. Louis Federals was the introduction of a local player named John Tobin. O'Connor was a product of the St. Louis sandlots himself and understood the quality of the city's amateur players. Among sandlot, or semi-pro, teams flourishing throughout the Midwest, the St. Louis Trolley League was said to provide the best competition. Tobin was playing for the Bell Telephone Company in the city when he signed with the Federals in 1913. O'Connor recognized a promising big league player in the smallish (5'8", 142 pounds) but speedy outfielder. Given the opportunity, the twenty-one-year-old Tobin batted .339 in 41 games and became a fixture in the St. Louis Terriers' outfield through 1915.[25]

Chicago was the early pace setter in the 1913 Federal League pennant race. As late as June 13, the Keeleys were in first place with a record of 20 and 13. Then the club was rocked by the news that the team's best hitter, right fielder Charlie "Silk" Kavanagh, was going to the White Sox, and their best pitcher, Tom McGuire, had signed with the St. Louis Cardinals. Kavanagh's batting average of well over .300 and his major-league-quality defense caught the attention of White Sox manager James Callahan. Charles Comiskey purchased Kavanagh's 1912 contract for $2,500 through a deal with the Green Bay (Wisconsin-Illinois League) club, which held the National Agreement rights to the player.[26]

The news of the players' defections arrived just prior to a series with Indianapolis. The Hoosiers were fresh off a five-game sweep of Pittsburgh that vaulted the Indy club past the Keeleys into first place. Although the National Commission ruled that Kavanagh and McGuire

William "Whoa Bill" Phillips, manager, Indianapolis Federal League club, 1914 (George Grantham Bain Collection, Library of Congress).

would have to finish the season with the Chicago Federals, the club never recovered.[27] After June 12, the Chicago Federals went 27–40 for the remainder of the season. Indianapolis never relinquished first place after taking the top spot in early June.

First place was not foreign to Indianapolis manager William "Whoa Bill" Phillips. Bill was a popular pitcher in Indianapolis prior to joining the Cincinnati Nationals in 1895 and he eventually returned to the Hoosier City as manager of the local American Association club. Bill began managing in the minor leagues in 1905 as a player manager with Indianapolis and he piloted the Wheeling, West Virginia, club to the 1909 Central League pennant. In the two years prior to his involvement with the Federal League, Phillips' clubs in Youngstown, Ohio, finished second, missing the 1912 Ohio-Pennsylvania League championship by mere percentage points.[28] One story attributed the origin of his unusual nickname to the time he attempted to break a wild bronco.[29]

When Phillips, formerly a pitcher for seven seasons in the National League, joined the Federals, his friend, President John Tener of the National League, said: "No matter where Bill Phillips goes, he will command respect. He's a credit to any league."[30]

On June 14, 1913, major league pitcher Elmer "Baron" Knetzer, Jack Lewis, infielder with the Boston Red Sox until they farmed him to St. Paul, and Tom Murray, a catcher from the St. Paul team, joined Deacon Phillippe's slumping Pittsburgh club. Knetzer was the Federal League's first quality and "name" major league player, having been a pitcher with the Brooklyn National League club. After Knetzer left Brooklyn during the 1912 season because of illness in his family, Manager "Bad Bill" Dahlen imposed a large reduction in salary on the hurler. Instead of playing for less money, Knetzer refused to sign his contract to play with Brooklyn in 1913. Because he was bound to that club by baseball's reserve rule, Knetzer's only choices were to play for Brooklyn, retire, or play with an "outlaw" team outside of the National Agreement.[31]

Known as "Baron" or "Kaiser," Knetzer was also nicknamed "Pretzel" because of the delivery on his main pitch, a hard-breaking curve ball. He also was not averse to using a wet one. Born in Carrick, Pennsylvania, Knetzer got his start in baseball with the semi-pro clubs of Pittsburgh. After pitching during the 1909 season for Lawrence, Mass., in the New England League, Elmer was sold to Charles Ebbets' Brooklyn club for $2,500.[32]

Brooklyn had a bad team during the time Knetzer pitched there and the Dodgers did not finish higher than sixth place. Still, his record was only three games under .500 after four seasons in the National League. Knetzer was twenty-seven years old when he walked away from the Dodgers following the 1912 season.

The day Knetzer joined the Filipinos, they lost a double-header to Indianapolis, dropping the Smoky City club's record to 13 wins, 24 losses. Deacon Phillippe tried to pull his club out of the doldrums by taking the mound himself for a game on May 31, but he got no run support and lost to St. Louis, 3–0. He tried again and again, but his luck was no better each time. Phillippe moved the youngster Mike Menosky to right field and installed newcomer Jack Lewis at second base. However, nothing seemed to help.

On June 20, Phillippe started the game for his slumping team against Cy Young's club in Cleveland and the forty-one-year-old ex–Pirates ace lost a pitching duel to Henry Miller, 2 to 0. One play cost Deacon the game. In the fourth inning he intercepted a throw from the centerfielder that allowed one run to score, then his third baseman let Deacon's throw get by and a second runner raced home.[33]

Phillippe would pitch again on June 28 at Exposition Park against Kansas City. His opposing number would be the opposition club's manager, Sam Leever, who took an occasional turn on the mound. The pair were teammates on the crack Pittsburgh Pirates' pitching staffs from 1900 through 1910 that brought the city four National League crowns. Leever left, trailing 2 to 1 after pitching five innings, but Kansas City rallied with three runs off Phillippe in the top of the sixth to send the Deacon to the bench. Kansas City went on to win, 7 to 5.

The Pittsburgh Federal League Club failed to meet payroll on the first of July, nor were paychecks distributed the next day. Filipinos pitcher Ray Ashenfelter refused to put on a uniform unless he was paid and witnessed his teammates play the game of July 2 against Kansas City from the grandstand. The players declared they would not play any more games unless they all received their pay. The Pittsburgh players were paid and a crisis was averted.[34]

The clubs' frustrations were manifest in a game before a large crowd at Exposition Park on July 14. Knetzer allowed only one run to Chicago, but the Filipinos could only manage one hit off opposing pitcher Whitey Timmerman; that one hit was made by Knetzer himself when he beat out a slow roller to second baseman Farrell.

On July 20, Ashenfelter lost a game to the Chicago Federals at DePaul Field, dropping the lowly Filipinos' record to 27 and 43. When the Pittsburgh club left town two days later, Ashenfelter wasn't with them, because he stayed in the Windy City as a member of the Keeleys' squad. The once promising southpaw of the Indianapolis Indians started for Chicago against St. Louis on the twenty-third and was pounded for four runs and eight hits in only two and a third innings.[35]

Late in the 1913 Federal League season things had reached a critical point for the Pittsburgh club. Following the season, Deacon Phillippe related the travails of managing in the bush leagues. Phillippe recalled:

> One trip we took to Kansas City last summer. I started out with a bunch of ball players, a railroad ticket as far as Chicago, and berths that far for my men. I was given $15 in cash to defray the expenses of the trip. I was ordered to stop off on the way and play two exhibition games to raise money enough to get to my destination. One of the exhibition games netted $22.25 and the other $25.75, and I had to dig down in my own pocket for the reminder of the expense money.
>
> Well, we got to Kansas City, and I telegraphed for more money. I was sent $50. We were not drawing anything, and all we got was the guarantee money. I found that by getting the Kansas City club to double up on a Sunday I could save one day's hotel bill, so I did that. Then I got all the railroad agents in the town to help me to figure out the cheapest way home. I found that by paying 75 cents per ticket more than a certain road wanted I could get home twelve hours sooner than by going over the cheaper route, but we did not have the coin, so we had to take the long route.[36]

Following the 1913 season, Deacon Phillippe moved to his farm and was never again involved with baseball on a professional basis. In January 1914, the former manager of the Filipinos prepared papers for the filing of a suit against the Pittsburgh Athletic Park Association, the title under which the local Federals did business in 1913. The suit was meant to recover $1,555.40, with interest at six per cent from July 15, 1913, which he claimed to be due him as part of his salary for that season.

After the Federal League received an infusion of new players following the breakup of the Inter-State League in late June 1913, the *Quincy Herald* quipped, "The Federal League must play some classy 'major league ball' with Prount, Myers, Mertens and Keupper all on one team [St. Louis] and making a fair showing. It would look like a Three-I roll call if all the aliases could be thrown aside and the real names would appear in the box scores."[37]

Initially, Organized Baseball adopted a policy to ignore the new independent circuit which was operating outside of the National Agreement. *The Sporting News* predicted the Federal League would quickly disappear like most of its predecessors. But before the end of the

1913 season, the outlaw Federal League would prove it must be taken seriously and a potential baseball war loomed on the horizon.

Back then, baseball was not exempt from federal antitrust laws, yet developments within this "baseball war" would have a significant impact on its interpretation. Early in the 1913 season, Western Telegraph refused to put the Federal League scores on its telegraph ticker. The Federal League dispatched attorney Edward Gates to appear before the Interstate Commerce Commission. Gates said that the Federal League had offered to pay Western Telegraph to carry the scores, but Organized Baseball coerced the company into denying the service to the Feds. The Federal League's attorney met with Representative Henry Gallagher, who had called for investigation of the "baseball trust" a year earlier. Gates implored the Illinois congressman to pursue a resolution in Congress to investigate whether Organized Baseball had violated antitrust laws because it had acquired certain privileges that other businesses lacked.[38]

At the end of June 1913, Lloyd Rickart, secretary of the St. Louis franchise, was chosen to replace John Powers after it was requested by the directors that the Federal League president take a "leave of absence." Rickart had strong baseball credentials. He had served as road secretary for the St. Louis Browns from 1907 through 1912. Willis Johnson, a sports writer for the *St. Louis Globe-Democrat* who became business manager of the St. Louis Federals in the spring of 1914, wrote, "There never was anyone who worked and fumed and fretted as much about work as Rickart. He knew figures, could look up at the sky and tell you all about the weather, and he knew, at the sixteenth of an inch, just how many miles the Browns traveled on each trip."[39] Though Rickart was recognized as one of the most efficient road secretaries in baseball, Browns owner Robert Hedges replaced him with the nephew of Mrs. Hedges before the 1913 season.

Rickart's first duty as chief executive was to oversee the placement of the Covington club in Kansas City. After posting a fourth-place 21–31 record, the Covington Federal League Club announced on June 23, 1913, that it would leave town because of low attendance. On June 26, the League voted in Indianapolis to transfer the Covington club to Kansas City, Missouri. Manager Sam Leever was notified the league would take over the salaries of his players.

The Covington ballpark reverted to creditors on June 25, 1913. Some boxing matches were later held at the park and Covington public school students also used the field for May Day athletic events. In March 1919 the ballpark was sold and torn down, and a tobacco warehouse was built on the site.[40]

Professional baseball had a long tradition in Kansas City. The city, located on the Kansas-Missouri line, had fielded teams in three different major leagues during the nineteenth century. In 1884, the Kansas City Unions (16–63) finished with the worst record in the Union Association. Two years later, the Kansas City Cowboys went 30–91 in the National League, and in 1888-89, another Cowboys team, this one in the American Association, struggled to records of 43–89 and 55–82.

George "White Wings" Tebeau, a former major league outfielder, purchased the Kansas City minor league franchise and joined Thomas J. Hickey's reorganized Western League in 1902. The league was renamed the American Association a year later. In 1903, Tebeau built a new ballpark, named Association Park, and it became home for the Blues for the next twenty years.[41]

The transition of the Covington club to Kansas City went remarkably smoothly. An adequate facility at 47th and Tracy was available, and there were only a few scheduling conflicts with the American Association Blues that had to be worked out. The ownership of the transplanted club was transferred to a group headed by Charles C. Madison, a local attorney who had once played ball on the same team as Joe Tinker.[42]

On July 12, 1913, the Kansas City Federal League team played its first game on the home grounds against Jack O'Connor's St. Louis aggregation. A large delegation of St. Louis rooters came to town along with Otto Stifel and Ed Steininger. A parade through downtown led to the ballpark, where Riley & Kelly's band, followed by the Kansas City and St. Louis players, marched across the field.

With approximately 5,000 looking on, "Mayor Jost went to the mound. After wetting the ball and rubbing his hands in the dirt he threw one wide to Hicks," noted the *Kansas City Star*.[43] Once the game got underway, Kansas City right-hander Pete Henning was the master of the St. Louis crew, allowing but three hits and striking out eleven of O'Connor's men in the locals' 3 to 1 win.

The club, dubbed the "Packers" for the city's main industry, played two games under .500 the remainder of the season and finished in fifth place. Manager and part-time pitcher Sam Leever wasn't around at the end, having been released on August 11. Hugo Swartling, a defector from Steubenville (Ohio) in the Inter-State League, replaced him as acting manager.[44]

On August 2, 1913, Federal League officials forced John Powers to officially relinquish the league's presidency and elected James A. Gilmore, president of the Chicago franchise, as the interim president. The league issued an official statement to the effect that Mr. Powers was granted a leave of absence until October 3, because he had been overworked in his "generous support of all things that have aided in the advancement of the circuit." Lloyd Rickart remained in actual charge of day to day affairs.[45]

The beginning of the end for Powers came on July 5, 1913, when the five directors of the financially strapped Chicago Federal League Club deposed current president Sherlock and elected a new set of officers. Gilmore, a newcomer to baseball, became club president and E.C. Racey was renewed as both vice president and treasurer.[46]

The Sporting News reported that Powers was ousted "because he is not considered 'big' enough for the ambitious plans that the Federal League magnates have laid out for next year." Powers's plan to put the Federal League on the same level as the International League and the American Association was not the vision of the owners led by James Gilmore. Powers was not enthusiastic about the league magnates' desire to expand into the East with two new clubs, then become a major league.[47]

Apparently, Powers's demise was precipitated by his attempt that summer to transfer a game between Pittsburgh and Chicago, scheduled in Chicago, to Sheffield, Illinois, the president's home town. Powers secured a large guarantee, and, after all the arrangements had been made, the new owners of the Chicago club refused to transfer the game. Then the powerful Chicago group engineered the removal of Powers at a meeting of league officials, although he nominally remained as president until October.[48]

Despite losses estimated at around $750,000 for 1913, the Federal League's directors declared their intention to continue operations in 1914. The magnates mutually agreed to ensure the basis of the league in the form of two bonds of $25,000 which all club owners were to sign before the final meeting of the organization on September 20. The first bond was to guarantee players' salaries and other expenses for the next season. The second bond was to ensure properly equipped playing fields, free of indebtedness. The league's leaders also decided to build new parks in Chicago, Indianapolis, St. Louis and Cleveland. Lloyd Rickart and William McCullough were named to investigate conditions for prospective franchises in Baltimore and Buffalo.[49]

The Federal League poked another thorn into the side of Mike Kelley's Indianapolis American Association club that August. The Indianapolis Federals signed twenty-two-year-old George Kaiserling on August 3, 1913, after the pitcher had been sold by the city's Amer-

George Kaiserling, Indianapolis Federal League club, 1913–1915 (George Grantham Bain Collection, Library of Congress).

ican Association team to San Francisco of the Pacific Coast League. Kaiserling, a spitballer, had been a top pitcher in the Central League a year earlier, and had joined the A.A. Indians for 1913. The Ohio-born right-hander lost his first start with the Hoosier Feds, falling to second-place Cleveland, 4 to 1, on August 6, but he soon became the ace of Manager Phillips's pitching staff.

Cy Young's Green Sox threatened to make a race out of the Federal League pennant chase in early August. Cleveland had pulled to within two and a half games of first place when the two teams met for the first of two crucial four-game series. In the first week of August, the clubs split the first series in Indianapolis, which meant the Green Sox probably had to win three of four in Cleveland a week later to have any hope of capturing the pennant. Instead, Indianapolis all but wrapped up first place.

After the Green Sox dropped the first two games to the Hoosiers at Luna Park, the third game on August 14 became a must win for Cleveland. In the very first inning, Indy's starting pitcher, Harry Billiard, faced only six batters. He walked three, hit one batter and gave up a hit before Bill Phillips pulled him and put in Kaiserling. Leading 4–0 with the Green Sox's sixteen-game winner, Henry Miller, on the mound for the home club, it appeared Cleveland had the game in the bag. However, Indy clawed back, eventually taking the lead and driving Miller out of the game. Cleveland tied it in the ninth, but Indianapolis eventually triumphed in the twelfth, 8 to 7.

That loss on the fourteenth finished the Green Sox. Indianapolis finished the sweep the next day to effectively settle the pennant race. At the end of the series, Indianapolis's record stood at 57–35, Cleveland 51–41, and the other clubs were all under .500.

So the home-town fans could honor their Federal League champions, St. Louis agreed to move its season-ending games with the Hoosiers to Indianapolis. The Hoosier Feds concluded their season with a double-header win over O'Connor's Terriers before 4,500 local bugs at Riverside Park. Al Kaiser was perfect in the two games, collecting five hits in five official plate appearances in addition to three walks.

The Indianapolis entry won the inaugural Federal League pennant by a wide margin and celebrated on September 13 with a big parade and a banquet given by chief owner Edward Krause following the final game. At the fete, first baseman "Biddy" Dolan was presented a silver bat and ball for leading the Hoosiers in batting. Dolan, who had spent 1912 in the Central League, did not join the club until the last day of May and his insertion in the lineup coincided with the Hoosier Feds surge that moved them to the top of the League's standings.

Final Federal League standings for 1913:

Indianapolis	75–45	–
Cleveland	63–54	10½
St. Louis	59–59	15
Chicago	57–62	17½
Covington/Kansas City	53–65	21
Pittsburgh	49–71	26

Once the Hoosiers were assured of the pennant, club president Krause proposed the idea of a post-season series between the champions and a group of all-stars from the league's other teams. The entire gate receipts would be turned over to the players with the winning team collecting an extra 20 percent. Sports writers would pick the all-stars from the other five clubs in the league.[50]

The best two games out of three series against the all-stars was supposed to begin on September 17, but because of postponements due to the weather, the contests had to be delayed for four days. When they were finally able to play on September 21, the teams agreed to play two seven-inning games because of the threat of rain. The Hoosier Feds made short work of the all-stars, taking the games by scores of 2–0 and 4–1. George Kaiserling hurled both games for Indianapolis and had thrown thirteen scoreless innings before the all-stars ruined his quest for a double-shutout with a single run in the final inning of game two. Because Indianapolis had already clinched the series, the third game, scheduled for the following day, was canceled. Most of the Indianapolis players, plus a few fill-ins from the all-stars, went barnstorming in the Midwest after the series.

Only a few players from the Federal League's inaugural season would return a year later to make important contributions after the circuit declared itself a major. Among that number were Elmer Knetzer, Jack Tobin, Pete Henning and George Kaiserling.

Manager Bill Phillips retained Kaiserling for his "major league" club the following season. George won 17 and lost 9 for the Hoosier Feds in 1914, and on July 20 of that season, the spitballer pitched a one-hitter against the St. Louis Terriers. On the other hand, Chicago outfielder Silk Kavanagh, the Federal League's batting leader in 1913, appeared in only five games as a pinch hitter for the White Sox in 1914.

2

A Challenge to Organized Baseball

Despite an initial season of significant financial losses (1913 attendance figures were not released), Federal League magnates nonetheless decided to expand for the 1914 season. The Federal League of Baseball Clubs proclaimed itself a "major league" with eight franchises, four in cities already with major league clubs and four in cities that had been abandoned by the major leagues.

James Gilmore, the new chief executive of the Federal League, came to the job as a former coal company salesman and president of a company that manufactured vending machines. He turned out to be a capable and persuasive league president and the position was soon made permanent.

James Alexander Gilmore was born on March 2, 1876, at Portsmouth, Ohio, where his father was in the dry goods business. The Gilmores moved to St. Louis soon after James was born and then to Chicago in 1882 where his father became connected with the coal business.

Young Jim Gilmore attended Chicago's Marquette School and played baseball as a change pitcher for the Wyandotte Nine, which played its games at vacant lots on the West Side. One of Gilmore's teammates on the Wyandottes was Jack Hendricks, who played for the Pittsburgh Pirates and was manager and part owner of the Indianapolis American Association Club during the time James was president of the Federal League.

Upon completing Marquette School, Gilmore became a messenger boy for Armour & Company earning $3.00 a week. After four months on the job, Jim's request for a dollar raise was turned down, so he asked his brother Charley for a job with the Crescent Coal Company for which he would receive $7.00 a week. Jim was working as a salesman for the coal company when war was declared against Spain in 1898.

The elder Gilmore had served in the Civil War and told Jim he was the one that should enlist in the Army since his brothers were married. Having never handled a gun, James enlisted in the 1st Regiment, Illinois National Guard, the next day. His unit was eventually sent to Santiago, Cuba. While serving on the tropical island, Gilmore contracted malaria and lost nearly seventy pounds over forty days.

After he recovered from the fever, Jim reenlisted at Fort Ethan Allen, Vermont, with the 43rd Volunteers, one of the forty regiments recruited for service in the Philippines insurrection. The volunteers departed by ship from New York in November 1899. Sailing by way of Gibraltar and the Suez Canal, Gilmore and his unit reached the Philippine Islands on January 1, 1900. Soon after his arrival there, Jim was appointed commissary sergeant. Following thirty-five months of military service, Gilmore was mustered out of the Army in San Francisco.

As result of his Cuban service, he became a member of the Society of Santiago, to which only veterans of the Spanish-American War were eligible.

Upon his return to Chicago, James resumed his work as a coal salesman and became associated with the Martin-Rowe Coal Company in 1908, the year his father died. Two years later, James Gilmore became president of the Kernchen Company, manufacturers of ventilators and ventilating engines, a position he still held at the time of his first involvement with the Federal League.[1] James married at age thirty-five in 1911. Since he had always been interested in sports, two of Gilmore's favorite haunts were the Exmoor Golf Club and the Chicago Athletic Association, where he loved to play three-cushion pool.

When the Federal League's Chicago club ran into financial difficulty during the 1913 baseball season, the money-strapped club owners called on the successful businessman for advice. Gilmore surprised the baseball men by offering to take charge of the local club's operations. James and a syndicate of his friends took over the Federal League club in July and nursed it through the remainder of the season although, according to Jim, it cost them $12,000.

Gilmore later told a reporter, "It was not until John T. Powers had been forced to quit because of failing health that I was attracted to the league. I was sealed in the Chicago A.A. at lunch when I was asked to become the president of the league. It startled me, but I sparred for a time, and when I finally accepted the position it was not with the idea of turning the baseball world topsy-turvy in the remnant of a season."[2]

The key to Gilmore's plan to build up the Federal League would mean a successful raid on the existing major leagues for established players, much the same as Ban Johnson had done in 1901. Gilmore and the Federal League's attorneys held that the major leagues' "reserve clause" was not valid. The league's direct challenge to the clubs of Organized Baseball was initiated at its board of directors meeting in Indianapolis on November 1, 1913.

"The board of directors of the Federal League here to-night decided to declare war upon the major leagues of Organized Baseball, admitted Buffalo, New York, and Baltimore to the circuit, making it an eight club organization...," reported the *New York Times*. The directors, in their decision to try to sign players of the two major leagues, voted not to ask any player in Organized Baseball already under contract to join their organization, but they held that any man under a reserve clause would be tendered a contract if he wished to play in the new organization.[3]

Since 1876, Organized Baseball's players were bound to their respective clubs by the "reserve clause." That clause meant that, at the end of each season, a player's contract could automatically be renewed by the management of his current club. This not only restricted a player's choice of teams for which he could play, but it also kept salaries low because owners could offer whatever wage they saw fit. The only recourse for a player was to refuse to play (hold out) until a higher salary was offered.

This controversial contract clause, which was known officially as Rule 10A, stated: "On or before January 15 ... the club may tender to the Player a contract for the term of that year by mailing the same to the Player. If prior to the March 1 next succeeding said January 15, the Player and the Club have not agreed upon the terms of such contract, then on or before 10 days after said March 1, the Club shall have the right ... to renew this contract for the period of one year."

The Federal League's Directors felt the contract of any player would be upheld in court, but they maintained that the reserve clause was illegal and would not be sustained if challenged in the courts. The Federals intimated that offers to players held under the reserve clause would include the majority of men in the National and American Leagues. Many players had not signed contracts for the 1914 season until demands they had made through the Players' Fraternity (a union) were achieved.

The directors warned, "The Federal League will take no further steps toward carrying on war upon Organized Baseball unless the major leagues attempt to retaliate, but if they do ... the organization is well supplied with money and will fight any attempt to disrupt its ranks." If such an attempt was made, the directors said, they had enough money to make tempting offers to the best players of the older leagues.[4]

Dumped by Ban Johnson's American League in 1902, Baltimore had been without a major league club since then. Twelve years later, approximately six hundred citizens put up $164,400, with another $36,000 raised through loans, for a Federal League franchise. The largest shareholder was Ned Hanlon, a local baseball hero, and the new club's secretary was Judge Harry Goldman, who was a large stockholder in the Orioles club that lost its place in the American League.

The second city awarded a new Federal League club was Buffalo, located on the New York shore of Lake Erie. Buffalo was a member of the National League for ten seasons until they were dropped after the 1885 season. Buffalo had a club in the Players' League, but it finished dead last with a 36 and 96 record. After that, the city had a team in three different minor leagues until Buffalo joined the newest major league want-to-be in 1914.

Upon completing the business of admitting the clubs of Buffalo and Baltimore, the magnates selected a new Federal League Board of Managers: C.C. Madison, Kansas City; E.A. Steininger, St. Louis; J.A. Gilmore, Chicago; J. Edward Krause, Indianapolis; C.X. Zimmerman, Cleveland; W.T. McCullough, Pittsburgh; Harry Goldman, Baltimore; and Dick Carroll, Buffalo.

Horace Fogel appeared at the meeting and presented the claim of a group of Philadelphia investors for a place in the expanded league. Fogel, a former president of the Philadelphia National League club, was banished from Organized Baseball by the National Commission in 1912 for charging that St. Louis manager Roger Bresnahan, John McGraw's former catcher, helped the New York Giants win the pennant by fielding weaker lineups against them. Fogel's request to join the Federal League was rejected.

The following day, it was announced that George Stovall, until recently manager of the American League's St. Louis Browns, had been signed to lead the Kansas City Federal League Club. The former Browns manager would receive a three-year contract at $7,000 a season plus a bonus. The Kansas City club was unusual in that it was owned by residents of that city. Lumberman C.E. Bancker was the leading stockholder with 200 shares, though President Charles Madison and Vice President S.S. Gordon, a wealthy clothing merchant, ran the operations. George Stovall received 60 of the club's 1000 shares of stock. After signing his Federal League contract, Manager Stovall departed on a recruiting trip.

Organized Baseball reacted slowly to the Federal League's challenge. The loss of Stovall caused little concern. At thirty-six he was past his prime as a first baseman and his pugnacity had gotten him involved in numerous scrapes. The final straw for George's previous employers came early in the 1913 season when Stovall spit on an umpire during a game.

The ruckus began when rookie umpire Charlie Ferguson called the ten-year veteran out on strikes. Stovall made a few disparaging remarks and then added some expletives, questioning the arbiter's parentage. Ferguson threw George out of the game and the affair appeared to be over. Before George left the field he sauntered over to first base, picked up his mitt, and walked slowly back down the base line toward the Browns' dugout on the third base side.

Browns third baseman Jimmy Austin remembered, "As George came around behind Ferguson on the way back to our dugout, the umpire told George to hurry up. I guess that was the straw that broke the camel's back, because George let fly with a big glob of tobacco juice — p-tooey! — that just splattered all over Ferguson's face and coat and everywhere. Ugh, it was an awful mess. It was terrible. George always did chew an uncommonly large wad, you know."[5]

On May 13, American League President Ban Johnson suspended the St. Louis manager indefinitely. The suspension was lifted May 24, but Browns President Robert Lee Hedges was fed up with his manager's antics. The former manufacturer of buggies and wagons turned baseball owner didn't do anything immediately, but bided his time. With the club mired in seventh place and thirty-seven games out of first place, Hedges fired the fiery Stovall on September 6. Jimmy Austin put it in perspective when he commented, "George spit himself out of a job."[6]

Stovall was still under contract to the Browns as a player, but Hedges told George he could go home and the balance of his salary due as a first baseman would be forwarded to him by mail. Stovall knew he was still liable for reporting to work and demanded that Hedges put the payment guarantee in writing. Hedges angrily refused, so George reported to the ballpark daily to safeguard the final month of his salary.

"There were several clubs that wanted me...," Stovall told *Baseball Magazine*. "I went to Hedges and asked for my unconditional release. He refused to give it. Then I asked him how much he wanted for it. He said $3,500.

"President Britton, of the Cardinals, wanted to take it at this figure, but I was determined that I would not be sold like a lot of furniture at the personal profit of the very man who had discharged me."[7]

Stovall secured an audience with the American League president, but Ban Johnson told George there was nothing he could do, as the player was still property of the Browns. He also refused Stovall his outright release, leading the ex-manager to quip, "After the experience I had I was sure no white man ought to submit to be bartered like a broken-down plow horse."[8]

George Stovall, 1912 (George Grantham Bain Collection, Library of Congress).

So, when the opportunity to join the Federal League came along, Stovall jumped at it. Upon signing, he was quoted as saying, "someone had to be first [to challenge the reserve clause] and it might as well be I."[9]

On November 2, 1913, the same day it was announced Stovall would manage the Kansas City franchise, the *Buffalo Express* proclaimed that Buffalo, New York, would have a Federal League team in 1914 and former major league player and minor league manager Larry Schlafly would be its playing manager. Larry played in the major leagues with the Chicago Cubs in 1902 and the Washington Nationals in 1906–1907, normally as a second baseman. Another fiery competitor, Larry was popular with players and fans. In 1907, Schlafly was named team captain by Washington manager Joe Cantillon and assumed the latter's duties when the manager was away from the club. Schlafly later served as manager of Toronto (Eastern League), and manager and part-owner of Troy (New York State League).

After leading the New York State League in batting, Larry was drafted by the New York Highlanders following the 1911 season. Schlafly did not return to the American League, because the lowly Jersey City Skeeters of the International League purchased his contract and made him manager for 1912. In each of the three preceding seasons, the Skeeters had finished at least 26 games out of first place. On July 10, 1913, the record of Schalfly's Jersey City team was 38–42, so management decided to sell off the best players. A disgusted Schlafly resigned that August.[10]

The new Buffalo Federal League franchise landed a capable business manager in Richard T. Carroll, a former major league pitcher. A product of the Cleveland sandlots, Carroll broke into baseball with Akron of the Pennsylvania-Ohio League in 1909, and was purchased by the New York Highlanders of the American League later that season. Carroll pitched only five innings for New York manager George Stallings, and found himself back in the minors the following season. Carroll bounced around in the bush leagues for three years, but when he was sent to Jersey City for 1913, he refused to report. Though Dick was only twenty-nine, the Federal League bosses recognized his talents and hired him for their push into the ranks of major league baseball.

At the Federal League's Board of Managers' annual meeting at the Hotel LaSalle in Chicago on November 15, 1913, James Gilmore's status of acting Federal League president was changed when he was elected full president. M.F. Bramley of Cleveland was chosen vice president, John George of Indianapolis was elected treasurer, and Lloyd Rickart was appointed secretary and assistant treasurer. Gilmore established the league's offices in the upscale Old Colony Building in Chicago and he reportedly would receive a salary of $15,000 as president of the Federal League for 1914.

While Buffalo and Baltimore were welcomed into the Federal League, it appeared Cleveland was on the way out. Cleveland was a charter member of the Federal League in 1913 and chief owner Fred Bramley expected to keep the club in the expanded league. He had already made plans to secure several of the local Americans players. However, President Gilmore and the other leaders of the league did not feel Cleveland's franchise was sustainable if the team continued to play games at Luna Park. Bramley was informed that Cleveland would not retain its franchise unless some other park, better located, was obtained. Bramley tried, but the Cleveland American League club's owner, Charles Somers, blocked his efforts at every turn. Bramley did manage to get an option on a site two blocks beyond the Cleveland Americans' park, but Gilmore would not approve it, fearing that the Naps, contenders for the pennant in 1913, would pull in the majority of the patronage if the Federals' fans had to pass Somers Park.[11]

The strategy employed by Ban Johnson in 1901 to bring his American League into direct competition with the Nationals was not lost on the newcomers. Like the American League, the Federal League went head to head with the existing major leagues in key cities, placing their strongest club in Chicago. As Johnson's league had done in 1901, the Federal League ignored baseball's reserve clause and signed major league players not under a current contract. Both the American and Federal Leagues had strong chief executives with the ability and single-mindedness to achieve the ultimate goal.

When Ban Johnson criticized the Federals for not respecting the reserve clause of major league contracts, Gilmore told the press, "No man should respect that clause. I don't think it is equitable to the ball player, because it is a clause that binds him practically for life without stipulating any salary after the first year."[12]

Gilmore's greatest success was in his ability to interest successful businessmen of considerable wealth to invest in his new major league. Sports writers nicknamed him "Glib Jim" and "Gabby Jim" because he had a remarkable gift of gab. *The Sporting News* wrote that Gilmore "could sell slices of green cheese out of the moon."

"Where Powers was perfectly contented to peacefully pass through the Federal League villages and review the respective teams in combat, Mr. Gilmore preferred to decorate his own battleground and seek his own amenities," opined *The Sporting News*.[13]

The *Washington Post* wrote of Gilmore's salesmanship, "Three minutes talk with him made the old dyed-in-wool, blown-in-the-bottle baseball scribes rub their eyes and wonder how a yelping baseball public ever got along without a third baseball league."[14]

During the ensuing months, Gilmore went about wooing wealthy businessmen to join the Federal League's chancy baseball venture. He sold them on the idea that baseball's recent prosperity, unprecedented attendance figures and profits, and construction of new ballparks, were proof that another baseball league was a solid investment. Among those enthusiasts that signed on for Gilmore's Federal League venture was Charles Weeghman, proprietor of a string of Chicago lunchrooms.

Neither the Federals nor the Americans years earlier could have gone forward without a wealthy investor to bankroll needy franchises. James Gilmore would find his "angel" in Robert B. Ward. Fourteen years earlier, Ban Johnson enlisted the support of Charles W. Somers, a thirty-year-old millionaire coal magnate. Somers bankrolled the Cleveland American League Club, invested in Connie Mack's Philadelphia Athletics, loaned Charles Comiskey the cash he needed to launch the White Sox, furnished money to put a franchise in Boston, and gave the Americans the financial capital they needed to sign many of the National League's best players. Somers was among the first in Organized Baseball to recognize the Feds' similarities with the American League's origins and view the newcomers as a serious threat.

"We're going to have our hands full," the Cleveland club owner told New York sports writer Frank G. Menke. "You fellows can spoof the Feds all you want. But to me it seems they aren't going about this business with any fly-by-night methods. They are building for the future. We'd better give them real consideration right now before this matter goes to a point where we'll be forced into some ugly position."[15]

Despite Somers' warning, through November and most of December the minions of Organized Baseball pointed out that the only Federal League signing of any note was the maverick ex-manager of the Browns, George Stovall, who at thirty-six, was over the hill as a player.

"I know the [Federal League] clubs lost something like $15,000 each during their 1913 season and suppose for this reason people are cheery about investing in the league," remarked George Tebeau, president of the Kansas City American Association club. "I believe if I were to offer $100,000 for the league — lock, stock and barrel — my money would be gobbled up in an instant, and the club owners would be glad of the 'chance' to 'come out' with their losses paid."[16]

Ed Cochrane of the *Kansas City Journal* editorialized, "When the Federal League hurled its 'bomb' at organized baseball in Indianapolis, the explosion was hardly as loud as we had expected, considering the amount of chatter that came from the various magnates previous to the occasion. They declared war, they said, but if the firing of the opening gun is a criterion of the battle which is to follow, the fans may settle back in their seats and prepare for a rather uninteresting comedy."[17]

The early perceptions about the "outlaws" would all change the day after Christmas, 1913, when one of the National League's most visible stars signed a large contract to play for the Federal League's Chicago club.

3

Lucky Charley

On Christmas Eve, 1913, Charlie Murphy, the brash owner of the Chicago Cubs, told a reporter that the Federal League was a joke and Charley Weeghman had told him he was not going to finance the local club. "I do not think Tinker will sign with the Federal League," Murphy declared. "All this talk of offering him $40,000 is nothing but a bluff."[1]

Only three days later, the joke would be on Murphy when Charles Weeghman was announced as the new president of the Chicago Federal League Club. The same day, Joe Tinker became the first big-name player to sign with the upstart league.

"Charles Weeghman has been a close friend," explained James Gilmore in March 1914,

> and when he told me he saw a chance to succeed if we could get money behind the other clubs, I assured him that money would come as soon as we showed the goods. The first great stroke of our career during the past winter was the signing of Joe Tinker. Weeghman's willingness to take a chance gave me confidence. Here was a restaurant and moving picture theater owner who had arrived in Chicago at the time of the World's Fair with $3.50 in his pocket, ready to pay out $36,000, a lump sum of $10,000 in cash, for the privilege of signing a player for a league that was just creeping. Otto Stifel, a millionaire brewer of St. Louis, went after Mordecai Brown and that helped in establishing my confidence.[2]

Joseph Bert Tinker's parents wanted their only son to have a "real" career as a wallpaper hanger. Instead, Joe defied his parents and became a professional baseball player at age nineteen. After only two years in the bush leagues, Tinker joined the Chicago Cubs in 1902 as a shortstop and became part of the most famous double-play combination in the history of baseball.

For eleven seasons, Joe Tinker was the shortstop immortalized in Franklin P. Adams's poem "Baseball's Saddest Lexicon" about the Cubs' double-play combination of "Tinker to Evers to Chance." Joe was an average hitter, possessed superior speed and played outstanding defense. He led National League shortstops four times in fielding percentage while playing in the same era as Honus Wagner and Mickey Doolan. Joe stole at least twenty bases each season he played in Chicago and tied a major league record on July 28, 1910, when he stole home twice in one game.

Ironically, Tinker didn't get along with his second base partner in the middle of the Cubs' infield. Johnny Evers, which rhymes with "weavers," was known as "The Crab" for the way he scurried around second base, as well as for his abrasive personality.

The keystone combination rarely spoke to each other after September 14, 1905, when they got into a fist fight during an exhibition game in Bedford, Indiana. There are several versions as to the cause of the feud, but according to the late Lee Allen of the Baseball Hall of Fame, the problem arose out of dispute over a ride from their hotel to the ballpark. Evers left by himself in a hack, leaving Tinker and others standing at the curb. Joe wasn't happy about it and when he finally made it the ballpark, the shortstop verbally assaulted Evers.

Tinker fumed over the taxi snub until the middle of the game, when the pair went at it right on the field. A day after the fight, Tinker told Evers they'd be better off just playing their positions and not speaking to one another unless it was absolutely necessary.

Evers was said to have replied, "That suits me!"

The players' strained relationship continued, season after season, through four National League championship seasons and two World Series victories. Tinker and Evers played side by side for the next five years, avoiding each other as much as possible.

After their playing days were over, the hard feelings softened. At Cooperstown in 1946, Evers and Tinker stood together one more time as they were inducted into the National Baseball Hall of Fame.

"Joe was there when I walked in," said Evers. "We hadn't seen each other for years. And do you know what we did? We rushed together, threw our arms around each other and cried like a couple of kids."[3]

Tinker reached his prime both as a hitter and fielder when he entered his thirties. In 1912 he achieved career highs in runs scored and runs batted in. Following that season, Cubs owner Charles Murphy appointed Evers to replace Frank Chance as manager. Tinker refused to play under his double-play partner, and on December 12 he was traded to the Cincinnati Reds as the cornerstone of an eight-player deal. As playing manager of the Reds, Joe achieved career highs in batting average (.317) and fielding average (.968), but his club finished with a 64–89 record.

Tinker's boss in Cincinnati was August "Garry" Herrmann, one of baseball's characters. He became president of the Reds in 1902 when the current president, Julius Fleischmann, became mayor of Cincinnati. Garry had been president of the board of the waterworks commission and a ward politician. The portly Reds owner was an entertaining fellow and his parties at the World Series and the National League's annual meetings were the centers of attraction. Herrmann was a connoisseur of sausage and he often carried his own whenever he traveled. He often included in his correspondence the comment, "I am sending you a package of sausage and hope that you will try it."[4]

Tinker had a frustrating season in 1913. He wasn't accustomed to playing on a team with a losing record. On the other hand, it was said the young Reds did not flourish under the Cubs' style of discipline employed by Tinker.

The losing ways began to grate on the manager. Tinker and Otto Knabe of the Phillies were suspended for five days and fined for a fight in Cincinnati that July. In September Joe was fined $50 for fighting with Rabbit Maranville and Hap Myers of the Boston Braves. Tinker was also suspended for three days for using abusive language to umpire Hank O'Day.

Following the seventh-place finish by the Reds in 1913, Tinker was sold to Brooklyn during the off season. The transaction started out as a joke between Herrmann and Brooklyn owner Charles Ebbets at the National League's annual meeting at the Waldorf-Astoria in New York that December. Herrmann was there in the dual role as president of the Reds and chairman of the National Commission. Garry didn't spend much time upstairs in meetings, but instead held court in the Waldorf's famous bar.

New York sports writer Fredrick Lieb described Herrmann's daily activity:

> Garry sat at one large table, surrounded by old-time baseball writers, fellow club owners who ducked the meeting, minor leaguers and other baseball cronies. As new arrivals came into the big room, Garry beckoned a waiter to push their table up to his, with the usual: "See what the boys will have."

From time to time, Garry grabbed a fistful of checks, and without ever looking at the amount, stuffed them into his pocket. When the meetings were over, he dumped them all out on the bar and told the head barkeep to bill him for the entire amount.[5]

The meeting that year was unusually quiet. No trades had been made, but a rumor made the rounds that Ebbets had offered to purchase Cincinnati's shortstop/manager Joe Tinker. Led by Bill McBeth of the *New York Morning Sun,* the sports writers goaded Garry to make a deal with Ebbets. Herrmann suggested a trade for Brooklyn's young star outfielder, Zach Wheat, but the usually tightfisted Ebbets told the Cincinnati owner he would buy Tinker for $25,000 instead. Garry promptly accepted. The two owners never imagined that their impulsive deal set in motion a chain of events that would cost Organized Baseball several millions of dollars.

An hour after the Tinker deal was done, the St. Louis and Pittsburgh clubs completed one of the biggest trades in National League history. The Pirates sent five players to the Cardinals for pitcher Bob Harmon, third baseman Mike Mowrey and first baseman Ed Konetchy. The key man in that trade was Konetchy, in another deal that would have ramifications on the war with the Federal League.

Unbeknown to Ebbets, Joe Tinker had already received an offer to manage the Federal League's club in Chicago. Tinker had long brooded about the restrictions baseball put on its players. He was a holdout in 1909 when he demanded a $1000 raise from the Cubs, but eventually settled for a $200 increase. With the offer from the Federals in his pocket, Tinker requested $10,000 of the purchase money in the Brooklyn deal. Herrmann at first thought his former manager was bluffing, but finally agreed to give up the $10,000.

The Tinker deal was further held up when the Fleischmann faction on the Cincinnati board of directors objected to giving a player part of the purchase price. The Chicago club's owner Charles Murphy stirred the pot by announcing he wanted Tinker back with the Cubs.

When he initially read of his trade to Brooklyn in the newspaper, Tinker was not happy. Days passed and Joe did not hear from the Dodgers. Wishing to ascertain his status with the club, Tinker sent two telegrams to Charles Ebbets. "I wanted to know where I stood, whether the story of the $10,000 bonus really went," he said. His wires went unanswered.

Finally, Tinker received a telephone call from Manager Wilbert Robinson, who said that Ebbets was angry because Joe had wired him and asked about the bonus and terms. Joe told reporter Bill Bailey of the *Chicago American* that the Dodgers offered him a salary of $5,000 a year for three years and bonus of $10,000.

"I was to go to the National League meeting in New York in February," said Joe. "The contract and the certified checks would be there. There would be a group of newspaper photographers. There would be a little party and the check would be photographed.... The deal with the Federal League had been completed and I had decided to cast my fortunes with them, even if the contract had not been signed."[6]

Eventually, the Cincinnati directors reluctantly approved the sale of Tinker to Brooklyn. Ebbets dispatched Wilbert Robinson to pay his new shortstop the promised $10,000. However, Tinker was dissatisfied with the $7,500 salary offer by Brooklyn and remained resolute about signing with the Federal League instead. When Robinson arrived in Chicago, Tinker was in Indianapolis and the newspapers were reporting Joe was a Federal Leaguer. When Herrmann refused to return the money he received for Tinker, Ebbets was out $15,000, though the Reds later shipped a couple of insignificant players to Brooklyn.

The day after Christmas, 1913, Joe Tinker signed a three-year contract for $36,000 to manage and play for Charles Weeghman's Chicago Federal League club. Unlike in Cincinnati, Tinker was assured he would have a comparatively free hand in obtaining players for the

Joe Tinker, manager, Chicago Federal League club, 1914–15 (National Baseball Hall of Fame Library, Cooperstown, N.Y.

club. Another bonus: Tinker would be able to play half his games in Chicago, where he had business interests and where he had wanted to play all along.

"I'm a Federal Leaguer from now on," he announced. "I'm a stockholder in the club, too."[7]

The signing of Tinker revived baseball interest in the Windy City and by the end of January a Chicago Federal League booster club announced it had a membership of 14,000.

On the heels of Tinker's defection, his former teammate, Mordecai "Three-Finger" Brown, joined the Federal League as manager-pitcher for the St. Louis franchise. At first there was disbelief among the organized major leagues, and many predicted that Tinker and Brown would come to their senses and return to the National League.

"I doubt very much that Tinker and Brown were foolish enough to sign with the Federal League," Ban Johnson commented. "If they really severed their relations with the National League they have acted unwisely, for I don't believe the Federals will be able to keep out of the ditch in mid-season."[8]

Charles Ebbets finally got his face-to-face meeting with Joe Tinker during an exchange at the La Salle Hotel in Chicago on January 16. The pair had a brief talk and parted amicably after Joe told the Dodgers' owner he was committed to the Federal League. Ebbets told the press that he would make no effort to prevent Tinker from joining the Federals, but if Joe decided to report to the Dodgers, he still would receive the $10,000 bonus."[9]

Probably no other city except Chicago could have produced a Charley Weeghman, backer of the City's new Federal League club. Known locally as "Lucky Charley" because of his rapid rise and willingness to take a chance, Weeghman did everything in a grand manner, and even his dress was dapper. Columnist Harry Neily wrote, "He might have served as an illustration for a collar ad — you know — the sleek fellow with goose-grease in his hair."[10]

The son of a German-born blacksmith, Charles Henry Weeghman was seventeen and working in a jewelry store when he decided to leave his family's home in Richmond, Indiana, and go to Chicago in 1892. He got a job for $10 a week as a waiter at King's Restaurant on the South Loop. King's was a fashionable place frequented by politicians, mobsters, gamblers, sports figures, and newspapermen alike. Weeghman was a good waiter and soon became captain and eventually assistant manager, for which he received $35 a week. Charley's cut of the tips at King's topped the salary of many professionals.

Charley married Bessie Webb, the restaurant's twenty-year-old cashier, in 1899. For years, Mr. and Mrs. Weeghman had a unique relationship. Bessie was a good businesswoman and was the calming influence to her husband's big ideas. Charley was the salesman and the dreamer, while she handled the details of their investments.

In 1901 Weeghman put $500 he had saved into a $2,800 investment with two other men in a counter lunchroom. They rented a small store at Fifth Avenue and Adams Street that could accommodate twenty-one customers at a time. The venture began with only a hired cook, Charley's wife behind the cash register and the young restaurateur behind the counter in an apron. While managing the lunchroom Charley became acquainted with William Walker, who had just embarked on his career as a fish wholesaler. The lunchroom endeavor expanded into six more locations over six years, but Charley wanted to go out on his own. He sold out to his partners for $50,000 and opened his own establishment on Madison Street.[11]

Charley's new restaurant, referred to in Chicago as the "gold mine which made Weeghman," was a version of the old "Baltimore Lunch," an operation that maximized space by providing one-armed chairs for patrons. The restaurant was open twenty-four hours a day and eventually utilized 108 chairs that would accommodate an average of 5,000 customers daily. They made money from the start and began opening new eateries all over the downtown district.[12]

As Charley grew in stature because of his "fast-food business," he began to mingle with the upper crust of society. Eventually, his business of thirty lunchrooms and several bakeries was worth several million dollars. He owned a motion picture house at 58 West Madison Street, opened a pool hall called "Weeghman's," and dabbled in the film production business.

After James Gilmore dropped some eight thousand dollars in 1913 without any visible returns for his investment in the Chicago Federal League Club, he sought new backers to boost the financially starved organization. Charles Weeghman's wealth, coupled with his interest in baseball and a reputation as a risk taker, led Gilmore to seek out the restaurateur.

Charley was not a baseball novice. In 1911 he attempted to purchase the St. Louis Cardinals of the National League after its owner died and left the ball club to a niece. "I had two or three talks with representatives of Mrs. Britton, but there appeared no disposition on their part to come to terms for the sale of the club," he said. "...It is a disappointment to me as I am anxious to get into the national game as a magnate, sincerely believing that I could 'make good.' I will bide my time and perhaps in the near future there will be a change of heart on the part of Mrs. Britton in regard to the disposal of her club."[13]

A year later, Charley told of his first involvement with James Gilmore's Federal League venture: "'Now, Weeghman,' he said, with the bland expression of a disinterested friend, 'I have a fine business opening for you, but we need more financial resources. We are going to reorganize the club with a capitalization of fifty thousand dollars. If you will take twenty-six thousand dollars' worth of stock, that will give you control of the club.'"

When Weeghman questioned that fifty thousand would not be enough to finance the club, Gilmore responded, "Oh, no, all we want is fifty thousand dollars. There won't be any other expenses. That will be all the money we shall require."[14] Within a few weeks the name Weeghman was all over the newspapers.

After Charley had to put in another seven or eight thousand dollars above his original investment, he sought help from a long-time friend and business associate. He went to William Walker, his partner in a string of movie theaters, one of which Weeghman boasted had netted $25,000 in one year.

"I had a very dear friend, Bill Walker, a man with sporting blood and money," recalled Weeghman.

> We had been associated in various schemes and they had generally proved successful, so I took the necessary time off from my duties to look up Bill. Walker is a full-blown bug and likes baseball almost as much as he likes the fish market.
> ...I outlined the proposition to him. He didn't know much about it, but he had been associated with me on other things that panned out well, so he was enough of a gambler to take a chance, and he did. That was how Bill became my partner.[15]

William Murphy Walker would become the Chicago Feds' vice president and treasurer. After moving to Chicago from New Jersey at age eleven in 1879, Bill began working as a butter and egg seller for his father to help support the family. At sixteen, he went into the fish and oyster business with a seafood stand and eventually controlled the largest individual fish business west of the Atlantic Coast.

Bill established W.M. Walker, Inc., in 1900 and he headed the company until four months before his death in 1941. "The business grew and now I suppose my place is the largest wholesale market in the West," Walker said in 1914. "They tell me it is, anyway, and I don't dispute them."

Walker had loved baseball since he played it as a boy on the sandlots and later as an amateur second baseman on Sundays. But he really got the baseball bug when he attended the famous "Merkle Game" that cost John McGraw's New York Giants the 1908 National League pennant won by the Cubs instead. Just as fellow Chicagoan James Gilmore gave Weeghman his opportunity to get into major league baseball, Weeghman provided that chance for Bill Walker.

Although Walker poured a large amount of money into the Chicago franchise, he was always content to remain in the background and let Lucky Charley garner all the publicity. "Nobody loves a fat man," he said, "so I keep in the background and let Weeghman do all the talking. I am interested in the venture as much as he and we both think we have a good proposition."[16]

The secretary and business manager for Weeghman's club would be Charles Green Williams, former treasurer and financial manager of the Chicago Cubs. Williams was well known in baseball circles for his mastery of *The Official Guide of the Railways,* and he was adept at arranging for players' Pullman cars to be attached to unscheduled mail trains. Williams was well respected by the players when secretary of the Cubs.

The Sporting News wrote that Williams "...did a great deal to smooth the way for [Frank]

Chance in handling them. He always had a chew of tobacco ready for a player when he was down in the dumps and a cheery word to brace him up."[17]

Fellow road secretary Willis Johnson of St. Louis once said, "Charley Williams, seemingly, not only knew everyone in Chicago, but most of the fans, theatrical people and hotel men around the country. He always wore a big smile, and had a good word for everyone."[18]

Williams's stepfather, John A. Brown, was treasurer of the Chicago National League Club for twenty-five years. Charles's mother was the club's official scorer from 1880 to 1890, in the days when the identity of the official scorer was carefully guarded. Even the league president did not know for years that the records were being kept by a woman.

Young Charles attended business school and went to work for Chicago National Bank, whose president, John R. Walsh, owned the local National League club. As a teller, Charles was entrusted with the ball club's deposits, which arrived after banking hours. In April 1898, Williams replaced his ill stepfather in the position of acting treasurer of the Chicago Nationals. Mr. Brown died on May 5 and Charley officially assumed the position. When the club was sold to Charles Murphy in 1905, Williams was named secretary-treasurer, a position he held until January 1914 when he resigned following a dispute with the owner.

Williams was the first active official of a major league club to jump to the Federal League. Though a businessman through and through, Williams went to work for Charley Weeghman without a contract. The ex-Cub official was told he would be "cared for" if anything happened to the new league. "That was good enough for me," explained Williams, "when I learned the caliber of the men with whom I was dealing."[19]

The Chicago Federal League Club had been known as "Keeleys" (for their manager) and Brownies in 1913, but neither nickname would survive after that first season. Though a newspaper competition was launched in early 1914 to suggest a name for the Chicago Federals, none of the proposals generated enough support to be adopted by President Weeghman. Suggestions submitted included Buns, Chics, and Pies, and someone nominated Whales. Eventually, the company name Chicago Federals was shortened to Chifeds and that became the favorite appellation among the press.[20]

4

"A Fifty Per Cent Raise Looked Too Good to Turn Down"

On January 5, 1914, it was announced that Otto Knabe, long-time second baseman of the Philadelphia Phillies, had signed a contract to manage and play for the Baltimore Federal League Club. Back in the fall, Knabe had been offered the job of manager with the Pittsburgh Federals, but he turned it down. Ned Hanlon traveled to Philadelphia determined to get his man and brought Knabe back to Baltimore with him. This time the money was right.

"I am very sorry to see Knabe leave the National League, but under existing conditions it is easy to see why he signed with the Federal League," President John Tener of the National League acknowledged.

> Knabe will receive $30,000 for three years. The situation in his case closely resembles that of Joe Tinker. Knabe is 30 years of age, and probably figured that he has not much more than three years left in which he might play in the majors. He is probably out to get all the money in this one and one can hardly blame him, although I am sorry to see him take the flop. He is a manly little fellow, a good ball player and a credit to the profession.[1]

Knabe was a player in the style of Hanlon's old Orioles teams. A roughhousing second baseman, Otto joined the Phillies in 1907 and he and shortstop Mickey Doolan played side by side in the middle of the Phillies' infield for seven seasons. With Knabe on one side of second base and Doolan on the other, opposing base runners entered their territory at their peril.

Upon his return to Philadelphia after a banquet with Baltimore Federal League officials, Knabe gave a statement to the press:

> The Baltimore stockholders treated me very liberally, and I can't lose out. I have half my money now.
> Signing with the Federals was simply a matter of business. Any other man in organized baseball, I think, if placed in a similar situation, would do exactly as I have done — better my financial situation.[2]

When Otto Knabe was announced as the new manager of the "Monumentals," as the press was already calling the team, the city of Baltimore was ecstatic. During a performance at the Maryland Theater, the audience erupted in an explosion of applause when one of the actors mentioned Otto. Then the actor turned to the audience and announced, "Wait till you folks see Knabe around second base. Take it from me, that boy is some ballplayer." The crowd responded with an even louder outburst of applause and whistles accompanied by the stamping of feet.[3]

The same day Knabe became the third big-name baseball star to sign with the Federal League, Garry Herrmann, National Commission Chairman, released Organized Baseball's first explicit warning to the Federals not to infringe on the rights of the clubs under the National Agreement.

"The Federal League, which operated clubs in 1913 in territory occupied by the national agreement clubs, did not attain prosperity or prestige," his statement read.

> A passive policy has been pursued by the Commission and the leagues directly affected by that organization, but if the contractive and reservation rights of the national agreement clubs are not respected by its promoters, it may become necessary to employ strenuous measures for the protection of the interests of major and minor league clubs.
>
> Rivalry will not be resented so long as league and club rights are not ignored, but illegal and unsportsmanlike interference with and utter disregard of established privileges of national agreement clubs will justify the adoption of vigorous defensive methods.[4]

Federal League chief counsel Edward Gates issued a response to Herrmann's declaration: "We have said over and over again that we will not attempt to get any player to break a contract in spite of the actions of the major league clubs last summer in trying themselves what they would term 'unsportsmanlike' on us."[5]

Gates apparently was referring to Organized Baseball's attempt in 1913 to prevent the Federal League's scores from being posted on the Western Telegraph ticker. The latest threat from Organized Baseball did little to deter major league ball players from talking with Federal League agents.

Mordecai Brown was regarded as one of the most celebrated pitchers in the game when he arrived in St. Louis the first week of January 1914. In the course of an interview with Sidney Keener, sports editor of the *St. Louis Times*, Brown remarked:

> Ball players in the organized field are disgusted with the movement of the American and National Leagues and for years the players have been waiting for just such a league as the Federal. The boys jumped years ago when the American League arrived because they were shown the money and they will jump for the same reason today.
>
> Organized base ball does nothing for the player. You don't know how long your job will last and when your salary is going to be cut. The contract of the Federal League is altogether different. The Federal League cannot release me and is forced to pay me the salary for three years. Who wouldn't jump at a chance like this?[6]

On January 8, Otto Knabe took a handful of Federal League contracts with him for a meeting with National League players Jimmy Sheckard, Runt Walsh and Enos Kirkpatrick in Pittsburgh. Meanwhile, Joe Tinker headed for Kansas City to talk with Pittsburgh Pirates hurler Claude Hendrix.

A day later, the Chicago Federal League Club announced the names of four players Manager Tinker had signed to three-year contracts: catcher Bill Killefer and pitcher Ad Brennan of the Philadelphia Phillies, pitcher Eugene Packard of the Cincinnati Reds, and pitcher Leonard "King" Cole of the New York Americans.

Philadelphia baseball columnist William Weart bemoaned:

> In the war [1901–02] with the American League, the Phillies were absolutely riddled. There was scarcely a remnant of the great team of sluggers left after the American Leaguers got through with the combination owned by the late John T. Rogers and A.J. Reach. It took two years to turn the trick, but it must be admitted that a mighty good job was made after the raiders got down to work.
>
> The Federals already have a big start towards making history repeat by signing Knabe, Killefer and Brennan and making offers to other members of [manager] Dooin's Daisies.[7]

4. "A Fifty Per Cent Raise Looked Too Good to Turn Down"

William Walker (left), James Gilmore and Charles Weeghman at the Chifeds' spring training site, Shreveport, Louisiana, 1914 (Chicago History Museum, SDN-009993. Original photograph has been cropped).

The Chicago offices of the Federal League were a hubbub of activity following the early signings of Tinker and Brown. Russell Ford and Ed Sweeney, battery mates on the New York Americans, showed up at the Feds' offices in the Old Colony Building to meet with Joe Tinker and Charley Weeghman. The same day, Philadelphia Phillies pitcher Howard Camnitz had a meeting with the Pittsburgh Federals' manager, Doc Gessler.

After George Stovall signed Art Kreuger of the Los Angeles Angels for his Kansas City Federal League team, Owen R. Bird of the *Los Angeles Times* had cause to write:

It is a well-known fact that every time a major league club secures a good Coast League player it costs the big league club about $5000 on the average, just for sale price. Now, the point is this: It does not cost the Federal League any such an amount for a starter; in fact, there is no sale price to be figured at all, so they can well afford to pay $3000 or more, for a good player and still be making money. The average salary in the Coast League is $2500 per season, so the Federal managers are getting classy ball players for $500 more salary and not cent of sale price.[8]

In addition to Krueger, Stovall's west coast trips landed Federal League contracts for catcher Ted Easterly, a five-year American League veteran who played in 60 games for the Chicago White Sox in 1913, Portland centerfielder Chet Chadbourne, New York Giants catcher Art Wilson, and twenty-two-year-old Angels infielder Claire Goodwin. It took only a $25 a month raise to get "Pep" Goodwin, a University of California product who had batted .275 in 104 games with Los Angeles in his only season of professional baseball.

Salaries promised by the Federal League money men shocked the owners of the existing major league teams. Regardless of the number and quality of the players Organized Baseball lost to the Federals, the strength of major league rosters undoubtedly suffered.

Organized Baseball's magnates, unwilling to allow their rosters to be depleted without a fight, made plans to thwart the raiders. National League club owners secretly met with President Tener in Pittsburgh and decided on a plan to tie up the Federal League's best players in legal entanglements that would prevent them from playing while the suits were pending. The same strategy had been used in the cases of Napoleon Lajoie and other Philadelphia Phillies players after they jumped to the American League in 1901. Organized Baseball also amended the rules of the National Commission to specify a three-year suspension for reserve-rule jumpers and a five-year suspension for contract breakers. Injunctions would be sought to prevent players from playing for the Federals, but eventually all were overturned. In the end, Organized Baseball had to upgrade its own salaries to keep from losing their best players.

Another problem for the National League was its rule requiring clubs to pare rosters to 21 men, although more than that number could be under contract. The roster reduction made it inevitable that players would be sent to the minors even though they would continue to receive their major league salary. A scenario would be played out on several occasions where players chose to jump to the Federal League rather than submit to a demotion to the bush leagues.

Although the Federals were unable to sign any of Organized Baseball's most dominant stars, it was not from lack of effort. Back in November, Eddie Collins said he turned down $50,000 for three years based on an annual salary of $15,000 plus interest. It was reported Honus Wagner was offered a $15,000 two-year contract by President John Barbour of the Pittsburgh Federals. Rebuffed by Wagner, Barbour then tendered a three-year deal to Brooklyn's star first baseman, Jake Daubert, for $30,000.[9] Baltimore's Otto Knabe unsuccessfully courted Philadelphia's Gavvy Cravath to join the Terrapins for two seasons at $6,000 per and a $4000 bonus. Washington's Walter Johnson and the Red Sox' Smoky Joe Wood declined three-year contract offers of $30,000 plus a bonus of $10,000 from Joe Tinker because each had already signed contracts with their current American League clubs. Sam Weller reported in the *Chicago Daily News* that James Gilmore sent Christy Mathewson an offer of $65,000 for three years, $25,000 to be paid in advance, but received no reply.[10]

Among the former major leaguers to play for the Federal League, several were past their prime, but well known to the average baseball fan. More players would have jumped to the new league but for the fear of not being allowed to ever return to Organized Baseball. Others merely used the Federal League threat as a bargaining tool to get better contracts from their current clubs.

Following the 1913 baseball season, Philadelphia's Connie Mack secured waivers on outfielder Danny Murphy with the intent to send the Athletics' former captain to Baltimore of the International League. Mack said he did not release Murphy and promised to do certain things for the twelve-year American League veteran if he would play for Jack Dunn. The Baltimore deal was kept secret until Danny sold his café, the "White Elephant," in Norwich, Connecticut. The fact that Murphy went to another club merely as a player rather than manager as some of Mack's faithful had done was not lost on the player. Instead of reporting to Baltimore, the thirty-seven-year-old outfielder signed a three-year contract with the Brooklyn Federal League Club that March.[11]

Arthur "Solly" Hofman, veteran of four Chicago National League champions, was another player to take the plunge. He batted .325 while the regular centerfielder on the 1910 champions. His baseball skills declined after he was hit in the head by a pitch in the summer of 1911 and Hofman was traded to Pittsburgh the following year. After playing in only 28 games for the Pirates in 1913, the outfielder refused to report to Kansas City of the American Association and asked to be sold to a team in the Pacific Coast League instead. A month later, Pittsburgh sold him to Nashville of the Southern League, where he played at a salary of $300 a month. On July 14, 1913, Hofman filed suit against his former Chicago club for the loss of his major league pay ($5,000 for the 1912 season) because he was sent to the minor leagues. Unhappy with the demotion to Nashville, Hofman signed a Federal League contract in March 1914 for $7,000. In 1915, an Illinois Court of Appeals granted the eleven-year major league veteran a judgment of $2944.47 in back pay due him from the Cubs.[12]

Al Bridwell was a nine-year National League veteran, mostly with the Giants and Braves, who signed with the Cubs in 1913 for $4,000 to fill the shortstop position vacated when Joe Tinker was traded to Cincinnati. That season, the light-hitting Bridwell hit his first home run in 3,246 major league at-bats with a round-tripper off Cincinnati's George Suggs. An offer of $6,500 following the season led him to join the St. Louis Federals in 1914.

Commenting about his decision to jump leagues, Bridwell said, "...a fifty per cent raise looked too good to turn down."[13]

Even journeyman players received Federal League contracts with compensation well above comparable wages in Organized Baseball. Boston Braves catcher Bill Rariden signed a three-year contract with Indianapolis for $6000 per season, although he had not appeared behind the plate in more than 87 games in any season, and had just completed his best year at bat, hitting a robust .236. Outfielder Vin Campbell, who had been out of the major leagues for a full year, was paid $8500 to play in Indianapolis.

Following a lengthy session of two committees of the Federal League on January 14, 1914, Charles Weeghman announced that 83 major league ball players would play with the league in 1914, and 44 additional athletes, including players from Class AA and smaller leagues, were also under contract to the new circuit. More important to the Chicagoans were the announcements that the local Federals had signed Rollie Zeider, a New York Yankees infielder, and Claude Hendrix, a pitcher for the Pittsburgh Pirates.

Claude Ray Hendrix was born in Oleathe, Kansas, where his father was a banker and sheriff of Johnson County. Claude played for the Wichita State Shockers in 1908 while he was a student at Fairmount Academy. Sports teams in the university's early days included athletes from the local high school level academy, which was part of W.S.U.'s predecessor, Fairmount College. Hendrix bounced between the minor leagues and semi-pro teams for the next three years. In 1910 Claude pitched with the touring club called the Cheyenne Indians at a salary of $175 a month plus expenses. The team barnstormed throughout Colorado, Wyoming, New Mexico, Texas and Western Kansas. Hendrix was credited with winning thirty-eight games for the Indians while losing only eight.

After gaining the attention of Pittsburgh manager Fred Clarke, Hendrix joined the Pirates in 1911. The Kansan fashioned a 24–9 record for the Pirates in his second season in the major leagues. During the Pirates' spring training in 1913, Hendrix injured his arm while playing soccer on a day when it was too wet to practice. Diagnosed with strained tendons in the elbow, the big right-hander found that his spitball wasn't as effective that season and his win total slipped to fourteen.[14]

Out of favor with the Pirates, Hendrix was receptive to the overtones from the Chicago Federals. In January Claude married his hometown sweetheart and elected to play for the Federal League. Claude was known as a dandy who was a flashy dresser and the additional income would help him with his wardrobe bills. The twenty-five-year-old spitballer was signed by R.D. Buckingham of the Chicago club for an annual salary of $7,000, with $5,000 paid in advance.

Joe Tinker also scoured the minor leagues for prospective gems. In late January he raided the St. Joseph Drummers and carried off two of their most popular players, Edward "Dutch" Zwilling and George "Tex" Westerzil. Westerzil was with the Detroit Tigers during the 1911 pre-season, but the promising infielder tore up his knee that spring and missed the entire season. Tex went to St. Joseph in 1912, and, after batting .305 in the Western League a year later, he signed with Tinker. When the Federal League divided its players later that spring, Westerzil went to the Brooklyn club and played 149 games at third base during the 1914 season.

As a twenty-one-year-old rookie in 1910, Zwilling played in 27 games with the White Sox and batted .184. Dutch played the next two seasons with St. Joseph, Missouri, of the Western Association. After batting .306 in 1913, he gave up his $250 a month job with the Drummers to sign with the Chicago Federals.

Amid all the good news for the Federal Leaguers there would be setbacks. Leonard "King" Cole of the New York Americans signed a contract to play for the Chicago Federal League Club and took $800 in advance. Unfortunately, it was discovered in February that Cole had signed a contract with the New York club back on December 23, 1913, for $3,000.

Cole returned to the Yankees and repaid the advance money to the Federals. A letter, purportedly from Cole to Charles Weeghman, accused President Gilmore of changing the date of his contract so that it would appear to have been signed before Cole accepted the Yankees' terms. Ring Lardner gave King Cole literary immortality by writing about him in articles for *The Sporting News* which later emerged as the "Alibi Ike" stories. According to Lardner, Cole was a slow-thinking poker player who was threatened with a $50 fine by New York manager Frank Chance unless he quit spoiling poker games with his erratic play during road trips.[15]

Chicago, Baltimore and Indianapolis got a jump on other Federal League clubs in signing players. By mid–January, in addition to Otto Knabe as manager, Baltimore claimed to have signed Enos Kirkpatrick (Brooklyn N.L.), Runt Walsh (Philadelphia N.L.), Guy Zinn (Boston N.L.), Mike Mowrey (Pittsburgh N.L.), Cozy Dolan (St. Louis N.L.) and Frank Smith, formerly of the White Sox. Ultimately, Mowrey and Dolan stayed with their National League clubs for the 1914 season.

Around the first of the year, Enos Kirkpatrick of the Brooklyn Dodgers inked a contract to play with the Baltimore Federals, getting $1,000 up front for his signature. Then in February, Enos met with Brooklyn Dodgers manager Wilbert Robinson and resigned with him. Three weeks later Kirkpatrick became king of the jumpers when he flopped again, notifying Harry Goldman that he was returning to Baltimore.

Though the new Baltimore Federal League Club practiced an unwritten rule not to tamper with players on the Baltimore Orioles, Hanlon's club exacted a large toll from other International League rosters. Among their recruits for the 1914 season, the Baltimore Federals signed the Internationals' reigning batting champion, Hack Simmons of Rochester, and Newark's Harry Swacina, whose batting average of .325 was only .004 of a point behind Hack.

After tying the New York Americans' club record with six home runs in 1912, Guy Zinn was released to Rochester of the International League late in the season. He refused to report and then was sold to the Boston Braves in August 1913. Returned to Rochester following the end of the season and then sold to Louisville, Zinn jumped to the Baltimore Federals instead of remaining in Organized Baseball.

Two days before the meeting of the Federal League Board of Directors in November 1913, the Indianapolis club had announced the acquisition of a site for a ballpark on Kentucky Avenue that was within four blocks of the downtown business center. Work on the new ballpark's grandstand began January 27, 1914, after Mayor Joseph Gill turned the first spade of earth on the construction site.

A hitch in the Federals' plans arose when the truce that existed between the Indianapolis American Association club and the local Federal League club was ruptured after the Feds announced they had signed Benny Kauff, an outfielder the Indians had recently purchased. In retaliation, James C. McGill of the American Association franchise said that he would block work on the Federal League ballpark. McGill claimed the current city ordinance dictated that grandstands had to be built of steel and concrete, but the Federals were using wood for their stands.[16] Fortunately the grandstand of heavy timber construction was approved by the city's building inspectors on February 13, 1914.

Indianapolis chose to recruit the best available talent rather than sign "name" major league players. Of course, they had the nucleus from their 1913 Federal League championship team to build upon. Indianapolis would retain more players from its 1913 roster than other any Federal League club for the circuit's first season as a major league operation.

During the winter, Indianapolis hired one of baseball's venerated veterans as business manager. William "Wattie" Watkins got his first job as a baseball manager with St. Thomas, Ontario, in 1881 and won the provincial championship. In 1882 and 1883 he piloted Port Hudson to the championship of the Michigan State League and led Bay City to a tie for first in 1884. Wattie was originally a third baseman, but in 1884, at the age of twenty-nine, he was struck in the head by a ball and hovered for some time between life and death. His hair turned white overnight as result of the beaning.

Watkins had Indianapolis in first place when the Western League disbanded in 1885. He finished the season with the Detroit National League Club and piloted that team to the league championship in 1887, then beat the St. Louis Browns of the American Association in the post-season "World's Series." When Detroit withdrew from the National League after the 1888 season, Wattie managed several minor league teams until he became part owner of the Indianapolis American Association Club in 1907 and remained in that position until he retired in 1910 at the age of fifty-one.[17]

On March 9, 1914, Watkins announced the roster of players signed to play for the Indianapolis Federals during the upcoming season. Among the pitchers named was one Frederick "Cy" Falkenberg, and he, along with another pitcher, former Detroit Tiger George Mullin, were already at the team's spring training camp in Wichita Falls, Texas.

Mullin, at thirty-three, was pretty much finished as a major league hurler. After going 1 and 6 to start the 1913 season with Detroit, he was waived to Washington, which, in turn, released the veteran with 196 major league victories to Montreal of the International League. George jumped the Montreal club and played independent ball in Detroit until he got the opportunity to pitch for Bill Phillips. On the other hand, Falkenberg, only six months younger than Mullin, had just experienced the best season of his career and was considered one of the top pitchers in baseball.

Upon learning of Falkenberg's deal with the Federals on February 1, 1914, his former Cleveland employers made Cy "a very attractive proposition" to entice the star pitcher back to the American League. When the Feds saw stories of the counteroffer in the newspapers, Dick Carroll, who resided in Cleveland, was told to keep the pitcher in the fold until reinforcements arrived. However, Carroll could not convince Falky to pledge that he would remain with the Federal League. Later in the afternoon of that same day, Larry Schlafly showed up and held a long conference with Falkenberg. The Buffalo manager made Cy such a lucrative offer, the pitcher vowed to stand by the Feds. According to Cleveland sports columnist H.T. McDaniel, Otto Knabe completed the deal by depositing a certified check for $10,000 to Falkenberg's credit in a Cleveland bank. Cy had already received $5,000, bringing the total advance money to $15,000 on the pitcher's $21,000 three-year contract. In addition, the Federals agreed to pay the expenses of his wife and two children for their trip to spring training.[18]

Fred Falkenberg came out of the University of Illinois to begin his professional baseball career with Worcester (Eastern League) in 1902, winning 18 games and losing 11. First coming to the major leagues in 1903, up until 1913 Falkenberg could be best identified as a journeyman pitcher. The most games he won in one season were 14 for Washington in 1906. Baseball men were concerned the slender pitcher's meager weight of around 180 pounds on his 6'5" frame did not provide him with the endurance needed for the long baseball season. Falkenberg's main stock in trade was a baffling slow ball, christened the "fade away," which he mixed with a passable fast ball. Falky led the American League in free passes in 1906, but with age, Cy's control improved.

After going 8 and 5 in a part-time role with Cleveland in 1911, Falkenberg found himself in the minor leagues a year later. At age thirty-one and apparently on the downside of his career, Fred had to decide whether to remain a professional baseball player. After eight seasons in the majors he had won only 68 games and appeared done as a big league pitcher.

While Cy was with Toledo of the American Association in 1912, a teammate introduced him to a pitch that would revitalize his career. Falkenberg practiced the pitch during that season in the American Association, and was so successful, Cleveland recalled him the following year.

Falky took the American League by storm, winning his first ten decisions in 1913. His new pitch acted like a spitball — the ball started out at the batter's shoulders then suddenly dropped below the knees. But Cy did not use a spitball, nor did he throw the rarely used knuckle ball.

"Kid Gleason [coach with the White Sox] used to watch me like a hawk," chuckled Falkenberg.

"I know you are doing something to that ball. You must be doing something to get it to break in that way."

Another man who was very suspicious was Clark Griffith. Grif had been a pitcher himself and thought he knew something about the workings of a baseball. I have seen him go on the field and examine two or three of the balls that had been in use, take them up and look them carefully all over to see how they differed from other balls. The "Old Fox" was pretty keen, but he never read their secret...[19]

After he won 23 games in 1913, *Baseball Magazine* named Falkenberg as pitcher, along with Walter Johnson, on that year's "All-American League" team. During the spring of 1914, Cy held several meetings with Cleveland owner Charles Somers regarding a raise. The pitcher did not feel his $3,250 salary was commensurate with the year he just had. When Cleveland offered only a $500 raise, Falkenberg decided to join the Federal League.

"I was whisked away from Cleveland to the minors when I possessed major league ability," Cy told reporters after it became known he was defecting to the Feds.

> I showed that by leading the American Association in 1912. In 1913 I came back and worked under a salary almost equivalent to that of a recruit pitcher. And I won twenty-five games and lost ten for Cleveland in 1913. I feel that my "come back" increased the profits of the Cleveland club $50,000, and yet the contract I was expected to sign for next season granted me an increase in salary of $9.38 a week.[20]

Falkenberg told *Baseball Magazine*:

> Mr. Somers is in financial difficulties, I understand, which is unfortunate, for he is undoubtedly a fine man.... If he had come to me and made a substantial offer there wouldn't have been any kick at all on my part, and I would have signed at once for terms far less than I afterwards received from the Federal League. But he didn't do so, and I took the only good offer I had ever had. I was getting on in years and owed something to my family and to myself.[21]

Cleveland pitchers George Kahler and Fred Blanding also dickered with the Federals, but both decided to remain with the Indians. Blanding even accepted a $3,500 advance to sign a contract to play with the Kansas City Federals before he jumped back to his former American League club. Cleveland flopped to last place in 1914 and both of the pitchers who passed on Federal League contracts were gone from the major leagues for good.

During the winter of 1914, the chamber of commerce from the town of Wichita Falls, Texas, solicited several major league baseball clubs to spend spring training in its city. Federal League officials were impressed with the town's proposal and in February assigned two teams to spend their 1914 training sessions in North Texas. The Kansas City Federal League club arrived in Wichita Falls by train the afternoon of March 10. The trip was uneventful except for some lost luggage and the cow that was hit by their train's locomotive. The Indianapolis club's private car was scheduled to arrive later that night, but the group of fans that awaited them at the station was disappointed when the team did not arrive until the next day. The Hoosiers would open spring training at City Park, where a clubhouse with baths and a dressing room had been added for the professionals. The Packers would practice seven miles from town in the park at Lake Wichita, to where the city's streetcar line had recently been extended.

Once the two teams were settled, the Wichita Falls Chamber of Commerce sponsored a dinner and dance for the players at Lake Wichita Pavilion. A beef barbecue dinner was provided by a prominent Kansas City citizen, Colonel Luke Wilson. Hoosiers outfielder Benny Kauff had too much to drink and started to undo his trousers to prove to the event's hostess that he was wearing his signature silk underwear. A couple of his teammates rushed Benny out of the building while Bill McKechnie "handled the ruffled feathers of their hostess."[22] Benny was put to bed at the team's hotel with the hope he would be sober in time for the following day's exhibition game against Kansas City.

Benny apparently had recovered by game time at 3:30 the following afternoon. Although he only managed one hit in five at-bats, the Wichita Falls newspaper reported that center fielder Kauff "raked in six drives, two of them being plenty hard enough."[23]

During the two clubs' spring training, they would meet for four successive Sunday afternoon games. The first of these exhibitions occurred on March 15 at the Wichita Falls City Park field. A record crowd for "those parts" paid fifty cents for grandstand or twenty-five cents just to get into the park. An estimated 1200 bugs and the curious filled the grandstand and bleachers, while 100 more watched from parked automobiles. Kansas City won the sloppily played contest and the Packers would go on to win all four games between the two teams.

The highlight of the teams' stay in Texas was a weekday visit to Luke Wilson's Sixty Six Ranch in nearby Archer County. Most of the players had never been on a ranch and appeared to have a good time despite the wind and dust that blew on the way down. Once the teams' twenty-car caravan reached their destination, they ate a hefty meal of barbecue beef, watched a few wild-west stunts, shot at jackrabbits, and "enjoyed themselves wholeheartedly."

A number of the visitors brought firearms and target shooting was one of the day's activities. Kansas City Manager George Stovall carefully explained to a young woman how to handle a rifle, check the sights, and so forth, before she "seized the rifle and proceeded to pour a stream of lead into the middle of the target."[24]

During the night of March 26, rain fell in torrents and swamped the practice field at City Park where the Hoosiers were scheduled to practice. Just before noon the next day, the groundskeeper rode into town on horseback to report the park was in no condition for baseball. Indianapolis manager Whoa Bill Phillips mounted the man's horse and started out to see for himself. While crossing a culvert the horse shied and when Bill tried to dismount, the animal backed off the side. The horse fell on its back, pinning its rider underneath. Bruised but not broken, Phillips finally pulled himself from underneath the animal, brought the horse to his feet and swung into the saddle. Bill rode to the grounds then returned to the hotel. Manager Phillips attempted to keep the episode quiet because of his discomforting nickname, but the groundskeeper leaked the accident to the press.[25]

In any event, Phillips was forced to cancel the day's practice, although the pitchers and catchers would work out at a vacant lot near the center of town. After a short session the position players were excused from work and several of them found a local who would take them hunting. They rented rifles and shotguns, purchased ammunition and made a short hunting expedition. The day turned out sour for outfielder Vincent Campbell when he discovered the loss of a diamond ring that was a $150 gift from his mother.[26]

Upon departing the city on April 9, Kansas City club secretary Harry Neily pronounced, "I've been South with six teams and you can say for me that Wichita Falls is the best training camp I've ever seen. I can't imagine a more ideal arrangement and the players are completely satisfied."[27]

5

The Baseball Players' Fraternity

At about the same time the Federal League became a thorn in the side of Organized Baseball, another problem for the major leagues emerged in a suddenly activist players' union. The union, called the Baseball Players' Fraternity, was created in 1912 by former player and attorney Dave Fultz out of an effort to organize professional baseball players. The Fraternity's stated aim was to combat contract violations and ensure that no major leaguer would be paid less than he could earn in the minors.

Following the 1913 baseball season, the fledgling players' union stipulated that unless the major leagues included in their contracts certain conditions demanded by the Fraternity, its members would refuse to sign contracts for 1914. The maneuver not only carried the implied threat that unsigned players might defect to the Federal League, but it presented an opportunity for the outlaw league to challenge the legality of Organized Baseball's reserve clause in court.

Baseball's reserve clause went back to September 1879 when the National League's club owners, in an effort to keep players' salaries low, agreed that each team would reserve five players who could not be signed by any other team. There would be penalties against clubs that played exhibitions against "reserved" players in non-league games.

Initially, the players did not object to the policy because becoming "reserved" meant one was a valued commodity. The reserve rule was soon written into the standard contract for every player, binding that individual to the first team with which he signed, unless he was traded, released or retired. John Montgomery Ward, president of the National Brotherhood of Professional Baseball Players and a future executive with the Brooklyn Federal League club, remarked, "Like the fugitive slave law, the reserve rule denies him [the player] a harbor or a livelihood, and carries him back, bound and shackled, to the club from which he attempted to escape."[1]

Though there were several attempts to unionize baseball, the Players' Fraternity was only the second effort to gain marginal success. The Union Association in 1884 was advertised as a crusade by St. Louis millionaire Henry Lucas to end professional baseball players' "bondage." However, that effort did not involve a players' union and was actually an attempt to organize a league around Lucas' strong St. Louis franchise. The league was unsuccessful because it employed only a few major leaguers and provided a non-competitive pennant race.

On the other hand, the National Brotherhood of Professional Players was a legitimate effort to organize major league baseball players into a union. The Brotherhood had its beginning as a benevolent organization that used dues of $5 a month to aid its sick and needy members. The players' revolt of 1890 came out of the Brotherhood's efforts on behalf of players' rights, and it posed a threat to Organized Baseball because it sanctioned a secession of players from the two existing major leagues.

Following the 1885 season, the National League and American Association (a major league then) set a ceiling on players' salaries at $2,000 and forbad cash advances during the off season. John Montgomery Ward, a player who was also a practicing attorney, led the fight against the salary scale. Although the limit was not enforced, it remained an official policy.

While Ward was on a world baseball tour in the fall of 1888, the National League announced that in 1889 no player would receive more than $2,500 in salary. Ward was a captive of the tour until March, but upon his return to the States, he proposed that financial backing be sought for a players' league for 1890 if the Brotherhood's demands were not met. The National League doomed any hope of annulling the threat by refusing to meet with the Brotherhood's grievance committee.

The Brotherhood published a Declaration of Independence on November 4, 1889. The players abandoned the reserve rule and allowed members to jump their clubs at will. Four out of every five National League regulars jumped to the new Players' League that began play in 1890. Among the players defecting to the outlaws were Charles Comiskey, Ned Hanlon, Pat Tebeau, Connie Mack, and Monte Ward, all of whom would figure in the Federal League story two and a half decades later.

The National League fought the "outlaws" by scheduling and rescheduling games to conflict with Players' League games in the same city. Rainy weather in the second half of the season hurt attendance and some of the nervous Players' League owners sold out to the National League. After losing much of their financial backing, the Brotherhood collapsed. The Players' League lost $125,000, another $125,000 was spent on plants and equipment, and $45,000 went toward legal fees. The National League revised the National Agreement to replace the hated reserve clause language on player contracts with an "option to renew" clause. All contract-jumpers, including Ward, were restored to their original teams without reprisal.[2]

A short-lived attempt to unionize players grew out of the American League's efforts to establish itself as a major league in 1901. While clubs from the American and National Leagues ignored player contracts and raided their opposites' rosters, astute players realized how easy it would be to play one league against the other to their advantage. The so-called Professional Protective Association evaporated in 1903 after the two warring leagues agreed to respect each other's contracts and reserve rights to their players.

David Fultz attended Staunton Military Academy (Virginia), Brown University and Columbia law school, passing the New York bar in 1905. He played in the major leagues with the Philadelphia Phillies, the Philadelphia Athletics and the New York Highlanders. After Fultz left baseball to practice law following the 1905 season, baseball players began consulting him about their contracts. He also helped them in their dealings with the National Commission, which did not always reply to player's complaints. Fultz was approached in 1910 about the leadership position in an organization to represent the players and, on August 6, 1912, he announced the formation of a "Players' Fraternity." In September, the organization was officially chartered as a New York State corporation under the name Base Ball Players' Fraternity, with Fultz as president, two players from each league as vice presidents, and a player as secretary. The Fraternity also featured a board of directors made up of player representatives from each of the sixteen major league teams. Dues were $18 a year. Within two months, the Players' Fraternity claimed a membership of 300 players and eventually had more than 1200 major and minor league members.

Among the Fraternity's vice presidents were Ty Cobb and Brooklyn's star first baseman, Jake Daubert. The Board of Directors included Cobb and Christy Mathewson, as well as future

Federal League jumpers Fred Beck, Cy Falkenberg, Bill Bradley, Davy Jones, and Mickey Doolan.

The Players' Fraternity assumed a more aggressive stance in the fall of 1913 after the Federal League announced its intention to become the third major league. On November 8, the National Commission and the minor leagues' governing board were handed a petition listing seventeen demands that was signed by nearly five hundred players who were pledged not to sign their 1914 contracts unless the petition was acted upon. Organized Baseball said it would respond to the demands after the first of the year. The significance of the Fraternity was not lost on the Federal League in their "declaration of war" against the existing major leagues that November.

"It was said that the action of the [Federal League's] Directors in deciding to make offers to any player held under the reserve clause would include the majority of the men in the National and American Leagues," reported the *New York Times*. "Those players, it was said, had refused to sign contracts for next season until the demands they had made through the Players' Fraternity were granted. The Federal League, the Directors intimated, was ready to grant these requests."[3]

The Federal League established a more liberal player contract policy than their Organized Baseball counterparts. Owners in the new league were required to increase the salaries of players by five per cent each year. The club still possessed an option on a player's services for the following season, provided it gave notice to exercise it by September 15 of the current season. In order to maintain its hold on their players, the Feds devised a formula in which a certain percentage of the profits generated by the league would be divvied up among the players at the conclusion of each season. Any player who spent any part of ten seasons in the Federal League could demand his unconditional release and become a free agent.

Two weeks after Joe Tinker signed his name to a Federal League contract, the Players' Fraternity squared off with the powers of Organized Baseball at the Sinton Hotel in Cincinnati. Representing Organized Baseball were Garry Herrmann and John E. Brace, chairman and secretary of the National Commission, along with representatives from the minor leagues' National Association. The players were represented by Fultz and five player representatives, Jake Daubert and Ed Reulbach of Brooklyn, Jack Miller of the Cardinals, John Henry of Washington, and Ray Collins of the Boston Americans.

The Sporting News called Fultz "an outlaw and a baseball anarchist." Though Ban Johnson declared the demands "blackmail" and called Fultz "a menace to the game," the owners agreed to eleven of the seventeen demands.

Following the conference, Fultz gave a statement: "We believe that in the Cincinnati Conference of January 6 the ball players won a victory which a year ago could not have been dreamed of.... Twelve of our requests were granted, though modified and two withdrawn. Eight or ten of them were opposed very vigorously, but with the utmost frankness and good feeling."[4]

The victories for the players were staggering upon consideration of Organized Baseball's position only a few months earlier. Prior to 1914, ninety per cent of major leaguers did not have copies of their own contracts, which was remedied. The major leagues agreed to publish waiver lists so players could learn of their potential dismissal. Veterans of ten or more years of major league service won their unconditional release (upon clearing waivers), enabling them to negotiate a new contract. The owners also agreed to pay for uniforms and travel expenses to spring training, and henceforth clubs would have to justify fines or suspensions in writing. Lastly, no player would be discriminated against for being a member in the Fraternity.

Baseball rejected out of hand the request that when a player was demoted to the minor leagues his salary would not be cut, as well as the request that waivers could not be withdrawn after once being asked.

In exchange for Organized Baseball's concessions, Fultz promised the National Commission that the union would not enter the fight between Organized Baseball and the Federals. The Fraternity announced it would expel members who jumped contracts without first submitting their grievances to its advisory board and those who went ahead after the board ruled against them would also be expelled.

When asked about the Fraternity's attitudes toward the Federal League, Fultz told reporters; "Absolutely neutral. The Fraternity will not advise players to sign with the Federals and will not advise them to go back to their old employers. This is a matter that concerns each player personally.... Officially, I have no opinion to express as to the Federal League movement."[5] Fultz couldn't admit how much of the credit for Organized Baseball's concessions to the players was due to the Federal League's presence, for his leverage was tenuous at best.

Following the regular season of 1914, John I. Taylor of the *Boston Globe* and a past president of the Red Sox editorialized that the Players' Fraternity shared a great deal of the responsibility for baseball's lean year. Taylor wrote:

> In January, when the National Commission granted the players' demands, practically as a whole, the ball players in the country had either received large offers from the Federal League, or had read what had been offered to players, and they had the opportunity for the biggest salary hold-up ever known in the history of the game....
>
> Men who were worth $1800 to $2000 a year as utility men got contracts of $3500 and $4000. Stars that were getting $4000 to $8000 jumped to 50 per cent and in some cases even more.
>
> Every player, good or bad, used the Federal League to the limit. Owners held out as long as possible, but in the end cut out the 10 days' release clause and signed men for two and three years.[6]

In early 1914, Organized Baseball and the Federal League found their dispute over player contracts in the courts. In mid–January, Philadelphia Phillies catcher Bill Killefer signed a three-year contract to play for the Chicago Federal League team for a total of $17,500, with a $500 advance. Killefer made $3,200 with the Phillies in 1913, and, under the rules of Organized Baseball, was bound to the Philadelphia club for the 1914 season because of the reserve clause in his contract.[7]

Though he had batted only .207 in 296 major league games, Killefer was already regarded as one of the National League's best defensive catchers. Upon hearing of his player's deal with the Federal League, Phillies President W.F. Baker decided to either resign Killefer or take him to court. Baker was confident that the decision in the 1902 Lajoie case was enough precedent to allow his club to hold on to Killefer despite any legal action taken by the Federals. In that case, star second baseman Napoleon Lajoie jumped the Philadelphia Phillies to play for the new American League club in the city, but the Pennsylvania Supreme Court upheld an injunction that barred the player from playing with the Athletics.

Baker wrote to Killefer's father, who was a probate judge in Michigan. The correspondence explained the Phillies' position and enclosed the player's contract as well as a copy of the decision of the Supreme Court of Pennsylvania in the Lajoie case.

On the heels of Mr. Killefer's advice to his son that the Phillies had the better case, the club's secretary, William Shettsline, traveled to see the catcher at his home in Paw Paw, Michigan. Shettsline convinced Killefer to return to Philadelphia, and then they made a side trip to Chicago to meet Ad Brennan, another Phillie who had signed with the Federal League.

Upon their arrival in the Windy City, Brennan would not join the pair as he was scheduled to be married that week.

When Killefer and Shettsline returned to the Chicago railroad station to catch the train to Philadelphia, Federal League President James Gilmore happened to be there and walked toward them. The Phillies' official positioned himself between the other two men until Gilmore boarded his train. As soon as the Federal League president found a reporter, he warned the Philadelphia club that the Federals would fight if Killefer and Brennan rejoined the Phillies.

Once he was in President Baker's office back in Philadelphia, it only took a few minutes to persuade Killefer that the reserve clause in his old Phillies contract was valid. Bill signed with the Phillies for three years and got a nifty raise in salary to $6,500 a season.[8]

The legal warfare between the leagues escalated when Chicago Federal League Club owner Charles Weeghman took his case to the Federal District Court in Grand Rapids, Michigan. On March 20, 1914, Weeghman asked for the court to restrain the catcher from rejoining the Phillies and compel him to play for no club other than the Chicago Federals on the grounds Killefer had fulfilled his obligations to the National League club; that he had now broken his contract with the Chicago Federals; and, because his services were unique, the catcher would be difficult to replace. The court was informed that the $500 advanced to Killefer was accepted by him, and was still retained by the defendant.

The case, *Weeghman vs. Killefer*, came before the Western Michigan Federal District Court and Judge Clarence W. Sessions in early April. The attorney for Organized Baseball, George Walton Pepper, argued that the Federals had "seduced" the Philadelphia club's employee and was not entitled to relief from the court.

On April 10, 1914, Judge Sessions denied the injunction's application because the petitioner came before the court with "unclean hands." He said the plaintiff knew Killefer was under a moral, if not a legal, obligation to play with the Philadelphia club when it induced him to repudiate his obligation by offering him a longer term of employment and much larger compensation. Moreover, the court said Killefer was "a person upon whose pledged word meant so little or no reliance can be placed, and who, for gain to himself, neither scruples nor hesitates to disregard and violate his express engagements and agreements."[9]

While the Federal League hoped the litigation would prove to be the crucial test of the reserve clause, Judge Sessions held the reserve clause was an unenforceable executory contract and it was "nothing more than a contract to enter into a contract in the future — if the parties can then agree to contract." He added that while a contract existed "if broken by either party, the courts were helpless to either enforce its performance or to award damages for its breach — because it lacked the 'necessary qualities of definiteness, certainty and mutuality.'"[10]

On April 14, 1914, President Gilmore demanded the Players' Fraternity expel Killefer, Earl Hamilton, Fred Blanding and other players who violated Federal League contracts. That same day, Killefer was expelled from the Fraternity for "contract jumping."

The U.S. Court of Appeals upheld Judge Sessions's decision and made the point that $750 of Killefer's 1913 pay was in consideration of his agreement to abide by the reserve clause, and Killefer, in return, had a moral, if not legal, obligation to bargain in good faith with Philadelphia before signing with someone else.

The decision was a Pyrrhic victory for Organized Baseball. It reeled Killefer back into the Phillies, but it also released the Federals from their self-imposed restriction to not negotiate with players under contract elsewhere. Accordingly, Charles Weeghman ordered manager Joe Tinker to wire players throughout the country: "You are invited to come to the Federal League quarters in Chicago and discuss terms. Even if you decide not to sign a contract, all your expenses will be paid by the Federal League."[11]

In reality, the Federal League's basic contract contained a clause containing language similar to the contacts used by Organized Baseball: "Party of the first part shall have the exclusive right and option of extending this contract from year to year upon like conditions, except that the compensation to be paid the party of the second part shall in every extension of this contract be not less than the sum named in this contract, provided that written notice of the exercise of such option shall be given to the party of the second part on or before September 15."[12]

Organized Baseball contracts differed from the Federal League's "reserve clause" in two significant aspects. First, the organized major leagues had until February 1 of the following season to exercise the option on renewing a player's contract, while the Federal League was compelled to notify its players whether a contract would be renewed before the current season ended. This gave a player ample time to negotiate with a new employer. Secondly, the Federal League stipulated that a player's salary could not be reduced in subsequent contracts, while the organized leagues could compel a player to accept a reduction in pay if the club so chose.

What the Phillies got for the extra $3,300 they paid Killefer for the 1914 season was a catcher who squatted behind the plate in 90 games and batted .234. He hit only four points higher a year later.

Killefer was not the first, nor the last Organized Baseball player to use the existence of the Federal League to his financial advantage. Johnny Evers probably would have joined ex-teammates Joe Tinker and Mordecai Brown in the Federal League following a clash with Cubs owner Charles Murphy, if not for the intervention by the National League. The Cubs failed to improve on their third-place finish under Manager Evers in 1913, and then lost the postseason city series with the White Sox. Despite Johnny's five-year contract, Murphy abruptly fired him, just as he had dumped Frank Chance the year before. The Federals offered Evers a substantial raise over the $10,000 a year he was earning in Chicago to sign with them for 1914. The former manager informed Murphy that if he did not get more money he would not play for the Cubs. Despite Evers's long-term contract, the angry owner gave Johnny his ten days notice, but had second thoughts and traded him to the Boston Braves instead. When Evers demanded his release, the executives of the National League were moved to action. They had already lost two league stalwarts, Joe Tinker and Mordecai Brown, to the Feds and were not about to lose another star. The National League guaranteed Evers $25,000 plus a bonus to play with the Braves.

Evers's guaranteed earnings with the Braves in 1914 made him the highest paid player in baseball—at least for a while. Charles Murphy's antics were the last straw for the National League. League President John Tener persuaded Charles P. Taft, brother of former President William Howard Taft, to buy out Murphy.

On paper, the loss of Bill Killefer did not adversely affect the performance of Joe Tinker's team. Three days after Killefer's defection back to the National League, the Federals signed Arthur Wilson, the New York Giants' twenty-eight-year-old backup catcher, to play in Chicago. "Dutch" Wilson was no slouch as a batter, having hit .303 in 1911 and .289 a year later in part-time work for John McGraw, though he slumped to only .190 the season before he jumped to the Feds.

Late in the 1914 season, Claude Hendrix, Chicago's pitching ace, would say:

> I consider Arthur Wilson of the Chifeds is the greatest catcher I ever saw. I say this with all due respect to Archer and Meyers and Simon. The latter two caught me when I was a Pirate and both were good, but I never saw a man handle any spitball pitcher like Wilson. He has made out of me what they call a low ball pitcher, because he handles and digs up the low-breaking spitter and gets the ball away again in a most amazing manner.[13]

6

The Federal League Survives a Crisis

A seminal event in the history of the Federal League occurred on January 17, 1914, when the league's magnates met in Chicago to discuss the future of the circuit. The fate of the league was in the hands of Charles Weeghman, who demanded that the six other franchises show him sufficient backing and players to make good. If the Chicago owner wasn't satisfied, he threatened to withdraw his support. Charley pointed out that only three clubs, Chicago, Baltimore and Pittsburgh, had any major league players under contract and warned that if the other clubs didn't get busy and sign quality players, it would be foolish to call themselves a major league. Earlier, Weeghman had been approached by an unnamed source and was offered the chance to purchase the St. Louis American League Club. This story gained credence when it was learned that Browns owner Robert Hedges was in Ban Johnson's private office that evening toasting the demise of the Federal League with the National League President, Garry Herrmann, and Detroit Tigers owner Frank Navin.[1]

"Baseball affairs passed through a turbulent storm yesterday," wrote Sam Weller in the *Chicago Daily Tribune*. "For hours the gale raged and a little craft labeled 'Federal League' was in great distress.... At four o'clock in the afternoon, it looked as if the small craft was lost, and sympathizers began to mourn."[2]

Sequestered with the Federal League magnates in a meeting room of the La Salle Hotel, Gilmore tried to assure his friend Weeghman the other clubs would be able to field quality teams. A little after ten o'clock on Saturday evening, Gilmore threw open the door of the private meeting room and invited the waiting reporters inside. Instead of reading the obituary of the Federal League, Sunny Jim announced they had a great baseball meeting and the Federal League was sure to go.

"I am with the league to the end," said Weeghman, "but at least six teams must show the first-class lineups that was agreed upon when I went into the organization."

Weeghman's friend, H.J. Murphy, told *Sporting Life* that Charley "quit the fold at that meeting only to be brought in again by Otto Stifel of St. Louis, who put up the necessary argument in the form of hard cash, and who, it is said, saved the Federal ship."[3]

The Sporting News reported that Stifel saved the day by tossing his check for $100,000 on the table and told President Gilmore to spend it for the immediate needs of the league. Otto urged the other magnates to do the same; Weeghman was pacified, and the crisis passed.[4]

Otto Stifel was a member of the St. Louis community of German brewers. His father established the family brewery in 1859 and Otto's share in the elder Stifel's estate was said to have exceeded three million dollars. He gained the controlling interest of the family brewery in 1906 and within a few years it was producing about 60,000 barrels of beer per year. In

Federal League officials: (top row, left to right) Weeghman, Walter Ward, Comstock; (middle row) L. Goldman, Robert Ward, Steininger, Gilmore, George Ward, Schleunes, Walker, Robertson; (bottom row) Krause, Ball, H. Goldman, Mullen, Rickart, Hanlon, Gates, George, Carroll, 1914 (George Grantham Bain Collection, Library of Congress).

addition to dabbling in professional baseball, Otto was big into horse racing. He owned the horse Colonial Girl, which won him a prize of $50,000 at the 1904 World's Fair. Otto was prominent in St. Louis Republican politics, was said to have been instrumental in the election of several of the city's mayors, and dropped a bundle in the unsuccessful reelection campaign of President William Howard Taft in 1912.

Stifel explained his interest in baseball and how he got involved in 1913:

> I have always been interested in baseball, and there was a time several years ago when I considered purchasing an interest in the St. Louis Browns.... Both the St. Louis clubs had been in a bad way and habitual losers for so long that the people were getting slightly sore, to say the least.
> I know I liked baseball enough to want my own town represented by teams a little higher in the race than the Cardinals and Browns. So a number of us clubbed together and started the St. Louis club of the Federal League.
> We organized a little club of fourteen members, every one of who was pledged to put in a thousand dollars to defray the expenses of the baseball team. We called ourselves the "Thousand Dollar Club," for it was well understood that we kissed good-bye to the thousand dollars when we invested it.[5]

When Stifel was elected president of the St. Louis Federal League club, it was understood that he would have larger holdings than the common members. After the club increased its capital stock from $20,000 to $135,000 in March 1914, it was disclosed that Stifel owned 334.32 shares, enough to retain controlling interest. Philip Ball held the second highest amount of stock and E.A. Steininger was the third largest stockholder.

6. The Federal League Survives a Crisis

As expected, Fred Bramley's Cleveland franchise was officially dropped at the meeting in Chicago, with the promise that when he was able to show the Federal League he had an advantageously located site for a ballpark, the franchise might be restored. The decision to dump the Green Sox also meant Cy Young's tenure as a Federal League manager was at an end. On June 15, the forty-seven-year-old baseball immortal signed to pitch with the Benton Harbor, Michigan, independent team. Six days later, old Cy pitched the Benton Harbor nine to a 16 to 4 victory over a team from Niles.

After Bramley was forced out of the league, a Canadian named Bernard Hepburn took over the Cleveland franchise. The league's newest magnate lived near Toronto, and Gilmore agreed to allow Hepburn to install the club in that Canadian city rather than Cleveland. Barney came from one of Ontario's oldest families, who had made a fortune operating steamboat lines in the Great Lakes. In addition, young Hepburn was one of the youngest members of the Canadian Parliament.

When the Federal League owners met again in Chicago on February 7, about half of the owners, led by Charles Weeghman, bitterly opposed putting a franchise in Toronto and supported the retention of Cleveland. Weeghman learned that while Hepburn had raised about $15,000 to back his club, no playing grounds had been secured; Bill Bradley, the prospective manager, had only conditionally agreed to enlist with the Federals; and no players had been signed for the Canadian club.

Gilmore did not like the idea of placing a team in Toronto either, but his options were limited. Charles Somers, owner of the American League's Cleveland club, had already made a preemptive move against the Federals by making arrangements to transfer his Toledo American Association team there to play at League Park when the Naps were on the road. Somers felt the Federal League would not invade Cleveland while baseball was being played there on a daily basis. The Mud Hens were already losing money, so Somers wasn't risking much by vacating Toledo.

The Federals' executive session evolved into a bitter exchange between the supporters of the Toronto franchise and those who opposed it. Gilmore pleaded with his opponents to be patient, pointing out the season was still ten weeks away and there was a good chance things would be worked out in the interim.

The meeting had reached a boiling point when Philip de Catesby Ball, a backer of the St. Louis club, walked in. It took Ball just a few minutes to size up the situation and determine that the venture was in danger of breaking apart. The fiery Midwesterner jumped to his feet and startled the other team owners when he began to disparage them.

"We've got the opportunity of a lifetime, but some of you fellows seemed to think too much of your bankroll," lectured Ball. "Some of you fellows seem to be showing the 'white feather.' Well, it's up to you to show your mettle. You've sunk a big bunch of money into this venture. Sink some more — you can't expect to win out in a big business enterprise against well-entrenched competition to the limit of your wad. Get busy! Don't be short sports. Don't be tight wads. Loosen up and we'll come out with flying colors."[6]

Ball's jeering attitude and his insinuation of cowardice with the "white feather" remark gave cause for the Federal League owners to sit back and analyze the situation.

"Ball certainly saved the league," declared Otto Stifel.

> Just before we went into the meeting, Weeghman had been offered the franchise of the Chicago Cubs for $400,000. It was a bargain price.
> ...with Weeghman gone it would have discouraged those that remained and perhaps others would have quit us. But just at the right moment, Ball came along, showed us our error, screwed up our courage and held the league together.[7]

The magnates finally agreed that Toronto would retain its franchise for now. But Gilmore knew he had to do something to repair the rift among the owners.

Six days following the volatile league meeting in Chicago, President Gilmore announced the Federals would field a team in the greater New York area for the upcoming season. After apologizing for his persistent denials during the previous week, he told reporters the newest club would play its games at the site of the Brooklyn National League club's old home, Washington Park, in South Brooklyn. The prospect of Toronto having a club in the league was finished.

Gilmore later said, "Toronto was not put in our circuit merely as a stall. We had intentions of locating here if grounds could be obtained under a suitable lease, but when I saw the Canadian city losing favor with the backers of the league, I met Robert B. Ward of New York. I was introduced to him by a mutual friend in Toronto, and did not talk, or even consider him as a probable investor in the new league until I met him again a few days later."[8]

Gilmore and the president of the Ward Baking Company struck up a friendship and Robert eventually became Gilmore's principal financial backer for his League. Ward owned over a million and a half dollars of stock in the bakeries and he had other investments of indeterminable value. His brother George was a partner in the bakery business and was convinced to go into the baseball venture with Robert. Publicly, Robert Ward was awarded the Toronto franchise, though he and Gilmore were secretly planning to place a club in Brooklyn instead.

Robert's father, Hugh Ward, came from Ireland to America in 1849 and opened a bakery shop on Broome Street in lower Manhattan. Robert was five years old when his parents moved to Pittsburgh, where he would someday begin his own bakery business. When the Ward's shop became short-handed during the Civil War, eight-year-old Robert worked in the bakery and delivered the "cakes" in a basket to the homes of customers.

After attending public schools and business college in Pittsburgh, Robert went to work in his father's business and, at twenty-one, became foreman of the bakery, making eighteen dollars a week. Hugh suggested Robert start his own business and the young Ward purchased a small grocery store in partnership with a future brother-in-law. Ward eventually sold out to the brother-in-law and in 1878 he purchased a small Pittsburgh bakery for $400. Thus began a business that revolutionized the bread-making industry.

Robert's younger brother George stayed with their father and at the older Ward's death, he inherited the family business. The two brothers soon joined forces in an enterprise which became the Ward-Mackey Company in 1897. In 1903, they erected one of the first large sanitary baking plants in Pittsburgh.

The Wards revolutionized the baked bread industry with the production of a loaf of darker-colored bread, weighing two pounds, which they called the Jumbo Loaf. The new loaf was produced from a lower grade of flour containing some of the coat of the kernel mixed with the finer grades. The prevailing price of bread at the time was about five cents per pound and the Wards were able to sell their Jumbo Loaf, double the usual size, for the same price. The idea helped make them rich.[9]

By the turn of the century, the Wards' bakery business had outgrown the limits of Pittsburgh, so they expanded into Chicago, Boston, Cleveland, New York, and Newark. In 1909 Ward selected locations for new Wards bakeries in Brooklyn and the Bronx.

"We invested two million dollars in our New York venture before we turned a wheel or gained the market for a single loaf of bread," he said. "The day we started our great plants we loaded a hundred wagons with bread and sent them out, instructing our salesmen to give the bread away as samples. The next day we sent them out again, this time to sell bread."

Ward, in one bold stroke, took the New York bread trade by storm. In 1913 his thirteen bakeries turned out a total of 249,992,335 loaves of bread. At the time of Robert Ward's first involvement in the Federal League, *Sporting Life* estimated his wealth at ten million dollars.

Ward explained his love of baseball in *Baseball Magazine*:

> For myself, I was always interested in baseball more than most things. When I was my father's foreman and working nights, I always set apart a sum of money to buy a season's ticket to the old Pittsburgh grounds and attended practically every game of the season. I am a member of golf clubs, but the only athletic pursuit in which I have ever had any concern has been baseball. Busy as I have been, I have always appropriated time when I could go to a ball game.
>
> I was in Toronto visiting a friend, and it so happened that Gilmore was also in the city at the same time. A friend of my son's knew Mr. Gilmore and introduced us. The next day Mr. Gilmore wished to see me. He outlined his proposition.[10]

Gilmore went about telling Ward why he thought his league would succeed.

"I called attention to the young players who are annually promoted from minor leagues by sale to major circuits," explained the Federal League president. "I showed him how we could deal directly with these players, get players of ambition and youth, pay them a portion of the amount that the magnates alone would have handled, and in the end build up a circuit that would be on a paying basis by reason of the great American public's interest in clean independent baseball. Mr. Ward was surprisingly willing to spend $200,000 for stands."[11]

"Mr. Gilmore, if you will put all your cards on the table and things are as you represent them, I will go into the scheme with you," Ward responded. "He did as I suggested. I investigated carefully and took the Brooklyn franchise."[12]

"I never expected to make any fortune in baseball," acknowledged R.B. Ward.

> No business man who has been in business as long as I have is carried off his feet by the visionary schemes of any promoter.... Baseball interest had grown, numerous cities outside the big league ranks had grown. Everything had grown but baseball. Major league baseball was stationary if the organized magnates had their will. I know of no business or of no public movement that can safely be curtailed or hidebound by the will of sixteen men.[13]

On February 13, 1914, the Federal Leaguers signed a ten-year contract for Washington Park and announced the existing grandstand would be replaced by a concrete and steel one that would seat 18,000 persons. The officers of the Brooklyn club would be Robert Boyd Ward, president, and his brother George Ward, treasurer. The former major league player, manager and champion of players' rights, John Montgomery Ward (no relation to the owners), was hired as club secretary and business manager.

The Wards attempted to lure the legendary Fielder Jones and Boston icons Jimmy Collins and Jake Stahl to Brooklyn as manager of their club, but all three turned them down. By default, the Wards accepted a man as manager who had no previous experience in the position. The prospective Toronto Federal League club's manager, William "Bill" Bradley, became the Wards' leader on the field for 1914.

Bill Bradley was perhaps the top third baseman in baseball when his career as a player was effectively shortened in 1906 when Bill Hogg of the New York Highlanders tried to brush him back by throwing at his head. Bill raised his right arm to protect his face and the ball shattered his arm. Bradley insisted the fractured arm interfered with his fielding, throwing and batting, before which he was on his way to a plus-.300 career batting average. Bill had played with Toronto of the International League the three seasons prior to his involvement with the Federal League.

Unfortunately, all of the Wards' money could not produce a winning team in Brooklyn. Hampered by their late start compared to clubs in Chicago, Indianapolis and Baltimore, the

Wards concentrated on acquiring veteran, well known ex-major league players. However, many of these expensive ball players had the disadvantage of age or baggage.

On March 10, 1914, the day Bill Bradley would become the Wards' manager, business manager John Montgomery Ward verified the signing of Danny Murphy of the Athletics, and predicted Murphy, Arlie Hofman and Steve Evans would give Brooklyn an outfield that would compare favorably with any in the major leagues.

With a straight face, Monte told reporters, "I think we have captured the best batter in the Federal League by getting Murphy, and now I think we have an outfield which will show a lot of speed all the way. Hofman and Evans have been classed among the best outfielders in the majors, and these two, with Murphy are going to make history in the National game, believe me."[14]

Ward must have forgotten that the pair of Murphy and Hofman, combined, played in only 68 major league games the previous season and both had been designated to the minor leagues by their former clubs. In addition, Murphy could not play in the outfield any longer because of a bad leg and a weak throwing arm.

Upon his assignment to the Federal League club in Brooklyn, Arlie Hofman boasted, "The Brooklyn fans will forget about Jake Daubert's fancy first basing after they watch me for a while."

Arlie's nickname was "Circus Solly" and *Baseball Magazine* once quipped, "He is serious only when asleep."[15] With Hofman and Steve Evans around, any manager would have his hands full.

During spring training in 1914, Solly and Evans volunteered to umpire an exhibition game between the Brooklyn Federals and the University of South Carolina baseball team. Prior to the game, the pair of novice arbiters snuck a dozen baseballs into their hotel kitchen, put half on ice and baked the rest. During the game, their teammates batted against the heavy frozen balls, while the collegians hit the lively baked balls much further than the professionals.[16]

In mid–March, Brooklyn announced the signing of another major league castoff. The Wards' first baseman would be Ralph "Hap" Myers. Hap stole 57 bases with the Boston Braves in 1913, but his lack of power led to his release to the Rochester minor league club. Instead of reporting to the International League, Hap jumped to the Federals. Myers would continue to steal bases at a high rate in the Federal League, but he would get on base only 111 times via hit or walk in 1914.

Another acquisition, a twenty-one-year-old reserve outfielder with the Giants named Claude Cooper, had only 27 major league games under his belt, but signed a contract with the Wards for $5,000 a season with one year's wages in advance. A year earlier, Cooper attracted the attention of the New York Giants after a sensational 1912 Texas League season at Fort Worth, where he was hailed as "another Speaker."[17]

"During my entire career as manager of the Giants," remarked John McGraw, "I have continually been looking for an outfielder of the Ty Cobb — Tris Speaker type, one of those gaunt, springy fellows, who do not have a weakness. I mean a player who can field, run and steadily hit over the .300 mark. I have found that person in Claude Cooper."[18]

Cooper turned out not to be the next Tris Speaker, but he did make the Giants' roster to start the 1913 season. He batted .300 in part-time duty, got into two games in the 1913 World Series as a pinch runner, stole a base, and went home with a full Series share.

R.W. "Ring" Lardner had quipped in his column of February 19, 1914, "Why not 'Ward's Tip-Tops' for the Federal League club in Brooklyn?"[19] On March 8, Brooklyn's treasurer Walter Ward released a list of players who would represent the club in the Federal League. The same report in the *New York Times* indicated the club would be known as the "Tip-Tops."

The Ward Bakery, which owned the club, put Tip-Top patches on the players' uniform sleeves to advertise the company's brand of bread.

For the most part, sports editors of New York newspapers would not go along with the Tip-Tops nickname for the Brooklyn Federal League Club. Writers who allied themselves with Organized Baseball ridiculed the Wards for so blatant a commercial advertisement. Robert Ward became so touchy about the nickname he told *Baseball Magazine,* "My club was nicknamed 'Tip Tops' by the sporting writers. They took the name from my favorite brand of bread, very true, but they did so without my knowledge or without consulting me. As far as I am concerned I am sorry they did, for it lays me open to some criticism. But a nickname is like a disease.... And once fastened on an individual or a club it is almost impossible to shake off."[20]

7

Ad Brennan and Tom Seaton

The Federal League was especially successful in luring players from the National League's skinflint operations in Brooklyn and Philadelphia. One of the first major league pitchers to join Tinker's Chicago team was Phillies left-hander Addison "Ad" Brennan, practitioner of the spitball. Brennan was also important in that he convinced a Philadelphia teammate, Tom Seaton, to also join the Federals.

Brennan began his professional career as a first baseman with Iola (Oklahoma–Kansas League) in 1908. He volunteered to pitch when his team suffered a shortage of hurlers and he was pitcher from then on, once striking out fifteen batters in a game. Brennan was purchased by the Phillies from Hutchinson of the Kansas State League in 1910. After winning three games and losing none in his rookie season, Ad split the 1911 season between Philadelphia and the Eastern League's team in Buffalo.

After joining the Buffalo Bisons in early June 1911, Brennan not only led the team in pitching (14–8), but also pitched two nine-inning, no-hit, no-run games. The first was on June 25 at Jersey City when he blanked the Skeeters, 1–0, and scored the only run himself. Two months and one day later, he pitched nine innings of no-hit, no-run ball against the same team, only to lose in the tenth, 1 to 0. In 1913, he was back with the Phillies.[1]

Brennan gained notoriety in July 1913 when he was fined $100 and suspended five days for punching Giants manager John McGraw after a game at the Baker Bowl. During the game of June 30, McGraw mercilessly abused Ad, calling him "yellow" with the objective of rattling the pitcher for his start the next day. Following the game, McGraw was walking toward the center field clubhouse talking to the Phillies' Mickey Doolan about joining his world tour. Reportedly, McGraw remarked within earshot of Brennan, "There's the fellow I want to fight!"

Ad was fed up with the abuse from McGraw so he turned and caught the approaching Giants manager with a left fist followed by a right. Both punches connected and McGraw went down, bleeding from his chin and cheek. Following the affair with McGraw, Brennan received over five hundred letters, mostly of congratulation. The Phillies' management paid the fine assessed by National League President Tom Lynch.[2]

When Brennan contracted diphtheria in 1913, his spitball was blamed. Philadelphia manager Charlie Dooin's antidote for "using the ball as a cuspidor" was to put disinfectant on it. The umpires warned him if he did it again he would be fined $50.

In January 1914 Brennan signed a three-year contract to play for the Chicago Federal League Club at an annual salary of $4300.[3] His short-term financial future secure, Ad married his fiancée, twenty-one-year-old Portia Durnell, the winner of a beauty contest for the most beautiful girl in Kansas City. Ad was promised an additional $500 bonus if he could convince Tom Seaton to also defect to the Federal League.

Fellow pitcher Seaton was Brennan's best friend on the Phillies. Tom emerged as one of the top pitchers in the National League in 1913, compiling a 27–12 record while appearing in 52 games. He led the National League in wins, innings pitched and strikeouts.

The pivotal game of Seaton's career with the Phillies came on August 7, 1913, when he took the mound against the Cubs in Chicago. Tom's wife Rene was suffering a difficult labor back in Philadelphia and was in danger of losing her life. Tom pitched seven innings that day and lost, 5 to 2. Immediately after leaving the mound he returned to Philadelphia, but his child had already died and even Rene's chance of survival was in doubt. Mrs. Seaton did recover, but she harbored a grudge against the Phillies and specifically Manager Red Dooin, whom she blamed for keeping her husband from being with her during the birth.

The Seatons claimed the manager withheld a telegram urging Tom to hurry to Philadelphia to be with his wife. Dooin maintained that he gave Seaton the telegram before the game and Tom had insisted on pitching, saying he would leave after the contest. Mrs. Seaton did not believe Dooin and when she got the chance for revenge, Rene urged her husband to quit the Phillies.[4]

Seaton was further displeased with Philadelphia owner W.F. Baker when his Phillies 1914 contract was mailed to him for his signature. Tom claimed that particular contract would make it necessary for him to take part in at least thirty-five games and win sixty percent of those games just to earn the salary stipulated.

Once on board with the Federals, Ad Brennan went to Pueblo, Colorado, to persuade Tom to play with him in the new league. Brennan and Seaton traveled to Chicago where, on February 18, Tom was signed to a three-year contract by Joe Tinker to pitch for the Federal League. He was to receive $7,000 per year, along with a $5,000 advance. The Phillies complained that Seaton had agreed by telegram to play for them in 1914 for a salary in excess of $6,000.[5]

Seaton thought he was going to play for Tinker in Chicago, but when the Federal League's players were distributed, he was awarded to Brooklyn, whose owner had given President James Gilmore a $25,000 check to be used to acquire a manager and a star player for his club. Almost the entire sum was used on one player, Tom Seaton.

However, Seaton wanted to play with Chicago and declined to join the Brooklyn club for spring training. Instead, he was on the Chicago club's train on March 8 when it departed for training camp in Shreveport, Louisiana.

In those days, major league teams rarely employed special coaches to assist the manager. Seaton, Brennan and Claude Hendrix worked with the younger pitchers on such things as holding a runner close to the base, working with runners on base, and covering up properly so the opponents could not distinguish what pitch was coming.[6] The three hurlers then honed their art against the team's reserves, "Jimmie Block's Blokes," and in a series of exhibition contests with the St. Louis Terriers who were training in Monroe, Louisiana.

Meanwhile, the Philadelphia National League club was not about to give up two of its pitchers without a fight. William Shettsline, the Phillies' secretary, slipped into Shreveport the evening of All Fools' Day and contacted Tom Seaton and Ad Brennan by telephone. The pitchers led the National League man right into an ambush.

When Shettsline arrived at the players' hotel, he was confronted by Joe Tinker. Several players and hotel guests surrounded the pair of antagonists as they sparred verbally. When the Phillies' secretary commented that the players had been treated well and prospered under Organized Baseball, Tinker leaped at the opportunity.

"You think they have?" he countered. "What did the Philadelphia club do to Tom Seaton last season? Didn't it keep a telegram away from him in Chicago, a message asking him to come home at once because his wife was dangerously ill? They kept the message away from him and made him pitch a game that afternoon and probably miss two or three trains for home."

The shell-shocked Shettsline professed ignorance of the incident, but Tinker continued with his diatribe against the National League, the National Commission, and the Phillies' mistreatment of Killefer. One remark was taken as an insult by the Phillies' official and he shot back angrily. Finally, some sportswriters pulled Shettsline out of the fray. The secretary told the scribes that he came to talk with Seaton because Tom had agreed to terms with the Phillies by telegram. "But it looks as if he's satisfied here and wants to stay."[7]

In an effort to convince Seaton to join their Brooklyn team, Manager Bill Bradley and the club's secretary, Walter S. Ward, were dispatched to Knoxville, Tennessee, where the Chifeds were playing an exhibition game. Seaton said he objected to his transfer to the Brooklyn franchise because he and his wife had already made plans to live in Chicago the next three summers with Ad and Portia Brennan and brother-in-law Jake Fournier and his wife. Ward tried to convince the Seatons to go to Chicago with him and speak with President Gilmore, but Tom refused. Young Ward even threatened the pitcher with a suspension, but Seaton knew he had an ironclad contract with Chicago and ignored the bluff.

All this led Chicago sports reporter Sam Weller to write, "Indications are that young Ward has had little experience in dealing with big league ball players, who sometimes have more temperament and business sense than drivers of bakery wagons and dough mixers."[8]

Tom Seaton, pitcher, Brooklyn Federal League club, 1914 (National Baseball Hall of Fame Library, Cooperstown, N.Y.).

Charley Weeghman even came to Knoxville to aid in the

negotiations. Chicago offered pitcher Claude Hendrix even up for Tom in an effort to settle the affair. When Ward talked to Hendrix about transferring to the Brooklyn club, Claude produced his contract, which contained a clause stating that he would play only on the Chicago club for the full term of his Federal League contract.

In a sidelight to Ward's business in Knoxville, Sam Weller reported, "Tom Seaton sat peacefully all day in the poker game right along with young Ward and enough others with money to make seven. Tom and the other boys thought it would be soft to take some of the Brooklyn baker's money in the P.G., but when the game was over the young magnate was way ahead of the game. He showed the boys a few new points on drawing the cards and now the athletes all are wondering how such a fellow can be opposed to Sunday baseball."[9]

Eventually, Seaton weakened and made the proposition to Secretary Ward that he would be ready to pitch on opening day for Brooklyn if something could be worked out for additional salary to cover his additional expenses due to a change in living conditions.[10] The younger Ward telephoned his uncle, Robert B. Ward, in Brooklyn and explained Seaton's demands. The Wards agreed to a salary increase to $8,500 a year for three years, and the team would pay Mrs. Seaton's expenses when she traveled with her husband on the road. Tom would pitch the Brooklyn club's first Federal League game, allowing only four hits in a ten-inning 1–0 victory over Pittsburgh at Exposition Park.

At six feet, Seaton was tall for the time and employed a menacing stare between pitches in an attempt to unnerve the batter. Tom was primarily a breaking ball pitcher with a sweeping curveball. Between 1913 and the end of 1914, all of those breaking pitches and 625 innings pitched took a toll on his arm.

In August of 1914, Seaton visited "arm specialist" Bonesetter Reese, who prescribed a good rest. Tom didn't pitch for two weeks in late August and early September. He then made ten starts in the final month of the season.

A Philadelphia reporter paid tribute to Seaton when it appeared the pitcher's arm had broken down due to overwork late in the 1914 season:

> It is hoped that the report of Seaton's pitching arm being "gone" is exaggerated.... It would be impossible to recall any twirler with the possible exception of Ed Walsh of the Chicago White Sox, or Jack Coombs, who was more willing to sacrifice himself for his team than Seaton. When with the Phillies, Seaton was always in condition. He thrived on hard work and he was always willing to go to the mound whenever called upon. He never hid behind the water bucket, and he never had an excuse when his manager wanted him to help out in an emergency. Seaton had similar trouble with his arm before he joined the Phillies, so that rest may prove a cure as it did once before.[11]

8

The World Tourists

After playing thirty-five games in thirty-one different American cities, two major league all-star teams set out from Seattle the afternoon of November 19, 1913, for Vancouver, where the players would commence a worldwide tour. The two baseball teams included stars from several major league teams, though the nucleus of the squads came from John McGraw's New York Giants and the Chicago White Sox of Charles Comiskey. The two teams would take major league baseball where it had not gone before. The foreign press and curious native populations experienced a glimpse into the never-before-seen American pastime as played by the likes of Jim Thorpe, "Turkey" Mike Donlin, Germany Schaefer, Buck Weaver, and Tris Speaker.

When the Philadelphia Nationals' shortstop, Mickey Doolan, agreed to join the tour, the Phillies told him he could not participate unless he took out a life insurance policy for $10,000 to protect the club. Doolan balked at the demand and maintained he was an unsigned free agent. In the end, John McGraw, who was interested in acquiring the slick-fielding shortstop to play for his Giants, paid the premium on Doolan's behalf.[1]

After barnstorming across the United States, the touring ball players set sail for Asia. The teams played baseball games in Tokyo, Shanghai, Hong Kong, the Philippines, Australia, Ceylon, Cairo, Rome, Nice, Paris and the final stop, London. During the trip, baseball's ambassadors met such dignitaries as Pope Pius X, tea magnate Thomas Lipton, and the last khedive of Egypt. The tour concluded with a game before twenty thousand curious English sports fans and King George V.[2]

During the trip, the St. Louis Cardinals' resident prankster, Steve Evans, walked through the players' train announcing to the ballplayers that there was free breakfast in the dining car. When the bill for the exorbitant breakfasts arrived, the players realized they were the victims of an Evans prank. After the tour reached Egypt, Steve stood on one side of the Sphinx to catch a baseball thrown over the monument by catcher Ivy Wingo. One of the best dancers on the team, Evans and Buck Weaver of the White Sox demonstrated the tango to a crowd at a fancy Egyptian hotel.[3]

Back in the States, Federal League officials recognized that eight of the touring all-stars — Tris Speaker, Sam Crawford, Lee Magee, Ivy Wingo, Ben Egan, Walt Leverenz, Mickey Doolan and Steve Evans — had not inked their baseball contracts for the 1914 season. The Federals were particularly interested in signing Speaker, Crawford, and Doolan.

Former Boston Red Sox manager Jake Stahl, who had been unsuccessfully courted by the Wards to manage their club in Brooklyn, agreed to use his influence on behalf of the Federals. He wired his former teammate Tris Speaker not to sign a contract for 1914 until after the touring players arrived in New York. Stahl's message apparently dissuaded the star center fielder from signing a new Red Sox contract despite the efforts of White Sox manager Jimmy Callahan, who had been deputized to keep Speaker in the American League.

Prominent executives of Organized Baseball, as well as a large group of Federal Leaguers, came to New York City well in advance of the World tourists' arrival there aboard the Cunard liner *Lusitania* on Friday, March 6. The Federal League delegation, in addition to President Gilmore, included club owners George and Robert Ward, Otto Stifel, and Ned Hanlon, and managers George Stovall, Mordecai Brown, and Larry Schlafly.

The afternoon before the big ocean liner was scheduled to dock at the port of New York, Gilmore sent wireless messages to the eight key passengers, telling them not to sign contracts until they had spoken to him. "They will be crazy if they don't accept what we are willing to give them," the Federal chief announced to the press.[4]

The declaration came only three days after Gilmore promised the greatest war in baseball history. The threat was precipitated by the news that pitcher Fred Blanding had forsaken his Federal League contract and jumped back to the Cleveland Americans. He joined Bill Killefer, Gus Williams and George Baumgardner, all of whom the Feds claimed had violated their contracts with the Federal League.

"If the American and National Leagues ignore our contracts and fail to appreciate the spirit of sportsmanship we have shown, we will start the biggest baseball war," Gilmore warned. "When it is over the Federal League will have the stars of the old leagues and will be the strongest in the game."[5]

Representatives of Organized Baseball outmaneuvered the Federal Leaguers by gaining passes on a custom boat and met the *Lusitania* at Quarantline, while the Feds' representatives had to wait on the dock for the ship to arrive later. Red Sox President Joseph Lannin and Vice President John I. Taylor waited anxiously as the revenue cutter pulled into the Hudson River docks with the valuable cargo. Upon the players' arrival, a falling snow did not dampen the planned festivities, and "...there was much noise of whistles and music by reception committees, formal and informal, and then a hustling of all hands to various hotels, where the contest over the rights to players was taken up in earnest..."[6]

Tris Speaker was spirited away by the Red Sox officials, who virtually gave the player the option of writing his own contract. However, the star center fielder had promised that he would not sign a contract for the 1914 season until he heard what the Federal Leaguers had to say. Tris went to the Knickerbocker Hotel that afternoon to meet with James Gilmore, the Ward brothers, and Brooklyn business manager John M. Ward. The *Boston Daily Globe* reported that Speaker was offered a three-year deal calling for $15,000 per season with a $15,000 signing bonus that was represented by a stack of $1,000 bills on a table in front of him.[7] Speaker left the meeting without committing to anything, but years later he told Lee Greene of *Sport Magazine* he would have signed with the Federals if they had been able to guarantee the multiyear deal.[8]

Following Speaker's dinner with Lannin at the Hotel Biltmore that evening, the Red Sox announced that Tris had signed a two-year contract. Though the particulars were not given at the time, it was learned that the total deal amounted to $40,000 in salary and bonuses.[9] In order to keep Speaker, Lannin made Tris the highest paid baseball player in the world, his annual salary of $18,000 topping Johnny Evers' recent National League contract.

A Saturday night banquet, honoring the returning players, marked the close of the festivities. Baseball magnates, players and men of sport from all parts of the county attended. It was close to ten P.M. before the coffee, cigars and speech making came to an end. Former White Sox manager Fielder Jones was a featured guest of Charles Comiskey at a grand dinner given in honor of the tour. Jones was given an engraved book commemorating the event even though he did not go on the trip. When Comiskey asked Fielder to return to Chicago as manager of his team, Jones turned him down. Comiskey would hear more of Fielder Jones a few months later.

Out of the eight targeted unsigned players, the Federal League signed two, but they missed the big prizes Speaker and Crawford. Soon after his arrival in New York, Mickey Doolan agreed to play for the Baltimore Federal League club for an annual salary of $6,000. Doolan's problem with the Philadelphia club went back years when he was not paid the bonus promised him for acting as captain of the team under the previous owner. Arguably the best defensive shortstop in baseball, Mickey felt little loyalty to the Phillies, for he had received only one raise since 1908, when owner William Baker raised his annual pay to $3,500 prior to the 1911 season.

Baker expressed surprise at Doolan's desertion. The Phillies' president said that his shortstop was tired of the continual "roasting" from the Philadelphia fans, so a deal had been arranged whereby Mickey was to be traded to the New York Giants as soon as he signed a 1914 contract. On the other hand, Mickey made it clear his grievance against Philadelphia was with the club rather than the fans.[10]

The other Federal League signee, erstwhile St. Louis Cardinals outfielder Steve Evans, went about town flashing three new $1,000 bills he had received from the Federals. The happy-go-lucky Evans was known as one of the National League's biggest pranksters for the five sea-

Brooklyn Tip Tops outfielder Steve Evans, 1915 (George Grantham Bain Collection, Library of Congress).

sons he played for the Cardinals. A lefty, both in throwing and thinking, Steve led the league in being hit by pitches each season he played in St. Louis.

The Sporting News downplayed the Evans defection and claimed the outfielder "was in the discard anyway. He was offered to a minor league club a month ago and its answer came back that it couldn't see him. Let Evans go to contest with Artie Hofman and a couple of unknown minor leaguers for places in the Brooklyn team's outfield...."[11]

However, St. Louis Cardinals President Schuyler Britton's comments to the New York press were not so vengeful. "We had completed arrangements for the sale of Evans to a team in the Pacific Coast League," he said. "But if he had agreed to our terms we would have kept him through the 1914 season anyway. He is a great man for a ball club, as his cheery disposition will keep any ball club in good humor."[12]

One of the more unusual stories of negotiations with an unsigned "tourist" involved Walter Leverenz, a pitcher who posted a mediocre 6 and 17 record with the last-place St. Louis Browns the previous season. Browns owner Robert Hedges invited Leverenz and his lady companion to dinner. During the meal, the player's girlfriend convinced the pitcher he should play for the Browns. Hedges didn't have a contract with him so he borrowed a pencil and drew up a one-year contract on the back of a menu card, which Walter immediately signed. After only one season in the major leagues, Leverenz now became one of the highest salaried players on the Browns.[13]

Leverenz' prospective Federal League employers made out well on their misfortune. Walt won only one of thirteen decisions for the St. Louis Americans in 1914, and that was exactly half the total of his major league victories after 1913.

Eventually, Ivy Wingo and Lee Magee would sign contracts with the Cardinals for $6,000 and the backup catcher Egan received a similar amount to play with the Dodgers for 1914. The Detroit Tigers retained Sam Crawford at a surprising low annual salary of $7,500, only a $2,500 raise over 1913. The signing of Wahoo Sam left Ty Cobb as the only Detroit player still unsigned. Tris Speaker would not be the highest paid player in baseball for long. Though major league officials regarded the offer as a publicity stunt by the Feds, Ty Cobb reportedly had an offer from the Federal League on the table for $75,000 for five years with the first $15,000 to be paid at once.[14]

9

Opening Day

The return of major league baseball to Baltimore was so popular the Maryland State House of Delegates voted to make April 13, 1914, an official half-day holiday in honor of the city's newest team, the "Terrapins." The *Baltimore News* gave the opening of the Federal League season front page coverage and published a late "Baseball Extra":

> At 3 o'clock this afternoon, as the *News* goes to press, the largest crowd ever gathered at a local ball game waited with bated breath for the umpire to call "Play Ball!" as Knabe's Terrapins and the Buffalo Federals lined up for the opening game of the new "big" league season.... So intense was the interest in "major league" baseball returning to the city, a line had formed at the gates to buy tickets at six o'clock in the morning, though the offices did not open until eleven.
>
> The city seemed baseball wild. Downtown this morning everybody seemed to be filled with the spirit of the day's game. The crowds that watched the ball players' parade adjourned en mass to the grounds, and all the trolley lines leading to the York Road were taxed to accommodate the swarms that were anxious to witness the ball game.... By 1 o'clock all north-east bound cars were filled inside and out long before they reached North Avenue. Determined fans clung to the platforms and steps of the cars and even stood on the buffers outside the rear vestibules.[1]

Baltimore had a strong tradition of major league baseball. The city fielded several fine amateur nines in the years following the Civil War. In 1872 Baltimore joined the first professional league, the National Association, a year after its formation. In 1874, the last-place Baltimores dropped out of the league.

Harry Von Der Horst, who owned a brewing company in partnership with his brother, brought major league baseball to Baltimore in 1882. He built Union Park, a double-decked grandstand that seated 6,000, a good-sized baseball park for that time. The Orioles played in the American Association, recognized as a major back then, from 1882 until the club transferred to the National League ten years later.

The person most identifiable with Baltimore baseball in the nineteenth century was Edward Hugh Hanlon. Known as Ned, Hanlon was manager of the Orioles' famous National League championship teams of the 1890s. After playing with Detroit for eight years, Hanlon managed Pittsburgh in 1889 and the following season Ned was one of the discontented players that formed the Players' League. Ned took over the Orioles in 1892 and remained with them through 1898.

Hanlon's Orioles finished first in the National League in 1894, 1895, and 1896, and those teams were well known for their aggressive tactics. Under Hanlon, his players perfected plays such as the "hit-and-run," the "Baltimore chop," and the "cut-off." These plays later were described as inside baseball, but back in the 1890s they were "Orioles baseball."

In the second half of the 1890s, syndicates of owners assembled enough stock to control more than one National League club. This was the case in St. Louis and Cleveland, Chicago and New York, and Baltimore and Brooklyn. In 1898, Brooklyn president Charles Ebbets purchased a substantial piece of the Orioles. In turn, Von Der Horst and Hanlon bought a large amount of stock in the Brooklyn franchise. Ebbets continued as president in Brooklyn while Hanlon remained president and manager in Baltimore. Hanlon and Von Der Horst apparently became involved in the deal because of lagging attendance for games in Baltimore and the recent annexation of Brooklyn into greater New York as its fifth borough.

The syndicate decided in 1899 that Hanlon and his top players would go to the Brooklyn club because it had more drawing power. Hanlon became manager of the Superbas and the players of his two teams were pooled for a draft. Brooklyn took the best players of both clubs, except John McGraw and Wilbert Robinson, who insisted on remaining in Baltimore. McGraw demonstrated his genius as manager with the Orioles by finishing fourth in the twelve-team league. Hanlon's Brooklyn team won two consecutive pennants, but the Orioles outdrew the Superbas' 1899 championship team at home.[2]

On March 8, 1900, the National League magnates met in New York and voted to downsize to eight teams. Despite earning a profit of $15,000 in 1899, Baltimore was one of four clubs dropped, along with Cleveland, Louisville and Washington. The league paid Baltimore $30,000 for its franchise with Charles Ebbets and Hanlon reserving the right to sell the Orioles' players.

McGraw was assigned to the Cardinals, but the stubborn ex-Oriole told the St. Louis owner that he would not sign a 1900 contract containing a reserve clause and would play there for only one season. After the National League pared down to eight clubs in the winter of 1900, a group of promoters organized by St. Louis sports writer Alfred H. Spink proposed to resurrect the old American Association. McGraw planned to return to Baltimore as a manager and part owner of a new American Association club.

Ban Johnson beat the promoters of the new Association to the punch when he transformed his Western League into the newly reorganized American League and began expansion into the East. When Johnson visited Baltimore, he sought out Judge Harry Goldman to discuss the future of major league baseball in the city.

Years earlier, Goldman had been a left fielder for a local amateur team known as the Pastimes, and he was a noted member of the "Eighteenth Degree Rooters" at National League games at Union Park. One author described Goldman as "a friend of Ned Hanlon's, to the extent the remote manager had friends. With his dark pompadour and his handlebar moustache and his ordered, businesslike face, he even looked like Hanlon. But Judge Goldman was a Baltimorean first. At base he was a crank."[3]

Judge Goldman suggested that McGraw and Wilbert Robinson meet with Johnson. The two former Orioles were persuaded to join Johnson's American League for the 1901 season. McGraw would be the new Orioles manager as well as a stockholder. Goldman became the club secretary. When the National League refused to recognize Johnson's league, his agents raided the older circuit of its players. The American Leaguers had little trouble getting players to ignore the reserve clause and sign with them because of the National League's salary limit of $2,500.

Baltimore had no park in which to play in 1901 because Union Park, vacated by the National League Orioles in 1899, was owned by Ned Hanlon, who refused to lease the park to the upstarts. In those days, though, wooden grandstands could be thrown up quickly. Goldman found a piece of property at 29th and York Road that the owner, Johns Hopkins University, agreed to lease for a ballpark. Ground for the Orioles' new park was broken on February 12, 1901, and was ready for the team's first scheduled game on April 24.[4]

At a meeting of the Orioles' stockholders on July 8, 1902, John McGraw negotiated his release from the club in order to manage the New York Giants at a salary of $11,000 a year. Conspiring with National League owners John T. Brush and Andrew Freedman, McGraw orchestrated the demise of the Orioles. John Mahon, a local contractor who only became club president a few months earlier, collected 201 of the 400 shares in the Baltimore Baseball Club — his own, McGraw's, those belonging to player Joe Kelley, and the stock Wilbert Robinson had traded for McGraw's share in a saloon they jointly owned. Mahon signed his shares over to a lawyer who was working for New York Giants owner Freedman for $50,000. Six of the Orioles' best players were released, whereupon four of them immediately signed with Freedman's Giants and two went to Brush's Cincinnati team.

After McGraw's defection, Ban Johnson told a meeting of the Orioles' minority stockholders, headed by Goldman and Sydney Frank, that he was taking over the Baltimore club to sustain the franchise and protect the rights of the minority stockholders. Wilbert Robinson was named manager of the Orioles and was supplied with a ragtag team of major league castoffs, minor leaguers, and semi-pros, guaranteeing the club would finish in last place. Late in 1902, President Johnson transferred the Baltimore franchise to New York. Johnson and Frank Farrell, the New York owner, made cash settlements with Goldman, Frank and the other stockholders who stuck with the club after McGraw pulled out.[5]

Meanwhile, Ned Hanlon wasn't satisfied in Brooklyn. His two championship clubs drew only fair crowds, then the franchise was hit hard by the loss of players during the war with the American League. Hanlon wanted to transfer the Brooklyn team into the recently vacated Baltimore market, but Charles Ebbets insisted on keeping the club in New York. The decision rested with Von Der Horst, who was ill and ready to get out of baseball. Hanlon tried to get enough money from Baltimore investors to buy Von Der Horst's stock, but failed. Ebbets convinced an associate to buy the key block of stock which assured the club would stay in Brooklyn.[6]

Rebuffed by Ebbets, Hanlon purchased the Eastern League's Montreal franchise and moved it to Baltimore. With Hugh Jennings as manager, the new Orioles did well in their first four seasons, but never won a pennant. They came very close in 1905, losing by a half-game to the Providence Clam Diggers, piloted by Jack Dunn. When Jennings left to manage Detroit in 1906, Ned hired Dunn away from Providence to manage the Orioles. Let go as manager after Brooklyn's last-place finish in 1905, Hanlon was hired by Cincinnati, which placed sixth in Ned's two final years as a manager. Ned grew weary of the Orioles' losing ways and sold the club to Jack Dunn for $70,000 during the winter of 1909–10.

Hanlon had just about given up the idea of ever bringing major league baseball back to Baltimore when the dreams of James Gilmore became his own. Though he was not an official officer of the club, Hanlon became the largest investor among the six hundred citizens who put up $164,000, with another $36,000 raised through loans, for a Federal League franchise. Another investor was Harry Goldman, who became the club's secretary. By 1914 moustaches were no longer in style, though Hanlon and Goldman kept theirs.

The site for the new Baltimore baseball park would be a vacant plot of ground that Ned Hanlon owned at the northwest corner of 29th Street and York Road. On the opposite corner was Dunn's Orioles Park, originally built for the American League in 1901.

Work on the Federal League Park that began on January 8 was finished and ready for the inaugural game. The cost of Terrapins Park was close to $195,000 and it was constructed of "wood above concrete" rather than entirely of concrete and steel, as were most new major league ballparks. This meant the grandstand would be cooler, but also more susceptible to fire. Baltimore's newest ballpark seated 16,000, including 2100 in the right field bleachers.

9. Opening Day

The left field wall, backed by East 30th Street, was only 300 feet away from home plate, but dead center was among the deepest in the league at 450 feet.

In mid–February, the directors of the new Baltimore club announced the team would be known as the "Terrapins." The players' jerseys would have a small diamondback emblem on the left side with head, foot and tail extended. The terrapin emblem would be enclosed in a field of gold outlined by a gold cord.

On opening day, the *Baltimore News* reported:

> Practically every seat in the great pavilions was filled long before 3 o'clock and the bleachers, after becoming overtaxed, turned hundreds into the field. Every inch of the stands are bedecked with red, white and blue streamers, while thousands of American flags made the spectacle one of brilliance....
>
> There was scarcely standing room in the Federal League Park, but just across the way in Oriole Park, the diamond of which could be seen from the Terrapin Park grand stand, John McGraw's famous New York Giants and Jack Dunn's International League Orioles, who had been pitted as a strong counter attraction to the Federal League opening, played before some 1300, even the bleachers being only one third filled. McGraw took it good naturedly, but it was galling to the erstwhile Baltimore favorites, whose personal popularity heretofore never failed to draw a big crowd in this town.[7]

The 27,692 fans who had paid to get into the Federals' park, combined with those who had gotten in on passes, pushed the total attendance for the opening game to 30,000. Seventy-five-cent tickets were being scalped for three dollars and the club's gate receipts were announced at $15,000.

"The advent of the ball players on the grounds was the signal for the first big demonstration," continued the *News*. "The men had been parading about town in carriages. The band that had accompanied them took a position on the field early in the afternoon and soon afterward the players themselves strolled out for preliminary practice. Each man got the glad hand and a lusty cheer, and some of the better known were quickly seized upon and heralded with particularly vociferous ovations."[8]

In those days there was no public address system or live organ music so club owners employed musicians ranging from mariachi to marching bands. Players' jerseys did not have names or numbers for identification and an announcer on the field used a megaphone to give line-ups and make announcements.

The visiting team appeared wearing a style of uniform shirt heretofore unseen in the major leagues. The Buffalo players sported a road uniform adorned with the word "Buffalo" angled across the shirt front in script lettering. Eventually, the style would become commonplace in baseball uniforms, but the Buffeds used the script logo for only that one season. It was not until 1930 that the Detroit Tigers revived it and the script lettering began to be adopted by other clubs.[9]

When Baltimore Mayor Harry Preston, with Mayor Fluhrmann of Buffalo standing beside him, tossed out the ball of the first major league game in Federal League history, President James Gilmore gave the signal for the raising of the American flag on the tall pole in center field. Before play began, Baltimore Manager Otto Knabe was presented with a loving cup by a group of his Philadelphia friends.

Buffalo's starting pitcher for opening day was Earl Moore, a thirty-five-year-old veteran with 150 major league victories, mostly with Cleveland and the Philadelphia Phillies. Manager Knabe decided to start the spitballer, John Quinn.

Quinn's own two-bagger, followed by a slashing double to left by Harry Swacina, broke the scoreless deadlock in the fourth inning. The Terrapins made it 3 to 0 after Mickey Doolan

Baltimore Terrapins' Benny Meyer slides into third base during Federal League opening game, April 13, 1914 (courtesy of the Maryland Historical Society, McKee Collection).

walked, stole second base, and scored on Jacklitsch's two-run double into the overflow crowd standing in the outfield. The Buffalos pulled within a run in the fifth largely due to left fielder Hack Simmons' muff of an easy fly ball. Charlie Hanford drove in Buffalo's two runs with a double, after which Quinn held the visitors scoreless the rest of the game to give the Terrapins a 3 to 2 win.

Like most pitchers in that era, Quinn used a short stride when he delivered a pitch and relied on his fielders to make plays rather than go for strikeouts. In doing so, a pitcher saved wear and tear on his arm and was able to work more often than modern hurlers.

The reason for this strategy was the ball itself. Baseballs were kept in a game as long as they were usable. Sometime, only one or two balls might be used for an entire game. As innings progressed, the ball became discolored and softer.

During the 1914 Federal League season, President Gilmore fined umpire Oliver Anderson $50 for violating a rule which provided that "old" balls must be kept in play as long as possible. Anderson, it was charged by players from Kansas City, kept throwing new balls into play during a game.[10]

"The ball wasn't wrapped tight and lots of times it'd get mashed on one side," recalled Edd Roush of the Indianapolis club. "I've caught many a ball in the outfield that was mashed on one side. Come bouncing out there like a jumping bean. They wouldn't throw it out of the game, though."[11]

Pitchers loaded the roughened misshapen spheres with spit, tobacco juice, or any foreign substance they felt would provide them with an advantage. Roush remembered that during the dead ball era "they threw everything. They'd spit on the ball or get some dirt and put it on and when they threw, the clod would go one way and the ball another."[12]

Though the period during the existence of the Federal League was known as the "dead ball era," one writer, Russell Wright, suggested that since the cork-center ball was already in play during the second decade of the twentieth century, that period between 1910 and 1919 should be called the "Dirty Ball Era" because of the dirt, spit and scuffs that collected on the baseballs.[13] Before the livelier ball of the Twenties a batted ball moved more slowly and seldom took high bounces, and it took a prodigious wallop to send a pitch over the outfield fence. Stolen bases, hit-and-run plays and bunts were important parts of the game. Batters choked up on heavy bats and tried to punch or place their hits past fielders rather swing for the fences.

Afield, large numbers of errors were common. Playing surfaces then did not resemble the well-manicured fields of today. Baseball gloves of the time would barely be recognized as such compared to current-day equipment. Catcher's mitts were large circular "mattresses" and a first baseman's mitt was of shovel-like design. Fielder's gloves were enlarged mutants of ordinary leather gloves, with a horseshoe of extra padding. The glove with a multi-thonged webbing between the thumb and forefinger was not developed until 1919 and its introduction coincided with a marked improvement in fielding averages.

While the Federal Leaguers were celebrating the gala renewal of major league baseball in Baltimore, the owners of the Boston National League Club filed a $25,000 conspiracy suit against James Gilmore, Edward Hanlon, Otto Knabe and John Picus, Quinn's real name. The Boston club maintained that several weeks before he signed with the Federals, Quinn agreed in writing to accept the Braves' terms and signed a National League contract that was approved by the president of the Baseball Players' Fraternity. On December 7, 1914, the Boston club withdrew its suit. The counsel for the plaintiff told the court that it would be difficult to collect damages for the loss of Quinn inasmuch as without him the team won the greatest possible honors in the baseball world, the 1914 World Series.[14]

10

"The Nerviest Proposition I Ever Saw"

In April of 1914, the St. Louis correspondent for *The Sporting News* wrote that St. Louis Browns pitcher Earl Hamilton "was one of the American League's best southpaws, young and with a bright future ahead of him." Hamilton utilized a great change-up to become the leading winner among the pitchers on the lowly Browns in 1912 and 1913. On August 30, 1912, the twenty-three-year-old lefty pitched a no-hitter against the Detroit Tigers.

On Wednesday, April 8, 1914, Kansas City Federal League club president Charles Madison and manager George Stovall met Earl Hamilton at a St. Louis hotel away from the city's business district and made telephone calls to several other Browns players. Outfielder Gus Williams and pitcher George Baumgardner of the Browns had previously agreed to play for Stovall but later refused to sign the Packers' contracts when they were presented to them. When Stovall first visited the Browns' spring training camp in Florida and encouraged Williams and Baumgardner to jump to the Federal League, he also exacted a commitment from Hamilton.

After Williams and Baumgardner again declined the Kansas City offers at their hotel, Hamilton began to waver on his agreement. Madison and Stovall laid five $1000 bills on the table in Hamilton's room and told the pitcher the train was about to leave for Kansas City so he had to decide to take the money and sign a three-year contract with the Federals. Hamilton finally agreed and he was rushed to a taxi that took the Federal Leaguers and their prize to the railroad depot.

Upon hearing of his pitcher's jump to the Federal League, President Hedges of the Browns declared he would go broke before he would let Hamilton go to Kansas City or anywhere else. Ban Johnson wired Hedges that the American League would spend every dollar in the league treasury to stop Hamilton.

Hamilton, reported *The Sporting News,* was working under a three-year contract with the Browns calling for $10,000, and said agreement still had two years to run. In addition, Hamilton's 1913 contract contained a clause whereby he was to receive a $500 bonus if he won fifteen games, which Hedges gave Earl although he won only thirteen. The Federal League contract offered by Kansas City was said to have been for three years for a total of $21,000.[1]

The evening of Hamilton's jump, Clem Clemens, a catcher in his first season with the Browns, said he was taking the train to Chicago and he would play for the Federal League club there. Throughout the day, rumors were rife that at least six other St. Louis major leaguers were considering Federal League offers.

Previously, it had been the announced policy of the Federal League not to sign major league players under contract to their current clubs. Though their league's policies hardly mattered to Madison and Stovall, President James Gilmore told the press, "Organized baseball tried to wreck Stovall's Kansas City club and took away Blanding and Baumgartner, who had signed legal contracts with him. Therefore I gave the Kansas City club permission to deal with members of the St. Louis team, whether they had signed contracts or not."[2]

While the St. Louis Browns considered what legal action it would take against the Kansas City club in the Hamilton matter, Hedges decided to pursue another strategy first. The Browns' chief might have found it hard to explain in court how this case was different from the time he "encouraged and harbored" contract jumpers in the days of the war between the American League and the National League.

Hedges decided to meet with Earl Hamilton's father, a Kansas businessman, who reportedly "was much distressed that his boy should show such scant regard for his signed contract...."

Hedges went to the elder Hamilton's home in Kansas City, to which Earl was summoned by his father. After a discussion with the Hamiltons, Hedges and the pitcher returned to the Browns' team in Detroit despite the fact that Earl was scheduled to pitch on Thursday in the Kansas City Federals' opening game of the season at Gordon and Koppel Field. Earl Hamilton issued a signed statement to the press pledging his loyalty to the Browns, declaring his fault and asking that "the public forget his break."[3]

Gene Packard, formerly a pitcher with the Cincinnati Reds, stepped into Hamilton's role as Kansas City's opening day starter. A capacity crowd of 9,000 jammed into the tiny Federal League Park for the revival of major league baseball in the city.

"Everything about the day was of big league caliber, except the crowd," wrote Sam Weller,

> and there were almost as many present as could be jammed into the little grandstand and bleachers. Perhaps another 1,000 might have been packed in, but the throng was more than double in numbers of the one which attended the opening game of the American Association club here two days ago.
> It is believed many of the fans went to the ballpark in a skeptical mood. They were slow in their applause. They seemed to be watchful, as if fearing a bunco game, but before the contest was three innings old they began cheering. Their applause grew as the game progressed, and when, in the eighth inning the home team became rampant and almost tied the score, the throng went into a bedlam of joy. So the Federal League magnates are sure tonight that Kansas City has been converted.[4]

After seven innings, the locals had only one hit off the baffling spitter of Chicago's Claude Hendrix. With the Packers down 3–0, Ted Easterly opened the eighth inning with a line drive single to center. Gene Packard guessed right on a fast ball and clouted a Hendrix pitch right through Joe Tinker at shortstop and all the way to the fence for a double, scoring Easterly. With one out, Stovall beat out a hit to third and Packard scored the local club's second run on Bill Kenworthy's single. Manager Tinker and catcher Wilson had a conference with Hendrix, after which Claude retired Pep Goodwin on a pop-up and Art Krueger grounded out. Chicago held on to win the game, 3 to 2.

Back with the Browns, Earl Hamilton took the mound in Detroit on Friday and pitched one of the best games of his career, besting the heavy-hitting Tigers of Cobb and Crawford, 2 to 1. That same day, Earl was made the defendant in a damage suit for $25,000 filed with the circuit court in Kansas City by the local Federal League club. The petition charged the pitcher with violating his contract for $21,000, of which $5000 had been advanced to Hamilton. The plaintiff, according to the petition, suffered a great loss through Hamilton's return to the St. Louis team, as "he is a wonderful pitcher and a great drawing card."[5]

Hamilton's father returned the five one-thousand-dollar bills that had been given to his son by Madison. However, the Packers' president took the money with the stipulation that such acceptance would have no bearing on any action taken against Hamilton and the pitcher would still be a defendant in the damage suit. Hamilton would win nineteen games for the Browns in 1914.[6] In the end, the Federal League's lawsuit came to naught.

When the Kansas City Federals came to St. Louis later that season for a road game, Earl Hamilton sought out Manager Stovall and asked if the Packers would return a trunk containing twelve suits he had left behind. The irascible Kansas City manager was reported to have said the trunk would be either burned or sold before he would return it to Hamilton.[7]

Only a few days into the 1914 National League season, George "Chief" Johnson pitched a losing game for the Cincinnati Reds against Pittsburgh. Five days later he would appear on the mound for the Kansas City Packers in a Federal League game in Chicago.

George Howard Johnson was born on the Winnebago Indian reservation in Nebraska. Though his degree of Winnebago blood is unclear, Johnson attended several Indian boarding schools, including Haskell and Carlisle, both of which he deserted. He began his professional baseball career in 1906 with a prominent barnstorming team known as the Nebraska Indians. Johnson bounced around the minors for a few years until he learned to throw a spitball. His success with the St. Joseph, Missouri, Western League club in 1911 and 1912 led the Cincinnati Reds to purchase his contract.[8]

By the time of his arrival in the major leagues, George Johnson was already known as "Chief," a nickname given to many Native American ball players, but taken by most recipients as a racial slur and disrespectful to the leader of their tribe. In his major league debut, April 16, 1913, Johnson shut out the St. Louis Cardinals 5 to 0. On August 26 of that year, Chief Johnson pitched a three-hitter against the Giants, but lost 1–0 to Christy Mathewson on a seventh-inning triple by Fred Merkle. Johnson won 14 games and lost 16 for Joe Tinker's seventh-place club in 1913.

An affront to Johnson's pride apparently was as much a factor in the pitcher's decision to jump the Reds as the money. Johnson was known to have a few drinks the night before a game he was to pitch, a predilection Joe Tinker had been prone to overlook. However, Tinker's replacement as manager of the Reds, Charles "Buck" Herzog, fined George fifty dollars during spring training for conditioning violations, a term often used in those days to disguise a player's excessive drinking. When Herzog found out Johnson had been drinking the night before a regular season game in Pittsburgh, he fined George $100 and sent him to the mound against the Pirates although it was obvious he was too hung over to pitch. Johnson was removed in the fourth inning after he was tagged for six hits and four runs. The pitcher felt the manager deliberately embarrassed him and George would not be humiliated in front of his teammates.[9]

The story of Johnson's defection to the Federal League began with a former Reds clubhouse boy named Johnny Schreckel. When Johnny was dismissed by the Cincinnati club when he asked for an increase in salary, he contacted Joe Tinker. The Chifeds' leader engaged his former clubhouse boy as a Federal League agent and asked the young man to persuade Reds players to jump leagues.[10]

Johnson had signed his first major league contract for an annual salary $1,650 in 1913 and received an increase to $2,250 after only thirty days with the Reds. His Cincinnati pay was bumped up to $3,200 a year later because of the baseball war, but the Winnebago was still receptive to Federal League offers.

Johnson and teammate Armando Marsans met with Charles Madison in a suite at the Sinton Hotel in Cincinnati. Marsans would not agree to sign with the Federals — at least for the time being. Madison and Johnson went to dinner, then returned to the Sinton, where the Federal League official pulled a stack of bills out of a valise and counted out twenty-five $100 bills. Johnson took the money, shook Madison's hand and headed for the railroad station to board the train bound for St. Louis.[11]

On the way to Kansas City, Madison and his prize detrained at Union Station in St. Louis. The Packers' president already knew the Chicago Cubs were scheduled to return home after a series in St. Louis about the same time Madison's train left for Kansas City. At about 8:45 P.M., Madison and a group of reporters spotted Mrs. Larry Cheney and Larry, Jr., at the station gate waiting for her husband, a pitcher who had won forty-six games for the Cubs over the previous two seasons. When Cheney arrived, he had a meeting with the Federal League executive in a baggage room and was offered a raise of $2,000 a year more to pitch for the Packers. The pitcher was known to have interest in playing for the Chifeds, but Charley Weeghman had a self-imposed policy to not tamper with players from the other Chicago clubs. Upon hearing the news of Madison's conference with his player, President Thomas of the Cubs telephoned Cheney at 2 A.M. and convinced him to remain in the National League.[12]

On April 21, 1914, the Kansas City papers announced that Chief Johnson of the Cincinnati Reds had jumped to the Kansas City Federal League club. In addition to his bonus, the pitcher signed a contract with Madison for $5,000 a year. As reward for his part in convincing Johnson to sign with the Federals, Schreckel received a groundskeeper position at the Chicago Federal League Park.

A more serious problem for Organized Baseball than increased payrolls was the threat the outlaw clubs posed in court actions to eliminate the ten-day clause. Most baseball contracts included a clause that a team was required to give a player ten days' notice prior to his release. Major league club owners never anticipated that the clause might be used by a player (or a rival league) to get out of a contract. According to Johnson's Federal League attorneys, the pitcher gave the Cincinnati Reds the same notice of his leaving the team that his contract required the club to give.

After joining the Packers, Johnson was scheduled to pitch for the first time when the club visited Chicago on April 23. Coincidentally, Johnson's former Cincinnati club was in Chicago at the same time playing the Cubs at West Side Grounds. Garry Herrmann arrived in the Windy City with an army of lawyers to arrange things so that Johnson and the Packers' president would be served with legal papers as soon as they got off the train in Chicago. By the time a judge was found who would take up the case, Herrmann could only hope to catch Madison and Johnson before the game at Weeghman Park. The papers to initiate an injunction request were not completed until nearly one o'clock.[13]

Upon their arrival at the ballpark, the deputies serving the papers expected to find Madison in the box with James Gilmore and Charles Weeghman. Gilmore, mistaking the visitors for inquisitive fans, arose and told them, "Boys, Mr. Madison isn't up here, but I think I can find him for you," and with politeness steered the process servers to their victim.

Pitcher Johnson was served with an injunction as he walked off the playing field at the end of the second inning. Although an injunction was served on President Madison as well, it didn't stop Federal League agents from invading the Reds' hotel and talking to players.

"This Madison is the nerviest proposition I ever saw," reported W.A. Phelon. "He had the calm nerve to walk into the LaSalle, where the Reds were staying, stroll around the lobby, and with Herrmann and his retainers standing beside him, call different players from their chairs for consultation! He made a special play for Marsans and Benton, but they rebuffed him...."[14]

On May 4 Johnson was expelled from the Baseball Players' Fraternity under the rules of that body. Long before Curt Flood challenged baseball's reserve clause, Johnson found himself at the center of a case against baseball's major league owners. The Federal League's case was based on the proposition that if management was allowed to use the ten-day clause to terminate a player while the player was not, the contract was voided and that player could sell his services to the highest bidder.

The court battle over Chief Johnson's contract began in the Federal Court of Chicago on June 3, 1914, and Judge Charles M. Foell upheld every contention of the Cincinnati National League club to make permanent the injunction that prevented the pitcher from playing in the Federal League.

The Federals took immediate steps to appeal Judge Foell's decision. President Gilmore announced that Johnson would not be used in any game until a final decision was reached on the validity of his contract, although the Federals' chief counsel, Edward Gates, interpreted Foell's decision to be effective only in Chicago.

Johnson worked out daily with the Packers' players and threw batting practice, but during his idle time the pitcher managed to get into trouble. Although Johnson carried a stout 200 pounds on his six-foot-tall frame, he came out on the short end of a barroom fight with Pittsburgh catcher Skipper Roberts in early May. "The Indian got off the reservation and went into Roberts, who came back and beat the Red man up to a fare-you-well," said a report from that time. "Services of a surgeon were necessary to repair his damaged nose. Roberts really got the worst of it though for the Pittsburgh club fired him."[15]

After two months of legal wrangling, the case involving George Johnson was finally settled in favor of the Federal League on July 16, 1914. A Chicago three-judge appellate court overturned the injunction issued by Judge Foell in superior count. The two-to-one decision held the ten-day clause in the ball player's contract "null and void."[16] On July 24, a petition of the Cincinnati club to grant a stay of dissolution to the injunction prohibiting Johnson from playing with Kansas City was denied by the court.

Johnson always had problem with his weight, and during his hiatus waiting for the courts to decide his case, the pitcher became woefully overweight and was unable to perform at his best. The following spring, Kansas City Manager Stovall introduced hoop-rolling as a training exercise, and *Baseball Magazine* reported that the Chief began the Federal League season in the best condition of his career.[17]

Once he returned to action on the field, the appearance of the Native American Johnson received "substantial attention" from fans and the

George "Chief" Johnson, pitcher, Kansas City Packers, 1914 (Chicago History Museum, SDN-059371. Original photograph has been cropped.).

press. Chief Johnson and others, Chief Bender and Chief Meyers for example, were curiosities to the press and were subjected to the stereotype of the time in which they played. Baseball writers of that period could hardly resist the urge to utilize racial clichés. Comments in a game report by J.J. Alcock of the *Chicago Daily Tribune* were typical of the time: "Chief Johnson and his Indian cunning knocked the Whales out of the lead.... The Redskin scattered six hits over as many innings."[18]

George Murphy Johnson pitched for the Packers through 1915, but he never received another major league contract. On June 22, 1922, Johnson was found shot to death in an alley on the south side of Des Moines, Iowa. The ex–Federal League pitcher suffered a fatal revolver wound to his right breast during what appeared to be a botched robbery attempt. He was thirty-six years old.[19]

During his years in the American League, George Stovall was notorious for run-ins with opposing players, umpires, management and the league's officials. George had few friends in Organized Baseball because of the dispute that caused him to leave the Browns and his part in the Earl Hamilton affair.

With Stovall obviously in mind, American League boss Ban Johnson issued a statement in May 1914 that read: "No player of the Federal League can ever play in the American League.... a man may be reinstated by the National Commission, but can never hope to get into the American League. The National and other leagues may accept him, but as for the American League, never."[20]

For the next two years, President James Gilmore was forced to deal with the troublesome manager in whom the Federals had invested so much. The first occasion came in July 1914.

Harry Neily, a personal friend of Stovall, resigned his position as sports editor of the *St. Louis Evening Times* in March 1914 to accept the position of secretary and business manager of the Kansas City Federals. In June, the club's directors decided to discharge Stovall's handpicked business manager and employ a different man for less money.

When the news reached Stovall the afternoon of July the Fourth that his friend had been discharged, the manager assembled his men in the clubhouse and informed them that their next game was off. "Neily has been fired and we won't go to Chicago unless he is reinstated," he told them.

The players were unanimous in agreement with their manager and President Madison and several directors of the club were called in. Madison informed the team that Neily had been discharged and that was all there was to it. When Stovall became hostile toward the owner, Madison beat a hasty retreat. The team finally decided to make the road trip, but Harry Neily would not be with them. Carl Lundsford went along as the new secretary.[21]

It was left to President Gilmore to settle the dispute. He acted quickly and decisively. Neily, who had been fired, was reinstated. "That's a question for Neily and Mr. Madison to settle," Gilmore asserted. "I will not stand for a ball player or manager threatening certain action unless he can have his own way. Fining Stovall $500 will make him think next time."[22]

Harry Neily was "suspended" by the Kansas City club for one week, after which he could return to his position as business manager but would lose a week's pay due to the suspension. The loss of pay made up the difference between his salary and what was to be paid a new business manager.[23] The Kansas City club dumped Neily after the season, after which the disgruntled reporter signed with *The Sporting News* to write a column disparaging the Federals, especially the Kansas City club's owners.

11

Three Finger Brown

The manager of the St. Louis Federal League Club for the 1914 season would be Mordecai Peter Centennial Brown, the ace right-hander of the great Chicago Cubs teams in the first decade of the twentieth century. Two days after Joe Tinker signed to play for the outlaw league, Brown affixed his name to a Fed contract for three years to manage and play for the St. Louis Terriers at $7,500 a season. Like Tinker's, his contract was guaranteed by a bonding company, which assured payment for the full three years regardless of what fate might befall the league.

Brown's lengthy given name came from an uncle named Mordecai, his father Peter, and the year of his birth, 1876, which was the United States' centennial. He was sometime called Miner Brown because he worked in the coal mines when he was a teenager, but is often remembered by the unusual nickname of "Three Finger," though he had four and a half fingers on his pitching hand. Brown lost the forefinger just below the second joint when he was five years old. Mordecai's older brother was operating a feed cutter (a machine that ground up hay or alfalfa with grain) when the younger Brown stuck his hand into the shaft on which the knives revolved. In addition to the damage to his forefinger, his index finger was mangled and broken.

While his hand was still splinted, young Brown fell one day chasing a rabbit and the fractured bone in his middle finger shifted. When the splint was eventually removed, the digit had healed in a malformed manner. Mordecai could still use his finger so no further treatment was considered. The result was a bent middle finger, a paralyzed little finger, and a stump where the index finger used to be. Brown's deformed hand enabled him to throw a ball which moved unpredictably during its flight to a batter.

In those days, the working class found relief from the daily grind by playing baseball. Mining towns near Brown's home promoted teams, and Mordecai played for Clinton, Shelburn, and Coxville. While playing third base for Coxville in 1898, Mordecai was called on to fill in for the team's regular pitcher against the neighboring town of Brazil.

Although throwing was a problem when Brown played the infield, his deformed hand was an asset when he pitched. Mordecai's pitching performance that day was so good, the Brazil manager offered Brown more money to play for his team. Once the Coxville season was completed, Brown joined the Brazil team.

In 1901 Mordecai joined the semi-pro Terre Haute Hottentots in the newly formed Three-I league. Brown posted a league-best 23 and 8 record to lead the "Tots" to the first Three-I League championship. Mordecai was picked up by Omaha of the Western League a year later and he became the ace of the pitching staff with a 27–15 record. It was in Omaha that the newspapers started calling him "Three Finger."

"I don't doubt that the hand injury gave me an advantage in throwing a curve," Brown reflected years later. "The stub gave support to the ball and with the rest of the finger gone, I was able to get more spin on the ball. The stub also was helpful in throwing a slow ball or floater."[1] Brown's pitching repertoire also included a pitch that later became called a "screwball."

After that season in Omaha, Mordecai joined the St. Louis Cardinals in 1903. Following one year with the Cardinals, he was traded to the Chicago Cubs, where he had his best years. Brown was the ace of the Cubs' teams from 1906 through 1910 that captured four pennants, and he won 186 games from 1904 to 1912. Mordecai's best years were 1906, when he threw nine shutouts while losing only 6 of 32 decisions, and 1908, when he missed winning thirty games by only one. Brown also won five World Series games.

Brown tore a cartilage in his knee during the Cubs' 1912 pre-season tour in Cuba. As he was attempting to make a quick throw to first base, his spikes caught on a board being used as the pitching slab. Thirty-five and pitching that season on one leg, Brown appeared in only fifteen games and fell off to a 5 and 6 record. Chicago's owner, Charlie Murphy, sold his former ace to Louisville (American Association), which offered the pitcher only $300 a month for the 1913 season. Brown's old friend, Joe Tinker, was named manager of the Reds that year and he asked Garry Herrmann to sign Mordecai despite the pitcher's injured knee. Tinker got his pal a $4,000 contract with the potential to win two $1,000 bonuses solely at the manager's discretion. Wearing a specially made leg brace, Brown won 11 and lost 12 with the second-division Reds.[2]

On December 29, 1913, Brown followed Joe Tinker's example and agreed to manage and play for the Federal League's St. Louis franchise. Mordecai took up temporary residence in the city's athletic club at 4th and Washington. St. Louis suffered its worst loss of life in a fire on March 9, 1914, when the Missouri Athletic Club was destroyed. Thirty men staying in the building perished, and among the missing was the famous baseball pitcher Three Finger Brown.

"I was supposed to have burned to death that winter," said Brown. "You see, I had a suite at the Missouri Athletic Club, but Mrs. Brown had come to St. Louis and I engaged a room at the American Hotel. In the M.A.C. fire, in which many were killed, I was reported missing and the story got out that I was one of the victims. The fire didn't get me, but I lost all my personal effects in it, including my knee brace."[3]

Also in the club at the time of the fire were the contracts of the St. Louis Federal League players that had been given to Brown for safekeeping. The charred remains of the baseball contracts were recovered from the debris, though Brown's knee brace was not found.

Philip Ball and Otto Stifel, the money men behind the St. Louis club, preferred to stay in the background in deference to the club's president, Edward A. Steininger. Steininger was president of the National League Cardinals until 1913 when Schuyler Britton was named the chief executive by the club owner, who also was his wife. The members of the Thousand Dollar Club that began the St. Louis Federal League club a year earlier eventually dropped by the wayside until only Stifel and Ball remained.

Like the Chicago franchise, the St. Louis club used a collegiate ball field for its games in 1913. A year later, the team needed a new ballpark that would be up to major league standards, and the club president just happened to be chief executive of the E.A. Steininger Construction Company. After Steininger negotiated a deal to build a ballpark in Handlan's Park, the *St. Louis Globe-Democrat* commented that the choice "is the one location in this city for a ballpark, accessible to all [street]car lines, and within fifteen minutes of any place in town."

Supposedly due to recent fires, the city rejected the Federal League club's initial plan for a steel and wood grandstand. A revised submission was approved that proposed a "temporary" grandstand estimated to cost $32,000. The new plan called for concrete footings for walls and reinforced concrete footings for piers and columns. A drop of fifteen feet for approximately 150 yards from north to south along Grand Street necessitated dumping more than 2500 loads of dirt on the site before work on the grandstand could begin.[4]

While the club owners went about securing a playing field, Manager Brown assembled a ball team. On February, 7, 1914, local product Bob Groom, pitcher for the Washington Senators, revealed he had accepted Brown's terms and would play for St. Louis. Aside from the very attractive terms, Groom wished to play near his home of Belleville across the Missouri River.

Groom's recruitment gave the St. Louisans five major leaguers under contract, the others being Edgar Willitt of Detroit, Al Bridwell (Chicago Nationals), Ward Miller (Chicago Nationals), and Manager Brown himself. A fastball pitcher who mixed in a spitball, Groom finished his rookie season with the last-place 1909 Washington Senators with a mound mark of 7–26, tying the American League record for losses. He found success in 1912, going 24 and 13.

After Manager Brown, the most recognizable ex-major leaguer on the St. Louis club would be the former New York Giants pitcher James Otis "Doc" Crandall. Crandall was born on October 8, 1887, in the tiny Indiana town of Wadena. He began playing baseball after he finished his chores on the family farm and at his father's store. By 1906 he made it to Cedar Rapids of the Three-I League. The New York Giants drafted Otis in 1907 because, as Manager John McGraw would later say, he had played for Cedar Rapids early in his own career and decided to pick Crandall on a whim.[5]

Otis was a second-line starting pitcher with the Giants until 1909 when he started only seven games and relieved in 23. He experienced his best season with New York a year later when he went 17 and 4 in 42 games. That September, Crandall stepped in for injured starting pitcher Red Ames and started seven games, winning six of them.

Damon Runyon of the *New York American* nicknamed him "Doc," writing that Crandall was "the physician of the pitching emergency" and "without an equal as an extinguisher of batting rallies and run riots."[6]

In the second decade of the twentieth century, it became the fashion to use a top pitcher both as a starter and reliever. In between starting assignments, a team's top pitcher could expect to be used late in a tight game. For example, included in Tom Seaton's 27–12 record for the Phillies in 1913 were five wins and five losses in relief. The same season, famed Athletics hurler Chief Bender was a relief pitcher in 26 games in addition to his 22 starts. The big Chippewa earned 6 of his 21 victories in relief and held the lead for his ball club in another twelve games.

Crandall led the league in relief appearances five seasons in a row while helping the Giants win three straight pennants, 1911–13. He led the National League in relief victories from 1910 through 1912, during which time he went 45–16 overall. In 1911, Doc not only pitched in 41 games, he filled in at shortstop six times in June when Al Bridwell was injured, then moved to second base for three games when Larry Doyle was hurt in a collision on the bases.[7]

During 1913, Crandall became the first pitcher to have more than thirty relief appearances, but on August 6, McGraw unexpectedly traded Doc to the last-place St. Louis Cardinals. Twelve days later, the Giants purchased him back from St. Louis. It was said the Cardinals balked at paying his Giants salary when the pitcher showed up in St. Louis with a sore arm. Crandall pitched for Brattleboro to get his arm in shape before he rejoined the Giants for the stretch drive.

The *New York Times* quipped in its edition of February 21, 1914:

"old Doc" Crandall had "jumped" to the St. Louis Federals. "Jumped" doesn't seem to be quite the word, because Crandall's "jumping" days are over, and the real truth of the matter is that he probably rolled over to the "Feds," or was carried.... Last season, Crandall, for want of work, fattened up considerably. He took jaunts before breakfast and wore a rubber suit, but he failed to get down to that weight where a hurried trip to second base would be anything less than an imitation of a truck going to a fire.

This year the Giants have so many young pitchers that Crandall's salary was not raised to the Federal League standard, so he decided to desert the Giants and play with Miner Brown, who also used to be a pitcher.[8]

Doc's favorite catcher on the Giants since 1911 was fellow Hoosier Grover Hartley, a journeyman backstop who was known for his intelligence in calling a game. The catcher had been traded by the Giants to Cincinnati in December and Crandall told the St. Louis Federals they would have to take Hartley too, or he would not switch leagues. After catching fewer than 100 games the prior four seasons, Hartley became the Terriers' regular backstop in 1915.

James "Doc" Crandall, pitcher, St. Louis Terriers, 1914 (George Grantham Bain Collection, Library of Congress).

Despite only two months' time between approval of plans and the first scheduled game, Steininger's Park was ready for the Federals' 1914 season opener. The park was in a residential neighborhood that gave it a similar feel to current-day Wrigley Field. There was seating for about 7,000 patrons in the single wooden grandstand on the corner of Laclede and Grand that curved toward a pavilion near the corner of Grand and Clark Streets. The bleachers behind center field were nestled between two barricaded rows of houses and could provide space for about 5,000 more people. The pavilion down the line in right field was capable of seating 2,600. The playing field featured a right field wall that was only 300 feet from home plate, an inviting target for left-handed batters.[9]

Club president Steininger calculated that the St. Louis Federals were already $250,000 in debt before the first pitch of the 1914 regular season. He put the cost of the ballpark at $50,000 and the club was out $200,000 for players' salaries and training expenses.[10]

The inaugural game of the St. Louis Feds, played on April 16, attracted a large crowd estimated at close to 23,000. The weather was ideal as the temperature barely rose above eighty degrees. Ten gates to the park were opened shortly after noon and the people that had been in line since 9 o'clock poured in. All reserved and box seats had been sold several days earlier so the throng had to scramble for places in the bleachers and grandstand. The outfield was roped off, furnishing standing room for about 3,500 of the overflow crowd that spilled onto the field.

When the "Brownies," as the press sometimes called the local Federal League team, arrived on the field a little after two o'clock, the pavilion was already filled and the grandstand and bleachers were nearing capacity. Manager Brown's players wore white uniforms trimmed in dark blue with the letters "St L" embossed on the breasts. The Brownies and the visiting Hoosiers from Indianapolis posed for photographs after which batting and fielding practice was held.

Missouri Governor Elliott W. Major walked out from his private box accompanied by his "catcher," St. Louis mayor Henry Kiel. The ceremonial first pitch flew so high, Mayor Kiel had to extend himself just to knock it down. The governor removed his Prince Albert frock coat and prepared to throw another pitch. The second throw was again wild. The governor wound up a third time and threw a pitch that bounced in front of the plate. The mayor attempted to catch it and in doing so "he fell forward on his protruding stomach, much to the merriment of the assembled electorate." Major finally provided a catchable pitch in his fourth attempt then the two executives strode from the field of play.[11]

As indication of his ace status with the club, Bob Groom took the mound for Brownies, but had to delay making his first pitch until the floral arrangement for Mordecai Brown was removed and a photographer was chased from behind second base. The first ball throw by Groom to leadoff batter Benny Kauff was called a strike by umpire-in-chief Bill Brennan. Benny grounded out, but the Hoosiers drew first blood with two first-inning runs.

The Brownies came right back against the former Cleveland ace, Fred "Cy" Falkenberg. With one out and a runner on base, St. Louis outfielder Fred Kommers hit a fly ball that went over the "short right field fence" for a home run. Two more hits led to another run that gave St. Louis a 3–2 first-inning lead. The locals had a chance to break the game open in the second, but Falky struck out Ward Miller with two out and the bases loaded.

Biddy Dolan sealed the outcome when he came to bat for the Hoosiers in the top of the third. With Kauff and Scheer on base, Dolan hoisted a high fly ball to right field. Kommers moved back to the garden wall, then watched helplessly as the ball went over the canvas stretched atop the fence for a home run.

After that, the lanky Hoosiers hurler pitched up to his American League reputation and retired the Terriers with only two hits the remainder of the contest. At the conclusion of the third inning, Falkenberg brought his daughter Doris from the nearby box seats to the Indianapolis players' bench. The little girl, who had just recovered from a bout with measles, watched the rest of the game from that vantage point.

As his batters, one after another, seemed helpless against Cy's slants, Manager Brown began to complain to the umpires that Falkenberg was using an illegal delivery. His complaint was that the Indianapolis pitcher did not toe the rubber correctly. Amid hollers from the crowd, Brennan walked to the middle of the diamond and talked to Falkenberg, after which the game resumed. The home town crowd was disappointed as Indianapolis defeated the Terriers, 7 to 3.

After losing their home opener, St. Louis reeled off eight straight victories, winning the final two games of the series against Indianapolis, sweeping three from Chicago, then three more in Indianapolis. After that, the team began to lose. By the end of June, the Terriers' record stood at 26 victories and 40 losses.

In the early going, only Doc Crandall experienced success. Crandall got off to a great start, winning his first eight games as a starting pitcher. Going for number nine on June 9 in St. Louis, the rotund hurler pitched shutout ball against Pittsburgh for five innings. In the sixth inning Doc was stung for four runs and he eventually suffered his first loss of the season, 7 to 2.

Crandall's season was turned upside down in mid–June when the Terriers' second baseman, Joe Mathes, was lost for the season due to blood poisoning in his injured leg. It was announced the St. Louis club would honor his contract and pay the fallen second baseman his full seasonal salary. Armando Marsans, an outfielder who had just jumped to the Feds from the Cincinnati Reds, played seven games at second base before an injunction secured by the National League club ended the Cuban's season.

Crandall had taken an occasional turn on the infield with the Giants and his hitting ability was well known. Doc was thrust into the position as the St. Louis second baseman for the remainder of the season. His old friend Hartley even helped out, appearing in 13 games at second, committing only 2 errors in 49 chances.

Doc had only four more pitching victories after his amazing start, but his batting numbers were remarkable. On July 19, he ranked sixth among Federal League hitters with an average of .333. He finished at .309 in 278 at-bats and among his hits were five triples. This was not a surprise since Crandall had batted over .305 three times with the Giants, registering a best of .342 in 73 at-bats in 1910. In the field, though, he had limited range and finished last in fielding average among the Federal League's second basemen.

Though the St. Louis club's attendance at home was miserable, the owners did pick up a good payday when they visited Doc Crandall's home town of Goodland, Indiana, for an exhibition game that June. Some 1,706 of Crandall's neighbors paid fifty cents each to watch the Terriers play the "home team."[12]

As the season progressed, a rare bright spot for the last-place Terriers was John Tobin, the young outfielder from the sandlots of St. Louis. According to St. Louis sports writer Willis Johnson, Tobin got his big break in 1914 when Terriers outfielder Del Drake got a sore foot from wearing new shoes that were too tight and Johnny had to fill in.[13] The diminutive right fielder became the Terriers' leadoff batter and the lefty hitter led the club that season in runs scored, hits, triples, home runs and stolen bases.

To thwart offers from the American and National Leagues to their promising outfielder, that July the Terriers extended Tobin's contract with the Federals for two more years. It was announced his new contract included a raise of $2000 to $5,500 for the 1915 and 1916 seasons.[14]

On May 6, 1915, at Brooklyn's Washington Park, Tobin made one of the most remarkable plays in the two-year history of the Federal League. The Terriers were in a tie game with the Tip Tops when the St. Louis pitcher, Doc Watson, put the first two runners on base. The next batter, Al Halt, clouted a pitch into the deepest part of right field.

The *New York Times*' correspondent described Tobin's play under the headline "Triple Play Stirs Brookfeds' Fans":

> Mike [sic] Tobin at the crack of the bat turned and raced toward the brick wall, and when a few feet from it pushed his glove hand up into the air and speared the ball. By the time Mike had brought down the long drive Evans had turned third and was dashing for the plate, and Myers was just about to turn into the home stretch. Tobin made a long throw to Johnson at short, who tossed the ball to Bridwell, doubling Evans, and the second baseman then threw to Borton, retiring Myers at first.[15]

Unfortunately for the Terriers, Brooklyn successfully plated a run in the seventh inning to win the game, 3 to 2. Tobin wasn't even known well enough at the time for the New York reporter to get his first name correct, but that would change.

12

Weeghman's "Edifice of Beauty"

While Joe Tinker went about assembling a team of players for Chicago's Federal League club, Charles Weeghman proceeded with plans to build "an edifice of beauty" for their games. Charley chose to erect his ballpark on the North Side in a residential district known as Lake View. The ball field would be named "Weeghman Park" after the flamboyant owner.

The land Weeghman selected for the Federals' ballpark was once the site of four buildings belonging to the Chicago Lutheran Theological Seminary. The elevated transit line that came to the area in 1908 promoted an increase in construction and population. That, plus the continual freight trains that steamed past the seminary, led the Lutheran professors to decide the atmosphere of "smoke, dust, grime, soot, dirt, foul gases, railroading by night and day; whistles, ding-donging of bells late and early and in between times, and the ceaselessness of undesirable traffic incidental thereto" was not a suitable environment for the seminary's students.[1]

The site proposed for the Chicago Federal League ballpark was bounded by North Clark Street, Waveland Avenue, Sheffield Avenue and West Addison Street, but a problem arose when it was learned that a lease on the land was held by members of Organized Baseball. In 1909 Charles S. Havenor of the American Association's Milwaukee club purchased an eight-acre tract of land from the Lutheran Church for $175,000. Havenor and the owners of another club, Mike and Joe Cantillon of Minneapolis, planned to use the site at North Clark and Addison for the baseball field of a new American Association franchise because the location would not interfere with the White Sox or Cubs. Their request for a franchise was denied, but they kept the rights for the land they had selected for a ballpark. Havenor gradually divested his share in the real estate to his Minneapolis partners.[2] The property sat idle for several years.

On December 2, 1913, Weeghman, Chifeds' co-owner William Walker, and Federal League President James Gilmore secured a one-month, $500 option to lease the North Clark and Addison property. Although the Cantillons had no plans for the grounds, negotiations for the property bogged down as the end of Weeghman's one-month option approached. According to Irv Sanborn of the *Chicago Daily Tribune*:

> The forces of organized baseball are said to have been working to block the scheme to locate a Federal League club on the Addison Street site with some prospect of success.
>
> As a countermove, the Federal backers obtained an option on the old White Sox park at 39th Street and Wentworth Avenue, occupied by the American Giants [a professional black team] since the erection of Comiskey Park.[3]

The threat of a Federal League club playing games just four blocks from Comiskey Park was just enough to persuade the major leagues to back off their opposition to the Lake View site. Just one day after Sanborn's article of December 30, the *Daily Tribune* reported that Mike Cantillon was on his way from St. Paul to sign the papers leasing the property to the Chicago Federal League club.

The terms of the lease were $16,000 for the first ten years, $18,000 for the second ten, and $20,000 for each of the remaining seventy-nine years. In addition to the lease, Weeghman and his partner, William Walker, shelled out $15,000 for a parcel of land, 15 by 100 feet, that was essential for completion of the ballpark. Weeghman had a verbal agreement for the small tract of land, but in the final stages of the deal, an anonymous buyer approached the owner of the plot with an offer of $25,000. Weeghman was confident the prospective buyer was from Organized Baseball. Fortunate for the nervous Federal League owners, no one showed up with the $25,000 at the time and place designated for the sale.[4]

The existing major leagues learned too late that the American Giants' owner, J.M. Schorling, knew of no agreement with Weeghman to lease the 39th Street Park. It would not be the last time Organized Baseball would be duped by Gilmore or Weeghman.

Mike Cantillon did not go home empty-handed. In exchange for his release of the property, Weeghman promised that no American Association players would be induced to jump to the Federal League for the 1914 season.[5]

The new Federal League baseball park was designed by Zachary Taylor Davis, who had been the architect of Comiskey Park, the South Side home of the Chicago White Sox completed four years earlier. Davis was contracted to build the Feds' ballpark on the newly acquired site for $250,000. It would have a single-decked grandstand and seat 13,000; the pavilions and bleachers would accommodate 4,000 more. In compliance with the fire codes of Chicago, Weeghman Park would be fireproof, being built of steel and concrete.

Construction crews began clearing the land of buildings and houses on February 23. On a chilly March 4, the ground-breaking ceremony for the facility was held. Consent of two-thirds of the property owners within 1000 feet of the ballpark was needed for city officials to approve it for sports activity. The Chifeds almost dropped the ball, assuming that only the owners on the facing street needed to be involved. At the last minute, representatives of the team had to smooth out community relations.

The Federals did not bulldoze all structures on the lease property. "Some of the buildings on the north end of the lot will be allowed to stand, as they bring in a rental of $6,000 a year," Weeghman acknowledged. The left field fence would be close to the rental properties, but at least for 1914, the buildings would remain. The *Daily Tribune* noted that the Federals' property would have "space enough outside the stands on the corner of Addison and Clark Streets for stores which would bring good rent," causing columnist Ring Lardner to quip, "What will you bet us that one of them won't be a restaurant?"[6]

By March 28, the steel infrastructure was complete. However, everything did not go along as planned. On April 2 the unionized construction workers went on strike. Fortunately for the club's owners, the strike was settled after only two days. Almost as soon as the ballpark was finished, a property owner behind the right field wall threatened a lawsuit, claiming that the club had violated a city ordinance by failing to get the consent of the property owners adjacent to the ballpark.

President Weeghman had not decided on a nickname for his team prior to the opening of the season, so the Chicago Federals would be known as the "Chifeds" for 1914. The local press used "Tinx" almost as often in their newspaper accounts to describe Manager Tinker's North Siders.

The first head-to-head competition between the new Chicago Federal League Club and an organized major league club occurred on April 12 when the Chifeds played an exhibition game against a semi-pro team in West Covington, Kentucky. The Chifeds' game drew 4,500 enthusiastic fans, paying major league prices, and another 1,000 saw the game from building roofs and elevated areas. Across the river in Cincinnati, the Reds played the Boston Red Sox before fewer than 4,000. A hit over the fence was ruled a ground rule double, and the Chifeds hit so many balls out of the park that the game was suspended while a messenger was dispatched for more. Chicago first baseman Fred Beck drove a hit over a six-story building that stood behind right field. Tinker's men pummeled the semi-pros, 20 to 1.[7]

In 1910 twenty-three-year-old center fielder Frederick Beck was the Boston National League club's top power hitter with 10 home runs, 9 triples and 32 doubles. He was sold to Cincinnati in March 1911, but got off to a bad start at bat and was traded to the Phillies. Fred was out of the majors for the next two seasons, playing with Nashville of the Southern Association and Buffalo of the International League, then got another shot in the big time with the Chifeds in 1914.

Joe Tinker's team played its first regular season game at tiny Gordon & Koppel Field in Kansas City on April 16, 1914, three days after a gala opening for the league in Baltimore. Claude Hendrix drew the start for Chicago and allowed only one hit up to the bottom of the eighth and survived a late rally by the Packers to secure a 3 to 2 victory for the Tinx. The batting star of the day was wee Al Wickland, Chicago's lefty-batting right fielder. Wick drove in all three Chicago runs with a double in the second inning and a bases-loaded single in the sixth.

Albert Wickland, who happened to be from the South Side of Chicago, became a major leaguer in 1913 when he came to the Cincinnati Reds from Dayton of the Central League. Al's major league initiation took place at the Cubs' West Side Grounds on September 5. Wickland was a sensation in the game, hitting a double and a triple. The following day, the 5'7" leadoff batter bagged a single and two doubles in four times up. After that, he cooled off considerably and finished the season with just 17 hits in 26 games for a .215 batting average. Al earned $230 a month as a Reds rookie before he followed his ex-manager to the Tinx in January 1914.

Since their home park was not ready, the Chifeds spent the first week of the season on the road, winning only two of seven games played. After Hendrix, the Whales' pitching staff was unremarkable. Ad Brennan, winner of 14 games a year earlier with the Phillies, was bothered by physical problems and started only 11 games for the Feds in 1914. Charles "Doc" Watson had only one major league game under his belt, a 7–2 win for the Cubs against St. Louis on September 3, 1913.

The ultimate success or failure of Tinker's pitching corps rested on the arms of three Chicago boys: Tom McGuire, a holdover from 1913; right-hander Erv Lange, a Forest Park native with only semi-pro experience; and Maximilian Patrick Fiske from the South Side's Roseland neighborhood. Fiske had gained the respect of the Chifeds' faithful on the final day of the 1913 Federal League season when he pitched both games of a double-header against Kansas City. The righty won the first game, 3–2, and then dropped the five-inning nightcap, 1–0, when Fiske's own error on an attempted sacrifice led to the only run of the game.

"This fellow Fiske has as good a spitball as I ever looked at," beamed Manager Tinker. "He needs a little polishing, but he's strong enough to pitch in either the National or American Leagues."[8]

A teammate remembered that Fiske had no special method for preparing his spitball. "Max went 'pah-tooie' and away the ball went."[9]

12. Weeghman's "Edifice of Beauty"　　　　　　　　　　　　　　　　　　　　87

"Fisk[e] was so great that one suspects trickery," wrote Sam Weller of the spitballer's first 1914 appearance at the local Federal League park. "He had Otto Knabe's heavy hitting batsmen doing whirligigs, and while the rain drizzled almost from the start to finish and while the little gathering of fans (by reports 1,000) clapped their hands, this husky Fisk[e] person continued to stage stuff that made one think of Ed Walsh in the good days."[10]

On April 18 construction of the Weeghman Park scoreboard was completed. The next day, final work on walls, plumbing, and the infield was finished and more than 4,000 yards of soil and four acres of bluegrass were brought in to seed the infield and outfield. Weeghman kept an old horse he called "Queen Bess" in a stable located under the left field pavilion. "She helped me a lot for more than ten years," he explained, "and now she hasn't got a thing to do but romp out here at the ballpark and pull the lawn mower when the grass needs cutting. Every night when the ground is not too soft she is to be turned loose on the field to roll and kick up her heels all she wants too."[11]

When the Chifeds played their opening game at Weeghman Park on Thursday, April 23, capacity had been set at 18,000 patrons, including 2,000 in the ten-cent bleacher seats in right field. A unique aspect to the park was the wind. If the wind blew off the lake toward home plate, it was very difficult to drive a ball in the air to the outfield. If the wind was blowing out, batted balls would soar over outfielders' heads and over fences at much a greater rate. Columnist Ring Lardner also noted in his column that day, "The North Side lacks the odors [from the stockyards] that have made the South Side so popular."

First game, Weeghman Field, Chicago, April 23, 1914. Note the large house behind the left field fence that would become part of the outfield wall a few days later (Chicago History Museum, SDN-059321. Photograph by *Chicago Daily News*.).

The Chifeds' opponents were the Kansas City Packers and Chicago turned out in large numbers to support the new team in town. Many people did not get inside the park because management had to close the doors a half an hour before the game. Since it was situated in a neighborhood, fans that couldn't get into the park could stand on top of the El or climb to the rooftops of houses behind the left field fence. The event was designated "cap day," and since the Chifeds gave out caps of different colors, the grandstand looked like "a huge floral horse shoe." Reports of the day noted the conditions: "A chilly wind was coming off the lake and one needed winter furs to be comfortable."

A group of Chifed rooters tried to stage a bullfight, but the bull was not cooperative. More successful was the presentation of a huge American flag by the Daughters of the Grand Army of the Republic. The ladies and their flag preceded the marching band and players of both teams to the tall flagpole in center field. Rockets and bombs were fired as the flag was raised to the song "Columbia, Gem of the Ocean." After the display of patriotism, flowers were presented to Joe Tinker and Charles Weeghman was given a large silver loving cup.[12]

With an estimated 21,000 in attendance, some of the crowd had to be allowed on the field behind restraining ropes. Dutch Zwilling took advantage of this in the second inning when he poked a ball into the crowd for a ground rule double. An infield out moved him to third and Dutch scored on Farrell's single. Catcher Artie Wilson's home run gave Chicago the early 3 to 0 lead.

The Kansas City pitcher, Chief Johnson, did not come out for the third inning. As he exited the field after completion of the previous inning, Johnson was served with an injunction sought by the Cincinnati Reds that restrained him from pitching for the Federal League. Dwight Stone replaced Johnson, but his spitter was not effective in the Chicago wind. Claude Hendrix did know how to throw a spitter in the breeze and allowed only one run in the first-ever game in Weeghman Park.

The hitting hero for Chicago in the 9 to 1 romp was Artie Wilson, who hit a pair of home runs. That same day, the Cubs played Cincinnati on the West Side of Chicago before only about 1000 of their bugs.

Joe Tinker and sons Roland (left) and Joseph Jr., 1914 (National Baseball Hall of Fame Library, Cooperstown, N.Y.).

After an off day, Kansas City and Chicago went at it again. The crowd was down from opening day, estimated at 12,000. The stands were about two-thirds full, but they were a noisy lot, largely due to the battalion of North Side rooters behind the bench that "rang cowbells and blew horns with boisterous abandon." Again baseballs flew out of the park. Artie Wilson and Joe Tinker each hit a home run over the left field wall and Manager Joe also added two doubles and a single to support the 7 to 2 Chicago victory.[13]

The Chifeds were caught unprepared for the huge crowd that showed up for the Friday game of the twenty-sixth. The circus seats added for opening day had been removed so a ring of people stood in the outfield and a lot of the fans ushered onto the playing field climbed onto the top of the left field fence. The crowd was said to be around 22,000.

In the first inning, Kansas City's William Kenworthy drove a pitch toward the top of the left field wall and a young man sitting on the fence stretched out his right arm and speared the ball. The two sides argued about whether or not the hit would have been a home run but umpire Bill Brennan eventually ruled it as such. In the third inning, Chicago's Art Wilson walloped one into the right field bleachers for his fourth home run of the series. Kansas City batters hit three home runs off the ineffective offerings of Ad Brennan in a 12 to 4 rout.

During the first three games at Weeghman Park, nine home runs were hit by Chicago and Kansas City batters. On his team's next off day, Charles Weeghman had the 310-foot distant left field fence moved back almost twenty feet even though it required the removal of the front porch on a three-story brick house that now became part of the wall. The left field fence now was 327 feet from home plate and left center would be nearly fifty feet deeper. The club announced that following the season, the big house in left field would be removed, the pavilion extended to the street and a new set of bleachers would be installed.[14]

A Chicago reporter noted that Art Wilson was sick in bed and required the attention of a doctor. "Art had heard about the fence moving," it was reported, "but upon investigation it was learned that that was not the cause of his sickness. He has a severe attack of tonsillitis and may not be able to take part in the national pastime for two or three days."[15]

To further combat the unwanted home run binge, Sam Weller wrote, "Along with the fence moving came the news from the baseball factory in the form of a telegram that five dozen balls would be shipped immediately to each Federal League club and the new batch would not have so much bounce in them. The manufacturer said the resiliency of the ball had been reduced 15 per cent."[16]

The Federal League received some criticism from the newspapers for the increased volume of home runs in the first month of the 1914 season. Although short fences in several Federal League ballparks were partly the reason, the initial focus fell on the baseballs provided by Victor Sporting Goods Company of Springfield, Massachusetts. Mindful of their lucrative contact to provide the official Federal League baseball, the company quickly readied a shipment of new balls with the resiliency of the ball reduced. No one had the foresight to predict the popularity baseball would experience with the upsurge of home runs during the 1920s.

Charley Weeghman brought many new ideas to the promotion of the baseball experience. One of the most enduring was implemented that first game at Weeghman Park. During baseball games, vendors had traditionally hawked their products by walking among the people throughout the stands. Many fans complained about the loud bellowing and constant obstruction of their view of the action on the field by the vendors. The *New York Times* would note in its report on the first Federal League game at Brooklyn's Washington Park, "The boys peddling peanuts and lemonade walk on your toes and get in your way just like in the big leagues." The astute Weeghman saw the problem as an opportunity and constructed concessionaire stations behind the stands.

Even the often cynical *Sporting News* managed to give Lucky Charley credit:

> Weeghman has shown the old clubs how to get rid of the peanut, popcorn and the nuisances that are considered a necessity. Being a restaurant man, with long experience in serving the public, he realized the fans resent having their view of the game ruined by some walking vendor, and that they object to having the peddlers yell in their ears.
>
> The service at the opening game at the Federal League Park was a revelation. A trained force of peddlers, each with stations near the back of the stands, furnished the necessary refreshments. There was extremely little interference with the patrons and little unnecessary noise, yet the crowd was served more rapidly and with a much higher grade of stuff than is usual.[17]

Particularly distasteful to fans in those days was the requirement at all ballparks that balls hit into the stands had to be turned over to an usher for return to the field. In his days as a National League owner, Weeghman was the first magnate to allow fans to keep balls hit into the stands. But in 1914 Federal League patrons who did not return a ball to the field could be thrown out of the ballpark and possibly arrested just like in the other two major leagues. Sometimes fans would go to great lengths to keep a foul ball. During a game between Kansas City and the Chifeds at Weeghman Park in 1914, "Occupants of the right field pavilion had some sport with a bluecoat over a foul ball that one of their number attempted to retain as a souvenir. The policeman and a park attaché surrounded the bug and the ball was finally produced, but tossed out of reach. Others took up the game and passed the ball back and forth for several minutes before it was lassoed."[18]

The big test for the Federal League came on May 10, when Weeghman's club went head to head for the first time on a Sunday against the other two Chicago major league clubs. The largest crowd of the three went to the Federal League Park, where "Mordecai Brown Day" attracted some 20,000 fans to see the Chifeds play Brown's St. Louis team. The St. Louis Terriers' owners, Otto Stifel and Philip Ball, brought a party of friends from Missouri to see the game. Four sports writers accompanied the Brownies to Chicago at a time when it was unheard-of in St. Louis to send that many scribes to a road game.

A Chicago paper reported, "There were two armfuls of American beauties for Brownie from his Chicago admirers. Ward Miller, another former Cub, got one armful. Joe Tinker's two little boys appeared as mascots for the Chifeds for the first time. They were dressed in regular Chifeds uniforms of miniature size."[19]

The bleachers at Weeghman Park filled up by two o'clock and up to 2,000 persons stood in the outfield. Another thousand stood in back of the stands and a number of persons watched the game from the tops of buildings across the street. A band was there to entertain between innings and a megaphone quartet advertised the popular songs of the day. At game time, the heat was intense, but around 2:30 the wind shifted and the breeze off the lake provided relief for the large crowd.

Things started off badly for the former Cub immortal when the Tinkers reached Brown for four runs in the second inning. Mordecai had yet to pitch a complete game for the Terriers, but he shut the North Siders down after that and by the eighth, St. Louis had pulled ahead 5 to 4. In the bottom of that frame, Brown walked the bases full, bringing the Chifeds' most dangerous hitter, Dutch Zwilling, up to bat. With half of the crowd cheering Brown and the other half rooting for the hitter, Zwilling flied out to end the threat.

Brown gave up a leadoff single to Wickland in the ninth, but induced pinch hitter Harry Fritz to bounce back to the mound with the tying run on third and two out. "Brownie tossed to first base and strode off the field, while everybody cheered."[20]

The day after the game, Sam Weller of the *Daily Tribune* commented that "Stifel spent his share of the day's receipts celebrating last night."

Several factors contribute to getting baseball fans to the ballpark — a winning team, good weather, an interesting opponent, superior facilities, and promotion by the local club. During the early decades of the twentieth century baseball clubs frequently advertised special days to honor individuals, usually players, to boost attendance. The clubs of the Federal League also adopted this well-tested major league promotion, but Charley Weeghman took the gimmick to new heights during the 1914 season. In addition to "ladies' days," Weeghman scheduled numerous "special days" aimed at particular segments of the local population. In order to pull in Cubs and White Sox fans, Weeghman Park played host to "special" days for Chicago baseball icons like Mordecai Brown, Joe Tinker and Fielder Jones, but there was also a "Max Fiske Day." Special days were designated for opposing players who had a particular ethnic following like Otto Knabe and Chicago native Cy Falkenberg. The Chifeds also held a "German Day," "Bravo el Toro Day," National Union Day, and a combined Flag Day/Masonic Day, during which 2,000 Masons, accompanied by their own fifty-piece marching band, paraded on the field before the game.[21]

A special day for women to get into the ballpark free (some clubs required they be accompanied by a paying male companion) was not really a new idea, but the National League had sustained a ban on ladies' day since 1909. In March 1914, Charles Weeghman announced the Chicago Federals would continue the 1913 Federals' policy of "ladies' day" at his ballpark: every Friday would be designated a special day for the new group of rooters who would come to be called "fanettes." The Chifeds also offered weekly discounts to women for general admission tickets. Ladies' days were important to a ball club because it was hoped the women would become hooked on the game and their presence would attract male fans.

When President Hempstead of the New York Giants inaugurated a plan to admit pupils of New York schools free into the Polo Grounds until every school in the city was included, Weeghman thought it was a good idea, adopted it for his Chicago Federal League club and announced the promotion would be kept until the pupils of the city's 225 primary schools all had seen a game.[22]

A year later, Weeghman took his promotion ideas to a new level, expanding on what was being done by Barney Dreyfuss in Pittsburgh. In July 1915, Charley offered a variety of circus and vaudeville acts at his Federal League park while the Whales were on the road. In order for the shows to run well into the evening, Charley installed a complete lighting system to illuminate the field, complete with a double spotlight. On the nights of July fourth and fifth, the hippodroming was followed by five thousand dollars' worth of fireworks, some forming the patterns of the Liberty Bell, the American flag and President Wilson.[23]

However, Organized Baseball's hatchet men did not let the Federal League's promotions go forth without ridicule. During the 1915 season, Weeghman came up with the idea of issuing numbered coupons to the customers of his twenty restaurants with the winners of daily drawings to receive free season tickets to the Whales' games. *The Sporting News'* Joe Villa chose that innocuous promotion to ridicule the Chicago owner. In his column Villa scribed:

> The exposure of the allotment of beanery season tickets has caused a big laugh here and incidentally it has opened the eyes of persons who were inclined for awhile, to regard the Lunch Room League with some favor. The scheme is so cheap and shoddy that it is surprising how the eminent Weeghman could have pulled such a terrible bane.
>
> Instead of calling his team the Whales, the King of the Flap Jack Trust should have dubbed them the Bean Bags, so that the struggle with the Gingered Tip Tops would have been sufficiently nourishing to the hunger of the handful of fans still going through the press gates....[24]

In another column, Villa took the occasion of the Baltimore Federals' signing of a reserve outfielder to bash that club's fans:

> So Johnny Bates has signed with the Baltimore Terrapins! Well, well! Orioles' fans have secured another minor leaguer. Canned by the Reds and Cubs, Bates had nowhere else to go. Otto Knabe, who is fighting hard to win the Corn Beef Hash pennant, grabbed Bates to strengthen his team. Baltimore fans didn't shed a tear when Jack Dunn sold Cree, Derrick, Twombly, Midhoff, Danforth, Ruth, Shore, Daniels and Egan! Why? Because they have gone away back in baseball knowledge. They went crazy when the Terrapins beat the ridiculous Chifeds the other day — the Chifeds who looked like bums in Brooklyn.[25]

A monthly publication, *Baseball Magazine,* edited by F.C. Lane, was essentially neutral in the war between the Federal League and Organized Baseball, but took note of the abundance of insulting articles. Without ever mentioning *The Sporting News* or any other publication, the magazine's editor wrote in the July 1915 edition:

> Certain scurrilous writers subsidized by organized baseball are fond of referring to the Federal League as the Lunch Counter Circuit. This ill-meant fiction, no doubt, had its origin in the restaurants of Charles Weeghman and the bakeries of R.B. Ward, two leading magnates of that league. Were there no undercurrent of ridicule the phrase might pass unnoticed.

On another page of this issue appears an article tracing the career of R.B. Ward, the principle representative of the "Lunch Counter League."

> No doubt the minions of O.B. can find some criticism of the man who, starting without a dollar, has built up the largest business of its kind in the world and completely revolutionized the bread making industry. The average fan ... might even suppose that baseball owners would prefer to have men of that stamp in the ranks to others who made their start at the race track, or in tricky contract deals, or cheap ward politics of one type or another [obviously a reference to Gaffney of the Braves and Murphy of the Cubs].
>
> ...if Ward and Weeghman are members of the Flap Jack League, Ward's bread is good and Weeghman's restaurants are wholesome, and the money they have is clean money, which is more than can be truthfully said for some of the financial resources of organized baseball.[26]

The same magazine reported that Chifeds owner Charles Weeghman encountered a particularly antagonistic sportswriter in the lobby of a New York hotel. Though *Baseball Magazine* did not mention the reporter by name, the usually polite and courteous Weeghman seized the tabloid columnist by the lapel of his coat and fumed, "You are either subsidized by Organized Baseball, or you are the damnedest liar in the world."[27]

13

The Emery Ball Specialist

"Russell Ford, star pitcher of the Buffalo Federal League team, is suffering from an injury to the spine and probably will not pitch again this season," wrote the *New York Times* on August 14, 1914. "Three weeks ago Ford was compelled to quit in the middle of a game because of a pain in the side. It continued to bother him, and this week he visited Bonesetter Reese at Youngstown, Ohio. He was told the injury to his spine was of long standing and that nothing but months of rest would benefit him, if he could be helped at all."[1]

The news about Ford disheartened the Buffalo club and its supporters. At the time he was disabled, Russ had a won-lost record of 15–5 with 80 strikeouts for the fifth place Buffeds.

Back in 1907, the Canadian-born Ford was an obscure twenty-four-year-old pitcher with Atlanta of the Southern Association. The spitball was increasing in popularity among baseball hurlers and Russ hoped that mastery of the pitch might be his ticket to the major leagues.

One day he was working on his spitball with a friend and catcher on the team, Big Ed Sweeney. One of the moist deliveries was so wild it flew past Sweeney and ricocheted off the grating of the grandstand. Ed retrieved the ball and threw it back to Ford. Russ grasped the ball on the same moist spot for the next pitch, threw it with the same motion, and watched the ball break sharply downward before it reached the catcher.

A puzzled Sweeney asked, "What did you do to that ball?"

Ford had not idea so he examined the relatively new baseball and found a scuffed spot from where it smashed into the grandstand. The scuff was strategically located in relation to the moist place on the ball from throwing the spitter and this combination gave his pitch an erratic movement on the way to the catcher.

Ford threw the pitch over and over, using the same grip, and the ball usually broke in that same manner. Russ had accidentally discovered that a baseball with a roughened surface, if held in a particular way, and thrown in a certain manner, would break drastically on its way to the plate. However, Ford had trouble controlling the pitch and many of his deliveries flew out of the catcher's reach.[2]

Ford continued to experiment with the new pitch, but it remained too unpredictable to use in a regular game. The next season, 1908, Ford was purchased by the New York American League Club, but was deemed too raw for the major leagues. The disappointed hurler was sent to Jersey City for further seasoning.

While in New Jersey, Ford concentrated on controlling the trick pitch he had discovered a year earlier. He attached a piece of sandpaper to his glove and used the scrap to roughen a spot on the ball. Russell worked on the pitch until he was able to throw it over the plate with considerable speed and control. Eventually, he learned how to make a pitch break where and when he wanted it to. When Ford could effectively control the pitch, he was practically unhittable.

Once he began using the pitch during games, Ford was a sensation for the Jersey City team. He was recalled to New York near the end of the 1909 season, but he got into only one game.

On April 21, 1910, Russ took the mound against the Philadelphia Athletics, a team destined to break the American League record for victories that season. Ford whitewashed the Athletics, 1 to 0. After that, Russell won game after game, purportedly with a sensational spitball. *Baseball Magazine* reported in 1911, "Ford's main stock in trade is a wonderful spitter that has three breaks. No other flinger in the big leagues today can boast of such a delivery, and Ban Johnson's stickers are almost universal in their declaration that Ford is the hardest man they face from one end of the season or the other."[3]

No one but Ford, his catcher, and a couple of friends knew the true nature of the pitch. Sweeney was Russell's catcher during his tenure with the New York club.

"It was a great advantage to have a catcher who knew something of the new type so that he could judge better of its odd breaks and not let so many balls get away from him," Ford explained. "Otherwise it was a very hard delivery to catch. And there lay one great defect of the emery ball."[4]

As time went by, Ford discarded the sandpaper in his glove and developed an even less detectible method of roughening the ball.

> I constructed a ring of leather which I used to slip on my middle-finger. On this ring was a circular disc of rubber with holes around the edge. This disc was about the size of a quarter. Every game, I used to sew a new piece of emery on this disc....
>
> I used the emery ball all the time I was with the Yankees.... I used it only when I felt that I was necessary to resort to heroic measures to extricate myself. But I had always at my command a delivery that no batter on earth could hit when it was going right, and I had experimented with it for years until I could control it as I could a curve.[5]

Earl Gardner, Ford's roommate in New York, played with the Toledo American Association club at the same time as Cy Falkenberg. The former Highlanders second baseman is said to have given Falkenberg the secret of the emery ball pitch.[6]

Ford won 26 games for New York as a rookie in 1910, and 21 more a season later. In 1912, the New York club descended into last place and Ford's record fell to 13–21. When he pitched his final season with New York in 1913, Russ was making $5500. Ford was the best pitcher on the team, the highest paid, and he threw the most innings. When his decline began, Ford was good for about three or four innings, then he seemed to lose his control and strength. New York club owner Frank Farrell criticized the pitcher to the team and suggested that after the season, Ford could expect a substantial reduction in salary.

"I felt certain that Mr. Farrell had meant what he said when he claimed that I would get my salary cut," reasoned Ford. "...I went to the Federal League offices and told them that I would pitch for them for a certain salary. They accepted my terms and I signed for three years. My contract with Farrell expired in any case, but even if it hadn't, it was subject to the ten-day clause and various other clauses to the benefit to the magnate...."[7]

During the off season, Farrell sent a contract to the home of Ford's in-laws in North Carolina. The contract stipulated that the pitcher was to receive only $4000 instead of the $5500 he had earned for the 1913 season, but specified that if Ford won twenty games he would draw an extra thousand dollars.

"Twenty games with that rotten ball club was the same as a hundred games, as far as any prospect of getting the bonus was concerned," growled Ford. "Walter Johnson couldn't have won twenty games for the Yankee team of that year."[8]

Ford ignored the contract offer from Farrell, but some time later, the New York owner, apparently unaware that Ford had signed with the Federal League, wrote to the pitcher that the club had withdrawn the original offer and now it was for $2,000 a year. There was no response to the second communication either.

Once Ford and Cy Falkenberg, the main practitioners of the emery ball, left the American League, there was no reason for the players who knew about the pitch to continue to keep the secret. Falkenberg had not been as careful with the secret as Ford and several pitchers with Cy's Cleveland team experimented with the delivery. As soon as the emery ball was exposed as a pitch different from the spitball, hurlers throughout the three major leagues began practicing it.

Catcher Ed Sweeney did not follow Russ to the Federal League. Buffalo President Walter Mullin stated that Ed wasn't signed because he "wanted the whole world for playing with us. He wanted a salary of $30,000 for three years."[9]

Ford was assigned to the Buffalo Federal League Club and when one of that club's officials urged Ford to deny he originated the emery ball, Russell replied. "Why should I deny it? The New York press, since I have left the city, have accused me of everything except polygamy and murder. Now that they accuse me of having an original idea, why should I deny it?

"...Even as it was, I could congratulate myself that I had had the use of so valuable a secret for so long."[10]

Like Baltimore, the city of Buffalo felt it had been betrayed by Ban Johnson in his play to make the American League a major league in 1901. Concerned about the future of the Eastern League, Buffalo Bisons owner Jim Franklin had cast his lot with Johnson's Western League in 1899. Ban changed the name of the circuit to the American League for 1900 and at the spring meeting of the owners, Buffalo's Jim Franklin made the motion to raise President Johnson's salary by $1,000. It was a favor Alderman Franklin would soon regret.

Months later, the *Buffalo Courier* editorialized, "Franklin was promised by that blubberous expounder of gaseous talk, Ban Johnson, that Buffalo would undoubtedly be a member of the new American League. Buffalo's impresario thought that the balloonish Johnson was a man of his word, but subsequent events inundated, so to speak, the dry land on which Franklin thought he stood."[11]

In early 1901 Johnson took his plan to gain equal status with the National League to the next level. A major factor in his plan was to invade key National League cities in the East. That move necessitated dropping the smaller population franchises from the league. Indianapolis, Kansas City and Buffalo were stripped of American League membership in a meeting in Chicago on January 28, 1901. The Buffalo press and fans were enraged when their club was formally dumped. The Eastern League, headed by the same Pat Powers who had managed the Bisons to a pennant in 1891, was happy to have Buffalo back following the Johnson double-cross.

Backing the Buffalo Federal League franchise were chief owner Walter Mullen, who at thirty-seven had "done wonders for the city in the real estate business," and businessmen Laurens Enos, Oliver Cabana, and William E. Robertson, who was chosen president. Former professional ballplayer Richard T. "Dick" Carroll, who had originally represented the Canadian investors, became business manager. John L. Kelly, brother of Billy Kelly, long-time sports editor of the *Buffalo Courier,* was secretary. The manager was Larry Schlafly, the former major league infielder.[12]

About $5,000 was raised in Buffalo for the franchise by placing subscription blanks in cafes, cigar stores, and hotels. In the spring of 1914, the local newspapers printed an advertisement from the Buffalo League Federal Baseball Company entitled "Share in the Profits of the Game You Patronize." The ad stipulated to potential investors that the local Federal League club had placed $50,000 of preferred stock in shares of $10 each on sale and, "With every purchase of preferred, one half the purchase price in common stock is given as a bonus.... This gives to even the smallest shareholder precisely the same terms as those extended to the officers and large purchases."[13]

Aided by assignments out of a central pool of players, Manager Larry Schlafly was able to assemble a representative team. Thirty-five-year-old Earl Moore won 22 games for the Phillies in 1910, but by 1914 he was unquestionably over the hill. William "Baldy" Louden had batted .241 as a fill-in at several infield positions for the Detroit Tigers the previous season. Buffalo's best and most recognizable major league player was Russell Ford.

When the Buffalo Federals advertised Russ Ford as "the greatest pitcher in the American League last year who jumped a $6,000 Yankee contract to play with Larry Schlafly's team," New York manager Frank Chance responded, "Let him go! We are glad to get rid of him." Then there were rumors that Ford's arm was "gone."[14]

Schlafly lured first baseman Joseph Agler and thirty-four-year-old catcher Walter Blair from his former Jersey City International League club. Harry Sandager of *The Sporting News* called "Heavy" Blair "one of the league veterans, a brainy backstop, a man who knew the weak points of rival hitters and his loss will be severe."[15] A product of Bucknell University, Blair joined the New York Highlanders in 1907, serving mostly as a reserve catcher the next four years. In 1911 the new manager, Hal Chase, named Blair the starting receiver for a young New York pitching staff that included Russ Ford, John Picus Quinn and Ray Caldwell. Unfortunately, Blair never hit major league pitching very well and spent the next two years in the minors.

Buffalo fans were familiar with Charles Hanford, who jumped from the city's International League club to play center field for Schlafly. Charlie proved to be a good acquisition as he led the Buffeds in hits, runs scored, doubles, triples, home runs and runs batted in. Lesser lights filled out much of the starting line-up: Agler, Thomas Downey, Frederick Smith and Ernest Luther Bonin.

Right fielder Luther Bonin's major league credentials consisted of exactly one at-bat with the Browns in 1913. Bonin was involved in an unusual play in Buffalo's second Federal League game. Bonin thought he had his first major league home run when he hit a ball into the bleachers during the game against Baltimore on April 17. As he rounded third base, Manager Schlafly patted Bonin on the back as he passed the coach's box. The umpire then ruled the runner out because of interference. Schlafly protested the game and Bonin was credited with a triple. Buffalo won the game anyway, 4 to 3. Bonin couldn't hold on to the right field job because of his anemic batting and finished his career without a single home run in his 21 major league games.

The "Buf-feds," a nickname actually chosen in a newspaper contest, scheduled their home opener for May 11, 1914. The date was remarkable in that it was less than two months after a Rochester contractor, Mosier & Summers, broke ground on a 500-by-500-foot tract at Northland Avenue and Lonsdale Road. At a cost of $130,000, the workers had the 20,000-seat steel and wood stadium sufficiently completed to play there on the scheduled opening date.

By the time of their home opener, the Buffeds had already lost ten out of their first seventeen games. Though the team was playing poorly, a clear pitching ace was emerging. A week before the Buffeds came back home, Russell Ford beat Indianapolis, 1–0, his first Federal League shutout.

On May 11, the day of Buffalo's home opener against Baltimore, a light rain fell almost continually and the new field was heavy with mud. An overflow crowd of 25,000 had been expected for the dedication of the new Federal League Park, but the miserable weather held attendance down to 14,286. Mayor Louis P. Fuhrman marched from downtown with a large procession and pitched the first ball to formally inaugurate the return of major league baseball to the city for the first time since the Players' League failed in 1890.

For a while, it looked like the game would be canceled because of the rain, then it was announced that a two-inning exhibition would be played to give the fans a reward for coming despite the miserable weather. The newly made outfield, uncovered by sod in many places, was a quagmire despite a liberal application of shavings.

Since there would not be a regular game, reserve pitcher Bob Brown was sent out to pitch for the home team. Remarkably, the sky cleared of rain clouds after play began and it was announced that the contest would become the regularly scheduled game. With one out in the eighth inning, Brown was relieved by Gene Krapp with the score tied at three.[16]

While with Cleveland, Krapp once led the American League in walks, and his old bugaboo of poor control cost the Buffeds. The spirits of the soggy home fans were further dampened when Krapp handed Baltimore the game via a bases-loaded walk in the ninth inning.

As for Bob Brown, that opening day was the only game he ever started in the major leagues. However, he wasn't Bob Brown at all, but was really Robert A. Smith, formerly of the Minneapolis American Association Club. Dick Carroll signed the pitcher to a two-year contract to play for the Buffeds that spring. However, the Federal League had a gentlemen's agreement not to tamper with any players in the American Association. Larry Schlafly didn't want the Cantillons to find out he had hijacked one of the Millers' players. So Smith agreed that he would play the 1914 season under the name "Robert M. Brown." During the season only two teammates, Frank Delahanty and Nick Allen, who also had played in Minneapolis, knew who Brown really was.[17]

The two emery ball specialists, Russ Ford and Cy Falkenberg, faced off against each other for the first time as Federal Leaguers in Indianapolis on May 3, 1914. A crowd of 10,000 was continually frustrated as the home team was unable to bunch more than one hit off Ford during any inning.

The *Indianapolis Star* reported that Ford had "his famous double-breaking spitball dancing around the plate and only five hits were made off his deceptive saliva slants." However, a fine fielding play by the Buffeds' second baseman thwarted a potential big inning in the early moments of the game. The Hoosiers' Bill McKechnie singled with one out in the home first and Benny Kauff drew a walk. The hard-hitting Frank LaPorte put solid wood on a Ford pitch and sent the ball on a fast ride toward right field. Buffalo's Tom Downey speared the hot bounder, tagged Kauff a few feet from the bag and threw to the first baseman to retire LaPorte.

Ford gained the distinction of scoring the game's only run after he walked in the sixth inning. The Buffalo pitcher stayed close to the bag as Falkenberg retired the next two batters. With Baldy Louden at bat, Russ made a sudden dash toward second base that was such a surprise to the Hoosiers that he made it in standing up. Ford's delayed steal paid off when he was able to score easily as Louden's ground ball took a high bounce over the second baseman's head.

Ford's defense may have saved the game in the home half of the sixth. With a runner on second, Russ knocked down Kauff's line drive and threw him out at first. Falkenberg was dominant except for the Louden hit and struck out eight of the "Black Hats." Cy walked in the eighth inning and departed for a pinch-runner, who was promptly picked off by Ford. With two out in the ninth Kauff took a Ford pitch in the ribs to get on base, but the game ended with Hanford's catch of LaPorte's long fly ball near the flagpole. Russell Ford won the match, 1 to 0.[18]

On August 3, Buffalo defeated St. Louis, 4 to 0, with the Terriers' manager, Mordecai Brown, the losing pitcher. Ford was compelled to leave in the middle of the game because of pain in his right side. The concerned pitcher traveled to Youngstown, Ohio, for a visit with Bonesetter Reese.

John D. Reese did not have a medical degree, but he did have a reputation as a manipulator of muscles and ligaments that made him somewhat of a miracle worker among Youngstown iron workers and later professional ball players. His nickname, "Bonesetter," did not mean he set broken bones, but it was a term the Welsh iron workers used for treatment of muscle and tendon strains.[19]

Ford at first denied any past injury, but under close questioning by Bonesetter the pitcher finally admitted that he may have received the injury in California during the winter of 1912 when he made an ill-advised dive into a water tank. Reese told Russ that he dislocated one of the joints of his spine when he hit the bottom of the tank. Ford was told that rest was the only treatment that might help his symptoms.[20]

Though it appeared his season was over in mid-August, Ford returned to the mound less than three weeks after he was disabled. On September 5, he pitched the Buffeds to a 4 to 2 triumph over the Terrapins. Russ finished the final third of the season as dominating as he had been the first two-thirds. Ford won five of his last six decisions, his final victory a sixteen-inning 1 to 0 whitewash of Pittsburgh in which he allowed only five hits and issued a single base on balls. The Rebels' Elmer Knetzer was touched for fifteen hits and gave up five walks, but the Buffs were unable to score until Heavy Blair crossed home plate with the only run of the contest in the sixteenth.

As more pitchers in all three major leagues began using the emery ball, baseball people began to demand that the pitch be banned. The American League was first, Ban Johnson announcing on September 22, 1914, that the emery ball was no longer legal.

After the conclusion of the 1914 season, the National and Federal Leagues also abolished the emery ball. President Gilmore let it be known that it was not sportsmanlike to permit a pitcher to deface the ball and announced a new rule. Federal League Rule 38 read, "The use of what is known as the emery ball is positively prohibited. If emery paper, cinders, or any other substance is used by any player to roughen a ball, the offender will be fined $200.00 and suspended for 10 days without pay."[21]

The year 1915 would be a different story for Russell Ford and Cy Falkenberg. Following the abolition of his emery ball and plagued by physical maladies, Russell Ford struggled.

14

The Terrapins Set the Pace

Right-handers Jack Quinn and George Suggs gave Baltimore the best one-two pitching punch during the Federal League's inaugural season as a major league. The pair accounted for 51 of the Terrapins' 84 victories while the rest of the staff, combined, won 33 and lost 44.

At five feet seven inches, George Franklin Suggs was short for a big league pitcher, even back then. While he was with the Memphis club of the Southern Association, Suggs pitched an eleven-inning no-hitter against Nashville on September 8, 1906, then came back in a second game that afternoon and shut out the Nashvilles on seven hits. The Kinston, North Carolina, native won sixty games over four seasons with Cincinnati Reds, including 18 in 1910 and 19 in 1912.[1]

Cincinnati sold the thirty-year-old Suggs to the St. Louis Cardinals in October 1913, but the pitcher jumped to the Federal League the following February, just days before he was to get married. George won 25 games for the Terrapins in 1914 despite allowing more hits than innings pitched. However, he did not walk many batters and had developed a unique ability to hold runners close to the base with a quick pick-off move. George missed a no-hitter against Boston in 1913 by one infield scratch hit. During the 1914 season, he walked only 57 batters in 319 innings pitched, 1.5 walks per nine innings.

John Quinn was always vague about his age, so various baseball record books place the year of his birth anywhere between 1883 and 1885. Born John Quinn Picus on July 5 in Janesville, Pennsylvania, he reversed his middle and last names in adulthood because he thought Quinn would go over better in the big cities. As a boy, John worked in the local coal mines picking slate before a mine fire caused him to change his vocation. He was in the lowest shaft when the blaze ignited and he had to fight his way more than a mile through suffocating smoke to escape.

His life changed when he attended a baseball game in Connellsville, Pennsylvania, in 1903. During the course of the contest, an errant throw rolled in John's direction and he fired it back to the catcher with such force and accuracy that the manager of the visiting Dunbar team offered him $5 if he would pitch and win the next game, $2.50 if he lost. John took him up on the offer. Though no records survive from the Pennsylvania State League, Quinn, who sometimes played under the name "Johnson," apparently was a successful pitcher in that circuit between 1903 and 1906.[2]

Playing under the name "Jackson," John pitched for Macon of the Sally League in 1907. At mid-season 1908, "Jackson" (Quinn) joined Richmond of the Virginia League and pitched the Lawmakers to the championship with a personal record of 14 victories, no losses and three ties. On August 8, the big right-hander pitched a no-hitter against Norfolk, winning 2–0.

Drafted by the New York American League club following the season, "Jack" Quinn found himself in the big leagues with the Highlanders (later known as the Yankees) in 1909. His first two seasons in New York were a success, as he posted 9–5 and 18–12 records with earned run averages of 1.97 and 2.37. In 1912, however, his earned run average jumped to 5.79 and New York shipped him to Rochester of the International League.

Quinn won 19 games for Rochester in 1913. Once, he pitched both games of a doubleheader against first-place Newark, but lost both for lack of support. Later, he threw a one-hitter against Jersey City. On August 23, the Boston Braves purchased Quinn's contract for $3,500. Quinn started seven games for the Braves the remainder of the season, winning four.

After his short stint with the Boston National Leaguers, the spitballer jumped to the Baltimore Terrapins of the newly formed Federal League for a promise of $4,800 a season for three years plus a $2,500 inducement.[3] Oddly enough, Jack enjoyed his finest major league season (1914: 26–14) and suffered through his worst (1915: 9–22) in the Federal League's two-year existence.

Baseball Magazine wrote that Quinn's "200 pounds is solid bone and muscle, or rather 'gristle,' as he calls it. The truth is, Quinn has a phenomenally powerful build. Nature endowed him with much more than average strength. And with that strength goes an even more pronounced endurance."[4]

Of his signature pitch, Quinn later said, "I didn't take up the spitter because I especially like it, although I learned to like it later. My fingers were so short I couldn't grip a ball well enough to throw an effective curve. With a fast ball and a spitter, however, I have developed a control that I think will rank as good as anybody's.... A spitter is thrown with exactly the same motion as a fast ball, and fast ball pitching is the easiest pitching there is."[5]

Jack Quinn defeated Buffalo on opening day of the 1914 season, after which Baltimore lost their next two games to the Buffeds. Then, the Baltimore club caught fire, winning 21 of their next 26 games. The Terrapins had every reason to believe 1914 would be their year following a game with Brooklyn on April 22. Trailing 7 to 0 against Tom Seaton in the fifth inning, Baltimore came roaring back, eventually overcoming the Tip Tops, 9 to 8. Otto Knabe's two-run double to right field plated the tying and winning runs.

During their marvelous start, the Terrapins had one winning streak of seven games and two of six straight. The high-water mark for the club was the sweep of a series with the Chifeds in Baltimore that May that drew close to 18,000 for the three games. Their victory in the finale of the three-game set on May 23 was especially electrifying.

"Baltimore fans turned out with loads of enthusiasm and in great numbers for the final fray," wrote a reporter. "The stands were almost filled and it looked as if at least 10,000 were present, which is a considerable throng for a town supposed to be a dead one in baseball. It was a swell day and straw hats and lawn dresses were prominent."[6]

The contest was tied at 3–3 when the home town came to bat in the sixth inning. Tom McGuire had kept the Terrapins in check after Fiske was driven out of the game during a three-run first. Vernon Duncan led off the sixth with a walk, then Harry Swacina raised a short fly to right. The wind carried the ball away from the Chifed second baseman and it fell for a single. McGuire tried to sneak the first pitch past Zinn for a quick strike, but Guy connected and drove the ball into the right field bleachers for a three-run home run. Baltimore won by the final score of 7 to 4.

On May 27, one day after St. Louis lost a game in Baltimore on a wild pitch by Bob Groom in the tenth inning, the Terrapins defeated St. Louis in a game that was suspended because of a windstorm in the sixth inning. After waiting twenty minutes, umpire Alfred Mannassau called the game with the score 4 to 3 in Baltimore's favor. The frustrated St. Louis players protested that it was light enough to play. During the argument, right fielder Fred Kommers, whose nickname was "Bugs," and who was one of three players ejected from the previous day's game, kicked Mannassau in the side. The umpire did not retaliate and Kommers was rushed off the grounds by his teammates.[7]

At the end of that stormy day, Baltimore was in first place with a record of 22 victories against only 7 losses, 7 games ahead of the second-place club. No other club in the Federal League was playing better than .500 baseball. That was about to change.

The May thunderstorm seemed to cool off the Terrapins, who thereafter went on a seven-game losing streak and won only eight of their next thirty-five games. Behind the scenes there were also problems among the players.

The first hint of disaffection among Baltimore players came in mid–May when pitchers Frank Smith and John Allen deserted the ball club and attempted to join the Montreal team of the International League. Allen was an insignificant substitute, but Smith was a symbolic, if not important, acquisition for the Baltimore Federals. At the time of his defection, Smith's record was three victories against no defeats.

Baltimore Terrapins manager Otto Knabe, 1914 (Chicago History Museum, SDN-059412).

Though past his prime, the thirty-four-year-old Smith (whose family name was Schmidt) had two career no-hitters and was owner of 119 major league victories, including twenty-five wins in 1910. However, the two-time twenty-game winner with the White Sox had a cranky disposition. After winning 23 games in 1907, he jumped the White Sox the following July, the second time he had left the club. Smith said he was unhappy with owner Charles Comiskey's complaints about his pitch selection and Manager Fielder Jones' early-morning workouts. Privately, the pitcher was upset with the criticism of his late-night drinking habits. Smith went home to Pittsburgh to take up his off-season occupation of piano moving. Frank's nickname was "Piano Mover," but the local papers reported the White Sox players began calling him "Deserter" Smith. Fielder Jones finally convinced Smith to rejoin the team and the pitcher won 11 games down the stretch of the 1908 season.[8]

During the 1909 season, Smith pitched in 51 games and threw 365 innings. A year later, he won only 4 and lost 9 games before Chicago sent him to the Red Sox. Boston sold him to

Cincinnati and, after pitching in only 7 games with the Reds in 1912, Smith was released to Montreal of the International League.

Terrapins officials acted quickly in reaction to the violation by Smith and Allen of their Federal League contracts. Following a special meeting of Federal League officials on May 23, the Baltimore club announced that Frank Smith would be fined $100 and suspended for forty-five days. Allen was fined $25 and suspended for fifteen days.

Smith told the press he quit the Federals because he was worked too hard and the club did not keep promises made to him. Furthermore, the length of his suspension was too severe because St. Louis outfielder Kommers received only a six-day suspension from the league for kicking an umpire. A forty-five day suspension would cost Smith $1,000 of his annual salary, so the pitcher threatened a lawsuit unless the penalty was reduced.

In the end, President Gilmore stepped in and restored Smith to the Baltimore roster, stating it was not within the powers of Manager Knabe to suspend a player for 45 days. Frank returned to the mound for the Terrapins in Indianapolis on June 11, only to be pounded in an 11 to 4 loss to the Hoosiers.

Baltimore declined an offer from the Brooklyn Federals to take Smith off their hands and the veteran right-hander finished the season with the Terrapins. Smith finally got out of Baltimore on June 28, 1915, when he was dealt to the Wards' Brooklyn club.

The Baltimore team's frustrations from their sudden losing ways boiled over on June 14, 1914, in Chicago during a double-shutout loss to the Chifeds. Five Terrapins were ordered from the field by umpire Garnet Bush and two of them, Runt Walsh and Mickey Doolan, earned three-day suspensions without pay from President Gilmore.

The Terrapins' chances of beating out Indianapolis and Chicago for the pennant were further damaged on July 12, when they lost one of their more important players during a meaningless exhibition game in Washington, D.C.

Local "blue laws" prohibited the playing of baseball on the Sabbath in the Federal League cities of Baltimore, Pittsburgh, Buffalo and Brooklyn. Often, following a Saturday game, clubs would travel to the visiting city where the blue law did not exist for the Sunday game of a series, then go back to the original city on Monday. If a league game was not scheduled on such a lucrative day for the gate, baseball clubs often scheduled exhibition games against semi-pro teams in cities where Sunday baseball was legal.

That Sunday in Washington, Baltimore was leading the Andrews Paper Company semi-pro team, 5 to 2, when the Terrapins came to bat in the top of the ninth inning. Left fielder Guy Zinn came to the plate with a teammate on base and drove a hit deep into the outfield that scored the runner. Instead of settling for a double, Zinn rounded second and charged into third base. The base runner's left foot caught the bag awkwardly, twisting his leg in such a manner as to snap the bone at the ankle.[9] The game was called at this point while Guy was hauled off to the hospital. Zinn would be lost for the reminder of the season.

The injury to Zinn was eerily similar to an occurrence two months earlier. On April 11, Baltimore third baseman Enos Kirkpatrick, the former Brooklyn National, broke an ankle sliding into home plate in an exhibition game against an amateur team.

The leg injury eventually ended Zinn's major league career at age twenty-eight. He played only 88 games in the outfield for Baltimore a year later, then disappeared into the lower minors.

After deciding to become a major league in 1913, the Federals toyed with the idea of placing a team in Philadelphia, and would revisit the proposition of a club in the City of Brotherly Love following the 1914 season. On July 20, 1914, the Baltimore Terrapins played an exhibition game in Philadelphia against a team of semi-pro "all stars" before more than

3,000 paying customers. Knabe, Doolan and Walsh, former Phillies, were presented with boxes of cigars as they each came up to bat.[10] Across town, the White Sox and the World Champion Athletics played to an announced crowd of 5,000.

A seven-game winning streak the third week in July moved Baltimore to within two games of Chicago in the Federal League standings. However, the lack of pitching depth and a marked decline in the team's batting for the remainder of the season eventually did the Terrapins in. Mickey Doolan, a notorious light hitter who batted above the .300 mark through mid–July, finished the year at .245. Harry Swacina's batting average fell from .314 on July 19 to .280 for the season, and the club's leading batter, Jimmy Walsh, dropped from .350 in July to .308 at the end of the year. Manager Otto Knabe batted only .226 for the entire season. Frank Smith, the club's third best pitcher with 8 wins and 5 losses at mid-season, won only one more game after July.

Across the street at Orioles Park things had not gone very well for Jack Dunn despite the fact that Baltimore was the only International League club immune from Federal League raids that season. Dunn lost only one player in the spring of 1914, when the veteran Danny Murphy bolted to the Feds after Connie Mack tried to ship his team captain to Baltimore. Behind the scenes, Ned Hanlon's purchase of stock in the Baltimore Federal League club had been conditioned on the Federals' promise to keep hands off the Orioles' players.[11]

Following the winter of 1909–1910, Jack Dunn, manager of the Orioles, then in the Eastern League, put together enough money to purchase the club from Hanlon. When he found himself in competition with his former boss four years later, Dunn assembled a very strong club of former major leaguers and talented youngsters who were destined for stardom. "With a team like that our fans won't be interested in those Federal League frauds," he predicted.[12]

Dunn tried to fight the Federals by scheduling exhibition series against major league clubs. Almost 30,000 paid to watch the Baltimore Federal League team's opening game of the 1914 season, but across 29th street in Oriole Park, only 1500 showed up to see Dunn's team play the vaunted New York Giants.[13]

The Orioles opened their season a few days after the Federals and drew 5,000, but after that it was all downhill for Dunn and the International League in Baltimore. On April 24, Dunn unveiled his star rookie pitcher, George Herman Ruth, at Orioles Park. The "Babe" pitched a shutout, but virtually no one was there to see it. Fewer than 200 fans saw the regular season debut of the man who would become baseball's most famous player. Though Dunn maintained that his players were better than the Terrapins, the fans undoubtedly preferred to see icons like Tinker, Chase, Brown, and the like from major league cities rather than lesser-known minor league teams from Providence, Montreal and Jersey City. Dunn's outstanding team outdistanced the other clubs in the standings, thus generating little interest in the pennant race. By the first of July, Dunn's team was running away with the International League pennant, but it couldn't draw flies to the ballpark.

On July 2, 1914, C.L. Schanberger wrote in *The Sporting News,* "...while there is no perceptible superiority of the Federals over the Internationals, they [the fans] nevertheless tell you that the Federals have placed this town on the map and for this if for no other reason they deserve consideration."[14]

On July 11, the Orioles staged a professional baseball game before what was probably the smallest paid attendance in the history of the International League. The club announced that there were only 26 paid admissions. Excepting the players, and including passes, gate keepers and ticket takers, there were not fifty people in attendance, reported *The Sporting News.* Across the street at the Federal League Park a crowd of 9,000 was witness to a double-header.[15]

On the verge of financial ruin, Dunn sought to move his Orioles franchise to Richmond,

Virginia. Community leaders, through the Richmond Business Men's Club, were enthusiastic about bringing a higher classification of baseball to the city. However, the Virginia League already had a club there. At their July 3, 1914, meeting, the Virginia League's directors decided Richmond was too important to the league and they would only permit the move of their Richmond club to another city if $15,000 was paid to the league in exchange for territorial rights to the city.[16] In an effort to save his team, Dunn and Edward Barrow, president of the International League, went to the National Commission in an attempt to convince the major leagues to stop their annual draft of minor league players.

"I dug deep this season," Dunn complained,

> and I gave Baltimore a team that I believe is as strong as a second-division major league team, if not stronger. I paid men like Cree, Midkiff, Derrick, Daniels, Egan and others major league salaries so that they would be satisfied to play in the International League.... I signed most of them to play for three years. That makes me personally responsible to them for their salaries for that length of time. I allowed for Federal League sentiment at the beginning of the season, but the novelty has worn off now and Baltimore is still not patronizing the Orioles. Why? Not because the Federals are better, but because the Orioles are in a so-called minor league, and a star player developed there can be taken away by draft and never be seen in Baltimore again. That's what I've been up against. I gave Baltimore a team that won 13 straight games, and on the thirteenth day I played to 150 people. And we were in first place, too.[17]

Rumors of the formation of another major league to be made up of the top American Association and International League clubs proved to be unfounded. The National Commission members, Herrmann, Johnson and Tener, procrastinated in responding to Dunn's request, then announced there would be no new major league and the draft procedures would remain as they were.

Without the approval of either the Virginia League or the International League, which originally voted to block the move, the deal to move the Orioles had to be canceled. Having already lost $28,000 on the season, Dunn had no other alternative but to sell his most marketable players. He returned to Baltimore and on July 7 began selling the Orioles' high-priced stars. Bridie Cree was the first to go, sold to Cincinnati. A day later, Twombly, the left fielder, and Derrick, the shortstop, were sold to the same team. In a deal worth nearly $25,000, Dunn sold Ernie Shore, Ben Egan and Babe Ruth to the Boston Red Sox on July 8.[18]

After he had dismantled his championship-caliber team, Dunn's Orioles went into a steep decline. Despite the great first half, the club's makeshift lineup of semi-pros and low level minor leaguers limped home in sixth place, five games under .500.

15

Rowdyism and Umpire Woes

Although Organized Baseball attempted to clamp down on "rowdyism" in the first decade of the century, it remained commonplace to see assaults on umpires by players, by managers, and even by fans. Umpires during this time enjoyed no assurance of employment and, with their activities under daily scrutiny, pressure from club owners could easily lead to an arbiter's termination. To prevent "cheating by competitors," two umpires were assigned to each Federal League game, the same practice as in the organized major leagues.

The Federal League's staff of umpires would operate under the direction of former National League arbiter Bill Brennan, an Irishman who was known for his wit and pleasant disposition. Only twenty-eight years old, William T. Brennan had umpired in the National League during the 1909 season and returned in 1913. Brennan ignored the National League's contract offer for 1914 that was mailed to his home in St. Louis and signed a three-year contract with the Federal League on January 20.[1]

Eight of Brennan's umpires during the Federal League's existence had previous major league experience, the most senior being James Johnstone, who worked in the National League for ten years. Still, umpiring in the two seasons of the Federal League was plagued by numerous arguments and ejections. Managers, players and the press openly berated the quality of the league's field officials. The Federal League started the 1914 season with eight full-time umpires: Brennan, Monte Cross, Al Manassau, Ollie Anderson, Stephen Cusack, Barry McCormick, Garnet Bush, and Steve Kane.

Many umpires of that period played professional baseball before becoming arbiters. The most well-known of these ex-players turned Federal League umpire was Monte Cross, who would officiate major league games for the first time in 1914. Cross was a National League shortstop that jumped to the "outlaw" American League in 1902. He became a star on Connie Mack's Philadelphia Athletics teams for six seasons. When Cross retired as a player in 1908, he became manager of the Kansas City American Association club. After leaving Kansas City, Monte officiated in independent, high school, and college baseball games until he joined Jim Gilmore's umpire corps.[2]

Questionable umpiring surfaced early in the 1914 season. On May 14, Chicago lost a game to Buffalo, 5 to 4, and Manager Joe Tinker lodged an official protest with the league office, requesting the game be replayed. The controversial play occurred in the bottom of the ninth inning with Buffalo's Walter Blair on first base, one out and the score tied. Buffeds pitcher Fred Anderson attempted to bunt and popped the ball up in the middle of the diamond. Anderson trotted a few feet from the plate, then turned off toward the home bench just as Chicago pitcher Fiske dropped the ball. Recognizing his teammates' screams, Max tossed the ball to first baseman Fred Beck, who tagged Blair, standing on the bag, and then stepped on first base. Anderson was already putting a sweater on when his teammates ushered him to first base, where he stood while the other players gathered around the umpires.

According to baseball rules, the play should have been a double play, but umpires Goeckel and Kane ruled that only Blair was out, claiming he was forced out when tagged. During the long argument that followed, the chilling wind coming off Lake Erie adversely affected Fiske. A single and two walks sent Anderson across the plate with the winning run.[3]

The rules, argued Tinker in his protest to President Gilmore, required the base runner to stay within the base lines while running to first base. Had the Buffalo man been declared out, he claimed, the winning run would not have scored. Umpire Ed Goeckel ruled against Tinker during the game, but on May 22, President Gilmore decided in the Chicago club's favor and ordered the game replayed.

Eddie Goeckel had only made his debut as a Federal League umpire on April 25. The former indoor baseball pitcher and umpire for Chicago area semi-pro games was signed as a substitute if one of the regular arbiters were unavailable to officiate a game.

Following a game in Chicago on June 14, James Crusinberry wrote in the *Daily Tribune*, "Rowdyism that approached a riot marked the afternoon of baseball at Weeghman Park yesterday.... The days of the old Baltimore Orioles, who harbored such famed scrappers as McGraw, Doyle, Jennings, and Joe Kelley, seem to have been revived by the new Baltimore Terrapins, who flew into such a raging rampage against the umpire in the second inning of the first game that order wasn't restored until at least seven of the unruly ones had been banished from the field."[4]

The row started when the Terrapins' Runt Walsh was caught off third base and went back into the bag feet first, knocking third baseman Rollie Zeider onto his back. The two players went at each other, but peace was restored. The situation deteriorated further after home plate umpire Garnet Bush banished Hack Simmons, the Terrapins' third base coach, for something he said. Manager Knabe and a flock of enraged Baltimore players flew at the arbiter. Simmons, Knabe, Walsh, Mickey Doolan, and Zinn were thrown out of the game. When Bush attempted to resume play, there were more yelps from the visitors' bench and two more Terrapins were ejected. With two outfielders playing in the infield and two catchers and a pitcher in the Baltimore outfield, the game resumed. Chicago won easily, 4 to 0, ironically, on what had been declared "Knabe Day" with a German band on hand to serenade the visiting manager. Federal League President Gilmore was in the grandstand and saw the whole fracas. Between games of the scheduled double-header, he delivered a lecture to the seven offenders and allowed them to play in the second game.

Gilmore received so many complaints about Garnet Bush, he gave the umpire his walking papers in mid-June and reinstated Mickey Doolan and Jimmy Walsh, who had been suspended for their recent row with that particular umpire.[5] Within days, umpire Stephen Kane joined Bush among the unemployed. Coincidentally, the pair, both of whom had prior major league experience, were among the highest paid umpires in Brennan's stable. Kane umpired in the Ohio State League in 1915 and on October 30 of that year he was found dead in a Louisville, Kentucky, hotel, victim of an apparent heart attack.

President Gilmore reinforced his stand against rowdyism on June 24 when he suspended Brooklyn manager Bill Bradley for five days and fined him $100 for his actions during a game at Indianapolis the previous day. Tip Tops pitcher Tom Seaton was fined $50 and received a three-day suspension for using abusive language to umpire Monte Cross. Cross was lost for a considerable time upon undergoing surgery in July after his foot was broken by a foul ball.[6]

William "Spike" Shannon joined the Federal League as an umpire on June 28, 1914. He had been a switch-hitting outfielder with the Cardinals, Giants and Pirates between 1904 and 1908 before he completed his playing career with Kansas City. Controversy didn't seem to follow the ex-player as an umpire, though his most publicized moment in the Federal League came in July 1915 when Brooklyn's Lee Magee started a fist fight with him after the rowdy Tip Tops manager was called out on a close play at home plate.

The most unlikely Federal League umpire was Bob Groom, who had the distinction of being the only person in major league history to umpire and pitch in the same game. On September 12, 1914, the Terriers were scheduled to play the Tip Tops in Brooklyn. As the 2:30 game time approached, umpires Cross and Anderson had not arrived. In order not to disappoint the Saturday crowd, the clubs each selected one team member to officiate the contest. Brooklyn selected pitcher Bert Maxwell, disabled because of an injury, and St. Louis designated Groom.

The missing umpires showed up at the field during the third inning and explained they thought the game started at the usual time, 3:30, instead of 2:30. The players substituting as umpires retired and the regular arbiters took over.

The St. Louis starting pitcher, Hank Keupper, faltered, was taken out of the game and replaced by Groom. Three hits off the substitute hurler netted the Tip Tops four runs which they parlayed into a 5 to 3 victory. The local newspapers joked that Groom unquestionably "jinxed" himself by taking the umpire job.[7]

Following the 1914 season, President Gilmore and Umpire-in-Chief Brennan went about reconstructing the league's umpire corps for the following year. Only three umpires who worked the 1914 Federal League season would be renewed for 1915 — Brennan, William McCormick, and William Shannon. In early December two former major league umps, American Association umpire Frederick Westervelt (A.L. 1911–12) and International League arbiter William E. Finneran (N.L. 1911–12), were hired to officiate Federal League games for the upcoming season. A few days later, umpires Monte Cross, Steve Cusack and Al Manassau were dismissed by Gilmore and were replaced by former American League pitcher Harry Howell, an umpire in the Texas League; Louis Fyfe of the Western League, who had also officiated for the Federal League in 1913; and Jim Johnstone. Johnstone came to the Federal League as its best known and experienced major league umpire.

Irish-born James Edward Johnstone was a minor league pitcher from 1894 through 1897, once throwing a no-hit, no-run game while with the Newark club of the Atlantic League. He joined the American League as an umpire in 1902. After only one season in Ban Johnson's circuit, Johnstone moved to the National League and umpired in the Senior Circuit through 1912. There he gained a great deal of notoriety for his battles with John McGraw and the Giants' players. Johnstone began a feud with league president Thomas Lynch in the fall of 1911 when he was rebuked for umpiring an unsanctioned off-season series between the Athletics and Phillies after the National League would not assign arbiters. Johnstone quit following the 1912 season over a salary dispute with Lynch.[8] The veteran umpire's resignation was not accepted for several weeks and Lynch ignored the request until the league's Board of Directors instructed the newly reelected President to accept the resignation.[9]

Johnstone worked in the American Association in 1914 until James quit after his jaw was broken by a punch thrown by Louisville pitcher Bill Burns. Johnstone gave his resignation to league President Chivington following the season because he was angry that Burns was not more severely punished for assaulting him.[10]

Johnstone signaled the Federal League's players that he would not be intimidated during a game in Newark on April 22, 1915. In the third inning, he ordered all the Tip Tops' players not in the game off the bench, because they refused his warning to stop making negative remarks. Later in the same game, the umpire threw Benny Kauff out of the game when the Brooklyn star kicked on a third strike call.

Even an experienced umpire like Johnstone did not escape controversy. On June 19, Chicago had the bases loaded with two out in the first inning when the Baltimore pitcher, George Suggs, threw a third strike past the batter, Fred Beck. However, the pitch got past catcher Owens and Beck made it safely to first. The Chicago runner on third apparently did not see the ball escape the catcher and walked to the visitors' bench. When he realized what had happened, the runner left the bench and ran to home plate. In the confusion that followed, Johnstone allowed the Chicago run to stand.

Manager Knabe of Baltimore protested the game on the grounds that the Chicago player, giving up the attempt to reach home plate, went to the bench, but later illegally got up and touched the base. Although that one run was all Chicago got in the disputed inning and they won the game 9 to 1, President Gilmore threw out the results of the game on July 8 and ordered it replayed.

Compared to most Federal League umps, Johnstone's one season in the circuit was generally unremarkable and controversy-free. Bill Brennan selected James to help him officiate the crucial final five games of the 1915 season between Chicago and Pittsburgh.

During the time Johnstone worked in the major leagues, the mask worn by catchers and umpires had a wire frame that did not prevent an occasional broken nose or broken tooth. In 1922, Johnstone developed a new full-vision design with a solid one-piece aluminum frame that was unbreakable yet lighter in weight than previous models. Called "The Original Full Vision Mask," it was distributed by the Johnstone Baseball Mask Co., located on Central Avenue in Newark. His mask was quickly adopted by major league catchers and Johnstone's original design was still in use when the hockey goalie-type mask came into vogue.

Following the death of his wife in 1927, James left his home in New Jersey for a European vacation. During the Atlantic Ocean voyage, the ex-arbiter developed an infection. Less than three weeks later Johnstone passed away in his native Ireland.[11]

John Mullin, who had been an American League umpire in 1911 and 1912, was hired as a Federal League arbiter in July 1915. He had been working Western League games and officiated his first Federal League game on July 22. It didn't take long for Mullin to get involved in a row with one of the league's raucous characters. During the third inning of a game between Chicago and Baltimore, Mullin called the Terrapins' Otto Knabe out on at attempted steal of second base. The veteran ball player flew into a rage. Mullin ordered him from the field and tried to walk away, but Otto pursued and jostled the rookie ump until he was persuaded to retire.

After being fined and suspended by President Gilmore for having a fist fight with umpire Tommy Corcoran in July 29, 1915, Kansas City Manager George Stovall announced he would refuse to play in any game officiated by Corcoran. Stovall had an expensive three-year contract with the Federals, so Corcoran was dismissed that August. When Baltimore pitcher Irvin Wilhelm refused to report to the Colonial League, President Gilmore made him an umpire since he was already under contract to the Federal League.

After the Federal League folded in 1915, Bill Brennan found himself shut out of the major leagues. One sports columnist lamented, "Bill Brennan, one of the best umpires who ever worked at that trade, had to take a job in a Class C circuit this year to get his bread and butter."[12]

Bill became the counselor and right hand man to Southern League President John D. Martin in 1918. Brennan died at age 47 in September 1933. On Sunday, September 10, he umpired a game on the final day of the Southern League season. The next day he had emergency surgery for a ruptured ulcer and the former boss of the Federal League umpires died two days later.[13]

William McCormick was one of only two Federal League umpires to return to the organized major leagues in that capacity. (The other was Fred Westervelt, a National League umpire in 1922 and 1923.) After serving one season, 1917, in the American League, McCormick umpired in National League from 1919 through 1929.

16

Washington Park

On February 13, 1914, Robert and George Ward of the Brooklyn Federal League Club signed a ten-year contract to lease old Washington Park, former home for Charles Ebbets' National League team, for ten years at the annual rate of $45,000. Bounded by Fourth and Fifth Avenues and Third and Fourth Streets, the ballpark was named for the site of George Washington's last stand before his retreat to Trenton during the Revolution. The Wards planned to refurbish and expand the rickety 1898 grandstand. However, Brooklyn building codes forced them to raze the existing wooden grandstand and erect a new one of concrete and steel. The contractors promised to complete new stands that could seat 18,000 persons in six weeks.[1]

Competition of the new grandstand did not go as smoothly as stadium constructions in St. Louis and Chicago. Union men refused to work at Washington Park because of the Ward brothers' reputation for using non-union workers in their bakeries. Union men not only refused work on the ballpark, but they would not attend the Tip Tops' games and encouraged their members to distribute literature outside the league's other ballparks attacking the Wards.

Work at Washington Park was interrupted in mid–March when a fifty-foot wooden tower used in the construction of the grandstand collapsed. Three riggers were working at the top of the tower that was one of two intended to support wire cable for the operation of an iron bucket containing concrete for the stands. A worker named Arthur Strauss was extricated from the ruins, but a short time later he died from broken bones and internal injuries.[2]

The last of the concrete was finally poured on April 17 and, despite accidents, problems with labor unions, bad weather, and city bureaucrats, Washington Park was ready for the Brooklyn Federals' home opener, which was pushed back to May 11. By the time the club played its first home game, the season was almost a month old and the team had sunk to fifth place in the standings.

The mediocre start by the team probably contributed to a below-capacity crowd of 15,000 that showed up for the Tip Tops' first home game. That did not prevent the local Federal League officials from putting on an elaborate ceremony for the event.

Pregame activities included a parade around the field with the Brooklyn players carrying a huge American flag. The Brooklyn flagpole had once been the mainmast of the America's Cup defender *Reliance*. A brass band dressed in uniforms of the Continental Army led the parade that also included Brooklyn team officials. "That tall fellow wearing a cane there in the front line there is one 'Sunny Jim' Gilmore," noted the *New York Times*. "Jim has been in so many opening parades this year he has developed a 'charley horse' and was woefully out of step."

16. Washington Park 111

Tip Tops players Claude Cooper (left), Felix Chouinard, Tex Westerzil, Hap Myers, Danny Murphy, Solly Hofman and trainer Joe Quirt standing in front of the grandstand at Washington Park, early 1914 (Library of Congress Prints and Photographs Division).

A candy firm put a sign on the outfield fence, offering a box of bonbons to any player "who knocks the ball over the sign." The purveyor of sweets did not have to worry about a drop of profits from the ad, for it was not until six games later that Bill McKechnie of Indianapolis cleared the thirty-foot outfield wall with the first fair ball to be hit out of the park.

A reporter for the *Times* wrote: "Gazing at the players of the two teams was like looking through an old baseball album. There were many familiar faces. Even Bill Brennan, the umpire, was 'cut into' the new league. Many of the age worn vets now in the Federal set have the edge on Lillian Russell when it comes to hiding their years. Davy Jones, Eddie Lennox, Rebel Oakes, Danny Murphy and Artie Hofman have all taken a bath in the fountain of youth and came up strong."[3]

A group of Danny Murphy's Philadelphia friends, "all dressed in new straw hats," presented the former A's captain with a gold baseball, silverware and a bunch of Killarney roses. Brooklyn's starting catcher, Grover Cleveland Land, celebrated the day's events by getting married a couple of hours before the game. He treated his bride to a noon breakfast and then took her to the ballpark.

Tom Seaton opposed Howie Camnitz of the visiting Pittsburghers in the actual game, and the Brooklyn pitcher's wildness at the onset cost the home team the game. The former Detroit Tiger, Davy Jones, was the first batter for Pittsburgh and Seaton walked him on four pitches. The next batter, Ed Holly, also walked and Rebel Oakes sacrificed the runners to second and third. The two Pittsburghers eventually scored on a sacrifice fly and Hugh Bradley's single. Brooklyn loaded the bases in the second inning but could not plate a runner. The Tip Tops did not threaten to score again, as the Kentucky Rosebud completed a 2–0 two-hit shutout of the Brooklyns.

After nearly 15,000 watched them play on opening day, the Tip Tops couldn't draw 1,000 for their games the following week and only 6,500 on Saturday (the Yankees/Browns game had a crowd of 15,000 that day). President Ward would not allow the Tip Tops to play on Sunday even when on the road.

On the field, only ace hurler Tom Seaton stood out, although the promising youngster Claude Cooper showed occasional brilliance in center field. When Cooper signed with the Brooklyn Federals, the *New York Times* speculated, "With Cooper and George Anderson, a rookie out of the New York State League, Brooklyn would have two of the fastest players in the League."[4]

Though he didn't hit much, Cooper did not disappoint in the field. In the first game of the season, he startled the Pittsburgh crowd with a sensational catch in center field to preserve the game for Brooklyn, which they won in the tenth inning, 1 to 0.

In a game against Chicago at Washington Park that May, the *Times* praised Cooper, who "cut off one run in the second inning by a beautiful throw to the plate when Wickland tried to score from second on Farrell's single. Cooper threw from deep left field just as Wickland was rounding third base and got the ball to Land in the air with a couple of inches to spare."[5]

Cooper was benched late in June because he was batting only .198. The Brooklyn outfielder consulted an oculist, after which he went on a batting tear. Between June 27 and the end of July, Claude hit .363 in 110 times at bat and raised his overall average 53 points. One reporter joked that Manager Bradley was thinking seriously of employing an oculist to work exclusively with his team.[6]

On Friday, July 31, Brooklyn was playing Indianapolis at Washington Park. With two out in the ninth inning and the game tied 0 to 0, Charlie Carr of the Hoosiers drove a long fly ball to center field that turned out to be a home run. Cooper misjudged the ball, first running in, then running backward without checking for the wall. In those days there was no warning track. The *Times* reported, "With an impact that could be heard all over the field, the Texan crashed into the center field bleachers and dropped as if he had been shot."

Cooper was unconscious for several minutes and was carried to the clubhouse, where he was examined by three physicians. Excepting a gash six inches long on the side of his face, Claude escaped serious injury. The surgeons indicated that if the blow had been one inch higher on the temple, the player might have suffered a fractured skull. As it was, Cooper would miss several games. He struggled for the remainder of 1914, but came back the following year to play in 153 games and bat .294.

On June 1 the Tip Tops came home from a road trip and played a game against the Terrapins before only 600 people at Washington Park. Despite a four-game winning streak that put the club's record above .500, attendance continued to be poor. On the last day of June, the Brooklyn club announced that admission prices would be reduced from 50 to 25 cents. (A day later the Pittsburgh Federals also reduced their fifty-cent tickets to a quarter.)

"The Philadelphia Athletics and the Boston Red Sox play 'twenty-five-cent ball' and there's no reason why the Tip Tops can't," announced Robert Ward. "Also, we shall abolish those barbarous bleachers. The man who can afford to spend only 25 cents for his baseball will be as comfortably shielded from the sun as his more fortunate brother in the higher-priced seat.... I am determined to give the people of Brooklyn good baseball, and at prices that will fit their pocketbooks."[7]

On Wednesday, July 1, Brooklyn's first home game with reduced prices brought 2,500 persons, including 1,500 school children, to the ballpark. It must be said that attendance was adversely affected by a light rain that fell throughout the game. It was overcast again the next day and only a thousand showed up to watch the six-inning rain-shortened contest with Buffalo.

The reduced ticket prices and an Independence Day double-header led the Brooklyn club to announce attendance figures for the first time since opening day. The Tip Tops claimed a crowd of 3,157 paid to see the morning game and 5,800 attended the afternoon contest. Brooklyn and Buffalo split the holiday set of games, both lopsided affairs.

A reporter at the game observed that the two clubs played like "they lacked interest," but praised the outfield performance of Claude Cooper. In the first game he made a running catch in left field, then made a "perfect throw" to double up a runner off second base.

"Cooper provided a couple of circus plays in the second game when he grabbed with one hand Downey's long fly off the fence in front of the left field bleachers in the fourth, and robbed the same player of another hit in the eighth when he made a diving catch of his low liner."[8]

During the Fourth of July games, the Brooklyn Federal League club passed out souvenir badges embossed with a $ sign. The badges bore the lettering: "Federal League Tip Top Agent."

The *New York Times* wrote, "On the way from the field one fan made immediate use of the badge making him an 'agent' by signing for five years a hopeful young player whom he found playing in a sandlot. The boy took the matter seriously when he saw the badge and will probably report to Manager Bill Bradley for work on Monday morning...."[9]

For the short run, Brooklyn's attendance improved. On Saturday, July 25, the *Times* estimated that 5,000 to 10,000 were in attendance at Washington Park. It was also "Joe Finneran Day," but it is undetermined how many fans were there to honor the Orange, New Jersey, native. There was a decided drop in attendance figures for the following Saturday when 4,000 persons witnessed Tom Seaton's victory over Indianapolis.[10]

Poor attendance was only one of several problems the Brooklyn owners had to deal with. A week into the season, club Secretary Walter Ward announced that the Brooklyn Federal League club would be the highest paid team in baseball, "upward of $100,000."

The *New York Times* reported in September that the Brooklyn Federal League team was carrying thirty players:

> The Federal League has been picking up players all through the season, and owing to the impossibility of dropping them to a minor league, has been forced to carry along many who are worthless to the team. As a result the salary rolls are stupendously large. Brooklyn, for instance, could probably dispose of at least ten of its players without weakening their strength, and these extra ten players are causing them a loss of at least $15,000 a season. The Federal League can't very well get out of carrying this burden, as the moment they let it be known that they are dropping their players, they will find it difficult to get others to leave organized baseball.[11]

Other than Tom Seaton, the pitching staff that Brooklyn assembled in the spring of 1914 was short on major league experience. Ed Lafitte had pitched only two innings in the majors since going 11 and 8 with the Detroit Tigers in 1911. Joe Finneran had lost his only two major league decisions. A Tip Top recruit named Bill Chappelle posted a combined record of 3 wins and 5 losses with the Boston Nationals in 1908 and 1909, Bert Maxwell won one game with the Giants in 1911, and Rudy Sommers pitched in one game for the Cubs in 1912. And that was it. Manager Bill Bradley used sixteen pitchers during the Federal League's inaugural major league season, but was unable to provide much support for Seaton, who won twenty-five games.

Most of the pitchers used by Brooklyn that year faded into obscurity almost as quickly as they appeared. One of those flashes in the pan went by the name John McGraw. Born Roy Elmer Hoar, this particular John McGraw appeared in only one inning of one game in his major league career. That one appearance happened to come in the longest game in the short history of the Federal League. McGraw worked a scoreless eighth inning of that game on July 29, 1914, against the St. Louis Terriers at Washington Park. He faced four batters, hitting one, and retiring the other three, two on strikeouts. McGraw was removed for a pinch hitter and the Tip Tops tied the score in the ninth. The two teams battled through one scoreless inning after another before Artie Hofman singled with two out in the eighteenth to end the contest after four hours and one minute of play. Brooklyn right-hander Rube Peters was the star for the day with his nine innings of scoreless relief pitching.

A pitcher that Manager Bradley had counted on for the season was Bert Maxwell. During a game that May, Maxwell was hit on his right arm by a pitch during an at-bat. Maxwell did not think the injury was serious, but within a few days his wrist became so stiff his pitching arm was almost useless. It was finally determined the pitcher had fractured his throwing arm. Although Bert eventually returned to the mound, he was never the same. He was replaced in the starting rotation by Joe Finneran, who was only on the Brooklyn roster because the Baltimore Terrapins decided they did not need him.

Joseph Ignatius Finneran would acquire the nickname "Happy" because of his sour demeanor. First coming to the major leagues at age twenty, the right-hander spent parts of the 1912 and 1913 seasons with the Philadelphia Phillies. When he was sold to Birmingham of the Southern Association in 1913, Joe declined to play in the South because he said it would be injurious to his health. After the Phillies refused to send him elsewhere, Finneran signed a contract with Otto Knabe in February 1914 to pitch for the Baltimore Terrapins.

On July 13, 1914, Brooklyn and Pittsburgh played a twelve-inning game at Exposition Park that was scoreless until Steve Evans of the Tip Tops homered over the right field wall in the final frame to secure the win for Brooklyn. Finneran pitched the twelve innings of scoreless ball for Brooklyn while Walt Dickson was the hard-luck loser for the Rebels. Joe won six of his next seven starts, including a rain-shortened two-hit shutout against the Terriers in St. Louis.

Finneran and Dickson squared off again in Brooklyn on September 8. There was no repeat of their earlier pitching duel. Pittsburgh scored two runs with the aid of a Westerzil throwing error in the first and the Tip Tops countered with four of their own in the home half. By the eighth inning, Dickson was long gone and Happy was coasting with a 7 to 3 lead, having allowed only three hits up to that point. When James Savage of the Rebels let the bat slip out of his hands while ducking back from one of Finneran's in-shoots, it almost hit the pitcher. Joe thought the batter had deliberately thrown the club at him and hurled it back at Savage, who barely got out of the way. Umpire Brennan immediately threw both players out of the game and Jim Bluejacket replaced Finneran. The 12–4 Brooklyn win ran Joe's won-lost record to 11 and 7.[12]

President Gilmore happened to be in the box seats at Washington Park when the bat-throwing incident took place. He promptly issued fines of $100 to Savage and Finneran. Joe said he wouldn't pay, but was eventually convinced to apologize and pay the fine.

Finneran's bubble burst in his next start when he was bombed by Indianapolis 9 to 2. A few days later, Joe gave up five runs in the first inning and lost to Kansas City. He would win only one more game the remainder of the season.

During the second year of America's participation in the World War, Finneran returned to the major leagues, splitting the 1918 season between the Tigers and the Yankees. Granted an unusual deferment by his New Jersey draft board to play baseball for the support of his wife and child, Joe won 2 and lost 8. After baseball, "Happy" went into business as a funeral home director.

Tip Tops pitcher Ed Lafitte was born in New Orleans and played college baseball under Coach John Heisman at Georgia Tech. He still holds the Georgia Tech record for shutouts in a season (4 in 1906) and career (6). On April 13, 1907, he struck out 19 batters in a ten-inning game against the University of Georgia.[13]

After winning eleven games for the Detroit Tigers in 1911, Lafitte told manager Hugh Jennings the following season that he wanted to leave early to attend dental school in Atlanta. Jennings told him if he left just keep on going. Lafitte did and became a dentist, though he continued to play baseball, even pitching in one game for the Tigers in 1912. He hurled for Providence of the International League in 1913.

The right-hander seemed to have a knack for flair during his first Federal League season. On June 3, 1914, Lafitte slugged a home run with the bases loaded against Baltimore. On September 11, Ed suffered a 1–0 hard-luck loss to the St. Louis Terriers and, five days later, costly errors by the Top Tops' porous defense cost the pitcher both runs in a 2–0 loss to Indianapolis. Then, on September 19, Lafitte pitched the Federal League's only no-hitter of the season in the opening game of a double-header against Kansas City at Washington Park. Lafitte's wildness in the latter part of the game prevented him from getting a shutout, and the final score was 6 to 2.

Lafitte gave up six bases on balls in his no-no, but Packers batters could not make solid contact when he did get the ball over the plate. Kansas City loaded the bases in the seventh on walks to Kenworthy and Perring and a hit batsman. Kenworthy scored when third baseman Tex Westerzil fumbled Johnny Rawlings' easy grounder. Kansas City's other run scored in the ninth after George Stovall walked and later came home on an out.[14] Though he led the Federal League in walks allowed, Lafitte won 16 games in 1914 and posted the lowest earned run average among Brooklyn's starting pitchers.

In July 1914 there was a lot of buzz around baseball about a Native American pitcher named Jim Bluejacket who had won twelve consecutive games in the Three-I League. He was a big and powerful hurler, measuring six feet three inches and weighing 212 pounds. In late July, John McGraw's New York Giants purchased the pitcher, who was described as a "natural athlete," from Bloomington. Bluejacket was scheduled to join the Giants on August 1, but the Wards surprised the National Leaguers by announcing that the star minor leaguer had signed to pitch for them.

Jim Bluejacket was born James Smith on July 8, 1887, in the Shawnee National Reservation near Adair, Oklahoma. Though most reports from the time said Jim was Cherokee, the *Washington Post* correctly reported that his parents were Shawnee.[15] James Smith did go to school at the National Cherokee Male Seminary for four years. After serving in the United States Navy, Jim caught on with a baseball team in Bartlesville, Oklahoma. The only clothing he had was his Navy uniform and his teammates began calling him "Bluejacket." Jim liked the nickname enough to adopt it as his own. Bluejacket played for Keokuk in 1910 and 1911, Los Angeles in 1912, and joined Bloomington a year later.[16] In 1913, the big right-hander led the Class B circuit with 23 wins and 189 strikeouts for a seventh-place Bloomers club that won only 65 games.

Jim Bluejacket made his inaugural appearance in the major leagues on August 6, 1914, at Washington Park in Brooklyn. Undoubtedly employing the publicity angle, the Federals matched him against Chief Johnson, the Winnebago pitcher of the Kansas City Packers.

The Tip Tops gave their rookie pitcher a cushion in the very first inning. Steve Evans doubled home Art Griggs, then Artie Hofman laced a hit past second base to plate a second run. Johnson settled down after his rocky first inning and pitched "splendid ball" thereafter, but the bad start did the Packers in.

The *New York Times* described Brooklyn's newest hurler as having a delivery "between that of Tesreau and Demaree of the Giants.... The Bloomington aborigine, who they say hails from the Cherokee tribe, had all the earmarks of a coming pitcher," wrote *The Times*. "He had great speed and excellent control. He passed one Packer, struck out three and held their allotment of hits down to six."[17]

The Brooklyn fielders were flawless behind the rookie. Second baseman Jim Delahanty pulled down a hot liner off the bat of Pep Goodwin in the fifth inning with his bare hand. Bluejacket made things easier for himself when he picked two opposing base runners off first base. The Brooklyn hurler was in difficulty only once. With runners on first and third in the sixth inning, he induced the Packers' most dangerous hitter, Duke Kenworthy, to pop up to the infield. Bluejacket went after it himself and corralled the ball near third base. With Brooklyn leading, 2 to 0, after completion of the seventh inning, the game was called by a prearranged agreement between both teams in order for the Western club to catch the train home.

His Brooklyn debut may have been the high point of Bluejacket's baseball career, although he pitched two more shutouts for the Tip Tops in 1915. Despite considerable hype, Jim was knocked out in his second Federal League start at Chicago. Chief Johnson got his revenge on August 20, when he benefited from the Kawfeds' pounding of Bluejacket for five runs in the first two innings.

That Labor Day, Bluejacket received official credit for winning a ball game without throwing a single pitch to a batter. With Pittsburgh ahead on the scoreboard in its half of the eighth inning, Jim succeeded Rudy Sommers on the hill with runners on first and third and two out. Bluejacket promptly picked the Rebels' Steve Yerkes off first base to retire the side. In Brooklyn's half of the eighth, the pitcher was lifted for a pinch hitter and the Tip Tops scored twice to take the lead. Happy Finneran pitched a scoreless ninth and Bluejacket got credit for the victory.[18]

After going 4 and 5 in 1914, Bluejacket's performance a year later was not much better and his strikeout total declined to only 48 in 163 innings pitched. He did shut out the eventual 1915 champion Chicago Whales on three hits that July, and blanked a good Pittsburgh team, 3–0, on September 10.

Bluejacket's contract reverted to Bloomington when the Federal League closed for business after the 1915 season. In 1916, he pitched in only three major league games with Cincinnati, losing his only decision. Jim bounced around the lower minor leagues with teams in Clinton, Columbus, St. Jo, Oklahoma City, and Enid until he finally hung up his glove in 1921. Bluejacket went on to have a successful post-baseball career in the oil business.[19] He was the great-grandfather of Bill Wilkinson, who pitched for the Seattle Mariners in 1985 and 1987–88.

17

Pittsburgh's Rebels

It was formally announced on May 7, 1914, that team captain Ennis "Rebel" Oakes had been named manager of the Pittsburgh Federal League club to succeed Doc Gessler. The manager was fired only one day after President Edward Gwinner assured local newspapermen that the manager would be retained. Actually, Oakes had been in charge for several days before his predecessor was officially deposed. The club stated that Gessler would be kept on as a scout and coach. Upon his dismissal, Doc told the Pittsburgh newspapers that he could not have won in a Class K league with the players given him."[1]

Doc Gessler was not the Pittsburgh club's first choice for manager. Not long after the 1913 World Series, the Federals offered Phillies second baseman Otto Knabe the job as manager of the new Smoky City club.[2] Knabe turned the offer down. Tommy Leach snubbed the Pittsburgh Feds after Chicago Cubs owner Charles Murphy told him about Deacon Phillippe's bitter experience with the outlaws. Said Murphy, "According to President Dreyfuss of the Pirates, Manager Phillippe is still trying to get $1,700.00 salary alleged to be due him from 1913."[3]

On the recommendation of Joe Tinker, the Pittsburgh bosses began serious negotiations with Jimmy Sheckard in late December. Three days after club secretary William McCullough announced that the former Cubs third baseman would be hired as manager for the Pittsburgh team, Sheckard sent a telegram to President John Barbour stating that the terms offered by the club were unsatisfactory. The sticking point was Sheckard's insistence that the Pittsburgh organization guarantee his salary for three years. A frustrated Barbour declared that no further overtures would be made to Sheckard.[4] Three days later, McCullough signed Gessler as manager.

Thirty-three-year-old Harry Gessler played in the major leagues for nine years with five major league teams, lastly Washington in 1911. Gessler actually was a physician, having received a degree from Johns Hopkins Medical School.

Barbour resigned as president of the Pittsburgh Federal League franchise on January 24 with the declaration, "I feel that in attempting to handle my business and the Federal League interests in this city I am impairing my health."[5]

Because of a limited amount of cash, the Pittsburgh club was at a distinct disadvantage compared to richer clubs in the league. The owners of the city's Federal League franchise were Barbour and William Kerr, who purchased the franchise from the men who held it in 1913. Kerr was a contractor and Barbour a stockbroker.[6] Neither was as moneyed as Gilmore would have liked, so the league president sought a large investor to breathe life into the Pittsburgh club.

Thanks to the advice of Robert Ward, the Federals found that man in fifty-nine-year-old Edward W. Gwinner, president of the Alleghany Traction Company. The son of a wealthy Pittsburgh businessman, Gwinner became interested in the Federal League three years after he sold the contracting business founded by his father. It was announced by President Gilmore on March 5, 1914, that Gwinner had taken over the majority holdings of the Pittsburgh club. He also stated that the new owner would immediately contract to build up the old wooden stands at Pittsburgh's Exposition Park and replace them with new concrete and steel stands for the upcoming season.

With Barbour out of the picture, Gwinner and New York architect C.B. Comstock became the principle backers of the local Federals. A new set of officers and board of directors was selected. Gwinner was elected president, Robert J. Kerr vice president, James Clark secretary and William Kerr, treasurer. The former secretary, William McCullough, was made business manager.[7]

The first act of the new controlling partner was to echo Gilmore's pronouncement that the stands at old Exposition Park would be remodeled and enlarged, and the playing field improved. Though he was hired before Gwinner assumed control of the club, Doc Gessler would be retained as manager of the team, which was scheduled to leave for training in Lynchburg, Virginia, in less than a week.

Club treasurer William Kerr boasted, "From now on we are going after every ball player that we can land. We are not going to stop at contracts or anything else. We have plenty of money and from now on it is going to be war to the end."[8]

Unfortunately, the Pittsburghers failed in their efforts to recruit big name major league stars at every turn. Honus Wagner and Jake Daubert had already turned down lucrative offers to play for the outlaws. First baseman Ed Konetchy had signed a 1914 contract with the Pirates and would not deal with the Federals.

Within a few days of the change in ownership, the Pittsburgh Federals acquired a bona fide major leaguer when Cardinals outfielder Rebel Oakes signed a contract to play in the Steel City. Ennis Talmadge Oakes was born in Louisiana, hence the nickname "Rebel," on December 17, 1886.

Oakes became a regular outfielder in the major leagues early in the 1909 season after he was purchased from the Pacific Coast League's Los Angeles club by the Cincinnati Nationals. The fleet outfielder became known as the "Dixie Flyer" while with the Reds. In February 1910 he was traded, along with Miller Huggins, to the St. Louis National League club. In four seasons as the Cardinals' regular center fielder, "Rebel" Oakes's batting average improved each season, reaching .291 in 1913. He once made six hits and scored six runs in a game against Boston. Out of respect for this friend and teammate of five years, Oakes wired Manager Miller Huggins to give him the news of his defection to the Federals.[9]

While the Pittsburgh club was in spring training, Manager Gessler made a side trip to Macon, Georgia, where the Boston Braves were in training. Doc registered as E.M. Empfield, Philadelphia, in the Dunker Hotel. However, Manager Stallings of the Braves was tipped to Gessler's ruse. The National League club was expecting such a visit from Federal League agents and had secured an injunction under the contract labor laws of the State of Georgia which provided imprisonment or fine for one seeking to influence a laborer under contract to violate it. Gessler scurried back to Lynchburg without talking to any of the Braves' players.[10]

Upon surveying the Pittsburgh players assembled at Lynchburg, the one most recognizable to baseball fans was outfielder Davy Jones, who played seven seasons in the Detroit Tigers' outfield that also included Ty Cobb and Sam Crawford. Thirteen years earlier, Jones had benefited from another baseball war to get a large salary for that day and time. Only a year out of Dixon College, Jones "jumped" the Chicago National League club to play with Milwaukee of Ban Johnson's American League. When the Brewers folded after the season, the Chicago Orphans' owner enticed the youngster to leap back to the National League. "Well, what could I do?" Jones recalled. "I was playing for $2,400, and here was a fifty per cent raise plus $500 in cold cash stacked up right in front of me. And, after all, I wasn't even twenty-two years old yet."[11]

Known as one of the best leadoff men in baseball, Jones played two seasons in Chicago, then went to Detroit, where he got into three World Series with the Tigers. Signed off waivers by the Chicago White Sox prior to the 1913 season, Davy played only ten games with Comiskey's club before he was sold to Toledo of the American Association. Jones himself admitted he was just about done as a player when he signed with the Federal League.

The fathers of the Federal League promised that each team would have at least one star pitcher from the major leagues. Pittsburgh's man was Howie Camnitz, a three-time twenty-game winner with the Pirates. A native of Covington, Kentucky, Camnitz attended Centre College at Danville, Kentucky, and he joined the Pirates in 1904. Howie's pitching skills deteriorated measurably in 1913 and that August he was traded to the Philadelphia Phillies.

When the "ace" of the pitching staff reported to the Federals' training camp in Lynchburg, Camnitz was not in "proper physical condition." At thirty-two, Howie was obviously on the downhill side of his career. Gessler sent the hurler to Hot Springs, Arkansas, to recuperate and also to delve in a bit of mischief involving the Pittsburgh Pirates, who were training there.

Members of the Pittsburgh Federal League Club, 1914: left to right, Elmer Knetzer, Jack Lewis, Claude Berry, Skipper Roberts, Ralph Mattis, Cy Rheam and Davy Jones (Library of Congress Prints and Photographs Division).

The Pirates alleged that Camnitz approached second baseman Jimmy Viox and made the young player an offer to jump to the Federal League. The Pittsburgh Nationals obtained a restraining order preventing the former Pirates pitcher and all other Federal League agents from tampering with its players, specifically naming Viox and pitcher George McQuillan.[12]

Things went bad for Gessler and the Pittsburgh Federals right from their opening day loss before 12,000 fans at old Exposition Park. Elmer Knetzer shut out Brooklyn with only three hits over nine innings, but the Rebels were not able to score off Tom Seaton either. The "Baron" began the tenth inning by walking Solly Hofman, after the former Cub fouled off six pitches. Hofman made it to second on an infield out and Danny Murphy was walked intentionally. The next batter, Brooklyn's third baseman Tex Westerzil, sent a hot grounder straight at a fellow Texan, Charles McDonald. The veteran of many games with the Reds and Braves was sure to start a double play, but the ball took a bad hop and went right between his legs. Left fielder Davy Jones charged in and fired the ball to home plate, but Hofman made a beautiful fade-away slide to score the only run of the game.[13]

Because of bad weather, the Rebels didn't play again until the following Saturday when they lost to Brooklyn again, this time before 8,000 patrons. Pittsburgh's batters managed to drive Tom Seaton from the game after six innings and took a 3–2 lead into the ninth inning. Knetzer relieved Cy Barger, gave up two runs and sent the home team to their second straight loss. As if things were not bad enough, Exposition Park was hit by a Sunday windstorm that blew down the entire left field fence and damaged the roof of the newly rebuilt grandstand.

After that first week, the city's baseball fans gave up on the newcomers. Wet weather caused the cancellation of three of the first five games of the season and when the Rebels finally played their third game the following Thursday, it was the day of the Pirates' home opener. Pittsburgh's Federal League team's record was 0–3 and they drew only about 700 people to watch their game. The next day, the Rebels held a double-header on a cold and windy day that was witnessed by about 2,000 brave fans.

After the club won only four of their first fifteen games, the Pittsburgh management decided a change had to be made. Manager Gessler wasn't the only one dumped by the Rebels. Catcher Skipper Roberts was released after his brawl with Chief Johnson. Two weeks later, President Gilmore ruled that Pittsburgh violated league rules in the Roberts case and the club had to take the catcher back. Eventually, Chicago took the former St. Louis Cardinals backstop off their hands.

At twenty-seven, Ennis Oakes became the youngest manager in the three major leagues. *Baseball Magazine* said of the Pittsburgh Federals' new field boss, "Oakes is an aggressive leader and an inspiring player, who is respected by mates and opponents, too."[14] Unfortunately, the rookie pilot was handed a bad team.

It has been suggested that the Pittsburgh Federal League club was nicknamed the "Rebels" after Oakes became the manager. However, contemporary newspaper accounts were already calling the team "Rebels" before the start of the season.

Obviously, the Pittsburgh club could no longer be the Filipinos, for its 1913 manager Deacon Phillippe. The name "Stogies"[15] was often used in newspaper stories about the team early in the 1914 season. Veteran reporters reclaimed that nickname from the 1884 Pittsburgh Union Association club. Oakes wasn't named team captain until the day before the season began, but Ralph Davis of the *Pittsburgh Dispatch* had begun calling the local team "Rebels" in his columns during spring training.[16]

The day Oakes was officially put in charge of the team, the Rebels were aided by the St. Louis club's eight errors and beat Three Finger Brown's Terriers by a score 15 to 7. Oakes celebrated his managerial debut by hitting a home run. Oakes and Gwinner visited several Cardinals players while in St. Louis, targeting Pol Perritt, Harry "Slim" Sallee, Ivey Wingo and Jack Miller with contract offers, but they had no takers.

The change in manager generated a temporary spark in the team, as the Rebels won 16 of their next 26 games and pulled within a game of .500 on June 8. However, Pittsburgh began to lose regularly in late June. Oakes's team just didn't have the talent of some of the other Federal League clubs. Any prospect for a winning season was doomed after the Rebels lost two of their most dependable starting pitchers when Elmer Knetzer had to have surgery for blood poisoning and Cy Barger came up with a sore arm.

The hitting of the veteran Ed Lennox was a bright spot for the club early in the year. On May 6, the Rebels' third baseman went five for five, including two home runs, a triple, double and single in the team's 10 to 4 win over Kansas City. A few days later, Lennox hit four home runs in an exhibition game against a semi-pro team in Akron.

"Eggie" Lennox played in six games for the Philadelphia Athletics in 1906, then he caught on as the regular third sacker for the Brooklyn Superbas in 1909, a season he led the National League in fielding at his position. Brooklyn attempted to send him to Louisville late in 1910, but Ed refused to report and was signed by the Chicago Cubs. The Cubs released Eddie to Louisville in mid-1912 after he had played in only 27 National League games that season. Lennox was transferred to Montreal in 1913 and batted .320, but was under suspension much of the time. He jumped to the Federals when the opportunity arose, signing a contract with Pittsburgh at $12,000 for two years. Despite missing three weeks with an injured ankle in August 1914, Lennox led the Rebels in home runs and runs batted in, and tied Manager Oakes for the best batting average (.312).

By 1914, however, Lennox had slowed considerably in the field. His loss of range is suggested by his 2.8 chances at third base per game that season. All other Federal League third sackers accepted at least 3.2 chances per nine innings.

In September 1914, former manager Harry Gessler secured a settlement with the Pittsburgh club ownership, reportedly getting a year's salary and a bonus for giving up a contract that had two years to run. As for his scouting job with the Rebels, Gessler quipped that "all the scouting he has done has been to look for his money" which he finally got.[17]

The local National League club was having its own problems. On Sunday, August 31, 1914, the *Pittsburgh Gazette Times* featured the sports page headline, "Greater Pittsburgh: first in coal, first in iron, but last in the National and Federal Leagues."

Though the Rebels eventually escaped the cellar, their draw at the gate was miserable. Estimates place the 1914 season attendance for Federal League games at Exhibition Park as low as 65,000. The Pirates finished seventh in the National League, and drew 139,620, still less than half their 1913 gate and the fifth consecutive year attendance at Forbes Field decreased from a high of 534,950 in 1909.

During a mid–August road trip an obscure nineteen-year-old rookie gave the Rebels a boost in Chicago. During their loss to the Chifeds in the first game of the series, second baseman Ed Holly was injured and outfielder Hal Savage had to play the infield. Manager Oakes decided to take a chance on the raw but talented Michael Menosky to fill the right field spot. It was "Ladies' Day" at Weeghman Park and the fair-sized crowd was made up largely of women.

In the second inning, the lefty hitting Menosky came to bat against right-hander Mike Prendergast and clouted a home run into the right field bleachers. The Chicago pitcher was more careful with Menosky in the fourth and gave him a walk. The rookie stole second and scored on Claude Berry's single. In his third at-bat, Mike's Texas League single to center drove in the run that put the Rebels ahead on the scoreboard, 4 to 3. Later in the inning he scored the Rebels' fifth run. Mike added another single in his fourth at-bat.[18]

The following afternoon, the youngest player in the league hit two doubles off Claude Hendrix and executed a perfect drag bunt that he had no trouble beating out. Menosky again was in the Rebels' lineup when the club moved on to Indianapolis, but after he made only one hit in the next two games, Mike returned to his accustomed spot on the bench.

Following the youngster's success against the Chifeds, Harry Kramer wrote of Menosky in *Sporting Life*, "He can cover miles of ground in the outfield and under the tutelage of Manager Oakes should develop into one of the best outfielders in the Country."[19]

Other than those two days at Weeghman Park, Mike did not experience a great deal of success during his time in the Federal League, but he did return to the major leagues three years later. "Leaping Mike," as Menosky would become known for his daring, fence-crashing catches, became a regular in the outfield for two American League teams, the Senators (1917 and 1919) and the Red Sox (1920–23). Menosky was one of the last surviving Federal Leaguers when he died at age 88 in 1983.

18

"I Will Pitch for the One That Gives Me the Most Money!"

Fresh off three straight losses in Baltimore, Joe Tinker's Chifeds stopped off in Washington on May 14 for a Sunday exhibition game before proceeding to Brooklyn for a series with the Tip Tops. A day later, the *Washington Post* reported: "Walter Johnson, the greatest pitcher in the World, will jump to the Federal League in 1915, provided he is tendered a suitable contract."[1]

Johnson met with the Chicago manager Sunday evening and said that Tinker would offer him a contract after the season was over. If it contained the salary mentioned (reportedly $25,000 a year), he would accept — unless the Nationals matched the offer. Johnson also intimated that two other Federal League clubs had made offers for his services.

"I will pitch for the one that gives me the most money," the Washington pitcher remarked.

At least for public consumption, Nationals owner Clark Griffith commented, "I am not worried. When the time comes, Johnson will do the right thing."[2]

The length to which parties on both sides of the baseball war would go to get players was demonstrated in the case of minor league pitcher Pete Schneider. In May 1914 the Chicago Feds wired $1,000 to Tim O'Rourke, their Seattle, Washington, agent, with the instruction to use it to sign a Pacific Coast League player. O'Rourke, an old-time baseball player who had played with several teams in the American Association and National League in the early 1890s, operated a saloon in Seattle that was a hangout for down-on-their-luck ex-ball players. Of the money provided by the Chifeds, $500 plus $71 for transportation to Chicago was to convince pitcher Pete Schneider to jump his Seattle (P.C.L.) contract and sign with the Federals. The eighteen-year-old phenom was planning to leave for the train station when Seattle club owner Daniel E. Dugdale got wind of the deal and tried to talk the pitcher out of going to Chicago. Schneider insisted he was joining the new "major" league.

Dugdale knew he would receive nothing in return if the right-hander signed with the Federals, so he wired John J. McCloskey, a major league scout for the Cincinnati National League club, who was operating in the area. McCloskey got to Schneider before he left town and convinced the young man that signing with the Cincinnati Reds would be a better option than the Federals.

Once Schneider was persuaded to switch from the Federals to the Reds, Cincinnati paid $7,500 to Seattle for the pitcher's contract. O'Rourke refused to take back the Federals' $500 bonus, so Pete left it with Dugdale.

When O'Rourke learned that Schneider was about to leave for Cincinnati with the Reds' scout, he rounded up some old friends from his saloon to prevent the prize pitcher from leaving town. According to McClosky, a "rummy" named Jack O'Brien had a gun, and the Reds' scout later said, "I came nearly getting my head shot off in Seattle when I escaped that night with Schneider."

After McClosky and his prize settled aboard the Great Northern train, he received a wire from President Dugdale warning that other Federal League agents might attempt to intercept them at Kansas City or St. Louis. However, the train arrived in Cincinnati without incident.[3]

Reds manager Buck Herzog immediately threw the young hurler into the fray with a relief appearance against the Giants on June 20. On June 28, the youngster made his first major league start and responded with a 1–0 shutout over the Pittsburgh Pirates. Schneider went 5 and 13 that season with a bad Cincinnati team, but three years later Pete would win twenty games and post a 1.98 earned run average for the Reds.

The Schneider incident was but a blip in the overall story of the baseball war. Meanwhile, Joe Tinker and the Federals had bigger fish to fry.

While the Washington Nationals were playing in New York on June 3, 1914, Walter Johnson was picked up at his hotel by the Tip Tops' Bill Bradley and Jim Delahanty, then driven to the mansion of Robert Ward. The Brooklyn owner offered the star hurler a three-year contract for $25,000 a year to play with the Feds. Upon hearing of the meeting, Griffith now became "concerned" and offered his "Big Train" a five-year contract at $16,000 a year and told the press that if his pitcher signed with the Federals, he would be breaking his contract on the grounds that the "reserve clause" bound him to Washington.[4]

Less than two weeks later, Keene Gardiner of the *Chicago Daily Tribune* broke the story that the Philadelphia Athletics' star second baseman, Eddie Collins, had been offered "the largest salary ever given to a ball player" if he would join the Brooklyn team of the Federal League. Collins, generally acknowledged to be the best second baseman in the game by that time, did not name the figure except to say that it was not less than $25,000 a year. The newspaper also went on to write that "the offer is said to be larger than the one reportedly offered Walter Johnson of $25,000 for three years and a $25,000 bonus."

Following the Athletics' game at Comiskey Park on June 14, Walter Ward, nephew of the Brooklyn Federals president Robert Ward, sought out Collins and invited him to dinner. Collins did not return to the A's hotel until late in the evening and when he arrived, Connie Mack was waiting for him. When quizzed about his activities that evening, Collins told his manager that he would not leave the Athletics until the expiration of his contract in October 1914. Ward indicated that the offer was open if Collins changed his mind in the future.[5]

The day Walter Ward met Eddie Collins in Chicago, Cincinnati Reds starting center fielder Armando Marsans joined the Federal League's St. Louis Terriers. A day later, Terriers business manager Willis Johnson issued the statement that another Red, pitcher Dave Davenport, had also signed a contract to play for the St. Louis club.

Two days after the Eddie Collins article appeared in the *Daily Tribune*, the news was bad for Organized Baseball. The *New York Times* reported on June 16 that five other players would follow the lead of Marsans and Davenport and cast their lots with the Federals. Named in the report were the American League's premier first baseman Hal Chase, Yankees pitcher Al Schulz, and three Cincinnati Reds: pitchers Rube Benton, Leon "Red" Ames and catcher Tom Clark.

When reporters located Ban Johnson, the obviously agitated American League president said the report of player defections was ridiculous: "I don't believe it. If, however, those players want to jump I would say let them jump. It would be a good riddance of bad rubbish. The Federals can't get sensible players to climb aboard a sinking ship. Hal Chase above all others. The Federals are running to cover. They're through!"[6]

After twenty-three-year-old pitcher Albert Schulz was drafted by the New York American League club in 1912, the city's main newspaper wrote, "In Al Schulz, the strapping, big, left-handed pitcher from Savannah, the New York Americans landed one of the most promising minor league pitchers who played in the South last season.... He proved a tireless worker in the South Atlantic League, and took part in forty-three games.... Schulz had a reputation of being an "Iron Man" and he was always waiting on the bench ready to go to the relief of any of the other pitchers on the Savannah club."[7]

An epilipetic,[8] Al "Lefty" Schulz pitched 371 innings for Savannah in 1912, threw 37 complete games and compiled a won-lost record of 25 and 12. He started 22 games on the mound for the "Yankees" in 1913 and signed a contract for the 1914 season calling for a salary of $2,400.[9]

Schulz started only four games during the first two and a half months of the 1914 season and was ineffective each time. Manager Frank Chance completely lost faith in the lefty and regulated him to the bench after Al allowed six runs in only four innings of work against the Athletics on June 1. Three days later, Schulz served ten days' notice to Manager Chance, indicating he would be leaving the Yankees. Upon expiration of the ten days, Schulz abandoned the club in Detroit and departed for Buffalo, where he would join the Federal League team in that city. Al gave no reason for leaving the American League and Manager Chance said he knew of no dissatisfaction on the pitcher's part.

Schulz made his debut with Buffalo on June 17 in Indianapolis, but was no more successful than he had been in New York, leaving after giving up three first-inning runs. After the Yankees sought an injunction against Schulz in Judge Charles Foell's court in Chicago, Buffalo decided not to take the big southpaw on their road trip to the Windy City for fear he might be served while there. Al finally became a member of Buffalo's starting rotation on July 6 and lasted only three and one-third innings against Pittsburgh. Over the remainder of the 1914 season, Schulz did not pitch much better in the Federal League than he did with the Yankees. His record with the Buffeds was 10 wins, 11 losses and a 3.57 earned run average. Things would be different a year later, when he would be one of the top hurlers in the league with 21 victories.

Though only a rookie, twenty-three-year-old Dave Davenport was a prized prospect. "The tall hurler was 220 pounds of finely muscled flesh distributed over an impressive framework," wrote *Baseball Magazine* about the Terriers' new pitcher. Dave won his initial start with the Reds in 1914, an easy 13–1 thrashing of the Cubs, and followed that up with a shutout of the Pirates. He then lost two one-run decisions before jumping to the Federal League.[10]

Unfortunately for Davenport, he would be playing for the St. Louis Terriers, the worst team in the league. Dave won 10 of 25 decisions for the tail-enders. However, three of the victories were shutouts and he held the lead in (saved) six other games for St. Louis. Davenport would thrive under the tutelage of Fielder Jones, who became the Terriers' manager later in the 1914 season. In the spring of 1915, Jones declared that Davenport had shown him more than any other young right-hander he had ever worked with and "predicted a career of startling success for the massive moundman."[11]

Baseball was a segregated game in 1913 and it would be more than thirty years before Organized Baseball would employ black players. An occasional "Latin" or "American Indian" managed to "pass" for white and play in the Major Leagues. In the second decade of the century, Cubans Armando Marsans and Adolfo Luque were light-skinned enough to be "allowed" into the major leagues despite suggestions of African heritage.

When the Federal League began signing players, African-American newspapers speculated that the shortage of qualified major league talent might open the door for "darker players" to play in the new league.[12] However, this idea was never a possibility because the Federal League's ultimate goal was to become a member of Organized Baseball. Furthermore, a move to use players from black teams would generate a backlash from the press, the players and the Caucasian fan base.

Armando Marsans had made a conspicuous entry into American major league baseball in June 1911. He was already a star in Cuba when he came to the United States along with another promising player, Rafael Almedia, to play for New Britain of the Connecticut State League in 1908. Cincinnati purchased the Cubans' contracts based on the recommendation of the club's secretary, Frank Bancroft, who remembered the players from the Reds' exhibitions on the island.[13]

The *Cincinnati Tribune* reported on June 23, 1911: "The Reds have signed two players from the Connecticut league who have Spanish blood in their veins and are very dark skinned. As soon as the news spread that the Reds were negotiating for the Cubans a protest went up from the fans against introducing Cuban talent into the ranks of the major leagues."

To appease their fans and the skeptical press, the Reds produced notarized paperwork from the Cuban authorities certifying that Marsans and Almeida were white and of unmixed blood. The Cincinnati newspapers were finally convinced, and one reporter wrote that the Cubans were "two of the purest bars of Castille soap that ever floated to these shores." Actually, Marsans was the son of Catalan immigrants to Cuba. Still, some modern writers have maintained that Marsans was part black and thus the first man of African blood to play in the major leagues during the twentieth century.[14]

While Almeida fizzled, Marsans was touted as one of the up-and-coming stars in the National League. No novice after several years of play against top-level competition in Cuba, Armando batted .317 and stole 35 stolen bases in 1912, his first full season in the majors. A year later, he hit .297 for rookie manager Joe Tinker and stole 37 bases. Armando was an aggressive base runner who was able to stretch hits into an extra base with greater success than most other players. He was a good enough fielder to appear in 25 games as an infielder for the Reds in 1913.

By 1914 Armando's Reds salary had grow to $4,400. Marsans spoke very good English and he was a successful businessman, managing a tobacco factory in Cuba and owning a cigar store in Cincinnati.

A dispute with Manager Buck Herzog led Marsans to quit the Reds during the first week of April. Herzog felt that Armando had not tried to get into condition during training and ordered the outfielder to play in a spring training game after Marsans said his shoulder was sore. After he was fined $100, Marsans left the team in Louisville and he said he was going back to Cuba or signing with the Federals if the fine was not rescinded. President Herrmann told Armando he would have to patch things up with Herzog, which he did and returned to the club.[15]

However, the temperamental outfielder never got along with Herzog and an argument between the two in June led to Marsans' decision to sign with the Federals. Though Armando listened to the Feds' offers on earlier occasions, he had turned them down.

According to *Baseball Magazine's* William Phelon, the final straw for Marsans came following a Reds game on May 31, 1914:

> During a tight game with Pittsburgh, the Cuban stole second. Seeing that the umpire was turning away, crafty old [Honus] Wagner suddenly jiu-jitsud Marsans off the base, slammed the ball on him, claimed the putout, and got it. Marsans went wild and trailed the umpire across the field, addressing him in fuming Spanish till the official ejected him. After the game, Manager Herzog gave him a call-down for so forgetting himself as to deprive the club of his services when impera-

tively needed. The altercation became red-hot, and Marsans, deeming himself unjustly scolded, proceeded to re-open communication with the very Feds he had rebuffed not long before.[16]

The St. Louis Federals promptly offered Marsans $21,000 for three years. Lawyers for the St. Louis Federal League club prepared notice of resignation letters for the Cincinnati jumpers, Marsans and Davenport. The documents were signed the day before Judge Foell's decision to sustain the injunction against Chief Johnson. The letters were in the handwriting of the respective players but were identical in wording:

Mr. August Herrmann,
   Dear Sir—As my alleged contract with you lacks mutuality and is avoidable for various reasons, including the ten-day reserve clause, I herby notify you that I now elect to cancel and void said contract, hereby offering, however, to render my services to you for the same salary proportionally for said ten days, including payment of expenses as in said alleged contract provided, but without in any manner or respect ratifying or adopting said alleged contract. Furthermore, if you desire expiration of said ten days, you must within two days after receipt of this notice offer the items satisfactory to me or I will after two days consider myself free of contract to render my services elsewhere after expiration of said ten days.
—Armando Marsans[17]

Herrmann at once turned the letters over to Manager Herzog and the latter told both players to turn in their uniforms and leave the club pending further communication. However, Herzog lifted the suspension on Davenport and agreed to forget the incident.

Though Marsans had the highest batting average among Reds players, Herzog was out of patience with him. Reportedly, Armando went over the head of Herzog to President Herrmann in a move for more money and a new contract. Herrmann told the player that the matter was in the hands of Herzog and he, the owner, could not take any action except as the manager requested. Herzog left Marsans at home when the team went on their next road trip. On June 13, Federal League President Gilmore announced that Armando would play for the St. Louis Terriers the next day against Buffalo.

Garry Herrmann chimed in that Cincinnati gave in to Marsans's demand in the spring for a two-year contract at $4,400 per season. The owner maintained that the Reds met the player's terms without any argument, which entitled the club to fair treatment in return.[18]

The Federals picked a Sunday game for Armando's debut because the courts were closed. Organized Baseball's spies estimated that only 500 St. Louisans showed up to watch Marsans's debut with the lowly Terriers while 20,000 attended the Browns-Red Sox game up the street. That night Marsans signed a contract to play for the St. Louis Federal League club at a salary of $21,000 for three years.[19] Meanwhile, the Reds were preparing to file suit against the player and the St. Louis Federals because their "property had been jeopardized."

The Terriers immediately employed Marsans in their depleted infield. After nine games, seven at second base and two at shortstop, the speedy Cuban was batting .350 with two triples and four stolen bases. After that, he would not appear in another Federal League game for over a year.

19

Prince Hal

If it were not for his unsavory reputation, Hal Chase would be in Baseball's Hall of Fame. Chase was one of the most talented first basemen ever to play the game and his wizardry around the bag is legendary. Many ball players from his time considered Chase to be the best-fielding first baseman ever. Babe Ruth, Walter Johnson, Napoleon Lajoie, and Ed Barrow named Hal as the first baseman on their all-time all-star teams.

New York baseball writer Frank Graham wrote in 1947, "Just as at shortstop there was only one Wagner, so at first base there was only one Chase, greater than Gehrig or Terry or Sisler or anyone you care to name."[1]

In 1904 a West Coast scout told Clark Griffith, the manager of the New York American League club, about a twenty-one-year-old sensation named Harold Harris Chase who was playing for the Los Angeles Angels. New York drafted Chase that October and Hal signed his first major-league contract for $2,000.[2]

Upon seeing Chase play for the first time the following April, the *New York Sun's* Joe Villa gushed, "He is a natural ball player, fast as greased lightning, easy, confident and brainy. He is that counterpart of Fred Tenney in the way he goes after grounders, widely thrown balls and bunts. Better still, he seems to know what is meant by inside baseball. As he is only a boy he will improve steadily from year to year and will always be a star."[3]

First baseman Chase soon became a popular figure both on and off the field in New York. Due to his spectacular fielding, Chase became known as "Peerless Hal" and "Prince Hal." He was especially proficient at defending bunts, often going to the third base side of the infield from first to throw the batter out at first. Hal soon became the lowly Highlanders' main gate attraction.

During the 1907 pre-season Chase jumped the club and demanded a raise to $4,000 a year. While the Highlanders' management procrastinated, Hal played for San Jose of the outlaw California League. He also managed the St. Mary's College baseball team to a record of 26-0-1; Chase's collegians defeated the Chicago White Sox and a Pacific Coast League all-star team in exhibition games. Management yielded to Hal's demands just before the regular season began and gave him a new three year contract.

Much of Chase's time with the Highlanders was filled with controversy. During the 1908 season, the city's press accused him of being "selfish and lazy" in his play. Hal blamed the club for planting the story, then he quit the team on September 3. Chase joined Stockton in the outlaw California State League, but the Highlanders decided they needed Chase more than he needed them, fired their manager, and convinced Hal to return in 1909.

New York was in pennant contention much of the 1910 season. After game in St. Louis that September, Manager George Stallings accused Chase of throwing games. After a loss in Chicago, Hal was involved in a fight on the team bus after some of the other players blamed him for their defeat that day.[4]

American League President Ban Johnson did not want the image of New York's star player tarnished and told the newspapers, "Stallings has utterly failed in his accusation against Chase. He tried to besmirch the character of a sterling player. Anyone who knows Hal Chase knows that he is not guilty of the accusations made against him, and I am happy to say that the evidence of the New York players given to Vice-President Somers this morning showed Stallings up."[5]

Angered that his club's owners backed Chase, Stallings quit as manager and Chase was named as his replacement. In Hal's first full year as manager, the team dropped from second place to sixth. Chase was replaced as manager in 1912 and the club finished dead last in the American League. In 1913, there was another managerial change in New York when former Cubs manager Frank Chance was hired. The appointment of Chance spelled the end of Chase's tenure with the Yankees. According to the *New York Press*'s Fred Lieb, who was the official scorer at Hilltop Park in those days, Chance also suspected Chase of throwing games.

Edd Roush explained how Chase would fix games:

He was the best first baseman I ever saw. He was also the worst if he wanted to lose a game. He'd cover the base late. A fellow would throw a ball tight to the base, belt high, and he'd be late getting there so it would go off his fingers and off to one side. You could tell after an inning or two whether he was in there to win or in there to lose. He was always alone; there was hardly anybody who roomed with him.... He was a great ballplayer if he wanted to win and he was a great ballplayer if he wanted to lose.[6]

Despite their first baseman's suspicious play, the New York club's owners felt they still needed Prince Hal to keep the franchise afloat. Without Chase's "magic glove" the team had no other attraction to fill the seats.

During the spring of 1913, Chance begged owner Farrell to trade Chase, but Hal's salary demands and reputation put off most teams. The final straw was Chase's mocking of the manager in front of his teammates. Hal would sit on the side of Chance's deaf ear in the dugout and mimic the tyrannical manager for the amusement of the other players. When catcher Ed Sweeney told Chance about the affront, the manager screamed to Chase, "Get out. Go to the clubhouse and take off that uniform!"[7]

That night, May 31, 1913, Chase was traded to the Chicago White Sox for first baseman Babe Borton and shortstop Rollie Zeider. Zeider was crippled because of his bunions and Borton was unproven. This led sportswriter Mark Roth to pen the immortal line: "Chance traded Chase for a bunion and an onion." In the June 5 issue of *The Sporting News* an enthusiastic Charles Comiskey, owner of the White Sox, gushed: "It means the pennant!"

Chase's most dubious moment with the Sox came on July 23, 1913, when his four errors in a game aroused suspicion among the baseball writers. Hal batted .286 for his new team, but Comiskey's pennant prediction came up well short as the White Sox finished the season in fifth place.

By 1914, Chase finally had tired of the overbearing Charles Comiskey and got into a dispute with the owner over his contract. Hal claimed the White Sox' boss cut his Yankees salary from $8,000 annually to $6,000. However, the New York owners had reduced Chase's salary two years earlier when they forced him out as manager.

Chase explained why he quit the White Sox: "At the time, Comiskey called me into his office and asked me to have the ten-day clause stricken from my contract. I demurred at this. A contract, it seemed to me, ought to bind both parties to the agreement. If that agreement allowed him to dispose of my services with ten days notice, I didn't see why I shouldn't enjoy the same privilege."[8]

On June 17, Chase told the *Chicago Daily Tribune*, "Yes, it is true the Feds have been after me and I have decided to serve the ten day notice on the Chicago American League owner."

Chase had claimed back in the winter that the Federals offered him a three-year contract with a material raise of salary and a bonus. However, Joe Tinker said the negotiations with Hal went nowhere; "We asked Chase what he wanted and if I remember correctly he asked for a three years' contract at $10,000 a year. Then he wanted a bonus of $10,000 for signing, and he wanted $20,000 of his three years' salary paid him in advance. He never got an answer."[9]

On Saturday, June 20, the Buffalo Federal League team played a game against the Chifeds in which Russ Ford allowed the local club only three hits and won a pitching duel against Claude Hendrix, 1 to 0. That day, the *Buffalo Express* ran a story with the banner headline "Chase Looks Sure to Come."

On Sunday morning, Chase cleaned out his locker at Comiskey Park and went to Weeghman Park. Upon hearing the announcement that Hal Chase would be playing first base for Buffalo, the 10,000 fans in attendance burst into a lengthy round of applause. During the game, Prince Hal's every move was rewarded with outbursts of cheers and hand clapping. Chase's double scored Everett Booe with the Buffeds' only run. However, Buffalo's Earl Moore lost a hard-fought decision to Chicago's Erv Lange, 2 to 1.

"I notice Chase played with the Federals on Sunday, in open disregard of his own statements to Mr. Comiskey," said American League president Ban Johnson. "As it was a Sunday, that could not be helped, but action will be taken to keep him from playing with the Buffalo team, which is equally culpable with Chase."[10]

The pronouncement that Hal Chase would play for the Buffalo Federal League Club in the first game of a home stand on Thursday was heavily advertised in the city. Furthermore, that first game back at home would be "Hal Chase Day" in honor of the player's first appearance before the local fans. Every person in attendance would receive a four-page souvenir booklet with a photograph and biographical sketch of "Prince Hal." Meanwhile, Charles Comiskey and a team of White Sox attorneys were in Buffalo seeking an injunction to keep Chase from playing with the Federals. Eventually, through a local attorney, they secured a temporary injunction from Justice Pooley of the state supreme court restraining Chase from playing anywhere in the state of New York.

President Robertson and Dick Carroll arranged for Chase and his wife to take the train to a resort at Niagara-on-the-Lake, Canada, where the player would remain so an injunction could not be served to prevent his debut at Buffalo's home park the following Thursday. Buffalo President William Robertson contacted the famous aviator Glenn Curtiss and asked if he could fly Chase to a field near Federal League Park before the game of June 25. Curtiss told Robertson he could not get a plane ready in time and the Federal League's latest publicity stunt was foiled.[11]

On Wednesday, the Buffeds' business manager, Richard Carroll, and club vice president Walter Mullen picked up the ball player and his wife at the Queen's Hotel and drove them to Black Creek, Ontario, where Hal spent the night aboard a motorboat at a boat club on Grand Island. Hal crossed the Niagara River the next morning, then was driven to a country club on the outskirts of Buffalo.[12]

That afternoon, wrote the editor of *The Sporting News*, "they dressed Chase in his wife's clothing and slipped him into the park as a dashing widow — or maid."[13] The *Buffalo Express* commented that "Hal made a very pretty looking girl — heavily veiled." Of course both reports were denied by the Buffeds.

Chase was not taken to the clubhouse, but to an empty tool shed down the right field line where he changed into a Buffalo uniform, then waited for the cue to make his dramatic entrance. Just after the scheduled game time of 3:30 P.M., the park announcer told the anxious crowd of almost six thousand that the game would begin a half hour late. At five minutes until four, a deputy sheriff arrived with a notification of injunction to be served on Chase, but he was denied admission to the ballpark by the club's attorney, Owen Auspurger.[14]

When four o'clock came, the announcer megaphoned the names of the batteries for the day's game, then added that "Hal Chase will play first base for Buffalo"–an announcement that evoked a great cheer from the crowd, announced as 6,443. The Pittsburgh team took the field, which meant Buffalo would bat first. As the first Buffed batter, Frank Delahanty, approached the plate, the tool shed door opened and out strode Hal Chase. Chase doffed his cap to the fans and followed a security guard to the home bench, where the player grabbed two bats, swung them over his shoulder and strode to the plate after Delahanty completed his at-bat. Upon emerging into the bright light after sitting in the dark shed for two hours, Chase didn't have a chance. He struck out on three pitches. "Even this won a laughing cheer," reported the newspaper.[15]

Meanwhile, Sheriff Frederick Becker arrived at the ballpark and Attorney Auspurger reluctantly accompanied him to the Buffalo bench. The Buffeds had already taken the field for the bottom of the first. The sheriff wanted to go onto the field and serve Chase immediately,

Hal Chase, Buffalo Federal League club, 1915 (George Grantham Bain Collection, Library of Congress).

but the Buffalo club's attorney persuaded him to wait until the inning was over. After the third out, Chase dropped his glove and headed for the bench, where he was met by a group of men. Robert B. McRoy, secretary of the National Commission, pointed at Chase and told Becker, "There's your man." The sheriff served the legal notice and Chase disappeared into the clubhouse amid "some hissing mixed with cheers" from the crowd.[16]

The case of the Chicago White Sox versus Hal Chase would be argued in the court of Judge Herbert P. Bissell in Buffalo. On July 9, the White Sox and Hal's Federal League bosses squared off in court. Organized Baseball would argue that Chase illegally broke his contract so he should not be allowed to play for any team other than the White Sox. Comiskey had previously indicated that Chase did not give ten day's notice, but his lawyers made no mention of that or the lack of notice during the proceedings.

While Judge Bissell was deliberating the Chase case, an appellate court in Chicago agreed with the Federal League's position on the ten-day rule in the case of Chief Johnson. Judge Bissell also felt the Federals' attack on the "ten-day clause" was valid.

In vacating the injunction secured by the Chicago club, Judge Bissell said:

The plaintiff can terminate the contract at any time on ten days' notice. The defendant [Chase] is bound to many obligations under the remarkable provisions of the national agreement. The player's contract, executed in accordance with its terms, binds him not only for the playing season of six months from April 14 to October 14, but also for another season if the plaintiff chooses to exercise its option, and if it insists upon the requirement of an option clause each succeeding contract, the defendant can be held for a term of years. His only alternative is to abandon his vocation. Can it fairly be claimed that there is mutuality in such a contract?

The structure of organized baseball would seem to establish a species of quasi-peonage unlawfully controlling and interfering with the personal freedom of the men employed. Organized baseball is as complete a monopoly of the baseball business for profit as a monopoly can be made....

This court will not assist in enforcing an agreement which is part of a general plan having for its object the maintenance of a monopoly, interference with the personal liberties of a citizen, and the control of his free right to labor wherever and for whom he pleases.[17]

As to the Feds' contention that Organized Baseball was in violation of the Sherman Anti-Trust Law, the judge would not agree that "the business of baseball for profit is interstate trade or commerce and therefore subject to the provisions of the Sherman Act."

The day after the injunction was set aside, Chase was back at first base in Buffalo's game against Kansas City. William "Baldy" Louden, who had been playing first before Chase joined the club, moved back to his old shortstop position. During Chase's absence, the club fell from the top position on June 16 (they held first place by percentage points for a few hours) to fifth place.

While the Feds were celebrating victory in the case of Hal Chase, Organized Baseball won a victory in St. Paul when Federal Judge W.H. Sanborn granted an injunction restraining Armando Marsans, the former outfielder of the Cincinnati Reds, from playing with the St. Louis Federals until the alleged breach of contract issue was tried in the United States District Court. However, the numerous court actions and injunctions did not dissuade the Federals from creating mischief within the ranks of Organized Baseball.

September 12, 1914, was proclaimed "Greater Buffalo Day" at the local Federal League Park, and more than 10,000 bugs turned out for a double-header with Chicago. Though the Buffeds lost both games that afternoon, the main excitement of the day was the presence of New York Yankees pitcher Ray Caldwell on the Buffalo bench. Later that day, Buffed business manager Dick Carroll announced to the curious press that Caldwell had been signed by the Federals for the 1915 season. Ray had been a teammate of Hal Chase and Russ Ford after he broke into the American League in 1910 and won sixteen games when he pitched for Manager Chase in 1911. Landing Caldwell would be a major coup for the Feds. Ray was a pitcher of immense talent though he had an appetite for the nightlife and a weakness for alcohol.

Caldwell was the Yankees' top pitcher in 1914 when he quit the team in August after a dispute with manager Frank Chance. Ray beat the Indians on July 31 for his seventeenth win, then, after a couple of losses, Caldwell jumped the team during a western road trip. Manager Chance had fined Ray on two occasions during spring training for violating curfew and missing practice. Chance suspended Caldwell for ten days on August 15 and refused to reinstate the pitcher when Ray said he would rejoin the Yankees if the manager would rescind the $200 fine.[18]

The presence of their star pitcher in the Buffalo Federal League Park stirred the New York owners to action. When Frank Chance learned that New York owner Frank Farrell had rescinded the fines on Caldwell, the manager resigned the same day Ray appeared at the game in Buffalo.

The action by the Yankees' management and Chance's resignation came too late. Buffalo business manager Dick Carroll, who pitched in two games for Farrell's team in 1909, offered Caldwell a cash advance to play for the Buffeds. Although he was still under obligation to the Yankees for the 1915 season, Ray signed a three-year contract with Buffalo on September 12, 1914, and took the $2,500 advance.[19]

A hitch in the deal was the pitcher's ironclad contract with the New York Americans. Caldwell's contract with the Yankees called for a 1914 salary of $4,500, of which $1000 secured an option on the pitcher for the succeeding season. The key release notice (ten-day clause) had been removed from Ray's 1914 contract.

The two sides in the affair engaged in a war of words in the newspapers. Farrell threatened to have Dick Carroll jailed for conspiracy because he enticed Caldwell to break a valid contract.

In October 1914, Caldwell played on an all-star team recruited by and starring Hal Chase. Caldwell's participation with the outlaws was an explicit violation of Organized Baseball's policy as set forth by the National Commission. However, Ray was too valuable a commodity to blacklist and lose to the Federals.[20]

In January 1915, the New York Yankees got new ownership when Jacob Ruppert and Tillinghast Huston purchased the club for $460,000. James Isaminger joked in the *Sporting Life* on January 23 that Ray returned to the New York club when he learned that a brewer (Rupert) bought the Yankees. However, the pitcher liked his new contract and new manager Bill Donovan more. Because of the Federal League actions, Caldwell's salary went from $2400 in 1913 to $4500 a year later. In early January 1915, Ray finalized a deal with the Yankees for four years at $8,000 a season.[21]

Buffalo demanded that Caldwell give back their advance money and threatened to jail him if he didn't. The Yankees sent $2,500 out of the pitcher's 1915 salary back to the Federals, but the Buffeds still sued Ray for breach of contract.

Years later, both Fred Lieb (*New York Evening Telegram*, January 15, 1922) and Joe Vila (*The New York Sun*, March 16, 1919) wrote that Washington Senators manager and owner Calvin Griffith "offered Walter Johnson to the new owners of the Yankees for Ray Caldwell during the time that both pitchers were flirting with the Federal League. American League president Ban Johnson advised the New York owners not to accept the deal because Ray was so talented and had so much potential."[22]

Hal Chase batted .347 for the 75 Federal League games in which he played in 1914, swiped 33 bases, and dazzled the fans with his play in the field. On September 7, Hal went five for five, including a home run and a double, in the first game of a double-header in Buffalo against Baltimore. Despite Chase's efforts, which also included a dazzling bare-handed stop of a grounder, the Buffeds lost, 11 to 8.

When the two foremost exponents of the emery ball met for the final time the pitch was legal on September 24, 1914, Hal Chase would play a key role in the outcome of the contest. Before only about 1,000 die-hard fans on a cool wet day, Russell Ford and Fred Falkenberg battled through twelve scoreless innings. Russ did not allow a hit until the seventh inning and Falkenberg was not in serious trouble until the twelfth.

Buffalo's Fred Smith reached the Hoosiers' lanky right-hander for a triple to lead off the twelfth inning. After Falky made a dazzling play on Blair's smash and threw the catcher out at first base, Manager Schlafly went in as a pinch hitter for Ford. He fanned and the Buffalo rally died when Smith was tagged out on his attempted steal of home on the third strike to Schlafly. Despite eleven strikeouts, only five hits allowed, and two walks, Ford would not figure in the decision. Al Schulz took over on the hill for Buffalo and blanked the Hoosiers over the next two innings despite walking three batters.

Hal Chase opened the home half of the fourteenth with a double down the third base line. The next batter, Charlie Hanford, bunted to Falkenberg, who threw too late to get Chase at third. Hal held third when Engle bunted Hanford to second. Fred Smith was up next and he hit a "screamer" to third baseman McKechnie, who threw to home to head off Chase. Prince Hal quickly switched direction and headed back to third. Hoosier catcher Rairden chased the speedy Chase and applied the tag a split second too late because the runner was on the bag. Bedford Bill then turned his attention to Hanford, who was returning to second base, but the catcher's throw sailed into center field and Hal danced home with the only run of the contest.[23]

20

Ty Cobb of the Feds

There didn't seem to be anything special about the Indianapolis Federal League team for the first two months of the 1914 season. The Hoosier Feds lost four of their first seven games before returning to Indianapolis for the home opener against St. Louis on April 23.

As in the other Federal League openers, there was a big parade to the new ballpark on Kentucky Avenue, just east of where the RCA Dome stands today. Prior to the season, the Indianapolis Federal League club conducted a fan poll to determine its new team's nickname. The results were announced a week into the season, "Hoosier Federals" being the leading vote getter. However, the club was most often referred to as "Hoosiers" or "Hoofeds" in the newspapers.

Indiana Governor Ralston threw out the ceremonial first pitch and then joined more than 15,000 fellow Hoosiers fans to watch a tight pitching duel between Cy Falkenberg and the Terriers' Hank Keupper. A number of young men watched the game from atop freight cars the "Big Four" switchmen left on the railroad tracks behind the right field wall. The contest was scoreless into the ninth inning when a double by pitcher Keupper drove in the run that sent the home team down to a loss.

Following a loss to Baltimore on Tuesday, June 9, the Hoosiers' record stood at 19 victories and 23 losses. However, the play of Indy's twenty-four-year-old right fielder, Benjamin Michael Kauff, began to attract the attention of the newspapers and fans. On May 11, Kauff, merely a utility player for the lowly New York Yankees two years earlier, banged out a triple, a double and two singles in the Hoosiers' 4 to 3 victory over Kansas City. The effort came in the midst of his twenty-three consecutive game hitting streak during which Benny accumulated 45 hits.[1]

On the other hand, Manager Whoa Bill Phillips was especially dissatisfied with the play of Biddy Dolan, who was batting only .223 after 32 games. Though Dolan had been the club's leading hitter in 1913, the Indianapolis club began the search for a replacement at first base. Their focus naturally fell on the city's own Charlie Carr.

Carr had parlayed his associations in baseball into a successful sporting goods manufacturing business in Indianapolis which supplied baseballs to several minor leagues. Carr's partner in the business was Bill Bradley, rookie manager of the Brooklyn Federals. Their store, Bradley & Carr Sporting Goods, was located at 724 Prospect Avenue in Indianapolis and was a popular hangout for ball players.[2]

Charlie Carr had spent parts or all of six seasons in the major leagues between 1898 and 1906 as a journeyman first baseman with five different teams. He also was the manager of the Indianapolis club that won the American Association pennant in 1908. At age thirty-six, Charlie played in 77 games and batted .266 for the Kansas City American Association club in 1913. That was enough to convince the Hoosier Feds that Carr was worth a contract offer.

The day Carr signed to play for his home town Federal League club, Indianapolis lost at home to Baltimore, 7 to 6, and fell to seventh place. The game against the Terrapins on June 10 was rained out and was rescheduled as part of a double-header on Thursday. With Carr playing first base, the Hoosiers went on a winning streak. Indianapolis defeated Baltimore in both games of the double-header and the Hoosiers would not lose again for two weeks.

After going hitless in his first game with the Hoosier Feds, Carr collected two hits in each of the next three games. Then on the fourteenth, before 8,500 bugs at Hoosier Park, he smacked four hits and scored four runs against Pittsburgh. Among his knocks were a double and a triple. Not to be outdone, Benny Kauff slugged a triple and a home run in Indy's 11 to 4 romp. A day later, Charlie got more three hits, one of them a triple, off the Rebels' Baron Knetzer in another Indianapolis victory. Carr's exceptional success at the bat led Indianapolis to release both of the veteran's predecessors at first base, Biddy Dolan and Frank Rooney.

Indianapolis took over first place in the Federal League race on June 20 by winning a double-header in Brooklyn, both on ninth-inning rallies. Four days later the Hoosiers beat Kansas City, 5 to 2, for their fifteenth straight victory. During the winning streak, Bill Phillips' club moved from seventh place to two games ahead of second-place Chicago in the Federal League standings.

The longest winning streak in the history of the Federal League came to an end on June 25 when Kansas City pitchers Ben Harris and Gene Packard combined to defeat the Hoosiers, 5 to 1. The setback was only temporary, as Indianapolis spanked the Packers, 10 to 6, two days later.

It was Benny Kauff's efforts during the Hoosiers' winning streak that thrust the left-handed slugger into the limelight. During his team's hot streak, Kauff batted .446 (25 hits in 56 at bats)[3] and his overall average sat at .460. Though he hit only .202 over the next five weeks, Benny was still batting almost .390 and leading the league in runs scored, hits, total bases and stolen bases at mid-season.

Kauff was complemented in the batting order by second baseman Frank Laporte, a proficient line drive hitter who had spent nine seasons in the American League starting with the New York Americans in 1905. His best season was 1911 with the St. Louis Browns, when he batted .314 with 37 doubles and 82 runs batted in. In 1913 the thirty-three-year-old infielder was sent to Kansas City of the American Association after playing in 79 games for Washington. Frank jumped to the Indianapolis Federals the following year and led the Federal League with 107 runs batted in while hitting .311.

The steadying influence on Phillips's club was catcher William "Bill" Rariden, who possessed a strong accurate throwing arm and had a reputation in the National League as a workhorse. After five seasons with Boston, the Braves offered Bill only $2,700 for 1914, so he inked a three-year deal with Indianapolis that January for an annual salary of $6,000. He also got to play near his home town of Bedford, Indiana. Though he batted only .235 in 1914, the twenty-six-year-old backstop caught 130 games at a time when few major league catchers caught more than 110 games in a season. While working behind the plate in 142 games for the Newark Federals in 1915, Bedford Bill established the existing major league record for catching assists in a single season — 228, breaking his own record of 215 set a year earlier.

An important stretch of the Federal League pennant race was the ten days between the second and twelfth of July, when Indianapolis played two series against a Chicago club that would be the Hoosiers' most serious rival for the flag. The standings on the morning of July 2, 1914 read:

Indianapolis	36–25	—
Chicago	36–26	½
Baltimore	33–27	2½

The Chifeds' first invasion of Indy's Federal League Park was delayed by one day because of rain, so the opener of the important four-game series began on July 2. The aces of the two clubs' pitching staffs took the mound, but an expected pitchers' duel did not materialize. Claude Hendrix was the master of Cy Falkenberg and the Hoosiers in a 7 to 2 Chicago victory. The game was close until Falky left for a pinch hitter in the eighth inning and his replacement gave up a three-spot in the ninth. Benny Kauff was tossed out of the contest by umpire Anderson after he jostled the smallish arbiter upon being called out at first base. Chicago reinforced its newfound hold on first the next day when the former semi-pro pitcher Erv Lange beat the veteran George Mullin, 5 to 2.

A crowd of more than 10,000 watched the two clubs battle for first place in a double-header at Hoosier Park on the Fourth of July. Indianapolis walloped the Chifeds in the opener, 12 to 3, but Max Fiske salvaged the day for Chicago with a heroic effort in the nightcap. With catcher Art Wilson sitting in the grandstand after being beaned in the head during the earlier game, Fiske was at his best in the clutch. Once, with the bases loaded and one out, he fanned Laporte and Carr in succession. Chicago triumphed 6–3 and left town in first place.

Now it was the Chifeds that were hot as Tinker's club returned to Weeghman Park for a series against Kansas City. On July 5, pitcher Claude Hendrix's third-inning home run high over the screen in front of the right field bleachers scored "Wee Johnnie" Farrell ahead of him to provide the winning margin in Chicago's 2–1 win over the Packers. Hendrix allowed only four hits while besting Nick Cullop before the Sunday crowd of between five and six thousand.

After taking two out of three games with Kansas City, Chicago played host to the Hoosier City club for another four-game series. A batting rally by the Chifeds in the eighth inning sent the first game into extra innings, tied at 3–3. The contest was settled in the eleventh when Chicago's Fred Beck walloped a home run into the right field bleachers, through "the teeth of the lake zephyrs which continue to hamper the swatsmen," noted the *Daily Tribune*. Hendrix went the distance to get the victory for the home team.

Trailing the Chifeds by four games in the standings, Phillips sent Cy Falkenberg out to stem Chicago's surge on July 11. The local club designated the day's event "German Day" and some 10,000 onlookers watched as the German club presented President Weeghman with a loving cup. Once the game started, it was Falkenberg who celebrated. He faltered only once, when a walk to Art Wilson and a home run by Dutch Zwilling gave the Chicagoans their two runs. The contest was tied at two in the eighth when Chicago pitcher Erv Lange made a wild throw after making a one-handed stab of Bill McKechnie's bounder. Deacon Bill raced all the way to second on the error and came home one out later when Laporte poked a single over the second baseman's head. Indianapolis held on for a 3 to 2 win.

The Chicago/Indianapolis series at Weeghman Park concluded with the clubs splitting a double-header before a crowd of 11,000. Hendrix won the first game in relief, 6–5, and Indy took the nightcap, 4–2. The two clubs combined for thirty-nine hits on the day, including five home runs. Two of the round-trippers were made by Benny Kauff, the second of the inside-the-park variety. At the end of the ten-day span, Tinker's club held first place, but Indianapolis remained within striking distance with victories in two of the final three games in Chicago.[4]

The Federal League standings after the games of Sunday July 12, 1914 read:

Chicago	44–30	—
Indianapolis	40–32	3
Baltimore	37–34	5½

On July 17, 1914, a syndicated column appeared in the *Washington Post* and several other newspapers across the nation that proclaimed Indianapolis outfielder Benny Kauff a second Ty Cobb:

> Kauff has been clubbing them out all season around the .400 mark, has been running the bases with the daring and dash of the wonderful Georgian, can cover a marvelous amount of territory in the outfield, and has an unerring arm.
>
> Kauff so far hasn't shown any batting weakness. He hits everything that comes his way, and it matters not whether the slants that are thrown up to him are from the arms of Tom Seaton, Russell Ford, Otis Crandall or some of the recruit pitchers in the new league. If Kauff, in his present form, had been uncovered in the American and National Leagues this year, his fame would be peering forth from the sporting pages almost daily.[5]

Russell Ford, the Buffeds' ace, had faced the greatest hitters in the American League many times and proclaimed, "That fellow [Kauff] will easily outshine Cobb, Jackson and Speaker. He's a natural hitter and base hits are everyday occurrences with him."[6]

Benjamin Michael Kauff was born January 5, 1890, in Pomeroy, Ohio. He was the oldest child of William and Hanna Kauff, descendants of German immigrants. It was assumed during his time as a player that Benny was Jewish, though there was no support for that conclusion other than the spelling of his name.

Like many of his contemporaries, Benjamin quit school at age eleven and worked in the coal mines. The hard work in the mines also made Benny unusually strong for his 5' 8" frame. "The work was very hard," Kauff told *Baseball Magazine*. "Seven years I worked in the dust and grime and baseball proved my way of escape from a lifetime spent in the same monotonous way."[7]

Kauff's father didn't want his son to play baseball so Benny went out on his own, playing on weekends for amateur teams. By 1909 he was the star of a local team called the Keystones. "In my first game I caught for three innings, pitched for three innings, and then caught for three more innings," he later said.[8]

Benny was good enough as a pitcher to get a shot with the Parkersburg, West Virginia, club of the Virginia Valley League a year later, and his father agreed that he could go. Kauff played outfield mostly, but pitched in eighteen games. The league didn't keep official statistics but Benny claimed a 14–4 record as pitcher, a batting average of .417, and 87 stolen bases.

Harry Young, captain of the Washington & Lee (Virginia) football squad, told a *New York American* writer named W.J. McBath that when Kauff came to the Virginia Valley League he pitched the first game of a double-header and caught the second.

Kauff was "discovered" by Arthur Irvin, a scout and once a manager in the National League. Irvin said Benny was "another Ty Cobb," but no one really believed him.[9] Because of Irvin's recommendation, Benny went to spring training with the New York Highlanders in 1911. However, Kauff was the odd man out among the outfielders and was not retained for the regular season. Manager Hal Chase sent the promising but raw player to Bridgeport of the Connecticut State League for more seasoning. The "Yankees" gave him another shot in 1912, but Benny appeared in only five games before he was farmed out to Hartford of the Eastern Association.

In 1913 Benny played with the New London, Connecticut, team, appeared in 135 games, and finished the season with a batting average of .354; his 176 hits lead the Eastern Association. In the off season, Kauff was drafted by the St. Louis Cardinals, who ordered him to Indianapolis of the American Association until they needed him. Benny never played in the American Association and signed with the Indianapolis Federal League Club for double his 1913 minor league salary of $2,000.

After 73 games with the Indianapolis Federals, Kauff had accumulated 100 hits and 35 stolen bases and was hitting .389, twenty-one points higher than the second best batting mark in the league. Baseball people were amazed at the amount of power Benny could generate, especially when he choked up on the bat as much as he did.

It was said that Kauff would sometimes walk to the plate at a critical moment in a game and inform the pitcher which pitch he was going to hit. Likewise, Benny sometimes would tell pitchers just when he was going to steal a base. He would take off on the pitch count he designated and more often than not make it safely. As the opposition caught on, he would cross them up by stealing on a different pitch than he had announced, or hit a pitch which he had not designated. (Benny stole 75 bases, more than any other major league player, in 1914. "Caught stealing" was not a statistic kept at that time.) Kauff's trickery at bat and on the bases did more than any other player in the league to disrupt and unnerve the opposition.[10]

Benjamin Kauff, "Ty Cobb of the Feds," Indianapolis Federal League club, 1914 (National Baseball Hall of Fame Library, Cooperstown, N.Y.).

"It's all in getting your lead and slide," Benny related to a reporter. "There are several players in the Federal League who are faster than I am, but they don't steal as many bases because they don't figure out their leads or don't slide properly into second base."[11]

Eddie Ash of the *Indianapolis Star* lauded Benny's ability in the report of the game against St. Louis on July 8:

> Benjamin Kauff was on deck with his usual electrifying performances, making a clean theft of home once, besides running wild in the outfield and bagging balls originally labeled "hits." The theft of home occurred in the fifth inning and it was so clean that there was not even an argument on the part of the Brownies. Benny surely did give a real demonstration of the "sprinting kid" and he proved his reputation of being the boldest base runner of the Federal League season to date.[12]

Among Benny's eight home runs in 1914, two came within a three-game span against a key rival in the pennant race. On July 27 Baltimore and Indianapolis were involved in a tight extra-inning affair at Terrapin Park. Hoosiers spitballer Harry Billiard held the home club scoreless after he entered the game in the eighth inning. In the thirteenth, Kauff connected with a George Suggs pitch for a home run into the left field bleachers with two runners on base to secure the victory for Indianapolis. Two days later, Kauff hit another three-run home run to tie a game with Baltimore, but the Terrapins managed to get the victory anyway with a run in the tenth. Before a home Sunday crowd of 4,500 on August 9, 1914, in six trips to the plate Benny collected five hits, three of them doubles, in a thirteen-inning victory over Baltimore.

In addition to his all-out play, the flamboyant Kauff had one thing other than his on-the-field performance in common with Ty Cobb. He wasn't particularly popular with his teammates, especially the married men and conservative players like McKechnie, Rariden and Roush.[13]

Nagging injuries finally caught up with the Indianapolis club in late July when the Hoosier Feds suffered their only prolonged losing streak since early in the season. On July 22 a two-run pinch hit by the Rebels' Tex McDonald in the seventh inning ruined a good pitching performance by Falkenberg and gave Pittsburgh a 2 to 1 victory. The loss sent the Hoosiers on a six-game losing skid during which five of the setbacks came against the lowly Rebels. An injury sidelined Frank Laporte, the club's best clutch hitter, for four of the losses. The bad stretch dropped Indianapolis 5 games behind first-place Chicago.

When Laporte returned to the infield at the end of the month, shortstop Jimmy Esmond went on the shelf for three games. The club got a big scare on August 11, when leadoff batter Vin Campbell was hit in the head by a pitch thrown by Baltimore's Jack Quinn late in the first game of a double-header at Indianapolis. The loss of the team's captain, center fielder, and leadoff batter, who happened to be hitting .337 at the time, would have been a serious setback for the pennant drive. However, Vin missed only the second game of the day's double-header and returned to his position in the lineup the next day.

Vincent Campbell almost wasn't in baseball at all in 1914. Immediately following the 1912 season he had spent with the Boston Braves, the twenty-four-year-old Campbell announced he was giving up baseball to get married.

There wasn't a question about whether Vin could play major league baseball. Campbell was a gazelle on the base paths and he batted .296 in an amazing total of 624 at-bats as the Braves' center fielder in 1912. Despite his offensive credentials, Vin wasn't considered a good fielder. The critics maintained that part of his fielding problem was related to his undersized hands, which became a handicap in snaring batted balls because the baseball gloves of that time were little more than mittens with fingers.[14]

The son of a St. Louis doctor, Arthur Vincent Campbell was an all-around athlete at Smith Academy and later attended Vanderbilt University. In January 1908 he was signed by the Cubs just days before his twentieth birthday. During the spring, Chicago sportswriters made a point of teasing the young dandy, commenting on his "champagne suit ... wine waistcoat, sherry hat and yellow chartreuse shoes."[15]

Campbell made the Cubs' roster as a back-up catcher, but got into only one game in 1908. Vin begged owner Charles Murphy to either play him or release him. Instead, Murphy wanted to "hide" his prospect, then draw a good price for the player in a future deal. The Cubs shipped Campbell to Wichita, but the manager there sent the player back to Chicago because of his "peculiar disposition." Chicago then optioned Vin to Decatur of the Three-I League, but later in the season the National Commission deemed the Decatur deal illegal and made Campbell a free agent. The Pittsburgh Pirates signed the Vanderbilt student late in 1909 and Vin batted .326 in 97 games for the Buccaneers during the 1910 National League season.[16]

During the off season, Vincent and Pirates president Barney Dreyfuss couldn't agree on a salary for the upcoming season. In February 1911, Vin sent a reply to Dreyfuss's contract offer that read, in part, "While I appreciate everything you have done for me I have decided not to play ball. I have taken a position with a brokerage and bond house and I believe it to be to my advantage to stay."[17]

Vin eventually acquiesced and returned to the Pirates, though he missed half the season. Campbell played with an independent St. Louis team to stay in shape and rejoined the Pirates on July 10, 1911, in Brooklyn. He also had another reason for wanting to return to the city of Pittsburgh.

Late in the 1910 season, Vin was introduced to an attractive young woman in the grandstand at Forbes Field. That young lady was Katherine Munhall of one of the oldest and wealthiest families in Pittsburgh.

"During his residence in Pittsburgh the blonde [sic] baseball player and the handsome Miss Munhall were together much of the time," the papers reported. "The young woman never missed a game when the team was at home and 'Vint' Campbell frequently was driven to the Munhall home for dinner in Miss Katherine's auto."[18]

Unfortunately for Campbell, another fleet footed outfielder had established himself in center during the time Vin held out. Max Carey, a future Hall of Famer, became the Pirates' regular center fielder in 1911 and there was no room for Campbell. Vin got into only 42 games, 21 in the outfield, and when he refused to sign a contract that winter, his days as a Pirate were numbered. On February 12, 1912, Campbell was traded to the Boston Braves.

Vint and Katherine were married at St. Paul's Cathedral in Pittsburgh on October 16, 1912, and he went into business in his home town as the agent for the St. Louis branch of an automobile supply company. A year later, a business opportunity to play baseball for the money he always wanted came in the form of a new baseball league.

21

Tinker's Invalids

In late June, Chicago's ineffective spitball pitcher Ad Brennan had his tonsils removed. A physician told him the trouble with his pitching arm was due to inflamed tonsils and the infection extended to the muscles of his shoulder. Brennan was of little value to the Chifeds the remainder of the 1914 season. Brennan's injured limb was a harbinger of the physical problems that would beset the Chicago team.

A month later, catcher Art Wilson was hospitalized with appendicitis at the same time another backstop, Jimmy Block, was out with a broken bone. With only one healthy catcher, the poor-hitting Clem Clements, left on the roster, the Chifeds acquired Skipper Roberts, who was out of favor in Pittsburgh after his bout with Chief Johnson. Fortunately, Wilson was not out for an extended period.

In the ninth inning of a blowout victory over Buffalo on July 28, Chifeds left fielder Max Flack attempted to score on a wild pitch and severely wrenched his leg in a collision with pitcher Earl Moore at home plate. Flack was carried from the field in agony and would obviously be lost to the club for an extended period of time. Career minor leaguer Austin Walsh would have to fill in until Max returned.

Third baseman and leadoff batter Rollie Zeider was also hurting. Zeider stole 49 and 47 bases in separate seasons with the White Sox and was on his way to swiping 35 in only 119 games for the Chifeds. Once called "Hook" because of his beak-like nose, Zeider became "Bunions" when he contracted blood poisoning after his foot was slashed by Ty Cobb's spikes.

Unfairly, Zeider thereafter became best known for being the "bunion" in the trade for Hal Chase in 1913. A converted pitcher, Rollie played every infield position for the White Sox during his term there from 1910 through 1912. He was not only one of the most popular players in Chicago, but the versatile infielder also served as team captain for the White Sox.

One thing Manager Tinker did have was a solid presence in center field. Day after day, Edward Harrison "Dutch" Zwilling patrolled the outfield and was the most dangerous batter in the lineup. Though only 5' 6" and 160 pounds, the stocky lefty hitter displayed surprising power. At mid-season 1914, Dutch was Chicago's leading hitter. The editions of the nation's newspapers on July 19 credited Zwilling with 96 hits in 77 games for a .332 batting average. Dutch had an unusual habit when playing the field. Each time Zwilling settled under a fly ball, he spread-eagled his arms just before making the catch.

On top of the team's physical problems, the Chifeds' hitters went into a funk that August. After splitting the first two games of a series with Pittsburgh at Exposition Park, the two clubs traveled to Weeghman Park for a Sunday game because of the Pennsylvania blue laws. The Rebels managed only one tally in Chicago but still won the game, 1 to 0. In the fourth frame,

Pittsburgh loaded the bases off Mike Prendergast. Rebel Oakes sent a grounder to shortstop and Davy Jones beat Stanley's peg to the plate by an eyelash. The Tinx' best chance to tie the game came in the eighth inning when Art Wilson straightened out a Knetzer fast ball and drove it deep to left field. Two feet further to the right the blast would have been a home run, but it ricocheted off the brick house that comprised part of the left field wall. One batter later, Wilson was thrown out at home when he attempted to score on a short fly to right fielder Cy Rheam.

A day later, back in Pittsburgh, it was same story as Chicago lost again, 1 to 0. The Rebels scored the only run of the contest in the top of the tenth inning to break up a pitching duel between Doc Watson and the Rebels' Walt Dickson. Dickson not only held the Chifeds to six hits, but it was his single in the tenth that drove home the game's only run. Zeider was absent from the Chicago lineup because of an injury diagnosed as two displaced vertebrae.

On August 4, Baltimore took the top spot in the Federal League standings for the first time since June 18 when Jack Quinn defeated Chicago, 2–1, before a crowd of 7,000 Terrapins fans. Baltimore managed only two hits off Max Fiske and Thomas McGuire, but won the game on errors. The victory pushed Baltimore ahead of Chicago by .004 of a percentage point.

Baltimore's position atop the league standings was short-lived. On August 5, Claude Hendrix pitched a five-hit shutout against the Terps, running his mound record to 18 victories against 9 defeats. However, George Suggs brought Baltimore back into first with a 5–2 victory in the finale of the three-game series with Chicago.

The Chifeds got a much-needed shot in the arm when a new acquisition, Adam Rankin Johnson, took the mound in the first game of a double-header with Brooklyn on August 8. Johnson did not allow a Tip Tops runner past second base through eight innings. Nursing a narrow lead into the ninth, a single, followed by George Anderson's double, put the Chifeds' 2–0 lead in jeopardy. One run scored on a long fly out, then, with the tying run on third and two out, Steve Evans, Brooklyn's leading hitter, rolled out to Tinker. When Prendergast's pitching and Zwilling's two-run home run into Sheffield Avenue propelled Chicago to victory in the second game, the Windy City club jumped back into first place after Baltimore split a double-header with Indianapolis.

Once a promising prospect for the Red Sox, Rankin Johnson gained rookie fame early in the 1914 season by beating Walter Johnson twice in just over a month, both on shutouts. Unfortunately, "Tex" Johnson's record against all other American League pitchers was 2 and 9. Rankin Johnson was traded by the Boston Red Sox along with Fritz Coumbe and Ben Egan to Cleveland for pitcher Vean Gregg on July 28, 1914. The rookie was making only $400 a month in the American League and rather than report to Cleveland, Johnson signed with the Federals. The Texan's flop was result of a visit to Cleveland by Jim Gilmore, Dick Carroll and Hal Case. They tried to get Egan and Coumbe as well, but failed. However, they also spoke with several players of the visiting New York Americans, and laid the groundwork for pitcher Ray Caldwell's negotiations with the Federal League.[1]

Johnson's second Federal League start came in the second game of a double-header after Hendrix lost a 2 to 0 duel to Brooklyn's Tom Seaton in the opener. Johnson won again, outlasting three Tip Tops hurlers, 5 to 3. The right-hander started 14 games for the Chifeds and his earned run average of 1.58 was the lowest in the league for 1914.

The addition of Johnson to the Chicago pitching staff meant that Doc Watson was the odd man out. Despite a 9 and 8 won-lost record, a 2.04 earned run average and three shutouts, Chicago sent the left-hander to last-place St. Louis. Since the Federal League did not normally allow outright sales between its teams, Watson was effectively "loaned" to the Terriers.[2] That decision would come back to haunt the Chifeds.

One of the toughest losses for Manager Tinker and Chicago came at Weeghman Park on August 16 in a game against Baltimore. Rankin Johnson pitched well, but the locals fell behind on Johnny Bates' sixth-inning home run into the right field bleachers. The score was still 1–0 when Chicago came to bat in the eighth.

With Dutch Zwilling at bat and one Chifed on base, first base coach Jimmy Block yelled to plate umpire Charles F. Van Sycle that Baltimore pitcher Bill Bailey had soiled a new ball just put in play. Van Sycle stepped toward the diamond to call time just as the pitcher was delivering the ball. Zwilling hammered the pitch into the right field bleachers for an apparent home run. While Dutch trotted around the bases, Baltimore manager Otto Knabe ran in and demanded the home run be disallowed because time had been called. Van Sycle seemed reluctant to render a decision and talked things over with base umpire Monte Cross. Tinker argued that two runs should be credited to Chicago, but the umpires finally ordered Zwilling to bat again. While many of the 4,000 home-town fans showered the field with garbage, the Chicago manager and his players lambasted the umpires. As a band on hand tried to soothe the hollering fans by playing popular tunes, Tinker argued and refused to order Zwilling back to the batter's box for eighteen minutes. Van Sycle called the time limit on Tinker several times, threatening to forfeit the game to Baltimore if Chicago did not send up the proper batter in "thirty seconds." Charley Weeghman and William Walker made their way to the Chifeds' bench and supported Tinker when the manager swore his team would not continue unless the two runs counted. Finally, Weeghman was convinced the umpire was correct and Charley told Tinker to finish the game, under protest.

Zwilling went to bat again and struck out. The inning ended when Fritz was caught attempting to steal on a third strike to Wilson. Former Browns southpaw Bill Bailey got the 1 to 0 victory and struck out twelve Chicago batters in the bargain. James Gilmore was in a field box at the game and declared the umpire was justified in forcing Zwilling to bat again. Though the Federal League did not grant the protest and order the game replayed, umpire Van Sycle was given ten days' notice of his release because President Gilmore said the umpire "did not properly enforce the rules...."

To make matters worse for Chicago, Indianapolis buried Pittsburgh, 21 to 6, to start a run of ten victories out of their next eleven games. Things began to look up for Chicago when Rollie Zeider returned to the lineup on August 18 following an extended absence. But the same day, second baseman Johnny Farrell showed up with tonsillitis and couldn't play. The following afternoon, Max Flack appeared in a game as a pinch hitter and a day later he started in left field for the first time since July 28.

On August 21, Indianapolis defeated Brooklyn in both ends of a double-header, pushing the Hoosiers into first place, .001 ahead of their Windy City rivals. In Chicago, Rankin Johnson reversed the earlier outcome in a second match against Bill Bailey and the Terrapins. The Texan got all the support he needed from Manager Tinker. Joe beat out a bunt in the third inning, which led to Chicago's first run; scored a run after Hack Simmons misjudged his fly ball that fell for a two-bagger in the fifth; and in the seventh another double contributed to two more runs. Johnson scattered five hits and two walks in his 4 to 0 shutout.

Chicago's fortunes sank the following afternoon against Buffalo before a festive crowd of almost 8,000. In the ninth inning, shortstop Joe Tinker dashed toward home plate to cover it on a wild pitch. The Buffed runner at third base, Charley Hanford, charged toward the plate and crashed into the Chicago manager. Despite the pain in his ribs and spike wounds to his knee and ankle, Joe finished the game, which Chicago lost 4–2. Later that day, the Chifeds' manager had such difficulty breathing that he decided to consult a physician.

The game against Buffalo on the twenty-third was rained out, but that was the best news of the day for the Tinx. The club announced to the press that Joe Tinker had a fractured rib and a splinter of the bone had penetrated his lung. For a time, the manager's return to the shortstop position in 1914 was in doubt. Joe's backup while he was disabled would be the light-hitting Jimmy Stanley.

Tinker did return to the lineup on August 31 in a game against St. Louis and in time for the Indianapolis series set to begin the next day. His presence on the field didn't seem to help.

On Monday, September 1, Chicago and Indianapolis played the first in a stretch of eight straight games between the two league leaders. Indy took undisputed possession of first place by beating Chicago, 4 to 0, in the first game, mainly due to Falkenberg's good pitching and Benny Kauff's hitting. The league's leading batter made four hits, including two doubles. The next day, Chicago was shut out again, this time by Earl Moseley, 2 to 0. Moseley pitched himself out of a big jam in the fourth inning when the Chifeds filled the bases with no one out. The Hoosier right-hander fanned Stanley, Beck hit into a force out at home, and Farrell struck out.

Falkenberg relieved Billiard late in the third game and stopped a Chifed rally to preserve a 5–4 Indianapolis victory. In the seventh inning, a three-run home run by Fred Beck pulled Chicago to within a run and, after Billiard gave up a walk and then threw three wild ones to Rankin Johnson, Manager Phillips called on his ace. Falky finished the walk to Rankin, then retired Flack and Zeider on infield taps.

Chicago salvaged one of the four games at Weeghman Park on September 4. The Chifeds were shut out until Kaiserling forced in the tying run by walking Tinker with the bases full in the ninth inning. Hendrix and Max Flack singled to start the Chicago tenth. Moments later, Hoosiers shortstop Jimmy Esmond made a wild throw on an attempted double play, allowing Hendrix to score the winning run.

After the two clubs moved to Indianapolis, the Tinx returned to their losing ways, falling 3 to 2. Chicago had a chance to tie it in the ninth after a tiring Cy Falkenberg walked two batters with one out. The rally fizzled when Tinker drove a fly ball that Benny Kauff corralled and Beck fanned on three straight pitches, all wide of the plate. At the end of the day, Indy's record stood at 70–52, four full games ahead of Chicago.

On the verge of falling out of the race, Tinker's men rallied to win the next two games. After Chicago built up a 9 to 4 lead in the Sunday game, Tinker decided to give the struggling Ad Brennan a chance on the mound. He faced only three batters, walking two and hitting another. Rankin Johnson was rushed in and he walked three more batters before the side was finally retired, but the Hoosiers had counted four runs that inning without the benefit of a hit. Johnson settled down and allowed only one more run the remainder of the game. About half of the 5,000 people in attendance left after the top of the ninth. Those who remained started throwing cushions onto the field to delay the game so Chicago's three ninth-inning runs might not count because of an Indiana law that forbade the playing of baseball after six o'clock on Sunday.

With the exception of a make-up game on September 30, the final games of the 1914 season between Indianapolis and Chicago would be played in a Monday double-header before 10,000 Hoosiers fans. The overworked aces Hendrix and Falkenberg struggled in the first game. The Chicago pitcher left after the seventh, but Cy went the distance. With the score tied at five in the ninth inning, Indy's Vince Campbell tried to make a shoestring catch on Tinker's line drive to right field. The ball eluded him and Joe hustled to third with a triple. Beck's single scored his manager with the lead run and Irv Lange retired the Hoosiers in the bottom of the inning for the win.

The combatants played to a 3–3 tie in second game. Indianapolis was two runs to the good starting the sixth inning when Bruno Block singled and Zwilling lifted a high fly ball over the right field wall to tie the contest. Chicago proceeded to load the bases with no one out on Wickland's single and safe bunts by Tinker and Beck. However, Indy Pitcher Kaiserling completed a Houdini act by getting out of the inning without allowing any further scoring. Claude Hendrix returned to the mound for Chicago and held the Hoosiers scoreless until the game was ended by darkness after the seventh.

Following the eight-game stretch between the two league leaders, Chicago's record stood at 68–56, two games out of first place. The hero of the week for Indianapolis had to be the veteran pitcher, Cy Falkenberg. Over a seven-day span, Falkenberg pitched three complete games against Chicago, winning two and losing one, and saved another with two and two-thirds innings of scoreless relief.

22

Fielder Jones

On Tuesday, June 16, 1914, the St. Louis Terriers defeated Brooklyn, 13 to 12, in twelve innings at Steininger Field. With the score knotted at 5–5, Brooklyn scored seven runs in the top of the twelfth inning off Manager Mordecai Brown, pitching in relief for St. Louis. Art Griggs ended the debacle by purposely swinging and missing three pitches from the thirty-seven-year-old legend.

Johnny Tobin led off the St. Louis half of the twelfth with a home run, then eight other Terriers batters safely reached base. Tom Seaton was relieved; Byron Houch came in to pitch, and he too was pulled after two more batters reached base. Rudy Sommers entered the game for Brooklyn only to give up the eighth run of the inning, and there was only one out when the winning run scored. Mordecai Brown got credit for the bittersweet victory despite his poor performance on the mound.[1]

The great comeback was one of the few highlights for the struggling St. Louis club that summer. As the club slid to the bottom of the Federal League standings, Brown was an obvious scapegoat.

In mid–July, St. Louis club president E.A. Steininger went to Chicago and had a discussion with Cubs catcher Roger Bresnahan about managing the Terriers. The Federal League executive reportedly offered the ex-manager of the Cardinals stock in the Terriers and a bonus equal to the amount the catcher might receive if the Cubs made the World Series. The offer was turned down.[2]

With the team ten games under .500, the St. Louis club announced a set of "blue laws," intended to increase the efficiency of the players. Steininger declared that manager Brown would be ordered to enforce the new rules:

> Players must retire at 11 o'clock each night. Extensive card playing or gambling of any kind [is] prohibited. Players must show up for practice at a specific time, and, if absent, good excuse must be given. All players "laying down" or failing to perform the plays called for will be subject to fine to be determined by the manager or president. Players making inexcusable errors will be subject to fine or suspension.[3]

Following the implementation of Steininger's blue laws, the Terriers dropped a three-game series to Indianapolis. The club lost seven of eight games it played between July 17 and the twenty-fourth, to all but guarantee a second-division finish.

Brown's lack of attention to detail nearly cost his team a game in Pittsburgh. With the bases full of Terriers in the sixth inning, batter Larue Kirby hit a grand slam home run. However, the Rebels complained that Kirby had batted out of order. The umpire called the proper batter, Delos Drake, out and took the four runs off the scoreboard. Then Kirby, batting in proper order, hit a single, driving home two runs. An error let in a third tally and St. Louis won the game anyway.

When the team failed to improve, Mordecai Brown was released from his duties as manager of the St. Louis Federal League club on August 22. Brown pitched his last game for the Terriers on the twenty-first, a 7–4 loss to Baltimore.

Following his dismissal as manager, Brown said that the Terriers' owners treated him shabbily and the failure of his team was due to the refusal of the ownership to spend money for players. Brown claimed he had arranged for third baseman Red Smith and second baseman George Cutshaw to jump the Brooklyn National League club, but his bosses were not willing to put out a year's pay in advance, amounting to $6,500 for Smith and $6,000 for Cutshaw. The owners obviously thought it wasn't worth that kind of money to add players that late in the season for a team near the bottom of the standings.[4]

"Mordecai Brown was one of the best fellows in the world personally," remarked co-owner Otto Stifel, "but as a manager he was not a success. He may have been too easy-going, too good in his treatment of the men, as I have heard it said. But he didn't get the results that he had hoped, and we secured the services of Fielder Jones."[5]

The evening of August 16, 1914, a beaming James Gilmore announced that Fielder Jones had been signed to manage the St. Louis Federal League club. Jones, legendary pilot of Chicago's "Hitless Wonders" World's Championship club of 1906, was one of the most highly sought-after managers by the major leagues. Though the deal was closed in St. Louis five days earlier, Jones did not want the news released until he officially resigned as president of the Northwestern League, which officially severed any connection he had with Organized Baseball.

When asked about the future of the current manager, Mordecai Brown, President Gilmore said that the league owed too much to the veteran not to take care of him. Brown indicated that he had not been notified of any change in the management of the team, but his days as pilot of the Terriers had been numbered for weeks. Brown immediately said he would not play for Jones.

The change of managers in St. Louis invalidated a pair of unofficial nicknames for the club heretofore identified with Mordecai Brown — the "Brownies" and "Miners." Thereafter, sports writers would be left with "Terriers" or "Sloufeds" for their reports.

"Mordecai is a good man and I would willingly keep him on the staff," Jones announced upon assuming the position of manager on August 23. "However, there would be a strained feeling between us, for Brown is too sensitive to take orders from a man who has just stepped into his shoes. If it is possible I will keep him, but if he wants to be traded I will do so. I will leave the matter for him to decide."[6]

Weeghman's Chicago club, in a tight battle for the Federal League pennant, inquired about making a deal for the deposed manager to fortify their pitching. However, Fielder Jones took the stand that a pitcher of Brown's experience was worth more to his club than the youngsters Fiske and McGuire, or Brennan, who was out of shape due to his illness. Brown finally got out of St. Louis the first of September when the Wards of Brooklyn took on the Miner's large contract.

Fielder Allison Jones was born at Shingle House, Pennsylvania, August 13, 1871. His parents named him after a great-uncle, Fielder A. Jones, a Civil War general of cavalry who became an attorney and newspaper publisher after his military service.

Jones began playing professional baseball with the Oregon State League in 1893 and by the fall two years later, he had made it to the Brooklyn Superbas of the National League.

Fielder played center field for Ned Hanlon's championship Brooklyn teams of 1899 and 1900. When Ban Johnson's new American League offered the opportunity in 1901, Jones jumped to the Chicago White Sox and played on yet another pennant winner. On June 8, 1904, White Sox owner Charles Comiskey appointed the thirty-two-year-old outfielder manager of the club.

Fielder Jones's place as a baseball icon was secured when he piloted the White Sox to the American League championship in 1906 despite a team batting average of .228. Dubbed the "Hitless Wonders," Jones's team then defeated the crosstown Chicago Cubs in the World Series after the National Leaguers had piled up a record 118 regular season victories.

Jones was renowned as the best tactician in the game, winning with a team that displayed little hitting prowess. He successfully employed the tactic of playing for one run and left the rest to a solid defense and strong pitching.

"Though not as personally popular as some baseball men, he had a keen knowledge of inside baseball which he was able to impart to his players," wrote *The Sporting News*. "With his quiet manner, he had a piquant sarcasm which aroused umpires' wrath when he ran to the diamond from his outfield position to protest decisions."[7]

For years Jones was an advocate for players' rights and, as time passed, he became frustrated with the way baseball was being run. He particularly disliked the reserve clause and felt that major league owners were not compensating the players fairly based on the amount of money they were making.

At the end of the 1908 American League season, Jones demanded to be allowed to purchase a significant minority interest in the White Sox which benefited at the gate because of his clever management. Charles Comiskey refused to sell any of his stock to Fielder and his brother. Jones shocked baseball when he refused Comiskey's counteroffer and went to Portland, Oregon, where he became a rancher and lumberman. Charles Comiskey made a trip to Portland in an effort to woo Jones back to Chicago. He offered Fielder $15,000 and again was turned down.

The lure of baseball was too strong for Jones and in 1910 he was named baseball coach at Oregon Agricultural College, later Oregon State. When Fielder decided to play for Chehalis of the Class D Washington State League after the college season, baseball's reserve rule dictated that he was still under contract to the White Sox so they had to give him permission to play. The ex–major leaguer led Chehalis to the championship, batting .358. The White Sox did not officially release Jones as a player until 1913, when he was forty-two.

Due to his popularity in Chicago, Jones was hired to cover the 1910 and 1911 World Series for a city newspaper. Comiskey made another offer for Jones to return as White Sox manager in September of 1910. Jones again turned down a "big salary."

The Northwestern League put a team in Portland for 1911 and late that year Fielder Jones was elected league president. In 1913 the Boston Red Sox offered Jones a job as their manager and the Brooklyn Tip Tops made a similar offer a year later. He turned them both down.

Finally, the Federal League made Fielder an offer he could not refuse in August of 1914. Jones came to St. Louis in early August and met with President Steininger, Otto Stifel and James Gilmore, who knew Fielder from his days with the White Sox. After a secret meeting that lasted several hours into the evening, Jones was induced to sign a contract with the Federal League. Estimates of Fielder's deal went as high as $50,000 though Jones revealed that he would receive $10,000 a season on his three-year contract plus a block of stock in the St. Louis club.[8] Rumors of the Federal League's coup gradually leaked out, but Gilmore refused to say anything about the matter except that the Federals would be glad to enlist the former White Sox manager in their service.

Fielder Jones, manager, St. Louis Federal League club, 1914 (George Grantham Bain Collection, Library of Congress).

Part of the Federal League's attraction for Jones was its limited reserve clause and the part of the agreement that gave him a minority interest in the Terriers. Sam Weller wrote in the *Chicago Daily Tribune* that Jones returned to baseball, "Not because he 'needs the money,' but because he sees an opportunity, after many years, to fight organized baseball, of which he always was an avowed and open enemy, even when connected with it."[9]

On Jones's first visit to Chicago as manager of the Terriers, the Chifeds designated a doubleheader "Fielder Jones Day" in honor of the former White Sox skipper. The crowd was disappointing as only 6,000 bugs came out on a cloudy "blue Monday." Mayor Thompson presented the legendary manager with a silver plate and pitcher that were inscribed "to Fielder A. Jones by his Chicago friends, August 1914." A movie camera recorded the festivities to exhibit in theaters around the country.[10]

Once the platitudes concluded, the local Federal League team was not very hospitable and beat Jones's club twice, 4 to 3 and 1 to 0. Claude Hendrix's two-hitter in the nightcap pushed Chicago into a tie with Indianapolis for first place in the Federal League pennant race.

The Terriers' record did not improve under Fielder Jones over the remainder of the 1914 season, as the club won only twelve of their remaining thirty-eight games. It didn't help that Fielder lost the club's most effective pitcher in former manager Brown. It didn't help that the leading hitter was also the second most effective pitcher, but he was playing out of position at second base, which kept him off the mound. To replace Brown, it was arranged that the Chicago club would "loan" pitcher Doc Watson to St. Louis.

On September 6, Chief Johnson's pitching and Bill Kenworthy's home run enabled

Kansas City to defeat St. Louis, 2 to 0. Manager Jones pinch hit for pitcher Dave Davenport in the ninth inning and singled cleanly to center. It was his first appearance as a player in a major league ball game in five years. Jones would pinch hit in five games with the Terriers that year, collecting one hit in three official times at bat.

Jones, the St. Louis owners, and the Federal League all committed to the proposition that the Terriers would field a competitive team for the 1915 season.

23

The Stretch Run

On Sunday, September 13, the city of Chicago saw its final triple clash of the 1914 baseball season when all three of its teams staged games. The Chifeds won a double-header in Buffalo on Saturday, but because of the Sunday blue law in New York, the two clubs took the train to the Windy City for another two-game set the next day. The Federals staged a special "Williams Day," in honor of the Chicago club's secretary, with a parade and a band. The Chifeds' game attracted 5,600 people to Weeghman Park while the Cubs played before only 2,800 at West Side Park and the White Sox were watched by 7,500.

Adam Rankin Johnson pitched a shutout against Buffalo in the first game of the Sunday twin bill and Ad Brennan managed to persevere in the nightcap, 7 to 5. The double victory gave the Chifeds a record of 73 victories and 58 losses, one game ahead of idle Indianapolis in the Federal League standings.

Back in August, Indianapolis swept three consecutive double-headers with the Brooklyn Tip Tops to vault the Hoosiers into first place. Bill Phillips' players were naturally full of confidence when the club rolled into Brooklyn on Monday, September 14. They had won their previous eighth meetings with the Tip Tops, Cy Falkenberg was set to pitch the first game, and Brooklyn's most effective pitcher had a sore arm.

By the final week of August, Tom Seaton's right arm had succumbed to overwork. After a session with Bonesetter Reese, the Tip Tops' ace was declared fit to pitch the opener in the Indianapolis series. For five innings, Tom set down the Hoosiers without allowing a hit. Then, in the sixth, he lost the lead, his cool and the game.

Seaton apparently became unnerved when Benny Kauff singled, stole second and scored the game's first run on a hit by Laporte. With the Indy shortstop, Jimmy Esmond, at bat, Seaton became enraged when umpire Ollie Anderson called a ball on a pitch Tom thought was a strike. Seaton walked up to the plate and hurled his glove high into the air to signify his displeasure with the umpire. Anderson promptly threw the Brooklyn pitcher out of the game. Upon his ejection, Seaton charged toward the umpire, but catcher Grover Land and Manager Bradley held the enraged pitcher at bay.

After Rudy Sommers came in to pitch, the Brooklyn team went to pieces. Two more hits and shoddy play by the Doughboys led to three more runs. Speedy Edd Roush got to first base on Hofman's error while Esmond held at third. Twice, Roush started toward second base on attempted double steals and twice was caught between first and second. The first time Edd slid back into first base, safely avoiding Evans' tag. On the second attempt, he ran back and forth in the run-down until Hofman made a hopeless play for Esmond at third, which gave Edd time to reach second.

Benny Kauff got into the act an inning later when he beat out a bunt, stole second, and eventually scored on a squeeze play. Falkenberg was the beneficiary of Brooklyn's collapse and completed a 10–0 shutout.[1] Chicago lost to Pittsburgh so, at the end of the day, Indianapolis and the Chifeds were tied for first place, with identical records of 73 victories and 59 defeats.

The following afternoon, Chicago's Claude Hendrix shut out Pittsburgh. Indianapolis had no trouble with the demoralized Tip Tops, winning 9 to 2, and the clubs remained tied atop the league standings.

On Wednesday, Indianapolis beat Brooklyn again when Earl Moseley threw a four-hit 2–0 shutout and again the Hoosiers' speedsters showed up the Tip Tops' defense. In the first inning with two out, Kauff got to first on a single and stole second. Laporte drove a hit to left field that went between the legs of Anderson and, while the outfielder was retrieving the ball, Kauff scored the game's first run. In the second inning, Roush punched a slow roller toward second baseman Hofman, who fielded the ball and threw it almost twenty feet over the first baseman's head. The Brooklyn pitcher, Ed Lafitte, wild-pitched Roush to third base, from where he scored on Bill Rariden's single.

Indianapolis completed a four-game sweep of the Tip Tops by beating Miner Brown. The game was tied 4–4 going into the eighth inning. With Hoosiers on first and third, Al Scheer pinch-hit for pitcher Kaiserling and chopped a grounder toward second base. The batted ball took a wild bound and escaped the grasp of Hofman as the runner on third scampered home. The Hoosiers reinforced their league lead when Pittsburgh's Howie Camnitz beat Chicago, 5–3, after Joe Tinker decided to save Claude Hendrix for the opener of their Baltimore series.

The Hoosiers' success against the Tip Tops was the big reason for their first-place status. During the season, Indianapolis defeated Brooklyn in nineteen of twenty-two games, including the last twelve.

On Saturday, September 19, Chicago played the first of a five-game series at Terrapin Park in Baltimore. The Terrapins were in third place, trailing the Chifeds by 2 games, although they had lost only one more game than Tinker's men. The Terps had just completed a series with Kansas City which drew such poor crowds the *Baltimore Sun* lamented, "The old guard who turned out every day became discouraged when they saw less than 2,000 persons in the stands two or three days in succession."

The large Baltimore crowd went wild in the ninth inning of game one when the Terrapins almost overcame a 7–3 Chicago lead. Four straight hits off Hendrix to open the final frame plated three runs and narrowed Chicago's lead to one. As the sun faded in the west, Claude retired Kirkpatrick on a foul fly to Beck, Doolan fanned, and Knabe's hard grounder was snared by second baseman Farrell, who threw him out. Although Chicago managed to escape town with three victories in the five games, the series revitalized the pennant race in Baltimore.

"Enthused by the game fight the Terrapins are making for the Federal League pennant," the *Baltimore Sun* noted on September 22, "the attendance at the local ballpark picked up considerably and more than 4,000 persons turned out. It was a pretty good crowd for a Monday, and the patrons gave the home crew plenty of encouragement. Chicago had no complaint to make regarding the attendance in Baltimore, for Saturday more than 6,700 persons paid admission to Terrapin Park."[2]

On September 25, Pittsburgh's Elmer Knetzer won a 1 to 0 pitching duel with Indy's George Kaiserling on a cold and windy day at Exposition Park. Up to the home half of the sixth inning, each club had garnered only two measly singles. A walk and a scratch hit put two Rebel runners on base and Eddie Lennox was given a free pass in order for Kaiserling to face Steve Yerkes. The former Red Sox infielder responded with a long sacrifice fly to score the lone run of the contest. Though he allowed but three hits, Knetzer walked five batters, but the Hoosiers couldn't cash in any of the passes for a run. The Chifeds moved into sole possession of first place after their victory over Three Finger Brown in Brooklyn.

On Saturday, Chicago reinforced its newfound hold on first place by sweeping a double-header at Washington Park. Fresh off a 1–0 shutout of Kansas City only four days earlier, Brooklyn's Tom Seaton was untouchable for four innings of the first game while his teammates drove the visitors' Ad Brennan off the mound with a six-run assault.

In the second inning of the contest, Chicago Manager Joe Tinker watched two of his players strike out, then he asked umpire Barry McCormick to check the ball. The ump examined the ball he had just tossed to Seaton and found that one side had been scraped as if with a file. Seaton denied using a foreign object, but Tinker found emery paper inside Tom's glove. Brooklyn manager Bradley rushed out and Seaton handed him the evidence. Bradley then refused to give the emery paper to McCormick, but the umpires allowed the game to continue.[3]

Chicago touched Seaton for a run in the fifth and another in the sixth, but Tom still held a 6 to 2 lead when he returned to the mound for the eighth inning. The overworked hurler suddenly lost his stuff and walked four Chifeds. Bradley went to the mound and motioned for Lafitte to come into the game. However, Seaton refused to leave the field and continued to pitch, though his deliveries were "walloped far and near" until Chicago took the lead, 7–6, the eventual final score.

The *New York Times* commented that the opening game "took the almost record time of two hours and forty-two minutes." Because of the length of the first game, the nightcap only went five innings. Bill Bradley introduced a new left-hander named Finis Wilson and again Chicago triumphed, 5 to 3. The Tinx did suffer one loss in Brooklyn, falling 9 to 5 on the twenty-eighth. Claude Hendrix allowed nine hits and five runs before he exited the game after only five innings.

Before making a flying dash out of the city on September 29, the Chifeds beat Brooklyn one more time. Dutch Zwilling drove a delivery from the "Unhappy" Finneran over the right field fence in the fifth inning that sent two runners home ahead of him. The three-run blast broke a 3–3 tie, then Max Fiske held the Brookfeds at bay the rest of the way to preserve the 7–4 victory.

During the Brooklyn series, Chicago's Dutch Zwilling put on a long ball-hitting exhibition for the Washington Park faithful. Over the course of the five games, the compact left-handed slugger banged out nine hits, including two doubles and three home runs.

At the same time Chicago was taking four of their five games with Brooklyn, the last-place Pittsburgh Rebels almost knocked Indianapolis out of the Federal League race by winning three of a four-game set at Exposition Park. After splitting the first two games with Pittsburgh, Bill Phillips decided not to take any chances in game three on the twenty-eighth. Leading 2–0 after seven innings, Indianapolis starter George Kaiserling gave up a single to Frank Delahanty and walked Menosky to open the eighth. Phillips summoned Cy Falkenberg to the mound and the Hoosiers' ace quickly disposed of the next two batters. The Rebels' Eddie Lennox worked a walk and Cy went to a 3 and 2 count on the next batter, Hugh Bradley. The Pittsburgh first baseman connected with Cy's next pitch and poked a safety to the outfield, driving in the tying run. An inning later, Pittsburgh's light-hitting backstop, Claude Berry, reached Falkenberg for a leadoff double and later scored the winning run on Menosky's grounder to second base.

A day later, League President Gilmore, Vice President Robert B. Ward and the entire St.

Louis Cardinals baseball team showed up at Exposition Park to watch the Rebels' game with Indianapolis. Earl Moseley would oppose the Rebels' top pitcher, Elmer Knetzer. In the third inning McKechnie tried to stretch a triple into a home run with two outs but was easily cut down at the plate. An inning later, Benny Kauff was thrown out at home trying to score when second baseman Steve Yerkes staggered after catching a pop fly in short right field. The game turned on one at-bat in the fifth inning when Pittsburgh manager Rebel Oakes came to bat with two outs and the sacks jammed.

"Moseley grooved one and it was a fatal groove," reported the *Indianapolis Star*. "...Oakes caught that grooved ball with his 'wagon tongue' and it hit the right center field wall for three sacks, every last one of those three Rebels racing over the plate with easily enough runs to win."

The three runs held up and Knetzer held the Hoosiers scoreless for the second time in the series. Knetzer pitched only three shutouts during the 1914 season, two within a four-game span against easily the best-hitting club in the Federal League.

Indianapolis players Bill McKechnie (left) and Fred Falkenberg (wearing jacket) on the bench during a game in Chicago, 1914 (Chicago History Museum, SDN-059578. Photograph by *Chicago Daily News*. Original photograph has been cropped.).

On the last day of September, the Hoosiers and Chifeds met for the final time in 1914 in a single make-up game in Indianapolis. A disappointing crowd of fewer than 5,000 watched a game with championship implications. Also in attendance was George Stovall's Kansas City team, on hand to watch their next two opponents battle. The Packers would play a crucial role in deciding the 1914 Federal League pennant.

Chicago's Rankin Johnson and Cy Falkenberg matched zeros on the scoreboard until the home half of the seventh inning. With one out, Jimmy Esmond drove a double between Zwilling and Wickland. Edd Roush slapped a pitch straight back at Johnson that was hit so hard the pitcher only had time to stick up his glove as the sphere buzzed past on its route to the outfield. Esmond scored the only run Falkenberg needed, but his teammates added some insurance an inning later with two more tallies, largely due to Benny Kauff's double that went all the way to the scoreboard. Cy was terrific, allowing the Chifeds only three singles.

The next day Tinker's men beat St. Louis, 2 to 1, at Weeghman Park, although the former Chifed, Doc Watson, almost did in his former teammates. He allowed Chicago only one hit over the first seven innings, but that hit by Rollie Zeider, a double in the first inning, led to a run. Watson was lifted for a pinch hitter in the eighth, and Chicago scored a second run off Doc Crandall. Mike Prendergast shut out the Terriers until St. Louis pushed across their lone run on an error in the ninth. Their victory added another half game to the Chifeds' lead over the Hoosiers, because Indianapolis had to settle for a deadlock with Kansas City when darkness halted the contest after ten innings. Baltimore kept its faint pennant hopes alive when John Quinn shut out Brooklyn, 3 to 0.

Baltimore was officially eliminated from the Federal League race on October 2. Old Miner Brown pitched his best game as a member of the Brookfeds and took a 3–0 lead into the ninth inning. An error by James Delahanty and a pair of singles with none out filled the bases with Terrapins. Hack Simmons hit back to Brown and Meyer was forced at home for the first out. After Kirkpatrick struck out, Swacina hit a routine grounder to shortstop but Holt fumbled it, allowing a run to score. With the tying run on second base, Brown struck out Jimmy Walsh to end the game and finish Baltimore's pennant aspirations.

The Federal League standings after the completion of games on October 2 showed Chicago in a good position to capture the Federal League championship:

Chicago	84–64	—
Indianapolis	81–65	2
Baltimore	78–67	4

Of the Chifeds' remaining six games, two were against last-place St. Louis, followed by a four-game series with Kansas City, which was in the midst of a seven-game losing streak. All of the games would be played at Weeghman Park.

Chicago made it two in a row over the Terriers in the Saturday game on Claude Hendrix's two-hit, 5 to 1 triumph. Joe Tinker sent his second best pitcher, Rankin Johnson, to the mound for the key third game on Sunday, October 3, and despite threatening weather, a festive crowd of 6,000 showed up in anticipation of their Chifeds' thumping last-place St. Louis. Opposing Johnson was the man he replaced in the Chicago rotation, Doc Watson, who was coming back to pitch for the second time in the series.

The two pitchers battled through five scoreless innings. The key play in the game for Chicago occurred in the fourth inning with one out and Rollie Zeider on first base. Art Wilson sent a line drive toward the left field wall. The Terriers' Ward Miller dashed back after the sphere, leaped at the last moment just as he crashed into the wall. The left fielder sprawled on the ground, but maintained the ball in his glove. By that time, Zeider was almost to third base and Miller recovered his feet to easily double the Chicago runner off first base.

In the St. Louis half of the sixth inning, light-hitting John Misse reached first base when shortstop Joe Tinker booted his slow roller. Watson bunted the runner to second, from where Misse scored on a double to right field by Jack Tobin. Watson was dominating after that and completed a 1 to 0 shutout. The Chifeds did not advance a runner past second base against the St. Louis mound doctor.

Meanwhile, Indianapolis won a double-header from Kansas City before 16,462 happy bugs on "Watkins' Day." In the first game, there was plenty of excitement in the fifth inning when Benny Kauff tried to steal home with Laporte at bat. Umpire Bill Brennan was on the right side of the plate to watch the play and Benny slid into him. The Hoosier outfielder got up smiling as the ump limped around in pain. The two exchanged a few remarks and the player was ejected. According to the *Indianapolis Star*, a squad of police were called and they did "minute duty" on the diamond near the dugouts. In addition to being lost for the remainder of the game, Kauff was slapped with the $25 fine stipulated by the Federal League for any ejection.[4]

Cy Falkenberg was in fine form until the ninth inning, when the Packers plated four runs. With the score 5–4 against them, Bill Rariden opened the Hoosiers' half of the ninth with a double. Surprisingly, Bill Phillips didn't pinch-hit for Falkenberg and sent the lanky right-hander to bat for himself. Nick Cullop fanned his opposing number, but Vin Campbell bailed his manager out with a single over shortstop to tie the game. Indianapolis won in the tenth inning when Johnny Esmond's triple scored Carr to send the huge crowd into a frenzy. Indy also won the second game, which concluded after four and a half innings because of darkness. Within the course of one afternoon, Chicago's lead in the pennant race had shrunk to a scant one half of a game.

Sixth-place Kansas City was the next team to visit Chicago and the Chifeds maintained their thin first-place margin with a 2–0 shutout of the Packers. During the course of the game, Kansas City's Nick Cullop had the ball so well "doctored" Chicago's Mike Prendergast had trouble controlling his pitches. In the third inning, Prendergast loaded the bases on an infield single and two walks. Joe Tinker begged umpire McCormick to put a new ball in play, but he refused. Tinker removed his starting pitcher and sent in Max Fiske, who threw a spitball and also had been practicing an emery pitch. Fiske enticed George Stovall to pop out to the second baseman and then struck out Otto Krueger to escape the jam. Fiske allowed only two singles over the final six innings to preserve the win.[5] The Chifeds' triumph marked their thirteenth victory in nineteen games with Kansas City. Indianapolis shelled St. Louis, 15 to 8, to stay right on the heels of Chicago.

In addition to having little at stake, the weary Packers had been on the road since September 7, when their park in Kansas City was badly damaged. Heavy rains that poured almost seven inches onto the city overnight turned Brush Creek from a stream into a rising torrent. The resulting flooding from the creek caused considerable damage to the Federals' ballpark. The raging waters washed away fences and the clubhouse was demolished, though not before the groundskeeper and his two assistants, who were asleep at the park, escaped. The team's bats, uniforms and other equipment were swept away. Manager Stovall sent a wire to Chicago, where the club was scheduled to play next, for new uniforms and equipment.[6] After their park was destroyed, Kansas City lost 17 of their next 24 games.

Chicago appeared to be in good shape for the first game of a double-header on Tuesday, October 6, with 29-game winner Claude Hendrix set to pitch against Kansas City. It was not as much of a mismatch as it appeared. With the exception of Art Wilson, the Chicago club's best hitters were left-handed and the team had struggled against southpaw tossers all season. Opposing Hendrix would be Gene Packard, one of the best left-handed flingers in the Federal League with twenty victories already to his credit despite pitching for a second-division club.

Packard employed several pitches that came out of different arm angles. He used a straight overhead motion for his big drop curve and had a good change of pace. But just when a batter settled in against him, Gene could unleash his rapid crossfire from an underhand or sidearm motion. Eugene Milo Packard first gained nation-wide recognition in 1908 while pitching for Independence of the Oklahoma-Kansas League. On August 5, he did not allow a Bartlesville, Oklahoma, batter to reach first base for a "perfect game." Gene finally made his big league debut at age twenty-five for the Cincinnati Reds with a victory over the Cubs on September 27, 1912. The *Chicago Daily Tribune* noted that "the left-handed stranger named Packard, who, it was learned, had been secured from the Columbus club ... was small, but displayed a lot of speed and cunning in his slabbing, and the Cubs could do little with him."[7]

A year later, Joe Tinker took over the Reds, and, employing several rookies, the club flopped to seventh place. Packard won only seven of eighteen decisions, but he became a successful recruit for the Federals.

Both Packard and Hendrix were on their game that October afternoon at Weeghman Park and the contest was scoreless going into the sixth inning. In the top of that frame, Kansas City pushed across a run to take the lead. Pop Chadbourne beat out an infield hit that second baseman Jack Farrell fumbled. He moved to second on an out and scored when George Perring picked out one of Hendrix's offerings for a run-scoring double.

In the bottom of the sixth, Farrell reinforced his hold on the goat horns for the day. He was on third base with one out when Zeider lifted a high fly to Chadbourne. Instead of tagging up, Farrell danced down the line, then was unable to score even though the center fielder's throw sailed ten feet up the line from home plate. Packard completed the 1–0 shutout and Claude Hendrix was denied a thirty-win season.

Despite pitching nearly seven innings the previous day, Max Fiske begged Manager Tinker to let him pitch the second game. Joe acquiesced and Max lasted only into the third inning when he was tagged for two runs. Lange replaced him and he gave up two more in the fourth. Chief Johnson was in control for Kansas City in every inning except the sixth, when Chicago scored their three runs in the loss. In the course of an afternoon, the Chifeds found themselves on the verge of elimination from the pennant race.

Many of the Chicago fans took exception to umpires McCormick and Cusack calling the second game after the seventh inning while there was still enough light to play. A "robust woman bug" who had been a steady and loud customer at Weeghman Park all season waited a half hour for the umps to leave the ball yard, then chased and berated them all the way to the "L" station.[8]

While Chicago was losing two games that day, Indianapolis defeated St. Louis for their sixth consecutive victory, moving the Hoosiers into first. When the second game in Chicago went final at 5 to 3 in favor of Kansas City, Indianapolis suddenly had a one-game lead. For Chicago to win the pennant, Indianapolis must lose its final two games while the Chifeds had to win its single remaining contest.

Without a game in Chicago the next day, the Tinx could only wait for the results of the Indianapolis-St. Louis contest. With Falkenberg, the Hoosiers' ace, ready to pitch against the last-place Terriers, Chicago's chances were slim. Maybe Falkenberg would be tired after pitching 43 complete games and 368 innings during the 1914 season. After all, he had blown a three-run lead in the ninth inning against the Packers four days earlier, only to have his teammates bail him out with a run in the bottom of the ninth inning to tie the game.

On this day the contest was never in doubt for the Hoosiers. Falkenberg retired the visitors in the top of the first, then his teammates went to work on tall Dave Davenport. The first batter, Vint Campbell, bunted and before he stopped running Indianapolis had a run. Catcher Harry Chapman fielded Vin's bunt and threw it high over the first baseman's head. Right fielder Tobin retrieved the sphere and pegged it to third, but the ball hit umpire Goeckel. As the ball rolled into left field, Campbell scurried home with the only run Falky would need. One batter later, Benny Kauff hit a ball off the scoreboard for two bases and scored from second when Laporte beat out a roller to the shortstop. "Benny covered ground in marvelous fashion and made the plate by a great elusive slide under Chapman," reported the *Star*.[9]

With a two-run advantage, Falkenberg took over from there. He struck out eight batters, allowed only one hit up to the ninth inning and finished with a three-hit 4–0 shutout. After the game, the champions' fans crowded onto the field and congratulated Manager Phillips and the players. Though Falkenberg and Benny Kauff shared the majority of the fans' plaudits, local sports reporter Ralston Goss attributed much of the club's success to catcher Bill Rariden.

"He has handled the steady Falkenberg, the erratic Moseley, the dependable Kaiserling and the wild Billiard so skillfully that he got the best results from each," wrote the *Indianapolis Star* sports writer. "His throwing and his general play place him head and shoulders above any other catcher in the league."[10]

Indianapolis and Chicago each won meaningless games on the eighth, and the Hoosiers finished the season a game and a half ahead of Chicago.

The final Federal League standings:

Indianapolis	88–65	—
Chicago	87–67	1½
Baltimore	84–70	4½
Buffalo	80–71	7
Brooklyn	77–77	11½
Kansas City	67–84	20
Pittsburgh	64–86	22½
St. Louis	62–89	25

By the conclusion of the season, the Hoosiers' Benny Kauff had undoubtedly become the Federal League's most notable player. He completed the 1914 season with a batting average of .370, twenty-two points higher than Steve Evans' second-best mark in the league. He was especially successful against left-handers, batting .422 in 116 official at-bats against southpaw flingers.[11] Benny led all three majors in batting average (Ty Cobb hit .368), in hits with 211, in total bases, and in stolen bases.

In an obvious publicity move on October 10, Indianapolis club secretary James A. Ross issued a formal challenge to the winner of the Boston Braves–Philadelphia Athletics World Series: "I hereby declare that failure on the part of the winners of the so-called world's series to accept this challenge precludes any right upon their part to lay claim to the title 'world's champions' or to the name of true champions."[12] Though they would not play for a mythical "world's championship," *The Sporting News* reported the Indianapolis players would go to the next spring training each driving a $4,000 automobile to be presented by President Gilmore for winning the Federal League flag.[13]

24

A Gloomy State of Affairs

There was speculation following the baseball season that the organized major leagues and the Federals would agree on a compromise to end the baseball bidding war. 1914 had been a tough year for all of professional baseball.

The founders of the Federal League made a miscalculation in ignoring a declining United States economy and a downward trend in per capita income by Americans that would drive down baseball attendance by mid-decade. Moreover, Federal League executives could not have predicted the brief but severe economic recession in mid–1914 that may have ruined any chance of making money that season.

After more than a decade of economic growth, attendance for major league games fell from 6,360,000 in 1913 to less than 4.5 million a year later, a decrease of almost two million patrons. The eight National League clubs drew just 1.7 million customers in 1914, the lowest attendance for that league since the settlement with the American League in 1903. The gate was even lower than some of the seasons during the depression-laden 1890s. The *New York Times* estimated that half of the American and National League clubs lost money in 1914 and those in the black only showed marginal profits. Attendance for the two traditional major leagues increased by 409,838 in 1915, but the numbers were still smaller than any season between 1904 and 1913.[1]

The reason for the drastic decline of baseball attendance in 1914 has not been fully explained. The portion of those attendance decreases attributable to the presence of Federal League teams in four major league cities cannot be determined, but it would be presumptuous to suggest the outlaws' impact was not significant.

Professor Harold Seymour disputes the rationale that a declining U.S. economy caused the decrease in baseball attendance that season and puts more of the blame on the Federal League intrusion:

> Another misconception passed along by a succession of writers is that the depression in 1914 and the onset of World War One caused attendance to diminish drastically and thus hastened the end of the baseball war ... the depression of 1914 was too brief to affect baseball attendance. And the outbreak of war in Europe soon brought a flood of Allied orders for munitions that pulled the United States out of its economic doldrums. The big 1914 decline in attendance was already apparent in May, whereas the World War did not break out until August, by which time the baseball season was two-thirds over.[2]

However, Seymour provided little explanation for the decline in baseball attendance other than to state that "some of this slack no doubt was taken up by attendance at Federal League games."[3]

Numerous reasons have been offered to explain the precipitous decline in baseball attendance. These include the rising popularity of movie theaters, ticker service to gambling establishments that allowed people to bet on games without being at the ballpark, labor unrest, people's malaise over the war in Europe, the Mexican situation, a partisan press that had taken sides in the baseball war, and the fans' disenchantment with the greed that led to excessive player salaries.[4]

"Baseball prices are too high," said Brooklyn's President Robert B. Ward. "Especially is this true where there is such a depression this year in industrial centers. The people, therefore, are willing to pay for it if they can afford to. The moving pictures have shown us that there is a demand, but only at popular prices. Almost all the big theatrical producers have seen the light and are catering to those who patronize the picture palaces. I think it is about time for the baseball magnates to consider the fan's pocketbook, too."[5]

St. Louis sports columnist J.B. Sheridan wrote of the disillusionment among fans at the salaries paid to baseball players:

> Salaries are out of reason. Traveling is too luxurious and expensive. Clubs carry too many players, assistant managers, coaches and trainers. It is clear that baseball is due for a great general reorganization. The clever energetic man who works hard for $50, $100, $200 a month becomes disgusted and disgruntled to when he sees some great lazy, hulking fellow whose sole asset is his ability to hit a baseball harder and oftener or to throw a baseball faster and more accurately than most men, getting from $1000 to $3000 a month for playing a few hours a day.[6]

The *New York Times* reported that the National League made a profit of $115,000 in 1914 and the American League had a net gain of $58,000, though only eight of the sixteen major league clubs made money. The *Times* placed the Federal League losses at $176,000, the International League was estimated to have lost nearly $150,000, and the American Association was in the debit column to the tune of $90,000.[7]

"Salary lists of the low-priced clubs jumped from $60,000 a season [before 1914] to $80,000 or $85,000 a season," wrote former Red Sox president John I. Taylor in the *Boston Globe*. "The higher priced clubs jumped from $90,000 to $115,000 or $120,000. The turnstiles at the majority of the ballparks did not click fast enough to keep up with the salary list, and the result was the poorest year in the history of organized baseball...."

"You can see who got the money this year," he wrote, obviously alluding to the increasing salaries paid to the players.[8]

Just after the World Series, rumors circulated that Charles Weeghman would buy the Chicago Cubs and the Wards of Brooklyn were going to purchase the New York American League Club. Upon the arrival of Federal League attorney Edward Gates in Chicago to discuss the upcoming league meetings with James Gilmore, the *New York Times* speculated, "The presence of Mr. Gates is believed to mean that he has been called here by President Gilmore with whom he was in conference most of the day to prepare legal papers for the proposed peace agreement with Organized Baseball."[9]

On Tuesday, October 20, the *New York Times* reported, "President Weeghman, owner of the Chicago Federals, will place before all the magnates at the meeting in New York, Friday and Saturday, details of his conference with Gary Herrmann, chairman of the National Commission, in New York."

Charley Weeghman and Herrmann met in New York to discuss suggestions that the Chifeds' owner might consider acquiring the Chicago Cubs. Organized Baseball's sources indicated that the history of negotiations with Weeghman dated back several weeks when Mike Cantillon, instrumental in the Feds' acquisition of the land where Weeghman Park stood, learned that Charley was concerned about the Federal League's future and would be receptive to purchasing the Cubs. Cantillon set up the meeting between Weeghman and Herrmann.

Weeghman expressed an interest in joining Organized Baseball, but he did not want to play the role of traitor to his fellow magnates in the Federal League. He asked of Herrmann that the way be made easier for his associates to join him in making peace.[10]

The price to persuade the Federal League to close up shop would be high. The Feds wanted to retain the rights to all players they claimed (contract-jumping players were to be forgiven and restored to Organized Baseball in good standing), they should have representation on the National Commission, and the Federals would be allowed to obtain control of the Chicago Cubs, a St. Louis club, and a franchise in the New York area, either the Yankees or the Dodgers. The Federal League franchises in Indianapolis, Kansas City, Buffalo and Baltimore either would assume the management of the local minor league club or dispose of their holdings for their cost of operations for the 1914 season.

At a subsequent National League meeting, several magnates joined the American League owners in opposition to negotiations with the Federals. Weeghman or the Wards might be acceptable individually for membership to the National League, but they had to come in without ties to the Federal League. Herrmann reported there was little hope of coming to satisfactory terms with Federals because they wanted too much.

After speaking with Herrmann by telephone about his meeting with the Chifeds' boss, American League President Ban Johnson immediately fed the story to Chicago sports columnist George Robbins. Johnson was quoted as saying in Robbins' column:

> This was the first intimation I had that the Federal League representatives had met anyone in the authority in Organized Baseball. It was Weeghman who sought Herrmann, though, and not Herrmann who sought Weeghman. Mr. Herrmann told me that Weeghman sent up his card when the Commission was meeting in the East, but that the chairman of the National Commission informed the president of the Chifeds that he could not talk with him in his official capacity but only in a personal conversation.
>
> You can say for me that the American League will stand pat and that we will make no overtures to the Federal Leaguers. They have lost a lot of money and are hard pressed, but they are trying to make it appear Organized Baseball is seeking peace terms.[11]

When his negotiations became public, an obviously irritated Weeghman told the press:

> I had a talk with Mr. Herrmann because of the stand I had taken in making public the peace conference in New York last week. I wanted Mr. Herrmann to understand that I agreed to remain silent in all good faith, and would never have allowed a word to escape my lips had Ban Johnson not told of the meeting in New York and accused me of seeking the conference and so tried to belittle me in other misstatements he made.
>
> I told Mr. Herrmann, I was tired of Johnson's abuse. Mr. Herrmann knows Johnson did not stick to the truth in his interview, and does not hold any ill feeling toward me for telling the facts about the meeting.[12]

Weeghman continued to exhibit interest in the Cubs and before the Federal League meeting in New York on October 21, Charley met with Cubs majority owner Charles P. Taft in Cincinnati to discuss the possibility of buying an interest in the National League club. Because of the condition of the ownership of the Cubs, the National League felt a Weeghman ownership of the club would be in the best interest of Chicago baseball. Furthermore, Charley's abandonment of the Federals to become an owner in Organized Baseball might deal a death blow to that league. However, negotiations were quickly terminated, presumably because Taft determined Weeghman was so tied up with the Federal League it would be impossible for him to disconnect from them as the National League insisted he must do to be allowed to purchase the Cubs.

When Organized Baseball's negotiations with Weeghman were broken off, Herrmann expressed regret, and, according to *The Sporting News*, "...tucked the peace dove away in its cage. There is no peace."[13]

On his way to New York for the annual meeting of Federal League owners at the Biltmore, President James Gilmore also squashed the possibility of any peace talks. The Federal League's owners reelected Gilmore president at their meeting on October 22, but the main concerns were stories that Weeghman and the Wards had offers to purchase the Cubs and Yankees respectively. After the Federals remained closeted for several hours, Gilmore emerged and read his annual report.

He reiterated that the Federals were satisfied with the fight they had made on Organized Baseball, and they were not seeking peace, but would accept it if the major leagues were willing to take them into the fold and remunerate them for all losses. On the story of Weeghman's being offered the Cubs, he stated, "The Wards will not think of buying the Yankees or Mr. Weeghman will not buy the Cubs while there is a Federal League."[14]

"I will admit that the Federal League this year did not come up to our expectations in attendance," said Weeghman.

> Some of the clubs were pretty hard hit, but the showing was indeed a fine one for the first year, and we are entirely satisfied and are ready to go on to next season without a hitch. I made some money in Chicago — not as much as I expected, it is true. I figured on about 200,000 paid attendance for the season to cover my expenses, and I calculated that I would get about 400,000 attendance. I fell short of this figure, however, and got about 312,000 paid attendance during the season.[15]

The Federal League declined to issue official attendance figures for its specific clubs. The league left it up to the individual clubs to give out attendance numbers, if they so desired. The Buffalo Federal League club set their 1914 season attendance at 185,326,[16] though Organized Baseball's counters estimated their gate at an unrealistically low number of just over 71,000. The Buffeds' best day at the gate was May 30, when the club drew 19,000 for a morning/afternoon double-header.

Based on information it received from Organized Baseball, the *New York Times* reported that the Pittsburgh Federal League club played to fewer than 65,000 paid admissions at home during the season, amounting to only about $30,000 in gross receipts, of which visiting clubs received less than $15,000. The expenses of that club were estimated at not less than $100,000, including $25,000 spent on renovating Exposition Park.

The *Times* also reported that the St. Louis Federals lost at least $60,000, "the Kansas City Federals were liable for a much larger sum, ... the Buffalo Federals ran far behind their expenditures, and the Brooklyn Federals dropped a bundle."[17]

Lloyd Rickart complained about misleading reports that the Indianapolis club had lost $76,000 in 1914. The Federal League secretary asserted, "Money was lost, but that was due to an outlay of $125,000 for the grounds, stands and improvements. However, as far as the team was concerned, the club had a profit of $50,000 over and above salaries and training and other expenses."[18]

The Sporting News scoffed at the Federal League's attendance figures provided by James Gilmore at their annual meeting: "Mr. Gilmore stated at the recent outlaw meeting that his total attendance for eight teams was 1,600,000. Mr. Weeghman boasts of 312,000 at home. Authentic information is that Pittsburgh drew 62,000, Kansas City 50,000, and St. Louis, we will say 60,000. That means 484,000 for four clubs in the Federal League. There is left

1,116,000 that must be made up by the remaining four clubs or an average for them of 278,000."[19]

The Sporting News' attendance estimates were provided by employees of Organized Baseball who estimated, or "clocked," the attendance at Federal League parks and fed the numbers to friendly sports writers. Using their questionable figures, *The Sporting News* printed a gloomy analysis of the Federal League's state of affairs: "It is estimated — by organized baseball — that the 786,327 paid admissions netted a total of $314,530.80 for the league, figuring on an average of 40 cents for each admission. The operating expenses of the league are estimated at $985,600. Thus a deficit of $671,069.20 is created."[20]

Organized Baseball's "counters" estimated the Chifeds' attendance at just over 200,000, Indianapolis 136,000 and Baltimore at about 125,000. Accepting those figures, the only major league teams of Organized Baseball that drew fewer fans than the Chicago Federals were Cincinnati (NL) 100,791, Brooklyn (NL) 122,671, Pittsburgh (NL) 139,620, Philadelphia (NL) 138,474 and Cleveland (AL) 185,997. Boston (AL), without direct competition from the Feds, had the largest attendance in baseball for 1914 (481,359) and the Boston Braves topped National League clubs.

During the final session of the Federal Leaguers' meeting in New York, the magnates decided that the Kansas City franchise would be transferred to another city. Philadelphia was mentioned as a leading contender for a club, though the lucrative New York City metropolitan area was the principle target for a team in 1915.

The League also focused on strengthening its weaker clubs, especially in St. Louis and Pittsburgh. Walter S. Ward of the Brooklyn club boasted to newspaper reporters that an "emergency fund" (said to be around $100,000) had been established to sign the stars of the organized major leagues who had not returned signed contracts for the upcoming season.

Rumors flew fast and thick, but the only announcement of a desertion from Organized Baseball was the revelation that William Fischer, a twenty-three-year-old backup catcher with the Brooklyn Dodgers, had signed with Chicago. Gilmore said that two star players had been secured from major league clubs, but mentioned no names. The *New York Times* repeated a report that Harry Davis, former captain of the Philadelphia Athletics, and Eddie Plank, Connie Mack's star pitcher, were seen in the corridor of the Hotel Biltmore during the Federals' meetings.

Within hours after their conference, Federal League officials announced the signings of two veteran National League players. Pittsburgh Pirates first baseman Ed Konetchy and pitcher William "Pol" Perritt were said to have inked deals with the Feds. On the heels of that report, it came out that Cardinals catcher Ivy Wingo had agreed to an offer from Buffalo.

Ed Konetchy (pronounced con-et-zy, with the accent on the first syllable) was a powerful right-handed hitter who usually batted cleanup, though his best season for home runs in the dead ball era totaled only eleven. F.C. Lane, editor of *Baseball Magazine*, wrote of the big first baseman, "For a man of his size he is very fast. He has blue eyes and a strong face showing an aggressive personality. But there is not the least bit of egotism in his disposition and he is universally frank, cordial and accommodating. He is deservedly popular among his fellow players; is never known to criticize while he is always ready to say a good word for any other of his teammates or members of another club."[21]

One of seven children, Edward Joseph Konetchy was born to immigrant Bohemian parents on September 3, 1885, in La Crosse, Wisconsin. At age fourteen, he left school to work in a La Crosse candy factory. By this time he was already 6 feet 1 inches tall. After working ten hours at the factory, Ed and other workers would walk two miles to a ball field. They would play baseball until it was too dark to see, then Ed would walk the twelve miles back home. The next day, he would repeat the process all over again.[22]

Konetchy was sixteen when he joined the factory baseball team as the left fielder. Four years later Ed tried out for and made the La Crosse team in the Class D Wisconsin State League, where he became a first baseman. In 1907 the St. Louis Cardinals were in need of a first baseman to replace the aging Jake Beckley. A Cardinals agent, Jake Huston, heard about "the next Hal Chase," who was batting around .350 and playing outstanding defense for La Crosse. Upon seeing the big Bohemian play, Huston recommended Konetchy to Manager John McCloskey and the Cardinals acquired the twenty-one-year-old first sacker that June for $1,000.[23]

Konetchy would lead National League first basemen in fielding eight times and batted .281 in 2,083 games. His 2,148 hits included 344 doubles, 181 triples (eighteenth all-time), and 74 home runs. By 1913 Koney and Jake Daubert were regarded as the National League's premier first basemen.

During the National League's annual meeting in December 1913, the Cardinals' new manager, Miller Huggins, traded Konetchy, along with third baseman Mike Mowrey and pitcher Bob Harmon, to Pittsburgh for five players. The Federal League approached Ed during the winter about playing for the outlaws, but he declined their overtures because he had already signed his 1914 contract.

After going 15 and 2 to start the 1914 season, the Pirates won only 8 of their next 29 games. As the team descended in the standings, Pittsburgh owner Barney Dreyfuss openly criticized his players and was particularly hard on Konetchy, who batted only .249. By August, reports out of St. Louis suggested Ed had spoken to a representative of the St. Louis Federals, but he decided to stay in Pittsburgh — for the time being. Mike Mowrey and Pirates outfielder Max Carey were also said to be talking with the Federals.

Dreyfuss later claimed that Konetchy acted as a Federal League agent long before the regular season was over. *The Sporting News'* Ralph Davis reported that when Mike Mowrey was released at mid-season, Koney reportedly said, "I will be the next one to go." The reporter further wrote that Ed "approached other members of the team, notably Cooper, Viox and one or two others and tried to get them to agree to make the leap with him."[24]

The Sporting News also reported John McGraw wanted Ed for the Giants and even offered $17,500 in cash and players for the first baseman and pitcher Marty O'Toole. Dreyfuss was disappointed in Konetchy and knew the player badly wanted off his club. Yet he wasn't willing to help the Giants win the pennant.

Ed had signed his 1914 Pirates contract prior to baseball's meeting with the Fraternity in spite of a promise by the players that they would not sign until told they should do so by union President Dave Fultz. Shortly after the start of the season, Konetchy went to President Dreyfuss and told him he wanted a new contract that conformed to the demands made by the Players' Fraternity.

At that time, Dreyfuss could hardly refuse Koney's request because the Pirates appeared to be a pennant contender. The new document did not contain the ten-day clause. Ed received $6,300 in salary from Pittsburgh for 1914 with a $300 option for the following year.[25] After the season, Konetchy went to the Pirates' president and asked for a three-year contract.

Dreyfuss told reporter Ralph S. Davis: "I tendered a contract to Koney, and he asked me to make it for three years. I told him to return the document, as he would not only not get a three-year contract, but that the document I had tendered him would not be given him again."[26]

Ed's lawyer examined the Pirates' final contract offer and insisted it was not valid because the ten-day clause was left in, whereas his previous contract with Pittsburgh did not contain the clause. He maintained that Pirate officials immediately broke the agreement when the clause in question was inserted in the new contract because Koney worked under an option clause in 1914 that stated the club must give him a contract the same in every detail for the coming season.

Satisfied that he was on firm ground, Konetchy met with Pittsburgh's Federals, who agreed to pay him $21,000 for three seasons. Aubrey Konetchy reportedly received $1,000 for helping convince her husband to change leagues.[27]

During a visit with Konetchy in St. Louis, Pirates manager Fred Clarke told Ed if he did not repudiate his Federal League contract, the National League would ensnare the player with an injunction to prohibit him from playing anywhere in 1915. Clarke promised that the Pirates would trade Ed to another team if he returned to the National League. On the spot for damage control, Jim Gilmore personally assured Koney the Federal League would take care of him and the player stood firm with the Federals.[28]

Rebel Oakes spoke out in defense of his new first baseman:

> Quite a few slams have been taken at Ed Konetchy by persons in organized baseball, simply because he has jumped to the Federal League. However, it is only a case of sour grapes, and such talk makes me sore.
>
> There is only one first baseman who can be mentioned in the same breath with Koney, and that is Jake Daubert.... And I'll tell you the name of one National League manager who would be highly tickled to get Koney, and that's John McGraw.[29]

In addition to Konetchy, the Pittsburgh Federals had apparently secured the services of the St. Louis Cardinals' outstanding young right-hander, William Dalton "Pol" Perritt, who was making $3,000 in the National League. Before the season, Cardinals President Schuyler Britton instituted a policy of players' bonuses based on the club's position in the final National League standings. When the Cardinals finished in a surprising third place, sixteen-game winner Perritt received his bonus, but he balked at signing a 1915 contract at the terms the club offered. Rebels manager Oakes, a fellow Louisianan and a former teammate of Perritt, offered the disgruntled Cardinals pitcher a lucrative Federal League contract. On October 13, Oakes announced the Rebels had signed Perritt and catcher Paddy O'Connor of the same club two months earlier. A report indicated that the pair had inked contracts that called for "large advances."[30]

"Pol Perritt is said to have been given a three year contract by Pittsburgh of the Federal League at $3,500 a year with one year in advance," reported *The Sporting News* on October 22. "Ivy Wingo is to get $6,000 a year from the Buffeds with a $3,000 bonus for signing."[31]

A week later, it was revealed that Pittsburgh native Marty Berghammer had jumped the Cincinnati Reds to play for his home town Federal League team. The twenty-six-year-old infielder later explained, "The reason I jumped was that I was getting $3,600 with the Reds and Pittsburgh offered me a three year contract at $6,000 a year. I also was given 5,000 one-dollar bills for signing. When you take everything into consideration, that was a lot of money in those days."[32]

In early December, Manager Oakes announced he had lured third baseman Jimmy Austin away from the St. Louis Browns.[33] The addition of the veteran of six years in the American League gave Pittsburgh six new players direct from the organized major leagues since the end of the previous season: Konetchy, Perritt, O'Connor, Berghammer, Austin, and Brooklyn left-hander Frank Allen.

Henry P. Edwards wrote in his *Sporting News* column, "Austin had been corresponding with Hedges and Rickey of the Browns for several weeks, and was reluctant to jump if he could get a long term contract with St. Louis. He waited two days for that contract and then signed with Oakes, getting a three year contract with advances in salary."[34]

"Mr. Hedges and Mr. Rickey treated me splendidly," Austin said, "but I have reached that state of my baseball career when I feel I must protect myself. The contract I have signed will protect me for three years. More I could not expect."[35]

In late November, it was said that Lee Magee would sign a contract to play for and manage the Wards' Brooklyn club as soon as his ten days' notice to the Cardinals lapsed. The Feds failed to sign Magee at the "Battle of the Dock" when the player returned from the Giants-White Sox world's tour the previous spring, but it appeared they would finally get their man.

James Gilmore promised Cleveland's Fred Bramley early in the year that when he was able to show the Federal League that he had secured an advantageous location for a ballpark, the Ohio city would be reconsidered for a franchise. Subsequently, Bramley acquired an option on a Euclid Avenue property which would be a good spot for a baseball park.

In the fall of 1914, Bramley convinced Gilmore, George Ward and William Robertson to come to Cleveland. The Federal League officials approved the site then they informed Bramley he could get back into the league by purchasing the Kansas City franchise for a price of $60,000.[36]

Since Bramley had not received a dime for his franchise when he was forced out of the league earlier in the year, he did not choose to pay for the expensive Euclid Avenue property as well as absorb the losses of the failed Kansas City franchise. The Cleveland amusement park owner decided on give up his aspiration of owning a major league baseball franchise.

In mid–December, President Gilmore and Charles Weeghman traveled to French Lick, Indiana, to meet with Colonel Jake Ruppert, who was negotiating to purchase the New York Yankees from Frank Farrell. Gilmore hoped to persuade the wealthy Gotham brewer to promote a New York Federal League franchise instead of joining Ban Johnson's circuit. The meeting was in vain, as Ruppert was committed to purchase the Yankees along with his partner T.L. Huston.[37]

Rumors about further defections by major league players to the Federal League were hot and heavy throughout December. Three Phillies, third baseman Hans Lobert, star hitter Sherry Magee and recently deposed manager and catcher Red Dooin, negotiated with the Feds, but eventually all three remained in Organized Baseball. Lobert and Magee were appeased by trades that sent the players to the Giants and Braves respectively.

The Federals signed thirteen players from the rosters of Organized Baseball's major leagues between the end of the 1914 regular season and mid–December. Though those defections were seen as serious, none would compare to the shock Organized Baseball experienced in early December when one of the top stars of the American League inked a 1915 contract to play in the Federal League.

25

The Big Train Almost Becomes the Federal Express

In late October 1914, St. Louis Federals manager Fielder Jones received the blessing of club owner Phil Ball in seeking a meeting with baseball's best pitcher, Walter Johnson of the Washington Nationals. The star hurler's contract had expired following the season just completed and he automatically became fair game for the Federal League. Johnson finished the year with American League highs of 28 victories, 10 shutouts, and 225 strikeouts. Since Walter won 32 and 36 games the two seasons prior to 1914, Washington club President Benjamin Minor remarked to Clark Griffith during contract talks that Johnson had a bad year and "doesn't warrant the $12,000 we're paying him now."[1]

On October 29, Jones accompanied the star pitcher on a train ride from Walter's home in Coffeyville, Kansas, to Fort Smith, Arkansas, where "Johnson's Kansas All-Stars" were to play an exhibition series. The Terriers' manager made Johnson a flat offer of sixty thousand dollars for three years, $10,000 of it in cash, to play for the St. Louis Federals.[2] Johnson said he would give the Terriers an answer later, then wired Washington manager and co-owner Clark Griffith, who not only refused to match the Federal League offer, but would not even come close.

At first, Johnson sought to use negotiations with the Federals as leverage to get a better contract from Griffith. Walter asked the Nationals for either a one-year deal for $15,000, a three-year deal for $36,000 or a five-year offer of $50,000. Griffith curtly told Johnson that he did not want to purchase the whole of Johnson's home state of Kansas. President Minor wrote Johnson that he was obligated to play for Washington because of the reserve clause and Walter would pitch for the previous year's salary of $12,000![3]

When Federal League magnates met in Chicago on November 28, Ball wired Johnson for an answer to his offer. He received no reply. The Terriers' owner then announced he was through with Johnson and said that anybody that wanted the pitcher could have St. Louis' rights to sign him. Federal League President James Gilmore had just taken the stance that his league would no longer go after the higher-priced stars of Organized Baseball and would undertake to upgrade the level of play through other means. However, the chance of getting Walter Johnson into a Federal League uniform would be too big a coup to drop.[4]

During the Federal Leaguers' Chicago meeting, Charles Weeghman said he would take Johnson at $20,000, but did not want him for more than two years. Ball then waived all claims to the strikeout king and agreed to aid Chicago in its efforts to sign the player.

Ball insisted, however, that if he waived his rights to Johnson, he should have the pick of other pitchers signed by the Federals. He agreed to take Eddie Plank, who had been slated to go to either Brooklyn or Chicago.

While several major league clubs worked behind the scenes to recover players defecting to the Federal League, the Philadelphia Athletics simply cut loose two star pitchers when Manager Connie Mack became convinced they were dickering with Federal League agents.

Blaming greed and intrigue for his players' discontent, which led to the loss of the 1914 World Series, Mack did not attempt to sell veteran southpaw Eddie Plank and right-handed ace Charles "Chief" Bender to another team, but released the pair. The Athletics tried to keep the waivers secret, but Detroit manager Hughie Jennings leaked the news on October 31.

Years later, Bender made a self-serving statement about the reason for his release: "It has been said that we were flirting with the Federal League before the Series and weren't prepared to give our best, but that isn't true. Not one of us had been approached by the Federal League. The Braves beat us because they were the better club."[5]

On December 2, 1914, Harry Goldman, treasurer of the Baltimore Terrapins, went to Gettysburg, Pennsylvania, and obtained the signature of Eddie Plank on a general Federal League contract. Though it was not definite at the time of the signing, Plank would pitch for Fielder Jones in St. Louis.

The evening of December 5, Chief Bender confirmed reports that he too had signed a contract to pitch in the Federal League with either the Brooklyn or Baltimore clubs. Harry Goldman arrived in Philadelphia earlier in the day and the former A's pitcher wasted no time in signing the agreement.

"The terms of the contract are very satisfactory, and it is the best thing I ever did in my life," Bender told reporters. "The contract is to run two years."[6]

Bender signed a contract with the Feds for a $5,500 bonus and an annual salary of $8,500. The contract was a windfall for the pitcher, who made $5,000 with the Athletics. A beaming James Gilmore concluded, "Connie Mack must have been completely off his balance when he asked for waivers on Plank and Bender, and the Federal League will give a contract for three years at a salary in excess of that he obtained from the Philadelphia club."[7]

Veteran pitchers like George Mullin, Earl Moore, Piano Mover Smith, and Three Finger Brown, who all signed with the Federal League before the 1914 season, were near the end or past their prime as major league pitchers. Although Bender had been a starting pitcher in the American League since 1903, he was only thirty-one and had compiled a 17–3 record with seven shutouts for the A's in 1914. Fifteen-game winner Plank, though 39, used an easy pitching delivery that relied on his superb control and finesse to fool the batters. The lanky left-hander won 285 games between 1902 and 1914 with the Athletics and was still a remarkably effective pitcher, as Federal League batters would discover in 1915.

On the day Bender signed his Federal League contract in Philadelphia, Robert B. Ward received a telephone call from New York Giants pitcher Rube Marquard asking for an interview. From 1911 through 1913 Marquard won 24, 26, and 23 games for three Giants pennant winners. In 1914, the temperamental southpaw slumped to 12 and 22. Marquard became irked at the Giants when he was refused an advance of $1500 on his two-year contract. Rube had his audience with Mr. Ward and suggested he was ready to jump to the Federals. After talking the matter over, the pitcher was told to go home and think about it.

At noon on December 3, Marquard came back to the Federal League office and satisfactory terms were agreed upon. Before giving Rube the $1500 advance money and signing him to a two-year Federal League contract at $10,000 a year, Ward had the pitcher sign an affidavit, stating that he was not legally bound to the Giants.

Before long, though, the Wards learned that Rube had lied about not being under contract to the Giants. At first, Robert Ward refused to believe that Marquard had made a false affidavit, but when assured, he accepted the situation that Rube was legally bound to the Giants and negated the contract.[8]

When Marquard was returned to the Giants, McGraw promised to "square" Rube's debt with Ward if he would not prosecute the wayward pitcher for fraud.[9] The New York club advanced Marquard $1500 so he could return to the Wards the money he worked them for and the payment would be withheld each payday until the Giants were reimbursed. The Wards did not prosecute the lefty and the incident was closed.[10]

On December 3, Chicago manager Joe Tinker went to Coffeyville and within only twenty minutes he completed a deal for Walter Johnson to pitch for the Chicago Federal League club. The Washington star signed a Federal League contract calling for $17,500 a season for three years and a $6,000 bonus.[11]

Federal League officials attempted to justify the large salary promised Johnson by pointing out that Chicago's road games in places like Kansas City, Buffalo or Pittsburgh would help make up some of the balance because of the increased number of people that would come out to see the "Big Train" pitch. A statistician friendly to Organized Baseball computed that based on an average of fifty cents per admission for which the home team received half, it would be necessary, if Johnson was paid $19,000, for the club to draw no less than 76,000 additional fans just to pay his salary.

Clark Griffith was not about to give up just yet and stated in a newspaper interview that he thought Johnson's Federal League contract was illegitimate based on Organized Baseball's "reserve clause" in the standard player's contract:

> There was a provision in the 1914 contract whereby I obtained an option on Johnson's services for the 1915 season. Twenty five hundred dollars of the $12,000 salary which he has received was given for the specific purpose of reserving an option in 1915 upon Johnson. I am convinced he has violated the agreement, and I will sue him to the end of the earth before I acknowledge his right to sign with the Federals.[12]

Attorneys had advised major league clubs against going to court in cases where a jumping player's contract had expired, so Griffith decided litigation might not be the most prudent thing to do. He asked Pittsburgh Pirates manager Fred Clarke, who lived not far from Coffeyville, to visit Johnson and set up a meeting between Walter and the Washington boss. Johnson agreed and Griffith traveled to Kansas City in an effort to convince Walter that he had always acted in good faith toward his ace hurler and deserved better. Johnson agreed, but felt that it would hurt the Chicago Federals if he were to jump back to his former club. Griffith argued that Johnson would ultimately hurt either Washington or Chicago, so he would have to make a choice. Swayed by Griffith's argument, Johnson agreed to return to the Washington Nationals, receiving only a $500 raise for all his trouble. Following his flop back to the American League, Johnson sent a certified check for the $6,000 bonus to Charles Weeghman of the Chifeds.[13] Johnson never threw a single pitch in the Federal League.

Without consulting his club, Clark Griffith had agreed to cover the repayment of the $6,000 bonus Walter received from the Federals. The Washington manager telephoned Ban Johnson at West Baden, Indiana, where the American League president and White Sox owner Charles Comiskey were taking in the therapeutic baths. Washington, D.C., sports writer Shirley Povich later published his account of Griffith's telephone conversation with his American League associates.

Griff told Johnson he needed $6,000 out of the American League's $450,000 reserve fund to pry Walter Johnson away from the Federal League. When Ban said it couldn't be done, the Washington owner told him, "Let me talk to Comiskey!"

Comiskey also told him the pitcher was Washington's problem, not his.

Griffith replied, "Well, then, how would you like to have Walter Johnson playing for the Chifeds next season and drawing all those fans away from the White Sox?"

Comiskey was said to have answered, "How much did you say you wanted?"[14]

In an interview with *Baseball Magazine* that spring, Johnson candidly admitted:

> From the first, I was always impressed with the Federal League. They looked to me like a game crowd, and I admired their courage. I do not see how anyone who has seen how they have fought against the greatest odds can fail to be impressed with their courage. I always hoped they would succeed, for I thought their success was a good thing for the ball player, and a good thing for the public.
>
> ...Whichever way I turned was wrong. I didn't treat the Federal League right. I broke my contract with them. But I did so only because I was convinced that by doing so I would be doing an even greater injury to Washington. It is a humiliating position to be in.[15]

Reeling from the loss of Johnson, Joe Tinker was faced with the job of rebuilding his pitching staff with less renowned candidates. By counting on Johnson, the Chifeds had lost out on Eddie Plank, now property of St. Louis.

Also gone was the spitballer Max Fiske, a starting pitcher with the 1914 Chifeds. The Chicago native won 12 and lost 9 that season, then rejected a five per cent raise for 1915. Both Fiske and Mike Prendergast held out and the club decided to renew the breaking-ball pitcher instead of Max. Erv Lange and Tom McGuire also did not return and Ad Brennan could not be counted upon because of a problem with his pitching arm. This left only Claude Hendrix, Rankin Johnson, and Prendergast set to pitch in 1915.

In the search for another premier starting pitcher to compliment Hendrix, the Chifeds' attention was drawn to a thirty-seven-year-old Tennessean named George McConnell, nicknamed "Slats" because of his 6'3" angular build. George was purchased by the Cubs from the International League's Buffalo club late in the 1914 season and started the second game of a double-header in St. Louis on October 3. He lost, 2 to 0, going seven innings in his only start for Chicago. The Cubs already had a number of pitchers under contract, so when the National League refused to budge off their 21-player limit per team for 1915 there was no room for McConnell. Chicago sold the spitballer to the Kansas City American Association Club only two weeks before the beginning of the National League season.

During his first year as owner of the Chicago Federal League Club, Charles Weeghman adopted the policy of not negotiating with players from either the Cubs or the White Sox. That course of action may have cost his team the 1914 Federal League pennant. Early in the season, Joe Tinker met with Chicago Cubs spitballer Larry Cheney in St. Louis. The newspapers reported that Tinker had reached an agreement with the pitcher, but Weeghman would not approve the deal.[16] Cheney went on to win twenty games, including a pair of one-hitters, for the Cubs. Weeghman's policy to not deal the other Chicago clubs' players had run its course by the spring of 1915.

Instead of reporting to the Kansas City Association club, George McConnell signed a one-year Federal League contract with Joe Tinker on April 5, 1915. Tinker had been tipped by a former associate on the Cubs that McConnell was as good as any pitcher on the team. A telegram from Buffalo Manager Larry Schlafly recommending the big hurler sealed the deal.

Cubs president Charles H. Thomas complained that $3,000 had been spent by the Chicago National League club on McConnell, $2,500 of which was paid to the Buffalo Internationals for the pitcher, plus $500 in railroad fares and training expenses. Thomas contended that McConnell refused to ascertain what offer would be made him by the Kansas City

Association club to which he was assigned by the Cubs.[17] The cordial relationship that Weeghman had established with Thomas was finished.

"McConnell told me he was a free agent," Charley explained to the *Daily Tribune.*

> I know absolutely that he was a free to sign with us anyway, for his contract with the Cubs contained a ten day clause, which made it illegal.
>
> Last season I said I wouldn't tamper with any Cub or White Sox players. I admit that, but I withdrew that resolution when agents of organized baseball kept me chasing all over the country last fall in an effort to settle the baseball war. They double crossed me then, and I lost all consideration for them. I'll keep McConnell, even if I have to fight for him in the courts.[18]

McConnell was originally a first baseman, became a spitball pitcher, and made the major leagues. He came to the American League's New York Highlanders in 1910. In New York, George rode the bench, pitching in only two games for manager George Stallings. "Demoted" to first-place Rochester of the Eastern League, George pitched a 5 to 0 no-hitter against Toronto on September 5. In 1911, McConnell posted the best record in the history of Rochester professional baseball. His thirty victories and .789 winning percentage for John Ganzel's pennant winner are still Red Wings records.[19]

After his outstanding 1911 campaign, McConnell earned another shot with the New York Americans at age thirty-five. That 1912 team, now being called "Yankees" by the press, was undoubtedly the worst in the franchise's history. George didn't pitch that poorly, compiling an 8–12 record and a staff-low earned run average of 2.75 for a club that lost 102 games. Among McConnell's teammates on that New York team were several future Federal Leaguers: Hal Chase, Russell Ford, Guy Zinn and Hack Simmons, as well Ray Caldwell, who also figured in the story of the outlaw league.

McConnell earned the nod of new Yankees manager Frank Chance to pitch the opening game of the 1913 season in Washington. With President Woodrow Wilson looking on, George allowed only six hits, but lost to Walter Johnson 2–1. Fifteen losses out of twenty decisions that season doomed George to the minors with Buffalo the following year. Slats made it back to the majors late in 1914 and started that one game for the Cubs.

At the February Federal League meeting of owners in Buffalo, the Tip Tops announced they would turn over Mordecai Brown's contract to the league. After the ex-manager made it clear he would not play in St. Louis under Fielder Jones, the Wards assumed Brown's contract in order to deflect criticism of the league. However, they refused to carry the burden of his salary into the 1915 season.[20]

Brown's contract with the Federal League as a pitcher called for a salary of $4,000, a $1,000 bonus in July 1914 and another $1,000 at the end of the season. Though he posted a 14–11 record between St. Louis and Brooklyn, the veteran hurler's 3.52 earned run average was 32 points above the league average. Fearful that he would have to pay Brown's salary out of the league treasury, President Gilmore attempted to shift Mordecai and another Brooklyn castoff, Bert Maxwell, to the championship Indianapolis club, but manager Bill Phillips refused to take them.[21]

Rebuffed in his offer to trade for Brown after Fielder Jones took over as manager of the Terriers in late 1914, Charley Weeghman now agreed to take the thirty-eight-year-old ex-Cub for the 1915 season. When Brown began spring training with the Whales, it appeared the veteran was finished as an effective starting pitcher, but Joe Tinker had not lost confidence in his friend. It would be a decision the Chicago Federals would not regret.

26

The Federal League vs. Organized Baseball

On January 5, 1915, the Federal League of Base Ball Clubs filed an antitrust lawsuit against Organized Baseball in the United States District Court of Northern Illinois, Judge Kenesaw Mountain Landis presiding. The Feds charged Organized Baseball with being a combination, a conspiracy, and a monopoly, in contravention of the Sherman antitrust law, and named as defendants the sixteen presidents in the organized major leagues and the three members of the National Commission. Federal League President James Gilmore contended that the monopoly enjoyed by the other two major leagues resulted in "illegal acts" that restrained free trade.

In eleven "prayers" for relief, the Federal League asked the court to declare the National Agreement, under which Organized Baseball operated, to be illegal and declare all contracts made under that agreement "null and void and of no effect." Point three claimed that the defendants conspired to injure or destroy the plaintiffs' business particularly by saying the Federals were financially irresponsible and threatening to "black-list" players under contract to the Federal League. Points four through six of the complaint addressed the status of players under contract to the Federals that were subject to court action or threat of injunction.[1]

The Federals specifically requested that the defendants be ordered to dismiss the various actions now pending against players George "Chief" Johnson, Harold H. Chase, Armando Marsans and Lee Magee. In addition, an appeal was made to restrain Organized Baseball from seeking "by injunctions, by threats, bonuses, promises or otherwise" to prevent players Fischer, Konetchy, Caldwell, Perritt, Wingo, O'Connor, Bedient, Austin, Allen, Berghammer, Bender, Plank and Marquard from performing contracts with the Federal League.

The text of the National Agreement, a copy of the pact between the Players' Fraternity and National Agreement clubs, and a copy of Walter Johnson's 1914 contract were among the exhibits appended to the bill of complaint. The plaintiffs added that "there are now in the United States 10,000 professional ball players, all of whom, with the exception of about 200 under contract to the Federal League, are under the domination and control of the National Agreement, rules and regulations of the National Commission and the National Association.... the defendants have claimed that a player under the National Agreement always continues to be a subject to the demands of the club subscribing to that agreement."[2]

In an addendum to the Federal League's eleven-point complaint, the league maintained it should share in the major league's World's Series to determine the eventual champion.

James Gilmore spoke to the assembled newspaper reporters about his league's motives,

"We seek help from the court in conducting our business, which is injured by the conspiracy of the members of organized baseball. We do not want to injure the game of baseball and we do not seek to benefit ourselves from the decision of the court, should it be in our favor. We have not brought the suit with the anticipation of getting all the players of organized ball set free by court action in order to grab them for our own use. We simply wish to protect what we have."[3]

With antitrust proceedings hanging over them, Organized Baseball and their agents presented a bold front, issuing statements condemning the Federals, and maintaining they welcomed the suit. Privately, they were worried.

American League President Ban Johnson issued the statement:

> This suit is the offshoot of the Gallagher resolution in the House of Representatives a few years ago to investigate the "baseball trust," which was pigeonholed. We said then we would welcome Congressional investigation, and we feel the same way about it now.
> When the American League was launched, we never voluntarily went into court to air our troubles. The American League never violated contracts or countenanced the violation of contracts. We are content to take the conditions as we found them and build up our organization on its merits. We fought our battle at the gate, not in the courts.[4]

Despite Johnson's selective memory, Clark Griffith, who helped form the American League, was once forced to admit to a Congressional committee that in 1901 they had ignored the National League's reserve clause and invaded its territory. He also acknowledged that the American League could not have succeeded without taking that direct action.[5]

Organized Baseball had considerable reason for alarm in that the Federal League's suit landed in the court of a notorious "trust buster" who had recently ruled that Standard Oil had been guilty of antitrust violations. Judge Landis set the hearing of the suit for January 20, ordered summonses issued against all of the persons named in the suit, and ruled the defendants must answer the Federal League petition before January 16, 1915. The Federals doubtless chose Landis's court because of his reputation as a trust buster. They did not know he was an ardent admirer of the existing major leagues.

The January 14 issue of *The Sporting News* led with the page-one headline: "Feds Pull Greatest Boner in All Their Erratic Career." Its New York correspondent editorialized, "You can be assured the Flap Jacks are going to have plenty of trouble before this crazy law suit has been either decided in favor of Organized Base Ball or thrown out of court because the plaintiffs have unclean hands...."[6]

Amid all the ballyhoo, Dave Fultz of the Players' Fraternity came closest to hitting the crux of the issue: "The dissolution of the National Commission would leave the players free to dispose of their services in the open market and to the highest bidder. Professional baseball, without proper organization and control, would result in complete disruption of playing and business standards. Such conditions would be the forerunner of baseball chaos."[7]

When the hearing got underway on January 20, more than 600 persons squeezed into the courtroom though there were seats for only 200. At least another 1,000 were turned away at the door. Seven attorneys, Garry Herrmann, Ban Johnson and John Tener sat at the table of Organized Baseball, and across the room James Gilmore and Robert B. Ward sat at the Federal League table with their three attorneys. Edward Gates was the lead attorney for the Federals, George W. Miller served as chief counsel for the American League, and George Wharton Pepper, later Republican United States Senator from Pennsylvania, represented the interests of the National League. A majority of major league owners were in attendance along with several Federal League executives, managers, players and umpires.

At the start of the proceedings, Leopold Hoernschemeyer (Lee Magee) asked the court to admit him as a party to the Federal League suit as a plaintiff "that he might be given an opportunity to secure justice and relief from prosecution at the hands of the alleged baseball trust." Hoernschemeyer filed an affidavit demonstrating how Organized Baseball dealt with him unjustly in that it had increased his pay as a player from $1,500 to only $7,200 in four years' time and had utterly failed to appreciate his true value as a performer.[8] When Magee entered the suit as a plaintiff, the injunction suit brought against him by the St. Louis National League Club before Judge Hollister in Cincinnati was indefinitely postponed.

After the Federals produced their "vast quantity of evidence," Attorney Keene Addington gave a speech focusing on the "system" that was Organized Baseball, which controlled the destiny, the salary and the abode of a player throughout his career. A particular target of his attack was Ban Johnson, who expanded his American League to major league status, secured peace with the National League, and created the National Agreement in order to ensure that no other organization could repeat what he had done.[9]

Affidavits by Joe Tinker and Mordecai Brown, favorites of Landis when they played for the Cubs, were read. Tinker expressed his objection to the ten-day clause and related that he had been traded or sold three times during his career in Organized Baseball without being consulted.

"Joe Cantillon, manager of the Minneapolis club of the American Association at one time traded a professional ball player for a bulldog," Mordecai Brown swore in an affidavit. He said he "also believed that Roger Bresnahan, while manager of the St. Louis club of the National League, traded a professional ball player, a pitcher named Hooper, to Richard Kinsella, then manager of the Springfield, Illinois, club in the Three-I League for a bird dog."[10]

Otto Knabe, Mickey Doolan, Secretary Lloyd Richart, and Indianapolis business manager William Watkins provided affidavits which were read by the Federal League attorneys. Employees of the Baltimore Federal League club attested that they saw a man perched on the grandstand of the International League Park across the street counting the Feds' attendance. A general answer to the Federal League's charges was made in an affidavit signed by Garry Herrmann, chairman of the National Commission, accompanied by declarations from Ban Johnson and Charles Comiskey.[11]

In his defense of Organized Baseball, National League attorney Pepper declared, "Their grievance is not that we prevent them from finding the young players on the "lot" and developing them through training in the various minor leagues as we do; they want to attain in one bound the advantage we have gained through ten years of labor; they want profit from the skill developed by our money."

When Pepper mentioned the word "labor" as applying to baseball players, Judge Landis expressed annoyance: "As a result of thirty years of observation, I am shocked because you call playing baseball 'labor,'" the judge snapped.

During the course of the hearing, Pepper made a statement that the theory of Organized Baseball's new reserve clause was not to hold the player except for one year following the contracted period. This statement suggested that the old reserve clause rule had not been fair since it gave an option on the player's services perpetually.

Landis exhibited surprise upon hearing that professional baseball no longer depended upon the reserve clause as the bulwark of a contract and that players who signed one-year contracts may become free agents following the one contracted for. Landis asked that Pepper repeat the statement, on which the attorney further elaborated.

"The player signing a 1915 contract agrees to terms with the club owner," the lawyer explained as he leaned confidently toward the judge. "Seventy-five per cent of the sum named in the contract applies as payment for the season and the remaining twenty-five per cent is an option on the player's services for the following year. If the player and the club owner cannot agree and come to terms for the 1916 contract ... when the 1916 contract expires the player is at liberty to negotiate where he wants. If he agrees to accept terms with the Federal League he is permitted to do so."[12]

Pepper's statements caused concern in the minds of the magnates and confusion among the press. Marvin Miller of the Baseball Players' Union applied similar logic in 1975 when pitchers Dave McNally and Andy Messersmith played the whole season of their option year without contracts. The players' contention that the reserve clause in their contracts could not bind them beyond the option year was upheld by an arbiter and the era of free agency began.

Thomas S. Rice predicted in the next issue of *The Sporting News*, "Whatever action Judge Kenesaw Landis may take in the Federal suit, the theory of base ball contracts as laid down by Mr. Pepper will remain fixed in the minds of the Players' Fraternity, and of the Federals, and his chatter is going to have a wide reaching effect."[13]

This ploy by Pepper was made solely to advance Organized Baseball's case and was not about to be adopted by the owners. Once the Federal League was dealt with, they would seek to render the Players' Fraternity impotent.

A good part of the morning session on January 23 was used by Judge Quincy Meyers, one of the Federal League attorneys, to show that the business of baseball was interstate commerce, which made it subject to jurisdiction of the federal court. Meyers cited the exclusive contract between the organized major leagues and Western Telegraph and the transportation of baseball paraphernalia from city to city to fulfill agreements to play games in those cities.

Early in the day's session, Landis interrupted the oration of Judge Meyers and demanded of the plaintiffs just what they expected him to restrain, if he should decide to issue the injunction as they had requested. Attorney Gates intervened to deny the intention of the plaintiffs was to bring hardship to the clubs of Organized Baseball. He contended that the purpose of the Federal League suit was to centralize the litigations being waged in other jurisdictions and bring them into one Federal Court.

"We are not seeking to stop the defendants from operating their usual business," said Gates. "We do not ask that they be prevented from carrying out their training plans, now, or in the end. But we do ask that they be temporarily stopped from going into various State courts and getting injunctions against our players."[14]

The judge took under advisement the request by the Federal League for a temporary injunction against Organized Baseball to restrain it from interfering with players the Feds had under contract. Landis gave Organized Baseball's attorneys twenty days to answer the charge of interference and other charges. After their answer was received, the court was to have decided whether to make the injunction permanent. The Federals then would have twenty-one days to reply.

Landis's procrastination in the issuance of a decision in the case gained him universal acclaim from friends of Organized Baseball. George S. Robbins wrote in *The Sporting News*, "Landis is a great fan and is conversant with baseball law and its relation to federal statutes, but is a stickler for justice. It is lucky for the game of baseball that the fate of the past time [sic] is in his hands."

Thereafter, the restraining order against Armando Marsans's playing for the St. Louis Terriers was tied in with the suit in Landis's court. The Federals grew weary of the judge's lack of action on their case against Organized Baseball and in late June, the Federal League's attorneys made a motion in Landis's court asking that Mansans be permitted to play pending the judge's decision in their antitrust suit. Landis refused to allow the motion, declaring that the player was not disadvantaged since he was being paid his annual salary of $7,000.[15]

Years later, J. Taylor Spink wrote in his biography of Judge Landis, "The end of the season and the Red Sox-Phillies' World Series passed and still no decision. I was one of the scorers at that Series, and I heard speculation about Landis' failure to render a decision. Obviously he [Landis] felt the Federal League had a case or he would have dismissed the case or given a ruling."[16]

27

Jumpers and Flip-Floppers

The new year of 1915 brought the resignation of one of the Federal League's most recognizable executives, John Mongomery Ward, business manager of the Brooklyn club. Actually, Ward had announced before the end of the 1914 regular season that his plan all along was to serve only one year in that position. Despite the failures of the team on the field, players jumping leagues, and the breach-of-contract lawsuits, Ward told reporters the only reason he resigned was that he had sorely neglected his law practice. He said his departure was not because he feared for the future of the league and called their battle "the most remarkable fight against tremendous odds that was ever chronicled in the history of the sport."[1]

The Wards hired Buffalo's enthusiastic business manager Dick Carroll to replace Ward. Despite the loss from the front office, the prospects for the 1915 season were looking good for the Buffalo club. On January 7, 1915, the Federals announced that Brooklyn National's outfielder Tolbert P. "Jack" Dalton had jumped to their club in Buffalo. Dalton signed a two-year Federal League contract without the objectionable ten-day clause.

A Tennessee native, Dalton honed his baseball skills at the University of Virginia. "Dalton knew the rudiments of the game before he attended the Old Dominion institution," wrote J.C. Kofoed for *Baseball Magazine*, "but his experience on the college squad served to polish the cruder portions of his playing. He developed into a deadly hitter ... who hit right or left-handed pitchers with equal facility. In one game against North Carolina he made the longest home run ever seen in those parts, and if the bucolic natives are to be taken at their word that ball is going yet."[2]

Dalton went to spring training with the White Sox in 1908, the last season Fielder Jones was at the helm of that club. At the end of training, Jones released the Tennessean. "A natural hitter," he said, "but he doesn't think quickly enough to nick a job with me. Besides that, he isn't fast enough in the garden."[3]

Jack played for Des Moines in 1909, batted .308 and scored 113 runs for the Western League club. A year later, he was hitting .300 after 50 games with the Iowa team when he earned a promotion to the Brooklyn National League club. In his second game with Brooklyn, Dalton made four hits off Giants pitcher Christy Mathewson. After 77 games in which he batted only .227, Jack returned to the minors. For the next three seasons, Dalton posted good numbers for Newark and Toronto. After batting .321 for Newark of the International League in 1913, he was summoned back to the National League.

Dalton won the center field job for the 1914 Dodgers and finished the season with the third-highest batting average in the National League. Jack only had a one-year contract and following the season he was contacted by Buffeds' manager Larry Schlafly, who knew Dalton from his time in the International League. Dalton gave Brooklyn owner Charles Ebbets until January 5 to meet his contract demands. After Schlafly again visited Jack with a solid offer to play for the Buffalo club, Dalton met with Ebbets. Reportedly, the Dodgers offered a $500 raise over Dalton's 1914 salary, but the player felt he was entitled to more money after leading the National League in batting for a good part of the season.

"It must be frankly confessed that we are sorry to see Jack go," wrote Brooklyn sports writer Thomas Rice. "He was a .319 hitter, a good man on fly balls and was full of fighting instinct. He was weak on grounders, but it must be remembered that he played nearly the all of last season with a festered finger that caused him pain whenever he threw or undertook to stop a smash that did not bound so he could get it in the palm of his glove."[4]

Ebbets responded to the defection of his centerfielder with the statement:

> Dalton's 1914 contract with Brooklyn expired on October 7 last, but in that contract was an option on his 1915 season for which we paid $750. He came here Saturday night, and in the presence of Edward J. McKeever and Larry Sutton, I officially handed him a letter which I read him, first notifying him that we had exercised our option on his services for 1915 at the salary stipulated in the 1914 contract.
> ...I heard later he had signed with the Buffalo Feds, receiving an advance of $4,000 in cash which he has deposited in a Newark bank.[5]

With each Federal League success, there seemed to be a setback. In February Ivy Wingo became the next contract jumper to follow Walter Johnson's example and return to the organized major leagues. Wingo spurned the St. Louis National League club in October to join the Federals, but after his flip-flop, Ivy did not play for the Cardinals. Wingo was traded to Cincinnati and signed a "wartime" contract to stay in the National League for an annual salary of $6,500, a raise of $2,000. Apparently, the Cardinals reached an understanding with Reds manager Buck Herzog that if he could secure Wingo's agreement to return to the Organized Baseball, a trade would be made in which the catcher would go to Cincinnati. Herzog went to Wingo's home in Georgia and convinced Ivy to return to the National League.[6]

In an ironic twist, a deadline for the Cracker Jack Company's Baseball Players Cards contributed to the distribution of cards mistakenly labeling two Organized Baseball stars as players for the Federal League. Cracker Jack issued 144 cards for their 1914 set and produced a supplement of 32 more cards for 1915. Of the 176 player cards available, 51 were Federal Leaguers, and two others, Rube Marquard ("Brooklyn Federals") and Jimmy Austin ("Pittsburgh Federals"), initially signed with but never played for the third league. These cards were widely distributed and the whole set could be obtained by sending in 100 Cracker Jack coupons or one coupon along with twenty-five cents. One card also came with each box of Cracker Jacks.

Just after the first of the year, Braves outfielder Les Mann stopped off in Chicago en route from his home in Nebraska to Springfield, Mass., where he coached basketball. After a lengthy conference with Chifeds manager Joe Tinker, Mann decided to continue his 1915 contract negotiations with President Gaffney of the Braves. It was reported that Mann wanted a $3,500 contract from the Braves with no ten-day clause. The Braves' owner offered the player $3,000 with the ten-day clause retained by the club and refused to budge off that proposition.[7]

On January 29, James Gilmore broke the news that third baseman Charley Deal of the World Series champion Boston Braves had defected to the Federals. Two weeks later, Charley Weeghman announced he had received Mann's signed contract to play with the Chicago Federal League Club for two years. Though he had already played two seasons in the National League, Mann was only three months past his twenty-first birthday.

Touted as one of the best all-around athletes ever to come out of the state of Nebraska,

Leslie Mann had earned seven letters in a high school career cut short by his decision to sign a major league baseball contract. His Lincoln High School honors included All-State in football for three years; he was a member of the basketball team that won the conference three straight years with a record of 46 and 7, including a 37-game win streak; and, as a sprinter, he won the 220 in a 1909 state track meet with a time of 22.2 seconds, only .8 of a second off the world record at that time. He also won the 50-yard dash, the 100-yard dash, the 440-yard dash and the 220-yard hurdles.

Mann gained the attention of major league scouts as a seventeen-year-old in 1911 when he led the Missouri-Iowa-Nebraska-Kansas Class D League in runs scored and averaged .328 in 95 games with Nebraska City. In a time when the rules regarding professional athletes were less strict, Les attended Springfield College in the baseball off-season and received All-American honors in football. Called up to the Boston National League club in 1913, he started in center field for two seasons and was a major contributor to the Braves' 1914 World Series championship.[8]

Chuck Deal, one of the heroes of the 1914 World Series, agreed to a two-year contract to play with Fielder Jones' St. Louis club. Deal signed with the Feds for $4,500 and a $3,000 bonus after the Braves denied him a $500 raise on his Boston salary of $2,400.[9]

A notorious light hitter, Chuck lost his job as the Braves' starting third baseman in 1914 after Red Smith was obtained in a July trade. When Smith broke his leg late in the season, Deal moved back into the starting lineup.

In the top of the ninth inning of the second game of the 1914 Series against the Athletics, Charlie doubled to right field off Eddie Plank, stole third base, and scored on Les Mann's single. Boston's Bill James completed the 1–0 shutout when he retired Philadelphia in the bottom of the ninth. For a while, it appeared both pitchers of that dramatic World Series game were headed for the Federal League in 1915.

Bill James was brilliant for the 1914 Miracle Braves, amassing a 26–7 record with a 1.90 earned run average in only his second major league season. In the World Series he threw that two-hit shutout in Game Two and won Game Three in relief. James was a holdout the following spring and spent a few days at the Brooklyn Tip Tops' training camp in Mississippi. The World Series star appeared set to accept Joe Tinker's $14,000 offer for two years to play with the Chifeds. James later said that he received a telegram from Braves manager George Stallings that read, "Come to Macon [the Braves' spring training camp]. I've always been your friend."

The big right-hander recalled: "Tears rolled down my cheeks. I had been to a sad movie and was feeling sad when I got the wire. If they had airplanes then, I would have flown down there."[10]

The real story was not quite so sentimental. When the Federals learned that James's National League contract did not contain a ten-day clause, they broke off talks with the Braves' pitcher.

"I still have some respect for the law," quipped Charles Weeghman, "even if I am a baseball owner."[11]

The Federals actually lucked out in the case of James, who came up with a lame arm later that spring and won only five more major league games. The same day it was announced James signed a three-year deal with the Braves, the Pittsburgh Federals learned that Pol Perritt had jumped his Federal League contract to sign with the New York Giants.

Perritt had sworn he would never return to the Cardinals, so the Brittons empowered John McGraw to negotiate with the pitcher and sign him for the Giants. The Southern farm boy became convinced his National League contract was binding and accepted a three-year deal to play in New York. The Cardinals completed the coup by officially selling the twenty-two-year-old 16-game winner to the New York Giants on February 18, 1915.[12]

When Perritt struggled with the Giants early in the 1915 season, Rebel Oakes was asked if the pitcher's sore arm was caused by cold weather. "That's not it," the Pittsfeds' manager quipped. "As a matter of fact, he's tied up with writer's cramp that he caught when he was signing all those contacts this spring."[13]

The news that Wingo and Perritt had gone back to their original clubs, following the example of Walter Johnson, Jimmy Austin and others who jumped their Federal League contracts, was the last straw for the Feds. "The Federal League has a war fund of $100,000," announced Charley Weeghman. "It was to be used only for emergencies, but the emergency seems to be upon us."[14] The threat was a hollow one. Deal and Mann were the last active members of the organized major leagues to sign with the Federals.

There was some good news left for the Feds. On February 18, *The Sporting News* reported that the Washington Senators had lost out to the Federal League for the coveted Los Angeles schoolboy wonder, Howard Ehmke. Ehmke was born in New York, then moved to Glendale, California, where his older brother was a high school baseball coach. Howard debuted in professional baseball in 1914 at age nineteen with Los Angeles of the Pacific Coast League. He pitched in forty games and finished with a record of 12–11 after winning his first eight P.C.L. games. Clark Griffith of Washington reportedly paid $7,500 for the pitcher, but Ehmke returned a contract offer for $3000 unsigned to the American League club. Howard had recently fallen heir to a large amount of money (reported by Harry Williams of the *Los Angeles Times* as $33,000) and was in no hurry to make a decision.

A veteran teammate of Howard's, Rube Ellis, explained the youngster's mid-season swoon: "Ehmke's arm simply went dead on him during the season from overwork. Now, he is showing more than at any time since joining the club. I may be overestimating him, but I am willing to go on record as declaring that he will in time be the superior of Walter Johnson. He shows a lot more than Johnson did at his age."

However, Ellis, a former major league outfielder with the Cardinals, warned, "Another year under [Angels manager] Dillon will make him a finished pitcher, and he will then have the physical development to stand the strain of a hard major-league race. A lot of promising youngsters have been ruined by going to the majors before they were ripe."[15]

Again it was Ehmke's brother who determined the young pitcher's fate. Now teaching in Buffalo, Howard's brother negotiated with the local Federal League club for $700 a week and the twenty-year-old pitcher signed to play for the Buffalo team on February 13, 1915.

At the meeting of the St. Louis Federal League club's directors in early February 1915, league secretary Lloyd Rickart was elected president of the Terriers to succeed Edward Steininger, who resigned to look after his private business. Though Rickart was the tentative president of the club, the money and strong personality of Philip de Gatesby Ball held the power.

On April 8, 1915, *The Sporting News* reported that American League President Ban Johnson and Philip Ball accidentally met and the pair had spent two hours in private conversation at McTegue's Café in St. Louis the previous Saturday.[16] Actually, their meeting had been arranged by J. Taylor Spink, editor of that baseball tabloid. Once the story surfaced, speculation about the possibility of peace negotiations between the warring baseball leagues began anew.

A few weeks later, Ball and Johnson were seen together watching a White Sox ball game in Chicago. During the game, Ball supposedly was heard to say that it was too bad baseball was not fought on the field instead of in stuffy courtrooms. Johnson reportedly agreed.[17]

"That story about a peace conference between the Federal Leaguers and representatives of Organized Baseball is one fine joke," Johnson told George S. Robbins of *The Sporting News*.

> You can say for me that there is absolutely not one word of truth in the story. I think the Feds are after some more cheap advertising.
>
> It is true that I talked with Mr. Ball here this week. Our subject of conversation did not relate to peace, however. We are good friends and the whole peace yarn seems to have spun around the fact that our paths crossed and we had a friendly conversation.[18]

Until he became the owner of a baseball club in St. Louis, the average citizens of the city had not heard of Philip Ball. Very private about his personal life, Ball was the archetypical self-made man.

Philip was born in Keokuk, Iowa, on October 22, 1864, the son of Charles J. Ball, a Union Army captain. The baby's mother Caroline wanted to name her son for his great-uncle Commodore Thomas ap Catesby Jones. However, she did not like the Welsh patronym "ap" so she changed it to de and gave him the name of Philip de Catesby Ball.

When Philip was fourteen, the Balls moved to Sherman, Texas, where his father was building an ice plant. There, Philip got his first job with a surveying gang. In 1879 the teenager started collecting bad debts for the ice plant at $15 a month, two-thirds of which was turned over to his mother for room and board. Ball did numerous odd jobs for his father, including driving an ice wagon.[19]

Phil worked for his father in the construction of ice plants for over ten years. Interested in baseball at an early age, Phil became an amateur league catcher and considered a career in the game. Ball's dream of a professional baseball career was dashed when his left hand was severely cut in an altercation with a man in a bar. Philip's hand bore the ugly scars the remainder of his life.[20]

At the time of his marriage in December 1885, Ball recalled that he had saved $1,011.00 and was earning $65.00 working for his father. "When I knelt down before the parson, I remembered I had on shoes that had just been half-soled."

Ball got a $10 raise after his marriage and continued to work on the road for his father until he returned to St. Louis for good in 1890. When the elder Ball decided to move to California, Philip took over the Ice & Cold Machine Company of St. Louis. "I paid him $20,000 for a few patterns and the company's good will," he said. "Then I set out to develop the concern."[21]

At the time of his Federal League dealings, Ball owned a ten-thousand-acre ranch in south Texas and was involved in the oil business, machinery plants, and St. Louis real estate. Philip was one of the "Thousand Dollar Club" that launched the St. Louis Federal League franchise in 1913. When the others jumped ship after the league decided to expand, he stayed with Otto Stifel to make the enterprise a success. In 1914, Ball generally let Steininger and Stifel do the talking then he began to take a more public role as time passed.

"It has been said that I inherited my money from my father," Ball later chuckled, "but I never got a nickel from anybody. When my father died, he left what little money he had to a brother, a sister and a third wife and I had to look after them."[22]

Harry Brundidge of the *St. Louis Star* wrote of Ball: "Shy, retiring and self-conscious, he has striven for years to cloak these attributes of his character, which he regards as shortcomings, in a mantle of brusqueness. In this he has been aided by a natural ability of stubbornness and independence of thought."

The Federal League had sworn to improve its St. Louis club following the 1914 season. When the Terriers traveled to Havana, Cuba, for spring training, Fielder Jones welcomed four important additions to his club: Eddie Plank, Charlie Deal, Ernest Johnson and Babe Borton.

First baseman William "Babe" Borton, formerly of the White Sox and Yankees, signed a contract to play for the St. Louis Terriers during the 1914 Pacific Coast League season. Borton was reported to have accepted a bonus and a $200 monthly raise over his Venice paycheck. Though it was known in September that he was under contract to the Feds, Babe finished out the Pacific Coast League season, batting .307 in 161 games.[23]

Twenty-seven-year-old Ernest Johnson led the Pacific Coast League's shortstops in stolen bases (37) and fielding in 1914. A native of Chicago, Ernie's major league experience consisted of fourteen games with the White Sox in 1912, but one at-bat endeared him to the South Side fans.

During the post-season city series against the Cubs that year, Sox third baseman Buck Weaver was injured during a game and Johnson replaced him. In the last of the ninth inning, the White Sox trailed 3 to 1 when Ernie came to bat with one out and Babe Borton on first. Cubs pitcher Larry Cheney tried to sneak one past the rookie, but Johnson drove the ball to right center, scoring Borton. Ted Easterly's double scored Ernie and the game eventually ended in a twelve-inning tie. Johnson went to spring training with the White Sox in 1913, but before the season began, he was sent to the Los Angeles club of the Pacific Coast League.

Following visits with George Stovall and Kansas City outfielder Art Krueger in January 1915, Johnson signed a three-year contract for $4,000 a season to play with the Federal League.[24] Three days later, Ernie walked into the Angels' office and signed a contract to play for them. When he went back home to Laguna Beach, Stovall convinced Johnson to change his mind again and it was announced he would play for the Feds after all. When he arrived in Chicago, American League President Ban Johnson had a conference with the player, but Ernie remained committed to play with the Feds.

"Ernie Johnson? Don't know anything about Johnson," growled Stovall, who was tired of the player's flip-flops. "I'm off them guys for life. To hell with them!"[25]

Awarded to Fielder Jones and the Terriers, Johnson batted only .240 with St. Louis in 1915, though he did lead the club in home runs with seven and smacked ten triples. His best day as a Terrier came on June 19, 1915, in a double-header at Washington Park.

In the second inning of the first game, Ernie greeted a pitch from Brooklyn's Finis Wilson "with a solid smash that sent it hurtling over the right field fence." Batting out of the eight spot in the batting order, Johnson added three more hits in the second game, including another home run.

Major league baseball teams began making post-season trips to Cuba after the Cincinnati National League Club went there in 1908. In 1915 Armando Marsans was instrumental in convincing the Terriers to become the only Federal League team to spend spring training on the Caribbean island. The team departed St. Louis on February 27, caught a steamer in Key West, Florida, and arrived in Havana on March 2. Accompanying the club to the Caribbean was J. Roy Stockton, a twenty-two-year-old sports writer on his first assignment for the *St. Louis Globe-Democrat*.[26]

"So warm is the weather that stiff sore arms are rarities," wrote Stockton in his first report from Cuba.

> The 18 ball tossers, Manager Jones, Secretary Johnson and three pencil pushers disembarked from the Steamer Gov. Cobb Tuesday evening and from 9 A.M. until the present the boys have been working at mid season speed.
>
> The Cubans received the Feds with joy. They are proud that their Armando Marsans "went up" from Cincinnati to the St. Louis club, for as they think, this move brought the charges of F. Alanson [sic] Jones to the island of cheap cigars, hacks and all-the-year around baseball.[27]

Later in his stay, Roy praised the selection of Havana for the Terriers' training site:

> The city has myriad places of interest, and in the evenings the players are so busy seeing the strange things that they forget any inclination to wander from the "straight and narrow." The streets are narrow and all are paved and the city reminds one of the streets at an exposition. There is more life and action, less dirt and dust and more quality parks and impressive buildings in Havana than the most ardent tourist or expectant visitor possibly could hope for.[28]

After a couple of days of practice, Stockton reported: "Fans used to think Jimmy McAleer [the Browns' manager from 1902 through 1909] strict with his club when he made them report at 10 o'clock in the morning. Now if the ball players are not in uniform and warming up on the field by 9 A.M. they—well they have managed to be on the job so far...."[29]

The players were aroused daily at 7:30 A.M. by a little bell in each room that was made to ring through its connection with the front desk.[30] Morning practice ran from 9 until 10:30 A.M., after which the players jogged around the 440-yard track and kept running until they reached the hotel. They had to be back at the park by two o'clock for another session of batting, fielding and sliding practice.

"After the clock strikes four the players repeat the jogging stunt of the morning," wrote Stockton, "and by the time the athletes perform their best little skit—playing the courses—Jones' other rule in regard to retiring by 11 P.M. is practically unnecessary."[31]

Jones quickly instilled the habit of hard work in his players and he pushed them to become skilled at the rudiments of the game. Stockton commented on the style of the previous manager of the Terriers: "In 1914 to listen to the prate of the men who worked under Mordecai Brown, attending to such a minor incident as training was out of the question. Some of the boys went fishing every other day while others went to practice every third day is the way some of the ball players describe last year's program."[32]

When the weather became brutally hot, Jones shortened the morning practice and allowed the players to ride on one of the trips to the field. Marsans was excused from most of the practices because "the Cuban is in great condition and doesn't need as much practice...."[33] Games were played every day and on days when a Cuban team was not available, Jones's regulars and Yannigans (a term used in those days for rookies and substitutes) would oppose one another.

After a week on the island, the Terriers played their first game and it came against Cuba's most accomplished team, Almendares. Babe Borton and Johnny Tobin each had a trio of safeties as the Americans prevailed, 5 to 4, with Marsans in center field for the Terriers against his former team. Jones used Willett, Davenport and Groom against three Cuban pitchers, the first of which was Jose Mendez. A day later, Jones' boys beat Havana 7 to 4 and Eddie Plank made his debut for the Terriers in actual combat, pitching three innings.

When word of the games between the Federals and Cuba's top professional teams reached the mainland, Philadelphia Phillies manager Pat Moran cabled the manager of the Havana Reds. He threatened that Organized Baseball would cancel sixty contests the Cubans had arranged with clubs in the United States if the Reds played any further games against the Terriers. Fielder Jones worked out an arrangement with a different Havana club.[34]

The Terriers suffered their first defeat to a Cuban club on March 18 when Almendares scored four runs off Doc Crandall in the fifth inning to beat St. Louis, 5 to 2. "Of course Crandall did not exert himself to any great extent," reported the *Globe-Democrat*. "The big boy is rounding too slowly and has instructions from the boss not to take any chances."[35]

After Juan Guerra hit a three-run home run in the fateful fifth, Bob Groom relieved Doc and did not give up a hit the remainder of the contest. Though Mendez did not pitch for the Cubans on that day, his sharp-breaking curve and rising fastball had impressed the Terriers and American reporters alike. Jones even urged his pitchers to emulate the pick-off move of the Almendares' ace.[36]

While Crandall was struggling, Plank was already in form. A week later, Eddie worked five innings against the Cubans and faced only eighteen batters. He allowed but three safeties "two of which would not have been hits on a better field," wrote one reporter.[37]

While he was in Cuba, Roy Stockton also covered the upcoming heavyweight championship boxing match between Jack Johnson and Jess Willard. Johnson warmed up with the Feds and, in turn, several of the St. Louis players visited the training site of boxing's first black heavyweight champion.[38] The Terriers were surprised at Johnson's indifference to the fight and his ultimate loss to the heavy underdog. Though none of the players got to see the fight because they returned to the States on the day it took place, some expressed suspicions that it was fixed because of rumors and conversations they overheard while in Havana.[39]

The Terriers played their final game in Cuba on April 4. As an added attraction a modified bullfight was held. Among those attending the day's contest was Jack Johnson.[40]

Jose Mendez pitched the entire game for Almendares and would have won except for one inning. "The Black Matty" walked Babe Borton to lead off the second inning and Miller followed with a single to left field. Chapman sent the two runners home with a double and the Terriers went on to add two more. Poor fielding and a pair of hits off Willett in the eighth led to two runs for Almendares and made the final score close, 4 to 3. Jones and his team departed for home the next morning.

The Terriers won seven of the nine games they played against Cuban teams.[41] The club experienced excellent weather while they were training, in contrast to some of the other clubs in the southern United States, where there were unusually cold temperatures.

As for J. Roy Stockton, he moved to the *St. Louis Post-Dispatch* in 1917 and, except for military service during World War I, his career as a sports reporter for that newspaper spanned forty-one years. Stockton died in 1972, and that same year he was honored by the National Baseball Hall of Fame with the J.G. Taylor Spink Award "for meritorious contributions to baseball writing."

28

"An Embarrassing Situation"

The Kansas City Federal League franchise, with its poor attendance record, shaky financial situation, and undersized park, combined with the distance from Eastern clubs, made it the logical choice for transfer to another city. In the league meeting back in October 1914, Philadelphia was favored for the new franchise, although Cincinnati, Cleveland and Toronto were prominently mentioned. However, the league's leaders knew that for it to achieve true major league status they would need a franchise in greater New York. That opportunity came in the form of fresh cash from backers interested in putting a club in Newark, New Jersey. By February 1915, the league's proposed plan to move the Kansas City franchise was set.

On February 9, 1915, President James Gilmore released a statement: "The league was anxious to stay in Kansas City, but, inasmuch as the club could not be properly financed by local people, it was necessary to make a change. I want to thank the people of Kansas City for their support given our club last year, and believe, when they are fully acquainted with the details of the transfer, they will not criticize the Federal League for taking this action."[1]

There was one problem. The team's owners and the Kansas City community would not go away quietly. Delbert J. Haff, a director of the Kansas City club, went to New York and declared he would do all in his power to get the officials of the Federal League to rescind the sale of the franchise. Haff expressed confidence that enough money could be raised to keep the club in Kansas City.[2]

On February 6, the Federal League announced that Pat T. Powers of Jersey City, a well-known sports promoter, along "with a prominent businessman from the West," would take over the Kansas City franchise. Powers had a long association with baseball. He served seventeen years (1893–1910) as president of the International League and in 1901 was elected as the first president of the National Association of Professional Leagues. He retired from baseball in 1911 after Ed Barrow defeated him for the presidency of the International League.

The "Prominent businessman from the West" turned out to be Harry F. Sinclair of Tulsa, Oklahoma, founder and president of Sinclair Oil Company. The oil baron began dabbling in professional baseball as a minority investor in the Kansas City Federal League Club, then became one of the league's chief magnates and investors in 1915.[3]

"Pat Powers was an old friend of mine," said Sinclair. "When he was in organized baseball he tried to get me interested in investments. I didn't follow his suggestion at the time. But when Powers left organized baseball it struck me that he had suffered a dirty deal, and when he tried to get me interested in the Federal League, I was ripe for action. I offered to back him up provided my name didn't appear in the transaction, but it leaked out."[4]

Powers told James Gilmore about his friend who was willing to invest in their baseball enterprise. A meeting was arranged in Robert Ward's New York office and Sinclair turned over a $25,000 check for the defunct Kansas City franchise.[5]

"Harry Sinclair didn't go into the Federal League with the exact idea it would be of great publicity," New York sports columnist Frank G. Menke reflected years later. "It was a gamble and Sinclair loved to gamble."[6]

Gilmore's man, Kansas City Club president Charles Madison, was ousted as the Packers' chief executive in January 1915 by wealthy banker Charles Baird. Baird was controlling owner of the Exchange Bank and director of the Inter-State Bank. Years earlier, Baird had been graduate manager of the University of Michigan football team, then became the university's first athletic director in 1898.

Baird immediately went to work as club president and placed 50,000 shares of a $100,000 stock issue to refinance the Packers into the hands of a syndicate of Kansas City businessmen. These sixty or so stockholders got together and eventually paid off the club's debt.

Especially prominent among the Packers' new stockholders was the German-born Conrad Mann, "a massive bear-like man with a brusque, unpolished manner" who had a reputation for knowing how to get things done. Mann began his career as a civic leader in Kansas City after he, as president of the Fraternal Order of Eagles, moved there in 1907. He organized and supervised a committee of 1,000 that drew up the largest local bond program ever in Kansas City for a variety of projects, including the construction of the Municipal Auditorium, City Hall and the courthouse.[7]

On February 22, President Gilmore returned to Chicago after a meeting with Federal League magnates in the East and reiterated that the Kansas City club would be relocated to Newark. Furthermore, a site for the New Jersey club had been acquired and $300,000 was set aside for construction of a park. The construction of the Newark Federal League's baseball park across the Passaic River in Harrison, New Jersey, did not begin until just 46 days before opening game of the 1915 season.

A day later, the Kansas City stockholders announced they had secured attorneys who were instructed to seek reimbursement of the $60,000 invested in their Federal League enterprise or the return of the club to the city. On February 25, 1915, legal papers were served on President Gilmore as he was boarding a train in Chicago. The Federal League suddenly became subject of a lawsuit filed on behalf of the Kansas City stockholders acting through Director Haff. The bill recited that under the franchise given by the defendant's league on February 28, 1914, it was understood that the Kansas City club would operate permanently as a member of the league, and that, consequently, the club assumed a great many obligations. The Packers' owners maintained that Gilmore's retraction of their franchise was illegal and they were seeking an injunction to prevent the club from being moved. March 3 was set as the date of a hearing on the suit.

President Gilmore left Chicago for the league's meeting in Buffalo with the statement that everything would be settled amicably and guaranteed that Newark would have a Federal League club. He also claimed Kansas City lost its franchise because the stockholders there failed to meet their obligation and the Federal League constitution provided that in event of such default a franchise was forfeited. The Kansas City people admitted being in debt, but said they would have cleared their obligations if given an opportunity. The plaintiffs stated in the suit that "although the club repeatedly asked for a statement of its account, being ready to pay any just claims, the league had refused any such statement though the league continues to claim a balance due from the Kansas City club."[8]

At the Federal League meeting in Buffalo, the Kansas City club was also faced with the forfeiture of one of its two best pitchers, twenty-eight-year-old left-hander Nick Cullop. The

Brooklyn owners claimed Cullop on the grounds of their financial investment late in the 1914 season that kept the Kansas City franchise afloat. The Wards did say they would ship their thirty-seven-year-old discarded manager, Bill Bradley, along with his large contract and a couple of other unwanted players to Kansas City in exchange for Cullop. Though his record was 14 and 17 for the sixth-place Packers, the hard-throwing left-hander with a baffling curve was considered one of the most talented hurlers in the Federal League.

Norman Cullop was born at Chilhowie, Virginia, and he still resided there in the off season on the fifty-acre farm owned by his mother. "The first professional game I ever saw," said Cullop, "was the day before I was sent in to pitch for Knoxville. The club was in last place. I had a good season that year and we won the pennant."[9]

In August 1912 Cullop was sold by Bristol of the Appalachian League to the New Orleans club. The young southpaw showed so much stuff in Louisiana, Pelicans manager Frank kept him on the bench until after the major leagues' draft of minor league players so the club could later sell Nick for a large price. That November Cullop pitched a twelve-inning no-hitter against a touring Cuban professional team, the Havana Reds. The Havana club's manager, Rafel Almeida, urged Garry Herrmann to purchase Cullop, but the price proved way too steep for Cincinnati. Eventually, Cleveland won the bidding war, paying New Orleans $15,000 for the Virginia pitcher.[10]

In 1913 Cullop appeared in 23 games for Cleveland, mostly as a relief pitcher, and had been assured by Charles Somers he would be with the big league club the following season. However, the owner insisted the pitcher have a tonsillectomy during the off season because the team physician said that Nick "would never be able to do himself justice" until his diseased tonsils were removed. Cullop accepted the money the Cleveland club gave him for the operation, but he did not go through with it.[11] Following the transfer of his American Association club to Cleveland so as to thwart the Federals' ambitions in that city, Somers attempted to transfer Cullop to the former Toledo team. Nick then became receptive to Federal League offers.

Though the Kansas City group was powerless to prevent the loss of Cullop, Newark owners Powers and Sinclair said they would not accept the transfer of the pitcher to Brooklyn; nor would they accept Bradley or Al Shaw and Bert Maxwell, the other two players offered by the Wards. Cullop was already at the Brooklyn club's training site when the league acquiesced and ordered the return of the Packers' hurler to Manager Stovall's team.[12] Then Cullop temporarily threw a wrench in the works when he refused to return to the displaced Kansas City team as the league had stipulated.

George Stovall, still manager of a team in limbo, and new owner Pat Powers ordered the Kansas City/Newark players to report at Marshall, Texas, on March 8 for spring training. Stovall had been in a unique situation after the league took over his team the previous September. Since then, he had taken his orders from President Gilmore. Without the assistance of even a secretary, Stovall took his team to Texas for training.

The hearing on the temporary injunction to prohibit the transfer of the Kansas City club got under way in United States Federal Court in Chicago before Judge Jesse A. Baldwin on March 3, 1915. In his opening statement, Federal League attorney Edward Gates said the agreement to transfer the Kansas City franchise was made on February 6, 1915. However, the club's former president, Charles Madison, testified he had been assured as late as February 10 that the franchise had not yet been transferred.

Letters from James Gilmore to Madison were introduced, both dated September 10, 1914, one giving notice that the Kansas City franchise had been forfeited because of a draft for $5,000 given the club to meet the payroll of September 1, and another letter advising Madison that the franchise would be protected if Kansas City could raise $20,000 to finish the season.

Gilmore testified that power to dispose of the Kansas City franchise was delegated to the executive committee on October 3, 1914. On November 18, an agreement was signed with Madison stipulating that the franchise would not be moved if the Kansas City people raised $100,000 to finance it. That money had not been raised by December 14, nor could Gilmore learn anything about the intentions of the Kansas City promoters, so the franchise was forfeited and the league went about finding someone to purchase it. That someone emerged in the form of Pat Powers and Harry Sinclair.[13]

The Wards, according to statements made during the proceedings, had put up $38,000 to keep the Packers afloat and of this the Kansas City people claimed an offset of $8,000 coming to them from the league, leaving $30,000 as actual debt.

After listening to the arguments by each side, Judge Baldwin announced that he would postpone the case until Monday, March 15, and by that date he would hear arguments and decide the issue. While delaying his decision, the judge made it clear that he would rule in favor of Kansas City on the ground the league executive committee had exceeded its authority in taking the team away from the people who owned it. The judge advised the league and the Kansas City stockholders to work out a compromise before he had to issue a ruling.

In the midst of the judge's remarks, James Gilmore turned and whispered to a friend, "We're beaten."[14] Upon leaving the courtroom, the Federal League officials hustled to Charles Weeghman's office to plot the league's next move.

The Kansas City stockholders remained resistant to any plan to transfer their club out of the Missouri city. With the situation stalemated, the Federals postponed their meeting scheduled in Pittsburgh on March 12, and planned a New York confab to settle the Kansas City issue. When the executives met Sinclair and Powers in New York, the Newark owners were asked if they would agree to keep the franchise in Kansas City. When Sinclair insisted that his club had to be situated in Newark, the Federal League asked if he would take the Indianapolis franchise instead. Sinclair agreed as long as the club was based in Newark.

Although Indianapolis won the 1914 Federal League pennant, *The Sporting News* reported that the club's debt was $102,000 more than it had taken in receipts. Prior to the 1914 season, the Hoosiers' promoters raised $50,000 from a stock issue, guaranteeing six per cent interest. The club leased a plot of ground at a fee of $4,200 a year and on it built stands at an alleged cost of $79,000. Although the Indianapolis stockholders did not own the ballpark, they had a five-year lease with an option to purchase it for $76,000.

Though only Chicago drew more people to Federal League games than Indianapolis, the Hoosier club's chances for a profit were burdened by its 394 stockholders. The club's stock was "peddled on the streets like bananas" and a prospectus was issued inviting people to buy shares at $25 and get annual passes. The result was that the Indianapolis club's gross attendance was burdened by a large pass gate for each game.[15]

The investors' capital was used up during the 1914 season and the club called on the league for help. The Wards contributed $10,000 and the Indianapolis club's directors managed another $26,000 on their personal account to keep the franchise going in the closing weeks of the season.[16]

On Friday, March 19, 1915, the Federal League's executive committee, comprising President Gilmore, William Robertson and Robert Ward, arrived in Indianapolis to make a "formal demand" that the local Federals surrender their club to Harry Sinclair and Pat Powers. The Feds' top officers met with officials of the Indianapolis club, including club Vice President F.L. Murray, John A. George (who held the proxy of former president J. Ed Krause), and Edward Gates, both a director of the club and the chief attorney for the league.

Gilmore interjected that Indianapolis should comply because of its failure to make good the money it had been advanced the previous season to keep it afloat. The Indianapolis owners refused to consider the transfer proposition and threatened to employ the same tactics used by the Kansas City franchise.[17]

Said Vice President Murray of the Hoosierfeds, "President Gilmore came to Indianapolis for the purpose of making the directors of the local Federal League club a proposition looking toward the sale of our franchise and players. He made it and we formally rejected it."[18]

Gilmore wasn't about to be taken in for a second time by the injunction ploy. That evening, Harry Sinclair stopped off at the Indianapolis railway station en route from St. Louis to New York and discussed the Hoosier club's situation with Gilmore and Ward. After the brief conference, Sinclair and Ward proceeded to New York, while Gilmore stayed over to take a later train to Chicago.

Meanwhile, the Indianapolis club's directors realized they were in an untenable situation. A $200,000 bond issue sought to place the club on financial footing necessary to make it through the upcoming season received no interest. Repeated appeals to the stockholders failed to elicit any favorable response and the directors had even been hard pressed to send the club to spring training and pay pressing debts. An eleventh-hour attempt by the chamber of commerce was made to raise enough money to continue the franchise for the 1915 season, but the effort was called off when a stockholder of the local club sued to have it placed in receivership.[19]

On Monday, March 23, Pliny W. Bartholomew, a former judge and holder of $500 in preferred and a like amount in common stock of the Indianapolis Federal League Baseball Club, brought suit in superior court against the club. His suit alleged that the Hoosier club was insolvent and asked that a receiver be appointed to conserve its assets for the stockholders and persons to whom the club was indebted. Bartholomew's action was within his right as a stockholder and was permissible under corporation law.[20]

The move prompted Harry Neily, the disgruntled former secretary of the Kawfeds, to write: "...one has to slip the prize to that Indianapolis stockholder who hauled the Fed outfit into court after it became known that Gilmore contemplated yanking the franchise away. By applying for a receiver, he just naturally threatened to trip up the whole works, so the league, via Angel Ward, came to bat and assumed some of the debts of Indianapolis."[21]

After notice of the suit had been served upon the attorneys for the club, the directors of the Hoosierfeds met for a conference with Judge Bartholomew and agreed to allow the suit to proceed to trial. On Tuesday, March 23, more than 300 of the Indianapolis club's 394 stockholders gathered at the local chamber of commerce to decide the fate of the city's Federal League club. Edward Gates presented a written proposition from James Gilmore. The Federal League boss proposed that the Indianapolis stockholders surrender their franchise and, in return, the league would assume $76,000 of the club's debts then in receivership proceedings. Another $26,000 in debts amassed by the Indianapolis board of directors would not be part of the deal. The Federal League also agreed to pay a year's rent amounting to $4,500 on the Hoosiers' ballpark. By unanimous vote, including that of J.E. Krause by proxy, the stockholders agreed to accept the Federal League's offer for the franchise.[22]

Ralston Goss wrote in the *Indianapolis Star*, "It seems self evident that the league did offer the local club a remarkably fair proposition, especially when it can be taken into consideration that it could have declared the franchise forfeited for nonpayment of dues and money owing the league. To all intents and purposes it places the league in the position of 'leaving a good taste' in the mouths of the Indianapolis sport-loving public."[23]

"I am decidedly pleased," said a relived President Gilmore, "that the stockholders saw fit to accept the league's proposition. It relieves me of an embarrassing situation caused by the

Kansas City tangle and permits the league to retain Harry Sinclair and Pat Powers among its club owners."[24]

That evening in Kansas City, the city's Federal League organization held a jubilee smoker to celebrate the official retention of their franchise. The injunction suit pending in Judge Baldwin's court was now rendered moot.

Three days later, the officers of the Federal League ratified the transfer of the Indianapolis club to Newark. While Federal League officials were celebrating the settlement of the Kansas City/Newark/Indianapolis issue, another crisis arose when Powers and Sinclair discovered that Indianapolis's two star players were to be transferred to Brooklyn.

The Newark club owners were happy to have gotten a championship team until they learned of the Wards' claim against the Indianapolis club for debt. In return for the $10,000 in advances made to the Hoosierfeds during the 1914 season, defending batting champion Benny Kauff and ace pitcher Cy Falkenberg were to be transferred to Brooklyn. The league had telegraphed Bill Phillips in Valdosta, Georgia, notifying him that all of the Indianapolis players would be transferred to the new Newark Federal League franchise with the exception of Kauff and Falkenberg. Powers and Sinclair would not consent to take the Indianapolis club unless it was turned over intact and for a short time it appeared they might drop out of the deal. A compromise was finally arranged.[25]

When it was shown that the Indianapolis club was under strong obligation to the Wards, the Newark owners agreed to the transfer of Benny Kauff to Brooklyn, but they would not consent to take the former Hoosiers team if they lost both players. The league decided to allow Falkenberg to play with Newark.

The retention of Falkenberg by the Newark club was not as significant as it appeared. Following the lead of the American and National Leagues, Jim Gilmore had already announced a ban on the use of Falkenberg's most effective pitch, the emery ball, in Federal League games.

On March 29, Pat Powers wired Falkenberg in Mississippi and ordered him to report to the Newark club in Valdosta despite the threat from Brooklyn manager Lee Magee that he would put up a fight for the pitcher. Powers also sent telegrams to Miles Main, Germany Schafer, Chief Brandon, and Ed Reulbach, who had been biding their time in Marshall, Texas, with the Packers, to join Bill Phillips' team without delay.

The Kansas City club continued to be a thorn in the side of the league when it objected to George Stovall's remaining as the Packers' field manager. The league decided to shift Stovall to the Indianapolis/Newark team as manager. This would entail dumping the current manager, Bill Phillips, whom the new owners had inherited. Phillips had irked the league's president when he refused to take Bill Bradley and Bert Maxwell after Gilmore attempted to shift those players to the Indianapolis club following the Kawfeds' rejection of the pair. However, Phillips had fortified his position as manager by negotiating a new contract with his previous Indianapolis club employers.

During his years as a manager, Phillips had never signed a contract with a club, preferring to allow his job security rest on the results he showed. However, in the spring of 1914, he recognized that the business of baseball had changed and asked for a contract. He later signed a three-year agreement to manage the Indianapolis Federal League club.

The Federal League's leaders could not ignore the loyalty displayed by Stovall since he had joined the league. Even when the future of the Kansas City club was in doubt, George spent the winter in Southern California trying to convince West Coast players to join the Federal League. Stovall worked hard, even spent his own money, but came away with just one player, Ernie Johnson.[26] After two days of negotiating among the principals, the status quo was maintained. Stovall would remain as manager in Kansas City and Phillips would go to Newark.

In case Kansas City defaulted on their debts during the 1915 season, Gilmore had the Hoosiers' former treasurer, John George, obtain the rights to the Federal League Park in Indianapolis. When Kansas City got off to a good start and was leading the league in attendance after the first month of the season, any plans to transfer the Packers to Indianapolis were shelved.[27]

Hoosierfeds' business manager William Watkins, who had spent years endeavoring to keep Indianapolis on the baseball map, made it clear that he would not go with the ball club to Newark. Following the departure of the Federal League from Indianapolis, their ballpark at Kentucky Avenue and South Street was utilized by the Indianapolis ABCs, a Negro National League team, through 1921. Today, there is no historical marker on the site of the Federal League Park that also was the location of the first official Negro League game on May 20, 1920.

After Charles Baird stepped down as the Kansas City club's president on May 27, 1915, Conrad Mann was rewarded for his support and was named to that post. Mann became a prominent fixture at Gordon & Koppel Field and continually offered support to Stovall by telegram when the team was on the road. On one occasion he even played the foil to authorities attempting to prevent a riot at the ballpark.

On September 19 the Packers were losing both games of a double-header to Newark, when, in the second game, Mann became part of a riot. The problem started when the umpire called a runner safe at home on a double steal attempt. The Newark runner appeared to be out and the decision threw the crowd into a "fit of anger."

"Joe O'Brien, one of Jim Gilmore's official guessers, may never forget the shower of soft cushions and pop bottles that fell in his direction," wrote the *Kansas City Times*. "...Manager Stovall and practically the whole Packer team protested the decision and surrounded O'Brien but they all left when the pop bottles came whizzing out of the grandstand."[28]

Eight policemen attempted to quell the disturbance, but when one officer attempted to detain a fan for throwing a bottle, President Mann refused to allow the arrest and ordered the policeman out of the stands.[29] The game was delayed about ten minutes by the crowd's demonstration and "after the field was cleared of weapons play was resumed."

After Mann died in 1943, the people of Kansas City were surprised to learn that Conrad was not a United States citizen. Instead, he had clung to the German citizenship of his birth.

29

Opening Day 2

The Federal League opened its 1915 season on Saturday, April 10, with games in Brooklyn, Baltimore, Chicago and Kansas City. Though there were gala opening ceremonies in each city, President James Gilmore chose to attend the game in Kansas City, considered the circuit's weakest franchise.

The early game in Brooklyn was typical of the festivities. "The crowd was big, the weather warm.... The park had on a spring dress of new paint and bunting," wrote a reporter. "Long streamers of flags waved in the breezes, which swept over the top of the stands. Headed by a band, the players of Buffalo in dark blue and the Tip Tops in white paraded around the field, carrying a big flag, that they afterward ran up to the top of a high pole in center field."

The *New York Times* complained:

> ...those who kept awake during the three hour ordeal will slumber tomorrow to get over it. Brooklyn won by a score of 13 to 9 before a crowd of about 16,000. There is no player limit in the Federal League, so the teams used an array of pinch hitters, pinch runners and pinch managers. Nearly everybody took part in the game except the members of the band and at one time it looked as if Brooklyn was going to call on the brass drummer to go in as a pinch hitter.[1]

Once the game began, Brooklyn's rookie manager, Lee Magee, lasted only one inning. He balked at a decision by umpire Louis Fyfe and was ejected from the game. Magee repeatedly returned to the coaching lines and had to be removed from the field on six occasions.

Said the *Times*, "If Magee is going to get mad at every decision that does not please him he will be able to spend all summer at the beach."[2]

A much better game was played in Chicago, where 16,000 turned out at Weeghman Park to watch a pitching duel between Claude Hendrix and Eddie Plank, the latter making his Federal League debut with St. Louis. As it had in 1914, opening day began in Chicago with a parade. Manager Joe Tinker, decked out in a sweater and a new Whales cap, rode in a car adorned with flowers. Several rooters had cars in the parade sporting pennants, garlands and other decorations. The local players wore new uniforms with cream-colored jerseys and pants, blue stockings and caps, and cherry-red sweaters. A blue whale likeness sat within a large blue C on the left breast of the jerseys.

In addition to new uniforms, the Chicago club had a new nickname. Weeghman revived the contest to select an official nickname for the Chifeds prior to the 1915 season and entries were submitted to Chicago area newspapers, the winner to receive a set of season tickets. Among the submissions were the Tinx, Chibuns (for Weeghman's restaurants), Bandits, and an assortment of animals: Colts, Eagles, Condors, Bunnies and even Rats. The *Chicago Herald* reported that Weeghman's choice of the entries was "Chix," but even the person who submitted the suggestion wrote the club and said he would never go see a team that could be mocked as "chickens."³

Charley decided to go with his second choice and announced his club would be known as the "Whales." The winning entry was submitted by D.J. Eichoff, a Federal League fan since 1913. Eichoff also included a drawing of a whale with its tail upturned, as if it had just conquered an enemy.⁴

Eichoff gave his reasoning for selecting the nickname: "The best commercial whales are found in the frozen north, which means that the North Side should have the best team; Whales lash and drub their opponents; and anything marked a 'whaler' is large and extraordinary."⁵

Writers quickly picked up on the new nickname and began calling the owner "Whale Oil Charley." But Weeghman liked the publicity and the new name.

Attendees to the 1915 opener noticed a number of changes to Charles Weeghman's ballpark. During the off season, Charley had the existing bleachers in left and right field torn down. At a construction cost of $17,000, a new, larger left field bleacher, fifteen to twenty

Large crowd on West Addison Street arriving for the game at Weeghman Field during the 1915 season (Chicago History Museum, SDN-059405. Original photograph has been cropped.).

rows deep, extended to center field. No seats remained in right field and a large brownish brick wall ranged all the way to the scoreboard. The infield dirt behind second base was changed from the usual box to a straight line. During the off season, a new firehouse for Engine Company 78 was built at 1052 Waveland Avenue and would become a neighborhood landmark that still stands.[6]

Newly elected Chicago Mayor "Big Bill" Thompson, reportedly a stockholder in the 1913 Keeleys, threw out the first pitch to Art Wilson. Managers Tinker and Fielder Jones received flower garlands from admiring fans and, finally, the game got underway at 3:15 P.M.

Eddie Plank's cross-fire delivery baffled the newly christened "Whales" for seven innings. The veteran pitcher was so dominant in the early innings that the Chicago crowd began to applaud him. The lefty fanned two batters in the first and added two more strikeouts in the second. Eddie's own double and a three-bagger by Johnny Tobin gave the Terriers a one-run lead in the fifth inning.

By the time the Whales came to bat in the eighth, Plank appeared to have the game well in hand. It was the opposing pitcher, Claude Hendrix, who started the rally with a solid double to right-center. In the key play of the game, Charlie Hanford pushed a bunt toward the pitcher's mound. Plank rushed in, scooped up the ball and slipped on the wet turf just as he threw to third base in an attempt to get Hendrix. The throw was late and the Whales had runners on first and third with none out. Fielder Jones pulled his infielders in close to make a play at the plate, but Mann's smash off shortstop Ernie Johnson's shin tied the score. A single by Wilson and a perfectly executed squeeze play with Rollie Zeider at the bat made the final score 3 to 1.

In Kansas City, Federal League President Gilmore received a surprising ovation from the 12,000 fans, the largest crowd to ever attend a game at Gordon & Koppel Field. By the three o'clock start time all the ticket holders were seated except for the overflow part of the crowd that lined up along the right field bleachers. Gilmore sat in a box with Pittsburgh Federals president Edward Gwinner and Packers director Conrad Mann. Up in the stands a band played the popular tunes of the day until the players, umpires and Mayor Henry L. Jost appeared around home plate. While two movie cameras and several photographers recorded the festivities, the band played the traditional "Dixie," then "America the Beautiful," before the Kansas City mayor threw the ceremonial first pitch.[7]

The Packers sent a strapping 6'5", twenty-one-year-old right-hander named Miles Main to the mound to oppose the Rebels' Frank Allen. Main was the only significant addition to a Kansas City ball club that had finished 20 games out of first place in 1914.

Also known as Alex, Main was a promising rookie pitcher for the Detroit Tigers in 1914 until he suffered a hand injury on the team's first Eastern road trip. Still, he started twelve games and posted a decent earned run average of 2.67. After jumping to the Federal League, Main was supposed to go to the Terriers, but after St. Louis acquired Eddie Plank, Miles seemed headed for Newark. Then, his assignment became Kansas City when Cy Falkenberg was transferred to the New Jersey club.

Main held Pittsburgh scoreless for four innings, but in the top of the fifth the Rebels broke the game open. An error by first baseman George Stovall, who dropped a throw, opened the floodgates. One of the league's new stars, Ed Konetchy, slugged a long home run over the fifteen-foot left field fence with plenty of room to spare, scoring two runners in front of him. The Rebels' Frank Allen kept the opposition's hits scattered and Pittsburgh won easily, 8 to 0.

In the spring, C.L. Schanberger wrote in *The Sporting News* of the anticipation for Baltimore's upcoming professional baseball season:

> All the reserved seats for the opening game have been sold at one dollar per, while there is every indication that a crowd similar to the opening last year will again file into new Terrapin Park. This plant, newly painted and looking good to the beholder, stands on a slight eminence on the other side of the street where the Internationals in games a gone were wont to gambol. Already Jack Dunn has removed the stands from old Oriole Park for erection in Richmond, while it is generally believed that this once beautiful ball field will be cut up into building lots.[8]

The 18,000 local fans at Terrapins Park for Baltimore's opening game were sorely disappointed as Jack Quinn displayed none of the talent that earned him 26 victories for the Terps in 1914. Newark batters made ten hits off Quinn before he was relieved by Piano Mover Smith in the eighth inning. Cy Falkenberg had a couple of shaky innings for the visitors, but the Newark nine prevailed 7 to 5.

After the Terps lost for a second time to Newark, Chief Bender finally took the mound for Baltimore on April 13, opposed by an old foe from the Detroit Tigers, George Mullin. Bender was not sharp. He gave up seven hits and despite his reputation for control the big right-hander walked five. Newark's Frank LaPorte touched the Chippewa pitcher for a home run and Baltimore lost its third straight game, 3 to 1.

It would be a long season for Baltimore.

Though the ballpark of the Newark Federal League club was not completed by opening day, an announced crowd of 26,032 packed Harrison Park to watch the "Peps" play Baltimore on April 16. An additional 5,000 fans reportedly were turned away.

"Newark and its surrounding hamlets were seized with a violent attack of baseball today, accompanied by a high fever and laryngitis," wrote the *New York Times*. "The ailment can be directly traced to the opening of the Newark Federals at their new roomy park in Harrison. The epidemic spread among nearly 25,000 Jersey folk who jammed the park to see 'Whoa Bill' Phillips' Peps make their home debut against Knabe's Baltimore Terrapins."[9]

"Everybody in Newark and its environs quit work when the whistle blew at 12 o'clock, put on their new spring spangles, and got ready for the big parade," reported the *Times*.

> Almost every boy and man in town walked in the parade carrying big banners welcoming the Federal Leaguers to New Jersey, and those who couldn't walk rode in automobiles. The long lines of baseball fans were punctuated with numerous bands and drum corps. When the parade squeezed into the ballpark after doing the double quick, right about face around Paddy McGuigan's Square, the big wooden stand and the centre field bleachers were already filled. There were enough floral horseshoes and shower bouquets to go around the whole Newark team.[10]

Pat Powers introduced a unique twist for the Newark Peppers' first home game of 1915. "It remained for the Federal League to introduce a real new one in having girl ushers in the grand stand," reported the *New York Times*. "That's why a lot of young men didn't see very much of the ball game."[11]

The revival of major league baseball in Newark was brought about by the administration of fifty-four-year-old minor league executive Patrick T. Powers and millionaire oil man Harry Sinclair. A New Jersey native, Powers had managed Rochester of the American Association in 1890, Buffalo a year later, and the New York National League Club in 1892. Powers became president of the Eastern League in 1893, a position he held for seventeen years (interrupted for one season in 1906).

The minor leagues were caught up in the war between the National League, which dominated most aspects of professional baseball up to 1901, and the new American League that encroached on their territory. Seven minor leagues decided to join together in a unified front to deal with the warring big leagues and they needed a veteran baseball man to deal with the major leagues. At their organizational meeting in Chicago on September 5, 1901, the seven minor league presidents selected Patrick Powers as their first chief executive. Powers gave the organization a name, "the National Association of Professional Baseball Leagues, Inc."[12]

Powers's first priority was to get the National League to restore the National Agreement, which gave protection to all signatory leagues in the areas of contracts and territorial rights. The National League had canceled the agreement when it was ignored by the American Leaguers in their pursuit of the older circuit's players.

Powers's Eastern League experienced a peaceful and profitable period after the big leagues made peace in 1902. Ironically, it was the Newark club's vote that ousted Powers from the presidency of the Eastern League following the 1911 season and put Ed Barrow in that position. In Barrow's first year as president, the circuit changed its name to the International League. Three years later Pat Powers would force the International League out of Newark. Because of the Federal League invasion, the Newark International League Club moved to Harrisburg, Pennsylvania, on July 2, 1915. Powers had his revenge.

Powers oversaw the construction of the Newark Federal League club's steel and concrete 20,000-seat stadium, located a block from the Passaic River in nearby Harrison. As the date for the first home game neared, President Powers told the *Newark Evening News* that the workers would have to demonstrate "pepper" to get the park finished on time, just as the team would have to demonstrate "pepper" on the field to win games.

The remark caught on with the press and they dubbed the club "the Peppers" or "Peps" for short. It was said that on the day of the club's home opener, one could not find small green or red peppers in any produce market in Newark because Peps fans had bought them all up and were wearing them on their lapels at the ballpark.[13]

Two days before opening day, the people of Newark held a "Dollar Dinner" in Krueger Auditorium in honor of the city's new baseball team. After the 900 or so dignitaries and fans were seated, Manager Phillips and his players entered in single file to a standing ovation from the audience. The crowd was entertained by the Peppers' new first baseman/coach/comedian, Herman "Germany" Schaefer, who mimicked Charlie Chaplin walking an imaginary circus high wire.[14] One of the zaniest characters in baseball history, Schaefer was well known for prompting a baseball rule change.

During a game between Detroit and Cleveland in September 1908, the Tigers' Davy Jones was on third base and Schaefer stood on first. The pair attempted a delayed double steal, but the Naps' catcher didn't throw through and allowed Schaefer to take second base. On the next pitch, Schaefer ran back to first base then shouted across to Jones that he was going to steal second again. This time, the rattled catcher threw to second and Jones was able to score. The maneuver was soon outlawed. By the time Schaefer became a Federal Leaguer in 1915, he was thirty-eight years old and had spent most of the previous season with Washington on the coaching lines, entertaining the fans along with his teammate and fellow clown, Nick Altrock. Clark Griffith wanted to keep Schaefer for his comedic talents, but the additional money the club spent to keep Walter Johnson meant Germany had to go.

A month into the 1915 season, the *Washington Post* wrote:

> Schaefer is a drawing card. Already he has won the hearts of the Newark bleacherites and hundreds of them go daily to the park, not so much because they want to see the ball game, but because they want to see Schaefer perform a few of his antics. Schaefer never goes to bat without getting a roar of greeting from the fans, and he never fails to respond to those greetings with a wave of his hand or a wave of his cap.[15]

Cy Falkenberg, ace for the Federal League champions of a year earlier, started on the mound in the Peps' home opener and the faithful went home happy when the local club won the game, 6 to 2. Most of the starters returned from that 1914 Indianapolis club — Rariden, LaPorte, Esmond, McKechnie, Campbell and Sheer — but conspicuous in his absence was star right fielder Benny Kauff. Fortunately, there was a capable replacement in the talented and speedy Edd Roush. Edd moved into the center field spot and Vin Campbell shifted to right.

Roush was a natural left-hander who learned as a youngster to play baseball right-handed because there were no left-handed gloves available to him. He began his professional career with Evansville of the Kitty League in 1912. A common myth is that a shoulder injury weakened Edd's right arm and caused him to switch back to a lefty. Actually, Roush returned to his natural throwing arm after he purchased his first left-hander's glove that first season in Evansville.[16]

Edd J. Roush and his twin brother, Fred, were born in Oakland City, Indiana, on May 8, 1893. Edd never revealed the reason for the unorthodox spelling of his first name, but said he was only given a middle initial so as not to offend his uncles Joseph and James. During his early years in professional baseball, Edd's name was often spelled "Rousch" in box scores and newspaper accounts.

Roush was batting .323 with Evansville in August 1913 when he was promoted to the Chicago White Sox. In Chicago, Edd came to bat ten times and made only one hit. That single off the Athletics' Chief Bender on September 9 would be the first of 2,376 hits in an eighteen-year major league career.

"I was with them for a month," Roush said of the White Sox adventure. "I left them in Washington, D.C., because the fellow who got hurt returned to the club. They sent me to Lincoln, Nebraska, to finish the season."[17]

Roush was unhappy with his demotion to the minors and with his unsatisfactory salary. That winter he got in touch with St. Louis, Chicago, and Indianapolis of the Federal League and applied for an outfield job. However, Manager Bill Phillips of the Hoosierfeds was the only one who made Edd an offer.

Edd's father Will, the former semi-pro player, chose to act as his twenty-year-old son's agent in negotiations with Phillips. When the Roushes arrived at the Indianapolis club's offices, business manager Bill Watkins had already taken care of Edd's Lincoln commitment and had drawn up a contract calling for a salary of $1,500 for the season. It was left up to Phillips to handle the negotiations with the outfield prospect. Will turned the contract down flat. The elder Roush said his son would play for $2,000 or they would return home to Oakland City. In less than a half hour Phillips agreed to the Roushes' demand for the $2,000. Young Edd would not forget the lesson, and several baseball club owners would pay the price in future contract negotiations.[18]

Edd spent the first few weeks of the 1914 season sitting beside Bill Phillips on the Hoosiers' bench. The youngster listened and absorbed every bit of baseball wisdom offered by the veteran manager. When Edd toyed with the idea of using a heavier bat, Whoa Bill agreed, "That bat will work for you because you have strong wrists and can swat it from the base."[19]

During 1914, Roush played 43 games in the outfield and was Phillips' number one pinch-hitter. Edd began playing more as the season progressed and in August Phillips released the Hoosiers' fourth outfielder, Al Kaiser, to open the door even more for his protégé. The little lefty batter compiled a .325 batting average in 166 plate appearances. Edd repaid his mentor during the off season by holding out for a 100 percent raise. The hold-out lingered into 1915 before the frustrated manager finally agreed to Roush's $4,000 salary demand.[20]

Once permanently installed in Harrison Field's spacious center field, Roush's over-the-shoulder grabs, shoestring catches and leaping one-handed spears made him an instant favorite among the fans. Edd studied the opposing batters so he could position himself properly when they came to bat and his outstanding speed enabled him to reach almost anything hit in the air to center field.

When Edd came to bat, he would shuffle about in an effort to outguess the pitcher and catcher. Roush was able to shift his feet after a pitch was on its way and punch the ball into an unoccupied part of the field. Throughout his career, Roush used one of the heaviest bats, weighing from 46 to 48 ounces. His bat was not long, but had a thick handle. He explained his reason for using a short and thick-handled bat: "Place hitting is in a sense glorified bunting. I take only a half swing at the ball, and the weight of the bat rather than my swing is what drives it."[21]

Roush was fast too. He would steal 215 bases in the major leagues with a high of 36 in 1920. Edd's major league career totals included 182 triples and 30 inside-the-park home runs. Before the final game of the 1914 season, the Indianapolis club held a field day where the players displayed running and throwing talents for the local fans. The *Indianapolis Star* reported that Roush "sprang the surprise of the day" in the bunt-and-run event when he bunted and ran to first in three and one fifth seconds "which is said to equal the world's record."[22]

During his two seasons in the Federal League, Roush's best friends were catcher and roommate Bill Rariden and third baseman Bill McKechnie, who, like Edd, was a student of baseball. On the day after Bill McKechnie became manager of the Newark team, Roush collected three hits to help the Peps to victory. The two friends were teammates on the Giants and Reds for two years after the Federal League folded, and after his days as an active player were over, Edd accepted only one baseball job, one year as a coach under Bill when he managed the Reds. Roush and McKechnie were elected to the Baseball Hall of Fame in the same year, and during retirement both men maintained their homes in Bradenton, Florida.

The 1915 season started off well for the Peps. On April 22, in the club's eleventh game, Harry Moran allowed only two hits to Brooklyn, and the 3 to 0 victory propelled Newark into first place.

Three days later at Harrison Park, the Pep's George Kaiserling won a sensational fourteen-inning pitchers' battle with Joe Schulz of the Buffalo Federals, 2 to 1. A double by Germany Schaefer, who got a start at first base, followed by Emil Huhn's safety to right, gave Newark the winning run with one out in the fourteenth.

The Peps' home field would be the toughest home run park in the Federal League, rivaling only Pittsburgh's Exposition Park in outfield space. It was not until the club's eighteenth home game, on May 9, that the Newark fans would see a home run. The four-bagger came off the bat of Chicago's Al Wickland and, naturally, it was an inside-the-parker. Wickland's long drive hit the center field fence and bounced far enough away from Edd Roush to allow Al to circle the bases. For the season, shortstop Johnny Esmond led the Peps in four-baggers with five and the club only managed 17 homers as a team. By comparison, Hal Chase led the league with 17 home runs by himself.

Because of the entertainment backgrounds of Pat Powers and Charlie Weeghman, the Newark and Chicago clubs were ahead of the other Federal League franchises when it came to promotions. In addition to his extensive baseball background, Powers had been active in the New York City entertainment business, which kept him in contact with many of the leaders in major league baseball. Powers operated out of Madison Square Garden and was involved in a variety of public amusement enterprises, including bicycle races.

"It is doubtful if the Fed promoters really expected to make money this year," a Newark newspaper editorialized.

...When they found people were not turning out fast enough they reduced the prices and invited many free. This was good business.

Mr. Powers also conceived the idea of permitting local athletic organizations to use the fine, new field. Track meets, football games, in fact a variety of sports have been conducted there and the appearance of the plant has been praised. This is cultivating among the people the habit of going to the park. This feeling of friendliness supplemented next year with car service over the Jackson Street Bridge, and possibly by spur tracks into the automobile space of the field, makes the outlook agreeable.[23]

Powers scheduled three unique double-headers against Brooklyn for the 1915 season. The morning game would be played in one team's ballpark and the second game at the other's park. These double bills were to take place on Memorial Day, July 5 (the Fourth was on a Sunday and Brooklyn did not play games on the Sabbath), and Labor Day. On July 5, the morning game of the set was to be played in Brooklyn, but it was rained out. The two teams traveled to Harrison, where they were able to play an afternoon game that was won by Newark.

30

Benny Kauff Goes Astray

On April 30, 1915, the *New York Times* reported: "Benny Kauff, outfielder and one of the sensational players of the Federal League, jumped yesterday from the Brookfeds to the New York National League Club, thereby creating the biggest commotion of the baseball season so far."[1]

This was yet another problem for the Wards. The Brooklyn rooters had been so optimistic just three weeks earlier. The local fans were introduced to their new star center fielder on opening day in a game against Buffalo. When Benny came to bat for the home team in the third inning, the score was tied 1–1, and two runners were on base.

"Kauff ambled up bearing his great reputation as a slugger modestly and also bearing a wicked looking bat," wrote the *Times'* reporter.

He faced Hugh Bedient, the Buffalo pitcher.... The ball whizzed at Kauff so fast that it whistled. Benny met it with a solid crash, and the ball rose into right field on a line like a shell from a 42-centimeter gun. Clearing the right field wall by a few inches, the ball landed in Little Italy, where the little Neapolitan cherubs playing in the street fought for the possession of it. Kauff trotted slowly around the circuit on his excursion trip, sending the other runners home ahead of him.

From that moment, Benny Kauff could have anything in Brooklyn. Twice after that he struck out, but what did that matter? He had batted his way into the hearts of 16,000 fans, and Brooklyn thinks that Benny is just as good as he was touted to be.[2]

During a game against Newark in mid–April, Benny added a double, a triple and a single to his resume. A reporter noted, "Benny Kauff, knowing that the weather will soon require a new straw lid, drove the ball against a hat sign on the brick wall in right centre and will collect a new hat for the feat."[3]

Noted New York columnist Damon Runyon wrote of Kauff in 1915:

Having seen him in civilian array we are undecided whether Benny Kauff of the Feds is a better show on or off.... On his hands Benjamin carries a couple of diamond rings that set him back about $3,500. In his necktie he wears a diamond horseshoe.... This pin cost Benny something like $1,500.

On days when he does not wear a four-in-hand tie Benny has the horseshoe pinned to his shirt bosom, and it cannot be denied that the effect is very striking. So much so, in fact, that the Brooklyn police have requested him to use dimmers on the display while in the city limits.[4]

As the season progressed, Brooklyn fell into the second division and Benny soured on his new club. During a loss in Newark on April 22, Kauff was thrown out of the game in the sixth inning for arguing with umpire James Johnstone on a strike call.

A week later, an Organized Baseball club escalated hostilities with the Federal League by signing Benny Kauff away from Brooklyn. Actually, by Organized Baseball's rules Kauff was still bound to the American Association club that held his contract when Benny jumped to the Federals in 1914. According to Jack Hendricks, manager of the Indianapolis American Association club, Kauff made advances to him late in the 1914 season, expressing the desire to return to Organized Baseball. Benny wanted Indianapolis to sign him to an American Association contract, then sell him to a major league team, preferably the New York Giants. However, Hendricks, an attorney as well as a manager, knew Kauff was legally bound to the Tip Tops for three years and refused to have any dealings with Benny.

The Giants' play for Kauff began in September 1914 when the club's president, Harry Hempstead, met with President McGill of the Indianapolis American Association club. McGill knew the Indians could never afford to sign such an expensive player and worked out an agreement with Hempstead by which the Giants agreed to give the minor league club two players and $10,000 if Benny could be signed to a legal contract then play the 1915 season with the New York club.

When the Indianapolis American Association club left for spring training in California on February 27, 1915, Kauff showed up and asked to be taken along. Again, Hendricks refused to have anything to do with the Federal League player.

Kauff was legally bound to the Indianapolis Federals, so when he was transferred to Brooklyn that March, the Wards' business manager, Dick Carroll, went to the club's training site at Valdosta, Georgia, to sign the player to a new contract. The player agreed to Carroll's terms, but later Benny said he didn't sign the contract because the Wards had not incorporated into it what their business manager had promised.[5]

Kauff reportedly signed a contract with the National League's New York Giants just before their game against the Boston Braves at the Polo Grounds on April 29, 1915. Nobody knew New York was going to sign Kauff until a scout named Kinselin informed reporters at the ballpark. When Boston Braves owner Owen Gaffney was told the news, he immediately called National League President John Tener.

Benny Kauff was inserted into the New York lineup that day as center fielder, but Gaffney, who was in attendance at the game, refused to permit his team to take the field against the Giants with a contract jumper and "blacklisted player" a participant in the contest. Umpire Ernest Quigley agreed and promptly forfeited the game to Boston by the score of 9 to 0.

Quigley's decision to forfeit the game before he spoke with his umpire partner Malcolm Eason, who had been on the telephone with President Tener, exacerbated the situation at the stadium. With 6,000 unhappy fans on hand and no game to watch, the parties finally resolved to play with Red Murray in center field for the Giants and Benny Kauff on the bench.

News that Kauff had appeared in a New York Giants uniform stirred Federal League officials into action. President Robert Ward of Brooklyn disputed Benny's contention that he had no contract with his Federal League club. Ward declared the player had been signed for three years and he would make a fight for him. The Brooklyn Federals disclosed that they were paying Kauff $6,000 a year, which was $2,000 more than he received in Indianapolis. Ward immediately wired President Tener and President Hempstead of the Giants, protesting New York's actions.

Federal League President Gilmore announced that Kauff was suspended effective immediately, and he was still under a valid contract to the Federal League. "If the organized baseball leagues begin taking players who have valid contracts with the Federals, professional baseball will soon go to pieces," said Gilmore. "The Federal League will fight to a finish to prevent Kauff playing with the National League, but I cannot now indicate just what procedure we shall follow."[6]

On his part, Benny Kauff said he had no intention of returning to the Feds because he had many offers to play independent ball around New York and had been asked to play with the same independent team in Pennsylvania as Frank Baker. Benny added that he had been offered $1000 a week to go into vaudeville and tell something he knows about "inside baseball" with the Federals.[7]

Kauff insisted he was through with the Federal League and applied to the National Commission for reinstatement, stating: "If I can't play with the Giants, I'll quit the game for good...."

On April 30, President Tener held an impromptu meeting in his New York office with several National League owners to discuss the Kauff situation. It was decided that the ironclad rules of the National Commission automatically prohibited the engagement of Benny by the Giants. As an "outlaw," Kauff could apply for reinstatement, but he could not be taken into the National League until three years after his offense of jumping to the Federals was committed — which extended through the 1916 season.

After the National Commission refused his reinstatement, Kauff was forced to eat his words and return to the Tip Tops. According to the *Times,* Kauff had a long talk with Brooklyn business manager Dick Carroll and indicated plainly that he was a penitent young man: "He is anxious to be forgiven and let by-gones be by-gones, which is probably what will happen."[8]

Kauff's version of his defection to the Giants differed from what was printed in the newspapers. Following the season he wrote in *Baseball Magazine*:

> When I went to Brooklyn I found that I was expected to work for two thousand dollars less than I found that I had been led to believe I was going to get. I had submitted a signed contract for six thousand dollars a year which was satisfactory to me, but when I was expected to take four instead I kicked. There is where this Giant business all started. Jack Hendricks, out in Indianapolis with the A.A. club that I was supposed to go to when I jumped to the Feds, had been at me all winter to go with the Giants....
>
> And so when McGraw got hot after me I agreed to go with the Giants if he could engineer the deal. The understanding was that I was to receive five thousand dollars to induce me to sign and I signed, keeping my part of the agreement in good faith. I did get into a Giants' uniform and that was about all, for the National Commission stepped in and stopped proceedings at this point. It seems Mr. R.B. Ward had signed my contract submitted to him and calling for $6,000 although I had no knowledge that he had signed it, as I had signed this contract myself all he had to do was to display the paper with my signature, showing that I was his property. That naturally quashed proceedings and I went back to the Federal League.[9]

Benny returned to the Brooklyn Federals' lineup at Washington Park on May 8. Despite two pretty catches in center field by the prodigal star, Brooklyn lost to Kansas City 8 to 5. After the Sunday off-day, Kauff assisted Kansas City's 4 to 3 victory at Washington Park on Monday when he threw the ball from deep center field into the visiting players' bench, allowing two runs to score.

Except for the games he missed due to suspension, the affair with the Giants had little effect on Benny's play. At the first of June, Kauff was batting .337 for the 60 games in which he had participated and he led the league with 25 stolen bases. Kauff was lost for another game when, on June 25, he was ejected from a game against Chicago by umpire Fyfe for arguing on an unsuccessful stolen base attempt in the first inning.

Upon receiving his monthly paycheck from the Brookfeds on July 1, Benny found that $500 had been deducted from his pay. Tip Tops business manager Dick Carroll explained that Kauff's contract provided that he was to pay the Brooklyn club in accord with the player's defunct Indianapolis Federal League contract on which he borrowed $1,500 to be repaid in $500 annual installments. Benny protested that his new contract with the Wards nullified his Indianapolis obligations, and immediately left the club in St. Louis.

The Wards' press agent announced that Kauff was fined $100 and suspended for ten days. If Benny attempted to play anywhere else, the Brooklyn Federal League club was prepared to take legal action against him.

On July 3, Benny was at Ebbets Field watching the Giants play the Dodgers. The flashy outfielder was decked out in his newest suit and all his jewelry. Upon hearing the news of his suspension, Kauff laughed and declared positively that if he did not receive his full salary he would never again wear a Federal League uniform. "I am not playing baseball for fame and glory and I want the money which is due me," he said.[10]

Kauff shook hands with John McGraw, but nothing was said about his joining the New York club. Manager McGraw said that the National Commission had decided Kauff could not play in Organized Baseball, and that's all there was to it.

While Benny was hobnobbing with the press and McGraw, his lawyer, John Montgomery Ward, was serving President Hempstead with paper on two suits, one for $5,000 plus interest, which Kauff said was promised him when he signed with the Giants in April, and the other for $18,000 salary for three years and $2,000 in counsel fees. Joe Villa surmised Kauff was the principal in a scheme to force the National Commission to allow him, in due time, to play with the Giants.

"There isn't a chance for the Whales to get Benny Kauff," responded Federal League President James Gilmore when asked about a trade Charles Weeghman of Chicago tried to engineer with Brooklyn. "Kauff is under suspension and fine now, and to trade him would be to acknowledge there is no way of enforcing discipline in our league. He'll play with Brooklyn or not at all. That is final."[11]

Once again, all Kauff got for jumping his team was publicity. In reality, he had no place to go but back to the Tip Tops. Benny served his ten-day suspension and rejoined the Brooklyn club in time to go on a batting rampage reminiscent of his 1914 work with Indianapolis. Benny's attorney, John M. Ward, interceded for him and convinced Brooklyn not to take the $1,500 loan Kauff got from Indianapolis out of his pay.

The player Brooklyn got for the remainder of the season was bitter and unhappy. "If my contract which I signed had been lived up to in the beginning there wouldn't have been any trouble," wrote Kauff.

> As it was it seemed to me that a lot of trouble had been caused and I had been put in a bad light with the public and all to no purpose. I was in bad with my own crowd, too. The Federal League umpires used to ride me after that. I never got any more close decisions. They all went against me. The players used to lay for me and try to show me up at the bat or on the bases. But while I was pretty well out of sorts with baseball for the balance of the season and had no great ambition to play my best baseball under such circumstances, I still led the league.[12]

As Benny's success grew, so did his ego. While holding court with reporters following the 1915 season he told reporters, "You asked me what my weaknesses was, didn't you? Well, I'll tell you. I ain't got any, what do you know about that?"

When asked about pitchers' attempts to intimidate him by throwing up and in, he bragged, "Let me tell you something. Earl Moore tried to knock my nose off with the 'bean ball' last season and do you know what I did? I just stepped back and tapped his bean ball right over the fence, that's how much afraid I am of any pitcher beaning me."[13]

Benny's explicit egotism caused considerable consternation among Federal League executives and players. A Brooklyn teammate, first baseman Art Griggs, said Kauff didn't appear to be bulging in the vicinity of the "bean."[14]

On the other hand, umpire Billy Evans reported in his syndicated newspaper column that during the 1915 season, Benny journeyed over to the Polo Grounds one afternoon to watch Detroit play the Yankees. It was the first time he had seen Ty Cobb in action.

After the game, Benny remarked to one of the players with him, "I must learn who dubbed me the Ty Cobb of the Federal League."

"Why?" asked the teammate.

"You saw Cobb play today, so did I. Now I realize what a compliment that scribe paid me," answered Kauff.[15]

Benny was a complex character.

While the Brooklyn club's officials were dealing with Benny Kauff another problem arose. The club's secretary, Walter S. Ward, was in hot water for his dalliance with a woman at a Pittsburgh hotel. Coincidentally, Walter was the son of co-owner George S. Ward and nephew of President Robert Ward in addition to his position with the club.

During the Tip Tops' first swing around the circuit in May 1915, Walter Ward met an attractive young woman when the team visited Pittsburgh. The team arrived in Pittsburgh on May 24 and that night the young brunette was introduced to Ward, who was known as a big spender and the life of the party. It was later reported by the local press that the girl lived with Ward at a hotel when the Brooklyn team was in Pittsburgh and was seen in his company constantly. The parties staged by Ward and his girlfriend became the talk of Pittsburgh's night life. When George Ward learned of his son's affair with the girl, he discharged the young man as the club's secretary and ordered him home.[16]

The affair came to light in 1922 after Walter Ward was charged with the murder of an alleged blackmailer in New York State. Martha Kendall, proprietor of a ladies' clothing store in Hollywood, claimed that Ward's father, George S. Ward, settled with her out of court for damages against the son in Pittsburgh. She was quoted as saying that Walter had broken into her apartment in 1915 and tried to kidnap her with the aid of his chauffeur and another man. R.H. Jackson, attorney for the Pittsburgh Rebels and former district attorney of Allegheny County, handled the case for the Wards, but when a search for a record of the action was made seven years later, no trace of it was found.

A Pittsburgh friend of the Wards told the press:

> I remember the Kendall girl very well.... I know she never missed a game when the Federal League played at old Exposition Park. She and another girl, who was the daughter of a former ball player, were close friends and traveled a great deal together. They were not only regular attendants at the Federal League games, but were on intimate terms with members of the Pittsburgh and Brooklyn teams of the Federal League. When Ward was in town they used to drop their own admirers and cling to him, for he was the gayest spender of them all, and was clever and attractive besides.
>
> The other girl tried to force Ward to pay for an alleged attack on her, but the Kendall girl had nothing to do with it. The part of her story which says that George S. Ward, Walter's father, paid $10,000 to settle the case out of court is absolutely false. The father was never brought into the case. It was adjusted by friends of Ward.[17]

On May 22, 1922, Walter Ward was arraigned in White Plains, New York, for the murder of a former sailor named Clarence Peters, whose body had been found on a deserted road two days earlier. Ward, then vice president of the Ward Baking Company and chairman of the New Rochelle Board of Police Commissioners, claimed that a gang of men threatened him and his children with death unless $75,000 blackmail was paid. Ward purportedly met the extortionists on a road near Kensico Dam and, following a shootout, one of the blackmailers, Peters, was killed.

During the summer of 1922, the New York newspapers were filled with stories about Ward and large gambling debts, blackmail conspiracies, and rendezvous with loose women at a Manhattan "love nest." Ward was freed of the murder charges the following January, then reindicted in July 1923 and held for trial without bail.

After months of legal maneuvering, Walter's trial for first degree murder finally went forth in September. Although the reason for the alleged "blackmail" by Peters was never disclosed, Ward was found not guilty by the jury on his thirty-second birthday, May 20, 1923.

The verdict was not the end of the strange story of Walter Ward. On May 5, 1926, Walter's damaged automobile was found abandoned in Trenton, New Jersey. No trace of him was found and it was feared he was a victim of foul play. A massive manhunt was initiated, but a few days later, the Ward family notified authorities that Walter had contacted them and the search was called off. Beryl Ward had stood by her husband during his murder trial, but following his disappearance, she filed for divorce. The whereabouts of Walter Ward remained a mystery until January 1927, when he arrived in Havana, Cuba, by ship from New Orleans. Walter immediately went to his father's Havana estate, where he went into seclusion from the press.[18]

31

Rebels Resurgent

Frank Allen of the Pittsburgh Rebels pitched the Federal League's first no-hit, no-run game of 1915 on Saturday, April 24, when he blanked the Terriers in St. Louis, 2 to 0. Allen was anything but sharp in the first inning when he walked three batters. But after the former Dodger escaped that frame unscathed, he faced only twenty-two men over the next eight innings. Allen did have some help behind him, especially in the outfield. In the sixth inning, Johnny Tobin cracked a fly to deep right field. Jim Kelly raced back and, while leaning against the fence, stretched out his left hand and secured the ball in his glove.

Pittsburgh did not score off the Terriers' Bob Groom until the seventh inning. Ed Konetchy opened the inning with a terrific clout over the center fielder's head for a triple. When Terriers catcher Grover Hartley spotted Koney cheating down the third base line, he whipped a throw toward third baseman Charlie Deal in an attempt to nab the Big Bohemian. Hartley's throw hit Ed and rolled far enough away for the Rebels' first baseman to score.

Allen still had not allowed a hit when the Terriers came to bat in the ninth inning. Leading off, Tobin tapped a ball in front of the plate that Allen grabbed and threw to first just in time for the out. Tobin and Fielder Jones hotly disputed the call and Johnny was ejected from the game.

With one out, the Terriers' manager was determined to prevent a no-hitter against his team if an all possible and sent Doc Crandall out to pinch-hit for the light-hitting second baseman Al Bridwell. Only about 500 local fans came out to see the day's game, but the ones remaining made their presence felt with jeers for Allen when the Rebels' pitcher issued an unintentional walk to Crandall with four straight wide ones. When the next batter, Del Drake, lined a pitch over shortstop it appeared Allen's no-hitter was lost, but Rebel Oakes came charging in "as fast as he could and made what looked like an impossible catch."[1] Allen completed his masterpiece when Babe Borton was enticed to ground to Berghammer, who stepped on second base for the force out.

Frank Allen was the first desertion from the organized major leagues to the Federal League in the fall of 1914. Less than forty-eight hours following the conclusion of his third season with the Brooklyn National League club, Frank signed a contract to play with the Pittsburgh Federals. That afternoon he sat in an Exposition Park box with the wife of Rebels manager Oakes during the game between Buffalo and Pittsburgh. Two days later, October 10, Allen took the mound for Pittsburgh on the final day of the Federal League season. He went seven innings and was the winning pitcher when the game stopped because of rain with the Rebels on top, 8 to 4.

"Frank L. Allen, our southpaw pitcher, who was one of the biggest disappointments of the [1914] season, has jumped to the Federal League," wrote the *Brooklyn Daily Eagle's* Thomas S. Rice.

> ...Allen's only feat of prominence was to win four games for Brooklyn on the first Western trip. He was worthless before that, and he won but four more games in the remainder of the campaign....
>
> Whether Allen signed with the Feds before the close of the National League season is not known, but it was rumored several times that he had. If such was the case, it may account for some of his poor pitching while drawing salary from Ebbets.[2]

One of Allen's biggest problems in Brooklyn was his propensity to give up a lot of bases on balls. Oakes thought the southpaw's wildness could be corrected through hard work. He also had a veteran catcher in Claude Berry, who was noted for his handling of pitchers. Berry had been in professional baseball since 1902 and once caught a remarkable 224 games during one season in the Pacific Coast League.

Allen's great start in the 1915 season stifled his critics in Brooklyn. He pitched a shutout in Kansas City on opening day and polished off the Packers again seven days later, 4 to 1, before 17,000 fans in the Rebels' home opener.

Largely due to Frank Allen's efforts on the mound, Pittsburgh made it through April two games over .500. On May 1, the Rebels began their first eastern trip of the year with the challenge to show they were not the pushovers of the previous season.

Allen would open the eastern swing at Washington Park against the Tip Tops. It was the pitcher's first appearance before the Brooklyn fans after jumping the Dodgers the previous October. President James Gilmore and all of the club owners in the Federal League were on hand for the contest.

Pittsburgh got the only runs Allen needed in the third inning. With two runners on base, Ed Konetchy redirected an Ed Lafitte offering and sent it to the deepest stretches of center field for a base-clearing triple. Allen allowed only four hits and pitched himself out of a major jam in the fifth inning after he walked a Brooklyn batter with the bases loaded. Pittsburgh won the game, 2–1, to give Allen his fifth victory of the season without a loss.

Allen's victory set the stage for a nine-win, one-loss road trip. The Rebels returned home ten games over .500 and the team would be a factor in the Federal League pennant race all season long.

The Rebels' new ace finally lost a game on May 14, when Chicago's George McConnell shut out Pittsburgh, 6 to 0, to end Allen's five-game winning streak. Among those watching the contest were members of the Kansas City Packers, who stopped over on their way from Newark to St. Louis. The two pitchers matched zeros on the scoreboard until Allen went to pieces in the top of the ninth inning after his teammates let him down. The breakdown began when third baseman Mowrey erred on Charles Hanford's easy bounder. After Zwilling walked, Allen and catcher Berry bumped into one another going after Les Mann's bunt and the bases were loaded. Art Wilson brought one run home on a single and the bases were again loaded. Joe Tinker hit a bouncer right back to the mound and Allen started what appeared to be a pitcher-to-home-to-first double play. However, umpire Barry McCormick declared Zwilling safe at home because Berry didn't have his foot on the plate when he took Allen's throw. Mann never stopped running from second base and slid home safely before Konetchy returned the throw home.[3]

Early on, Manager Oakes's pitching rotation came up short-handed because of the ineffectiveness of Howie Camnitz and the incapacity of Elmer Knetzer due to an attack of malaria. Knetzer had been the ace of the Rebels' pitching staff the previous season with nineteen victories and he did not start a game in 1915 until May 25. The Baron did not win his first game until June 3, but he still won eighteen games and was the club's most dependable starting pitcher in the second half of the season.

Despite Allen's early season success, the Rebels would have been severely handicapped if not for the emergence of a rookie right-hander named Francis Clinton Rogge. A product of Adrian (MI) College, "Clint" had posted a win-loss record of 17 and 12 with the Toronto Maple Leafs of the International League in 1914.

Rogge began to match Allen's success on the mound as the weather warmed up in May. The rookie made James Kelly's first-inning home run hold up in a 1–0 shutout of the Blues at Federal League Park in Buffalo on May 11. Kelly made solid contact with the first pitch of the game from Spitball Fred Anderson and the long drive to left field took a sharp turn before disappearing over the pavilion fence. The locals threatened in the first inning when hits by Dalton and Louden landed the former on third base, but Rogge held him there. Pittsburgh completed a three-game sweep in Buffalo to extend the Rebels' winning streak to eight games.

First-place Pittsburgh returned home on May 14 to play the team that would be the Rebels' main competition in the fight for the 1915 Federal League championship. The first game against Chicago saw the ninth-inning meltdown by Frank Allen in the visitors' 6–0 victory. The next day, Saturday, Claude Hendrix did not allow the Rebels a hit in the 10 to 0 Whales' rout.

Since Sunday baseball was illegal in the Smoky City, the two clubs took the train to Weeghman Park for a game on the sixteenth. It would be up to Rogge to salvage a victory in the series for Pittsburgh.

"Clint Rogge's curve ball proved baffling to Chicago's batters when hits would have scored runs today," a contemporary report said, "and Pittsburgh downed the Whales, 4 to 1. A steal of home by Steve Yerkes, whose work was a factor in Pittsburgh's victory, and Ed Konetchy's home run were features."[4]

The Rebels did, however, experience one loss that day. Shortstop Marty Berghammer broke the small bone in his right leg sliding into home plate during the first inning. Jack Lewis, a holdover from the 1913 team, would take over at short until Marty recovered. The absence of their shortstop was a big loss for the club, and the Rebels played under .500 baseball while he was out of the lineup. Though a light hitter, Marty was an experienced major league shortstop with a good throwing arm, having played in 151 games for the Cincinnati Reds over the previous two seasons.

"Marty's absence shot the infield to pieces," explained William McCullough, the club's business manager. "The smoothness and steadiness that featured the team's playing went when Marty was hurt.... What he lacks at bat he makes up in the field, and can surely cover a large plot of ground. He was fielding brilliantly and it was his wonderful defensive work that helped the Rebels to rise up to the high position they held."[5]

Amazingly, Berghammer returned to the field in less than a month, though he still wasn't fully healthy and could not play every day for a while. Although he batted only .243 for the season, Marty's 83 walks were the third-highest total in the league and, despite missing twenty-one games, Berghammer's 96 runs scored was only one tally off the league lead in that department.

The early season success of newcomers Rogge and former National League pitcher Bunn Hearn made the veteran, Howie Camnitz, expendable. Overweight and out of shape, the Kentucky Rosebud had posted only a 14–19 record against sub-par Federal League competition in 1914 and struck out only 82 batters in 262 innings.

On May 21, 1915, the same day Clint Rogge defeated Baltimore on a soggy field at Exposition Park, the Pittsburgh management notified Camnitz that he was unconditionally released.

The pitcher's contract contained a clause which allowed the club to release him on ten days' notice and the Rebels' official reason for the player's dismissal was Howie's violation of team rules. To that point in the 1915 season, he had started only two games for the Rebels and lost them both. Camnitz also got into an altercation with another guest at the team's New York City hotel during a road trip the first week of May. The pitcher was then sent home after a run-in with Manager Oakes.

Oakes responded to reporters' questions with a short press release: "I do not care to discuss the real reason of Howard's release, but it started in New York."[6]

Usually one of the toughest critics of the Federal League, Pittsburgh sports columnist Ralph Davis supported the Rebels' decision to release Camnitz: "No one conversant with the pitcher's case blamed Oakes and Gwinner for letting him out. He was absolutely worthless to the team, for he would not keep himself in condition. Through remorse for leaving Organized Baseball or some other reason, Cammy has been going the pace for some time, and it looks now as if he had come to the end of his string so far as the national game is concerned."[7]

Howie did not go away quietly. Camnitz wrote a letter to club President Edward Gwinner stating that he would continue to report to Exposition Park every day to fulfill his contract. If he was not paid the salary due, he would sue the Pittsburgh club. Gwinner ignored the pitcher's threat and commented that Camnitz had not "been in condition to pitch" all season and was of no further use to the team. The Kentucky pitcher decided to give up and return to his home in Louisville. He would not pitch professionally again.[8]

Some of the slack due to Camnitz's failures was taken up by left-hander Bunn Hearn. Hearn had attended Elon and the University of Mississippi, and pitched parts of three seasons for the Cardinals and Giants between 1910 and 1914. A good hitter, he once hit three home runs in a game, two in the same inning, for Springfield (Three-I League) during the 1912 season. While with Toronto in 1913, Bunn pitched 20 innings of scoreless ball in a game that ended in a 0–0 tie. After starting two games

Pittsburgh Rebels outfielder Mike Menosky (left) and Manager Ennis "Rebel" Oakes, 1915 (Chicago History Museum, SDN-060164. Photograph by *Chicago Daily News*. Original photograph has been cropped.).

for the Giants in 1913, John McGraw took him along on the celebrated world tour that off season. Hearn was on the sidelines during an exhibition game before a crowd of 60,000 in London when King George V asked to be shown how a pitcher held a ball. Bunn was summoned to the royal box and he explained the various pitcher's grips to the King of England.[9]

Hearn went 6–11, with a 3.27 earned run average for the Rebels in 1915. The North Carolinian's only Federal League shutout came on April 25, 1915, a 3–0 whitewash of the St. Louis Terriers.

Cy Barger got into the Rebels' shutout column on May 28 with a 4 to 0 victory over Buffalo at Exposition Park. Cy Rheam, the first Pittsburgh batter in the game, turned a Russ Ford pitch around for a home run and Barger held the Blues to only two hits. Manager Rebel Oakes drove in the other Pittsburgh runs with his three hits.

Barger's parents gave him the impressive name of Eros Bolivar Barger, but to his baseball teammates the Kentucky-born right-hander was known as Cy. A University of Kentucky alumnus, Barger had his best season in Organized Baseball in 1909 when he won 23 games with an earned run average of 1.00 for Rochester, then in the Eastern League. That performance with John Ganzel's league champions earned Cy a regular spot in the pitching rotation of the Brooklyn National League club. Barger won fifteen games for sixth-place Brooklyn in 1910 and got a raise to $2,700 for the following season. However, a horrible record, 1 win, 9 losses and a 5.46 earned run average, two years later seemed to finish Cy's major league career at the age of twenty-eight. That is, until the Federal League came along.

Barger labored through 1913 with Newark of the International League for only $400 a month, then he signed with the Pittsburgh Federals for 1914. He went 10–16 with a bad Rebels club that season, completing 18 of his 26 starts. In 1915 Cy became the Rebels' late-inning rescuer. He started 13 games and relieved in 21, registering 4 of his 10 wins in relief, and he held the lead for his club in five other games. Barger's 2.29 earned run average led the Pittsburgh pitching staff.

Only two starting position players on Pittsburgh's 1914 club retained first-string jobs a year later: catcher Claude Berry and manager/outfielder Rebel Oakes.

Pittsburgh had actually begun revamping the 1915 club the previous August, when it had signed twenty-six-year-old infielder Steve Yerkes, late of the Boston Red Sox. The 1912 World Series was the high point of Steve's career. He drove in the winning run for the Red Sox in Game One with a two-run seventh-inning single, and he scored the Series' winning run in the tenth inning of Game Eight (eight games were played that year because of a tie).

Yerkes was in his third season as the Red Sox' second baseman (he had been their shortstop in 1911) when the relationship between the Boston club and player began to deteriorate in 1914. After the team, with high expectations of a pennant, floundered that summer, Yerkes suffered much of the blame, not only because of a batting average around .200, but for his rumored dealings with the Federals. *The Sporting News* reported on August 20, "There are several men of no use to the team pulling down fat salaries and these President Lannin will release outright. One or two of these men have been flirting with the Federals and will have their chance to go to the outlaws."

As the Red Sox fell farther and farther behind the Philadelphia A's in the pennant race, Boston owner Joseph Lannin let it be known that several players, including Hendrickson, Bedient, Engle, and Yerkes would not be back with the Red Sox in 1915.[10]

Though only twenty-six years old, Yerkes was given his unconditional release by the Red Sox on August 31, 1914. Steve planned to join the Federals anyway once his Boston contract expired and quickly found a place with the Rebels.[11]

After earning $3,500 a season with the Red Sox, Yerkes signed with the Federal League's

Pittsburgh club for $6,500. Steve found himself at third base because of Eddie Lennox's injured ankle. In the final six weeks of the 1914 season, Yerkes batted .338, and was shifted back to his accustomed position of second base a year later.

The Rebels' new third baseman, Mike Mowrey, was only considered by Pittsburgh after Jimmy Austin ignored the Federal League contract he signed and jumped back to the St. Louis Browns before spring training began. Mowrey had been without a job in Organized Baseball since he was cut by the Pittsburgh Pirates the previous summer.

After being traded by the Reds to the St. Louis Cardinals in 1910, Mowrey gained a reputation for defending the bunt and was touted as one of the best-fielding third basemen in baseball. Mowrey employed an unorthodox, though efficient, method of fielding ground balls. He would slap a batted ball to the ground with his glove, quickly pick it up with his bare hand and throw the runner out. Employing this technique, Mike led National League third basemen in double plays three of his four seasons in St. Louis.[12] Though only a lifetime .256 hitter, Mike had a reputation as a good batter in the clutch.

Hampered by injuries, Mowrey played in only 79 games for the Pirates before he was put on waivers in July 1914. At the time of his release, Mike's fielding average at third base was .960, seventeen points higher than the eventual National League leader at the position. The Chicago Cubs made an offer to Mike later in the season, but he decided to play independent baseball for the remainder of the year. A late addition to the roster, Mike joined the Rebels at their training site in Augusta, Georgia, on March 22.

Mike's 1915 season in the Steel City made Rebels fans forget all about the loss of the light-hitting Jimmy Austin. Mowrey played in all but two of Pittsburgh's 153 games, led the Federal League's third basemen in assists and fielding percentage, and batted .280.

In addition to right fielder Oakes, newcomers Jim Kelly and Al Wickland gave Pittsburgh a serviceable major league outfield. Kelly, whose real name was Robert John Taggert, played 32 games with the Pirates in 1914 and assumed center field duties for the Rebels in 1915. One of his biggest hits as a Rebel came on July 3, 1915, in Chicago. Pittsburgh and the Whales were deadlocked at 3–3 in the eighth inning when the Rebels managed to load the bases against Claude Hendrix. Lewis cleared the bases with a three-run triple to give Pittsburgh the 6–3 victory.

When Les Mann joined a solid Chicago Whales outfield that also included center fielder Dutch Zwilling and right fielder Max Flack, Al Wickland became the odd man out. After managing only a .244 batting average in 86 plate appearances with Chicago in 1915, the lefty-hitting Wickland was sold to the Pittsburgh Federals in June. In his return Weeghman Park for the first time as a member of the Rebels, Al was generously cheered by the 5,000 or so in attendance, then he stung his former employers with three hits. Al became a regular in the Rebels' outfield, batted .310 in 109 games, and was a key component in Pittsburgh's drive for the Federal League pennant. After Buffalo got off to a very bad start and was essentially out of the pennant chase by the first of July, the Blues offered to trade outfielder Jack Dalton to Pittsburgh, but the Rebels' budget couldn't accommodate the former National Leaguer's hefty contract.

The heart of the Rebels' team was the big first baseman, Ed Konetchy. Koney was a powerful right-handed hitter who stood upright in the batter's box, choked up on the bat, and was noted for his vicious line drives to the outfield. In his only season in the Federal League, Konetchy posted his career highs in batting average (.314), hits (181), and triples (18), finished in the top five in almost every offensive category, and won the fielding triple crown. With the steady presence of Koney at first base the Rebels posted a team fielding average five points better than any other club among the 24 major league teams. Konetchy, Marty Berghammer and Mike Mowrey led the Federal League in fielding at their respective infield positions in 1915.

By winning the final game of a four-game series in Kansas City on Saturday, June 8, the Rebels improved their record to 25–18. They did not win another game until June 15. The club was not done in by opposing teams, or by the weather, but by the outrageous schedule devised by the Federal League.

James L. Long wrote in *Sporting Life* after the team left for the road trip on May 29, "The Gwinnites will travel 3851 miles on the trip — not counting exhibition jumps on the side — and will spend nine nights on sleeping cars. With 20 persons in the party, railroad and sleeping car fare will exceed $2000 and hotels and meals about $4000 more, making the trip cost $8000."[13]

The Rebels won the game in Kansas City on the eighth, then hurried to the railroad station to catch the train for a Sunday game at Weeghman Park. After being blown out by the Whales, 10–5, Pittsburgh had five straight scheduled off days. Manager Oakes sent his team barnstorming around Illinois until the schedule had them in St. Louis. There, the Rebels lost three straight to the Terriers over two days. They returned to Exposition Park on July 8 upon completion of a 33-game, 37-day road trip! When the trip ended in Chicago on July 5, the Rebels' record was seven games over .500, exactly where they were when the team left Pittsburgh on May 29. Upon their arrival home from Chicago, bad weather handed the Rebels five consecutive days off.

A bright spot during the Rebels' bizarre June was Clint Rogge. On Sunday, June 20, a crowd of nearly 10,000 watched the rookie throw a 2–0, one-hit shutout against the Peps at Harrison. Rogge walked only one and the only hit he allowed was a single by Newark's first baseman Emil Huhn. Al Wickland's triple off Earl Moseley in the third drove in Berry and Berghammer with the only runs in the game. The Rebels then were shut out themselves in the nightcap by Newark's George Kaiserling.

On July 25, Frank Allen ran his record to 14 and 6 with a victory over Dave Davenport in St. Louis. Allen and the Rebels trailed, 1 to 0, going into the eighth inning. Mowrey opened that frame with a triple and scored the tying run on Yerkes's single. Pittsburgh's next two batters reached to load the bases and an obviously rattled Davenport forced in a run by walking Al Wickland. Rebel Oakes grounded a pitch back to Davenport, but the Terriers' pitcher fumbled it and another run scored. Berghammer scored the fourth run of the inning on a sacrifice fly by Konetchy, and Allen shut the door on the home team in their final two at-bats to preserve a 4 to 1 Rebels victory.

32

The Top Whale Goes Down

On May 9, 1915, the nation's sports pages headlined the news that "Joe Tinker, manager of the Chicago team of the Federal League, has suffered a rupture in his right side and will be out of the game as a player for a month, if not for life."

In the course of pre-game practice in Harrison on May 7, Tinker felt something give in his side. He became nauseated and left the field, but directed the game against the Peps from the bench. Joe inserted himself into the game in the ninth inning as a pinch hitter with the tying runs on base. Newark's Harry Moran threw an inside curve ball that struck Joe on the knee, but umpire McCormick declared that Tinker had swung at it and called him back to the batter's box. The Whales' manager protested so vigorously that he was ejected from the game. Chicago lost, 5–4.[1]

The disputed check swing apparently aggravated Tinker's problem. Following the game, the pain in his side was so severe Joe consulted a physician and was told he had a rupture. Tinker was warned to rest and disobedience would mean an operation.[2]

Saturday was "Joe Tinker Day" at Peppers Park and the Chicago manager was presented with a gift from his admirers. Joe was limping and visibly in pain as he approached home plate to accept a floral arrangement. Tinker admitted his future as an active player was none too bright due to his injury. As for the game itself, Newark's Earl Moseley whitewashed Tinker's team, 6 to 0, Chicago's sixth straight loss.[3] Meanwhile, Pittsburgh was in the midst of an eight-game winning streak that moved them past Newark and Chicago into first place.

Only four days after his injury in New Jersey, Joe returned to the field in the bottom half of the ninth in Brooklyn after shortstop Jimmy Smith was pinch-hit for in the top of the inning. He next appeared in the field as a late-inning replacement at third base during a game in Pittsburgh on May 14. On June 17, Tinker started at shortstop in the second game of a double-header in Buffalo and went 0 for 3. Just a month shy of his thirty-fifth birthday, Joe was through as a player. He would only appear as an occasional defensive replacement over the remainder of the season.

Tinker appeared in only 31 games in all of 1915, partly due to the fact the manager did not play his first game at shortstop until two weeks into the season. Manager Tinker had decided to play the youngster Jimmy Smith at shortstop so he could devote his attention to coaching the team. This idea was sidetracked on April 23 in Kansas City, when Smith was badly spiked by Grover Gilmore. Gilmore overslid second base on a stolen base attempt, and, in his effort to get back to the bag, his spikes tore a two-inch gash in Smith's hand. As Jimmy was being taken to a doctor for stitches, Tinker assumed the shortstop position.

The loss of Tinker from the lineup twenty games into the season severely handicapped the Whales' offense and infield defense. Due to the earlier Jimmy Smith injury, Rollie Zeider had to move from third base to shortstop and Harry Fritz was plugged in at third. Back in March of 1914 Monte Cross, former American League shortstop and newly hired Federal League umpire, recommended Fritz to Tinker. After batting .313 and stealing 50 bases with Wilmington of the Tri-State League in 1913, Harry finished the season with Connie Mack's team in Philadelphia. After Cross maintained that the Athletics' rookie infielder was a "young Lajoie," Tinker sent Fritz a Federal League contract, which was accepted. As it turned out, Fritz was not even close to being the next Lajoie.

Light-hitting Jimmy Smith returned to shortstop duties on May 12, but the club's infield woes did not end there. Harry Fritz wasn't satisfactory at third base and first baseman Fred Beck was struggling at the plate, destined to bat only .223 in his final major league season. Zeider, who was batting in the low .200s, missed some games due to the illness of his wife, and the injuries suffered by his teammates forced him to alternate between three infield positions (83 games at second, 30 at third base and 21 at shortstop). In contrast to the team's struggling offense, the Whales' three leading pitchers had higher batting averages than most of the infielders. Mordecai Brown batted .293, former first baseman McConnell hit .248, and Hendrix posted a .265 batting average. Between them, Hendrix and McConnell were used as pinch hitters seventeen times.

Pitcher Claude Hendrix was a good hitter. He batted .322 during his 23-game-win season for the Pirates in 1912 and would finish his career as a .241 lifetime major league hitter (in the dead ball era), with 39 doubles, 17 triples and 13 home runs. He also was used as a pinch hitter 49 times.

On May 15, Claude Hendrix did not allow the Rebels a hit during a 10 to 0 shutout at Exposition Park. The Chicago ace gave up three walks, but none of the resulting base runners advanced further than first base. After the seventh inning, the 8,000 or so in attendance at Pittsburgh's home park began to cheer for Hendrix. After Mann corralled James Savage's long foul fly for the final out, many of the fans poured onto the field to congratulate the former Pirates hurler.[4]

Just when everything seemed to be getting better for Tinker's Whales, bad weather contributed to the team's woes. Eight home games between May 18 and May 30 were rained out. On May 28, the Chicago Weather Bureau reported that it had rained 21 days that month. Chicago would play 31 double-headers (20 at home) in 1915, largely because of the weather. Only three of the home twin bills were on the regular schedule, May 31, July 5, and September 27, and they had one pre-arranged double-header, in St. Louis, on September 6. In comparison, Chicago had only played seventeen double-headers during 1914. After being atop the league with a 12–5 record on May 3, Chicago lost 17 of their next 28 games.

After losing three straight games to rain, the Whales returned to action against the Tip Tops at soggy Weeghman Park on May 21. Hendrix blanked Brooklyn in all except the first inning and led, with a triple and a home run, the attack on Tom Seaton that resulted in a 9 to 2 victory for Chicago. In the third inning, Brooklyn's shortstop Al Halt booted a sure double-play grounder, and the next batter, Hendrix, drove a triple to center that scored the two Whales on base. Brooklyn manager Lee Magee dropped an easy pop fly off Jimmy Smith's bat to open the fourth inning and two outs later Hendrix drove a Seaton fast ball off the noggin of a fan in the left field bleachers for a two-run home run.

Hendrix's win seemed to inspire the Whales, as they won five of the next six. Then the rains returned. Chicago lost five games to the weather from May 25 through the twenty-ninth.

On Friday June 4, George McConnell was hit hard and lasted only three innings on the mound against St. Louis. The 8 to 3 loss to the Terriers sent Chicago into the second division of the league standings. The Whales went on to lose all five games of the weekend series to St. Louis.

Infielder Rollie Zeider was severely spiked during a game in Kansas City on June 13, but received a break when bad weather idled the Whales for the next two days. Then Rollie became ill and the desperate Whales purchased Tex Westerzil from Brooklyn. Unfortunately, the third baseman showed up in Chicago with a lame leg.[5] First baseman Beck was benched for a couple of weeks after an argument with Manager Tinker and Bill Jackson, a notoriously weak hitter, had to fill in.

To this point in the season, pitchers Rankin Johnson and Ad Brennan were plagued with sore arms and were of marginal usefulness. The Whales attempted to dispose of its two sore-armed hurlers in late June. President Weeghman intended to ship Ad Brennan to Springfield of the Colonial League in May, but the veteran right-hander balked and the Whales eventually had to retain him. On June 25, the Baltimore Federals announced the purchase of Rankin Johnson from Chicago. A day later, Johnson pitched a complete game, a 5 to 3 Terrapins victory over St. Louis. Johnson won his first four starts with Baltimore, then succumbed to the depression that overwhelmed the Baltimore club and won only three of fourteen decisions the rest of the season.

Catching, which wasn't considered an offensive position back then, was a Whales strength. Though limited to 87 games behind the plate because of various ailments, Art Wilson batted .305 and hit 7 home runs. Wilson's defense was hampered by a problem with his throwing arm, leaving the brunt of the catching duties that summer to Bill Fischer. Fischer squatted behind the platter in 80 games and batted a robust .329. After riding the bench for over a month, Wilson made the trip to Youngstown for a visit with Bonesetter Reese in late August. The expert of manipulation snapped a couple of misplaced cartilages in Wilson's right arm back into place and told the catcher to play ball at once.[6]

On Saturday, June 26, Manager Joe Tinker replaced Farrell at second base late in the second game of a double-header in Brooklyn. During the eighth inning, a Brooklyn batter sent a hot grounder to Tinker. Joe had plenty of time to toss the ball to shortstop Smith and force the runner coming from first base. Instead, Tinker remembered that the runner, Hap Myers, had spiked him a couple of years back. Joe jabbed the ball into Hap's stomach as he neared second base. Myers went right through to the bag and waited until he was called out before he said anything. As Myers walked back to the bench, he made a disparaging remark to the Chicago manager, prompting Tinker to hurl the ball into Hap's face. When Myers went after Tinker, Jimmy Smith jumped on the much larger Brooklyn player's back. Members of both teams spilled out onto the field and it was hard to determine whether they were helping their respective teammates or trying to separate them. President James Gilmore happened to be at the game and issued suspensions to the two antagonists.[7]

On July 5, Charlie Weeghman attempted to return Tex Westerzil to Brooklyn on the grounds that the player was damaged merchandise. Brooklyn's Lee Magee wired Chicago that he wouldn't take Westerzil back. The Whales maintained they had taken Tex on a trial basis, but President Gilmore interjected that Brooklyn made a straight deal and Chicago had to keep the player. Weeghman thought he was off the hook on July 16 when Fielder Jones accepted the third baseman to play in St. Louis, where a replacement for the ill Charlie Deal had not been found. After Tex managed only four hits in 24 at-bats, St. Louis returned him to Chicago and the Whales' owner was again stuck with the unwanted player's salary.

Westerzil went on to play 49 games with Chicago and his performance was little improvement over Fritz's. Tex did sparkle against his former club. After Chicago beat Brooklyn 3 to

1 on August 5 at Washington Park, the *New York Times* noted, "When the Chicago team was here some weeks ago Tex Westerzil was purchased from the Brookfeds, and yesterday he showed that he was just as lively with the willow as ever. He accumulated three hits in four times up, and one of these was a two-bagger that paved the way for the first run."[8]

33

Buffalo's Got the Blues

The city of Buffalo had high hopes for its Federal League club going into the 1915 season. The directors of the club put in an additional $75,000 to finance the franchise for the upcoming season. The team would have Hal Chase and former Boston Red Sox infielder Clyde Engle for a full year, plus they had added the Cardinals' young catcher, Ivy Wingo, the International League's best shortstop in Wilbur "Roxey" Roach, former Red Sox pitcher Hugh Bedient, and the minor leagues' latest pitching sensation, Howard Ehmke.

Bedient first gained national attention while pitching for a semi-pro team from Falconer, New York, when, on July 25, 1908, he struck out 42 batters in what was heralded as a world's record. He accomplished the feat in 23 innings against Corry, Pennsylvania, his team finally winning the game by a score of 3 to 1. When the wire services picked up the story, Bedient received offers from nineteen professional baseball teams. The Boston Red Sox drafted Hugh from Fall River (New England League) in 1911, then released him to Providence (Eastern League). In January 1912, the Jersey City International League club bought Bedient's contact for $750 and made a handsome profit two months later when the Red Sox paid $6,000 for Hugh and four other players.[1]

Bedient won twenty games as a Red Sox rookie in 1912 and picked up another victory in the World Series when he beat Christy Mathewson 2 to 1 in the fifth game. He also pitched the first seven innings of the final game, won by the Red Sox in the tenth. After besting the World Champion Philadelphia Athletics in his first start of the 1914 season, Bedient fell on hard times and struggled to an 8–12 record. Boston planned to release him to Providence during the off season because of the pitcher's "poor form and poor health." However, Hugh announced on October 18, 1914, that he had signed a two-year contract to pitch for the Buffalo Federal League club. Two days later, Boston owner Lannin officially released Bedient to his International League club though the move was pointless at that juncture.

Just when things looked brightest for the 1915 season, Buffalo business manager Dick Carroll was hired away by Brooklyn, Ivy Wingo jumped back to the National League, and Roxey Roach decided to stay in Toronto. The weather at the Buffeds' spring training site in Athens, Georgia, was the coldest in fifty years, leading to an abbreviated training season. The team's pitchers did not get enough work and were not ready when the season began. On the way north for the club's opening game in Brooklyn a driving rod on their train's locomotive split in two. Disaster was averted because the train was going slowly at the time, and nobody was injured.[2] The mishap was a precursor to the first half of the 1915 season.

Hugh Bedient's inaugural Federal League start for the newly anointed "Blues" came on opening day and he was bounced around in a 13 to 9 loss. Things got so bad that on April

12, Brooklyn base runners stole ten bases against Buffalo's catcher Walter Blair and three Blues pitchers. Brooklyn's Benny Kauff stole second, third and home in one inning. Buffalo starter Gene Krapp walked four batters in only one and two-thirds of an inning before he was relieved by Howard Ehmke, who was making his major league debut. The shaky twenty-year-old rookie was pulled following the third inning after he walked four Tip Tops and hit two others. Buffalo lost, 7–5, in the sluggish contest that featured 21 bases on balls and saw 27 runners stranded on the bases. Twenty-five players appeared in the game that took two hours and forty-five minutes to complete.

The Blues played their first home game on April 17 after a day's delay because of rain and lost. The opening day crowd was announced at 18,281, a figure disputed by friends of Organized Baseball. Russell Ford pitched his first game without the benefit of his emery ball on April 24 and last-place Baltimore routed the emery paper-free Ford, 10 to 4.

After a fourteen-inning loss in Newark on April 25, Buffalo's star first baseman, Hal Chase, was assaulted that evening as he was walking down South 2nd Street in Harrison. A Newark fan, Billy Quinn, began heckling Chase about the Blues' loss and the pair exchanged blows. Paddy McGuigan, a former pugilist and saloon keeper, joined the brawl and landed a couple of blows on Chase before police arrived and broke up the fight. Chase pointed out the antagonist Quinn to a policeman, but the gathering mob prevented his arrest. To make matters worse, Chase went into a prolonged batting slump after the scuffle.[3]

Howard Ehmke made his first appearance as a starting pitcher for Buffalo against Pittsburgh on May 13 and the phenom was pounded in a 12–7 loss. The promising rookie would start only one more game in 1915. Due to an elbow injury, Ehmke was used sparingly, appearing on the mound in only 54 innings for the entire season.

On May 24, the Blues lost in fourteen innings to the Whales in Chicago. Present on the Buffalo bench that day was the former captain of the Chicago White Sox, Harry Lord. "I accepted terms from the Buffalo club because there were no other offers to accept," Lord said.[4] Three days later, the thirty-three-year-old veteran of eight American League seasons became Buffalo's regular third baseman.

Lord had inspired his teammates in Chicago with the hustle that earned him the White Sox captaincy. However, his play became inconsistent. After a career high of .321 in 1911, Harry's average declined in the three succeeding seasons. As an infielder, Lord had little range. In 1913, he set single-season American League records for fewest chances accepted and fewest assists by a third baseman that played in 150 or more games.

The White Sox sank to seventh place after a 3 to 2 loss to the Nationals in Washington on May 12, 1914. In the sixth inning, Clyde Milan of the Nationals tripled to right field. First baseman Hal Chase took the relay from the outfield, spun around and fired a throw right over the third-base bag. Unfortunately, Lord was not on the base. Milan scampered home with the deciding run and Chase was charged with an undeserved error.[5]

After the players had gone to bed that night, Lord packed his bags, said goodbye to roommate Hal Chase and left for a midnight train out of Washington. Chase reported Lord's departure to manager Kid Gleason the next morning.[6] Though it was surmised that the captain of the Sox left because of the team's poor play and his mental mistake in the Washington game, his batting average of .188 for the 21 games he had played probably had something to do with his "retirement." Chase jumped to the Federal League six weeks later.

The following May, Lord went to Comiskey in search of a job, but the White Sox had no openings. Charles Comiskey and Lord discussed the possibility of the player's purchase of an interest in the New England League team in his home town of Portland, Maine.

"He was a free agent and at liberty to go where he could make the best bargain," acknowledged Comiskey upon hearing of Lord's association with the Buffalo Federals. "When he asked for his release he said he wanted to buy into the Portland team. I gave him his release with no strings attached. I suppose he couldn't buy into the Portland Club and found Buffalo offered the best thing in sight."[7]

The Buffalo directors' $75,000 in fresh money did not last long once the 1915 season got underway. The team's poor showing, combined with the miserable weather, reduced attendance to a mere trickle. Desperate for cash, the Blues (as did other Federal League clubs) reduced their prices. Pavilion seats that had cost 75 cents became 35 cents, and a spot in the bleachers was a dime. By the end of the season, the club was over $50,000 in debt, and it was announced that $100,000 would be needed to keep it afloat going into the 1916 season.[8]

The Blues continued to play poorly and by June 1 they were in the cellar. From April 23 to June 4, Hal Chase batted only .182, bringing his overall average down to .217. Solly Hofman came to the Blues in a trade with Brooklyn, but the former Chicago Cubs outfielder batted only .234 in 109 games.

If things weren't already bad enough for Manager Schlafly, he was disabled by a case of influenza in May.[9] The manager was the first to pay the price for the club's failures and he "resigned" on June 4. Schlafly was replaced for one day by catcher Walter Blair and then third baseman Harry Lord took over.

Sporting Life editorialized on June 5: "Larry Schlafly has a contract with the Buffalo Federal League club which runs for another year.... It was he who induced many organized baseball players to make the long and uncertain jump, and if their institution does keep on going

Larry Schlafly, manager, Buffalo Federal League club, 1915 (George Grantham Bain Collection, Library of Congress).

ahead and they profit in better salaries probably they will not forget the man who worked indefatigably to make the independent organization a success."[10]

Schlafly served as playing manager of the Bradford, Pennsylvania, Drillers in the class D Interstate League in 1916. The following year, Larry was diagnosed with pulmonary tuberculosis, though he was still able to play semi-pro ball in Canton, Ohio. In 1918, Schlafly acted as a scout in the Western League and on the Pacific Coast for the St. Louis Cardinals. The following baseball season, Schlafly umpired in the Western League until early June, when he took a leave of absence and went home to Beach City, Ohio, for a rest. On June 19, he was diagnosed with tubercular spinal meningitis. The former Buffeds' manager died on June 27, 1919, at the age of forty.[11]

The Blues experienced marked improvement under Lord's managerial leadership, winning 60 of their 107 remaining games, and the team almost made it into the first division. Hal Chase returned to his 1914 form, batted .291 and led the league in home runs with 17. The Buffalo club finally got the quality shortstop it wanted when the coveted Roxey Roach jumped the Toronto Internationals to finally join the Blues on June 21.

When Whales pitcher George McConnell told Joe Tinker that Roach would be receptive to offers from the Federal League, the manager was obviously interested, considering Chicago's problems at shortstop. Since Roach had signed a Federal League contract with Buffalo during the off season and then reneged on it, Tinker contacted President Robertson of the Blues to reach a deal whereby the Whales could negotiate with the International League player. However, Buffalo needed a shortstop as well and offered Roach a proposition that he accepted.[12]

The Blues' top starting pitchers during the 1915 season were not Ford, Bedient or Krapp as one would suspect, but Al Schulz and Fred Anderson. Schulz won 21 games, five of them shutouts. He came close to getting a no-hitter against Pittsburgh on August 6, the only safety a double by Rebels catcher Paddy O'Connor that went right over first base.

Hugh Bedient was a bust as a starting pitcher, going 12 and 17 in 30 starts, but he was the league's leading relief pitcher. In 23 games in which he performed as a substitute hurler, Hugh won three, lost one and held the lead in ten other games (saves) for his club.

Conversely, star pitcher Russell Ford fell on hard times after his main pitch was declared illegal. With the emery ball legal in 1914, his record was 20–6; without it in 1915, he won 5 and lost 9. On July 13, Buffalo gave Ford his unconditional release. President Robertson told the press, "Ford has won but two games for us this season and we could not afford to carry him any longer at the salary he was getting."[13]

Ten days later, Ford was re-signed by Buffalo, but only for about half of his original salary of $1,000 a month. Russ would be released again before the end of the season.

34

"This Season You Are Playing for Me"

On Sunday, June 1, 1915, Kansas City's one-run victory over St. Louis moved the Packers into a first-place tie with Pittsburgh atop the Federal League standings. The win was left-hander Nick Cullop's eighth straight, while Eddie Plank of St. Louis was the loser, 3 to 2. A day later Kansas City took over sole possession of first place after Gene Packard won a pitchers' battle with the Terriers' Dave Davenport. Davenport allowed only one safety until the eighth inning, when the Packers' Al Shaw reached Dave for a triple and Pep Goodwin drove in the game's only run with his single. Kansas City would run its winning streak to five before losing to Chicago on June 11. Who would have thought just three months earlier, when the club's stockholders were fighting just to save the franchise for Kansas City, that this team of career minor leaguers would be fourteen games over .500 on July 1?

The Kansas City club's position at the top of the standings also paid off at the gate. On June 13, more than 15,000 watched a double-header with Chicago, the largest crowd ever to attend a baseball game in Kansas City up to that time. Ropes were strung all around the field and special ground rules were necessary. *The Sporting News* reported, "Kansas City boasts that it is the best drawing crowd in the Federal League and figures show it." On Sunday, July 3, 3,657 turned out for the game against St. Louis, and the next day four times that number attended two games at Gordon & Koppel Field.[1]

Looking back, beat reporter E.W. Cochrane observed, "[In 1915] a party of men got together and paid the club's debt. They said they would give Kansas City a chance to show that it would support that kind of baseball. It did support it better than any other town in the circuit, but not enough to make it a paying proposition. It likely would have paid, except for the weather."

The Sporting News reported:

> The salary list ran to almost $68,000. Men like Bill Bradley were getting salaries equal to some stars in the National or American Leagues. Several members of the team were getting more than $5,000 each and outside of Gene Packard and Nick Cullop there was not a man on the club worth that price unless it was George Stovall, who might have been worth it as a manager, but not as a player.[2]

After the Packers were made almost a unanimous choice to finish last in the 1915 Federal League standings, Manager Stovall told his charges, "Boys, last year you were all playing for the Federal League and yourselves. This season you are playing for me and I've got to make good." The players apparently took his thinly veiled threat seriously.[3]

"I don't care so much about batting," Stovall explained to *Baseball Magazine* editor F.C.

Lane. "Of course a winning club must make hits, but give me a club of fast young players with good arms, and that is the main thing."[4]

George Stovall actually started his professional baseball career as a pitcher. "I worked on the farm until I was twenty-two," he explained. "It is true that I played baseball the large part of the playing season until after I was twenty, but the farm was always the base of supplies.... I worked long hours and the only amusement I had was to play baseball on Saturday afternoon and Sunday. I used to slip into town on those days and play with the other kids."[5]

George became a member of a Kansas City area amateur team known as the Hagan Tailors. Alumni of that team included Joe Tinker and Johnny Kling, both of whom became major league managers.

"I went to Seattle in 1901, when I was twenty," Stovall remembered, "...I pitched two games there and threw my arm out. When I found I could not pitch any more I tried other positions, particularly first base."[6]

George played with several different teams in the Northwest over the next two years. During the time he played in the Pacific Coast League, Stovall established his home in Southern California and became involved in the orange growing business.

In June 1904 George was named player/manager of the Burlington team in the Iowa State League and a month later he was sold to the Cleveland American League club. He just missed playing with his older brother Jesse, who was a pitcher with Cleveland in 1903. On October 7, 1904, George hit a home run off Jesse, who was pitching for the Detroit Tigers. Stovall would be the Naps' regular first baseman for eight years.

Often forgotten within all the rhetoric about Stovall's irascible personality and sometimes volatile behavior was that he was a good manager. When Nap Lajoie voluntarily stepped down as manager of the Cleveland club in May 1911, team captain Stovall was picked to replace him.

"A winning manager is the rarest treasure in baseball," editorialized F.C. Lane, "...but there is one rarer. That is the case of a manager who makes good who far exceeds all expectations which were held of him.... George Stovall, all inexperienced as he was in the difficult role of a manager, raised the shattered [Cleveland] club from hopeless seventh to aspiring third. And then he was deposed and his place given to another."[7]

During the off season, Cleveland dumped George in favor of Harry Davis, the highly regarded Athletics captain. George was dealt to the Browns, and by mid-season 1912, Davis was out in Cleveland and Stovall had replaced Bobby Wallace as manager in St. Louis. The St. Louis club had little major league caliber talent, but under Stovall, the Browns finished out of the American League cellar for the first time in three years. A year later came the publicized spitting incident with umpire Charlie Ferguson that ultimately led to George's association with the Federal League.

A quick look at the Kansas City Packers' 1915 team statistics confirm that the starting pitching of Packard and Cullop, with frequent assists from Chief Johnson and Alex Main, was the Packers' saving grace. The Packers were last in runs scored and was tied for the worst batting average in the league.

Cullop almost wasn't with the Packers at all in 1915. The "trade" engineered by the Wards the previous winter, in which Nick was to go to Brooklyn, was finally straightened out on the eve of the regular season. Bert Maxwell was returned to Brooklyn and Cullop rejoined Kansas City. The contracts and salaries of two other former Tip Tops, Bill Bradley and Al Shaw, were assumed by the Packers.

With the exception of the lefty-hitting catcher, Ted Easterly, and first baseman Stovall, there was very little major league experience in the Packers' lineup. Partly due to nagging hand injuries, the thirty-six-year-old Stovall played only 129 games at first base and batted .231, the lowest average of his twelve-year major league career.

Easterly, at thirty, was a veteran of five American League seasons with Cleveland and Chicago before he joined the Kansas City Federals in 1914. He batted over .300 three straight American League seasons before slumping to .237, mostly as a pinch hitter, in 1913. He rebounded a year later to finish third in the Federal League batting race with an average of .335. Ted finished his seven seasons in the major leagues with a career batting average right at .300 in 704 games.

If the Packers had a batting star it was second baseman William Jennings Kenworthy. Kenworthy attended Muskingurn College and signed his first professional baseball contract with Beaver Falls, Pa., in 1907. He bounced around between minor league clubs in Ohio until late 1910, when he was purchased by the Boston Red Sox, then sent to Denver.

The Denver Grizzlies were the class of the Western League in 1911 and 1912, winning successive pennants. In 1911, Kenworthy was a second-line pitcher, winning 9 and losing 3. However, he hit so well, Manager Jack Hendricks began to use Bill as a substitute outfielder. In 65 games (178 at-bats), Kenworthy hit .315. A year later, he played well enough in the outfield to receive a call up to the Washington American League Club. He debuted in the major leagues on August 28, 1912, but batted only .237 in what was left of the season.[8]

Kenworthy played with Sacramento of the Pacific Coast League in 1913 and became a second baseman. Though he was never a great fielder at second, Bill's hitting was well above par for the position. During 1913, he batted .297 in 177 games for the Solons with 104 runs scored, 16 triples, and 60 stolen bases.

In August 1915 Kenworthy revealed that he was heir to a million dollars from the estate of his uncle, Joshua Kenworthy of London, England. The Englishman had burned to death in a hotel in Connecticut while touring the United States the previous year. The story went that Bill hit a home run on the day he learned of his windfall. Joshua Kenworthy's fortune, said to be fifty million dollars, was divided among relatives in England, Ireland and the States. Because of the onset of the World War, the disposition of the estate was delayed and Bill kept his good fortune secret until he received definite word that his claim had been allowed.[9]

Bill signed with the Federal League in 1914 and batted .317 for Kansas City that season. He was joined on the Packers by two former Denver Grizzlies teammates, pitcher Ben Harris and outfielder Grover Gilmore.

Kenworthy's greatest day in the Federal League came on June 13, 1914, during a game between Kansas City and Brooklyn at Gordon-Koppel Field. In the second inning of the first game, Bill drove a home run over the wall with a runner on base, but by the time he came to bat in the eighth inning his team trailed by one run.

The report in the *Kansas City Star* read:

> Tomas Seaton, whose advertising agent says he is the premier pitcher of the Federal League, strutted out to save a wavering ball game yesterday afternoon. The bases were bowed down with much weight when Thomas ascended the hill and Judge William Kenworthy was at the plate. And the very first ball that came sailing up to the judge went sailing right over the fence, carrying four runs with it ... before the crowd had ceased cheering Stovall kissed another one over the boards.[10]

The two round-trippers gave Kenworthy the league lead in home runs over Ed Lennox of Pittsburgh, 8 to 7. Bill would finish the year with 15 home runs, tied with Chicago's Dutch Zwilling for the most in the circuit.

In its first year as a major league, the Federal League advised its clubs not to tamper with players claimed by Minneapolis of the American Association, because of that club's arrangement with Charley Weeghman. After the Cincinnati Reds sold rookie second baseman Johnny Rawlings to Minneapolis during the summer, he refused to report to the minor league club. The St. Louis Federals were interested in signing Rawlings, but yielded to the league's wishes and backed off the player. George Stovall had no such compunction. As he saw it, no club in Organized Baseball was any better than any other.

On July 28, 1914, the Kansas City Federals announced that Rawlings had accepted $500 in cash and signed a two-year contract to play for the Packers. Rawlings became the Packers' starting shortstop for the remainder of the club's existence in the Federal League.[11]

When asked why he picked up Rawlings after the Reds sent him to the minors, Stovall, in his characteristic manner, replied: "Well, some of my boys had played with him in the winter league out on the Coast, and they recommended him, but then I just had a hunch that he was a good man because Garry Herrmann was willing to let him go. You know; Garry always turns loose the best ball players."[12]

Rawlings would have a successful major league career that lasted until 1926, but in his days with the Packers Johnny was overmatched by big league pitching, batting only .212 and .216 in his two seasons in the Federal League. His backup, Pep Goodwin, who once stole third base with the bag already occupied by a Kansas City base runner, wasn't much better at .236.

Rawlings returned to the major leagues with the Braves in 1917 and became a dependable infielder. He played on three World Series champions and, while the starting second baseman on the 1921 New York Giants, Johnny batted .333 in the eight-game World Series of that year against the New York Yankees.

The Packers' third baseman was George Perring, a teammate of Stovall's in Cleveland, 1908 through 1910. Incidentally, Perring was the shortstop in Addie Joss' perfect game for Cleveland in 1908. He batted .278 and .259 in his two Federal League seasons. Stovall's backup at third was thirty-seven-year-old Bill Bradley, who was just riding out his lucrative contract. Bill got into 61 games and batted only .192.

Center fielder Chet Chadbourne was a career minor leaguer whose major league experience amounted to only 48 games other than his two seasons in the Federal League. Chet never could adapt to major league pitching although he stayed around long enough to accumulate 3,216 hits in the minors, mostly in the Pacific Coast League. Chadbourne's main assets were his speed and range in the outfield. He led the Federal League in outfielders' assists with 34 in 1914 and in fielding average in 1915.

Chadbourne's ability in center was especially crucial because left fielder Al Shaw was a slow and unreliable fielder. Shaw's glove work was too much of a liability for the organized major leagues, but he stuck with the Federals because of his bat. Al had the fourth-highest average in the league in 1914 when he batted .324 with Brooklyn.

It wasn't expected that the upstarts from Kansas City would remain in first place long and would soon drop to the wayside as Newark had done after a brief stay at the top in the first week in June. However, the Packers' pitchers kept Stovall's team in pennant contention until the middle of August.

Because the Fourth of July fell on Sunday, the Kansas City club chose to celebrate the holiday with a double-header on Monday. Some 4,761 fans turned out for the morning game and saw Alex Main beat Bob Groom of St. Louis, 1–0, on a ninth-inning run. A much larger crowd, reported to be 9,783 strong, squeezed into Gordon and Koppel Field for the afternoon contest. St. Louis gained a split for the day with a four-run fifth-inning rally after Eddie Plank had to be relieved by Doc Crandall with the Terriers down, 3 to 0.

On July 6, successive singles in the seventh inning by Easterly, Packard and Chadbourne produced the only run of the game as Cullop and Packard combined to shut out St. Louis in the finale of the series. For the second time within a month, Dave Davenport lost a game to Kansas City by a 1–0 score.

In the first game of a July 12 double-header in Chicago, Kansas City fell victim to a pair of home runs to right field by Dutch Zwilling in a 7 to 2 loss. For the second game, George Stovall called on southpaw Gene Packard, who had worked three innings the day before. Packard faltered only once, in the third inning when Max Flack hit a home run with two on. Gene nursed a 4 to 3 lead into the ninth inning. To open the final frame, an error by Rawlings and a single put the tying and winning runs on base. The Whales' Bill Fischer attempted to sacrifice, but Packard made a quick throw to third just as he stumbled on the base line. The umpire called the runner out, only to reverse the call when third baseman Bradley dropped the ball. With the bases loaded and no one out, Joe Tinker sent the right-handed-hitting Charles Hanford up to bat for the Whales' leading batter, lefty Dutch Zwilling. Despite the encouragement of the 7,000 bugs on hand, Charlie popped out and the bases remained loaded. Harry Fritz hit one of Packard's pitches on the nose and drove a liner to right field, but Grover Gilmore caught the ball before it came to earth. Zeider was off third base and had to go back and tag up. Gilmore spotted Flack off second base and threw to second to complete a double play before Zeider crossed home plate and settled the contest in favor of Kansas City.

The following afternoon, Cullop shut out Pittsburgh 1 to 0. Kansas City scored their only run in the top of the first off Frank Allen on a one-out walk to Johnny Rawlings, and two singles. The Packers' lefty escaped a bases-loaded jam in the second inning, aided by a Pittsburgh base-running gaffe. With runners on first and third, the Rebels' James Kelly hit a high infield fly near first base. Stovall, in the game despite a tightly bandaged hip, corralled the fly, but Kelly brushed the ball out of his glove as he ran toward first. Stovall picked up the ball, ran to the bag and tagged Mike Mowrery, who had stayed on first and became the victim of a force play. Cullop walked the next batter to load the bases before he got the opposing pitcher to roll out to third.[13]

Cullop's unusual pitching motion, which the *Kansas City Times* referred to as "his own peculiar and nefarious left handed way," contributed to his success. "When Cullop pitches," a *New York Times* report later said, "he winds up like the spring of a watch. Then, as he untangles himself, the ball shoots out and comes up to the batsman looking about the size of a pill. Nick has several times displaced a rib or two in negotiating his pretzel delivery."[14]

One of the Federal League umpires told National League ump Billy Evans about Nick Cullop. "He is a great pitcher, has plenty of speed, a fine curve and one of the queerest breaking fast balls you ever saw. Acts pretty much like the emery ball, but Nick doesn't use any emery, because we have given him the once over a half dozen times.... We are pretty sure he is roughing the ball at the seam with his thumb nail."[15]

Nick didn't deny the accusation. He explained, "Now the batters are positive that every time I rub the ball with my thumb, I am using my nail to roughen the surface. Well, I have done such a thing, so why not make the batter believe I am doing it all the time? It doesn't help to increase his confidence."[16]

On July 20, Kansas City sat in first place with a 48 and 34 record. In the fourth inning of the game that day against Newark, starting pitcher Alex Main was trailing 2 to 0, due to two separate instances where a Packers fielder had not properly covered his base. With two out and a runner on first, Peps pitcher Moseley hit a line drive directly at Main, who took the ball right in his stomach. The tall pitcher doubled over, but he still attempted to recover the ball. As Main reached it, he collapsed to the ground. The base runner, Emil Huhn, never stopped running, rounded third and headed for home. Kenworthy grabbed the ball and shot it to home ahead of the runner, but catcher Drummond Brown dropped the throw. The fallen Kansas City hurler was carried from the field and the Packers went on to lose the game, 6 to 0.[17]

The incidents of the twentieth seemed to signal a change in the fortunes of the club as Stovall's charges lost five games in a row. A third straight loss to Buffalo on July 23 toppled Kansas City from the top spot and Chicago replaced them in first place.

Main returned to win his next start and stop the losing streak on July 25. Then, on August 16, Main got credit for a no-hit, no-run game against Buffalo. The Packers scored five runs off Russell Ford, but the only semblance of a hit off Main came in the third inning when Blues catcher Walter Blair hit a dribbler toward shortstop. Johnny Rawlings knocked it down with his gloved hand, picked it up and made no effort to throw to first base because he didn't have a good grip on the ball. Blair was a very slow runner and most of the writers viewed the play as an error, but the official scorer credited Walter with a hit. Other than that play, only one other opposing player reached base. Main walked the very first batter to face him, Benny Meyer, and Benny again reached base in the ninth when second baseman Kenworthy booted his slow grounder.

The *Kansas City Times* reported, "The big fellow [Main] had everything in the world this afternoon. His fast ball was hopping into Ted Easterly's pad with a zip that could be heard in the remotest corner of the bleachers and his curve ball snapped past the bats of many a Buffed."[18]

After talking to umpires and players after the game, the official scorer changed his decision, giving Rawlings an error on the disputed play and Main had a belated no-hitter. Rawlings admitted, "It was an error. I should have thrown the man out by twenty feet." And umpire in chief Bill Brennan agreed, "The play was an error. There was little room for doubt."[19]

The Packers planned a special day to honor Manager George Stovall at the local park on July 31. However, the festivities were put on hold after Stovall was suspended indefinitely for fighting with umpire Tommy Corcoran the previous Tuesday.

"Once more 'Stovall Day' has spelled disaster to George Tracey Stovall," reported the *Kansas City Star*. "...The affair was called off this morning when the announcement was made the firebrand had been suspended indefinitely and fined $150."

Two previous "Stovall Days" had been scheduled and each time the Packers' manager was suspended the eve of the event. During 1914, the Baltimore Terrapins scheduled a day to honor Stovall. However, as the *Star*'s reporter recalled:

> They named a day for him and got up a fine little party, but a couple of days before the celebration George Tracey got fresh with Ollie Anderson and when time rolled around for the big affair he was serving time on the bench. But the day was held just the same.
> Then again the Kansas City bugs named a day for him and once more he ran into Ump Anderson and this time he again was on the bench when the big day came.[20]

With a good gate at stake, President Gilmore lifted the suspension so George could play on "Stovall Day" in Kansas City on Saturday. In tribute, Stovall was presented with an all-leather wallet with a load of legal tender and a bag of golf sticks. But the best gift was a double-header victory over Baltimore that pushed the Packers back to the top of the league, tied with the Whales for first place.

Stovall's success with the Kansas City Federals led his former boss, Charles Somers, to remark to a *Cleveland Plain Dealer* reporter, "Ever since I have been in baseball, I have been looking for a man of the caliber of Connie Mack. You can count such men on the fingers of one hand. George Stovall came closest to the mark and I made an error when I failed to keep him...."[21]

35

The Colonial League

At the Federal League's meeting in Chicago on November 18, 1914, a twenty-player limit was adopted for the 1915 season, a significant problem for clubs that had 35 to 40 players under contract. Lacking minor league connections in 1914, the Federals had been compelled to carry these extra players at considerable expense. In June it was rumored that the Atlantic League might become affiliated with the outlaw Federal League, but nothing ever came of the story and that Class D league went out of business following the season. Using money supplied by the Wards of Brooklyn, the Federals assumed operation of their own minor league in early 1915 by signing an agreement with the Colonial League of New England. That league had only begun operation a year earlier.

As far as Organized Baseball was concerned, the Colonial League was a unique operation. The league was the only circuit in the country pooling all receipts and paying all expenses from one headquarters. Located in territory owned by the New England League since 1902, the Colonial League had teams in Brockton, Mass., Fall River, Mass., New Bedford, Mass., Pawtucket, R.I., Taunton, Mass., and Woonsocket, R.I. The Colonials' attendance was less than half that of the New England League, but the new circuit's expenses were also about half of the older league's.[1] Each club in this economically operated Class C "trolley league" traveled by interurban transit to its games and returned home by nightfall to cut down on hotel and food expenses.[2] Unbeknown to Organized Baseball, the league had a secret "angel," and that benefactor was Robert B. Ward. In August 1914, *The Sporting News'* New England correspondent gave much of the credit for the Colonial League's success to the "league's general director, a clever young man named Al Bannwart."[3]

Swiss-born Alexander W. Bannwart came to Boston as a boy and became a naturalized citizen. Following his graduation from Princeton University in 1906, Bannwart decided to try his luck at professional baseball during the summer. When he first joined the Lowell, Massachusetts, club of the New England League, the team was in the midst of a losing streak. Fred Luke, the team's manager, declared that he would call the new recruit "Winn" and the name stuck. "Al Winn" gained considerable fame playing for Lowell and later obtained control of the club. Alexander was known by the name Winn the whole time he was manager and owner of the Lowell club, and as well when he organized the short-lived Greater Boston League in 1912.[4] Undoubtedly, John Montgomery Ward, business manager of the Brooklyn Federal League club, became familiar with Bannwart when the former was president of the Boston National League club in 1912.

On June 3, 1914, John E. Blake, owner of the Brockton franchise in the Colonial League, told the press he was quitting the league because Bannwart was the one-man power of the league and was receiving his funds from the Ward brothers of the Federal League. Blake maintained that Bannwart secured the lease on the Brockton baseball park for $700 and deposited $1000 in each league city for use by the clubs as working capital.

"Fully $9000 was spent by Bannwart in putting parks into shape for the season," claimed Blake. "...I am satisfied that so far Bannwart has put nearly $25,000 into the new league."

"I was opposed to this syndicate baseball," added the disgruntled owner, "but they roped me in when they secured the grounds ahead of me. When I became satisfied that the Federal League was behind Bannwart, I got out, as I do not care to jeopardize myself with organized baseball by helping the Federals."[5]

Stories of the Federal League's dealings with the Colonial League caused the Boston Red Sox to cancel an exhibition game with Woonsocket in August of 1914.[6] Still, the Colonial League experiment was successful enough in its first season for the Federals to become interested in pursuing it as a farm league for its excess players. With Bannwart as their front man, the deal went through without a hitch.

In January 1915, Federal League President James Gilmore and Robert Ward met with representatives of the Colonial League in New Haven to formalize an agreement whereby the Wards would officially finance the circuit. Following the conclusion of the conference on January 30, Gilmore said the reorganized Colonial League would have eight teams, each to be financed locally. Each club would be provided with six Federal League players as a nucleus for building a team. The Colonial League's teams would pay to the Federal League $200 a month for each player, the parent league (in the form of Robert Ward) paying the difference when the player's salary was in excess of that amount.[7]

Robert Ward's son, William S. Ward, was named treasurer of the revamped league and Charles B. Coppin was elected to the largely figurehead position of Colonial League president. Once again, the actual operations of the league would be handled by the thirty-four-year-old league secretary, Alexander Bannwart.

Woonsocket was dropped from the league and three new clubs were added, New Haven, Conn., Hartford, Conn., and Springfield, Mass., all from the disbanded Class B Eastern Association. A potential problem arose because the Colonial League co-opted the three clubs from the New England League's territory without the approval of Organized Baseball.

The Colonial League began the 1915 season with eight clubs: New Haven, Hartford, New Bedford, Springfield, Pawtucket, Brockton, Fall River, and Taunton. On May 21, one day after the opening games of the season, Colonial League officials notified the National Association of Professional Baseball Clubs that the league had decided to withdraw from Organized Baseball. The decision was inevitable because of the Federal League's financial backing and the number of that league's players on the minor league's rosters.

The Federal League used the teams in their minor league much as the arrangement between the majors and minors today. On May 13, pitchers Courtney Woodman and Robert Smith, and outfielder Delbert Young, were released by Buffalo and went to the Colonial League. Three days later, the Pittsburgh club released James Savage and Frank Delahanty to the Springfield club. Rarely used Rebels outfielders Mike Menosky and Ralph Mattis were sent to New Haven of the same league.

The Wards had been looking for a place to send pitcher Bert Maxwell since he was disabled with a fractured arm in May 1914. Maxwell had a long-term contract with the Wards and started only eight games on the mound in two seasons with the Brooklyn club. In addition to Maxwell, the Brooklyn Federal League club shipped four other hurlers to the minor league circuit: Rudy Sommers (13–7 record for Pawtucket), Byron Houck (14–6 at Pawtucket), Oscar Peters (19–10 with Fall River and Brockton), and Bill Chappelle (6–5 with New Haven).

Several of the players sent to New England were not has-beens or rejects. Some, like twenty-year-old Menosky, needed more seasoning. Mike joined Pittsburgh's Federal League club as an eighteen-year-old with high expectations in 1913 and got into 68 games for the Rebels a year later. After batting only 21 times with just two hits in the spring of 1915, he was sent to New Haven. Though he batted only .258 in 77 games, Mike did steal 47 bases in the Colonial League. Two other Pittsburgh players, Edward Holly and Hugh Bradley, refused to go to the minor league when ordered there in June. Rebels President Gwinner then gave the veteran players their unconditional releases. Other former major league players also refused to report to the Colonial circuit when ordered there, Ad Brennan of the Whales and pitcher Irvin Wilhelm (who was made a Federal League umpire instead) being the most prominent examples. Danny Murphy, former captain of several of Connie Mack's great Philadelphia Athletics clubs, did go to New Haven when ordered there by the Wards and batted .299 in 28 Colonial League games.

On June 14, the Brooklyn Federal League team made a quick trip to New Bedford for an exhibition game before a "large crowd." Less than two weeks earlier, Hartford had defeated the Baltimore Terrapins in an exhibition game and Brooklyn's Lee Magee was not about to allow the bush leaguers to pull than stunt on his team. The Tip Tops used their regular lineup throughout the game. The Whalers' best pitcher, John Tillman, started on the mound for the home team against Joe Finneran for the big leaguers. The Federal Leaguers scored four runs in the first inning and whipped the Colonials, 10 to 0, with Benny Kauff and Claude Cooper each collecting four hits.[8]

The Colonial League's chances for success at the gate were severely hampered when the Wards refused to yield on their position regarding Sunday baseball even for the minor league teams they promised to bankroll. *The Sporting News* wrote, "The Wards, Methodist gentlemen who are backing the Colonial League offered a reason why one of the Colonial teams was allowed to play on Sunday and the other seven teams are not. Walter Ward says the eighth club, New Haven, is owned by Bert Maxwell, a pitcher they sent there as manager. Therefore, they cannot insist it should be idle on Sunday."[9]

By mid-season, the Colonial League had reached a crisis point. Secretary Bannwart proposed that the circuit be abandoned unless money was forthcoming from its Federal League backers. The Wards put up an additional $10,000 to keep the league going.[10]

On July 8, the league announced that two clubs, Fall River and Taunton, were to be dropped. In addition, Pawtucket had drawn so poorly at home it would play its remaining games on the road, which led to the team's being dubbed the "Orphans." The best players on the disbanded teams were to be distributed among the other six clubs and former Buffed outfielder Del Young was named manager of the Springfield team. Play resumed with a six-club league on July 11, but without much improvement in attendance.

The conclusion of the Colonial League's pennant chase mimicked that of the Federal League. The race went into the final day of the season, September 7, with three teams still in contention for the flag. Hartford clinched first place by winning a double-header from New Haven. Trailing 4 to 0 going into the bottom of the eighth inning of the second game, New Haven rallied for three runs. After pitching a shutout in the first game, Hartford's Fred Trautman came on to get the final two outs of the eighth inning, after which the game was called because of darkness. Hartford finished in first place by .003 of a percentage point, despite the fact that second-place Brockton and New Bedford each won more games.[11]

Former Brookfed Jim Delahanty managed the Harford team and led the Colonial League in hitting with a .379 average in 76 games. Harry Billiard came to Connecticut from Newark after contributing nine victories to Indianapolis's 1914 Federal League champions and helped

Hartford to a championship with eleven wins out of fifteen decisions. Harry also pulled a Bert Maxwell on June 21 in a game with Fall River. When no umpire showed up to officiate the game, Billiard was pressed into service as the sole arbiter in a contest that his club, Hartford, lost, 15 to 5.

Brockton's Merwin "Jake" Jacobson, who batted .320 and stole 28 bases in 98 games, was signed by the New York Giants following the Colonial League season. (Jacobson became a star for Jack Dunn's great Oriole teams of the 1920s.) Gil Whitehouse, Hartford's center fielder, was the league's leading "slugger" with 49 extra base hits and batted .344. Whitehouse, who was contributed to the Colonials by Newark, had played for the Boston Nationals briefly as an eighteen-year-old catcher in 1912.

New Bedford's John Tillman led the league's pitchers with a record of 23 games won and 6 losses. After the minor league season ended, Tillman joined the St. Louis Browns and won his only career major league start on September 22 with a 3 to 1 decision over the New York Yankees at the Polo Grounds.[12]

Ultimately, the Colonial League became just another fatality of the Federal League war when it went out of business following the peace agreement in December 1915. Organized Baseball had forty-two minor leagues starting the 1914 season. Of that number, twenty-nine circuits that were members of the National Association folded before the end of 1915. One of those leagues no longer in business was the Colonial's chief competitor, the New England League, though a league with the same name was resurrected for part of a season in 1919 and again in 1926.[13]

The Colonial League venture appeared to end Alexander Bannwart's baseball ambitions and he turned to politics. He became part of the pacifist movement that gained momentum as the president was about to request a congressional declaration of war against Germany in 1917.

Bannwart became a Massachusetts delegate to a peace gathering in Washington, D.C., to demonstrate during President Woodrow Wilson's address to Congress. The ex-minor league executive was among a small delegation that visited Massachusetts Senator Henry Cabot Lodge at his Capitol office the day of President Wilson's war speech. There was an angry exchange of words between the senator and the pacifists. Bannwart reportedly called Lodge a coward and the lawmaker responded, "You are a liar!" A shoving match erupted among those present and the sixty-seven-year-old senator knocked Bannwart to the floor with a single punch to his jaw.[14]

Bannwart was carried off to jail, but Lodge refused to press charges. After hearing Wilson's address, Alexander revised his views and decided to support the president. That May he enlisted in the Reserve Officers' Training Corps. A year later, Bannwart sued Senator Lodge for $25,000 and the case was eventually settled out of court.[15]

36

Lee Magee Style

The *New York Times* once wrote that Cincinnati native Lee Magee was "considered one of the best of the younger players in the major leagues."[1] The Federal League unsuccessfully attempted to sign Magee to a contract in the spring of 1914 after Lee returned to the United States from the world tour. He had played in the Cardinals' outfield with Rebel Oakes and Steve Evans the previous two seasons, but with their departure to the Federal League, Lee moved to center field, performed remarkably, and also played 40 games at first base, where Miller Huggins was having a hard time replacing Ed Konetchy. With only five major league seasons under his belt, the brash Magee made it known in late 1914 that he was willing to jump the Cardinals for a managerial position. Though Lee was only twenty-five, the Wards decided it was worth the risk to hire an unknown quantity as manager to get such a highly regarded player for their Brooklyn team.

Rumors circulated at the Federal League's Chicago meeting late that fall that Tip Tops player Artie Hofman would be the Wards' manager for 1915. The Cardinals' owners didn't think Magee's managerial aspirations would be taken seriously and surmised that he would stay in St. Louis when the Federals would not employ him as the Tip Tops boss.[2] However, on December 1, 1914, Robert B. Ward confirmed he had signed Magee to a three-year contract and denied that Hofman had ever been considered as the Brooklyn manager. This appeared to mean that the manager job was open to Magee.[3]

"Yes, I've signed with the Federals," Magee announced to the press, "and I'm going to play with them and I don't care whether they make me a manager of a ball club or keep me as a plain player — I'll stick. My salary at St. Louis was $6,000. I'd have remained there for $8,000 and that was the price I set. Couldn't get it; went where the money grew thickness. Sorry to quit on a club that was run by one of the best boys on earth, Miller Huggins, and where I had so many friends."[4]

While Robert Ward was in Chicago attending the meeting of the Federal League executive committee in mid–December, Lee Magee was in the same city having a conversation with Cubs manager, Roger Bresnahan. The press circulated a story that Lee was ready to return to the organized major leagues if he was not made manager in Brooklyn. The nervous Tip Tops boss promptly announced that Magee would be his manager for the 1915 season.[5]

With all other options gone, the Cardinals prepared to file suit in U.S. District Court in Cincinnati on January 2, 1915, restraining Leopold Hoerschemeyer (Magee) from playing with the Federal League. Judge Hollister set the date for the hearing of the plea for injunction for January 9.[6] However, the Federal League's antitrust action in Chicago ultimately put all other litigations on hold.

Right from the start, Magee clashed with Tip Tops business manager Dick Carroll over the location of the team's spring training camp. Then he allowed his players to practice on Sunday, contrary to the Wards' policy. Magee said players should no more be allowed to be idle on Sunday and get cold and stiff than a baker's oven fire should be allowed to go out over the day.[7]

After alienating the Brooklyn club's business manager and owners, Magee went after several of the veterans on the team. Lee announced that Hap Myers would not be his first baseman in 1915 and the other "minor leaguers" on his infield would not do. Magee said Jim Delahanty and Danny Murphy were too slow and Houck hadn't the required class to satisfy him as a pitcher.[8]

On April 6, the *New York Times* reported, "A state of war exists between Manager Lee Magee of the Brookfeds and Artie Hofman and if one should take the remarks of both manager and player seriously, there is very little likelihood of their squabble ever being smoothed over."

The genesis of the dispute came during training when Hofman, a twelve-year major league veteran, failed to follow Magee's instructions to wait out the pitcher instead of swinging at the first pitch. Artie claimed he was playing "Johnny Evers style" baseball and the rookie manager insisted that "Lee Magee style" ball would be played as long as he was in charge. A fine assessed Artie for smoking cigarettes brought the conflict to a climax. Hofman turned in his uniform and announced he was going home to Akron.[9]

"If Robert B. Ward calls Hofman to Brooklyn he can have my resignation," said Magee. "It will be a question of the Brooklyn club having my services or those of Hofman. I shall stand by the fine of $10 which I levied on Hofman when I caught him breaking one of the most stringent rules I have laid down for the players, that of smoking a cigarette."[10]

The feud escalated after Hofman declared he was a free agent and Magee responded that he had the power to prevent Artie from playing baseball for the next two years inasmuch as his contract with the Brooklyn club was for that length of time. Hofman eventually rejoined the team two days after the season opener and was immediately suspended. The rookie manager refused to back down and Artie was shipped to Buffalo, leaving the Tip Tops with Hap Myers as their first baseman. This was the same player just weeks earlier Magee said would not be his first baseman.

On the day Hofman was suspended, Magee was notified by President Gilmore that he had been fined $50 and suspended for two days on charges of misconduct in the season's opening game in Brooklyn. In his statement, Gilmore declared he would tolerate no rowdyism and he would support his umpires.[11]

Magee returned to play second base for the Tip Tops on the fourteenth in a home game against Newark. The player-manager collected four hits in five trips to the plate and missed a fifth hit when his long drive was picked off the fence in front of the left field bleachers by Al Scheer. In the first inning, Magee tripled and stole home, although it took several minutes for umpire James Johnstone to convince the Newark players just where Lee's spikes hit the plate in his slide.

Brooklyn was trailing 7 to 5 when Magee came to bat in the ninth inning. He sent a hit into left field and flew around first base, sliding into second base in a cloud of dust. Benny Kauff drove a long fly to right field and Steve Evans drew a pass. Hap Myers sent a stinging single to left, scoring Magee. After Myers stole second, Tex Westerzil brought victory to Brooklyn when he smacked a pitch over second base into center field, sending Evans and Myers home.

Upon Kauff's temporary desertion to the Giants, Brooklyn recalled Felix Chouinard, one

Lee Magee, manager, second baseman, Brooklyn Tip Tops, 1915 (George Grantham Bain Collection, Library of Congress).

of the "minor leaguers" Magee had released. Both Kauff and Magee returned to the club on May 10, after the boy manager's enforced absence because of an injured finger.

In late June, Magee suspended Tom Seaton for five days without pay and it was rumored the pitcher would follow Kauff's example and jump the ball club. The Brooklyn club issued a report that Seaton was not with the team because he was suffering from an attack of malaria and would report as soon as he was well.[12] Another pitcher in Magee's doghouse was Ed Lafitte, who had thrown the league's only no-hitter in 1914. Although he won his first start of the 1915 season, "Doc" Lafitte walked eleven Buffalo batters in seven and one-third innings. By midseason, the pitching dentist had won only six of his sixteen starts and had the highest earned run average among Brooklyn's starters.

Magee continued to have problems dealing with veteran players that had more experience than he had. When he couldn't get along with one of the league's best hitters, Lee engineered a trade that sent Steve Evans and his $6,000 contract to Baltimore for pitcher Piano Mover Smith. Another player the manager couldn't get along with was third baseman Tex Westerzil. Despite a batting average of .311 after 31 games, Westerzil was sent to Chicago on June 22 in a cash deal engineered by President Gilmore.

Then there was the case of pitcher Jim Bluejacket. Entering the season, he was in Brooklyn's starting pitching rotation. The Shawnee hurler had two unremarkable performances, then sprained a ligament in his left calf during a game in Buffalo. Bluejacket claimed Manager Magee's insistence that the pitcher change the angle of his delivery caused the injury. When the club returned to Brooklyn, Jim was given a few days off to allow his injury to heal. When the Tip Tops went to check on Bluejacket at Hotel St. George, they found that his room had not been occupied for several days. Magee and Dick Carroll surmised that Bluejacket had gone home to Adair, Oklahoma, but Jim's wife responded that he was not there. Weeks passed and finally Carroll received a telegram from Jim, asking that he be allowed to rejoin the team. The pitching starved Brooklyn club took him back without any repercussions.[13]

On the first of July, center fielder Benny Kauff left the team for the second time. With Evans already departed, Magee started an outfield of Anderson in center field, Cooper in left and pitcher Lafitte in right. With this setup, the Tip Tops lost a double-header to Kansas City. Brooklyn was forced to bring Danny Murphy back after Magee had earlier "fired" the former Athletics captain and sent him "scouting" in the minor leagues.

Magee must not been impressed with Lafitte's outfield skills, because he fired the Louisiana hurler and sent catcher Larry Pratt packing as well. Lafitte signed with Buffalo and Pratt caught on with Newark. The club's poor performance in the field prompted Magee and the club to make several more changes. Lee signed a pair of Lafayette Collegians, Ty Helfrich to play the infield, and catcher Dick Wright, who played in only four games and exited the major leagues with a batting average of .000. George Wiltse, former New York Giants pitcher and later Jersey City manager, even played a game at first base and "he danced around that bag, pulling down all kinds of throw, just like a youngster," according to the *Times*.[14]

Ultimately, Magee's player deals came back to haunt him. On July 9, the Tip Tops lost a double-header to Buffalo at Washington Park. In the second game, Ed Lafitte, released by Magee ten days earlier, allowed but one run to his former teammates and pitched the Blues to victory, 9 to 1.

Despite all his flaws as a manager, there were few complaints about Magee the player. On July Fourth, traditionally considered the mid-point of the baseball season, Lee was leading the Federal League in hitting with a .354 average. On the negative side, he had played in only 45 of Brooklyn's 71 games, partly due to his frequent suspensions.

In the fourth inning of the second game of a double-header in Baltimore on July 14, Magee was called out at home plate on a close play. Lee took a swing at umpire Spike Shannon and further fisticuffs were averted when Terrapins catcher Frank Owens, a former Tip Top, separated the belligerents.

Magee's volatile temper resurfaced in a double-header in Kansas City on July 28. Tom Corcoran, a former major league shortstop turned umpire, had only recently come from the International League, and Tommy had problems with both managers during the day. In the first game, won by Brooklyn, 4 to 3, Corcoran called two runners safe on what the Packers contended was a perfect double play. The argument that ensued reached a climax when Packers Manager George Stovall threw his glove and it struck Corcoran in the chest. The umpire hit Stovall with a fist to the jaw and George retaliated. Umpire Bill Brennan and four policemen restored order, after which Stovall and his second baseman, Pep Goodwin, were banished to the clubhouse.[15]

In the second game, both teams objected to Corcoran's strike calls while Benny Kauff was at bat and the tying run on third. When a pitch thrown by the Packers' Nick Cullop was called a ball that he thought was a strike, the pitcher threw down his glove, went to the bench for a drink, and returned to the hill. In the meantime, Stovall and his catcher raised a kick about the umpire's ball and strike calls. The next pitch was called strike three on Kauff and he put up a vigorous protest. Magee rushed out to assist his player and kept on coming when Corcoran waved him back to the bench. The directing arm of the umpire grazed Lee and he responded with a wild swinging fist. Corcoran retaliated, striking Magee in the mouth, drawing blood. Kauff came to his manager's rescue and both players were ordered off the field.[16] It was the second time within a month the Brooklyn manager had assaulted an umpire.

"Umpire Corcoran hit me first in our mix-up, and I couldn't let him make a fool out of me," whined Magee. "I have schooled my players into being aggressive, and I am not going to play ladylike baseball just to please some umpires."

A day after the incident with umpire Corcoran, President Gilmore announced fines of $250 for Kansas City manager Stovall and $150 for Magee. Furthermore, both managers were suspended indefinitely. Kauff was fined $50 for getting involved in Magee's fight with the umpire.

"I'm going to communicate with the Brooklyn club's owner and tell him unless we get better umpiring and better breaks on the decisions, I'm going to resign," Magee threatened. "I was put out of the first game of the season, and I have been the butt of every umpire's anger since that time. They've been after me because I'm known as an aggressive player and manager. Every time I open my mouth on the field I am sent to the clubhouse."[17]

On August 4, the Tip Tops were in Pittsburgh where they split a double-header with the Rebels. That evening, about midnight, Magee was arrested following an altercation with Harry Kramer, a reporter who also happened to be the former press agent for the Rebels. The Brooklyn manager was also charged with being insulting to patrons of a downtown hotel. When he appeared before Magistrate Sweeney at the Central Police Station, the local official scorned Lee, calling him a "bully" and a "smart aleck." Magistrate Sweeney threatened to send the Brooklyn manager to jail if he appeared before him again. Magee was fined $25.00 and costs.[18]

Magee's days as manager in Brooklyn would soon be over. Patronage at Brooklyn's games had been very light and the receipts for two games in the final week of June amounted to only $146. Manager Magee had run most of the veterans out of town and the club was in disarray. Artie Hofman, Danny Murphy and Lafitte were past their prime when let go, but the trade of Steve Evans for the washed-up Frank Smith was puzzling. Evans finished the year with a batting average of .308 and led the Federal League in doubles with 34. The club's biggest name players, Benny Kauff and Tom Seaton, were unhappy and openly expressed an interest in getting out of Brooklyn. And the manager was out of control!

Attendance was so bad at Washington Park, the Wards sought to attract a new fan base by giving away free tickets to the Tip Tops' games. On Thursday, June 24, the Tip Tops offered the holders of special newspaper coupons free admission to Washington Park for the game with Chicago. When the gates opened, about 4,000 people with the required coupons were admitted. After a lull, the club officials decided to invite everybody left in the streets to enter for free. *The Sporting News* reported that 10,000 people came into the park, of which 5,000 were children and 130 were women. Joe Villa estimated that a day later not more than 250 paid for tickets and at the following Thursday double-header "with Kansas City's 'Sinkers,' the gross receipts, so the clockers said, were $154.50."[19]

The Wards liked the big crowd of the twenty-fourth so well they offered another free game, designated "Fans Day," the following Monday in commemoration of the opening of the new Fourth Street Avenue subway. Business manager Carroll said the actual turnstile count was 14,394, but according to the seating capacity of the grandstand and bleachers, which was 19,000, the newspapers declared there were no fewer than 18,000 persons in the park. The extra numbers went untabulated because the Tip Tops did not expect such a throng and did not have enough men at the gates, which were not opened until forty-five minutes before game time. When the fourteen turnstiles could not handle the crowd, one of the big gates was thrown open to clear the crush and thousands passed through it. Despite the huge crowd, the results on the field were the same as the earlier free game. Brooklyn lost to Chicago.[20]

In early August 1915, officials of the Newark Federal League Club announced that admission prices would be reduced at Harrison Park effective August 10. The new scale would be 15 cents for the bleachers, instead of 25 as heretofore, 25 cents for seats in the extreme section of the covered stands for which 50 cents had been charged, and for seats in the main section of the grandstand the price would be 50 cents, a reduction of 25 cents. Box seats remained a dollar.

The idea of reducing admission prices originated with Harry Sinclair. "Since baseball is an amusement and it is," reasoned Sinclair, "why not treat it as other amusements? ... there are thousands of young fellows just getting started to whom baseball is an obsession. They can't pay big prices for seats. But they could pay ten cents."[21]

James Gilmore said that the official attendance at Newark Park the first Sunday of ten-cent ball (in the bleachers) was 21,000. Newark newspapers estimated the crowd at "about 15,000." Organized baseball's spotters indicated the cheap bleacher seats only held about 500 the next day.[22]

Three days after Newark reduced its admission prices, Robert Ward announced that ten-cent baseball would begin at Washington Park. Attendance at the Tip Tops' home field had gradually decreased until a daily average of only 250 patrons came to the ballpark on weekdays. The substantial increase in attendance at Newark's game on Saturday convinced the Brooklyn management to make the change. The Wards would set apart 2000 outfield seats for the low rate of admission, while seats in the grandstand would be 25 cents excepting the two front rows, which would be 50 cents.

Cut-rate baseball was inaugurated at Washington Park on Thursday, August 12, and those who came to the park were rewarded when Brooklyn pulled out a ninth-inning victory over Kansas City. Down 6 to 4 in the final inning, the first two Tip Top batters worked Packers pitcher Pete Henning for walks. With the crowd cheering for Benny Kauff to hit one out of the park, the league's leading hitter almost pulled it off. Benny lifted a fly ball to right field that just missed clearing the wall. One run scored on his blast and two more came home on consecutive singles by Myers and Halt to make Brooklyn a 7 to 6 winner.

The *New York Times* reported that the ten-cent section of the park attracted 984 of the 2,500 persons that attended the game: "In the pavilion and in the grand stand there was not such a large increase so it was argued that the gain in the bleachers indicated that the low price had attracted an entirely new crowd to the park."

The same article discredited Organized Baseball's ever-present "clockers" who fed deflated attendance figures to the press. "Clockers, said to be in the employ of organized baseball, said that the total attendance was 1,511 ... 507 in the bleachers, 375 in the 25-cent stands, eighty-five 75-cent admissions, twenty-four in the boxes at $1 each and 157 passes. This, however, much underestimates the crowd which saw the game."[23]

Baltimore became the third Federal League club to reduce rates a week later. St. Louis opened its "ten-cent baseball" policy on August 27 and the fans got their money's worth with an extra-inning game won by the Terriers when Kansas City's Gene Packard wild-pitched home the winning run in the thirteenth inning.

Despite the temporary success the reduced admissions gained for the Federal League, publications unfriendly to Organized Baseball ridiculed the Federals' "Bush League experiment." Mouthpieces for the established major leagues claimed that the reduced rates "cheapened the game."

The Federal League's most ardent critic used the occasion of the reduced prices to ratchet up his attacks on the third league. "The Lunch Room League started to provide the public with major league ball at major league prices, which was a total failure," wrote Joe Villa. "Like the bankrupt clothing dealer who cuts the price of coats and vests, the Lunch Room League has hung out the red flag and the public has at last come to the point of realizing that the whole thing was bunk."[24]

Brothers Robert and George Ward finally found an experienced manager to handle their dysfunctional team with only six weeks left in the 1915 season. After being turned down by Fielder Jones, Jimmy Collins and Jake Stahl in 1914, the club settled for Bill Bradley, then made possibly the worst choice for a field boss in Lee Magee the following winter. Late that summer, the Wards found one of the most successful managers in the history of the International League receptive to an offer to pilot the Federal League Club.

John Henry Ganzel was one of five brothers to play professional baseball. He was a good-fielding, light-hitting first baseman with five major league clubs in first decade of the century. John was the first baseman for the 1904 Highlanders' team that lost the pennant to Boston on the last day of the season.

Ganzel purchased the Grand Rapids (Western League) franchise in 1904, and that winter he paid the Highlanders $3,000 for his release so he could play for the club he owned. After returning to the majors with Cincinnati in 1907, he was player-manager for the 1908 Reds and led the National League's first basemen in fielding.

Charles T. Chapin, owner of the Rochester Eastern League franchise, hired Ganzel in 1909 to rebuild and manage his team. Under John's leadership Rochester won three straight pennants from 1909 through 1911. Known as "Big Jawn," Ganzel became a popular figure in Rochester and his new-look team was dubbed "Ganzel's Hustlers." At one point Ganzel was the highest-salaried minor league manager and he earned a share of his team's profits.

The Hustlers' championship streak ended in 1912 when Chapin infuriated his manager by selling two of his best players to the Yankees three weeks before the end of the International League season.[25] His club finished in second place for 1912, as well as the two ensuing seasons. Prior to the 1914 season, Ganzel's Hustlers lost heavily in players to the Federal League. Despite his success at Rochester, Ganzel wanted to return to the majors and reportedly was miffed because he was passed over for the managerial position with the New York Yankees.[26]

With only days left in the 1915 International League season, Ganzel resigned as manager of the Rochester club and, on August 18, was hired to direct the Brooklyn Federal League club for two years at $5000 per season.[27] Lee Magee had tendered his resignation to President Ward a day earlier and said he would continue with the club as a player.

According to the *New York Times,* Magee expressed a desire some weeks earlier to resign as manager, but it was not until the day before Ganzel was hired that his resignation was accepted by Robert Ward. Magee contended that the worry of managing the team affected his health and he would be of more service as a player if relieved of that responsibility.[28]

The first official act of Ganzel as manager of the Tip Tops was to complete the trade of the unhappy Tom Seaton, along with his $8,000 contract and private car arrangements, to Newark for Cy Falkenberg. Both hurlers had been among the top pitchers in the Federal League in 1914, but the pair had fallen on hard times a year later. Seaton obviously had not recovered from the tired arm that plagued him late the previous season, and the barring of the emery ball hurt both pitchers.

Seaton pitched his final game for Brooklyn on September 19. Tom gave up eight hits to the St. Louis Terriers and exited after seven innings, trailing 4 to 3. Despite not being at his best, Eddie Plank preserved the one-run victory, stranding Tip Tops runners on third base in both the eighth and ninth innings. St. Louis catcher Grover Hartley threw out six Brooklyn base runners attempting to steal.

At the time of his trade, Seaton had only ten wins out of twenty-one decisions after winning 25 games for the Tip Tops a year earlier and 27 for the Phillies in 1913. Tom declared he was well pleased with the trade and told reporters that he "will show those people who think he is all in that they are mistaken and that he will pitch Newark to the pennant." *The Sporting News* suggested, "His failure to make a better showing with the Tip Tops was because of poor support when he was on the mound and that with a better fielding team he will be able to win more games without having to work so hard."[29]

Ganzel's first game on the bench for the Tip Tops came in Baltimore on August 23. Falkenberg took the mound for Brooklyn and he beat the hapless Terrapins, 5 to 2. The club did well under Ganzel until the Tip Tops dropped eleven of thirteen games in the final two weeks of the season.

In early September, Tom Seaton faced his former team for the first time since joining the Peps. Seaton was matched against the man he was traded for, Cy Falkenberg, in the second game of the Labor Day double bill. After Brooklyn beat Newark in a morning affair at Washington Park, the two teams traveled to Newark's park for an afternoon game. Seaton held the Tip Tops to only three hits, but a walk to George Anderson in the sixth inning did him in. The speedy Brooklyn center fielder moved to second on an infield out and scored on a two-out single by Benny Kauff. Falkenberg scattered five hits and walked three in his 1 to 0 shutout of his former club.[30]

After the Federal League closed for business in December, John Ganzel remained out of the game in 1916, but returned a year later to manage the Kansas City American Association club. He spent three seasons at the helm of the Blues, adding another pennant to his resume in 1918. John quit baseball after the 1919 baseball season to enter the oil business, but was again drawn back to the game. He managed at Laurel and Orlando in the minors and scouted for the Washington Senators before he retired.[31]

37

"My Resignation Was Wired to Mr. Ball This Afternoon"

During spring training, Fielder Jones stressed baseball fundamentals, especially defense, and molded the St. Louis Terriers into his style of baseball team. Over the course of one season, St. Louis improved from sixth in fielding percentage to second, from seventh in on-base percentage to first, and from eighth in earned run average to third. Over the course of one season, the Terriers improved in areas that were important to playing inside baseball: pitching, defense, sacrifices, walks and stolen bases.

A twelve-game winning streak by Jones's club between the twelfth and twenty-third of June propelled St. Louis into pennant contention. On July 2 the Terriers returned home trailing the first-place Kansas City Packers by only one-half game in the standings.

The Terriers would play a single game against the Packers on Saturday, then the clubs would travel to Kansas City for four games at Gordon & Koppel Field. "At last, after months of fighting," stated a report from St. Louis, "the Federal League is attracting more attention than the other two big leagues. Rooter clubs have been formed in all parts of the city and bands boosting both the Packers and Terriers will be on hand."

Saturday was designated as "Missouri Day" at the St. Louis Federal League Park and a large crowd was expected to turn out to watch the two clubs battle for first place. A contingent of Packers fans was expected to come down from Kansas City and "a big crowd of St. Louis bugs" have made arrangements to go to Kansas City and see the second game."[1]

The Terriers won the game in St. Louis and the Packers rebounded to capture a victory on the Fourth of July. The July 5 morning-afternoon double-header between the two clubs in Kansas City was punctuated with fireworks on the field.

Fielder Jones was in a good mood after the first game. The pitching duel between the Packers' Miles Main and Terriers' Bob Groom was scoreless going into the ninth inning. In that frame St. Louis scored the only run of the game on a single by Babe Borton, Miller's sacrifice, and a double by catcher Grover Hartley.

Things turned sour for Jones in the afterpiece and at the conclusion of the holiday double-header, Fielder announced he was through and telegraphed his resignation to President Ball. The trouble began in the third inning of the second game. The Terriers were trailing 2–0 when Kansas City's Johnny Rawlings attempted to steal second base. After initially calling the base runner out, umpire Harry Howell ruled Rawlings safe because shortstop Ernest Johnson dropped the ball. Ernie claimed he just released the ball while pulling his hand away from the runner's foot to avoid Rawlings' spikes. Johnson protested and was thrown out of

37. "My Resignation Was Wired to Mr. Ball This Afternoon"

the game, after which Manager Jones was chased by umpire Howell when he took up his player's case.

Jones turned on the second umpire, Bill Finneran, with whom he had had a recent dispute in Baltimore and a subsequent clash in Buffalo. When confronted, Finneran informed the legendary manager, "I will suspend both of you indefinitely and I will go through with it."[2]

Fielder walked over to the bench, took his glove over to Finneran and announced, "See that glove? It goes into my pocket for the last time if such umpires as you stay in the league. I'm through."[3]

On his way to the clubhouse behind the outfield stands, Johnson had to dodge a soda bottle thrown by a spectator in the overflow crowd standing in right field. When the spectator called the Terriers' player a "vile name," Ernie knocked the fan down. Players from both teams and several policemen rushed out to protect Johnson from the crowd, after which they ushered him to the clubhouse.[4]

"I have nothing to say," Jones told a cluster of reporters. "My resignation was wired to Mr. Ball this afternoon, and any comment concerning the case must come from him."

"Did the umpires have anything to do with your action?" he was asked.

"Yes," he replied, and then repeated, "I have nothing to say!"

Though he did not mention it to the reporters, the Terriers' manager was particularly irritated when umpire Finneran supposedly told Jones he would suspend him.

The St. Louis players were not so reticent. "The umpires are the cause of it all," one of them said. "We have had Finneran and Howell in our last several series, and they have decided several close plays against us — yes, and some that were not even close. Fielder has fought them gamely and fairly. He knows baseball thoroughly, and on every decision to which he has objected he has known he was right and that the umpires were obviously wrong. He simply tired of arguing for the right in vain."

The players felt Jones would reconsider his resignation. "He is the finest man to work for in the world," another one added, "and every player on the club has the highest respect for him."[5]

While he was an umpire for the National League, Bill Finneran was involved in one of the most notorious incidents of rowdyism in the history of the major leagues. During a dispute over a third strike call in the third inning of a game in St. Louis on July 10, 1911, Philadelphia Phillies outfielder Sherry Magee grabbed Finneran, then leveled him with a left cross to just above the jaw. The umpire fell to the ground, out cold and blood spurting from his face.

The base umpire, Cy Rigler, and Phillies manager Red Dooin rushed to assist Finneran while Magee was hustled off the field by his teammates. When the fallen arbiter came to, he pulled off his chest protector and challenged the whole Phillies bench. The enraged umpire was restrained until he calmed down, and only then the bloodied Finneran went to the hospital for treatment of his broken nose.[6]

Manager Dooin interjected that the rookie umpire had been too aggressive all season, often bragging about his ability as a fighter and threatening to lick players, including Dooin himself during a June series in Boston.[7] A year later Finneran reportedly challenged the Cubs' Johnny Evers, Heinie Zimmerman, and Frank Chance to a fight under the stands after a game that August. Finneran was not retained by the National League for the 1913 season and it came as no surprise when he was involved in the most publicized incident between an umpire and a manger during the two seasons of the Federal League.

"Any announcement regarding my resignation should come from Mr. Ball in St. Louis," stated Jones. "It is not as hasty as it seems. I have been a victim of bad umpiring for several weeks and I have been tired of it long before this. I hate to see a good ball club broken up by bad decisions."[8]

After the local Federal League officials implored him to stay on, Jones modified his decision and agreed to remain with the club until it returned home from the current road trip. Fielder also indicated he might continue as manager if President Ball would "back him up" and President Gilmore would give him some "satisfaction" regarding the league's umpiring.[9]

President James Gilmore was in New York when he heard of Jones's statements. Gilmore hurried to St. Louis to add his persuasive abilities to those of Philip Ball and convince the Terriers' manager to withdraw his resignation. In a statement designed to save face for the league, Gilmore announced that Jones was suspended indefinitely and St. Louis shortstop Ernie Johnson was suspended for three days and fined $50 for his part in the argument with umpire Harry Howell.

It has been said that another factor in Jones's resignation was the manager's annoyance that the league wanted its club owners to pay for league operations based on the amount of stock an individual owner held. Fielder was a minority owner in the St. Louis club because of the stock he received upon becoming manager and he was personally against paying anything back to the league. Only after the officials of the St. Louis club promised Jones that the assessment would not affect his holdings did he agreed to continue as manager.[10]

"Fielder Jones left St. Louis for Pittsburgh with his club last night," Gilmore announced to the press on the eighth. "After a conference with Phil Ball, Jones withdrew his resignation as manager of the club. He will stay with the St. Louis club until his contract runs out, at least, and probably long after that. Jones told Ball before he left St. Louis that he was going to work the limit to win the Federal League pennant for the Mound City."[11]

On the Terriers' next visit to Newark, a well known Peps rooter known as "Strawberries" gave Fielder Jones a particularly hard time. When the St. Louis manager went out to second base to dispute the umpire's decision, Strawberries put a megaphone up to his mouth and shouted that another "resignation" would be in order for Fielder. An agitated Jones tried to convince a policeman to eject the noisy fan from the ballpark.[12]

Soon, Jones had more than his problem with the umpires to worry about. The Terriers rallied to win the second game of the double-header in Kansas City on the fifth, but dropped their next three games. The game of July 6 in Kansas City was especially tough. Davenport pitched well enough to win but lost 1–0. In the seventh inning, Packers pitcher Gene Packard (who had taken over for Cullop in the fifth) singled with Easterly on base and the Kansas City catcher scored on Chadbourn's hit. Packard retired the Terriers in order over the final two innings.

The news got worse. The final game of the Kansas City series would be the last time Charlie Deal, the team's leader in batting average, would ever play for the Terriers. While the team was in Pittsburgh the Terriers' third baseman was stricken with typhoid fever.

While Deal was hospitalized in Pittsburgh, the Terriers' management desperately sought a replacement for their fallen third baseman. Vaughan, Bridwell and the lame Westerzil all auditioned at the third sack with unsatisfactory results.

Frank "Home Run" Baker, a star third baseman who did not return to the Philadelphia Athletics following the 1914 World Series, was contacted by the Terriers. The club telegraphed a contract offer to Baker, asking him to name his price for the remainder of the season. Baker wired back on July 19, "Sorry, can't come this year; will be glad to talk business with you in October."[13]

On July 26, the league announced that one of Jones's tormentors, umpire Harry Howell, and George William Fyfe, George Stovall's sparring partner, had been released. After a short vacation, Howell was reinstated as a Federal League umpire to replace Tom Corcoran, who was fired.

Before a game against Buffalo on August 1, Fielder inserted himself into the lineup as the Terriers' starting right fielder. Batting seventh, Jones went hitless against the Blues' Gene Krapp, though he scored a run after reaching base on a force out. St. Louis lost, 6 to 2, and a great performance by Doc Crandall was wasted when the second game of the double-header was called after the eleventh inning because of darkness and rain with the score 1 to 1.

A few days later, the news out of Pittsburgh worsened when it was reported that Mrs. Charles Deal was dangerously ill in the hospital. After nursing her husband through his crisis with typhoid, she was stricken with a severe fever. Both the Deals recovered, but Charlie would not play baseball again in 1915.

The affair with umpires Howell and Finneran would not be the end of Fielder Jones's problems with Federal League umpires. Later in the season, Jones was suspended for three games and fined $50 for arguing with umpires during a game with Kansas City.

"I'm going to win this pennant for St. Louis and then quit the Federal League," Jones announced following the game of September 30.

> President Gilmore and Chief Umpire Brennan have got my goat. Gilmore is a smart business man, a first class promoter, but he doesn't know how to run a baseball league.
>
> The umpires have been rubbing it into St. Louis from the jump. Take the case of Umpire O'Brien today, for instance. He put me out of the game for merely suggesting that he merely run his own part of the game and allow McCormick to call the balls and strikes. I noticed him running in every time the pitcher tossed the ball in the seventh and told him where he got off.
>
> "Why don't you mind your own business and let McCormick run the plate," I said.
>
> "Get off the field," snapped O'Brien.
>
> He put me off, too. I had to sit in the coop and saw wood while Stovall did as he pleased. George fights on the field and isn't suspended. But the moment I open my mouth, Gilmore suspends me for three days for talking.

Stovall walked up while Jones was talking to reporters and gave the Terriers' pilot a good-natured slap on the shoulder.

"Quit? You're kidding," offered Stovall.

"I never was more serious," replied the angry Jones as he walked away.[14]

The injunction restraining former Cincinnati Reds outfielder Armando Marsans from playing with the St. Louis Federals was finally rescinded in Federal District Court in St. Louis on August 19, 1915. Sidelined since playing in a Federal League game on June 22, 1914, Marsans did play in the Cuban League the previous winter, although he went by the assumed name "Mendromedo," because the National Commission threatened to ban any player who played against outlaws. In Cuba, Marsans was visited by New York Giants Manager John McGraw, who offered to trade for Armando if he would return to Organized Baseball. Marsans turned him down, partly because the New York press treated him badly. The New York writers "always thought it funny to poke jokes at me," he explained.[15]

Back on July 28, 1915, the Federal League's attorneys appeared in Judge Landis's court in Chicago and pointed out that Marsans was the only one of seventeen players who had been enjoined from playing for the Feds and was still idled. Landis refused to dissolve the temporary injunction, but promised a quick decision in the case. However, the judge procrastinated for two more weeks, at which time the Terriers sought a different course of action.[16]

On August 10, Marsans's attorney, Charles Madison, petitioned Federal Judge David Dyer in St. Louis to dissolve or modify the Cincinnati club's injunction against the player. Judge Dyer, in deciding the case, considered only one of the three points raised by the Federal

League attorneys in their petition. That point was that Marsans's contract with Cincinnati was not binding after October 14, 1914. The two points not considered by the court were the charge that the Cincinnati club did not comply with its contract with Marsans and that the contract was not binding because it lacked mutuality. Technically, the decision of Judge Dyer was a modification and not a dissolution of the injunction against Marsans. The judge did not decide the entire question raised in the injunction suit, but allowed that "clause eight" of the contract applied only to the season of 1914. The court held that this clause did not bind Marsans to play for the Reds during the 1915 and 1916 seasons, and set forth that the three-year claim of Cincinnati to the player could not be grounded on this clause.[17]

Judge Dyer's decision, in effect, set aside the reserve clause, because Marsans was to receive $1100 from Cincinnati as an "option" on his services for 1915 and 1916. This $1100 was included in his $4400 salary, but the contract read that the "total compensation for the season herein contracted for" was $4400. Under the judge's ruling "the season contracted for" terminated October 14, 1914.[18]

Once the decision was issued, the counsel for the Reds filed a motion to set aside the Federal Court's decree modifying the injunction. This motion was denied by Judge Dyer, although he did grant an appeal to the Circuit Court of Appeals, pending which Marsans could play with St. Louis. Phil Ball, principal owner of the Terriers, said that if the case was definitely settled in favor of St. Louis his club would file suit against Cincinnati to recover money advanced to Marsans.[19] As part of Organized Baseball's settlement with the Federal League that December, Cincinnati owner Garry Herrmann agreed to pay Phil Ball $2500 in damages for keeping Armando Marsans from playing with the St. Louis Terriers.

The August 19 court decision meant that Marsans was at liberty to play ball with the Terriers. Armando immediately left St. Louis to join the team in Brooklyn.

The return of the star Cuban outfielder to the Terriers' lineup did not provide the spark they hoped. In his first game back with St. Louis, Marsans had a single in four times at bat and he accepted two chances in center field. Unfortunately for the Terriers, Brooklyn had begun to play good baseball under new Manager John Ganzel and thumped St. Louis, 8 to 1. The Terriers also lost the next two games in Brooklyn. The following Tuesday in Chicago, Marsans was seriously spiked.

During the fourth inning of the game with the Whales on August 25, Marsans stole second base, but the foot of Jimmy Smith landed on the Cuban's right leg after the shortstop leaped for the high throw. Smith twisted his foot just as his steel spikes cut into Armando's leg and a made a gash clear to the bone.[20] Although the physicians predicted the outfielder might be out of action for two weeks, Marsans returned to the lineup against Pittsburgh on September 5.

The long layoff and the legal battles both defined and ruined Marsans's major league career. After a decent performance in 1916 with the Browns, he was batting only .230 a year later when St. Louis traded him to the New York Yankees for Lee Magee on July 15. However, the star-crossed player suffered a broken leg that ended his season. After batting only .236 in thirty games during the 1918 season, Marsans returned to Cuba and was finished with his major league career at age thirty.

Marsans returned to the United States in 1923 for a brief stint with Louisville of the American Association. Late that year, he played with the Cuban Stars of the Eastern Colored League, becoming the only player until 1947 to play in both the organized major leagues and the Negro major leagues. Marsans became the first Cuban manager in the minor leagues, serving as player-manager of the Elmira Colonels of the New York-Penn League in 1924. In 1939, Armando became one of the first ten inductees in the Cuban Baseball Hall of Fame in Havana.

38

"The Belgium of Baseball"

In January 1915, outgoing Brooklyn Tip Tops business manager John Montgomery Ward likened the relationship between the minors and majors to "Belgians drawn into the fight between the big fellows." Ward blamed the self-limiting policies of the National and American Leagues for forcing minor leaguers to toil in tank towns even though there was "crackerjack talent all around the minors."[1]

The minor leagues, for the most part, were privately owned, and only a few of their players had contractual ties to major league teams. However, they were part of "Organized Baseball," so the major leagues could draft players from the minors' rosters during the off season and pay a set sum for each player. Shrewd minor league owners could make more money by selling off their best players before the draft got them. Minor league magnates received nothing for players who ignored existing contracts and signed to play in the Federal League.

In the two years of the Federal League's existence as a major league, 25 players broke minor league contracts to play for the Feds, and another 115 ignored the minor leagues' reserve clause to sign with the outlaws.[2] The International League's Rochester club lost heavily in players to the Feds in the spring of 1914. John Ganzel's "Hustlers" lost the league's 1913 batting champion Hack Simmons, veteran catcher Fred Jacklitsch, Ralph "Hap" Myers, and pitchers Walt Dickson and Kaiser Wilhelm to the Federals. After reporting on March 16, 1914, that the Montreal Royals had lost ten players to the outlaws, C.L. Schanberger commented in *The Sporting News*, "In the camp of the Royals the Federals have left a blackened waste."[3]

The National League loaned the International League $35,000 during 1914 to keep it afloat, and Ban Johnson made a personal loan to the Buffalo International League Club to help it compete with the Buffeds. The *New York Times* estimated that the International League lost close to $150,000 in 1914, and the American Association $90,000.[4] Joseph Lannin, owner of the Boston American League club, purchased the Providence club on July 31, 1914, and it essentially became a Red Sox farm club. Though Buffalo's International League club survived the 1914 season, the local majority owner gave up just before spring training in 1915 and sold controlling interest in the Bisons to Lannin. In the three cities where Federal League teams competed against International League clubs for attendance, only Buffalo remained in business for the full two years of the Feds' existence, and only because of major league ownership.

In October 1914, Stanley Milliken of the *Washington Post* spoke for supporters of the minor leagues when he wrote: "It is the time for organized baseball to lose some of its false dignity, and frankly acknowledge a situation for which Ban Johnson and some of his allies are more to blame than anybody. Organized ball realized conditions as they are, but must face the issue squarely, and meet the Feds half way if the minors and baseball as a whole are to be saved."[5]

At the International League's winter meetings, the owners reversed their earlier position on Jack Dunn's request to move the Baltimore Orioles to Richmond for the 1915 season. The Virginia League accepted $12,000 for the territorial rights to Richmond, opening the way for the Orioles to move there for the 1915 season. Known as the "Virginians" or the "Climbers" while in Richmond, Dunn's club finished in seventh place. Following the Federal League's demise in December of 1915, Dunn took the best Richmond players and organized a new Baltimore International League club.

After the Federal League moved into Newark for the 1915 season, the city's International League team shifted operations to Harrisburg, Pennsylvania, at mid-season. All these developments earned the International League the nickname of "the Belgium of Baseball," alluding to Germany's invasion and occupation of that small country in August 1914.

Expensive contracts and the problem of players' jumping back to the organized major leagues after signing with the Federals led the outlaw league to focus its recruiting efforts on the class AA circuits for 1915. The Federal League ceased serious negotiations with major league players in the spring, and thereafter courted receptive players in the upper minor leagues.

After the Cantillons of the Minneapolis club released their option on the land where Charles Weeghman built his ballpark, there was an understanding that no American Association players would be induced to jump to the Federal League in 1914. The Feds felt no such obligation a year later. Agents for the Federal League began their raid on Association players that July.[6]

The Feds' first target was Kansas City Blues center fielder Pete "Bash" Compton, a former St. Louis Brownie (1911–13) when George Stovall was manager there. Compton had a decent season in 1912, batting .280 in 100 games, but slumped badly a year later and was shipped back to the minors. It was reported that Charles Madison, former president of the Kansas City Federal League Club, acted as agent for the St. Louis Federals in getting the "crack slugger" to buck Pat Tebeau's Blues.[7] When he signed to play for the Terriers, Bash was leading the Association in batting average, extra base hits, and runs scored. After playing in a Blues game on July 23, Compton left the club without notifying his teammates.

Compton admitted he had an American Association contract without a release clause, but said he was not paid promptly as required in his contract. The Federal League maintained that the player was a free agent because his salary due from Kansas City's A.A. club was more than two weeks late. The Blues' owners sought an injunction to prevent the defecting outfielder from playing in the Federal League.[8] However, Pat Tebeau's court action did not immediately dissuade Federal League agents from making offers to several other Kansas City players in an apparent effort to wreck the first-place Association club and give the Feds free reign in the city.

When the Tebeaus learned that Compton planned to play in a double-header with the St. Louis Federal League club on the twenty-fourth, a deputy sheriff showed up at the Terriers' ballpark to serve the injunction on the defecting player. However, the lawman bowed to the authority of the Federal League umpires and watched the game from stands as the Terriers won two games from Brooklyn.

Compton played center field in the first game and most of the second. While the deputy waited on the sidelines to deliver the court papers, Pete was spirited away in the eighth inning and Delos Drake was put in his place.

Compton did not appear in the Terriers' next three games, then a circuit court in St. Louis made permanent the injunction restraining Bash from playing with the Federal League. At the hearing on the Compton injunction, attorneys for the Federal League acknowledged that the outfielder was bound by a legal Association contract and surrendered him to Organized Baseball without a fight.

Two days after Compton's Federal League debut, Manager Jack Hendricks of the Indianapolis American Association club announced from Louisville that pitcher Sanford Burk had jumped to the Pittsburgh Federal League club. Burk's record was 14–6 with an earned run average of 3.37 for Indy to that point in 1915. Sandy had played for the St. Louis Cardinals in 1912 and 1913 during the time Rebels manager Oakes was with that same club.

"I have not heard that Burk of the Indianapolis team has jumped to the Pittsburgh Federals," said James Gilmore, "but I understand that clubs in our league have offered places to several Association players, whom we contend are free agents."[9]

The Fed chief contended that certain American Association players became free agents because of the failure of their clubs to pay their salaries for a month or six weeks. A day later, Burk went the distance for Pittsburgh in a ten-inning game against Baltimore at Exposition Park. With the score tied 1–1 in the last half of the tenth, the Rebels' Jim Kelly singled, went to second on Mowrey's sacrifice, and, after Yerkes walked, scored the winning run when Paddy O'Connor singled.

Meantime, the Federals didn't forget about the International League and created mischief among discontented players in that circuit as well. A month after Roxey Roach jumped from the International League to the Buffeds, Art "Dutch" Kores defected to the St. Louis Federals. His last game with Rochester was July 20. When C.T. Chapin, president of the Rochester club, purchased Art from the New York Giants for $2,500, the player's contract had a five-day clause and the Rochester club did not protect its investment by signing him to a new contract. After Kores jumped to the outlaw league, Chapin wrote a letter of protest to the Terriers' owners, but took no court action. Kores became the eventual replacement at third base for the ill Charlie Deal, batted only .234 in 60 games, and never made it back to the major leagues after that one season.

James Gilmore expressed sympathy for the minors, but answered their complaints about the Feds' tactics by saying, "It is the fault of the minors themselves that they are victims of war's ravages. The minors hold the whip hand; the majors are unable to exist without them, but for the foundation, which is the little fellows, who Atlas-like, hold up the whole structure of the baseball universe."[10]

Pete Compton returned to the Kansas City A.A. team on Friday, July 30, and played center field as if nothing had happened. President Tebeau of the Kansas City club did not notify the National Commission that he intended to play Compton after the player had, in the eyes of Organized Baseball, been "outlawed," and should not have been able to play for three years. Two weeks later, Compton was sold by Kansas City to the Boston Braves.

In late September, George Tebeau sued the Boston National League club, alleging he sold Compton to the Braves for $4,000 in cash and two players. The complaint read in part, "Boston is using Compton, but has refused to make payment, having been informed, it is stated, that Tebeau entered into an agreement with the St. Louis Federals that he would recognize their claim to Compton for next year as a result of the contract signed with the outlaws."[11]

Hardly had the courts given Compton back to the Kansas City Association club when it was learned another promising outfielder, Sammy Mayer, had left the Blues the evening of July 28 and was headed to the Brooklyn Federal League club. Tebeau had only recently recalled the young outfielder from Topeka of the Western League. Sammy, brother of Philadelphia Phillies pitcher Erskine Mayer, had played seventeen games and was batting .361 in 61 at-bats for the Kaws. Kansas City again went to court and got an injunction against Mayer's playing for Brooklyn, but the Feds maintained the restraining order was only effective in Missouri.

On Friday, July 30, the same court in Kansas City that granted the Compton injunction, issued a temporary injunction against President James Gilmore and owners of Federal League clubs, restraining them from tampering with any players under contract to the Kansas City American Association team.

Mayer never played for the Tip Tops, for he leaped from the Federals to Washington of the American League. Sammy, whose real name was Samuel Erskine, claimed he never signed a Federal League contract, while the Brooklyn club insisted he did. When Benny Kauff heard that Mayer had "jumped" to Washington, he repeated his intention of playing for the Giants in 1916.[12] Sammy Mayer's major league career lasted exactly eleven games, all of them with Washington at the tail end of the 1915 season.

While President McGill of the Indianapolis Association club procrastinated about what to do in case of pitcher Sanford Burk, Sandy pitched Pittsburgh to a 4 to 2 victory over Brooklyn on July 31, his second victory in a Federal League uniform.

McGill met with American League President Ban Johnson on August 2, then immediately headed for Pittsburgh to seek action against Burk. McGill said he had given Burk money in advance, had paid off a mortgage the pitcher owed on a moving picture theater, and had done various other favors for him.[13]

The Burk injunction prevented the Pittsburgh Federals from selling the player or transferring him to another club. Though failing to hold on to Burk, the Rebels had better luck with another minor league acquisition.

Pittsburgh quickly recovered from the loss of Burk by recruiting Ralph Comstock, a right-handed pitcher the Boston Red Sox had sent to Joseph Lannin's club in Providence. Despite a record of 15 and 6 with 113 strikeouts for the Grays, Comstock brooded about his demotion to the International League after winning two games in relief for the Red Sox early in the year. Comstock jumped to the Federals even though Lannin belatedly sold the recalcitrant right-hander to the Cincinnati Reds in an effort to appease him.[14]

Comstock signed a Federal League contract presented by Rebels business manager William McCullough, on August 16. The newest Rebels pitcher didn't have long to wait to prove his worth. A day after he signed his new contract, Comstock pitched Pittsburgh to a 5 to 2 victory over Brooklyn. He spent the remainder of the season with the Smoky City Federals, pitching in 15 games down the stretch, seven as a starter.

39

The Deacon Takes the Pulpit

An early-season surge put Newark in first place in late April 1915, but after that Whoa Bill Phillips' team fell on hard times. After the Peps beat St. Louis on May 21 to push their record to 19 and 12, Newark won only seven of its next twenty-two games. With each loss attendance declined. Three weekday losses to St. Louis in mid–June drew only 1,700 total admissions. After the Peps were pounded by St. Louis, 12–2, for their fifth consecutive loss, Bill Phillips was dismissed as manager.

The money man behind the club, oil tycoon Harry Sinclair, made the decision that Phillips had to go. The Peps' recent losing streak was the last straw. "I want a winner or nothing," Sinclair demanded.

"Sinclair himself wished to make no comments on the case," reported *Baseball Magazine,* "but it is known that his chief objection to Phillips was his easy going way with the players. Sinclair is a man who demands fire and dash and enthusiasm in a ball club. While in the west he hired two Pullman coaches and took a party of friends to Kansas City to see his team play."[1] Newark dropped three in a row to the Packers with the unhappy owner in the stands.

On June 18, William McKechnie, the Peps' twenty-eight-year-old third baseman, was named manager. Though he didn't flaunt his Christianity, third baseman McKechnie was a man of strong convictions and was dubbed "Deacon," supposedly because he sang in the choir of his hometown church in Williamsburg, Pennsylvania. Bill began his baseball career by playing semi-pro ball in the Pittsburgh area and for Washington, Pa., of the Pennsylvania-Ohio-Maryland League in 1906. Even though he didn't hit much, Bill made the little black book of Pirates owner Barney Dreyfuss as a youngster that was "smart" and "well worth watching."

McKechnie had a cup of coffee with Pittsburgh in the fall of 1907 and returned to the Bucs in 1910. He spent three years sitting on the Pirates' bench behind shortstop Honus Wagner and third baseman Bobby Bryne.

Bill said he learned a lot about baseball at the knee of the great Wagner. "Honus seemed to take a fancy to me when I first came up," he said.

> Maybe it was because Honus, like I, came from the outskirts of Pittsburgh. He taught me to watch other National League ball players, see where they were most likely to hit, and other peculiarities. He told me what men were likely to steal and our best defense against the hit-and-run maneuver.
>
> He also tried to teach me his batting knack and really put across his lessons. I knew just what he wanted me to do, but I could not execute properly. But, subsequently in my managerial career, I taught Honus' old batting hints to some of my players and they worked.[2]

Convinced that McKechnie would never hit much, the Pirates gave up on him in 1912. The Boston Nationals drafted him from St. Paul of the American Association that September and Deacon was the Braves' opening day center fielder in 1913. That was the only game Bill played for Boston because he was sold to New York Yankees on April 15 for the waiver price. He batted only .134 in 44 games for Frank Chance, then was again demoted to St. Paul.

Along with Bill Phillips, six players were cut by Newark in the June 1915 purge. Among those dropped was the thirty-four-year-old veteran pitcher, George Mullin, owner of 228 major league victories. Mullin had always been a power pitcher who relied on the fast ball to set up a passable curve. After winning a couple of games during April, Mullin completely lost his stuff. Allowing only three runs in his two victories, he gave up nineteen runs in his next three outings, which consisted of fourteen and a third innings pitched. Mullin signed on in 1916 as manager and pitcher for a semi-pro team in Kokomo, Indiana, and played for various Ohio town teams over the next three seasons. After a job with the Rockford, Illinois, club as assistant coach in 1920, George retired from baseball.

Bill McKechnie instituted one change in his first game as manager. He installed Ed Reulbach in his pitching rotation, and the former Cubs star put an end to the club's losing streak in a game against Pittsburgh. Ed was dominant after the Rebels scored two runs in the first inning and Edd Roush helped him out with three hits in Newark's 4 to 2 victory.

A statuesque 6'1" right-hander, Reulbach employed a high leg kick that allowed him to hide the ball from the hitter for a moment before a pitch was delivered. Edward Reulbach began playing baseball professionally at age eighteen under the name "Lawson" with Sedalia of the Missouri Valley League, then enrolled at Notre Dame University in the fall of 1901. No one at the university knew that the Lawson who pitched for Sedalia in the summer was Reulbach, the Irish's star center fielder and pitcher during the collegiate baseball seasons of 1903 and 1904.[3]

Ed was elected Notre Dame's baseball team captain for 1905, but while pitching in Vermont's outlaw Northern League under the name "Sheldon," he met and courted his future wife. Instead of playing his senior year at Notre Dame, Ed enrolled in medical school at the University of Vermont. He played baseball there and was the star of the team, playing left field when he wasn't pitching. After shutting out Syracuse University on May 12, Reulbach received a lucrative offer from the Chicago Cubs. Four days later he made his major league debut for Chicago against the New York Giants at the Polo Grounds. The rookie tossed a complete game five-hitter, but lost 4 to 0.[4]

Reulbach didn't lose often in his years with the Cubs. He won eighteen games with a 1.42 earned run average as a rookie and thereafter was a dominating pitcher in the National League. In 1906 he pitched a one-hitter against the crosstown White Sox in the second game of the World Series. That win started a 17-game personal winning streak that finally ended on June 29, 1907. On September 26, 1908, Reulbach became the only pitcher in major league history to pitch two complete game shutouts on the same day. In 1909 he compiled a fourteen-game winning streak, during which he threw five shutouts and five one-run games.

The poor health of his young son undoubtedly contributed to Ed's decline as a pitcher and he won only twelve games in 1910. Ed never returned to his pre–1910 form and his record was a mere 1 and 3 when the Cubs traded him to Brooklyn in July 1913 for cash and an obscure pitcher named Eddie Stack.[5]

Reulbach rebounded in Brooklyn, pitching a sixteen-inning two-hitter in his first start, en route to a 7–6 record and a 2.05 earned run average over the remainder of the season. He was selected as Brooklyn's opening day starter in 1914 and defeated the eventual National

League champion Braves. He threw 256 innings for a bad Dodgers club and had a record of 11 and 18. Ed's earned run average was among the lowest on the pitching staff.

Reulbach's fate in Brooklyn was sealed by his involvement in the Baseball Players' Fraternity. As an officer in the fraternity, he fought for player salary increases, a very unpopular stance with his bosses.

In 1914, Brooklyn owner Charles Ebbets offered first baseman Jake Daubert a $500 raise for the following season. Daubert sought Reulbach's advice during a train ride to a series in Chicago and Ed told the star first baseman to wait for an offer from the Federal League because that would strengthen his bargaining position. Daubert eventually got a big raise, but Reulbach was released by Brooklyn on January 29, 1915. No other major league club would offer a contract to Ed, although he would only be thirty-two when the ensuing season began.[6]

Reulbach told *The Sporting News* that the real reason Charlie Ebbets let him out was that, as secretary of the Players' Fraternity, he took up claims of players on Brooklyn's club who were unpaid at the end of the season. Ebbets admitted the players didn't get their pay in full, but cited Ed's pitching record as the reason for his release.[7]

David Fultz, president of the Players' Fraternity, issued a statement denouncing the release of Reulbach as

> another evidence of the unfairness of the present waiver rule as operated by organized baseball.... Reulbach was not notified that waivers had been asked, or of the club's intention until January 27 this year, three days before the club either would have to send him a contract or release him. On this day he was released unconditionally after all clubs had virtually completed their rosters for the coming season.... Any regulation which permits a man to be held for months at the will of another, when that other has already decided not to employ him, is vicious and should be done away with.[8]

Reulbach had turned down previous Federal League offers, but now he had no other alternative. James Gilmore announced on February 8, 1915, that Ed had signed a Federal League contract for one year. Assigned to the prospective Newark club, Reulbach was sent to spring training with the ex-Kansas City players in Texas. After the deal to transfer the Packers to Newark fell through, Ed insisted that he signed to play in Newark and would not pitch for any other Federal League club.

Reulbach made his Federal League debut on April 17 at the new ballpark in Harrison. Though he was wild at times on the bitterly cold afternoon, Ed defeated the Baltimore Terrapins, whose starting pitcher that day was Chief Bender, the former Philadelphia Athletics ace.

Bill Phillips did not employ Ed much in the early part of the season, preferring to use the pitchers who had won the Federal League pennant in Indianapolis the year before. When Reulbach did pitch, he was rusty and ineffective. After Phillips was fired by the Newark owners in June, Ed got his chance under the team's new field manager.

Ed Reulbach's curve ball was once regarded as one of the best in baseball, but Fielder Jones knew something was different about the break on his pitches during the Terriers' game against Newark on July 27. Earlier in the season, it appeared the former Cubs ace was about done as a front-line starting pitcher, but in his last few starts the right-hander appeared to have received a dose from the Fountain of Youth. On that afternoon at the St. Louis Federal League Park, Reulbach toyed with the Terriers' batters as the Peps cruised to an 11 to 3 victory. It turned out that Ed's success was partly due to a new pitch he had been working on that was probably against the rules.

On August 1, Reulbach beat Claude Hendrix, 4–3, in the first game of a Sunday double-header in Chicago. Ed's inability to control his new pitch cost him a run in the fourth.

Max Flack singled and worked his way around to third on two outs. Flack raced home when Reulbach uncorked a throw that flew past the catcher and banged off the grandstand. Newark scored three runs off Hendrix in the seventh inning and the game went to the ninth with a tie score. The Peps' Edd Roush beat out a grounder when the Whales' first baseman slipped just as he started for the bag. After walk and a force out, Huhn's single sent Roush home with the winning run.

After the game, the Whales complained that the Newark pitcher had broken the rules. During the game, Reulbach would spit tobacco juice in his glove and rub in sand or mud to make a sticky mush. Once it was applied to the ball, the pitcher achieved a better grip on the sphere.[9] By changing the pressure on a pitch, Ed could make the ball break at varying angles, similar to the emery ball. The so-called "mud ball" was thrown like a regular fast ball with an overhand delivery, but it was very difficult for a batter to pick up the movement on the pitch. Reulbach had also used his "mud ball" to defeat St. Louis in his previous start.

The afternoon Reulbach used his mystery pitch to beat the Whales, Cy Falkenberg unveiled his version of the pitch in the second game of the double-header. For eight innings Cy worked his "dry spitter," so called because of the wet spot on the ball covered in dirt that produced a significant break when thrown. However, the Whales' Ad Brennan pitched shutout ball for the first eight innings of the nightcap and Chicago led 1 to 0 when the Peps came up for their final at-bat. Despite leading on the scoreboard, the Whales had managed only four hits and Falky's breakers had set nine of their batters down on strikes.

Newark catcher Bill Rariden doubled to start a ninth-inning rally and Manager McKechnie sent himself up to pinch hit for Falkenberg. The Deacon came through with a run-producing double and the game plunged into extra innings. Brennan and Harry Moran, who relieved Falkenberg, matched scoreless innings until Newark reached Ad for a pair of runs in the twelfth on two infield hits and a double by second baseman Frank LaPorte. Chicago countered with one run in the bottom of the frame to make the final score 3 to 2 in favor of Newark. Meanwhile, Kansas City took a double-header from Baltimore to push past Chicago into first place.

The game at Weeghman Park on Monday was remarkably similar to the twelve-inning game of the day before. Again the Peps trailed by a run going into the ninth inning, and again they tied the score on three singles. The game would have ended in the twelfth had not McKechnie stabbed Hanford's swat over third with the bases full. The contest remained deadlocked into the sixteenth inning. In the top half of that frame, McKechnie singled and Esmond sacrificed Bill to second. Deacon went to third on Roush's infield out and dashed home when the Whales shortstop fumbled Al Scheer's slow bouncer on a do-or-die attempt. Earl Moseley, who pitched the whole game for the Peps, retired Chicago in the bottom of the inning for another extra-inning 3 to 2 victory.

Within the space of three days, the Whales lost three games in the standings to first-place Kansas City. However, later that week it was the Packers' turn to face the red-hot Peps in a four-game series at Harrison.

Federal League standings at the end of play, August 2, 1915:

Kansas City	57–40	—
Chicago	54–43	3
Pittsburgh	51–41	3½
Newark	52–44	4½
St. Louis	50–46	6½
Brooklyn	44–54	13½
Buffalo	45–56	14½
Baltimore	34–62	22½

Things had not gone well at home for the Peps since early in the season. By midsummer, the club was mired in the Federal League's second division and attendance was so poor there was talk the team would be leaving New Jersey. To get to Harrison Park from Newark, people attending the game had to squeeze onto the narrow footpath of the Centre Street Bridge.

"Harrison Park was across the Passiac River from downtown," explained Mrs. Edd Roush. "We had to walk across the bridge to get to the park. It was an ugly, smelly river because of the dye water from the silk mills north of Newark. You had to hold your nose as you went across."[10]

The Freeholders of both Essex and Hudson Counties responded to the problem by voting to permit the Public Service Railway to lay tracks over the Jackson Street Bridge. This would make the Peps' ball ground accessible from all parts of Newark, thus remedying what was regarded as the club's greatest handicap.

Upon returning home from their successful Western road trip, the Peps found that admission prices had been reduced at Harrison Park for the bleachers and grandstand. According to statements by the Peps' management, attendance averaged between 6,000 and 7,000 after the reduction of admission price for the bleachers.[11] However, the Peps' eight-game winning streak that thrust them back into the pennant chase undoubtedly had an impact on the increase in attendance.

When the Peppers played on Saturday, August 7, they were greeted by a crowd the club announced as 15,000. On the field, it was the same old story—another extra-inning affair.

Bill Rariden, catcher, Newark Peps, 1915 (George Grantham Bain Collection, Library of Congress).

The Packers' Gene Packard and Newark's Ed Reulbach engaged in a remarkable pitching duel that kept the game scoreless for twelve innings. Runners were cut down at home on perfect throws by Kansas City's center fielder Pop Chadbourne and the Peps' Al Sheer.

In the top of the thirteenth inning, Kansas City broke the scoreless tie with a pair of runs. Down 2 to 0, Newark had them right where they wanted 'em. Amazingly, it was birthday boy Bill McKechnie again who began the comeback with a single. Jimmy Esmond doubled and one run scored when the Packers' Pep Goodwin erred on Roush's grounder. The tying run came home on left fielder Al Shaw's error. Then things got interesting.

Frank LaPorte hit a grounder that should have been an inning-ending double play, but Goodwin was unable to complete the throw to first base. The Kansas City shortstop protested that Sheer, coming into second, interfered with his attempt to complete the throw to first. Roush, who had been on second, kept on running around third and scored the winning run while Goodwin held the ball.

The Packers were incensed and Kansas City catcher Ted Easterly attempted to strike umpire James Johnstone. When the Newark fans began pouring onto the field, the hostilities ended there as the Packers made a hasty retreat. Newark went on to take all four games of the series with Kansas City to run its winning streak to eight. The next few weeks saw five teams jockeying for the top position in the Federal League pennant chase. On August 12 four teams had the same number of losses at 45 and only 2 games separated fifth-place St. Louis from the top spot, shared by Kansas City and Chicago.

The actions of the Newark pitchers' "mud ball" were not lost on other teams' hurlers. On August 5, George McConnell of Chicago used his own mud ball to beat Brooklyn, 3 to 1. "McConnell has worked on the new delivery for less than a week," reported J.J. Alcock, "but he had the ball almost talking in his first trial with it in a real game. Brooklyn bunched two hits off him in the first inning before he got the new wrinkle working. After that he had the Tip Tops tamed absolutely."[12]

On August 10, Federal League President James Gilmore officially added Reulbach's "mud ball" to the list of pitches banned by the Federal League. The league dictated that any pitcher using the "mud ball" would be subject to a $50 fine and umpires would now be required to rub the gloss off balls before putting them into play.

At Harrison Park that afternoon, Ad Brennan had his best outing as a Federal Leaguer when only three Peps reached second base in his 7 to 0 shutout. There were about 8,000 who paid to see the game and a good part of that number shelled out four bits for grandstand seats.

A day later, Chicago became the first club to face Reulbach after his mud ball was made illegal. Before about 3,000 fans at Harrison Park, Reulbach responded with his best performance of the year, blanking the Whales, 8 to 0. Chicago managed only two singles off Ed, and the only Whale to reach second base got there on an error. Chicago Manager Joe Tinker claimed Ed was still using his "mud ball," but the umpires could not find evidence of the illegal pitch.

In the Peps' next game on the twelfth, they went into the ninth inning tied 1–1 with Chicago. The Whales' Leslie Mann tripled with one out and Joe Tinker sent Hanford to pinch-hit for shortstop Arnold Hauser. On a perfectly executed squeeze play, Charlie pushed a bunt down the first base line and beat it out for a hit. The run made McConnell a winner and ended Moseley's personal six-game winning streak. More importantly, the Whales' victory put Tinker's team back into first place.

Newark attained first place on August 22 by taking a Sunday double-header from Pittsburgh. The Peps won the opener in the bottom of tenth on Edd Roush's inside-the-park home run. Newark ended the day atop the Federal League standings by one percentage point over Kansas City. Pittsburgh was in third place and Chicago fourth with only one-half game separating the four clubs.

Two days later, Newark lost its short-lived hold on first place following a 3 to 0 loss to Buffalo. St. Louis got back into the pennant mix with a seven-game winning streak, and over the next few weeks five teams jockeyed for the top position in the Federal League standings. Newark was the first contender to fall to the wayside. An eight-game losing streak in early September doomed McKechnie's scrappy club and the Peps finished the season in fifth place.

No one could blame Ed Reulbach for the Newark Peps' failure to win the pennant. He compiled a 21–10 record with four shutouts and a 2.23 earned run average. Ed pitched the Peps' final game of the season, beating Baltimore, 6–0, in the second game of a double-header on October 3.

Following a loss to Buffalo on September 4, Manager Bill McKechnie left the team in the hands of Bill Rariden and went to Youngstown, Ohio, for treatment of his injured shoulder. At the time of Deacon Bill's enforced absence, the record of the second-place Peps stood at 67 and 53. Following manipulations by Bonesetter Reese, McKechnie returned to the club, but he did not again play at third base. The Deacon would only appear as occasional pinch hitter over the final four weeks of the season. Minor leaguer Johnny Strands, who had spent the previous year in the New England League, filled in at third base, but he proved to be an anemic hitter. Germany Schaefer was somewhat better, although "his wild throws to first were expensive." Ted Reed, a recruit from the New York State League, hit for a higher average than the other two, but he too was unsteady in the field.[13] After sweeping a double-header from Baltimore on September 5, the Peps won only eleven of their final thirty games and slid to fifth place.

40

The Tribune's Amateurs

In July 1915, the *Chicago Daily Tribune* sponsored a contest open to Chicago's amateur baseball players under the age of twenty-one. The entrants would be evaluated by scouts and the three best performers would each be assigned to join the Cubs, the White Sox, or the Whales on those clubs' final Eastern road trips of the season. Always on the lookout for new talent, Whales President Charles Weeghman and Manager Joe Tinker joined the contest's chief scout Jimmy Ryan as interested spectators throughout the tryouts at the Federal League Park.

Early on, one of the brightest young stars-to-be was a slick-fielding third baseman named Charles Pechous who played on the Western Electric Company's baseball team. The day before the four hundred amateur players were to be pared down to two teams at Whales Park, Pechous planned to travel to a game at Michigan City aboard the lake passenger steamer *Eastland*. The eighteen-year-old infielder overslept that morning and rushed to the Clark Street Bridge on the Chicago River in an effort to board the excursion steamer before it left the dock.

That morning of July 24, the *Eastland* loaded passengers in drizzly weather at the Clark Street Bridge dock. The excursion vessel's capacity was supposed to be 2,570 people, but it is believed that at least 3,200 were on board that day.

The overflow crowd, Western Electric Company employees and their families dressed in their best summer attire, crowded onto the decks, waving handkerchiefs and calling out to friends still on shore. The ship eased away from the dock and immediately began to list. As more passengers pushed toward that side of the deck, the boat tilted dangerously. The steamer's crew emptied the ballast compartments to provide "stability" for the craft. The *Eastland* righted herself, listed again and slowly rolled over on her side and settled on the muddy bottom of the Chicago River. Passengers on deck were dumped into the water and others jumped clear of the ship. Nearly all the passengers who were inside the steamer when it got underway were doomed.

Standing on the dock was Charlie Pechous, who arrived at the dock with his two sisters just as the boat rolled over.[1] The final death toll rose to 844 men, women and children, and twenty-two complete families were wiped out.

Both the Whales and the Cubs announced that games scheduled the day following the tragedy would be canceled in respect to the city's official day of mourning for the *Eastland* victims. Always conscious of his club's position in the community, Charles Weeghman decided to make the game against Buffalo on Thursday, July 29, "*Eastland* Sufferers' Day." It was hoped that $10,000 would be raised for the victims, but weather conditions were so bad fewer than 3,000 persons turned out for the benefit. After the heavy rain of the morning, no one thought the game was possible. Under normal circumstances, neither team would have permitted its players to play on such a sloppy field, but no one complained due to the special event.

All proceeds from the game, including concessions, were to be given to families of the *Eastland* victims. In order to increase attendance for the relief effort, the Whales lowered ticket prices to a quarter for the grandstand and fifty cents for box seats. The pass gate was closed and even reporters and league president James Gilmore had to pay to get into the park. The Cubs and the New York Giants were in town and several of their players paid to attend the event.

The *Daily Tribune* reported, "Chorus girls from two loop theaters worked like beavers persuading the fans to purchase flowers or programs, and their efforts accounted for $201.04 of the total.... The pretty girls ... held Weeghman up for $10. One of them placed a flower on his coat and got a five spot and another sold him a score card at the same price. The admissions netted $754.10." Not a single fan was in the bleachers, because the reduced prices induced everyone to gather in the grandstand.

Mordecai Brown, pitcher in games that drew some of Chicago's greatest crowds, was advertised to pitch for the Whales, but Claude Hendrix was substituted due to the condition of the field. Chicago used a three-run first against Gene Krapp to win, 4–2, and jumped back into first place in the bargain.[2]

Charlie Pechous made the finals of the *Tribune*'s contest on the twenty-fifth and the finalists were divided into two teams which would play at Comiskey Park the morning of August 1, proceeds of the game to go to the *Eastland* disaster victims.

Pechous, Harry Rasmussen, pitcher, and John McKittrick, shortstop, were selected as the best of the amateurs. As determined by lot, twenty-year-old Rasmussen was chosen to accompany the Whales on their next road trip. In eight games with the Illinois Steel Company, the youngster had struck out 113 batters. Before that, he once struck out 21 batters in a single game while pitching with an amateur team called the Fairviews.[3] Pechous would join the Cubs for a road trip.

"Heinie" Rassmussen got into only two regular season games for the Federals, but he did manage to get thrown out of a game and fined $25 after he was sent in to coach third base. However, it was the veteran players on the Whales who set the youngster up for the fall through a pre-arrangement with umpire Barry McCormick. The prank began when Bill Fischer kicked on a called strike. Rassmussen finally worked up enough nerve to shout something to the umpire, "For the love of Mike, call 'em right in there!" McCormick tossed him, which also carried an automatic fine. The Whales continued to rib the boy after the game and informed him the fine must be paid before he could play again. Finally, Heinie had heard enough of the taunts and asked trainer King Brady to lure McCormick into the dressing room before the next day's game so he could give the ump a "good trimming." Only then did the culprits hand Rassmussen a phony telegram that said the *Tribune* would pay the fine and Heinie could finish the trip.[4]

During Rassmussen's eastern trip with the Whales, Manager Joe Tinker became involved in a bit of intrigue involving one of the American League's most prominent players. While the Cleveland Americans were in New York to play the Yankees, Indians outfielder Joe Jackson sought out Tinker at the Somerset Hotel and expressed interest in jumping to the Federal League. "Shoeless Joe" explained that the Cleveland club was several weeks behind in his salary. Joe was particularly miffed that he asked the club for $25.00 on account and was refused.[5]

Tinker wasn't sure about the player's story and he wanted more information before he offered the Indians' best player a deal. He soon became convinced that the Cleveland club owed Jackson six weeks' back salary and that invalidated his contract.

After Tinker returned to his team's Baltimore hotel following a double-header with the Terps on Saturday, August 14, he read a telegram that arrived that afternoon and ten minutes later the Whales' manager was on a train headed west. Upon his arrival in Cleveland, Tinker went to the house where Jackson was boarding. Unfortunately, several Indians players had been tipped that the Fed manager was coming and were also there. When Tinker attended the Indians' Sunday game at League Park, he was immediately recognized. *Sporting Life* noted, "As Joe had on the family jewels and his Sunday clothes he naturally attracted more than usual attention, especially when he shoved a quarter into the ticket window with those diamonds of his glistening on his hand."[6]

Joe sat in the bleachers and during the course of the game Jackson waved to him several times. After the game, Tinker went back to the Jackson home and appeared to have a promise from the player that he would leave on the train with the Whales' manager. Jackson's teammates had been alerted to keep an eye on him and when Joe packed his uniform after the game a plot was suspected. Several team officials soon arrived at the Jackson abode. Tinker beat a hasty retreat, but believed Jackson might still defect to the Feds. However, the Whales' manager was concerned because Mrs. Jackson was opposed to leaving Cleveland and would convince her husband to remain with the Indians.[7]

It was reported a year earlier that Jackson and his wife spurned Federal League offers to play for Cleveland at $6,000 a season because they liked the city and the club's owner.[8] Four days after Tinker's visit with Jackson, the financially strapped Charles Somers sent Shoeless Joe to Charles Comiskey's White Sox for $31,500 and three journeyman ball players.

Charley Weeghman jumped on the 10-cent admission bandwagon in August. "I came to the conclusion to cut prices after having a long distance talk with President Gilmore," said the Whales' owner.

> He told me there were over 18,000 paid admissions at the Newark ballpark Sunday and over 10,000 on Monday and the amount of money taken in was not as small as one would suppose. I always have been convinced that it is better to have three fellows at the game at 50 cents apiece than one fellow at 75. It will be better to have three fellows at 10 cents than one at a quarter, too.[9]

Twelve thousand fans flocked to Weeghman Park on Sunday, August 22, the first day of the reduced ticket prices. Coincidently, it was "Brownie" day at the ballpark in honor of Whales pitcher Mordecai Brown. The legendary hurler rose to the occasion with a two-hit 4–0 shutout of Buffalo. One of the hits was tainted because Brown and Beck both went after a bouncer in the second inning and the first base bag was left uncovered. The only legitimate hit came in the sixth when the Blues' catcher, Walter Blair, stroked a double.

Pittsburgh went into first place in the Federal League pennant race by taking a doubleheader from Kansas City on August 24. However, the Rebels lost shortstop Marty Berghammer in the second game when he was seriously spiked on the finger. He would be out of the lineup for the upcoming six games against Chicago. The veteran Jack Lewis would fill in until Marty returned.

Prior to his starting assignment in the important Pittsburgh series, ailing Chicago pitcher Claude Hendrix made a flying trip to Youngstown for a visit with Bonesetter Reese. According to Art Wilson, who accompanied his pitcher, Reese found nothing wrong with Claude's arm, but told him he was carrying his slippery elm in the wrong pocket. Hendrix indicated "Bonesetter" found a muscle twisted in his hip and straightened it, relieving the pain which troubled him at times.

On the twenty-seventh, Hendrix took a 2 to 0 shutout into the eighth inning and no Pittsburgh runner had advanced past first base. To open the fateful eighth, Mike Mowrey touched the Chicago spitballer for a single. Steve Yerkes rolled an easy double-play ball to Jimmy Smith, but the Whales' shortstop fumbled the ball and both runners were safe. After catcher O'Conner sacrificed the runners into scoring position, Manager Oakes called on the veteran Eggie Lennox to pinch-hit for pitcher Frank Allen. Lennox sent a Hendrix fast ball on a line toward a vacated part of the Exposition Park outfield. Both runners on base scored to tie the game at 2–2. Most runners would have had an inside-the-park homer, but Lennox was so winded he fell flat on his face when he reached third base. Mike Menosky pinch-ran for Eggie and was thrown out at the plate when Lewis rolled to third baseman Tex Westerzil.

In the ninth, left fielder Les Mann tried to snare Ed Konetchy's line drive, but it got away for a double. Kelly beat out a bunt as Koney moved to third. Mowrey was walked intentionally to load the bases and Manager Tinker called the infield in close for a play at the plate. Yerkes sent a short fly to Mann, whose throw toward the plate held Konetchy at third. Bill O'Conner fouled off nine pitches from Hendrix then poked a 3–2 pitch high in the air to Mann. It appeared Konetchy had no chance to score, but Big Ed tried for home.

Mann's throw beat Konetchy to the plate, but umpire Bill Brennan called the runner safe, feeling that catcher Bill Fischer's bare-handed tag was late. While the Rebels celebrated, Tinker, Fischer and other angry Whales players surrounded Brennan. Fischer displayed a spiked hand which had held the ball that he used to tag Koney, but the arbiter had no sympathy for the injured backstop.

Joe Weiss, first baseman for a Chicago area amateur team called the Magnets, joined the Whales for the double-header against Pittsburgh on August 29. Joe was a candidate in the first tryouts held by the *Tribune*, but he was disqualified from the competition because of the age limit and the fact he had played minor league baseball. However, Joe Tinker was impressed enough to take a closer look at the player in an amateur game, after which he signed Weiss to a contract. On his first afternoon with the Whales, Weiss handled fourteen chances in the double-header and managed a single in the second game.

More than 8,000 turned out, despite frigid winds and a threat of rain, for the Sunday twin bill between two pennant contenders. Slats McConnell earned his twenty-first victory of the season by besting Pittsburgh's Elmer Knetzer in the first game. In the afterpiece, Chicago's Mike Prendergast pitched out of jam after jam to match Clint Rogge's dominance of the Whales' batters. In the fifth, the Chicago pitcher struck out Konetchy and Kelley with runners on second and third, and Max Flack saved the game in the third inning with a good throw that nailed O'Conner at home plate on Lewis's sharp single to right. After that play, Mike walked Al Wickland to load the bases, but Oakes grounded out to end the threat. The game was still tie at 0–0 when it was called after six innings.

That evening the two clubs hopped the train back to Pittsburgh to continue the series. Weiss did not know he would be accompanying the team on the road until Tinker decided the youngster's performance in the double-header warranted an additional trial.

Pittsburgh beat Three Finger Brown on Monday the thirtieth. Brown was obviously weak from a month-long bout with nephritis, but he pitched the entire game despite giving up fifteen hits and seven runs. Weiss again looked good at first, got one hit, and made two great stops on poor throws by Westerzil.

The long series finally came to a close with a double-header on Tuesday and, as the *Daily Tribune* remarked, "Rebel Oakes and his Federal League pennant aspirants stuck a harpoon into the Chicago Whales in two places this afternoon." Chicago took 2–0 leads in both games, but neither Hendrix, in the first game, nor Brennan, in the twilight contest, could hold the lead. In the opener, Frank Allen allowed only three hits after the Whales got their runs in the first inning, and scored the lead run himself in the seventh after Mann missed a shoestring catch on the pitcher's drive that rolled to the fence for a triple. Pittsburgh added insurance runs in the eighth to make the final score 6 to 2.

Much to the glee of the 7,000 Pittsburghers on hand for the twin bill, Jimmy Smith's error with the bases filled in the fourth inning of the nightcap gave the Rebels the tying and lead runs. Although the Rebels' Ralph Comstock had to be warned several times about a balk move, he held Chicago scoreless after the third inning in Pittsburgh's 5–2 win. The completion of the six-game series between Pittsburgh and Chicago found the Rebels in first place, a game ahead of Newark. The Whales dropped into a tie for fourth place with Kansas City, five games behind Pittsburgh.

On July 31, 1915, President James Gilmore issued an open letter to Federal League players that warned "indifference and insubordination will be no longer tolerated, and a way will be found to cancel even mutual long-term contracts unless their possessors render full value in return for the emoluments and privileges enjoyed."[10]

As the season moved into its final stages, the Baltimore Terrapins developed plans to further reduce expenses after the institution of cut-rate baseball. On August 28, the last-place club began a general reorganization of its roster supported by President Gilmore's order to club presidents to suspend players "who are not giving their best efforts to their clubs."

The Baltimore club announced the unconditional release of catcher Fred Jacklitsch and first baseman Harry Swacina, as well as the pending sale of third baseman Jimmy Walsh. A day later, the Terrapins released their highest-paid pitcher, Chief Bender, whose four and sixteen record was not good enough to offset his big salary. According to the official position taken by the club, Bender was released "for not being in condition." That fall, Swacina and Bender each sued the Baltimore Federal League club for breach of contract. Swacina contended he had a contract for $3,500 a year with a year yet to run and he wanted payment from the date of his release to the end of the 1915 season.[11]

These roster moves by Baltimore, and later by other clubs, presented a problem for the Federal League in future efforts to convince the players of Organized Baseball to switch leagues. The Federal League had at least the passive support of major league players from the start, but once they began to release men with long-term contracts, that support would wane.

The desperate Baltimore franchise continued to dump payroll by offering other players for sale to the highest bidder. Third baseman Jimmy Walsh was hitting well over .300 when he wrenched his ankle and had just returned from a visit to Bonesetter Reese on the day he learned of his sale to the St. Louis Terriers.

A replacement player employed by Baltimore was David Hickman, reported to be the property of the Detroit Tigers, who jumped to the Terrapins at the end of the North Carolina League season. Asheville's Hickman was the leading slugger in the league, driving out 14 home runs, 13 triples and 30 doubles in 118 games. He also stole 65 bases. The arrival of the twenty-one-year-old North Carolina prospect signaled the exit of another Baltimore outfielder. Guy Zinn was released on September 20.

Hickman played 20 games with the Terrapins and batted only .210. He went to the Brooklyn Dodgers in 1916 and played four years there as an outfielder. However, Dave never figured out major league pitching and compiled a career major league batting average of only .217.

In Chicago manager Joe Tinker was dissatisfied with the shortstop play of Jimmy Smith and Pee Wee Hauser, and he coveted the Terrapins' Mickey Doolan. The Whales had taken a chance on the 5'6" Hauser. Three years earlier, when he was with the St. Louis Cardinals,

Pee Wee was described by the editor of *The Sporting News* as "one of the cleverest and fastest short fielders shown in big league circles in years." Then, in 1913, his personal world collapsed; Hauser injured his knee, his mother committed suicide, his two small children died in a fire, and his wife died. The shortstop was institutionalized with what was described as religious mania.[12]

Hauser played his first game for Chicago on August 12, and displayed enough of his old skill to become Tinker's day to day shortstop. After a few games, though, it became obvious Pee Wee would not be the solution at the key infield position. Hauser batted only .204 in 54 at-bats. The Whales' other shortstop, Jimmy Smith, was almost as anemic, hitting .217, and he was leading the league's shortstops in errors.

Rumors were rampant before a meeting of the Terrapins' Board of Directors on September 1 that there would be no Federal League team in Baltimore after the 1915 season. Following their meeting, the directors had nothing to say about the team's prospects, nor would they discuss an eminent trade involving Mickey Doolan.

Chicago and Baltimore eventually negotiated the price for Doolan and the trade was finalized on September 3. Jimmy Smith and third baseman Harry Fritz went to Baltimore in the deal. Combined, Smith and Arnold Hauser made 57 errors in 476 total chances during the season compared to Doolan's 40 miscues in 703 chances. In Chicago's last game before Doolan joined the club, Hauser made three errors that all led to runs in the 4 to 0 Whales loss in Kansas City.

Doolan, who was born Michael Joseph Doolittle in Ashland, Pennsylvania, was thirty-five when he joined Tinker's Chicago club and was recognized as the best-fielding shortstop in the league. He led the Federals' shortstops in putouts, double plays and fielding average in 1914 was again leading in double plays and fielding percentage when traded to Chicago.

Acknowledged to have one of the most accurate and strongest throwing arms in all of baseball, Mickey Doolan was the rock in the Phillies' infield for nine years (1905–13). He led the National League in putouts four times, assists five times, double plays five times, and fielding percentage once. One must remember that he played in that league at the same time as Honus Wagner, the legendary shortstop of the Pittsburgh Pirates. Doolan and Wagner played when infielders' gloves were just enlarged mutants of ordinary leather gloves, with a horseshoe of extra padding. Webbing between the thumb and forefinger had not yet been developed.

"Doolan credits his ragged glove for the base hits he kills off every day," wrote a contemporary reporter. The covering on Mickey's unusual glove was ragged and the lining frayed, but a batted or thrown ball conspicuously stuck in a manner uncommon to regular gloves of the day. The center of the palmless glove was similar to a doughnut. Beneath the doughnut was the fielder's heavily calloused palm.[13]

Mickey claimed that his famous "snap" throwing motion came about after he broke an arm as a youngster and had to drop down to a three-quarters motion. "When the break mended there was some stiffness in my arm and I was unable to make the long overhand throw," he told a reporter during the World Tour. "I had to snap the ball to first and long practice made me proficient in that. If it hadn't been for that break in my arm, I never would have been anything probably but just a fair throwing shortstop."[14]

Mickey played college baseball at Villanova College, 1901–02, and pursued a degree in dentistry. After coming to the major leagues from Jersey City in 1905, Mickey plied his trade as a dentist in the off season. Following his retirement from baseball, Dr. Doolan practiced dentistry full time. Inevitably, his baseball nickname was "Doc."[15]

Doolan never was much of a hitter. His career major league batting average was only .230. Although he batted .245 and stole 30 bases for the Terrapins in 1914, Mickey was having a woeful season in 1915, hitting only .186 when traded. Rejuvenated after the trade, he batted .267 in 24 games with the Whales.

When Doolan first appeared at shortstop for the Whales, Chicago was only six games over .500 and seemingly out of the race. They would win 19 of their final 24 games.

Federal League standings at the end of play, September 4, 1915.

Pittsburgh	71–54	—
Newark	66–54	2½
St. Louis	68–58	3½
Kansas City	67–59	4½
Chicago	67–61	5½
Buffalo	63–68	11
Brooklyn	59–69	13½
Baltimore	42–80	27½

Chicago received help in the pennant race from an unexpected source when the rejuvenated Tip Tops of John Ganzel took three out of four games from Pittsburgh in a mid–September series at Washington Park. When the Doughboys returned home to play the Rebels on September 10, Brooklyn was fresh off a sweep of a five-game series with Newark.

The Rebels' Cy Barger pitched well enough to win the first game of the Brooklyn series — except for one inning. With two out in the home half of the third, Hap Myers slapped a single to right and stole second base. After Magee walked, Benny Kauff slashed a single to center, scoring Myers and sending Lee scurrying to third base. Kauff and Magee executed a double steal to produce a second run. That was all Brooklyn got, but it was all they needed as pitcher Jim Bluejacket allowed only five hits and shut out Pittsburgh, 2–0.

A day later, Brooklyn almost knocked the Rebels out of first place in a Saturday double-header. Manager Ganzel sent Cy Falkenberg to the mound in game one and he pitched masterful baseball. Pittsburgh managed only two hits while the Tip Tops pounded opposition hurlers Allen and Dickson in their 5 to 1 victory.

"Benny Kauff ruffled the feelings of the Pittsburgh men in the second inning, when he bumped the ball into the centre field bleachers for a home run," wrote the *Times*. "This started Fred Smith off on the same trail. The home run habit was still with the team the next inning. After Anderson walked, Lee Magee was nipped by the home run mosquito and lifted the ball over the right field wall."[16]

Later that afternoon, Ganzel's charges won their tenth straight and seventeenth victory in twenty-two games when they took the nightcap in ten innings by a score of 2 to 1. After taking Sunday off, Pittsburgh salvaged the final game of the series on Monday.

On September 14, President Charles Weeghman announced that the Whales had traded pitcher Dave Black to Baltimore for veteran southpaw Bill Bailey. Bailey broke into the majors at age eighteen with the St. Louis Browns in 1907. After six seasons in St. Louis, he spent 1913 with Providence of the International League then signed with the Baltimore Federal League club. He had a record of 5 wins and 19 losses with the last place Terrapins at the time of his trade to Chicago.

The day of the Bailey deal, the Whales signed one of the three winners of the *Chicago Tribune*'s amateur baseball contest. It wasn't the pitcher Rasmussen, who made the eastern trip with the club in August, but third baseman Charlie Pechous, who had taken his road trip with the Cubs. Manager Joe Tinker offered to take Rasmussen to training with the Whales in 1916, but the young hurler signed with the Cubs instead. The local National Leaguers had earlier tried to sign Pechous, but the teenage infielder said he wanted to finish school before playing professional baseball. Joe Tinker convinced him to change his mind.

"Tinker says Pechous will be a marvel if he can hit at all, and I sure hope he can hit," said President Weeghman. "...I understand Bresnahan offered Pechous $1,800 to join the Cubs. That's a pretty good salary for an untried youth but I am leaving the matter to Tinker, and Joe says there will be no hitch over the price if Pechous can show just a little hitting ability."[17]

After an off day, Pechous was thrown into the lineup as the Whales' starting third baseman, giving Chicago two of the *Tribune*'s amateurs in its infield. An announced crowd of 17,000 showed up at Weeghman Park on September 19 and got their money's worth when they saw one of the former amateurs, Joe Weiss, start a triple play in the Whales' double-header sweep of Buffalo.

The Whales' triple play began with Roxey Roach's line drive over first base that appeared headed for the right field corner. Weiss was close to the bag because of the base runner and made a stab for the ball, which stuck in his mitt. He stepped on the bag for the second out and turned to see the other base runner, Baldy Louden, heading for third base. Joe tossed the ball to second baseman Zeider to complete the triple play.

Chicago moved within two and one-half games of first place Pittsburgh with a double-header sweep of the Peps at Weeghman Park on September 21. The Whales piled up fifteen runs in the twin bill and center fielder Dutch Zwilling collected a single, two doubles, a sacrifice, a stolen base and a home run in the second game. *Daily Tribune* reporter J.J. Alcock called a catch by the little center fielder one of the "best I ever saw." He wrote, "With LaPorte on first in the fourth frame, Esmond slammed a terrific fly almost to the fence in left center. Zwilling dug back at full speed, but with apparently no chance to catch the drive. He was on the hill that leads to the bleacher when with a desperate lurch forward he just got his glove under the falling sphere. The ball stuck and a double-play would have followed but for a bum play by Doolan."[18]

After the two clubs played to a fifteen-inning 4–4 tie the next day, they got together for another double-header on the twenty-third. The pitchers figured prominently at bat in both games. The Whales won the first game in the second inning when Three Finger Brown hit a high fly ball with two runners on base. Newark outfielders Scheer and Roush let the easy fly drop between them and both runners scored. Earl Moseley was the hard luck loser to Brown, 2 to 1. Tom Seaton won the afterpiece when, with the score tied 1–1 in the seventh, he knocked a George McConnell pitch over the right field fence to provide the margin in Newark's 2–1 victory. Chicago, Pittsburgh and a suddenly red-hot St. Louis club would battle for the Federal League pennant in a race that would not be decided until the final inning of the final game of the 1915 season.

The major league careers of Joe Weiss and Henry Rasmussen consisted entirely of the games they played with the Chicago Whales late in the 1915 season. Charlie Pechous hung on with the Cubs for two years as a rarely used reserve. A graduate of Loyola University of Chicago, Pechous was a practicing physician for over fifty years. He died at the age of eighty-three in 1980.

41

Davenport and Plank

Fielder Jones's St. Louis club emerged as a factor in the 1915 Federal League pennant race with a twelve-game winning streak from the twelfth through the twenty-third of June. Of all the managers in the Federal League, Jones had the easiest decision when it came to selecting his starting pitcher for the day's game. He had the Big Hoss, Dave Davenport, and then three capable major league veterans, Eddie Plank, Doc Crandall and Bob Groom.

Big Dave Davenport's most remarkable performance with the Terriers was his two complete games in a double-header against Buffalo on Saturday, July 31. St. Louis was in fifth place and there was little reason for the fans to come out to the Federal League Park on a brutally hot afternoon. Dave won the opener, 1 to 0, but lost the second game by the same score. The feat was more amazing in the face of the dangerously high temperatures. During the course of the first contest, home plate umpire Fred Westervelt was overcome by the heat and had to retire for the rest of the day. The other umpire, William McCormick, assumed a position behind the pitcher and finished that game, then officiated the nightcap by himself. In the Cardinals' game across town, third baseman Bobby Byrne also had to leave the field during a game because of the heat. In the very first inning of game one, Terriers catcher Grover Hartley had his right little finger broken by a foul tip and his backup, Harry Chapman, had to catch both games.

Davenport was masterful in the opener, allowing four harmless singles, two of which were negated by double plays. He walked no one and struck out eight Buffalo batters. Despite Dave's dominance, Blues pitcher Al Schulz also had not allowed a run when the Terriers came to bat in the bottom of the eighth inning. Ward Miller opened the home half of the eighth with a single, was sacrificed to second and took third on an infield out. There was a two-strike, two-ball count on the right-handed-hitting Chapman when Miller made his move. While Schulz was winding up, the fleet Terriers outfielder made a dash for home. The pitch was high and wide and Ward slid safely across the plate. A pair of hits in the ninth landed Buffalo batters on second and third with one out, but Big Dave retired the next two batters, getting Hal Chase on a pop fly for the final out. "Prince Hal" would get his revenge later in the day.[1]

Over the first seven and a third innings of the second game, the Terriers touched Buffalo's Ed Lafitte for six hits, including three doubles, but could not plate a runner. Hugh Bedient relieved Lafitte and slammed the door on the Terriers the remainder of the game.

Davenport allowed only two hits in the afterpiece, but a questionable ball call with Tex McDonald at bat in the eighth inning cost him the game. Dave was sure the pitch called ball four was a good one, but didn't complain much because of McCormick's difficult position behind the mound. With a count of two and two on Chase, McDonald took off for second. Hal reached out with the bat in one hand and punched the ball toward third base. The force of Davenport's pitch knocked the bat out of his hand, but when Hal realized the ball was fair he took off for first. The ball bounced past the startled St. Louis third baseman and rolled all the way to the fence. McDonald stopped at third and Chase took second. Davenport made a good play on Engle's grounder and threw McDonald out at home for the first out. The next batter, Solly Hofman, lifted a fly ball to the outfield and John Tobin made a good throw to Chapman, but Chase made a "great slide" to score the only run of the game.[2] In the eighteen innings he pitched that day, Davenport allowed but five hits.

Arthur David Davenport was born in Alexandria, Louisiana, but spent most of his boyhood in southern Texas. He began his baseball career in amateur ball for the town team at Runge, Texas. Dave was pitching for independent teams in the Lone Star State when a scout for San Antonio signed him for the Texas League club in the closing weeks of the 1912 season.[3]

In 1913, Davenport won 15 games and lost 16 for San Antonio and showed so much promise he was drafted by the Cincinnati National League club. The Reds had themselves a muscular six-foot-six-inch 220-pound hurler of raw but unlimited ability. With only one season of minor league ball, the twenty-one-year-old right-hander debuted in relief in Cincinnati's second game of the 1914 season with Chicago. Dave's first victory as a starting pitcher also came against the Cubs, a 13 to 1 rout at Chicago's West Side Grounds. His next major league victory came on May 30 when he shut out the Pirates, 3–0, at Forbes Field.

Dave's salary with the Reds was only $225 a month, so he was naturally interested when the Federals offered him a contract for $4,500 and a signing bonus of $1,000.[4] In 1914, Dave compiled a record of two wins and two losses in the National League, then won 8 and lost 13 for the Terriers' miserable last-place club.

During the Terriers' 1915 spring training in Cuba, Manager Fielder Jones declared that "Dave" showed him more than any other young right-hander he had ever worked with and predicted a successful career for the massive pitcher.[5]

On September 5, 1915, the Terriers made Lloyd Rickart Day (for the president of the club) one of celebration with a victory over first-place Pittsburgh. With two runs already home in the second inning and runners on first and second, Jack Tobin all but clinched the game by smashing the first ball offered by the Rebels' Ralph Comstock far over the right field wall. That was all Davenport needed as he handed the Rebels a coat of whitewash, 6 to 0. Only one opposing base runner advanced as far as third base.

After only one day of rest, Davenport pitched a no-hit, no-run game to beat the Chicagoans, 3 to 0. Two of Tinker's men reached first base on bases on balls, but each was retired on a double play. The Whales' Tex Westerzil also reached base when catcher Hartley made a bad throw to first on his bunt. Four of Dave's offerings were hit to the outfield, but all fell into outfielders' gloves for outs.[6]

In his next start, on September 10, Davenport gave up only two hits (both to Vin Campbell) in beating Newark, 3 to 0, his third shutout within a week. On the seventeenth, Dave threw yet another gem, this time against Cy Falkenberg and the Tip Tops. With the game a scoreless deadlock, Davenport suffered a lapse in the eighth inning and loaded the bases with Brooklyn runners. With two out and the sacks full, Dave reached back and struck out Hap Myers. In the home half of the eighth, Ernest Johnson worked Falkenberg for a walk and Davenport sacrificed him to second. Johnson scored on a two-base hit by Miller, who then scurried home himself when second baseman Lee Magee made a bad throw on Marsans's grounder. Davenport retired the Tip Tops in the top of the ninth to preserve yet another shutout.

On the twenty-fourth, Big Dave allowed only three hits as St. Louis whipped Buffalo, 6 to 1. The Terriers' winning streak had reached nine straight when Davenport took the mound in front of the home fans against the visiting Kansas City Packers on September 29. In only one hour and twelve minutes, the streak was over as Davenport lost, 1 to 0.

Davenport had an incredible year for any level of baseball. During the 1915 season, Dave threw ten shutouts and struck out 229 opposing batters in an amazing 393 innings pitched. No other major league hurler since the cork center ball was introduced in 1910 has thrown that many innings in a single season. Due to poor run support, Davenport lost 18 of his forty decisions despite a 2.20 earned run average.

After facing Davenport, opposing batters had to deal with the veteran Eddie Plank, who came to the Terriers following the 1914 season. Connie Mack signed Edward Stewart Plank fresh off the campus of Gettysburg College in 1902, and over the next thirteen seasons, Eddie won 284 games and lost 160 for the Philadelphia Athletics. Though he would be forty years old by the time the 1915 season ended, Eddie was still a remarkably effective pitcher. He had superb control and mixed a fast ball with his "cross-fire," a sidearm curve that bisected the plate at an angle which made it difficult to be hit hard. Plank loved to brush batters off the plate and he led the American League in hit batsmen twice. The lefty was noted for being annoyingly deliberate on the mound, irritating fans, sportswriters and batters — an effective part of his game because he knew impatient hitters swung at bad pitches.

On Sunday afternoon, May 2, 1915, St. Louis shut out Newark twice at Peps Park in Harrison. Eddie Plank won the opener 1 to 0, on a three-hitter, all singles. Newark's Cy Falkenberg was also in good form and the game was scoreless into the ninth inning. Babe Borton's triple scored Delos Drake with the game's only run, and Plank polished off the Peps in the bottom of the ninth.

It was inevitable that when St. Louis played Baltimore the first time in 1915, Plank would pitch against his former Athletics teammate Chief Bender. The two were first scheduled to face one another in the opener of a double-header in Baltimore on June 26. The game matching the two old war horses was heavily advertised and Baltimore's best crowd of the season turned out to see it. Eddie's parents came to the game, as did his brother, a Baltimore policeman. It was only the second time the elder Plank had seen his son pitch.

Chief Bender pitched well enough to win, but Plank was better. Eddie allowed only three hits and walked no one. The left-hander struck out the first two batters he faced and fanned seven more to run his total for the game to nine. Terrapins third baseman Jimmy Walsh was able to crack the veteran's slants with a pair of doubles, but he was thrown out trying to stretch one of the two-baggers into a triple. Walsh's second double opened the eighth inning but he was stranded when the southpaw retired the next three batters. As Eddie completed his 2 to 0 shutout, most of the 10,000 fans in attendance stood and cheered him.[7]

Plank and Bender met again when Baltimore came to St. Louis. Howard Tyler of *Baseball Magazine* wrote that 9,000 bugs watched Plank and Bender in a double-header while only 300 showed up at Sportsman Park to see the Browns play the Yankees. Gettysburg Eddie again prevailed, this time 5 to 1. Plank held Baltimore hitless until the seventh inning, when the Terrapins scored their only run of the game on an error.[8]

Eddie Plank pitched a remarkable game against Chicago on July 13 before a St. Louis crowd close to 3,000. The game was played under a sweltering sun and the temperature was near 100 degrees. Both pitchers had to be groomed between innings to keep them fresh. Eddie held the Whales to one hit over thirteen innings, a double by opposing pitcher Hendrix in the third. A fifth-inning error by second baseman Bobby Vaughn allowed the only other base runner against the Terriers' lefty until the fourteenth inning, and Plank's breaking pitches set fourteen Whales down on strikes. However, Chicago's Claude Hendrix had also not allowed a run, despite permitting nine hits.

Plank had not allowed a base on balls when the Whales' light-hitting first baseman, William Jackson, drew a pass in the top of the fourteenth. Eddie bitterly complained that a ball was called on what he thought was the third strike. Les Mann singled to put two runners on base and the next batter was the opposing pitcher. Hendrix lifted a fly ball to left field for what should have been the third out. However, left fielder Ward Miller lost the ball in the sun and it fell in safely as both base runners scampered across home plate. Moments later, Miller made a great running catch on Zeider's fly, but the damage had been done.

The fans had stuck with the game thus far, but it was fast approaching seven o'clock and they began moving toward the exits. People leaving the ballpark stopped in their tracks when Babe Borton and Miller opened the home half of the fourteenth with singles, then Hartley walked to load the bases with none out. Hendrix bore down and fanned Ernest Johnson for the first out. Fielder Jones called on Doc Crandall to bat for Bridwell. Crandall had gained a reputation as a pinch hitter, but on this day he did not get solid wood on one of Hendrix's spitters and grounded it at Zeider. Rollie touched second and pegged to first baseman Jackson to end the classic pitchers' duel. Plank was a hard-luck 2–0 loser.

Sam Weller wrote that "some of the women in the grandstand, and there were many as it was a free day for them, cried when they saw Ward Miller misjudge Hendrix's long fly, realizing it probably spelled defeat for their idol. They think as much or more of him here than the fans in Philadelphia ever did, they say."[9]

Plank won his 300th major league pitching victory on September 11, 1915, against Newark at Handlan's Field. Ed Reulbach pitched for the Peps, but lasted only three innings. Plank didn't have to work hard, leaving for a pinch hitter in the eighth inning in the 12 to 2 St. Louis rout. He became only the eighth player in major league history (since 1876) to earn 300 victories.

Baseball Magazine wrote in 1915, "...we have personally seen Plank pitch as good a game for the Federal League as we ever saw him pitch, and that no lesser authorities than Home Run Baker personally told us they thought Plank was as good right now as he had ever been."[10]

Plank experienced a rare breakdown at home against Brooklyn on September 16. Eddie relieved Crandall in the tenth and an inning later he was reached for a double by Lee Magee. The next batter, Benny Kauff, drove a home run over the right field fence and Brooklyn went home with an 8 to 6 victory. Two days later, Eddie would be the winning pitcher in both games of a double-header against Brooklyn.

Plank took the mound against the Tip Tops in the tenth inning of the first game and threw three innings of scoreless ball, allowing only one hit. St. Louis made the veteran a winner with a run in the twelfth. Doc Watson, who had also started the first game, again took the hill for the nightcap and took a 4–0 lead into the fourth inning. With two runs in and the bases loaded with Brookfeds, Fielder Jones summoned Eddie to again save the game. Plank retired the Tip Tops without further damage in the fourth and held the visitors to two hits the rest of the game. When darkness halted the proceedings after the seventh inning, Plank received credit for his second victory of the day. The double victory vaulted the Terriers over Chicago into second place after the Whales were shut out by Buffalo's Hugh Bedient.

Doc Watson started the Terriers on a nine-game winning streak by pitching a 5–2 win over Baltimore on September 21. Watson's win kept St. Louis four games behind first place Pittsburgh. During the winning streak, Plank beat Baltimore, 10–2, though he missed a complete game by retiring after the eighth inning. Three days later, the lefty beat Buffalo, 5 to 0, on a three-hitter in the second game of a Sunday double-header in Buffalo.

1915 St. Louis Terriers team. Standing, left to right: Borton, Watson, Hartley, Deal, W. Miller, Drake, Davenport, Groom, Crandall; sitting: Chapman, Johnson, Vaughn, Tobin, unidentified youth, Fielder Jones, Bridwell. Conspicuously absent is Eddie Plank (National Baseball Hall of Fame Library, Cooperstown, N.Y.).

Eddie would attain another milestone later in the season with his twentieth win. He achieved that on September 30 with a 4–2 victory over the Kansas City Packers in St. Louis. It wasn't easy, though, as Chief Johnson kept the Terriers in the doghouse for six innings. Kansas City tied the score at one in the fifth and took the lead in the top of the seventh when Plank was victimized by a triple steal. After Bill Kenworthy laced a one-out triple, Perring was purposely passed to set up a potential double play. Stovall attempted a squeeze but his bunt was popped up to the third baseman. Eddie intentionally walked Johnny Rawlings in order to pitch to pitcher Johnson instead. However, in pitching to the Chief, Plank returned to a full wind-up. As he slowly and deliberately went into his pitching motion, Kenworthy broke for home and slid in safely before the catcher could apply the tag. Plank proceeded to strike out Johnson, but now the Terriers trailed 2 to 1. However, Kansas City threw the game away in the home half of the inning when three errors led to three St. Louis runs. The win kept the Terriers one-half of a game behind first-place Pittsburgh in the standings with two games to play.[11]

Plank pitched one more time in 1915, taking over for Doc Crandall in the third inning of the team's final game, and received credit for the victory, his twenty-first. The veteran Terriers left-hander led Federal League pitchers in fewest walks (1.81 per nine innings), finished second in earned run average, 2.08, and was second (to Dave Davenport) in shutouts with six. Davenport and Doc Crandall each won twenty-two games for St. Louis; six of Doc's wins came in relief. The forgotten man on the club's pitching staff was the fourth starter, Bob Groom, who pitched 209 innings, won twelve games (four of them shutouts) and lost eleven.

42

The Pivotal Series

The 1915 Federal League pennant chase came down to the final six games of the season in a series of games between Pittsburgh and Chicago beginning on September 29. There were single games scheduled Wednesday through Friday, then a double-header on Saturday to be played at Exposition Park. Because there was no Sunday baseball in Pennsylvania, the teams would travel to Chicago for a single game that also would be the final game of the season for both clubs. Despite Chicago's hot streak that saw them win sixteen of twenty-one games in September, Pittsburgh seemed to have the advantage. The Rebels only needed to break even in the six games to capture the pennant and had the additional benefit of playing five of the six in their home park.

The Rebels started fast against George McConnell in the opening game of the series on Wednesday. Pittsburgh was leading 3 to 1 in the fifth inning when Rebels starter Frank Allen suddenly lost his control and walked the bases full. He gave way to Ralph Comstock, who walked the only man he faced to force in a run. Walt Dickson came in to pitch and walked Joe Weiss to force home the tying run. The Rebels' nightmare inning continued when center fielder Jim Kelly dropped Mickey Doolan's fly ball and two more runners scored. McConnell came out of the game with a strained arm in the seventh, and, without any particular warmup drill, Three Finger Brown shut the Rebels out the remainder of the game to preserve Chicago's 6 to 3 win.[1]

Meanwhile in St. Louis, the Packers' Gene Packard personally derailed the pennant aspirations of Fielder Jones's Terriers, much as he had done to the Chifeds a year earlier. Dave Davenport allowed only four hits through eight innings and only one Kansas City batter advanced farther than first base. However, that one batter was Packard, whose sixth-inning home run cleared the right field fence to account for the only run of the game and disappoint the six thousand pennant-stricken local bugs in attendance. In winning his twentieth game of the season, Gene walked one and allowed only four scattered hits, all singles.

On Thursday in Pittsburgh, the Rebels drove Chicago's Bill Bailey from the game with a five-run outburst in the third inning. Marty Berghammer's leadoff single was followed by a four-base knock off the bat of Al Wickland. Rebel Oakes and Ed Konetchy followed with singles, and both scored on Kelly's triple that bounced up the hill in front of the right field fence. After Hendrix relieved Bailey, Kelly tallied when Chicago's catcher dropped the throw from Pechous on Mowrey's squeeze bunt. Pittsburgh added two more runs on Clint Rogge's triple off Hendrix in the sixth to take a 7 to 2 lead.

A pair of walks and two hits pulled Chicago to within 7–4 in the seventh inning. Cy Barger relieved Rogge with one out, retired Zwilling and Fischer to end the threat, and set the Whales down the rest of the way without allowing a hit or walk. Their victory allowed the Rebels to maintain the lead in the pennant race by a half game over St. Louis after Eddie Plank beat Kansas City, 4 to 2.

The Friday game in Pittsburgh was rained out, so the 1915 Federal League season came down to its final weekend. Saturday, October 2, was a gloomy day in Pittsburgh, but baseball would be played. Before the day's play, the Federal League standings stood:

Pittsburgh Rebels	85–64	.571
St. Louis Terriers	86–66	.566
Chicago Whales	83–65	.561

The difference in games played among the contending teams was due to rainouts that would not be made up. On the slate for the day were a Pittsburgh-Chicago double-header and a St. Louis-Kansas City single game. St. Louis had put itself in the race during a torrid stretch which saw the Terriers win ten of eleven games prior to the final Saturday of the season.

Twenty-four hours of almost continuous rain at Exposition Park stopped the morning of the Saturday game, but the sky remained overcast all day. Due to the threat of precipitation in the Pittsburgh area, the first game was started a half-hour early. The miserable weather held attendance down to 6,000 for the key Saturday games at Exposition Park and only about 15,000 bugs came out for the three days of games in Pittsburgh.

The Whales sent the legendary Three Finger Brown to the mound to face the former Dodger Elmer Knetzer in the initial contest. Brown had been the "big-game pitcher" for the Cubs a few seasons earlier, but at this point in his career he was just about done. During his prime, Brown could shut down the best lineups in baseball, but on this day he didn't have to. After surrendering a run to the Rebels in the first, Chicago pushed across a pair of scores in the second, two more in the third, and then four in the fourth for an 8–1 lead. Brown was not at his best, allowing sixteen hits, but his teammates gave him plenty of support and the Whales cruised to an 8–5 victory.

Going into the bottom of the ninth inning of the second game it looked like a sure sweep for Chicago. The Whales reached Cy Barger for three runs in the second inning and Chicago's starting pitcher, Mike Prendergast, was working on a one-hitter when Pittsburgh came up to bat in the ninth. Marty Berghammer raised the Rebels' hopes with a leadoff walk, but the next two batters were retired. Pittsburgh was down to its last out, but the Rebels didn't go quietly.

Konetchy hit a ball to the Chicago third baseman that should have ended the game, but Charlie Pechous couldn't handle it for an error. Jim Kelly strode to the plate and scorched a triple to right-center, driving home two runs. Kelly was injured sliding into third and was replaced by Cy Rheam. Rheam tied the contest at 3–3 when he came home on a single by Mike Mowrey. Prendergast took care of the next batter to end the inning, but his shutout was long gone. The teams plunged into extra innings.

Following a scoreless tenth, Les Mann started the eleventh with a double off Barger. He scored on a Doolan single, and after another single and a double, Doolan also scored. The Whales went to the bottom of the eleventh with a 5–3 lead and Prendergast retired the side for the victory.[2]

In St. Louis, the Terriers still had a chance for the flag if they won out and Pittsburgh split the remaining two games with Chicago. Two of the best pitchers in the Federal League, Nick Cullop, a twenty-one game winner, and Dave Davenport would oppose one another in the crucial game. Both pitchers were on their game and Big Dave carried a 1–0 lead into the visitors' half of the fifth inning. The Packers put two runners on base in that frame due to a Bobby Vaughn error and a Perring single. The runners moved up a base when George Stovall rolled out to first base for the second out of the inning. With the light-hitting Johnny Rawlings at bat, Fielder Jones ordered Dave to intentionally walk the shortstop and pitch to Cullop instead.

"The bases were full and Nick could hardly wait until Davenport wound up," wrote the *Kansas City Star*. "He hit the first ball pitched. He hit it with the accent on the hit and it traveled. The bases emptied rapidly and hope fled from the hearts of the sixteen thousand sad-eyed bugs. It was the hope of twenty-seven years that fled, for with that blow went all chances of a 1915 pennant for the Sloufeds."[3]

Suddenly down 3 to 1, the Terriers had four more innings to save their season, but each time they threatened to score, Cullop rose to the occasion. Every method was used to unnerve the Packers' hurler. The St. Louis fans in the box seats behind home plate waved newspapers, score cards and coats. Hundreds more screamed and taunted the visiting pitcher, but Cullop never lost his poise.

In the seventh, the Terriers put runners on second and third with two out and Fielder Jones sent Runt Walsh to bat for Davenport. After one strike, Jones rushed out with the accusation that Nick was using something to scuff the ball. The whole St. Louis team gathered around as umpire Joe O'Brien examined the baseball. O'Brien threw the suspect ball out of the game and tossed a new one to Cullop, which he used to strike out the pinch hitter.

The Terriers again tried to rally in the eighth when two men reached base with no one out. Armando Marsans smacked a hopper between short and third. Rawlings sprinted over, dug the pellet out of the dirt and fired quickly to Goodwin to retire the runner coming to second. The double play was completed when the second baseman's throw beat the speedy Marsans to first.

The 4 to 1 loss officially eliminated Fielder Jones's team from the pennant race. The Packers' win also spoiled the plans of the St. Louis club for a big crowd on the season's finale on Sunday. A few months later the *Chicago Times* broke a story that there was an attempt to "fix" the October 2 game between the Terriers and Packers.

"Before the deciding game," revealed Kansas City manager George Stovall,

> certain people came to me and offered a big sum of money if I'd promise not to work Cullop. You bet I pitched Cullop, and I told all the players, and they did their best to win. We took the game and deprived St. Louis of what chance it had of winning....
>
> I don't mean to infer [*sic*] that the club owners had any knowledge of the attempt to frame the game, but the people who made the proposition were around the ballpark almost every game.
>
> After the game some of the smaller stockholders seemed peeved that we didn't lay down, but the big men in the club were sportsmen and took what they got and were satisfied.[4]

Chicago's double-header sweep in Pittsburgh had shaken up the Federal League standings. On the morning of October 3 the standings read:

Chicago Whales	85–65	.567
Pittsburgh Rebels	85–66	.563
St. Louis Terriers	86–67	.562

There would be a Pittsburgh-Chicago double-header at Weeghman Park to decide the championship. Pittsburgh protested that there should only be one game in Chicago, as the schedule dictated, to end the season. The Whales' management insisted on two games to make up the game rained out on Friday in Pittsburgh, because Chicago would only have to win one of two if a double-header was held. President Gilmore settled the Rebels' protest by declaring that the game postponed at Pittsburgh was "automatically" transferred to Chicago. The Rebels were warned that if they refused to play the double-header, the games would be forfeited to Chicago.

It would be a perfect Sunday for baseball in Chicago. At noon, long lines of fans began to make their way through the turnstiles. By one o'clock a mob of fans had swamped the ticket booths and at two o'clock the gates had to be closed. Every seat was sold well before game time and the Chicago club was forced to close the gates, much to the dismay of another 10,000 who voiced their protests outside the park. On the field, extending from the Whales' bench clear around the park and back to the bench occupied by the Rebels, there was one giant horseshoe of vocal fans only separated from the field of play by a rope that stretched across the outfield. At its thinnest point, the horseshoe was six or seven people deep, while in the more favorable spots there were fifteen lined up in each row. People stood in the aisles and the press box was stormed by three hundred anxious bugs looking for a place to watch the game. An estimated five thousand milled around outside of the stadium, following the game on the scoreboard.[5]

The Chicago club's officials were not prepared for the huge crowd. The *Chicago Daily Tribune* wrote, "Weeghman is lamenting the fact that he did not know how to distribute the fans, for he believes he would have broken the record for attendance at a ball game if he could have crowded in everybody who tried to get inside the grounds."

While the Whales reported 34,361 paid admissions for the season-ending double-header, on that same day the White Sox drew under 3,500 at Comiskey Park and fewer than 2,000 watched the Cubs play on the West Side.

In the first game, Pittsburgh's surprising rookie right-hander, Clint Rogge (17–12), would

Chicago Whales 1915 pitchers (left to right) Brown, Bailey, Hendrix, McConnell, Brennan, Prendergast (Chicago History Museum, SDN-060451. Photograph by *Chicago Daily News*. Original photograph has been cropped.).

oppose Chicago's 25-game winner, George McConnell. With the loss of Kelly due to an injury on Saturday, Manager Oakes would move to center and the light-hitting Cy Rheam would be in right field. Kelly was batting .294 with 17 triples and 38 stolen bases for the season. His loss could be crucial.

McConnell was warned by Bonesetter Reese a day earlier that he would have trouble throwing his curve, but the veteran was great for eight innings. By the ninth inning of the opener, the Whales were up 4 to 1 and it looked as if the Whales had the game in the bag. McConnell was tiring, but seemed to have enough stuff to win the game and put a lock on the pennant. The Chicago spitballer walked Mowrey to open the frame, then quickly got two outs on a foul out and a strikeout to bring the Whales within one out of the championship. But like the day before, Pittsburgh did not go down tamely. The Rebels sent Jack Lewis up to bat for Rogge, and he came through with a single that sent Mowrey to third. The next batter, Marty Berghammer, lofted a lazy fly ball into left-center. The game should have ended then and there, but just as the ball settled into the glove of Dutch Zwilling, Les Mann barreled into the center fielder and knocked the ball loose. Berghammer got credit for a double and Mowrey scored on the play. Former Chifed Al Wickland worked the count to 3 balls and 2 strikes, then drove home the two runners with a single. What a few minutes earlier had been a sure thing was now gravely in doubt. The game was tied at four. A walk stirred concern in the crowd, but the Whales survived the ninth without any more damage as relief pitcher Mike Prendergast finally retired the side. Elmer Knetzer, scheduled to be Pittsburgh's starting pitcher in the second game, was sent out by Rebel Oakes to finish the game.

Neither team scored in the tenth, but in the eleventh the Rebels' pitcher reached base on a single. Berghammer sacrificed Knetzer to second, then Wickland came through again. Al's wicked smash caromed off the shins of Chicago shortstop Mickey Doolan and Knetzer scored to give Pittsburgh the lead. The Rebels held fast in the bottom of the eleventh for a 5 to 4 victory.

Though mathematically eliminated from the championship, St. Louis rolled to a 6–4 win over Kansas City to clinch second place. Even if Chicago and Pittsburgh split their double-header, St. Louis would finish .001 behind the Whales. Prior to the outcome of the second game in Chicago the Federal League standings stood as follows:

Pittsburgh Rebels	86–66	.566
St. Louis Terriers	87–67	.565
Chicago Whales	85–66	.563

A win for Pittsburgh in the season's final game would mean the Federal League title for the Rebels. A Whales victory would give Chicago the flag over St. Louis by the barest of margins. If the game could not be completed due to darkness or weather, the Rebels would be the champs. Chief Umpire Bill Brennan said before the start of the game that the contest would be terminated when whatever half-inning was completed after 5:24 P.M., the predicted time of sundown.

Pittsburgh sent Knetzer back to the mound for the all-important second game. The Baron had pitched the last three innings of the first game for the victory, and also had started the day before, lasting but two and two-thirds innings. Chicago put its fate into the hands of veteran hurler Bill Bailey, the late-season pickup from Baltimore. Against these same Rebels on Thursday, Bailey had been knocked out of the game in the third inning after giving up five runs. However, the southpaw had not pitched since then, while the rest of the Whales' staff had seen duty. Despite a 7–20 record for the season, on this day Arkansas Bill delivered. The Browns' castoff decimated the Rebels inning after inning.

Up to the sixth inning, both Bailey and Knetzer were in good form. The Whales' hurler had allowed but two singles and both those runners were picked off first base by the lefty. The Baron had not allowed a runner past second when Chicago came to bat in the bottom of the sixth.

"The team that could squeeze over a solitary run would most likely be in possession of the bunting, as the game might be called any minute," wrote one reporter. "It was already too dark for the spectators to follow the gyrations of the ball as it played hide and seek between the pitcher and the catcher or gamboled off the shinbones of some groping infielder."[6]

The Chicago crowd came alive when Mickey Doolan shot a single between second and third to open the Chicago sixth. The runner was sacrificed to second by pitcher Bailey and then Doolan advanced to third on Zeider's infield out. Max Flack was up next and with darkness imminent, the Whales might not get another chance. If Flack was retired and Pittsburgh kept the game tied until darkness forced the game to be called a draw, the Rebels would be awarded the flag by .001 of a percentage point.

"Two balls and two strikes had been called on Max," wrote special correspondent G.W. Alexson.

> The roars from the stands, bleachers and field had died down to a whisper, as a blurred, round object started on a journey for the fence in right center. Flack had collided with the ball and the noise of the blow carried around the Federal League circuit, as the wallop put Pittsburgh and St. Louis out of the pennant race. Oakes finally dug the sphere from out among the latest trouser patterns, but there was no profit in the digging as Doolan had crossed the plate and Max had been given the credit for a two-bagger.[7]

It had been so close. The Pittsburgh outfielder was able to get some leather on Flack's drive, but the webbed glove that might had ensnared the ball was still four years away from use. The ball ricocheted off his glove and into the crowd assembled behind the outfield rope. Flack's two-out hit opened the floodgates for the Whales. Dutch Zwilling followed with another run-scoring ground rule double into the crowd in right, and he came home with a third run on Art Wilson's Texas league single. A Pechous single spelled the end for Knetzer. Frank Allen came in and retired Mann on a pop-up.

The umpires allowed the game to continue into the top of the seventh inning, but there would be no comeback for Pittsburgh this time. Bailey continued his mastery as he set the disheartened Rebels down in order. Ed Konetchy became the final batter in Federal League history when he flied out to Dutch Zwilling to end the top of the seventh. Before the sides could exchange places, umpires Brennan and Johnstone ended the game because of darkness at 5:25 P.M. The Whales were 3–0 victors to take the pennant and the final inning in Federal League history had been played.

As soon as the signal to end the game was given, the crowd behind the outfield ropes rushed the diamond in order to celebrate with the players. The bugs in the grandstand expressed their joy by tossing their seat cushions onto the playing field. Fans mingling on the field took to throwing the cushions back and the scene soon degenerated into a huge pillow fight. The park's attendants and police finally got the celebrants off the field and the large crowd made its way onto the street and for the elevated railroad cars.[8]

Though Max Flack got the headlines, the Chicago hero of the day was the late season pickup, Bailey, who held the Pittsburgh batters to only two hits and did not allow a runner to advance past first base.

Two rainouts that were not made up enabled the Whales to win the pennant by .000854 percentage points. The next day, Owner Charles Weeghman challenged the American and National League winners to a three-way series to determine the best baseball team in the world. His offer was declined. Weeghman's challenge in the form of a telegram read in part, "I believe that we must all admit that to make baseball truly the American pastime it must be conducted on a truly American principle of absolute fairness to all, and that the champion team of the country must be the team that defeated the champions of our league." That evening the Chicago City Council passed a resolution directing Mayor Thompson to ask the proper baseball officials to give the Chicago Federals a chance to play for the world's championship.

Weeghman did receive a response from the chairman of the National Commission, Garry Herrmann, acknowledging, "I am in receipt of your telegram of Oct. 4 and have sent a copy thereof to my colleagues for their information and consideration."

Charley mused, "Well, I'm glad they recognized the challenge, at any rate."[9]

The "Whales" (with a lineup of mostly second stringers) then went on a barnstorming tour playing the top amateur clubs in the Chicago area. The Whales' subs ignored a challenge from Rube Foster's American Giants, Chicago's top Negro baseball team.

Final Federal League standings:

Chicago Whales	86–66	.565789	—
St. Louis Terriers	87–67	.564935	—
Pittsburgh Rebels	86–67	.562	½
Kansas City Packers	81–72	.529	5½
Newark Peppers	80–72	.526	6
Buffalo Blues	74–78	.487	12
Brooklyn Tip Tops	70–82	.461	16
Baltimore Terrapins	47–107	.305	40

43

The Big Bluff

Despite a close pennant race, Federal League attendance figures for 1915 were disheartening. Even the reduction of ticket prices in most Federal League cities didn't attract enough additional fans to warrant another season. Though the Federals kept their attendance figures even closer to the vest in 1915 than in their inaugural season, it was obvious the league lost a considerable amount of money. That, coupled with hefty players' contracts that the clubs were bound to honor, spelled doom for the league. James Gilmore, as well as the club magnates, hoped to recoup some lost capital rather than fold their tents and disappear from the scene.

Attendance for the American and National Leagues increased by 409,838 in 1915, but the numbers were still smaller than any season between 1904 and 1913.[1] Even more distressing to the major league owners than attendance numbers were the astronomical salary increases among the players. In 1913 twenty select players from clubs in the two traditional major leagues received a total of $76,350 in salaries, and average of $3,817.50 apiece. In 1915 the same players were paid $146,550, an average of $7,327.50, a salary increase of almost 92 per cent. During the Federal League war, Tris Speaker's pay doubled to $18,000 a season and Ty Cobb's increased from $12,000 to $20,000, the largest contract of the "Dead Ball Era."[2]

Several major league magnates were ready to negotiate with the outlaws, but there were a few powerful men in Organized Baseball who swore they would never sit down with the Federal Leaguers. Consequently, James Gilmore and a couple of his key owners proceeded to orchestrate the biggest bluff in baseball history. Their efforts succeeded enough to extract a generous settlement from Organized Baseball, seemingly impossible only a couple of months earlier.

As they had following the 1914 season, the Federal League sought to settle their war with Organized Baseball in October 1915. Gilmore and Charles Weeghman stuck close to the big men of the organized major leagues during the World Series as it moved from Philadelphia to Boston.

Late Friday Night, October 8, a Federal League delegation of Gilmore, Harry Sinclair, Ed Gwinner, and Philip Ball met with National League President John Tener and National Commission Chairman Garry Herrmann in a room reserved at the Bellevue-Strafford Hotel in Philadelphia. Ban Johnson was having supper with Colonel Jacob Ruppert of the New York Yankees when the American League President was requested upstairs. Ban refused to enter the discussion with Gilmore present and the Fed chief was induced to leave.

Johnson said, "Tie a can to him [Gilmore] and send him out," reported the *Times*.

With the three members of the National Commission present, the representatives of the Federal League made their pitch. The Feds freely admitted that they were weary of carrying on their struggle and proposed that the National and American Leagues expand to ten teams, taking in the Federal League clubs in Brooklyn, Pittsburgh, Baltimore and Buffalo or Kansas City. They also proposed that Charles Weeghman and Harry Sinclair be allowed to buy existing major league clubs.[3]

Following the meeting, Johnson said: "The meeting served no purpose except to give a wrong impression to some of the fans and the press regarding our relations with the Feds. It made it appear to some that a peace conference between the Feds and Organized Baseball was on when such is not the case."[4]

Organized Baseball took the position that owners of the outlaw league could buy stock in National League clubs, but they must abandon all Federal League connections, square up their obligations with players they had under long-term contracts, and acknowledge the claims of Organized Baseball clubs on those players before they jumped leagues. The point regarding player contracts was a problem for the Feds. The Federal League money men had the idea that a settlement of their obligations relating to player contracts would be a matter to be taken over by the National League.[5]

President Tener favored ending the baseball war, but he could not get his owners in Pittsburgh, Brooklyn, Chicago and New York to support the ideal of two leagues with ten clubs each. Barney Dreyfuss of Pittsburgh met with Tener and Herrmann on Friday following the Series and refused to hear of any compromise with the Federals.[6]

Following the final game of the World Series on October 13, Ban Johnson went directly home from Philadelphia without meeting again with the belligerents. Without the support of Johnson and Dreyfuss, the compromise plan had little chance of success.[7]

On October 18, 1915, the Federal League's fortunes were dealt a devastating blow. Robert Boyd Ward, league vice president and president of the Brooklyn team, died at his country home in New Rochelle. Ward had been diagnosed with pneumonia a week earlier and by the following Monday evening the sixty-four-year-old Brooklyn club owner was dead. When Robert Ward passed, much of the heart and fight of the Federal League died with him.

Patrick Powers paid tribute to his friend with the memory of one of his final meetings with the Tip Tops' magnate. "Mr. Ward insisted upon me sitting in the sun with him along toward the middle of the season. He was ill then and wore an overcoat, but he was good-natured, and it seemed to be his sole ambition to see his boys win. I almost rooted against my own team. Newark lost, 1–0. I have never seen a man more pleased."[8]

The *New York Times* editorialized:

The death of Robert B. Ward removes from the Federal League one of its staunch supporters. He was ever an active force in promoting the welfare of the league, and on several occasions came forward with loans of money to tide over the difficulties of clubs less firmly entrenched than his own. In view of the position which he held, his death naturally entails consideration of what affect his loss will have on the future of the league.[9]

Almost one-half of Robert Ward's estate, estimated at $3,000,000, was left to be divided among his nine children. Robert's brother George, though not as active in the league, was an equal partner in their team. On October 31, George Ward officially became the new president of the Brooklyn Federal League club.

When the appraisal of Robert Ward's estate was released by Westchester County, New York, in May 1917, it was revealed that he lost an estimated $1,000,000 because of his association with the Federal League. The appraisal showed that Ward held promissory notes of the Brooklyn club amounting to $220,800; he paid $373,000 for 1,347 shares of preferred stock and 2,373 shares of common stock in Federal League clubs that became worthless after

1915; and he advanced the league $50,000 on contracts the club made while he was president. He also was said to have advanced the league other large sums that were not included in the estate records.[10]

A few days after the death of Robert Ward, the name of Harry Sinclair, owner of the Newark Federal League franchise, began to show up a lot in the newspapers. *The Sporting News*' Joe Villa wrote in his column of November 11:

> Garry Herrmann, apostle of peace in baseball, hunted up N. Ashley Lloyd, the late John T. Brush's former partner in the ownership of the Giants, and made a proposition in behalf of Sinclair, which finally went up in the air.
> ...Garry told Lloyd that Sinclair and Ward were proved to pay about $1,000,000 for a controlling interest in the New York club. But several days after Lloyd had received this proposition and had been urged to exert his influence with the Brush heirs, Mr. Ward passed out of this life and Sinclair refused to go ahead.[11]

It had been widely reported that Sinclair was interested in purchasing one of the New York clubs, but Lloyd, the current treasurer of the Giants, denied Villa's story and said he never met Sinclair and had not tried to exert his influence with the Brush heirs to consent to a sale of any kind.[12]

A week earlier, Villa had written, "This is a true story of the plan to throw the Feds' hooks into the Giants. I can prove it if necessary." Villa printed Lloyd's denial in his column, but *The Sporting News*' chief propagandist did not mention any of his "proof."

Rumors continued to materialize over the next few days. On October 27, Chicago newspapers ran a story that peace terms had been reached under which the Federal League and the National League would unite. The story, which hit the papers just when Charles Weeghman and William Walker returned to the city, reported the possible purchase of the New York Giants by Harry Sinclair and the union of the National and Federal teams in St. Louis, Pittsburgh and Chicago. It was all pure speculation.

The dismal state of the Federal League was apparent at their annual meeting in Indianapolis the first week of November. Baltimore, Buffalo and Kansas City were run by stockholders and all three clubs were in financial trouble. President Robertson of Buffalo admitted that an appeal for public funds to bail out his ball club had failed. The Baltimore Terrapins borrowed $50,000 from a trust company by pledging the club's stock and physical property just to pay its debt. However, Baltimore's stockholders vowed to continue in the league and warned against any peace plan that did not leave Baltimore a "major league" city.[13]

Robert B. Ward, president, Brooklyn Federal League club, 1915 (National Baseball Hall of Fame Library, Cooperstown, N.Y.).

Other than in Kansas City and Buffalo, Federal League owners were prepared to continue the league unless a satisfactory deal could be made with Organized Baseball. The magnates insisted that in any arrangement they must be recognized as a league and be taken care of as a whole.

James Gilmore was reelected Federal League president and after the meeting he confirmed that the Federal and National Leagues had been unable to reach an agreement about consolidation. He also announced that the Federals' Kansas City club, whose franchise was declared forfeited, would be moved to New York and strengthened so that it "will merit the support of the New York fans." He added that plans had been submitted for stands to seat 55,000 persons and the league would be ready to operate in New York at the beginning of the 1916 season.[14]

The forfeiture of their Federal League franchise did not come as a surprise to the Kansas City club. According to a report made at a stockholders' meeting on October 25, the Packers showed a loss of $35,000 on the season's operations and the club was in debt to the league to the extent of $8,300. To add to the Packers' woes, the club was being sued by a woman for $10,000 on the grounds that a foul ball which hit her in the face on April 25 destroyed her eyesight.[15] Notwithstanding the financial loss, the club announced that paid attendance at Kansas City's Federal League park the past season was 82,060, a marked increase over 1914. Club President Conrad Mann said that only two other cities in the Federal League turned in greater attendance than Kansas City. The home receipts of the Packers amounted to $82,060.60 and the Packers paid visiting clubs $32,355.57, while the Kansas City club only collected $21,234.42 from its road games.[16]

The guarded optimism of Gilmore and the other Federal League magnates before their meeting in Indianapolis was gone by the time they adjourned. The *New York Times* reported on November 12 that the peace negotiations had fallen through as the three major leagues could not agree on any settlement that would be suitable to the parties involved. It seemed that both sides were in agreement that peace would be best for all, but the only peace proposal submitted by the Federals involved ten teams in each of the two major leagues and was unacceptable to the older circuits.[17]

President Tener reluctantly declared that there was no possibility of any Federal League men buying into Organized Baseball. Editorialized the *Times*, "As this was the supposed basis of peace negotiations, it is presumed that the difficulty is no nearer solution than a year ago."[18]

Early on, James Gilmore wanted to move the Feds' Newark franchise to New York City, but was blocked by the Newark investors. However, the Feds did not give up the dream of challenging two of baseball's top franchises, the Giants and Yankees. At the time, the Giants were the toast of New York City and the Yankees had just received a fresh infusion of cash from their new ownership. Though the plan to place a club in New York City did not prove feasible, Gilmore, with the assistance of Newark owner Harry Sinclair, came up with the idea of using a proposed New York Federal League club as a bargaining chip in their dealings with Organized Baseball.

The story got a great deal of publicity when Sinclair got into a battle of words in the newspapers with some of Organized Baseball's owners. When critics maintained that the oil man did not have the revenue to establish a club in the city, Sinclair reacted with a proposition.

Frank G. Menke revisited the story of Sinclair's challenge to the magnates of Organized Baseball in his column of November 9, 1933:

> Sinclair lost money, but he gained more publicity out of the old Federal League than any man identified with it. There was constant talk about Sinclair having millions and millions. This

caused eventual scoffing by magnates of Organized Baseball and Sinclair's ire was aroused by this to such an extent that he made this proposal:

"I'm not saying I have all the money I'm supposed to have. And I'm not denying it. But what I say is this. I'll get into a boat with the club owners in Organized Baseball and we will go about fifty miles out into the ocean where it is very deep. And then, for each silver dollar that each of the magnates drops into the Atlantic, I will also drop one. In other words, I'm saying that I'll drop ten dollars for each one by each of these magnates. So you hear any acceptance?"[19]

A different version of the story was oft retold by J. Taylor Spink and columnists of *The Sporting News:* "I'll stand at the Battery [New York's waterfront] and for every dollar the major leagues want to toss in the North River, I'll toss in another," pronounced Sinclair at the time. "And I won't be the first to run out of dollars."[20]

Years earlier, Harry Ford Sinclair's father wanted his son to replace him as the druggist in his Kansas home town, so young Harry sought a pharmacy degree at the University of Kansas. Harry ultimately inherited the drug store from his father when he was nineteen, but he lost the business in a speculation at age twenty. Sinclair spent a year traveling around the country for a drug company, managed to save a couple of thousand dollars, and headed for the oil fields.

"I went into the oil business on a shoe string," Sinclair related, "buying leases and selling them. Later I was able to develop the leases and produce oil on my own account."[21]

Sinclair first sold lumber for oil derricks, buying and selling leases on the side. Harry traveled by train and buggy throughout southeast Kansas and the Osage Indian territory of Oklahoma, buying drilling rights, then reselling them for small profits. He organized small companies around single leases, with himself as salaried manager and treasurer. He also acquired a few shares of stock for his effort in each venture. Sinclair's propensity for sniffing out lucrative oil fields, plus his managerial talents, attracted wealthy speculators to invest with him. Sinclair insisted upon absolute control of the operation, though his salary for supervision was sometimes as low as $75 a month. With control, he could buy and sell any oil leases he chose.[22]

Sinclair's instincts paid off in 1904 when he made $100,000 at Kiowa, Oklahoma, for his drilling syndicate. A year later, Harry developed another Oklahoma field with 100 wells. The profit from this venture was put into Glenn Pool, Oklahoma's first large producer. By 1907, Sinclair was the richest man in Kansas and within six years Sinclair was managing 62 oil companies.[23]

Sinclair was one of the first oil men to establish his residence in Tulsa, Oklahoma, soon to become known as "Oil Capital of the World." He and his brother founded the Exchange National Bank in the city. The bank became known worldwide for doing business with oil men and petroleum companies and within nineteen years, the assets of Sinclair's bank grew from $700,000 to fifty million dollars.[24]

The Federal League's operation in deception actually began in early August 1915 when Gilmore announced,

We are going to pay no further attention to Judge Landis, but we will proceed to raid organized baseball as soon as we can induce such stars as [Grover Cleveland] Alexander, Eddie Collins, Stuffy McInnis and others to jump. We will invade New York City right on Manhattan Island where we have secured grounds within five minutes of Broadway and 42nd. We are prepared to keep on losing big money for a dozen years to come, for we have millions behind us.[25]

In mid–August James Gilmore, Robert Ward, Harry Sinclair and C.B. Comstock were guests of Boston Braves owner James Gaffney for dinner, a Red Sox game, and a tour of his brand-new ballpark that would seat 40,000 when it opened the following week. Reportedly, the Feds asked the Braves' owner if his contracting company would accept a contract to build the new Federal League Park in New York City.[26]

On September 3, 1915, the *New York Times* reported that the office of the New York Federal League club would be in the Longacre Building, Broadway and 42nd Street, open for business about September 15. "The headquarters of the Federal League prior to this have been in Chicago, but will now be transferred to this city, occupying the same offices as the phantom New York Federal League club," the writer added.[27]

The *Times'* use of the term "phantom" was prophetic. James Gilmore later revealed that in order to convince Organized Baseball to offer better peace terms, they took out an option on grounds for a New York City ballpark as well as a two-year lease on executive offices for the mythical New York Federal League franchise. The Feds made sure the newspapers found out about the Federal League's application to the city for permission to close off streets and prominently displayed an architect's plan for a 40,000-seat stadium in the storefront window of their 42nd Street office.[28] The Federals even announced the hiring of a business manager for the prospective New York club, Edward W. Harter, a boxing match and bicycle race promoter.[29]

On November 29, 1915, Gilmore announced his league had acquired the option on property at the corner of 145th Street and Lenox for the magnificent sum of $1,250,000. Gilmore estimated that they could build a new stadium on the site for about $475,000. He produced a blueprint which called for a stadium that could hold 55,000 patrons and figured it could be completed in just a few short months. It was to be a design similar to Shibe Park in Philadelphia, with a two-tier cantilevered grandstand that would offer an unimpeded view of the field. "It is estimated to be about one-third larger than the Polo Grounds and will give ample room for the building of additional stands," wrote the *Times*.[30]

When a reporter sought out Johnny Evers in Spokane and asked him about the rumor he had been offered the job of managing the New York Federal League club, Joe Tinker's former teammate with the Cubs responded:

> I have nothing but respect and warm feelings for the Federals. They have come in and made a grand fight against mighty big odds. Ball players generally like the Federal League for it has done one thing, if nothing more, and that is boost salaries for all if us. When a player in Organized Baseball says he don't like the Feds he says so because he's afraid or because he don't know any better.... They have had a tough road and I am afraid it will be even tougher from now on....[31]

Needless to say, *The Sporting News* and other publications favorable to the organized major leagues condemned the veteran second baseman for his traitorous remarks even though Evers was under contract to the Braves and had no intention of jumping leagues. Evers and other players in Organized Baseball ran a risk when speaking publicly about salary inequities and making favorable comments about the Federal League.

The new Tip Tops president, George Ward, got into the business of deception by announcing that lights for night baseball in 1916 would be tested by the Brooklyn Federal League club. The lights would be installed on five steel towers, each eighty feet high. There would be one at each coach's box, one at the end of each foul line in the outfield and one in center field.[32]

The first trial of the new lighting system for playing night baseball was made at Washington Park the evening of October 25 and the Brooklyn club reported satisfactory results. Dick Carroll assembled a number of semi-pro players who played several innings. A local newspaper reported, "While there were some faults which may be easily remedied by adjusting the screens in front of the lights, the scheme generally worked out well."[33]

While all this was going on, Federal League agents continued their campaign to sign top minor league players to contracts for the upcoming season.

"The engagement of John Ganzel of Rochester as manager of the Brookfeds has taken a sinister aspect," whined *The Sporting News* on October 14. "Pitcher Erickson of the Hustlers and Charley Pick, Richmond's hard hitting third baseman, were lured away by the wily chief of the Wards' ball club."[34]

The Sporting News wrote that Ganzel was also courting International League home run champion George Whiteman of Montreal, former White Sox infielder Morrie Rath of Toronto, Harrisburg's Clarence "Big Boy" Kraft, second baseman Joe McCarthy of Buffalo, and first baseman Walter Holke of Rochester.[35]

George Stovall was again at work in the west. Following the Federal League's regular season, Stovall's Kansas City club barnstormed in the southwest against teams composed of Western Association players. There seemed to be no attention paid to the rule that forbade players of Organized Baseball to participate in games against "outlaws."[36]

In early November, Stovall made a trip to San Francisco at his own expense and secured a pair of the Pacific Coast League's top players, Jimmy Johnston and Joe Gedeon. James "Jimmy" Johnston of the San Francisco Seals was known as a hustler who could play anywhere in the infield or outfield. He held the Organized Baseball record for stolen bases in a single season with 124 while playing with San Francisco in 1913. Shortly after the 1915 Pacific Coast League season closed, Johnston signed a two-year contract to play for Newark of the Federal League for $4,000 a year with a $1000 signing bonus.[37]

Joe Gedeon enjoyed a spectacular 1915 season with Salt Lake City. For the extended Pacific Coast League season, the 21-year-old played 190 games at second base, banged out 234 hits, scored 133 runs, and finished with a .317 batting average. His 67 doubles set a league record, and his fielding percentage was .962, a pretty good mark for the times, especially for his first season as a full-time second sacker.

Gedeon had been outfielder with the Washington Senators in 1913, but was unhappy there so Clarke Griffith allowed him to play ball out west until he was ready for him.[38] Griffith planned on Gedeon's playing second base for the Senators in 1916. Instead, Joe agreed to a lucrative two-year contract to play for Newark of the Federal League. After signing Gedeon, the Peps sold second baseman Frank LaPorte to Brooklyn.

Another question for the Federals was how long Chicago's Charles Weeghman would remain loyal and resist the temptation to bolt to Organized Baseball. Since the end of the 1914 season, the prospect of Weeghman's abandoning the Feds to purchase the Chicago Cubs haunted the Federals. Despite all the rumors and off-the-record negotiations, Charley remained faithful to the Federal League.

The Chicago Whales' owner was temporarily removed from the peace discussions by the death of his father, August W. Weeghman. On November 18, 1915, the 65-year-old former blacksmith committed suicide in the home of his son, with whom he and his wife lived. A coroner's inquest held that the cause of death was "nervous unrest."[39] Upon his return to the spotlight, Charles Weeghman said he wanted the baseball tangle settled and he believed all the men in baseball desired to accomplish the same end.[40]

After a conference of several Federal League magnates in New York on November 22, 1915, Gilmore announced they would soon reveal the identity of a Boston millionaire who was to back the new club in New York.[41] Six weeks later *The Sporting News* reported that, based on information received from John Montgomery Ward, the "Boston millionaires" mentioned by Gilmore were Percy D. Haughton and Arthur Wise, who purchased the Boston Braves in early January 1916.[42]

Charles Somers became a casualty of the Federal League war when attempts to preserve his position as owner of the Cleveland American League club failed. By 1915 Somers had lost almost two million dollars in real estate and the coal business, and the Indians were in dire financial trouble. The team finished last in 1914 and attendance continued to decline the following season.

Somers had been in on the beginning of the American League in 1900 and his money helped bankroll Johnson's league. All that didn't help him in the fall of 1915. After meeting with Somers' bankers in Cleveland the second week of December, Ban Johnson said that the Indians would soon be in the hands of new owners because the creditors of the current owner had declined to accept any other proposition and insisted upon a sale of the club's holdings.[43]

On December 15, 1915, Federal League President James Gilmore declared that peace in baseball must be reached no later than December 21, because the Federal League's option on the property for the ballpark in New York City expired on the twenty-third. Unless there was an understanding between all those concerned in baseball before that date, he stated, the Federals would purchase the park property and include it in the assets of the Federal League at such a time a peace agreement might be reached.[44]

The Federal League's pursuit of a baseball park in New York pushed the heretofore resistant National League owners into changing their mind about further negotiations with the outlaws. However, American League boss Ban Johnson was not fooled. Johnson had made inquiries about that selfsame plot of land for his new league in 1903. Ban knew that there was nothing he could do if the city decided to put a street right through the heart of the property, so he rejected the land. Johnson tried to convince the Senior Circuit to stand strong, that Sinclair and Gilmore were only bluffing, but his National League colleagues were ready to end the war.

44

Peace!

Talks between representatives of Organized Baseball's major leagues and the Federal League inaugurated during the World Series laid the groundwork for further negotiations aimed at ending the baseball war. National League owners, gathered in New York for their annual meeting, met with James Gilmore and Harry Sinclair in President John Tener's office on Monday, December 13, 1915. That evening, representatives of the National League and Federal League had dinner together at the Republican Club. Jointly, they drew up a tentative draft of a peace agreement. The National League owners were not prepared to proceed until they found out whether the American Leaguers would go along.

Pittsburgh's Barney Dreyfuss, who was respected by the American Leaguers for his efforts in settling the war between the leagues in 1902, was dispatched to take the plan to them during the junior circuit's meeting in Chicago. Dreyfuss went from the Nationals' assembly room to the railroad station without even taking the time to collect his toiletries.

Ban Johnson dismissed the mission of the Pirates' owner: "Dreyfuss is not coming with peace plans.... He has been opposed to peace all along and simply wishes to know which way the wind is blowing in the American League."

Dreyfuss arrived in Chicago at two o'clock and went immediately to the Congress Hotel where the American League magnates were meeting. Without even a fresh collar, Barney entered the American League meeting two hours earlier than expected. All league business was dropped to allow the Pirates' owner to make his pitch.

"The eloquent and convincing speech of Dreyfuss won the day," wrote George Robbins from Chicago. "It is difficult to fathom the diplomacy that caused the American League, including its chief, to be transformed in a twinkling from a bellicose lot to pronounced pacifists. The wild side, rampart eloquence of Barney Dreyfuss turned the trick. Had President Tener or Garry Herrmann made the trip to Chicago things might have been different. Dreyfuss was the man of the hour."[1]

The National League's envoy also brought an implied if not stated warning that it was up to the Americans to jump into the breach, "lest terms would be made that would give the Feds a chance to say they had won something."[2]

"I had just stood up to read my report on the Federal League when Dreyfuss blew in," Johnson told the press. "You know the nature of my report. It was lengthy and would have required two hours to read it. I had shown in this report where the Feds didn't have a leg on which to stand on. Dreyfuss came in with his report and it upset everything."[3]

The National League's delegate took over an hour to make his case, then retired to the hotel barber shop to shed his day's growth of beard. While awaiting the owners' decision,

Dreyfuss was surrounded by a large group of newspaper hounds and a few curious parties, all wanting a story about the meeting upstairs.

"Peace is better than war," Dreyfuss told the reporters, "and I told the American League magnates so.... I laid the terms before the American League at its meeting here, and can say no more about it. I can give out no details. My work is over and I expect to leave for Pittsburgh tonight."[4]

The American Leaguers discussed Barney's proposition for over an hour, then sent for the Pirates' owner, who was waiting in the hotel lobby. Dreyfuss reentered the meeting room to find Ban Johnson and his owners unexpectedly agreeable to a settlement with the Federals.

After the meeting was adjourned for the afternoon, Johnson emerged and announced to the assembled reporters that the American Leaguers had accepted the draft of the National League's peace proposition. Ban and his owners would hold a night session to finish their business so they could meet with the National Leaguers in New York as soon as possible. The American League selected a committee consisting of Johnson, Charles Comiskey, Joseph Lannin, Benjamin Minor and Jacob Ruppert to meet with the other interested parties at the Waldorf-Astoria Hotel in New York and arrange a settlement.

The next morning, the *New York Times* and newspapers all around the country printed similar stories of the news out of Chicago: "The end of the baseball war came in sight tonight when American League club owners, at their annual meeting here, agreed to the peace terms arranged at New York between the Federal and National Leagues. Within a few days, according to President Johnson, the details of the agreement which would abolish the Federals as an independent league will be arranged."[5]

All of this was news to the owners of the Baltimore Federal League club, who insisted they had no idea of what was going on until Gilmore summoned the Terrapins' president, Carroll Rasin, and principal owner Ned Hanlon to a meeting at the New York Biltmore the morning of December 17. There, Hanlon and Rasin learned that the Federals were about to throw in the towel and no arrangement had been made for the Baltimore interests, because Gilmore and Sinclair claimed they did not have the authority to negotiate for that club.

Baseball historian Harold Seymour wrote, "Baltimore officials had been suspicious of the intentions of their colleagues, and some Baltimore leaders had made a special trip to Chicago toward the end of 1914 to satisfy themselves about Weeghman's and Gilmore's intentions. Although they received assurances that there was nothing to rumors of flirtations with Organized Baseball, they left with their suspicions unalloyed. At the New York parley at the end of 1915 their worst fears were proved well founded.... Baltimore had been given the 'dinky-dink.'"[6]

Another problem arose when the National Leaguers could not make good on a promise they had made to St. Louis Federal League owner Philip Ball. The peace committee felt they would be able to deliver the St. Louis National League club for Philip Ball to purchase, but they forgot to seal the deal with the Cardinals' owner. It was known that Helen Britton was ready to get out of the baseball business after five years as owner of the St Louis club. She had owned the Cardinals since her uncle, M. Stanley Robinson, died in 1911, and in his will left 75 percent of the club to his thirty-one-year-old niece, Helen, and 25 percent to her mother.[7]

When Mrs. Britton arrived in New York, she discovered a beautiful floral bouquet in her room at the Waldorf-Astoria. She went to the National League conclave fully prepared to sell the Cardinals if the price was right, but when President Tener and the seven male owners attempted to pressure her, she called in the option to sell and returned home still in possession of the club.

"In the early minutes of the meeting, Mrs. Britton informed us that she named her price to the peace committee to sell and it was reported the Cardinals had been sold to Ball," reported Phil Keener in the *St. Louis Times*:

>...The switch remained a secret until the lady told the story herself.
>When the magnates tried to force her to sell instead of trying to persuade her, and informed her that "it would be for the good of the game for her to get out of baseball," she stood toe-to-toe with them and won the night.
>The National League made the mistake of telling her what she "must" do.[8]

When the Cardinals were pulled off the market, a key component of the deal with the Federal League was in jeopardy. Now the onus shifted to Ban Johnson. Soon after the American League's December meeting in Chicago, Ban Johnson contacted his friend Philip Ball.

Ball recounted the story of his deal with Johnson to *Sporting News* columnist Harry Brundidge a year after Ban's death:

>Ban Johnson, then president of the American League, wired me, I wired Sinclair, and we three, with Charles Comiskey, late owner of the Chicago White Sox, met in the Union Club in Chicago. Johnson discussed ways and means of dissolving the Federal League. One of my first propositions was that if this was done, all players who had jumped from the other two leagues to the Federal be reinstated. Ban agreed and asked if I would be interested in buying the Browns of the American League, and I told him I would at the right price.[9]

With Ball's assurance, Ban Johnson went about securing an option from Robert L. Hedges and his fellow owners to sell the St. Louis Browns before the peace agreement was finalized. Hedges had owned the Browns since purchasing the Milwaukee Brewers and moving them to St. Louis in 1902. He was one of Johnson's staunchest supporters, but he had grown weary of the inability to build a winning team in St. Louis. Selling out at this time might be his best chance to cash in on his initial investment of $30,000 fourteen years earlier.

Hedges agreed to sell his 60 percent of stock in the St. Louis American League club, so Ban Johnson was able to attend the preliminary peace conference with the "Browns in his vest pocket, so to speak." Outgoing owner Hedges was believed to have realized $765,000, counting salaries and dividends over thirteen years, on his original investment.[10]

In addition to Johnson's American League committee, the men who would determine the fate of the Federal League at a meeting room in the Waldorf included the National League committee, consisting of President Tener, James Gaffney, Garry Herrmann, Barney Dreyfuss and Charles Ebbets. National Association Secretary John H. Farrell and President Ed Barrow of the International League represented the minor leagues. James Gilmore, George S. Ward, Charles Weeghman, Harry Sinclair, and Carroll W. Rasin spoke for the Federal League.

"Harry Sinclair was much gazed upon by the magnates and the curious crowd," wrote W.A. Phelon.

>Any man who has 40 millions is sure to attract a great deal of attention from the throng. Mr. Sinclair, to the apparent surprise of the multitude, proved to be anything but a Coal Oil Johnny. He turned out to be a very quiet, unassuming man of medium size; pale of face, looking hardly like the published pictures and dressed in solemn black. His only fad seemed to be the toting of a little cane, with a hooked handle, which hung over his arm whenever he walked around the lobby.[11]

Organized Baseball required that the Federal League withdraw its antitrust suit before Judge Landis immediately. However, the Federals considered their suit a strong bargaining point and would not consent to dropping it until Organized Baseball agreed to some basic demands.

The discussions proceeded amicably until the issue of player contracts came up. When the Federals stood firm on their demand that Organized Baseball assume all the Federal League's player contracts the American Leaguers balked. It became obvious that negotiations would not go smoothly.

Charles Comiskey of the White Sox nearly doomed the peace discussions when he stood and announced, "Not for me. I'm through here and I am going back to Chicago!"

Other American League representatives appeared ready to join him, when, of all people, it was Ban Johnson who saved the conference. "One minute, gentlemen," he said. "Maybe we can reach an agreement on this point. Let us try anyway, before we do anything hurriedly."[12]

During informal discussions, Baltimore's Carroll Rasin surprised the delegates by proposing that his club should have the opportunity to purchase a major league franchise, preferably the St. Louis Cardinals, and move it to Baltimore.[13] The Baltimore representatives maintained their city was deserving of a major league team. They pointed out that the Maryland city's population was greater than four other major league cities.

When the Baltfeds' attorney said his clients were willing to pay $250,000 for a franchise, Charles Comiskey sarcastically remarked to the delegates that it was just the right price for a minor league franchise: "Baltimore is a minor league city and not a hell of a good one at that."[14]

During negotiations, it was suggested the Baltimore Federal League club could be taken care of through amalgamation with the city's International League club. Jack Dunn exploded. "After what I've been through, I'm not amalgamating with anybody. Nobody is horning into my club." Ed Barrow, the International League's president, echoed Dunn's objections from New York: "They won't take care of the Baltimore Federals at our expense or at the expense of one of our clubs. We were no party to this peace agreement." The National Commission had no way of imposing this proposition on a minor league club so it was dropped. The Baltimore club left the conference with no promise to take care of it or the stockholders.[15]

On Saturday, committees of the three leagues, upon finding it difficult to arrive at an equitable plan, decided to suspend talks and reconvene in Cincinnati on Monday. The matter that threatened to complicate the whole matter was still the Federals' proposition that Organized Baseball take care of $385,000 worth of Federal League players' contracts. Ebbets of Brooklyn, the Pirates' Dreyfuss, and Gaffney of the Braves refused to take back any players who jumped contracts or violated the reserve clause to join the outlaws.

On Sunday, the story broke in Chicago that Charles Weeghman had reached an agreement whereby he would purchase the Cubs. During a discussion with reporters just before he left for Cincinnati, the Whales' owner announced that Joe Tinker would manage the Cubs and they would play their games on the North Side in 1916.

"I will have them [the Cubs] as soon as the peace agreement is signed," Weeghman stated. "...I think there is no doubt now that there will be peace, and it will be very soon after we all get together down in Cincinnati."[16]

Actually, Weeghman's arrangement to purchase the National League club could not be finalized until he met with Cubs owner Charles P. Taft, who was on a hunting trip in Texas and would not return to Cincinnati until after the first of the year. The Federal League had always been concerned with the prospect of Weeghman's deserting the league for a club in the organized leagues, but he had stayed with them for two years. It would be impossible for the Federals to remain viable with the loss of both Charles Weeghman and Robert Ward. With the pressure now on the Federal Leaguers, they modified their demand that Organized Baseball assume all of the Federals' player contracts.

On December 23, the *New York Times* led with the story:

Cincinnati — The most disastrous war that the baseball game has ever experienced came to a close here tonight when a treaty of peace between the Federal League and both parties to the national baseball agreement, known as Organized Baseball, was signed.... The agreement gives immunity to all men who have jumped their contracts from both the major and minor leagues of Organized Baseball, as well as all other Federal League players....

That there will be a wild scramble for some of the best Federal League players was clearly indicated by a provision in the treaty that the Federal League, as a league, and which, in so far as actual baseball playing is concerned, ceases to exist. The agreement does not go into the distribution of any players, and it was announced that the bars have been thrown down, and that inasmuch as all are eligible, those who are for sale will probably go to the highest bidder.[17]

By terms of the agreement, Charles Weeghman was to take controlling interest of the Chicago Cubs of the National League from Charles P. Taft, and Philip Ball and his associates with the St. Louis Terriers would gain control of the St. Louis Browns. Organized baseball agreed to assume control of the baseball parks in Newark, Buffalo and Pittsburgh, "which may be abandoned and they could not be used for baseball purposes except as may be agreed to by the power in control."

When asked what disposition would be made on the Federal League's antitrust suit against Organized Baseball pending before Judge Landis in Chicago, President Tener of the National League said: "The suit will be withdrawn."

Minutes after the peace treaty was signed, Garry Herrmann, who was known as somewhat of a jokester, put one over on James Gilmore. The magnates were gathered around a large circular table when the reporters were allowed in. Most of them headed for Herrmann, who was sitting with Gilmore. With a straight face, Garry read the terms of the peace agreement to the scribes and then remarked: "All Federal League magnates, players and umpires are hereby made eligible for Organized Ball. We would also make the fans eligible, but there weren't any." W.A. Phelon noted that "Mr. Gilmore, with a low cry of anguish, ordered refreshments for the crowd."[18]

Histories of Major League Baseball often present the impression that the Federals had thrown in the towel, but terms of the agreement between the leagues were far from a "total victory" for Organized Baseball. The price of peace with the Federals came high. In effect, Organized Baseball bought out the Federal League.

Organized Baseball would pay $600,000 in exchange for the dissolution of the Federal League and amalgamation of two of its clubs into the major leagues. Of that total, George S. Ward[19] and the heirs of his brother would receive $400,000 in twenty annual payments of $20,000 each; $100,000 went to Henry Sinclair in ten annual payments; Edward Gwinner of Pittsburgh was given $50,000 and the right to sell his players to the highest bidder. The National League threw in $50,000 toward Weeghman's purchase price for the Cubs.[20]

The Feds could not get their rivals to assume the Federal League player contracts, at least not in theory. Under terms of the peace pact, Organized Baseball recognized the Federal League's right to the players it had signed and that league's authority to dispose of them even if those players had violated contracts or had ignored the reserve clause. Furthermore, Organized Baseball also agreed not to prevent such players from signing with any team that wanted them. Clubs in the American and National Leagues would be forced to bid for the return of Federal League players who had violated the National Agreement and the clubs from which the players originally jumped had no claim on them. By selling the players they had under contract, the Federal League would be able to get out of the long-term contracts they were legally obligated to honor.

In one additional concession to the Federals, Philip Ball was to receive $2500 in damages from Cincinnati's Garry Herrmann, whose injunction kept Armando Marsans from playing with the St. Louis Terriers.

The only thing not settled at the time of the peace pact was the Federal League's demands relating to the International League; that issue was postponed until January. Among all of the rumors swarming around the conference was one that Pittsburgh's Ed Gwinner would take over the Cleveland Indians franchise from the financially strapped Charles Somers. The story was not founded in fact. The Pittsburgh Rebels joined the Baltimore, Buffalo and Kansas City clubs in the belief they had been sold down the river.

"Whenever I get kicked out of an organization it is time for me to quit and that is what I am going to do," an embittered Gwinner told reporters.

> I was willing to go along until the Federal League became a paying proposition, but when my partners saw fit to "feather their own nests" and drop me overboard, I decided that baseball politics were too much for me, and so I am out. I do not want a franchise of any kind, neither major nor minor league. As soon as I have sold my players I want to forget that I was ever in the baseball ownership game.[21]

The agreement between Organized Baseball and the Federal League did nothing for the Kansas City and Buffalo investors, who lost everything. On July 21, 1916, the Buffalo club went into bankruptcy, listing debts of $89,793, most of which was money advanced by officers and directors to pay the bills.[22] James Gilmore telephoned the Baltimore directors and told them the best he could get for that club was a $50,000 settlement. The Baltfeds flatly rejected the offer and made plans to initiate the most famous litigation in baseball history.

Upon meeting Charles Ebbets in Cincinnati for the very first time, Charles Weeghman and the irascible Dodgers owner engaged in a friendly banter. "Glad to shake hands with you," said the Brooklyn magnate, "even though you did take Tinker away from me. You know, they blamed me for causing the Federal League."

"It was an injustice," replied Charley, "for it was Charles Webb Murphy who really caused the Feds. He gave Mordecai Brown such a raw deal that I agreed to subscribe $5,000 to put a new Chicago club in the field, and, by the way, I've been putting up money ever since."[23]

Organized Baseball did not make the first payment of their $550,000 obligation to the former Federal Leaguers until February 23, 1918, when National League attorney John C. Toole presented a check for $55,800 to James Hindman, attorney for the Federals. Of the payment, $25,000 went to the Pittsburgh Trust company, receiver for the Pittsburgh Rebels; $20,000 to the Robert Ward estate for two years' rental of Washington Park; and $10,000 to Harry Sinclair for two years' rental of the Newark ballpark.[24]

On the surface, the biggest loser in the Federal League settlement seemed to be the defunct league's president, James Gilmore. As a consequence of the peace, there was no place in baseball for Gilmore. He established residence in the Hotel Biltmore in New York and became interested in promotion of the Sinclair Oil Company as well as extramarital activities. On August 31, 1916, Genevieve Gilmore filed suit against the former Federal League president for separate maintenance in the Chicago Circuit Court of Judge Charles Foell, the same Judge Foell from the Chief Johnson case.

"Mr. Gilmore has engaged himself to marry another woman, at one time a dancer in the 'Floradora' sextet and now the rich widow of a successful manufacturer," the suit alleged, "as soon as he can arrange and have carried into effect the collusive divorce desired by him, which his wife has always and still continues to refuse to grant him."[25]

Judge Foell issued a divorce decree to the couple on November 8, after the parties agreed to a settlement in which Genevieve would receive $250 a month as long as she lived, a cash sum of $2,500, and furniture.[26] Never again involved with baseball, James Gilmore slid into obscurity, working in a brokerage firm until the mid–1930s. The Spanish-American War veteran died in a New York veteran's hospital at age 71 on March 19, 1947. His obituary gave his home address as Downey Veterans Hospital, where he had been confined because of a stroke since December 1945. He was survived by his widow, Marie Boura Gilmore.[27]

45

The Big Auction

Hardly had the ink dried on the peace document between Organized Baseball and the Federal League when Harry Sinclair and Pat Powers collected a reported $5,000 from Garry Herrmann's pitching-poor Reds for Newark pitcher Earl Moseley, a thirty-two-year-old right-hander who possessed a good fast ball and a fast breaking curve. The former Red Sox pitcher posted the Federal League's best earned run average in 1915. It was said Herrmann became the first to welcome a contract jumper back as a gesture of good faith.

"I have the disposition of the Kansas City, Buffalo, and Newark Federal League players," announced Harry Sinclair the day after the peace agreement, "and I hold the contracts of Benny Kauff, Lee Magee, and George Anderson, all of the Brooklyn Federals."[1]

In the name of the Federal League, Sinclair took over five "star" players of the Kansas City Packers to satisfy the debts owed to the league by that club. The former Newark owner also announced he had assumed the contracts of five Buffeds, Hal Chase, Al Schulz, Fred Anderson, Hugh Bedient and Nick Allen, presumably for the same reason. Sinclair declined to say how he acquired the three players from Ward, or how he happened to have the Kansas City and Buffalo players on his hands. He did deny that he was the liquidating agent of the Federal League. The oil man announced that if he couldn't dispose of Chase, he would make him the first baseman for the Tulsa Western Association team.[2] Sinclair eventually would sell the contracts of seventeen players for $129,150.00.

Harry Sinclair also pursued his interest in acquiring the National League club in New York. Joe Villa reported that when James E. Gaffney and Robert Davis sold the Boston Braves to a syndicate on January 8, 1916, they were to join hands with Sinclair in the purchase of the New York Giants because he was short of Harry Hempstead's asking price by $200,000.[3]

After several meetings with New York Nationals President Hempstead, the oil man became frustrated with the Giants' owner and his demand of $1,400,000 for 62 percent of the stock in the club. Upon being asked by a reporter in Tulsa on December 31 if he had bought the Giants, Sinclair snapped, "I have other uses for my money!"[4]

Ban Johnson had said several times no Federal League jumper would ever play in the American League again. However, at the time of the settlement, the new owners of the Yankees let it be known that several former Federals would be playing for the 1916 New York American League team.

Two weeks into the New Year, the New York Giants stole a march on the other clubs of Organized Baseball when they grabbed the Federal League's best player, its best catcher, and one of the circuit's most desired pitchers. On January 14, 1916, the Giants' John McGraw charged into the Federal League's New York office and had a long talk with Sinclair and

Gilmore. They arranged a formal meeting the following evening that would also include Giants President Hempstead and club's secretary, John B. Foster. After only a half-hour discussion, Sinclair was paid $65,000 for Brooklyn's Benny Kauff, Bill Rariden of Newark, and Buffalo hurler "Spitball" Fred Anderson. It was said the price for Benny Kauff alone was $30,000.[5]

Benny Kauff had said the Carolina dentist, Fred Anderson, was the hardest pitcher to hit in the Federal League. In two seasons with Buffalo, the former Red Sox spitballer had a record of 31 and 29 with seven shutouts. Regarded as one of the best two or three available pitching prospects in the Federal League, Anderson was quickly snapped up in Sinclair's auction of players. The lanky right-hander became an important component of John McGraw's pitching staff until he departed for military service in midsummer 1918. Fred often became McGraw's heroic saver in relief and during New York's National League championship season of 1917, Fred's earned run average of 1.44 was best among the Giants' pitchers.[6]

When the New York Americans learned the Giants were offering $21,500 for Lee Magee, the former Tip Tops manager/second baseman, co-owner Tillinghast Huston upped the Yankees' offer to $22,000. Sinclair was not in a hurry to deal with the Giants because Hempstead was dragging his feet on the Gaffney-Davis-Sinclair syndicate's offer to purchase the New York National League club. The Feds agreed to sell Magee to the Yankees and Huston rushed to Cincinnati and sign the player.[7] Magee's contract with the Yankees called for a salary of $8,500, which was $1500 more a season than was made by established major league stars such as Honus Wagner and Joe Jackson.

The New York Americans added three more ex-Federal Leaguers on January 21: the Packers' left-handed pitcher Nick Cullop, Joe Gedeon, on whom the Newark club held the rights, and the Peps' Germany Schaefer, who was to be used by the Yankees as a coach and comedian. After the Yankees made the deal with Pat Powers to purchase Gedeon's contract for $7,500 (a considerable amount for a minor leaguer), Clark Griffith protested to Ban Johnson that the player's contract was owned by Washington. The American League president sided with New York and ordered Gedeon to report to the Yankees.

While other major league owners sought to acquire the best free agent talent available, Charles Weeghman's deals seemed to be driven by his loyalty to his former Federal League associates. Joe Tinker persuaded Weeghman to purchase Steve Yerkes from Pittsburgh because of his ability to crack out the long ball. Consequently, the Cubs paid $6,000 for Yerkes and assumed his $5,000 annual salary as stipulated in his Pittsfed contract.[8]

Even more puzzling was the Cubs' purchase of Tom Seaton, who had consulted a specialist for arm trouble at the conclusion of the 1915 season. Nevertheless, Sinclair was able to sell Seaton's contract to the Chicago Cubs for $7,500. Tom's three-year contract with the Federal League had one more year to run. However, Weeghman balked at Seaton's peculiar demands, saying he would furnish travel expenses for only one of the Seatons, and that one would be the Seaton who was assigned to pitch for him.[9]

An opportunity to pare the Cubs' bulky roster came as result of a visit from John Holland, owner of the St. Joseph Drummers. Holland was a savvy baseball man who was grooming several of his players for sale to the major leagues, but got nothing in return when Federal League agents swooped in and signed his best players prior to the 1914 season. At the time, Holland had completed an agreement with the Boston Braves for Tex Westerzil at a price of $4,000, and expected to realize about $5,000 for Dutch Zwilling before he signed with Weeghman's Chifeds.

In late January 1916, Holland, who had been Joe Tinker's roommate when they played together with Denver in 1900, came to Chicago to seek reimbursement for the players he had lost two years earlier. Weeghman and Tinker gave the Drummers Westerzil and first baseman Bill Jackson, and promised to send Holland a pitcher later. By the peace agreement, the Cubs' new owners owed Holland nothing, but instead they got rid of a couple of extra players the club didn't need and gained a bit of good publicity.[10]

In late February, the new-look Cubs took Kansas City Packers pitcher Gene Packard off Sinclair's hands for a stated $10,000. To make room for Packard on their inflated roster, the Cubs released pitcher Addison Brennan.

On May 1, Brennan signed to pitch for the Atlanta Crackers of the Southern Association, thus becoming a teammate of former Federal League players Eddie Lennox, Tex McDonald, Ed Lafitte, Finn Wilson, Al Bridwell, and the almost Fed Sammy Mayer. After being plagued with a sore arm during his two seasons in the Federal League, Brennan became rejuvenated in Georgia. He completed the 1916 season with an 18–6 win-loss record and returned the following year to help pitch the Crackers to the Association championship. Brennan was named team captain for 1918, but he was sold to the Washington Senators in June when the Southern Association contracted to six teams due to the World War. Ad finished the season with Cleveland, where he pitched his final inning of major league baseball on July 27, 1918.[11]

As president of the Pittsburgh Federals, Ed Gwinner shouldered practically all the club's financial losses, which chiefly consisted of players' contracts and the lease on Exposition Park. At the time of the settlement, Gwinner had sixteen players under contract to the Rebels for 1916, with salaries amounting to over $60,000. The largest obligation was to Ed Konetchy, whose Federal League contract called for $8,500 a year and ran through the end of 1917. The monetary settlement Gwinner received from Organized Baseball only amounted to enough to pay for the $50,000 in improvements he made on Exposition Park.[12]

In January 1916, Gwinner wrote a letter to Garry Herrmann and asked if the Reds' president would be interested in taking any of the contracted players off his hands. In it he explained the current contract status of the players still under contract: Pitcher Frank Allen's contract for $5,500 without a ten-day clause ran through 1916; Konetchy's was due $7,000 for each of the next two seasons and did not have a ten-day clause; Knetzer's contract called for $4,500 in 1916, but did not have a ten-day clause; Berghammer's agreement contained a ten-day clause and he was owed $3,500 for each of the next two seasons; and Comstock was contracted for the next two seasons for $3,500 each with a ten-day clause.[13] Herrmann replied to Gwinner's inquiry later that month and expressed little interest in the players, especially the ones who had contracts with the ten-day clause eliminated.

After Gwinner sold Steve Yerkes to Weeghman, the Pittsburgh owner had little success peddling his former players to major league clubs. Ed Konetchy was one of the leading hitters in the Federal League during 1915, but his expensive three-year contract and a high price set by Gwinner for the player's services deterred most clubs from bidding for the star first baseman.

Frustrated about the lack of takers, Gwinner offered to transfer player contracts to any club that would take on their Federal League salaries. He offered Rebel Oakes and Al Wickland to Barney Dreyfuss, but the Pirates declined the players. Fed up with the whole affair, Gwinner turned over the remainder of the former Rebels under contract to the defunct league for disposal.

Former Rebels outfielder Jimmy Kelly received a letter from Gwinner notifying him of his unconditional release and gave him the name of a Federal League agent "who will attempt to place you." Kelly consulted the chairman of the National Commission, Garry Herrmann, who ruled Kelly was not the property of the Pirates from which he originally jumped and was a free agent.[14]

Pat Powers managed to sell several former Federal League players at the annual National League meeting at the Waldorf-Astoria in New York on February 9. The new owners of the Boston Braves purchased the contracts of Frank Allen, Baron Knetzer, and Ed Konetchy for $18,000. The price for Big Ed alone was $12,000.[15] That same day Powers transferred the contracts of catcher Emil Huhn and shortstop Jimmy Esmond of Newark, as well as a Buffed pitcher, Al Schulz, to the Cincinnati Reds.

The Braves needed the thirty-year-old Konetchy because Butch Schmidt had retired, and the "Big Ethnic" did not disappoint. Though Koney's batting average fell to .260 in 1916, it still was good enough to be the best on the Braves. He led the third-place Braves in hits, doubles, triples and runs batted in, and again sparkled in the field, leading National League first basemen in put-outs, assists, and double plays. Knetzer didn't work out and was sold to Cincinnati in April, but Frank Allen became a valuable addition.

Allen started only one game for the Braves before July 7, which he lost, 1–0, to the Cubs' Gene Packard at Weeghman Park. Manager George Stallings decided to give him another shot at the Cubs in the fourth game of the same series. This time, Allen came out on top, beating Prendergast 1 to 0. In a third start against the Cubs, Frank lost again, 1–0, this time bested by Hippo Vaughn. Allen pitched in 19 games, 14 of them starts, had a record of eight wins and two losses, threw two shutouts, and posted an earned run average of 2.07.

On January 19, 1916, the National Association released a list of former Federal League players who, as result of the peace pact, were free agents. These players had been released by their Federal League clubs and presented little or no value on the open market. There were many recognizable names on the list: Chief Bender, Charles Carr, Howard Camnitz, Fred Jacklitsch, Davy Jones, Earl Moore, George Mullin, Danny Murphy, Harry Swacina and Hack Simmons. As explained by National Association secretary John H. Farrell, these players, since they were not under contract, automatically reverted to their original club in Organized Baseball.

"If the club holding title to the player's services when he left organized baseball does not desire to secure said player's services," explained Farrell, "then such player shall be permitted to negotiate for his services with any other club. All players must be tendered contracts on or before March 1."[16]

The players from the International League who signed Federal League contracts after the close of the 1915 baseball season were ruled to be Federal League property as part of the peace settlement. That group included Eric Erickson, George Whiteman and Ken Nash of Montreal, Joe McCarthy and Mickey Lalouge of Buffalo, Charlie Pick of Richmond, and veteran Cuban pitcher Dolph Luque of Toronto.

Eric Erickson was highly coveted by the major leagues and had been drafted by the St. Louis Browns in the fall of 1915, but the deal was canceled when the American League learned the pitcher had signed with John Ganzel of the Feds. Erickson came to the Detroit Tigers indirectly from the Wards in a sale that also included the Giants, who were to reimburse Rochester the money paid for the pitcher.[17]

The International League, stung badly by Federal League raiders the previous two years, employed very few former Fed players for 1916. On the other hand, the American Association, which enjoyed an uneasy truce with the outlaws for much of the war, loaded up on former Federal League players. Indianapolis picked up Clint Rogge and Al Wickland. In Minneapolis, the Cantillons signed Sandy Burk, Mike Menosky, Frank Owens and Walt Dickson. Toledo employed Stovall, Rawlings, Evans, Bedient, Kaiserling, and Main. St. Paul opened the season with eight former Federals on its roster, including Ernie Gilmore, Happy Finneran and Marty Berghammer.

Berghammer said that he could have returned to the Reds at a salary reduction, so instead he accepted a two-year contract with St. Paul. He remained in St. Paul until 1925, when he became manager of the Western League's Tulsa Oilers. There he won three pennants in four and one-half seasons. Marty later managed Milwaukee and Sioux City before retiring from baseball after the 1936 season.[18]

"I've sold all my players except one, and I'm through with baseball," Harry Sinclair told reporters on his way home to Tulsa in February 1916. "And the best part of it is that I have made money, instead of losing the large sums I read of every day."[19]

On May 1, 1916, Harry Sinclair formed Sinclair Oil from the assets of eleven smaller petroleum companies. Now among the big powers of the oil industry, Harry established his headquarters in New York City. By the end of 1918, the stated value of his corporation exceeded $110 million. Sinclair was still months shy of his fortieth birthday.

Hal Chase was the player without a 1916 contract that Sinclair referred to in his farewell to baseball. As late as February 2, 1916, Ban Johnson declared that Hal Chase and George Stovall were banned forever from the American League. "There's no blacklist," the American League chief announced, "but Stovall and Chase are not the kind of men the American League wants."[20]

Detroit's Hughie Jennings wrote in his newspaper column that spring that the Tigers could win the American League pennant with a player of Hal Chase's ability at first base. However, the Detroit manager said he would not risk employing a star player with "such a bad disposition" that would be a bad influence on the team.[21]

Chase remained unwanted by the major leagues for over a month. Pat Powers became concerned because the former Feds were obliged to pay Hal the sum of $8,000 for 1916, whether he played or not.

Finally, Chase signed a three-year contract with Cincinnati for $8,333 on April 6, 1916. Gary Herrmann was desperate for a first baseman and hoped Chase would jump-start the Reds lineup after a disappointing fifth-place finish in 1915. On April 16, Chase made an impressive National League debut. He smacked a double his first at-bat, stole third, and then home. At thirty-three years old, Hal led National League hitters in 1916 with a .339 batting average. As for rumors about his play, 1916 was the year Chase proved he was still one of the best players in baseball.

On Sunday, April 16, 1916, the *New York Times* reported: "In all, we have a record of 137 former members of the Gilmore circuit having signed to play in Organized Baseball this year. Fifty-seven Federals have joined major league clubs, 36 being in the National and 21 in the American. The Chicago Nationals and St. Louis Americans, which were combined with the Federal League clubs in those cities, naturally have the greatest number of Feds on their roster."

Actually Chase wasn't the last Federal League player to sign with the major leagues for 1916. On the eve of the opening of the National League season, Harry Sinclair received a desperate telephone call from John McGraw. The Giants' starting third baseman, Hans Lobert, had injured his knee during an exhibition game against Yale on April 11. Now without an experienced third sacker, McGraw wanted to know the status of former Newark third baseman Bill McKechnie, who was still unclaimed but had stayed in shape by working out with Philip Ball's Browns during the spring. McGraw closed a deal with Sinclair over the phone and ordered his new third baseman to report to the Giants in Philadelphia. Bill was in a Giants uniform and in the starting lineup for New York's third game of the season on April 15.[22]

The major leagues had no place for George Stovall because he had convinced so many players to jump to the outlaws. Sinclair and Weeghman guaranteed the Federal League's financial obligations due the Kansas City manager whether he found a job or not. Stovall signed on with Toledo, where owner/manager Roger Bresnahan found spots for former major leaguers unwanted elsewhere. George got a job managing the Pacific Coast League club at Vernon, California, in 1917. During World War I, Stovall worked in the shipyards, but after the war he found himself outside of Organized Baseball. George returned to baseball in 1922 as manager of Jacksonville in the Florida State League. He managed semi-pro teams in the California oil fields, then in 1933 he became baseball coach for Loyola University of Los Angeles.

Stovall was a president of the Association of Professional Base Ball Players of America, a players' aid association originated in California in 1924. George sought to become secretary of the organization in 1937 and was elected to that post in a mail-in vote as prescribed by the association president. Baseball Commissioner Kenesaw Landis stepped in, nullified the election and ordered a new poll. The incumbent, Win Clark, was selected instead in a second election held in early 1938.[23] After scouting for Pittsburgh from 1935 to 1941, Stovall left baseball for good and worked in the shipyards until his retirement in 1946.

Rebel Oakes was not offered a major league job for 1916, but surprisingly went to work for J.C. McGill, owner of the Indianapolis American Association Club. The previous summer, one of McGill's pitchers, Sandy Burk, was enticed to jump his Indianapolis contract and sign with Oakes's club. Less than seven months later, Oakes was made manager of the Western League's Denver club, also owned by McGill. The Denver job did not work out for Oakes and he was released during the 1917 season.

Oakes was out of baseball in August 1919 when a Standard Oil Company test well came in as a 7,000-barrel gusher on Oakes's land in Claiborne Parish, Louisiana.[24] With oil revenues coming in at a rate of $15,000 a day, the suddenly wealthy ex–Federal League manager made an offer in February 1920 to buy a controlling interest in the Pittsburgh Pirates. Barney Dreyfuss declined.[25] Oakes was out of the game for three years before the lure of the playing field brought him back into baseball with Jackson of the Class D Mississippi State League in 1921. He ended his baseball career with Greenwood of the same league at the end of the season.

Vin Campbell couldn't find a baseball job with a salary to his liking in 1916 and announced his retirement to go into the automobile business. Vin sued the Newark Federal League Club for breach of contract and sought a judgment of $8,268. The case went to trial in New York City in October 1917. Despite a claim by the defense that Campbell, upon his release, refused to accept service with the St. Louis or Cincinnati National League clubs, the jury awarded payment of $5,957 to the player for the third and final year (1916) of his Federal League contract.[26]

Another player who didn't find a job in major league baseball for 1916 was thirty-five-year-old Frederick "Cy" Falkenberg. The former Brooklyn and Newark hurler caught on with Indianapolis of the American Association and posted a record of 19–14 in 1916. That was good enough for Cy to earn a shot with the pitching-poor Athletics of Connie Mack a year later. Falkenberg went 2 and 6 in his final season in the major leagues. Cy pitched two more years in the minors before he retired following the 1919 season.

Federal League magnate Harry Sinclair remained interested in sports, being heavily involved in horse racing. "Once Harry asked me how much money I lost last season with the Browns," Phil Ball chuckled during an interview in the 1920s. "I told him it was about $200,000 and he told me I was crazy to waste that much money. I told him baseball was my hobby and then I asked him how much he had lost with his string of race horses the previous year. Sinclair said he was $300,000 crazier than me."[27]

Sinclair did gain success in the horse racing business after the purchase of a yearling he named Zev. In 1923 Zev won the Kentucky Derby, was named Horse of the Year, and also was that season's leading money earner with $272,008 in winnings. The "Brown Express" won twenty-three of forty-three starts for Sinclair's Rancocas Stable, earning $313,639, which surpassed Man o' War to become the all-time leading equine money earner at that time.

While his thoroughbred was burning up the racetracks, Sinclair was occupied in the controversy that would eventually become known as the Teapot Dome Scandal. A contract to develop the Elk Hills and Teapot Dome U.S. Navy oil reserve lands in Wyoming was awarded in 1922 to Mammoth Oil, a company organized by Harry Sinclair to operate in the reserve. When Sinclair returned to the United States from the Soviet Union where he met Lenin and negotiated for oil rights in Siberia, the oil baron learned that he was named as a key figure in a government scandal.

Alleging fraud in the awarding of the Teapot Dome contract, the government sued in 1924 to abrogate the arrangement with Mammoth. It was charged that Sinclair bribed U.S. Secretary of the Interior Albert Fall with a payment of $100,000 in exchange for the rights to the Elk Hills and Teapot Dome Navy oil reserves. The court held Mammoth Oil's lease legal and dismissed the complaint. Upon appeal in 1927, the U.S. Supreme Court voided the contract on technicalities, though it found "no direct evidence of fraud." After only forty minutes of deliberation, a jury acquitted Sinclair of the charge of conspiracy to defraud. However, his use of private detectives to keep the jury under observation during the trial drew the oil man a conviction for contempt of court. During the ongoing controversy, Sinclair testified before twelve legislative committees, disdaining the Fifth Amendment. For refusing to answer one question that his attorney considered not pertinent to the legislative inquiry, Sinclair was held to be in contempt of the Senate. On the contempt citation, he spent six and a half months in the Washington, D.C., House of Detention in 1929.

During the seven years of the Teapot Dome scandal, Harry continued to serve as chairman and chief executive officer of Sinclair Consolidated, with the support of his directors, who tendered him a unanimous public vote of confidence as he left New York to serve his jail sentence.[28] Many of its competitors folded during the Great Depression, but Sinclair Oil doubled in size. The legacy Harry left was $700 million in assets for 99,500 stockholders and 21,000 employees.[29] Sinclair died in 1956 at the age of eighty.

46

The Aftershock

Organized Baseball offered the Baltimore Federal League franchise a settlement of $50,000 at the time of the peace agreement, but the club's investors demanded more. They wanted the right to purchase a major league franchise, which they planned to move to Baltimore. The major league owners rejected their demands out of hand. Then the former Terrapins asked for an International League franchise in Baltimore, but were again rebuffed. Though the Federal League settlement stipulated that all lawsuits brought against Organized Baseball be withdrawn, the Baltimore club's objections to portions of that arrangement postponed dismissal of the Federal League's antitrust suit against Organized Baseball in Judge Landis's court.

On Saturday, February 3, 1916, the Federal League and Organized Baseball finally appeared in U.S. District Court in Chicago to end the antitrust action. The proceeding came to a halt following a declaration by Stuard L. Schwartz, Federal League attorney, who stated, "There is the matter of which I think the court should be informed. Understand that the Baltimore club of the Federal League is dissatisfied with the arrangements made regarding the dissolution of the Federal League and that it may oppose this motion."[1]

Judge Landis declared that under the circumstances, he would postpone the matter until the following Monday to give Baltimore a chance to state its reasons for opposing dismissal of the suit. The Baltimore litigants were notified by telegram to be in court at that time.

Attorney Stuart S. Janney represented Baltimore in federal court on February 5. The attorney threw the courtroom into a tizzy when he announced that Baltimore was waiving its objection to the dismissal of the suit. Apparently, the Baltfeds received a promise of concessions from the National Commission if in return Janney would withdraw the objection to dismissal of the Federal League suit.

Judge Landis ordered the dismissal of the Federal League's antitrust suit without prejudice. Within his decision, Landis revealed that he had no intention of ruling in favor of the plaintiffs regardless of the merits of their case. Landis declared, "The court's *expert* knowledge of baseball obtained by more than thirty years of observance of the game as a spectator convinced me that if an order had been entered it would have been, if not destructive, at least injurious to the game of baseball."[2]

After the order was entered, Janney said that if a satisfactory settlement was not made with the Baltimore club it had ample opportunity to seek redress in the courts either in a suit for damages or under the provisions of the Clayton Act prohibiting restraint of trade. The Baltfeds' attorney said that Garry Herrmann promised the Baltimore franchise remunerations for any damage it might suffer by having been left out of consideration when the peace pact was signed. "Unless remuneration was forthcoming," added Janney, "a new suit would be instituted by the Baltimore club with all the other Federal League officials and those of Organized Baseball included as defendants.[3]

With no hope of fielding a franchise for 1916, the Baltimore Federals canceled the contracts of players still under obligation and announced that those players were "free-agents." These new free agents suddenly on the open market were Otto Knabe, Steve Evans, Duke Duncan, Jack McCandless, Dave Hickman, Yip Owens, Enos Kirkpatrick, Jack Quinn, Rankin Johnson and George Suggs.[4]

Surprisingly, outfielder Steve Evans failed to get an offer from any of the major league clubs despite being only thirty-one with batting marks of .348 and .308 in his two Federal League seasons. Perhaps an issue was his reputation as a prankster and flake.

Eventually, Evans was hired by his former manager, Roger Bresnahan, to play with Toledo of the American Association for the 1916 season. Evans batted .298, scored 101 runs, and hit 33 doubles, 16 triples and 10 home runs. Still no major league offers came his way. Following the 1917 season, Evans retired from baseball and returned to his home in Cleveland.

Not surprisingly, Baseball made no concessions to the Baltimore club after the antitrust suit was dropped in Landis's court. The Baltimore interests now decided to ignore the peace agreement and pursue their grievances in court. When the Federals held their final league meeting in Chicago on February 19, 1916, to settle affairs, the Baltimore club refused to attend. The Maryland club recouped $25,000 through the sale of Terrapin Park to Jack Dunn, and the stockholders raised some $50,000 to finance legal action.[5]

On March 29, 1916, the Baltimore Federal League club's owners sued Organized Baseball and former Federal League officials Gilmore, Sinclair and Weeghman in the United States District Court in Philadelphia under the Sherman Antitrust Act and the Clayton Act. The bill of complaint filed by Philadelphia attorney William A. Glasgow alleged the Baltimore club was not considered in the negotiations the previous winter which resulted in the so-called agreement between Organized Baseball and the Federal League owners, and that in consequence it suffered a loss of $300,000. The plaintiffs asked for triple damages under the federal antitrust laws.[6]

The suit was withdrawn in June 1917, because the defendants intimated a settlement might be reached. When a settlement was not offered, Baltimore reinstated their suit that September in the Supreme Court of the District of Columbia.

Following a two-week trial in 1919, Associate Justice Wendell Stafford found on April 12 that the activity of Organized Baseball constituted an attempt to monopolize the business of baseball exhibitions within the meaning of the Sherman Act. The jury fixed damages at $80,000, and the court tripled the judgment to $240,000 plus $24,000 in attorneys' fees. Organized Baseball's attorneys immediately appealed the decision.[7]

The District of Columbia court ruling stunned the major leagues. If the Baltimore decision was upheld by the courts, Organized Baseball felt the reserve clause and the ten-day clause could no longer be part of a player's contract. Major league clubs would also see an additional $240,000 plus attorneys' fees added to the balance left on the $600,000 in payments due to the other owners of the Federal League.[8]

Particularly worried was Boston Red Sox owner Harry Frazee, whose team had not drawn the type of crowds he expected after purchasing the club from Joseph Lannin in late 1916. Lannin and Frazee argued over who was responsible for Boston's $30,000 share of the legal settlement with the Federal League. Ultimately, the repercussions of the Baltimore Federal League lawsuit played into the sale of Babe Ruth to the Yankees.

His baseball debt and precarious personal investments led Frazee to default on his

$262,000 payment to complete his purchase of the Red Sox from Lannin. Frazee had to pay an additional $30,000 annually in rent on Fenway Park, which was owned by Fenway Realty Trust, controlled by Charles Taylor of the *Boston Globe* with Lannin as partner. Frazee said he would complete his payments for the Red Sox if Lannin would pay the Federal League bill and allow him to proceed with his purchase of Fenway Park.

A way out of Frazee's financial problems without dipping into the money he held in reserve to operate his theatrical interests was to accept an offer from the New York Yankees for his star outfielder, Babe Ruth. In 1920 Ruth was a problem in the clubhouse and off the field. He agitated for a new contract, a new manager, and special consideration. Frazee was out of patience with his recalcitrant star and considered the pitcher turned outfielder a prima donna who just had a career year. Frazee decided to settle his debt to Lannin with a $300,000 loan that Yankees owners Ruppert and Huston tendered as part the deal that sent Ruth to New York for $100,000 in January 1920.[9]

Judge Stafford's decision in favor of the Baltimore club in the 1919 case was reversed in appellate court on December 6, 1920. Chief Justice Smyth reversed the decision on the grounds that a baseball exhibition was not in the category of trade or commerce since "it affects no exchange of things." Not until the players come into contact with their opponents does a baseball game come into existence, reasoned Judge Smyth.[10]

The Baltimore plaintiffs appealed Smyth's decision to the United States Supreme Court, but the ruling was reaffirmed by the high court in 1922. This was the famous Supreme Court decision where Justice Oliver Wendell Holmes agreed with George Wharton Pepper that the game of baseball was the national pastime, the actual games were not interstate commerce, and thus, the antitrust question did not need to be reviewed. Though Organized Baseball won in the end, the fight with the Baltimore Federal League club cost the major leagues $80,000 in attorneys' fees.[11]

The Federal League venture was the last time Ned Hanlon was directly involved in baseball, though he occasionally attended events at the former Federal League Park, renamed Oriole Park. In 1916 the city's mayor appointed Hanlon to the Baltimore parks board and he became its chairman in 1931. One of Baltimore's most prominent citizens, Hanlon died there at age 79 on April 14, 1937, and joined Orioles teammates John McGraw and Wilbert Robinson in the New Cathedral Cemetery.

The Federal League's opposition to the National Agreement had given the fledging players' union leverage it needed to achieve some concessions from the owners on playing conditions and player contracts. The players discovered what could be achieved in salaries through the threat of free agency. More than one writer has suggested that the salary structure the magnates restored in 1916 motivated the disgruntled players in the direction of the corruption and scandals that occurred at the end of the decade.

The executives of major league clubs hated the Players' Fraternity with as much fervor as they held for the Federal League. They not only blamed the Fraternity indirectly for the two-year life of the Federal League, the players' union shared the blame for the loss of baseball income in 1914 and 1915. Once the Federal League was out of the picture, the American League, National League and National Association of Professional Baseball Leagues (the minors) were determined to crush the Players' Fraternity before its power expanded and spread discontent among the players.

In a November 1916 report issued by the National Commission, August Herrmann, chairman, left no question about the owners' objective: "Club-owners were compelled to make extraordinary concessions to players in order to placate them and prevent them from deserting to Federal clubs. Salaries were virtually dictated by players, long-term contracts became common and in some instances, the player could be retained only by eliminating the renewal clause from his contract. Base Ball must be brought back to its normal basis."[12]

Baseball players undoubtedly became big losers in the demise of the Federal League when the owners began slashing salaries to the pre–1914 levels. Tris Speaker, one of the three or four best players in the American League, earned $18,000 a season during the baseball war, but in 1916, the World Series Champion Boston Red Sox offered Speaker only half that amount. Tris held out for $15,000 and was traded to Cleveland, which had new ownership.[13] Even the newcomers to Organized Baseball, Charles Weeghman and Phil Ball, quickly adapted to their new associates' tactics by slashing salaries of players who now had no recourse but to play with the major league team that owned their contracts.

The case of infielder Jimmy Johnston was a classic example of the owners' tactics in dealing with players. Shortly after the 1915 Pacific Coast League season closed, Johnson signed a two-year contract to play for Newark of the Federal League for an annual salary of $4,000. Harry Sinclair, who held the Federal League rights to Johnston, learned that the Dodgers' owner, Charles Ebbets, had made a trade with Oakland for the player the previous fall. Sinclair relinquished any claim on Johnston and Ebbetts returned the player's $1,000 advance plus $250 for expenses incurred by George Stovall in his trip to California.

After the Brooklyn owner offered Johnston only $3400 for the 1916 season, Jimmy stayed home in Oakland. Johnston maintained he would report to spring training as soon as Ebbets assumed the contract he signed with Newark.[14] Charles Ebbets announced that if his players held out for more money, "We'll fill their places with ambitious youngsters."[15] Jimmy finally acquiesced, reported to Brooklyn and became a mainstay in the Dodgers' lineup for ten years and two World Series.

During the course of the antitrust hearing before Judge Landis in January 1915, National League attorney George Pepper surprised everyone in the courtroom with the statement that the theory of Organized Baseball's new reserve clause was not to hold a player except for one year following the contracted period. His statement suggested that the old reserve clause had not been fair since it contained an option of retaining the player's services perpetually. The magnates had no intention of adopting their lawyer's interpretation of players' contracts that he made in an attempt to gain support for Baseball's case.

A November 1916 National Commission memorandum to all major league club presidents outlined a new player contract. The document noted that as a result of the Federal League war, some players were able to procure contracts which did not contain a renewal clause and that such contracts no longer would be approved. The Commission reasoned that the reserve clause was not only a bulwark of professional baseball, but it assured the players regular employment at salaries adequate to their expertness. The Commission declared that the major league club to which a player was under contract at the close of the season was entitled to retain him for the ensuing season, if it so desired. The memo concluded that the Commission would not approve or recognize any contract not containing the reserve clause.[16]

Following the dissolution of the Federal League, the Players' Fraternity urged that its members be allowed to rejoin Organized Baseball and supported Jimmy Johnston and other players in their contract disputes. In 1916, the union again presented a list of demands to Baseball, this time on behalf of the minor leagues. When the union was turned down out of hand by the minor leagues' National Board and the National Commission, President David Fultz announced that the Fraternity's players would refuse to sign their 1917 contracts until the demands were met.

The strike threat unleashed an all-out assault on the Fraternity by baseball's owners and their allies. Since the Federal League was no more, no reasonable alternative baseball employment outside of Organized Baseball existed. This made Baseball's decision to rebuff the Fraternity's demands an easy one. Major league players began to renege on their strike promise, not willing to risk their careers for the "bush leaguers." The two major leagues officially abrogated the 1914 agreement with the Fraternity because the union had "violated the letter and spirit" of it. Fultz called off the strike, but his Fraternity, to all intents and purposes, was history.

The press shed no tears for the demise of the Players' Fraternity. "When Ban Johnson ... turned the hose on the Fraternity," editorialized Joe Villa's *New York Sun,* "it vanished like old newspapers on the way to a sewer."

Following the United States' entry into the European war in 1917, Organized Baseball got its chance to get even with *Sporting Life* for its passive support of the Federal League. During the World War, Baseball gave financial assistance to *The Sporting News,* but refused to support *Sporting Life.* Francis Richter's sports tabloid gave up publication later in 1917.[17]

The owners got their first big opportunity to exert their renewed power in 1918 after the regular season was terminated on Labor Day due to the draft for the World War. The owners released their players with ten days' notice in order to avoid paying the entire season's salaries. Technically, the players were free agents and could sell their services to the highest bidder, but the magnates entered into a "gentlemen's agreement" not to sign another club's player. The National Commission quickly announced that all players were bound to their former clubs. "Thus the owners had it both ways," wrote Harold Seymour. "They saved an estimated $200,000 in payrolls and at the same time retained their monopsony control over their players, pending the reopening of business."[18]

It got worse. In April 1921, Baseball implemented a rule that players under the reserve rule who failed to report to their clubs within ten days after the opening of the current championship season would be placed on the "general ineligible list." Applications for reinstatement had to go through the Commissioner.[19]

The Federal League has been condemned for disrupting the established major leagues' monopoly and restrictive player policies. It has also been suggested that the Federal League "caused" the collapse of the Players' Fraternity. Actually, the gains the union achieved during the Federal League years led to the organization's own downfall. As it turned out, the Federal League would not have been able to sign as many major league players as it did without the Players' Fraternity and the Fraternity would not have been able to persevere without the presence of the Federal League. The Fraternity overestimated its strength in 1917 and called for a strike on behalf of minor league players when there was no Federal League type alternative to use in negotiations with the owners.

Though it was far from obvious at that time, the eventual aftershock from the baseball war of 1914–15 would claim Organized Baseball's most powerful figure. At the end of the war, Ban Johnson appeared to be as powerful as ever and the National Commission functioned with little controversy until a series of decisions between 1918 and 1920 threatened to blow the two major leagues apart.

The seeds of discontent were sown in 1915 when Garry Herrmann voted to award first baseman George Sisler to the St. Louis Browns instead of Barney Dreyfuss's Pittsburgh club. The irate Pirates owner demanded that Herrmann be replaced by an independent, neutral chairman. Though he was ignored at the time, Dreyfuss continued his campaign over the ensuing years, complaining about having an executive of one club rule on matters affecting his competitors.[20]

The National Commission quietly went about its business until 1918. When both the Boston Braves and the Philadelphia Athletics claimed a pitcher named Scott Perry, the National Commission awarded the player to the National League club. Instead of complying with the decision, Philadelphia obtained an injunction to block the transfer. National League owners blamed Ban Johnson for encouraging the lawsuit and National League president John Tener was so enraged he wanted to cancel the World Series. When his owners refused to go along with the boycott, Tener resigned his presidency in disgust. The other National League owners now sided with Dreyfuss in his campaign to replace the National Commission.[21]

A second dispute cost Ban Johnson one of his principal backers in the American League. After the Pacific Coast League suspended operations on July 14, 1918, because of the World War, Charles Comiskey signed Vernon pitcher Jack Quinn for the White Sox. The former Baltimore Terrapins hurler won five out of six decisions for Chicago over the remainder of the American League season. After the season, the New York Yankees protested that they had purchased Quinn before he signed with Chicago. When Ban Johnson awarded Quinn to New York, Comiskey was livid.[22]

At the January 1919 winter meetings, the National League endorsed a neutral party as a sole commissioner, while the American League voted 6–2 to continue the current National Commission. The two leagues finally agreed to search for a new National Commission chairman and Herrmann would retain the position in an interim capacity.

The tide turned against Ban Johnson during the 1919 season. After Red Sox pitcher Carl Mays jumped his team on July 13, Boston traded him to the Yankees for a pair of journeymen pitchers and $40,000. Instead of sanctioning the deal, Ban suspended Mays indefinitely for contract jumping. An angry New York Club responded by seeking a court injunction to overturn Johnson's suspension. The owners of the Yankees and the Red Sox joined Charles Comiskey as sworn enemies of Johnson.

At their January 1920 winter meetings, the National League forced Herrmann off the National Commission by requiring him to choose between the chairmanship of the National Commission or presidency of the Reds. American League owners overrode Johnson and ordered the reinstatement of Carl Mays. Ban Johnson's power was further restricted when his owners appointed Jake Ruppert of the Yankees and Clark Griffith of the Senators to review all penalties and suspensions of more than ten days.

The two leagues could not agree on Herrmann's replacement as chairman of the National Commission. One of the early choices was former President William Howard Taft, but he turned it down. Another finalist was Judge Kenesaw Landis, already a favorite of Organized Baseball for stalling the Federal League's antitrust suit until the outlaw league folded. As a result of the stalemate, the National Commission was left with only two members during the greatest scandal in baseball history.[23]

Rumors that the 1919 World Series was fixed made the rounds even before play began, but the National Commission proved impotent. The White Sox' owner wouldn't confide in Ban Johnson, who initially dismissed Comiskey's suspicions as "the yelp of a beaten cur." When the Black Sox scandal exploded in the final week of the 1920 season, Organized Baseball realized that something had to be done about the weakened National Commission.[24]

On October 18, 1920, the National League's Board of Directors met with Yankees owners Ruppert and Huston, Charles Comiskey, and Boston's Harry Frazee in New York. The group elected to scrap the National Agreement and selected a committee to draw up a new accord along the lines of the Lasker Plan, proposed by a Chicago advertising executive who was a small shareholder in the Cubs. Albert Lasker proposed the National Commission be replaced with a three-man board of eminent citizens with no connection to baseball. This board would have total authority over every aspect of Organized Baseball. *The Sporting News* identified the leading candidates for a proposed three-man board as Judge Landis, General John J. Pershing, and Senator Hiram Johnson of California.[25]

The five American League clubs still backing Ban Johnson were given an ultimatum: join them by November 1 or the Yankees, White Sox, and Red Sox would pull out of the American League and join a twelve-team National League (a new team in Detroit would be added to fill out the league). The American League's "Loyal Five" rejected the Lasker Plan, citing the folly of putting their entire industry under the control of men with no baseball experience.[26]

On November 8, 1920, the National League magnates, the three American League defectors, and Clark Griffith, acting as representative of the Loyal Five, met at the Congress Hotel in Chicago settle things. As a result of the meeting, the three anti–Johnson clubs withdrew from the American League and a new National League was formed.

Four of the five loyal American League owners finally threw in the towel and agreed to attend a joint meeting on November 12 in Chicago. In the end, only Philip Ball remained loyal to Ban Johnson. During that meeting, the sixteen major league clubs voted to accept Judge Landis as a sole Commissioner. Landis was finally rewarded for his stonewalling in the Federal League lawsuit with his appointment as "Commissioner for Life." Ball, faithful to Johnson to the end, was the only owner not to affirm the election of Landis, though he did allow Bob Quinn, his vice president, to cast the vote for the Browns that made it unanimous. Later that day, Landis accepted the $50,000 annual position, with the stipulation the Commissioner's decisions were all encompassing, final, and could not be challenged by the clubs in court.[27]

Ban Johnson remained American League president, but Landis curtailed his power and humiliated him at every opportunity. After Johnson promoted an investigation looking into charges that Ty Cobb and Tris Speaker had been involved in game fixing by gamblers in 1919, Landis felt Ban had intruded on the Commissioner's power and became determined to isolate the American League president even more.[28]

In January 1927, Landis bullied the American League owners (except Phil Ball) to issue a document censuring Johnson. Johnson continued to condemn Landis publicly and ruffled the feathers of the club owners until the founder of the American League was persuaded to resign as its president on October 17, 1927. In the end, it was Kenesaw M. Landis who proved to be the biggest winner among all the big names involved in the Federal League war with Organized Baseball.

47

The Browns/Terriers

Once the peace treaty was finalized between the Federals and Organized Baseball, the same publications that referred to the outlaw league's owners as "anarchists" and "traitors to the game" who should be "cast into outer darkness," welcomed the "sportsmen" Weeghman and Ball into the organized major leagues because they were "in the game for love rather than money." *The Sporting News* even editorialized that there should be a place in the major leagues for Harry Sinclair, because he too was a "real sportsman."

Despite large personal losses for the 1914 and 1915 seasons, Philip Ball was still anxious to continue in the business of major league baseball. After the deal for the St. Louis Browns was finalized, Ball told the press that the Federal League venture cost him $88,000 in 1914 and he lost about $94,000 a year later.[1] Said Ball:

> My option on the Browns provided that I was to pay $30,000 before Christmas of 1915, and one of the stockholders came to St. Louis to get that money. While he was there, news broke out that the Federal League was no more and he began to welch on the option. I had gone to the bank, obtained gold certificates and met the stockholder at the office of my lawyer. The man stalled until 4 P.M. and then said he was going back home — that he had to be home for Christmas.

When Ball produced the $30,000 deposit, the Browns' agent still refused to take it and shoved the money off the desk and onto the floor. "It's o.k.," Ball replied. "If you don't take it, the woman who cleans up this place will.

"I walked out," said the prospective Browns' owner. "He gathered it up."[2]

The transfer of the Browns to the Ball interests required the purchase of two separate corporations, one holding the franchise of the club, and the other controlling the real estate. The price for the St. Louis American League franchise, players and ballpark was $525,000. That sum was paid by Ball, James W. Garneau and Otto Stifel for 800 shares of stock in the ball club and Dodier Realty Company, the owner of Sportsman's Park. Upon completion of the club's sale, Philip Ball became president of the Browns and Garneau, a "meat packer" and a newcomer to baseball, was head of the real estate company that owned Sportsman's Park. Ball was by far the largest stockholder with 2350 shares, Stifel held the second most with 733, and Garneau held 109 shares. Otto Stifel, Ball's original partner in the Terriers, was one of three vice presidents. Fielder Jones was another vice president because of the amount of stock he had in the Terriers. Jones took over Branch Rickey's desk at the team's offices at five o'clock the morning of January 2, 1916.[3]

By terms of the treaty between Organized Baseball and the Federal League, the new

Browns owners were privileged to use what players they chose from their Federal League team and the St. Louis American League team. A story made the newspapers that the new Browns owners were considering renaming the team "Terriers," but ultimately "Browns" was retained.

As the new manager of the Browns, Fielder Jones was responsible for trimming a preseason roster that totaled 57 players. The one returning Browns player Jones really liked was George Sisler, whom the new manager said was the best young player he had ever seen. *The Sporting News* suggested that Branch Rickey preferred to use Sisler as a pitcher, but Jones wanted George in the lineup everyday in the field.[4] Former manager Rickey did not get along with the new owner, and when the crosstown Cardinals offered him the team's presidency that spring, he jumped at the opportunity.

When the former Terriers players were transferred to the Browns, Eddie Plank held out and declared he was a free agent. The basis of Eddie's claim came from Baseball's agreement with the Players' Fraternity whereby players with ten years of service would win their unconditional release upon clearing waivers. Since the defunct Federal League had no further claim to his service, the veteran pitcher hoped to negotiate a contract with the highest bidder. However, the National Commission disallowed Plank's request in early February because the pitcher left the Athletics before waivers had been obtained and before he had had been released by the Philadelphia club. With no other recourse except retirement, the southpaw reported to St. Louis.[5]

Dave Davenport married his home town sweetheart, Lillie Calloway, in Runge, Texas, on February 23, 1916, then announced he was a holdout for spring training because his Federal League contract had expired.[6] Eventually, he did sign with the Browns and pitched in an American League–high 59 games that season, winning 12 and losing 11.

Some 10,000 people were turned away from the Browns' season opener, in which Bob Groom beat the Indians, 11 to 1. After that, the season turned sour for Jones and his ex-Federals. Fielder kept thirteen of the former Federal Leaguers on the Browns' roster and his loyalty to them hurt the team, as Hartley, Johnson, Deal and Tobin did not fare very well against American League pitching. The Browns sank to seventh place. By June the team started to jell after Jones shuffled his starting lineup. In the field, outfielders Armando Marsans and Ward Miller were the only ex-Terriers to remain starters for the entire season. However, the additions of ex-Federal Leaguers Plank, Davenport and Groom helped the pitching staff improve from fifth-best in 1915 to third in team earned run average.

Though only twenty-seven when he pitched his last Federal League game as a member of Fielder Jones's "big three" with the Terriers in 1915, Doc Crandall did not last long with the Browns. After retiring only four of thirteen batters in two relief appearances, Crandall went to the Pacific Coast League, where he would pitch for thirteen years, mostly with the Los Angeles Angels. On April 7, 1918, while pitching for Los Angeles, Doc had a no-hitter with two outs in the ninth inning against Salt Lake City when his brother, Karl Crandall, spoiled it with a base knock. Doc led the league in 1918 with a 16–9 record (the season was called on July 14 because of the World War), and in 1919 he won 28 and lost 10. He is a member of the original Pacific Coast League Hall of Fame, winning 230 games and losing 151 in that circuit.[7]

Big Dave Davenport heated up in the summer, just like he had the previous season. On July 29, Dave duplicated his 1915 feat of pitching two complete games in a double-header. After beating the Yankees' Ray Caldwell, 3–1, in the first game, Davenport again took the mound for the second contest in the extreme summer heat of St. Louis. Dave was trailing, 1–0, when the Browns came to bat in the fifth inning. Fielder Jones was preparing to substitute a pinch hitter for Davenport, but the crowd began to chant, "Let Dave hit!" Jones allowed his pitcher to bat, and Dave sent the first pitch he saw from Allan Russell on a line drive to the right field fence. Davenport's hit scored two runners and he went on to pitch a complete-game 3 to 2 victory.[8]

Davenport's two victories came in the midst of a fourteen-game winning streak that thrust the Browns into the pennant race. A 21–9 record during August moved the club into fourth place, just four games out of first. However, St. Louis faltered in September and October and the Browns finished in fifth place. The club improved only one spot in the standings from 1915, but raised the team's win-loss percentage from .409 to .513, the Browns' best record since 1908.

The Browns had become a Jones-style team in the second half of the season and they had high hopes for 1917. However, some of the original Browns soured on Jones's demanding brand of baseball. Jones was not one to coddle players and the breach gradually widened. Among the holdovers, only George Sisler openly supported the manager.[9]

The highlight of the 1917 season for the Browns was Bob Groom's no-hitter against a strong Chicago White Sox club in the second game of a double-header on May 6. Groom's feat was more remarkable because he pitched two scoreless innings in the Browns' first-game victory that day at Sportsman's Park. At the end of the day, the Browns' record was 11 wins and 8 losses. That would be the club's high-water mark for the year.

By mid–July, the team had fallen into last place. Only first baseman George Sisler sparkled, batting .353, but almost everyone else slumped. Dave Davenport led the team's pitchers with 17 victories, but he also lost 17.

Eddie Plank won 16 games for the Browns in 1916, then, after losing an eleven-inning 1 to 0 decision to Walter Johnson on August 6, 1917, he quit baseball. Despite a 1.79 earned run average to that point in the season, his record with the punchless Browns was only 5 wins and 6 losses. Plank retired to Gettysburg, Pennsylvania, and in February 1926, at age fifty, the former pitching great suffered a stroke and died a short time later. In 1946, he and Joe Tinker became the first ex–Federal Leaguers to be elected to Baseball's Hall of Fame.

In July 1917, Manager Jones severely disciplined several players for a crap game, further alienating the holdovers from the Branch Rickey regime.[10] That August rumors surfaced that the Browns were throwing games. After a 13 to 6 loss on September 4 to the league-leading Chicago White Sox, a St. Louis newspaper quoted owner Phil Ball as saying that some of his players were "laying down" during games.

Responding to a phone call from Manager Jones, Ball hurried to Sportsman's Park the next morning to head off a potential players' revolt. The players asked the owner if the statements printed in the paper were true and did Ball say that he would "cut salaries $100 for every $1000 the club lost for the season." Ball explained that some of his friends had told reporters the players were lying down, but that he was not competent to judge. However, the owner declared that he meant what he said about the cuts in salaries.

"I will pay for the kind of ball I receive," he told the assembled players. "That's fair, I think you will agree."[11]

The Browns' keystone combination of Doc Lavan and Del Pratt felt they were being singled out and they sued Ball for libel. The stubborn owner said he would not trade the players until they dropped their lawsuit. Though the newspapers reported that Pratt and Lavan received a $5,400 settlement, Ball maintained the payoff to the players did not cost him a cent. It was suggested that the American League paid the bill.[12]

The Browns played better baseball after Ball's accusation, but they could only manage a seventh-place finish. At the end of his second season with the Browns, Jones's three-year contract with Phil Ball expired, but Fielder reluctantly agreed to manage St. Louis in 1918. Partly due to her husband's heart problems, Jones's wife refused to return to St Louis in protest of Fielder's decision to continue as manager of the Browns.

The Browns hired Bob Quinn to handle personnel decisions and Jones instructed him to rid the team of all players who did not fit the manager's definition of "team players." Disgruntled players were traded away and military service took several others.[13] The Browns started the 1918 season slowly, but achieved a winning record the first week in June. Jones, however, remained frustrated with his team and the stress was affecting his health. After a game on June 12 in which the Browns blew a five-run lead in the ninth, Jones informed Quinn and Ball that he was through. Philip Ball sent his manager a letter thanking him for his services and wished him the best.

After Jones's death from heart disease on March 13, 1934, the *New York Times* ranked him with McGraw and Mack as "one of the three greatest baseball managers." Alfred Spink, editor of *The Sporting News*, called Jones the "greatest exponent of 'inside' baseball that ever played." George Stovall said of Jones, "He ranks right with McGraw and Connie Mack. He had an inspiring personality and his teams played flashing, dashing, and smart baseball."[14]

Dave Davenport, the Federal League's top pitcher in 1915, did not live up to the promise his manager Fielder Jones predicted when he called the 6'6" right-hander the best pitching prospect he'd ever worked with. Dave had decent seasons in 1916 and 1917 for mediocre Browns clubs, winning 12 and 17 games respectively, but his earned run average increased and his strikeout total decreased each succeeding season he was in St. Louis.

The beginning of the end for Davenport in St. Louis began with the departure of his mentor, Fielder Jones, and the selection of Jimmy Burke as manager. The big hurler had a record of only 3 and 11 in 1919 when he was suspended indefinitely after a fight with Burke and General Manager Bob Quinn.

On August 30 of that year Davenport started the second game of a Saturday doubleheader against Detroit at Sportsman's Park. The Browns amassed a 7–0 lead before Dave and his successor, Ernie Koob, blew the game, losing 8–7. Four days later, the Browns made their last home appearance before a road trip.

After the game, Davenport, who had been absent without leave for a couple of days, walked into the clubhouse while the Browns' players were preparing to leave for the train station. Dave expected to make the road trip, but Burke informed Davenport that his misconduct had drawn a fine and suspension without pay for the rest of the season. Harsh words led to a scuffle between the pitcher and manager, whereupon "Bobby Quinn quelled it by calling a couple of coppers."

The Browns went to Detroit without Dave and his running mate Urban Shocker, who also was suspended. Davenport was fined $100 and suspended for the remainder of the season by Manager Burke, leading *The Sporting News* to speculate, "As for Davenport he is done as a Brown. Koob and Wright are also done."[15]

Dave was working for a Cleveland electrical concern in February 1920 when he learned of his sale to the Washington Senators. The still-suspended pitcher demanded part of the purchase price, then refused to sign a contract with Washington. Senators owner Clark Griffith canceled the deal.

After Davenport refused to play in Washington, he went to the wilds of Idaho and Utah to play independent ball. By ignoring the reserve clause in his major league contract Dave technically "outlawed" himself for two years.

Dave was so good with Ogden of the North Utah League he was fired. On July 4, 1921, Davenport pitched a perfect game against Tremonton. The big pitcher won all seven games he pitched for Ogden, averaged sixteen strikeouts per outing, and threw a one-hitter and a three-hitter in addition to his no-hit game. In July the opposing teams rose up in protest and declared that if Davenport was not released, they would "bust" the league.[16]

Big Dave wound up with the Independent Mid-West League in Colorado. *The Sporting News* reported:

> He found things so pleasant there he proclaimed with sarcasm that instead of asking reinstatement at the end of his two years suspension he would ask that it be extended so he could continue outside the fold. Since then..., the outlaws have collapsed and the league will be organized as an Organized Baseball circuit.
>
> Had he behaved and played with them [Browns] the past season he might have been quite a factor in their pennant chase, for Dave can pitch, no denying that. The fault with him is his temperament. He's one of the kind that never grew up mentally....[17]

In 1922 Davenport pitched for the elite Beloit team in Chicago's powerful semi-pro Midwest League. Dave joined former major league hurlers "Hippo" Vaughn and Wynn Noyes on the league champion Fairies' pitching staff.

Dave was reinstated by Organized Baseball in 1925 when he was thirty-three and his best years behind him. He played with Wichita (Western League) and in Colorado before retiring from baseball.

One ex–Terrier who would star for Ball and the Browns in the post–Federal League years was outfielder Jack Tobin. After batting .213 and sitting on the Browns' bench the second half of 1916, Tobin found his batting stroke at Salt Lake City the following season. He led the Pacific Coast League in runs scored and hits while posting a batting average of .331.

Johnny was back with St. Louis in 1918 and would remain in the Browns' outfield through 1925. A lifetime .309 hitter, the smallish, lefty-batting Tobin excelled at dragging a bunt for a base hit. He could also hit away with authority, averaging 32 doubles and 12 triples a year from 1920 through 1924. He hit two grand slam home runs off Walter Johnson, including the first ever off the Washington hurler on August 6, 1922. Tobin had four straight 200-hit seasons and batted well over .300 each year from 1919 through 1923, hitting a career-high .352 in 1921 when he led the American League with 671 at-bats.

Johnny was the leadoff man for Ball's best club, the 1922 Browns, that finished one game behind the pennant-winning Yankees. Tobin coached for the Browns from 1944 through 1948 and then scouted for the club. Along with the likes of Rogers Hornsby, Stan Musial and George Sisler, Tobin was named as an outfielder on the All–St. Louis All-Star team as selected by the St. Louis chapter of Baseball Writers of America in 1958.[18]

Former Terriers part owner and Browns stockholder Otto Stifel had fallen on hard times by 1920. His extravagant lifestyle had sapped his fortune, Prohibition put his Union Brewery out of the beer business, and the conversion of the plant to the manufacture of oleomargarine did not produce near the profits it had realized when beer sales were legal. By December of 1919 Otto had divested himself of his Browns stock. Things appeared on the upswing in June of 1920 when Stifel sought and received the Republican Party's nomination for congressman of the 11th (St. Louis) District of the state of Missouri.

Then, on August 18, 1920, Otto committed suicide by shooting himself in the mouth at his Valley Park Farm. He was fifty-seven years old. Stifel left several rambling suicide notes, blaming Prohibition and money problems caused by allegedly unscrupulous family and business associates for his despondent state. Apparently, large gambling and other debts, plus the potential loss of his lifestyle after losing much of his inheritance, became too much of a mental burden for Otto to handle. Otto's son Carl continued to run the family's plant until Prohibition was repealed in 1933 and the brewery was leased to Falstaff. Falstaff rented the South

Side Brewery until February of 1944, when it was purchased from Carl and the Stifel estate for $600,000.[19]

Unlike Stifel, Philip de Gatesby Ball was a content man. He rarely missed a game at Sportsman's Park, and his main regret was that his Browns never won a pennant.

He told Harry T. Brundidge in 1932, "The Browns made money for me in 1922, not since. As president, I get no salary, and I run the club for the pure fun of it. The Dodier Real Estate Company, which owns the ballpark, has paid a couple of five per cent dividends, but the Browns owe my real estate company around $100,000 and haven't paid any rent for two years."

In response to the question about how much he had lost on the Browns, Ball answered, "About $300,000."[20]

About a year after his team just missed winning the 1922 pennant, Ball was diagnosed with a critical illness and told he only had a short time to live. Philip sold his Ice & Cold Machine Company for a price in excess of five million dollars. However, after two years Ball was still very much alive and the doctors were proven wrong. He returned to the business as a stockholder in the company's 150 ice plants.

Ball was plain-spoken, cantankerous, and a ruthless businessman, but he was also honest and commanded an affectionate loyalty from his small group of friends and associates. One person not counted among his friends was Kenesaw Landis, whom he considered an interloper and a nonessential presence in the game. Ball's clashes with the Commissioner of Baseball culminated in 1931 when he sued in federal court to restrain Landis from interfering with the transfer of a Browns player to the Milwaukee minor league club in which Ball held an interest. Ball lost in court, but threatened to take his case all the way to the Supreme Court until the other club owners prevailed on him to drop the suit.[21]

Philip Ball contracted septicemia (blood poisoning) in 1933 and after only a few weeks died at St. John's Hospital in St. Louis on his birthday, October 22.

John "Jack" Tobin, outfielder, St. Louis Terriers, St. Louis Browns. The photograph is from the early 1920s (National Baseball Hall of Fame Library, Cooperstown, N.Y.).

48

The Cubs/Whales

Page one of the December 30, 1915, issue of *The Sporting News* featured a large photograph of Charles H. Weeghman with this caption: "Weeghman is a splendid sportsman in Chicago. He's a man who has made himself, having started as a waiter in a restaurant, and now he owns a dozen or so of his own. He is a baseball enthusiast, satisfied with nothing less than a winner, and a new era is promised for the Cubs with him at the head of them."

On Wednesday, January 5, 1916, Weeghman, William Walker and Harry Sinclair went to the Cincinnati office of publisher Charles P. Taft, the principal owner of the Cubs, who had just returned home from a hunting trip in Texas. The ex–Federal Leaguers arrived at 10:30 A.M. and the men remained sequestered until midafternoon.

Taft wanted $500,000 for 90 percent of the stock of the Chicago National League Club and he would not budge off that price. "I was young—and cocky—and decided that I could afford to sink half a million or so in the Cubs," Charlie recalled twenty years later. "My string of restaurants were paying big and, to the best of my figuring, I was worth between eight and ten million dollars."[1]

Taft instructed Weeghman to deposit $500,000 cash in the Corn Exchange in Chicago by January 20 at twelve o'clock noon in order to secure his ownership of the Cubs. The magnates shook hands to seal the deal, then parted company.

Weeghman went about assembling a group of investors that would ensure he would be able to meet Taft's price and retain personal control of the club. Among the new shareholders in the Chicago National League club were meatpacking magnate J. Ogden Armour, and William Wrigley, head of Wrigley Gum Company, each earning a seat on the Cubs' board of directors for their investments of $50,000. Other investors in Weeghman's club included several other wealthy Chicagoans including Charles A. McCulloch, manager of the Thompson's restaurant chain, a competitor of Charley's.

McCulloch and John Hertz had gone to Taft after the team had been promised to Weeghman and offered him $750,000 for the Cubs. As Weeghman recalled, "Mr. Taft, I was told, had informed them, in effect, 'I have given my hand to Charley Weeghman and the Cubs are his, if he produces the purchase price within the specified time.'"

Weeghman added, "Charlie Taft, there was a man for you. He wouldn't give me a scratch of writing, and he passed up $250,000 extra profit to keep his word with me."[2]

A few days later Weeghman admitted to James Crusinberry, "Last Thursday when we paid the $500,000 for the Cub stock I found that a little before noon two checks from our association had failed to arrive and we were $78,000 short of the required amount."[3]

Weeghman telephoned his friend George Reynolds, president of the Continental Bank,

311

and in just eight minutes a man arrived from the bank and handed Charley seventy-eight $1,000 bills. Weeghman placed the cash and checks in his inside coat pocket and quickly walked down La Salle Street to the Corn Exchange Bank. Weeghman plunked his payment in full down on assistant cashier John Wakefield's desk just before 12 o'clock in time to thwart the efforts of anyone else to cut in on the deal.[4]

The official exchange of ownership ceremony was conducted at 2:30 P.M. and was witnessed by William Walker, several minor stockholders in the club, outgoing Cubs President Charles Thomas, and Charles Schuttler, secretary to Charles Taft. Weeghman handed over a check for $500,000 to the Corn Exchange Bank and in return Charley was handed all the stock formerly owned by Taft.[5] The payment was the largest price paid for a major league team up to that time, because Ball's $525,000 deal for the Browns also included a ballpark whereas Weeghman's did not.

At the end of January, Weeghman's syndicate purchased the stock of Harry Ackerland, ten shares in all, for $75,000 to complete the sale of the club to its new owners. The sale netted Ackerland a profit of $35,000 on the stock he purchased from Frank Chance when the long-time manager left the club after a spat with Charles Murphy.[6]

Once he became owner of the Cubs, Weeghman moved their home from the West Side Grounds into the Federal League facility at the corner of Clark and Addison. The merger of the Cubs and Whales also brought Manager Joe Tinker and club secretary Charles Williams back to the National League. When he retired from the Cubs in 1917, it was said Williams had traveled some 500,000 miles on the railways. Ironically, at the time of his death on January 12, 1938, Williams was aboard a New York Central train en route from Cleveland to Chicago.[7]

Joe Tinker opened the 1916 season with thirteen ex-Federal Leaguers on the Cubs' roster: Les Mann, Max Flack, Rollie Zeider, Bill Fischer, Steve Yerkes, Dutch Zwilling, Mickey Doolan, Gene Packard, Claude Hendrix, Tom Seaton, Mike Prendergast, George McConnell and Three Finger Brown. Because of the large number of players under contract on the Cubs and Browns, the National Commission ruled that the two clubs were exempted from the limit of twenty-one players in the National League and twenty-five in the American League until 1917.

A parade of motorcars over a mile long preceded opening day festivities on April 20, 1916, at Weeghman Park. There was a donkey from the 25th Ward Democrats and greeting fans on the Addison Street side was JOA, a bear cub owned by Cubs minority owner J. Ogden Armour. Over 20,000 came to see the opener and the crowd overflowed onto the field.[8]

The former Whale Claude Hendrix started for the Cubs, and the Reds countered with an almost–Fed, Pete Schneider. Both pitchers gave up a pair of runs in the first, and going into the bottom of the eighth, the Cubs were on the short end of a 6–3 score. The Cubs scored twice in the eighth to pull within a run. In the ninth Max Flack doubled and scored the tying run on Heinie Zimmerman's double. The Cubs won in the eleventh inning on Vic Saier's run-scoring double.

The high-water mark for Tinker's club was April 28, when Hendrix shut out the Cardinals, 7 to 0, to give the club an 8–4 record. They managed a .500 record on Packard's 1–0 shutout of the Braves on July 7, then lost five in a row and did not achieve a winning record again that season.

William A. Phelon complained in *Baseball Magazine* that Tinker should have been able to select 21 out of the 60 athletes available in the spring to assemble a pennant-contending team. "Players came and went all summer, and this continual alteration of the club seemed doubly strange in consideration of the army that Tinker had at hand before the schedule opened."

By 1916 Steve Yerkes had slowed down considerably in the infield and on June 7 he was released to the Atlanta Crackers. The Atlanta Club would pay only the part of the player's salary based on the Southern Association's scale and Weeghman would pay the balance in accord with Steve's Federal League contract.[9] Yerkes sparkled in the Georgia city, accepting 127 consecutive chances afield before committing an error, and he batted .332 in 86 games there. The Cubs reacquired Steve via the draft in September, but released him to Indianapolis the following spring.

The Cubs were four games under .500 when, on July 29, Chicago traded outfielder Wildfire Schulte and catcher Bill Fischer to Pittsburgh for the return of Art Wilson and former Terrapins second baseman/manager Otto Knabe. Then, on August 28, they sent third baseman Heinie Zimmerman, serving a ten-day suspension for "lying down," and Mickey Doolan to the Giants for Larry Doyle and two others. Among the players parading through Weeghman Park that season was Arlie Hofman, brought back from oblivion for five games.

Charles Weeghman, president, Chicago Federal League club, 1913 (Chicago History Museum, SDN-058980. Photograph by *Chicago Daily News*. Original photograph has been cropped.).

Including Manager Tinker, who appeared in seven games, forty-five different players appeared in the Cubs' lineup at various times during the 1916 season. Just over half, twenty-six, were ex–Federal Leaguers. An eight-game losing streak in early August doomed any lingering pennant aspirations the club had.

Tom Seaton was a spot starter and reliever for the 1916 Cubs, finishing 5 and 6 with a 3.27 earned run average. Seaton started his first game for the Cubs in Cincinnati on April 15, but he lost a complete-game two-hitter, 2–0. He also pitched in the Cubs' first game at Weeghman Park, striking out the Reds' Bill Louden with the bases loaded and two out in the seventh inning.

Tom started out well in 1917, and even had a 1–0 shutout of Brooklyn on May 12. However, Seaton's right arm grew weaker with each outing and he lost four out of five starts in late May and June. His final major league appearance came on June 23, 1917. Despite a 5–4 record and a 2.53 ERA in 16 games, Seaton was dealt to the Los Angeles Angels, where he pitched in 22 Pacific Coast League games over the remainder of the season.

Edward "Dutch" Zwilling, the Federals' leading home run basher, was used mostly as a pinch hitter for the Cubs in 1916, batted only .113 in 53 plate appearances, and did not return to the majors after that season. Dutch had a long and successful career with the Kansas City

Blues of the American Association, first as a player and then as manager. He managed several minor league teams, lastly Oakland in 1938. Dutch scouted for the Cleveland Indians and worked for the Kansas City Athletics in the 1950s. In the 1960s and 1970s he was employed by both New York clubs. After scouting for Casey Stengel's Mets, Zwilling retired from baseball in 1973 at eighty-four years of age.[10]

Joe Tinker did not return as manager of the Cubs following the 1916 season. He went on to become president and manager of Columbus in the American Association. Due to his wife's poor health, Joe left as president of the Columbus team following the 1920 season and moved to Orlando, Florida.

During the 1920s, Tinker made a fortune purchasing and selling Florida real estate. In 1921, the old shortstop bought controlling interest in the Orlando Gulls, a Florida State League team which he would also manage. Joe bought sixteen acres for $5,000 and built the Orlando club a new ballpark on the land. Joe later sold the baseball field for $28,000 to Garry Herrmann, who used it as a spring training site for his Reds. After the Reds deserted Orlando, the city purchased the facility in 1932 for $1,500. Tinker's ballpark later became the spring training home of the Twins, Cubs, Dodgers, and Senators at various times. It is now part of a multi-venue complex in Orlando that includes the Florida Citrus Bowl and a music hall. The park is still known as Tinker Field.[11]

Joe Tinker became so successful in the real estate business, he was once estimated to have $170,000 in cash deposited in several local banks and was said to be worth a half million dollars. Then the bottom fell out of real estate boom because of the Depression and Tinker lost all the financial gains he had amassed. In order to make a living, he was forced to return to baseball in 1930, serving as assistant manager for the Buffalo Internationals. He finished that season as manager of Jersey City in the same league.[12]

Following the baseball season, Joe returned to Florida and opened a billiard parlor that became so popular he did not have to go north for a baseball job the next spring. On his sixty-eighth birthday, Tinker died from complications of diabetes.

Otto Knabe was signed by the Pittsburgh Pirates three days into the 1916 baseball season. He was batting a paltry .192 when traded to the Cubs in late July. Knabe hit a respectable .276 (well above his .247 lifetime average) over the remainder of the season.

When Jack Dunn took Richmond's best players and returned to Baltimore following the 1915 season, the Virginia International League franchise was left in shambles. The club got off to a bad start and on May 24, 1917, Knabe, former manager of the Federal League's Baltimore Terrapins, was hired to manage and play second base for the hapless Climbers. He could do little with the talent on hand and Richmond finished in last place. The city lost its place in the International League before the next season.[13] The stronger teams in the league decided to disband and form a "new" International League.

Knabe returned to the Cubs in 1918 and 1919 as a non-playing coach and assistant manager to Fred Mitchell. After eleven years as a player, Otto finally experienced a pennant as a coach with Chicago in 1918. Knabe was manager of the Kansas City American Association club from June 1920 until June 14, 1923, and then returned to Chicago as a coach for the Cubs in 1924.

The Cubs, still employing a number of former Federal Leaguers on its roster, won the National League pennant in 1918. Former Feds Les Mann, Max Flack, Charlie Deal and Rollie Zeider graced the starting lineup; and Claude Hendrix, a 16-game winner for the 1915 Federal League champion, won 20 games for the National League champs that year. Hendrix became the only pitcher to win twenty or more major league games before his Federal League sojourn, during his stay with the Federals, and after rejoining the organized major leagues.

On August 31, 1920, Hendrix was scheduled to pitch for Chicago against the Philadelphia Phillies until Cubs President William Veeck Sr. received six telegrams and two phone calls saying Detroit gamblers were betting heavily that the last-place Phillies would beat the Cubs, a first-division club. Veeck ordered manager Fred Mitchell to scratch Hendrix because of the insinuations, and use the team's best pitcher, Grover Cleveland Alexander, instead. The Cubs lost the game anyway.

On September 2, 1920, the *Chicago Herald and Examiner* reported the story of an alleged attempt to "fix" the August 31 Cubs-Phillies game. A letter appeared on the front page of the sports section written by Jim Crusenberry calling for an investigation of the August 31 game and the 1919 World Series.

Five days after the *Herald and Examiner*'s article, a grand jury of Cook County, Illinois, began to investigate the suspicious game. A Kansas City sportswriter named Otto Floto appeared with the claim that, on August 31, a gambler named H.A. "Frock" Thompson received a telegram advising him to bet heavily against the Cubs. Floto said he couldn't remember for sure, but he "thought" the telegram was signed by Hendrix. The grand jury apparently disregarded Floto's accusation after Hendrix and Thompson both denied the assertion. Veeck said that none of the messages implicated Hendrix or any other player, and suggested that gamblers might have started the rumor to make Alexander, the Cubs' best pitcher, unavailable for his next scheduled start.[14]

During the initial investigation, the grand jury expanded its investigation to include the 1919 World Series. Suspicion also fell on Cubs first baseman Fred Merkle, infielder Buck Herzog, and pitcher Paul Carter, relating to the possibly tainted Cubs-Phillies game. However, no conclusive proof was found to indicate Hendrix, Carter, Herzog or Merkle conspired with gamblers. The grand jury never issued a decision on whether the August 31 game was fixed.

On February 8, 1921, the Cubs unconditionally released Claude Hendrix. Veeck issued a statement that the pitcher's release had nothing to do with the rumors surrounding the Cubs-Phillies game of the previous season. Claude's 1920 pitching record of 9 wins and 12 losses with a 3.58 earned run average just wasn't good enough to retain the pitcher for another season. Veeck's statement gained credence when the Cubs also released veteran players Dode Paskert, Fred Merkle, and Buck Herzog.

A few days later, Oscar C. Reichow expanded on Hendrix's release in *The Sporting News:*

> Hendrix is clean as far as the Cub officials are concerned. They had nasty reports about the game of August 31 and put in a lot of time investigating them. Not only did they attempt to uncover facts, but President John Heydler of the National League also strived to run the reports to the ground. He got nowhere and the Cubs' officials got nowhere. Hendrix, therefore, was not dismissed from the team because of any evidence secured against him.... Hendrix's pitching last season ... was too inconsistent and unsteady. Besides, he did not know what it was to keep his self [*sic*] in the best of shape. He was always pounds overweight.[15]

Hendrix moved to Allentown, Pennsylvania, and became a cafe proprietor. In 1924, Claude joined a semi-pro team (which operated under the auspices of the Commissioner of Baseball) in the Lehigh Valley of Pennsylvania. The question of Hendrix's status in baseball arose, but Judge Landis indicated Hendrix was a free agent. Four years later, Claude pitched for a semi-pro team in exhibition games against two major league teams, which would not have been allowed if he had been on baseball's ineligible list.

The allegation that Hendrix was guilty of corruption and was banned from baseball by the Commissioner appeared in the 1947 biography of Judge Landis written by J.G. Taylor Spink, publisher of *The Sporting News*. Hendrix had died on March 22, 1944, childless and a widower, so there was no one to defend his name and Spink's invalid claim went unchallenged.[16]

Just before the United States entered the World War in 1917, Cubs owner Charlie Weeghman took out significant bank loans to fund a number of business ventures. The influenza epidemic that swept across America in the summer of 1918 had dire consequences for Weeghman's restaurant and movie theater businesses. He also lost a sizable amount of money in the commodities market and owed the banks a lot of money. Unable to raise significant capital, Charley borrowed money from one of the Cubs' minority investors, William Wrigley, giving Cubs stock as collateral.

Wrigley told sportswriter Harry Neily how he forced Weeghman out of the Cubs' presidency. The chewing gum magnate reportedly told Charley, "If I help you out, you must retire from baseball and devote all your time to business."[17]

With all the leverage he needed, Wrigley presented Weeghman's resignation as club president at the stockholders' meeting in December 1918. Wrigley assumed full control of the Cubs in 1919.

Weeghman later mourned his losses:

> I suppose I should have stayed out of the Federal League which ultimately cost me $3,000,000, and should have let Hertz and McCulloch have the Cubs. I might have stuck to my string of restaurants — why, you know my one place on Madison Street, near the old Tribune Building, paid me for years as much as $11,000 per week profit. But I wanted to spread out all over the country, and I did, with what result is history now.[18]

Some said that Weeghman's luck ran out when he and wife Bessie split up and he entered the movie theater business. Charley and Bessie officially divorced in 1920, Mrs. Weeghman gaining custody of their eight-year-old daughter Dorothy Jane.

Charley's old friend and partner in the Chifeds, William Walker, stayed on with the Cubs, ascending to the club presidency upon the death of Bill Veeck in 1933. However, Walker and P.K. Wrigley never agreed on how to run the club and the young heir of William Wrigley took the presidency himself in 1934.

On August 13, 1920, Charley Weeghman's chain of Chicago restaurants was thrown into receivership. That followed the filing of a petition in bankruptcy court by three creditors whose claims totaled $12,000. As Weeghman plunged from the pinnacle of success into the depths of comparative poverty his sobriquet became "Unlucky Charley."

By the time Charley remarried in 1922, his large number of enterprises in the Windy City had dwindled to one restaurant and a night club until he gave those up, too. The name of Weeghman faded from the Chicago scene and he moved to New York City.

Backed by Colonel Jacob Ruppert of the Yankees, Harry Frazee, and Harry Sinclair in 1927, Charley opened a bar and grill on Fifth Avenue in New York City. The business did not prove to be a success, but undeterred, he opened Weeghman's Restaurant on East Fifty-Eighth Street. This effort failed too, as did Weeghman's Yacht Club, which he opened later the same year. Despite all the failures, Charley stayed in the restaurant business and was serving as associate manager of Ben Marden's Riviera at Fort Lee, New Jersey, at the time of his death.[19]

Ironically, Weeghman died in Chicago. On November 2, 1938, he suffered a stroke at Chicago's Drake Hotel while on a stopover from a trip from New York to Hot Springs, Arkansas. Charley was survived by his widow, the former Carol Osmund, and a daughter.

Harry Neily eulogized the former Chicago Whales and Cubs owner:

> Probably no city except Chicago could have produced such a character.... Weeghman wasn't a New Yorker. He was as typical of Chicago as the stockyards or Lake Michigan. His breezy style was fitting for the mid–West and totally out of place in New York.

Charley Weeghman was a showman and lived by the standards of that picturesque profession. He ran a shoestring into a million and when luck turned, nobody ever heard him complain.[20]

Weeghman Park was renamed "Cubs Park" in 1920. Then, in 1926, it became "Wrigley Field" for William Wrigley Jr., the team's owner. Wrigley Field underwent major renovations in 1937, including expanded bleacher seating, magnetic controls in the hand-operated scoreboard, and the planting of the ivy that eventually covered the outfield wall. The Cubs did not play a single night game until 1988, when lights were finally added to the stadium. The current seating capacity is more than double the seats as when it opened in 1914.

49

The Outcasts

During August of the 1918 National League season, Hal Chase was suspended from the Cincinnati Reds without pay for the remainder of the season. Reds President Garry Herrmann did not offer an explanation for the suspension. Chase did: "Let's not beat around the bush. I'm accused of betting on ball games and trying to get a pitcher [Jimmy Ring] to throw a game for money."[1]

Chase's reaction to his suspension was to sue the Reds for unpaid back salary and demand a formal hearing on the charges, which would be conducted by National League president John Heydler. The accused's former manager, Christy Mathewson, was unable to appear since he was serving with the U.S. Army in Europe, so his testimony was submitted in an affidavit.

The official finding of the National League president was announced on February 5, 1919: "...after full consideration of the evidence, is that it is nowhere established that the accused was interested in any pool or wager that caused any ballgame to result otherwise than on its merits, and that player Hal H. Chase is not guilty of the charges brought against him."[2]

Two weeks after the hearing, Chase was traded to the Giants for Walter Holke and former Federal League catcher Bill Rariden. Late in the 1919 season, outfielder Benny Kauff and pitcher Fred Toney each told Manager John McGraw that third baseman Heinie Zimmerman and Hal Chase offered them bribes to throw games. Once McGraw learned of his players' supposed treachery, Zimmerman was suspended, ostensibly for "breaking curfew," and he never played in the major leagues again. McGraw claimed the Giants wanted to avoid legal entanglements with the player and offered him a contract for 1920 at only $2,100, far less than the $6,500 Zim made the previous year.

"I had absolute confidence in Chase when I signed him to play last year," McGraw testified under oath in 1920.

> When he was declared innocent of Matty's charges I felt sure he had done no wrong and was a victim of circumstantial evidence. But after I learned of his connection with the 1919 World Series scandal, I became convinced that he purposely made dishonest plays that enabled the Reds to beat us in the four out of six games at the Polo Grounds last August.
>
> Chase, it will be remembered, muffed a throw from pitcher Neff in one of those games that resulted in three Cincinnati runs and the Giants' defeat. Later in the series, Chase slide into third base, and, declaring that he had sprained his wrist, remained out of the games, although the New York Club's physician could find no trace of such an injury. In my opinion, Chase deliberately threw us down.[3]

Chase sprained his wrist on September 4 and next appeared in games on the fourteenth and fifteenth. With the Giants out of the pennant race, McGraw left the team for the final two weeks of September. Christy Mathewson took over the club for the rest of the season and even employed Chase as first base coach. On September 25, 1919, Hal Chase made his final appearance in a major league baseball game, as a pinch hitter. He smacked a double that drove in a run.

"Later when I heard from Arthur Fletcher that Benton [a Giants pitcher] had been offered bribe money by Chase," continued McGraw, "I resorted to the same methods that retired Zimmerman. Chase received a new contract which named such a small salary that he quit of his own accord. The indictment of Chase by the Chicago grand jury has vindicated the New York Club's action."[4]

On March 23, 1920, Lee Magee, who played with Chase on the Reds and who was released by the Cubs prior to the 1920 season, announced to the press: "On Saturday, I shall make public the charges on which the National League bases its action in barring me from its circuit. I'll show documents both in my favor and against me.... If I'm barred I'll take quite a few noted people with me. I'll show up some people for tricks turned ever since 1906. And there will be merry music in the baseball world."[5]

On April 14, Magee filed suit against the Cubs for his 1920 salary plus $5,000 extra in lost World Series pay if the Cubs won the 1920 pennant, a total of $9,500. Lee's lawsuit began in United States District Court in Chicago on June 7, 1920. Magee admitted during his testimony that while with the Reds he made a bet on the first game of a double-header with Boston, July 25, 1918. He stated Chase placed the bet and Lee swore he was not aware the wager was against his own team until Hal told him after the game. After a three-day trial, the jury ruled against Magee in his suit against the Chicago National League club.[6]

Meanwhile, Hal Chase was playing for San Jose in California's Mission League. That August, he was barred from all parks in the Pacific Coast League after having allegedly tried to bribe Salt Lake City pitcher Spider Baum prior to a game in Los Angeles. That incident and allegations that he tried to bribe an umpire led to Chase's banishment from the Mission League as well.

During a Chicago grand jury investigation of the suspicious Cubs-Phillies game (August 31, 1919) and the 1919 World Series, Giants pitcher Rube Benton testified that Hal Chase won as much as $40,000 betting on the World Series between the White Sox and Reds.[7] On March 26, 1921, the Chicago grand jury handed down indictments against eighteen individuals, players and gamblers, charging them with fixing the result of the 1919 World Series. One of the men indicted was Hal Chase, and he was arrested in California on April 25, 1921. A month later, Chase was released on a writ of habeas corpus and a bail of $3,000, then was exonerated on the grounds that a proper warrant for his arrest had not been sent from Chicago. No further attempts to extradite Chase to Illinois for the trial were attempted.[8] Chase always said he knew about the fix in advance, but had not profited from it.

During the last two weeks of the 1919 Pacific Coast League season, there were rumors that bribes were paid to ensure Vernon the pennant. In October 1920, the deputy district attorney of Los Angeles County took his case before a grand jury, arguing that at least five of eight clubs in the league were involved with gambling interests. When Vernon's first baseman, William "Babe" Borton, was brought before the grand jury, he claimed that Vernon won the 1919 pennant because at least six players on the clubs in question had conspired to deliberately lose games. Borton testified that twenty of his teammates, including the team's manager, contributed to a $2000 "slush fund" that was used to pay off Portland and Salt Lake City players to guarantee a championship for Vernon. Although the grand jury dismissed the indictments against three players and a known gambler, Pacific League President William H. McCarthy suspended Borton and Salt Lake City outfielders Karl Maggart and Bill Rumler for gambling and conspiring to throw games during the 1919 season. The charges against the indicted players were dismissed on Christmas Eve because the judge in the case reasoned that fixing ball games was not a crime under California law. The players would be banned by Organized Baseball the following January, although Rumler would be reinstated in 1928.[9]

Another player who was caught up in the Pacific Coast gambling scandal was former Brooklyn Tip Tops hurler Tom Seaton. Seaton joined the San Francisco Seals in 1918 and pitched there for three seasons. He had an outstanding record in 1919, winning 25 games and losing 16 with a 2.84 earned run average in 354 innings.

After pitching in ten games for San Francisco in 1920, Seaton, along with fellow Seals pitcher Luther "Casey" Smith, were released that May. The club's president, Charles Graham, said, "From time to time rumors of the most serious nature have reached me regarding these players, their practices and their associates.... whether true or untrue, for the best interests of baseball, Seaton and Smith should be released."[10]

Though no mention of gambling or consorting with gamblers was mentioned by President Graham or Pacific Coast League President William H. McCarthy, the assumption was the pitchers' releases were a result of such associations. The Associated Press reported at the time that "one of the pitchers was involved in a similar affair last year, but the news of the scandal was suppressed."[11]

Seaton joined the Manford team in the industrial San Joaquin Valley League, but after pitching in only three games Tom was released when the club was told it would be thrown out of the league if it kept Seaton. Tom attempted a return to Organized Baseball by joining Casey Smith with Little Rock, but Southern League President John Martin refused to approve the contracts, citing the pitchers' questionable conduct in the Pacific Coast League. The Arkansas club was determined to use the pitchers anyway, but several teams in the league said that they would not play Little Rock if the two players were on the roster. The Little Rock club appealed to the United States District Court to set aside President Martin's edict and allow the pair to pitch in the Southern League. Finally, in December 1920 the Little Rock club filed a motion to dismiss the suit and dropped the two pitchers.[12] By that time Seaton had accepted a lucrative offer to play industrial ball.

Seaton pitched for a team in Poplar Bluff, Missouri, in 1922 and then he moved to the southwestern part of the United States. Tom settled in Tucson, Arizona, and pitched for the Tucson Motive Power team in 1923. In 1925 Seaton was working for the Southern Pacific Railroad in Tucson when the Juarez, Mexico, Copper League baseball team signed him to a player contract.[13]

The El Paso club protested that Juarez could not use Seaton because he was an "ineligible player." One week later, it was reported that Seaton had produced a letter from the San Francisco Seals that indicated he was released from that club and did not mention any ineligibility.[14]

Seaton pitched in the Copper League for three years. In June 1925, Tom was named manager of the Juarez club. Juarez won the second-half championship with a 15–11 record, then played the first-half champion, Douglas, in a best-two-of-three games for the championship. The Juarez team won the two games pitched by Seaton, 4 to 2 and 6 to 1. Douglas was no pushover either. It had 42-year-old player-manager Hal Chase at first base, and two banned White Sox players, Chick Gandil at second and Buck Weaver at shortstop.

Douglas persuaded Chase to become its manager in 1926. Serving as both manager and pitcher, Tom Seaton led the team from Juarez, composed of an all–Mexican contingent other than himself, to the first-half championship with a record of 25 and 12. Pitcher Seaton topped the league with a record of eight wins and only one loss. Juarez ran into financial problems during the second half of the season and its players were distributed among other teams in the league.

The El Paso team of the Copper League posted mediocre records in 1925 and 26, and hired Seaton as their pitcher and field manager for the 1927 season. After the Copper League season, Tom joined former Black Sox pitcher Lefty Williams on the Juarez all-star team, organized from Copper League players to play a touring team of Cuban stars.[15]

After baseball, Seaton permanently settled in El Paso, worked as a foreman for a smelting company and continued to pitch semi-pro ball for several years. He gained a reputation as one of the top bowlers in the El Paso area. Tom died of lung cancer on April 10, 1940, and was buried in El Paso.

Hal Chase was unable to play baseball in 1927 due to a knee injury suffered during the recent Copper League season. Chase ultimately returned to the diamond and became a legend playing in the "outlaw" leagues of California, Arizona and Mexico. Always a heavy drinker, Hal became a wandering alcoholic. The man who at one time was considered to be baseball's greatest first baseman, worked in a pool hall, in a bar, as a plumber's assistant, and as a car salesman. He was hospitalized in California in 1941 for the treatment of beriberi, a disease often associated with chronic alcohol ingestion. Prince Hal was totally destitute and had no means to pay his hospital bills. Hal Chase died of alcohol-related maladies on May 18, 1947, in Colusa, California.[16s]

50

The Benny Kauff Story

Benny Kauff craved publicity and longed for the chance to hold court before New York's sports reporters. Before playing an inning of baseball with the New York Giants, Benny was already contemptuous of National League pitching. "If Larry Doyle hits .320, I'll hit .375," Kauff boasted to reporters in December 1915. "...if I don't steal forty bases up there next season, you can have my year's salary, boys, I'm not kidding you. I want to play in New York. I'd do anything for McGraw. He's treated me white."[1]

After his Federal League contract was purchased by the Giants, Benny notified the club, through his attorney John Montgomery Ward, that he had conditions before he would play baseball in New York. He would not play for his Federal League salary of $6,000 a year unless he got a $5,000 bonus from Giants President Hempstead plus $5,000 from Harry Sinclair, because his original contract with the Indianapolis Federals did not contain a clause giving the club the right to assign his services.

When the Indianapolis Federal League club was transferred to Newark for 1915, Kauff claimed he became a free agent. After the first time Kauff signed with the Giants in April of 1915, Hempstead refused to pay the "promised" $5,000 bonus or a cent of salary after learning Benny would not be removed from baseball's ineligible list. The Giants were willing to pay a $5,000 bonus in the spring of 1916, but Benny ignored McGraw's order to report until he got the $5,000 from Sinclair, who was paid $35,000 by New York for his release. After much haggling, Sinclair finally agreed give Benny the $5,000.

Following negotiations conducted by John Ward on behalf of Kauff, the outfielder signed a new contract with New York the morning of March 10, 1916, then departed by train for spring training at Marlin, Texas. The "Feds' Ty Cobb" would receive $7,500 per season, instead of his old Federal League guarantee for $6,000, and it would run through 1918. Benny got his $5,000 bonus in cash and pocketed a month's pay in advance.[2]

When Kauff arrived in Marlin "he was wearing an expensive suit, a loudly-striped silk shirt, patent leather shoes, a fur-collared overcoat and a derby hat. He had a huge diamond stickpin, an equally huge diamond ring and a watch encrusted with diamonds. His luggage consisted of three bags and four trunks — and he had $7,500 cash in his pockets."[3]

One of the trunks reportedly contained 52 bats, though Benny told reporters he had thirty-five new ones. "Charley Carr made me some new ones and they're pippins. If I strike out it will be because I don't take my bat off my shoulder. Nobody could ever bat any better than I can."[4]

Despite the newcomer's boasting, legendary Giants pitcher Christy Mathewson said of his new teammate, "From what I have read of Benny Kauff before I had met him enough to know him at all well I imagined he would be hard to get along with and a player who would have to be taken down by us old timers frequently. But Benny, in spite of his belief in himself, is very likable, and I look for him to make good. Kauff is egotistical without being fresh, or offensive."[5]

New York sports reporter Sid Mercer wrote of Kauff in the spring of 1916:

> In conversation Benny is quaint and picturesque, but he has determined to be more careful, as he realizes now that boastful bursts of confidence which he uttered with boyish abandon were picked up and retailed.
> As a matter of fact, Benny Kauff has great respect and admiration for men like Cobb and Mathewson, and he never loses an opportunity to praise Cobb and express a wish that he may deserve some day such a reputation as Ty has earned.[6]

On the field, highlights for Benny were few and far between during his first summer in the National League. One Eastern critic even began to haunt brash Benny with the taunt, "Benny Kauff, the Ty Cobb of the Feds and the Ping Bodie of the National League."[7]

A seventeen-game winning streak in May pushed the Giants into second place, but after catcher Bill Rariden suffered a broken finger the Giants sank in the standings. When Bedford Bill returned to the lineup, the club caught fire.

On September 7, 1916, the Giants were three games under .500 and all but out of the National League pennant hunt. Then, over the ensuing three weeks, the Giants were unbeatable, reeling off the longest winning streak in baseball history, 26 games (actually they were unbeaten in twenty-eight games because of two suspended contests). Benny Kauff was Mr. Clutch during the streak, driving in 24 runs. Within two days, he hit home runs in three consecutive games during the streak.[8]

Though the second game of a double-header against Pittsburgh on September 18 ended in a 1–1 tie, Benny saved the Giants from a loss in fifth inning. The *New York Times* reported, "Benny Kauff laced the ball on a wild, tearing trip to the fence in right centre field. Benny gathered up speed like a race horse, and just got over the plate as Carey's wide toss arrived."[9]

Under the sub-heading "Two More Homers for Modest Benny," the same newspaper wrote:

> Benny Kauff is coming nearer to the expectations of Benny Kauff every minute.... Benjamin got two monstrous home runs yesterday, one in each game.... In the first game, when the Giants were overcoming the unlucky No. 13 jinx, Benny did his share with a four-station clout into the right-field stand, and in the second game he slammed the ball so hard that it fell limp and breathless into the upper tier boxes.
> So Mr. Kauff's opinion of Benjamin Michael Kauff's baseball ability, which he expressed so forcibly early in the season, wasn't so far wrong after all.[10]

In the second game of a double-header at the Polo Grounds on September 28, Benny achieved a rare inside-the-park grand slam home run. It came in the third inning against the Boston Braves' veteran right-hander Pat Ragan.

"Don't let it slip your mind the bases are jammed," reported the *Times*.

> Ragan pitches ball after ball at Kauff until high upon the score board these 35,000 or more spectators see that the count on Benjamin Michael is two strikes and three balls....
> The ash bat on Kauff's shoulders is poised as Ragan's tangent approaches. There is a mighty swing and a crash. If you watch closely you can see the little white ball in its wild flight over the head of Fred Snodgrass in centre field. On and on it sails to the centre field fence....
> Around the base paths four runners go like mad. It resembles a merry-go-round and when three of them have crossed the plate, little Benny is tearing around toward third base. Manager McGraw, coaching at third, gives him the high sign and Benny dashes for the plate. The crowd is on its toes, the din of the tumult and the shouting stunning 70,000 ears.

Look, the ball is being relayed in from the outfield and Benny is not at the plate yet.... Then a moment's silence as the ball lands in the glove of Pat Ragan with a thud. Pat turns about and soaks it at Hank Gowdy at the plate. All of a sudden, Benny leaves the ground. He hurls himself, feet first, at the little rubber plate which spells glory for him. The toe on one of Kauff's shoes just touches the outer edge of the platter, as the ball lands in Gowdy's mitt. Umpire Charley Rigler is looking on with wide open eyes. "Safe" cries Rigler.

Benny rose from a cloud of dust, panting like a hunted deer, and half a dozen Giant players rushed from the bench and began to slap Benny on the back.... Benny just smiled a smile of contentment as much as to say, "Well, I told you I'd do it some say, and I'll be blamed if I didn't."[11]

Despite the heroics, the season did not end well for Kauff and the Giants. After the 26-game winning streak ended on September 30, the Giants lost four of their five remaining games, and finished in fourth place. Benny's batting average actually dropped ten points after September 7, the day the steak began.

Benny batted only .264 for 1916, but did finish second in the National League in stolen bases (40), was second in triples, and fourth in runs batted in. In 1917 he improved to .308, which was the third-best batting average in the league, and stole 30 bases as the Giants won the pennant. Of concern, though, was the decline in his extra-base hits, 15 fewer than the year before. In the 1917 World Series, which the Giants lost to the White Sox, 4 games to 2, Kauff hit only .160, but he did homer twice in New York's fourth-game victory.

In March 1918 Benny received notice from his local draft board and was ordered to report for military duty on June 14, 1918. On June 22 Kauff played his last game for the Giants before going into the Army. To that point in the season, Benny was having his best season since coming to the National League. After 54 games, the twenty-eight-year-old Kauff was batting a robust .324. Manager McGraw and the Giants' players presented the departing player with a gold watch. In mid–August Benny played a few games with New York during his furlough, but after he left the club in June, the Giants played only two games above .500 and finished in second place behind the Chicago Cubs.[12]

Benny Kauff spent his military service with the 158th Depot Brigade at Camp Sheridan, Ohio. Corporal Kauff was mustered out of the Army on February 14, 1919. One month later, the renowned New York "dandy" married Irish-born Hazel Cassley, the daughter of a Pennsylvania Railroad engineer.[13] He was one of the last players to report to Giants training camp in Gainesville, Florida, that spring. Benny not only had a new bride, but he also was joined by a new teammate, Hal Chase.

When he came to the Giants in 1916, Benny had been the most heralded newcomer to the National League in a generation. When he returned from the Army, the luster had faded. Ross Youngs had emerged as the Giants' bright new star, and the newcomer out-hit Benny in 1919, .311 to .277. Kauff did finish second in the National League in home runs with 10 and placed fourth in runs batted in.

Aware of Benny's personal problems with his automobile parts business, teammates Heinie Zimmerman and first baseman-coach Hal Chase offered Kauff money to throw games late in the 1919 regular season. Kauff refused the money and informed his roommate Christy Mathewson, one of the most respected players in the game, and Manager McGraw.

"Kauff and [Fred] Toney were loyal to the New York Club when they came directly to me with information that Zimmerman had offered to pay each $225 to play dishonestly," McGraw told *The Sporting News*. "For their willingness to expose crooked methods in baseball they not only deserve praise, but set a fine example for other players in the profession."[14]

After Zimmerman's case became linked to the White Sox' plot to throw the 1919 World

Series, the names of Kauff and other Giants were also mentioned. Billy Maharg, one of the conspirators in the Black Sox scandal, even claimed Kauff had taken part in the fix, and Arnold Rothstein, the gambler who bankrolled the scheme, "reportedly" told Ban Johnson that Benny Kauff had asked him for $50,000 to pay off the White Sox players prior to the World Series.[15]

In late February of 1920, Kauff was arrested and arraigned on a grand larceny charge involving a stolen automobile. The charge stemmed from his partnership in the Manhattan auto parts business he had started the previous year with his half brother and Giants pitcher Jesse Barnes. Kauff, free on bail, went south for spring training with the Giants in Texas.

Kauff was batting a respectable .274 after 55 games for the Giants in 1920 when, on July 2, Benny was traded. He did not go to another major league club, but to Toronto of the International League, along with cash, for the unheralded Vern "Tubby" Spencer, whose major league career consisted of 45 games.

Kauff's first game after joining Toronto was an exhibition game at Maple Leaf Park against his former teammates. The International League club beat the Giants, 4–3, and Benny got some measure of satisfaction by hitting a home run on the second pitch of the game from Jesse Winters, a pitcher with whom he had traded blows during spring training.

Batting second in the Maple Leafs' lineup, Kauff hit .343 in 79 games, tops on the club, and he stole 28 bases. However, as Louis Cauz wrote in his history of baseball in Toronto, *Baseball's Back in Town*, "unfortunately, Kauff's reputation — and the auto story — followed him to rival parks. He would be greeted by fans armed with automobile horns. One day in Jersey City, the groundskeeper left the steamroller in deep left. A fan bellowed, 'Hide that machine quick, here comes Kauff.'"[16]

In late September 1920, John McGraw gave testimony before the grand jury in Chicago investigating the Black Sox scandal. McGraw said that he released Hal Chase after National League President Heydler told him that the first baseman had offered Cubs outfielder Lee Magee a bribe to "lay down" in a game against the Giants. He also stated that Zimmerman was released because Kauff and Toney turned him in. The grand jury asked McGraw if he could come back and bring Benny Kauff with him.[17]

That same day, the reports out of New York said that a private detective of dubious reputation named Val O'Farrell said that Benny Kauff, former minor league pitcher Bill Burns, and a gambler named Orbie approached Arnold Rothstein at the Hotel Astor in New York with a scheme to "fix" the 1919 World Series between the White Sox and Reds. The famous New York gambler turned them down flat.

O'Farrell said his friend Rothstein told him, "Can you beat it? Trying to put over a deal like this with Benny Kauff in it. They are the kind of fellows that are killing baseball. I could never listen to any such proposition as that."[18]

Furthermore, O'Farrell intimated that McGraw sent Kauff to Toronto in July because Rothstein had told McGraw and that he heard Kauff was "telling his friends all over the town how the series had been fixed."[19] Historians have treated O'Farrell's accusations with trepidation and the comment about "killing baseball" does not ring true coming from the man who became infamous for fixing the World Series.

When he returned to testify on October 5, McGraw denied that gambling had anything to do with the release of Kauff to Toronto that summer and said the demotion was due to a slump in Benny's play when he began to worry over the charges of receiving a stolen automobile.[20]

Kauff testified about the bribe offer by Zimmerman: "I listened to what he had to say and immediately reported the matter to Manager McGraw. I refused to have anything to do with Zimmerman. In fact, I think I got three or four hits in that particular game."[21]

Fred Toney, Giants president Charles Stoneham, second baseman Larry Doyle, and trainer J.L. Mackall, substantiated Benny's testimony. The next day, indictments came down against Heinie Zimmerman and Hal Chase for bribery. McGraw told the press he held nothing against Kauff because of his alleged involvement with suspicious automobile deals, but did concede that Benny's situation was an embarrassment to the Giants.[22]

Kauff appeared in court for the automobile theft charge on February 21, 1920, and trial was set in two weeks. Kauff's lawyer, Emil Fuchs, requested a delay for the trial because his client was scheduled to go to spring training with the Giants on February 26. Rumors of a trade that would send Kauff to the Boston Braves made the rounds, but only a few days into spring training, 1921, Benny's baseball career was put on hold.

Kauff reported to the Giants' training camp in San Antonio, then, unexpectedly, he received a telegram from the newly appointed Commissioner of Baseball, Judge Kenesaw Mountain Landis, on March 7. Landis insisted Kauff come to Chicago for a meeting and Benny departed that evening. Landis wanted to talk to Benny about a claim made by an apparently vindictive Heinie Zimmerman. Heinie accused Kauff of auto theft and said Benny associated with gamblers during the final Giants-Cubs series in 1919.[23]

One part of the affidavit was particularly interesting for Frederick Groehl, a district attorney who was part of a special task force investigating auto thefts. The same day Kauff was meeting with Landis, Groehl was attempting to secure Zimmerman's testimony against Benny on the grand larceny charge.

During his meeting with Kauff on the ninth, Landis "requested" the outfielder not to return to spring training, nor play with the Giants, until the auto theft charges against him were "cleared up." No transcript of Benny's meeting with Landis exists and it is not known what he told the Commissioner, if he said anything at all. The next day, Landis placed the eight Black Sox players on the "Permanently Ineligible List." Landis also said he had sent Kauff to New York to await the outcome of his case.[24]

Six days before opening day of the 1921 National League season, Judge Landis ruled Benny ineligible to play in Organized Baseball. He said Kauff's indictment "does imply that, in the judgment of the Grand Jurors, there is probable cause to believe the accused guilty," and more damningly, "more than thirteen months have elapsed since the filing of formal charges of the commission of a felony.... It is perfectly apparent that earnest insistence on a hearing by the defendant would before this have brought the matter to finality."[25] Landis apparently decided Kauff was guilty because his attorney, Judge Emil Fuchs, requested a delay so his client could go to spring training with the Giants.

To justify his suspension of Kauff for conduct detrimental to baseball, Judge Landis cited Section 2 of Article 4 of the Major-Minor League Rules, which stated that players who participated in a game with or against a club containing a player under indictment for shall be considered ineligible.[26] The commissioner's interpretation of this rule seemed to indicate Benny was suspended so his teammates would not become ineligible.

The case against Benny Kauff went to trial in New York on May 10, 1921. The two auto thieves, James Shields and James Whalen, testified that they had dined with Kauff on the night of December 8, 1919, and Benny told them he had a customer for a Cadillac automobile. The car thieves testified that they walked down Broadway with Benny and failed to find a car with the desired make, but eventually found one on West End Avenue, which they stole. After they changed the tires and repainted the body, the car was sold for $1,800. The profits were split three ways.[27]

The next day, Kauff was preceded to the stand by his wife. On the night the prosecution witnesses said Benny was dividing money with them, Hazel Kauff said that she and Sadie

Levy dined with the outfielder. Kauff said he had business to transact and left the women at an uptown store. Returning in half an hour, Benny informed the women he had disposed of an automobile and they returned to their hotel, where Mrs. Kauff said her husband immediately turned over the proceeds of the sale to her. Under oath, Benny asserted he bought the car from William Dorst of the Cumberland Hotel in October 1919 and testified he had a valid bill of sale for it. Kauff said he refunded the purchase price to the man who purchased the stolen automobile when detectives alleged the car was stolen. Benny's former partner and teammate, Jesse Barnes, told the jury that he and Kauff failed in an automobile accessory business and had to borrow money from the club to pay their debts when the business failed. They still owed the Giants money on the deal.[28] McGraw and Giants outfielder George Burns were called as character witnesses for Kauff.

In the end, the jury did not buy the testimony of the confessed thieves and stayed out less than an hour before returning a "not guilty" verdict on May 13. Benny Kauff was innocent in the eyes of the law, but was still banned from Organized Baseball.

On June 1, Landis told the *New York Times* that he had received Kauff's application for reinstatement and that it would be considered shortly. Landis procrastinated for three months without rendering a decision. He later would say that his review of the trial transcripts made it clear that Kauff was guilty, and called his acquittal "one of the worst travesties of justice" he had ever come across.[29]

Benny went to the New York Supreme Court on September 12 and obtained a temporary injunction from Justice Isadore Wasservogel dictating that he be reinstated as a player pending a full hearing of his case in court. In his affidavit to the court Kauff said the commissioner set himself up as a "czar" in his case and, "although receiving the most severe criticism of the Congress of the United States, continued to hold his judgeship and entered into a business contract for $40,000, and arbitrarily, without justice, reason or sense of justice, had continued to deprive me of my livelihood and the practice of my profession."[30]

Benny's lawyer told the press that had tried unsuccessfully to persuade Landis to reconsider Kauff's suspension. Landis said that Kauff could not be reinstated because he had admitted in court "sitting with a couple of men who claimed to have lost money through the purchase of a stolen automobile." Landis also felt Benny had tried to buy off the car owner, because the ball player testified that he offered compensation to the owner of the stolen automobile. However, it was attorney Fuchs that advised him to settle "as one in good faith had guaranteed the cars and not as one who was in any way culpable criminally."[31]

That December Justice Edward Whitaker heard arguments to make the temporary injunction permanent. It was stated the New York Giants wanted to re-sign Kauff, but were prevented from doing so by the commissioner and the National League. On January 17, 1922, Judge Whitaker ruled in favor of the commissioner by rejecting Benny's request to make his temporary injunction permanent. Kauff, he said, could only sue under his contractual rights and his contract with the Giants had ended in October of 1921. As it was now January, he could not rule for Kauff, even though the judge admitted that an "apparent injustice has been done the plaintiff."[32]

Landis responded to the news by stating that Kauff "could not be restored to good standing without impairing the morale of the other players..." and his "mere presence in the line-up would inevitably burden patrons of the game with grave apprehension as to its integrity."[33]

Kauff would never be reinstated by Organized Baseball. In 1927, Benny sued the Giants for lost salary in connection with his 1921 contract. That suit was settled out of court a year later.

After baseball, Kauff dropped out of sight and occasionally made the newspapers when he ran afoul of the law for minor offenses. Benny spent his post-baseball life in the Columbus area with his wife and their only child, Robert. He died on November 17, 1961, of a cerebral hemorrhage. The Federal League's most illustrious player is buried in Columbus's Union Cemetery.

51

Back into Good Society

"The Federal League amalgamation worked out just about as all close critics thought it would," wrote William A. Phelon in *Baseball Magazine* after the 1916 season. "All through the season, the ex-Feds and the 'loyal element' of last year worked together in the greatest harmony and good fellowship. There was no clannishness and no Federal or anti–Federal cliques were formed. The boys simply forgot all about what happened last season, and went along together as good fellows ought to go."[1]

All in all, forty-three ex-Federal Leaguers appeared in at least one National League game during 1916. Of course, about half that number was with the Cubs. Boston, Cincinnati, and New York each employed six of the former outlaws and only one National League club had none, the last-place Cardinals. On the other hand, only eight former Fed players found roster spots on American League clubs other than Philip Ball's St. Louis Browns, which used eleven former Terriers.[2]

In early 1913, a young outfielder named Edd Roush, playing in the Central League, caught the eye of several major league scouts. In late May, Garry Herrmann of the Reds wrote a letter to the owner of the Evansville, Indiana, club to inquire about a price for the raw but talented player. The Evansville owner replied that he had already made a deal with Charles Comiskey for $3,000 and Roush would be called to the White Sox whenever they needed him.[3]

Following the settlement with the Federal League, Newark owner Harry Sinclair set a price of $10,000 for Edd Roush's contract, but the high amount put off bidders. The break came when John McGraw learned that the Giants' right fielder, Dave Robertson, would miss at least the first six weeks of the 1916 season due to a hip injury. Germany Schaefer, Roush's former teammate at Newark, suggested to McGraw that he get Edd, who "was the best outfielder in the [Federal] league. He's a better outfielder than Kauff.... I tell you he's the best buy in the lot and nobody knows it — not even Sinclair."[4]

McGraw offered $7,500 for the young outfielder. Sinclair had grown tired of the whole matter of disposal of players and agreed. About the same time, Cincinnati's Garry Herrmann sent a letter to Sinclair asking about Roush, but it arrived two days after McGraw finalized his purchase. For the second time, the Cincinnati owner's procrastination cost him the services of the coveted outfielder.

Prior to the 1916 spring training, the Giants sent Edd a contract for the same salary he had received in Newark, $4,000. The brash young outfielder resealed the envelope and returned it to New York. Roush finally agreed to a $500 raise. Perhaps more important to him, he had managed to miss three weeks of spring training.[5]

McGraw started the 1916 season with four former Federal Leaguers in his starting lineup, Kauff and Roush in the outfield, McKechnie at third base, and Rariden behind the plate. A fifth Federal, pitcher Fred Anderson, would be a member of the starting rotation.

Roush hated playing for a demanding manager like John McGraw. "I didn't like New York," Edd told Lawrence Ritter. "...It was really McGraw I didn't like. John J. McGraw. I just didn't enjoy playing for him, that's all. If you made a bad play he'd cuss you out, yell at you, call you all sorts of names. That didn't go with me."[6]

Roush got off to a slow start and was hitting just .188 on July 20, 1916, when the Giants sent him to the Reds in what later became known as the "Hall of Fame" trade. McGraw sent three future Hall of Famers, Christy Mathewson, Bill McKechnie and Roush, to the Cincinnati Reds in exchange for Buck Herzog and William Killefer.

New Reds manager Christy Mathewson told Edd he would be his center fielder from then on. The rest is history. Roush won National League batting titles in 1917 and 1919. He batted .333 in 1918, but lost the batting championship by two percentage points to Zack Wheat. With the explosion of offense in the 1920s, Roush averaged .350 over a four-year period, 1921 through 1924.

Roush generally skipped spring training, holding out as an excuse not to report until just before the season began. He felt he stayed in good enough shape hunting in the off season and did not need the six weeks of workouts. In 1922 he held out all the way into July.

In February 1927 the Reds traded Edd to the New York Giants for George Kelly and cash. Remembering the abuse he had received from McGraw in 1916, Edd tried to get out of New York by holding out for a salary of $30,000. McGraw had always regretted trading Roush and Edd finally signed with the Giants just before the 1927 season for three years at $70,000.

During the 1928 season, Roush suffered torn stomach muscles diving for a line drive, played only 39 games in the outfield and had to have surgery that July. In 1929 he batted .324 in 115 games, but his legs were giving him trouble. The Giants cut Edd's salary to $15,000 for the following season and added a clause to his contract that reduced his pay even more if his abdominal injury recurred. Roush refused to sign the contract and sat out the entire season. The Giants released Edd in the spring of 1931 and he returned to the Reds for one final season.

The Reds wanted Roush as a drawing card so Edd said he would play for $15,000, but "they would be damn fools if they paid it." Edd explained that he was out of shape and "even if I hit .500, they would still finish last again because they didn't have any players."[7]

Although Edd Roush, Benny Kauff and John Tobin became the most prominent of the ex–Federal League players, several former "outlaws" experienced prolonged major league careers.

Two former Chicago Whales outfielders had lengthy and productive National League careers. After batting .352 for Peoria in 1913, twenty-three-year-old Maximillian Flack joined the Chifeds in 1914. During spring training, Max established himself as the Chicago Federals' fastest runner in trials instituted by Manager Tinker. He stole 37 bases in each of his two Federal League seasons and Max became known as one of the surest-handed fly chasers in the league. The left-handed hitter retired after the 1925 season with 1,461 hits and 200 stolen bases during his major league career. At the time, Flack's .974 lifetime fielding average was the highest ever for a right fielder and was only a point behind the record for all outfielders. Unfortunately, Max is known more for his error in the third inning of the final game of the 1918 World Series that allowed two runs and cost the Cubs the game.

Les Mann played most of his sixteen major league seasons as a platoon player against left-handed pitching. While he was with the Cardinals between 1921 and 1923, Les hit .328,

.347 and .371, mostly against southpaws. Mann played his last major league season as a teammate of Edd Roush with McGraw's Giants in 1928.

As the Cubs' player representative, Mann headed a player revolt demanding higher shares for the 1918 World Series. In 1922 Giants pitcher Phil Douglas wrote a letter to Mann, his former roommate at Chicago, offering to "disappear" if the Cardinals would make it worth his while rather than help John McGraw win the pennant. Mann turned the letter over to Manager Branch Rickey, who in turn sent it to Commissioner Landis.

During the baseball off seasons, Mann served as coach of the University of Indiana freshman basketball team and was named head basketball coach on December 6, 1922. Upon the announcement, he "formally declared a secret practice for this afternoon." He held the position for one year in which his team compiled a record of 8 wins and 7 losses. Mann also held an off-season job as physical education director at Rice.

Mann served as the secretary of the United States Amateur Baseball Congress and was the manager of the team that the United States sent to Germany for the 1936 Olympic Games. Other countries had promised to send baseball teams to compete in the games, but none showed up. Mann's U.S. team was then split into two squads and a demonstration game was conducted before a huge crowd of puzzled Germans, estimated at 125,000.[8]

Mann was well known for his work in establishing baseball schools. A member of the Nebraska High School Hall of Fame, Les passed away in January of 1962.

After his one-year stint in the Federal League, Big Ed Konetchy played with the Boston Braves and the Brooklyn Dodgers. He remained one of the most dependable fielders in the game and led the National League's first basemen in fielding for the 1917, 1918 and 1919 seasons. In 1920, Ed batted .308 for the National League champion Dodgers. Following his major league career, Koney became a home run slugger in the minor leagues. As player-manager of the Petersburg, Virginia, club in 1924, he batted .340 with 38 homers and 98 RBIs in 125 games. At age thirty-nine, he signed with the Fort Worth Panthers, one of the most formidable minor league clubs in the nation. In addition to leading the Texas League in fielding in 1925, Konetchy batted .345, had 213 hits, hit 41 homers and drove in 166 runs.[9] After winning their seventh straight Texas League championship the Panthers defeated Atlanta in the Dixie Series. Ed had 21 home runs and 104 runs batted in with the Cats in 1926. Edward Konetchy was posthumously inducted into the Wisconsin Sports Hall of Fame in 1961.

Former Kansas City Packer Nick Cullop took the American League by storm in 1916. He was almost unhittable in winning his first nine games for the Yankees before suffering a loss to the Tigers on a twelfth-inning double to Ty Cobb. Then, during a game on July 18, Nick pulled a muscle just below his lower rib as he threw a fast ball and collapsed on the field. Cullop eventually returned to the mound and ran his record to 12 and 1. Nick lost some tough games late in the season, but his earned run average of 2.05 was the lowest on the Yankees' pitching staff. A year later, Nick suffered a mysterious loss of control on his curve ball, which allowed American League batters to concentrate on his fast ball. After winning only five of nineteen decisions, he was traded to the Browns. Cullop seemed to lose interest in baseball after that. In 1918 he decided to stay on his farm in southwest Virginia and did not pitch for the Browns. St. Louis sold him to Salt Lake City in December 1919. Nick reported to the Pacific Coast League club in 1920, but, after pitching two shutouts in his first three games, he left to play independent baseball in Idaho. Salt Lake City sought an injunction against the pitcher and he eventually rejoined that club. Nick got one more shot at the majors in the spring of 1921. After losing two decisions for the Browns, Cullop was released to Louisville.

The most successful of the ex–Federal League pitchers were Jack Quinn and Howard Ehmke. Former Baltimore Terrapins spitballer John Picus Quinn compiled a 247–216 win-loss record over his 23-year major league career. At its annual meeting in December 1919, the National League voted to ban the use of the spitball. A year later, both major leagues decided to permit the use of the spitball indefinitely for active major-league users who were registered by their ball clubs. Quinn was one of seventeen hurlers who were "grandfathered."

Howard Ehmke, who spent an injury-plagued season with the Buffeds in 1915, was the top pitcher in the New York State League with Syracuse a year later. He led the league with a 31 and 7 record and in strikeouts with 195. Sold to the Tigers for $4,000, the lanky hurler added three more wins with Detroit at the tail end of the 1916 season. Ehmke went on to win 167 major league games, but none was more significant than the first game of the 1929 World Series for the A's, when he struck out a record thirteen batters in his 3 to 1 victory over the Cubs.

Other former Federal Leaguers who performed yeoman service in the major leagues after 1915 included catchers Bill Rariden (1909–1920) and Art Wilson (1908–1921), Rebels outfielder Mike Menosky (1916–1923), Whales shortstop Jimmy Smith (1914–19, 1921–22), Kansas City Packers shortstop Johnny Rawlings (1917–1926), and Terriers shortstop Ernie Johnson (1916–18, 1921–25).

Ernest Johnson spent three seasons with the Browns following the failure of the Federal League. He returned to the White Sox in the spring of 1919, but Chicago sold Ernie to Salt Lake City of the Pacific Coast League. Johnson began his managerial career with Salt Lake City in 1920, but after batting over .300 two straight seasons in the Coast League, he was summoned back to Chicago in 1921 to replace shortstop Swede Risberg, who had been banned from baseball in the wake of the Black Sox scandal. That year, Ernie had his best season in the major leagues when he batted .295 with 28 doubles, 7 triples, and 93 runs scored. Johnson was waived by the White Sox on May 31, 1923, but it turned out well for Ernie when he was signed by the New York Yankees, the eventual World Series Champions. Johnson appeared in two games in the 1923 World Series as a late-inning replacement at shortstop and as a pinch runner.

In a substitute role with New York in 1924, Johnson batted .353 and hit 8 triples in only 119 at-bats. After spending 1925 with the Yankees, Ernie became player-manager of the Portland club of the Pacific Coast League and remained in that position through 1928. He managed Seattle in the same league from 1929 until his release in June 1932, after which he hung up his uniform.

Johnson was the West Coast scout for the Boston Red Sox during the 1930s and he was instrumental in sending Ted Williams, Bobby Doerr, Johnny Pesky and other stars to the American League. Ernie's son, Don, was an infielder with the Cubs from 1943 through 1948.

Though he never hit much, former Whale Jimmy Smith's fielding and ability to play several positions keep him in the major leagues with five different National League clubs through 1922. He was a teammate of former Federal Leaguers Edd Roush, Bill Rariden, and Nick Allen on Cincinnati's 1919 World Series championship team. Smith got into one game in the Series that year against the Chicago "Black Sox" as a pinch runner.

The last appearance of a former Federal League player in a major league game occurred in 1935. That season, former St. Louis Terriers catcher Grover Hartley, a journeyman backstop for six major league teams, appeared in five games while serving as a player/coach for the St. Louis Browns.

William "Bill" McKechnie got his first shot at managing with the Newark Federal League club during the 1915 season. The Peps won 53 games and lost 48 under the twenty-eight-year-old player-manager. Bill returned to the National League as a player, closing his active major league career as a utility infielder with the Pittsburgh Pirates in 1920. After playing the

1921 season with Minneapolis of the American Association where he batted .321 in 156 games, McKechnie returned to the Pirates as a coach the following year.

The Pirates were in sixth place on July 15, 1922, when club owner Barney Dreyfuss promoted Coach McKechnie to the manager's position. Deacon brought the team up to fourth place by season's end, and set on course a managerial career that would culminate in the National Baseball Hall of Fame. The Pirates won the 1925 World Series under McKechnie, but he was fired after a mutiny of veteran players that may have cost the club the 1926 pennant.

Deacon Bill signed on to coach with the Cardinals and was named manager for 1928. When his team lost the World Series that year to the Yankees in four straight, Cardinals President Sam Breadon demoted McKechnie to manager of the Rochester farm club in the International League. Bill was brought back to the Cardinals at mid-season in 1929, but when Judge Emil Fuchs offered him a five-year contract to manage the Boston Braves beginning in 1930, he accepted. The Braves were a poor organization, but McKechnie managed to finish fourth in 1933 and fifth two years later. In the latter season, Bill was named by *The Sporting News* as the "Number 1 major league manager."

McKechnie left the Braves in 1938 to manage another tail-ender, the Cincinnati Reds. In his second and third seasons in Cincinnati, the Reds won National League pennants, then added a World Series title in 1940. He gave up managing following the 1946 season and retired to Bradenton, Florida.[10]

McKechnie was lured back to the major leagues in 1947 as bench coach and advisor to Lou Boudreau, the twenty-four-year-old playing manager of the Cleveland Indians. Bill was instrumental in the Indians' 1948 World Series championship. During his three seasons in Cleveland, Deacon Bill also was influential in the development of Larry Doby, the first African-American player in the American League.

Irvin Key Wilhelm received the nickname "Kaiser" years before the German Kaiser became a hated figure in World War I. Wilhelm the pitcher debuted with the Pirates in 1903. Joining the Brooklyn National League club the following year, he compiled a pitching record of 39–84 with Ebbets' perennial doormat club through 1910, losing more than twenty games in three of those seasons.

Wilhelm had an undistinguished record as pitcher with the Baltimore Terrapins before his arm went dead and he became a Federal League umpire. Irvin retired from baseball after a short stint as a coach and scout for the Cubs, but came back into baseball as an assistant to Jersey City manager Bill Donovan. When Donovan became manager of the Philadelphia Phillies in the spring of 1921, Wilhelm went with him as a scout and coach. That August, Wilhelm replaced "Wild Bill" as manager of the last-place Phillies. Field boss of the seventh-place Phillies in 1922 was the Kaiser's last job in the major leagues. Wilhelm managed and scouted in the minor leagues and in 1930 he became baseball coach at the University of Rochester. He died at the age of 58 in 1936.

Baltimore Terrapins pitcher Charles "Chief" Bender never regained the pitching form he had before his thirtieth birthday. Though Bender was a trim healthy specimen during his playing days, he was plagued by various stress-induced maladies and issues with alcohol. Too often, poor health and sore arms interrupted his mound duties for the Athletics.

"My arm was so weak," complained Bender, "I couldn't get anyone out in the Federal League."[11]

After winning 180 games prior to his thirtieth birthday (May 5, 1914), Bender went 32 and 28 in his thirties, finishing with 212 major league victories. Pitchers of that era often wore out in their early thirties since off-season conditioning was virtually unheard-of and sore arms became more frequent as a pitcher aged.

Bender spent 1916 and part of the 1917 season pitching for the Phillies, then won another 94 games in the minors. Bender coached the United States Naval Academy baseball team from 1924 through 1928, managed seven different minor league clubs, and served as pitching coach for the White Sox, Giants and Athletics.

Another ex-Terrapins player, Fred Jacklitsch, coached collegiate baseball teams at Amherst (1919–25) and Rutgers (1926–31). Ex-Buffalo catcher Nick Allen won the American Association pennant as rookie manager of St. Paul in the 1924 and piloted Tulsa to the Western League title five years later.

In 1916, a team from New London, Connecticut, won the Eastern League title, setting league records for wins and percentage, 86–34, .717. Interestingly, the team served as a home for several veterans of the defunct Federal League. The Planters' top pitcher was former Pittsburgh Rebel Charles Bunn Hearn. Bunn not only had a record of 22 and 7 for New London, the lefty also had the second-highest batting average on the team at .279. Bunn earned two trips back to the majors, both with the Boston Braves, in 1918 and 1920. Including his 6–11 record with the Federals in 1915, Hearn had a major league mark of 13 and 24 in six seasons.

In 1921, Hearn returned to Wilson, North Carolina, where he had made his pro debut eleven years earlier. Bunn managed Wilson to the Virginia League pennant in 1922 and he pitched for that club through 1927. During his playing career in the minors, pitcher Bunn Hearn won 247 games.

It was as a college coach, however, that Hearn achieved his greatest success and fame. He was head baseball coach at the University of North Carolina, 1918–19, and returned to the Tar Heels in 1932 for fifteen more seasons. His North Carolina teams won six Southern Conference titles and two Big Four championships. Hearn suffered a stroke in 1947, but he remained with the team in an advisory capacity for another ten years. Bunn Hearn became a member of the American Association of College Coaches Hall of Fame in 1966.[12]

Former Kansas City Packers second baseman William "Duke" Kenworthy played and managed in the Pacific Coast League from 1916 through 1924, except for a five-game stint with the St. Louis Browns in 1917. Duke later served as freshman baseball coach at St. Mary's College in Murago, California, and returned as a coach with Portland in 1939. On September 21, 1950, Kenworthy and three companions went on a fishing trip in Humbolt Bay near Eureka, California. The men were last seen in their eighteen-foot motorboat at 4 P.M. At about ten o'clock that evening the former baseball player's body was found on a beach and a half hour later the overturned boat washed up on shore nearby.[13]

Kenworthy was not the only former Packers player to meet an untimely end. Grover Gilmore died of typhoid fever in November 1919 at the age of thirty-one. Pitcher George "Chief" Johnson was found murdered in a Des Moines alley in June 1922. And Chet Chadbourne, a long-time Pacific Coast League umpire, shot and killed himself in 1943. But none these ends were stranger than the story of former Federal League player Jack Dalton.

Former Buffalo Blues outfielder Tolbert Percy "Jack" Dalton was without a job in 1916 until he reached an agreement with Garry Herrmann's Reds on April 13. But after only one day, Herrmann called off the deal because Dalton "tried to get us to pay him more than we had agreed to."[14]

On the opening day of the 1916 season, Dalton signed with the Detroit Tigers, but after collecting only two hits in his first eleven at-bats in the American League, Jack was sold to San Francisco of the Pacific Coast League. In 1917 Dalton was playing manager of Joplin in the Western League until he was released in August. So far had the Brooklyn Dodgers bright star of 1914 fallen in less than three baseball seasons.

On Sunday, July 4, 1948, Tolbert Dalton left his home in Catonsville, Maryland, for the service at his church, the Columbia Primitive Baptist Church in Burtonsville. Dalton, who had just turned sixty-three the previous day, never arrived at the church. The husband and stepfather of three children was never seen or heard from again.[15] Dalton is still considered a "missing person."

Edd Roush was the last surviving Federal League player when he passed away at age ninety-four in March 1988. Ironically, he suffered a heart attack while attending an exhibition game at Bradenton's Bill McKechnie Field, named for Roush's former running mate when the two played for the Federal League's clubs in Indianapolis and Newark.

Epilogue

Marc Okkonen may have summed it up best in his short history of the Federal League, published in 1989, went he concluded, "Even in retrospect, who can judge if the final outcome of the Federal League adventure was the best in the long run for the future of the game?... For the promoters of the new league, the outcome was for the most part a costly failure and a deterrent for future entrepreneurs with ideas of challenging the status quo of baseball's establishment. But from a historical point of view it was a fascinating gamble — a case history in the ongoing saga of the free enterprise system in America. Failure or no, those men had a dream and they pursued that dream in the best tradition of visionaries with a conviction to take great risks to realize their dreams."[1]

Following the collapse of a well-financed Federal League, no major league pretenders have taken the field in opposition to teams under the auspices of the American and National Leagues. Although the staggering financial losses suffered by the Federal League served as a powerful warning for future promoters of a third major league, the earlier failures did not prevent ambitious baseball dreamers from hoping to become the next Ban Johnson.

In December 1926, William T. McCullough of Pittsburgh explored the possibility of establishing a six-team "major league" outside the auspices of Organized Baseball. By the end of the year, McCullough claimed to have enlisted four cities and investors for his new major league, as well as two playing venues, Pitt Stadium and the Sesquicentennial Stadium at Philadelphia. McCullough revealed that Pittsburgh, Cleveland, Detroit and Baltimore had received charters in the league and Philadelphia, New York, Milwaukee and Chicago had applied for the not-yet-named league.[2]

McCullough had invested in the Pittsburgh franchises of the U.S.L. and Federal League and served as business manager for the Rebels in 1914 and 1915. He was well known in circles around Pittsburgh for activities outside of his association with the Keystone Commercial Company. During the World War he went overseas as a member of a quartet to sing for the soldiers in France, and when the local Communists held a memorial meeting for Lenin at the Lyceum Theater, the uninvited McCullough broke up the event when he rose at a key point of the meeting and requested that they all sing "America" in honor of President Wilson, who had died that day.[3]

The latest outlaw major league never made it past the formative stage, for on February 9, 1927, the fifty-six-year-old McCullough collapsed in a downtown Pittsburgh office building and died shortly thereafter of an apparent stroke.[4]

Years later, a serious effort to establish a third major league came out of the abandonment of New York City by the Giants and Dodgers in order to relocate on the West Coast.

In November 1958, an article in the *New York Daily News* indicated that "New York is going to promote a third major baseball league. Stymied in its efforts to get the National League to return to the city, the mayor's baseball committee, headed by Bill Shea, yesterday announced it would begin immediately to attempt formation of a new major league."

The following year, Branch Rickey, a long-time baseball executive who had been manager of the St. Louis Cardinals during the Federal League years, announced his intention to form the new league. It would be known as the Continental League and would have teams in New York, Atlanta, Buffalo, Dallas, Denver, Houston, Minneapolis-St. Paul, and Toronto.[5]

The proposition of a new league brought back memories of player raids and the escalation of players' salaries that had marked the Federal League war of forty-five years earlier. This time, the club owners acted preemptively. Major League Baseball decided to expand by two teams in each league, targeting the key cities in Rickey's proposed circuit. The Continental League was dead before it could get off the launching pad.

Though the Supreme Court decision in the 1922 case brought by the Baltimore Federal League club exempted Baseball from the antitrust laws, later generations of major league magnates found that judges decisions were not irrecoverable. The Federal League's court cases proved to be a harbinger of what would plague baseball in the second half of the twentieth century.

The validity of Organized Baseball's "reserve clause" was not settled in court actions during the Federal League war, and another thirty-two years passed before the contract restriction was assaulted. Danny Gardella was an outfielder with the New York Giants who joined the Mexican League in 1946 rather than accept assignment to the minors. In April, Baseball Commissioner Happy Chandler imposed a ban of five years on all players who had violated the reserve clause of their contract and jumped to the Mexican League. In 1947, Gardella sued Baseball, seeking $300,000 in damages. He argued that Baseball was depriving him of his livelihood and violating antitrust laws because of the reserve clause that bound him to a club until he was released or traded. A federal judge dismissed Gardella's case in 1948, but it was sent back to district court the next year. Rather than risk a battle in court, Chandler offered amnesty to the players who had gone to Mexico. Gardella dropped his lawsuit in lieu of a $60,000 settlement.[6]

Major league pitchers Andy Messersmith and Dave McNally played in 1975 without a signed contract and after that season claimed to be free agents because they were not bound to their respective clubs by a contract. As prescribed by the "Basic Agreement" with the Players' Union, the dispute went to an arbitrator. The arbitrator ruled in favor of the players and declared them free agents because, in his opinion, the reserve clause only bound the players for one year after the expiration of a contract.

The owners had used the same tactic as in the Federal League cases (claiming that baseball was not a business), but the arbitrator was no Judge Landis. Before spring training of 1976, the owners locked the players out and the cycle of player/management disputes was set in motion.

Since 1915, the debate has raged among baseball historians whether the Federal League should be granted major league status in official baseball records. One of the first comments on that subject came from the editor of *Baseball Magazine* in July 1915:

> *Baseball Magazine* has never commented on the comparative merits of the Federal League and the major league of Organized Baseball. But we will say, now that the subject has been broached, that we have seen as good baseball in the Federal League this season as we have seen in the National League and that we have seen as poorly played games in the National League as we have seen in the Federal League. Furthermore, we will say that, in our opinion, and that opinion is not, like that of the writers, in the slightest degree biased, that the Federal League is playing a full 50 percent, better brand of baseball than it did last season.[7]

For the next fifty-eight years, it was left to individual publications to determine whether and how the Federal Leaguers' records would be considered. For years, *The Sporting News* refused to recognize statistics of the two Federal League seasons in its record books. Eddie Plank is credited with 327 pitching victories in most current record books, but *TSN* set his total wins at 305. Edd Roush had 219 fewer hits in *TSN* record books because his Federal League records were not included in their totals.

The Official Encyclopedia of Baseball, edited by Hy Turkin and S.C. Thompson, received the endorsement of the Major League Executive Council prior to its release in 1951. The volume provided Federal League records on equal footing with those of the American and National Leagues.

During the mid–1960s, a Special Baseball Records Committee was formed by Major League Baseball to standardize the erratic records from the period prior to 1920. Members of the special committee included, among others, Jack Lang, secretary-treasurer of the Baseball Writers Association, Joseph Reichler from the office of the Commissioner, and Lee Allen of the Baseball Hall of Fame. The committee met twice in 1968 and resolved seventeen key issues related to record-keeping procedures. The committee decided which leagues would forthwith be defined as "major": National League (1876–present), American League (1901–present), American Association (1882–91), Federal League (1914–15), Players' League (1890) and Union Association (1894).[8] Since the landmark *Baseball Encyclopedia* (Macmillan) was released in 1969, Federal League records have been given the same consideration as those of the American and National Leagues.

Today, the Federal League is little more than a footnote in the long history of major league baseball. Brooklyn's Washington Park was converted into a public park. In 1922, a neighborhood movement to save it as a "playground and national memorial" failed and in June the Brooklyn Edison Company purchased the property for a warehouse. A portion of Washington Park between 1st and 3rd streets along 3rd Avenue survived into the twenty-first century. The players' clubhouse wall, its red brick now covered by a gray paint, was once behind the left field wall. It was preserved by Con Edison as a barrier between the street and its storage house for trucks and equipment.[9]

An effort was made to convert Federal League Field in Buffalo into a city recreation facility, but without success. Eventually, the structure was sold for $5,500 by the bankruptcy court. It was then torn down for salvage, and the land (which had been leased) was converted into building lots. St. Louis's Federal League Park was used by the St. Louis Giants of the Negro National League for games in 1920 and 1921. After that, "Handlan Park" served as the site for an occasional circus or carnival until the "temporary" grandstand fell into disrepair in the 1950s.

Newark's Harrison Park sat idle for six years until the city's International League club began playing games there in 1921. On August 18, 1923, Harrison Field burned down and the Bears had to return to old Meadowbrook Oval, which was being used by the Newark Eagles Negro National League team. Organized Baseball actually came out okay because they held a $90,000 insurance policy on Harrison Park. The Baltimore Federal League park experienced a better fate when it became home to the International League Orioles for many years. It too succumbed to fire on July 4, 1944.

The site of the grandstand and pavilion of the Federal League park in St. Louis is now occupied by Saint Louis University's Marchetti Towers. On October 17, 2007, the St. Louis chapter of the Society for American Baseball Research (SABR) dedicated a free-standing marker at the site to recognize the Terriers and Steininger Field.

After Pittsburgh's Exposition Park was torn down, no vestiges remained and its memory

Exposition Park in 1915, home of the Pittsburgh Federal League club (Pittsburgh City Photographer Collection, Archives Service Center, University of Pittsburgh).

disappeared. The exact location of the historic park was unknown until members of SABR marked the location of the old park in a parking lot near Three Rivers Stadium. A state historical marker located at the site of the old ballpark's home plate was dedication in 1998. When Three Rivers Park was demolished, the site was obliterated and the marker disappeared. In October 2002, fans and SABR members returned to the site to remark the site. During the 100th anniversary of the first World Series, a new historical marker was installed along the river walk near PNC Park. The home plate and base marks of old Exposition Park are in parking Lot 2, just outside Heinz Field. The left field line ran toward the river and the right field line ran along General Robinson Avenue.[10]

A number of players, managers, and executives associated with the Federal League have been inducted into the National Baseball Hall of Fame in Cooperstown. Former Federal League players, with the year they were elected, are Joe Tinker (1946), Eddie Plank (1946), Mordecai Brown (1949), Chief Bender (1953), Bill McKechnie (1962, as a manager), and Edd Roush (1962). Ned Hanlon, former director of the Baltimore Terrapins, was elected to the Hall of Fame in 1996 and Brooklyn Tip Tops business manager John Montgomery Ward entered the Hall in 1964.

The most enduring legacy of the Federal League isn't an individual, nor the records, but a ballpark. Wrigley Field means a lot of things to today's baseball fan — the ivy-covered outfield walls, the bleacher bums, and its place as the last of the neighborhood ballparks. However, the home to the Cubs was built originally on the North Side for the Federal League's Chicago club in 1914 that was merged with the city's National League club two years later. In those days it was known as Weeghman Park after its Federal League owner. After William Wrigley took control of the club, the ballpark was eventually named for the owner and it has been known as Wrigley Field ever since.

Chapter Notes

Introduction

1. Amber Shaw, "The Impact of Francis Richter upon the Development of Baseball," www.uga.edu/ 2003/shaw.html.
2. "Third Major League Status," *Sporting Life*, November 6, 1915, p. 4.
3. J.G. Taylor Spink, *Judge Landis and 25 Years of Baseball* (St. Louis: Sporting News, 1974), p. 220; "C.C. Spink Claimed by Death," *Chicago Daily Tribune*, April 23, 1914, p. 18.
4. Spink, p. 40.
5. John P. Rossi, *The National Game: Baseball and American Culture* (Chicago: Ivan R. Dee, 2000), p. 81.
6. David Quentin Voight, *American Baseball: From the Commissioners to Continental Expansion* (State College, PA: Penn State University Press, 1983), p. 65.
7. Marc Okkonen, *The Federal League of 1914–1915: Baseball's Third Major League* (Garrett Park, MD: Society for American Baseball Research, 1989), p. 3.
8. *The Washington Post*, May 28, 1912, p. 8
9. Harold Seymour, *Baseball: The Golden Age* (New York: Oxford University Press, 1971), p. 206.
10. Ibid., p. 196.

Chapter 1

1. Okkonen, p. 3.
2. James A. Ross, "The Champion of the Federal League," *Baseball Magazine*, no. 1 (May 1914): p. 21.
3. "Blames it on Dreyfuss," *New York Times*, January 22, 1914, p. 9.
4. *The Sporting News* (*TSN*), November 26, 1914, p. 1.
5. "Federal Ball League Formed," *New York Times*, March 9, 1913, p. 45.
6. "Owners of the St. Louis Feds," *Baseball Magazine* 15, no. 6 (October 1915): p. 69.
7. *Washington Post*, April 7, 1913, p. 8.
8. "Covington Blue Sox," www.cincysports.net/BlueSox.htm.
9. *Chicago Daily Tribune*, May 4, 1913, p. C2.
10. William Brashler, "Jake Beckley," www.baseballlibrary.com.
11. *Chicago Daily Tribune*, July 30, 1913, p. 4.
12. "Covington Blue Sox."
13. "Fans Pronounce New League O.K.," *Indianapolis Star*, May 11, 1913, p. 32; May 10, 1913, p. 10.
14. "Filipinos Hand Out Blank to St. Louis," *Indianapolis Star*, May 15, 1913, p. 10.
15. "No-hit, No-run Game Pitched by Federal," *Indianapolis Star*, May 17, 1913, p. 11.
16. "Federal League Makes Bow Here," *Chicago Daily Tribune*, May 24, 1913, p. 13.
17. Ibid., p. 13.
18. *TSN*, November 25, 1937, p. 3.
19. *TSN*, November 8, 1937, p. 8.
20. "O'Connor Awarded $5000," *Boston Daily Globe*, May 13, 1913, p. 6.
21. *Washington Post*, June 13, 1913, p. 8.
22. *Kansas City Star*, June 29, 1913, p. 12.
23. "O'Connor Battles Ump," *Chicago Daily Tribune*, June 19, 1913, p. C3.
24. "Must Pay Umpire McNulty," *Washington Post*, July 18, 1914, p. 8; *TSN*, April 23, 1914, p. 2.
25. Steve Steinberg, *Baseball in St. Louis: 1900–1925* (Mount Pleasant, SC: Arcadia Publishing, 2004), p. 109.
26. *Chicago Daily Tribune*, June 21, 1913, p. 3.
27. *Chicago Daily Tribune*, June 22, 1913, p. C1.
28. James A. Ross, "Champion Club of the Federal League," *Baseball Magazine*, May 1914, pp. 21–30.
29. Susan Dellinger, *Red Legs and Black Sox* (Cincinnati: Emmis Books, 2006), p. 46.
30. "Silent Bill Phillips," *New York Times*, April 10, 1915, p. 9.
31. "Knetzer Joins Outlaw Team," *New York Times*, June 14, 1913, p. 12.
32. "Pretzel Knetzer," 1912 T207 card set; www.zazzle.com/collections/products/gallery/, *New York Times*, June 23, 1913, p. 5.
33. "Phillippi in Defeat," *Indianapolis Star*, June 21, 1913, p. 10.
34. *Washington Post*, July 3, 1913, p. 8.
35. *Chicago Daily Tribune*, July 24, 1913, p. 13.
36. "Phillippe Says the Pittsburgh Fed Club Owes Him $1,555.40," *Indianapolis Star*, January 19, 1914, p. 8.
37. *TSN*, July 17, 1913, p. 1; July 24, 1913, p. 1.; August 14, 1914, p. 4.
38. "Federal League Protests," *New York Times*, June 16, 1913, p. 7.
39. Willis Johnson, "Long Line of Road Secretaries Has Kept Club Traveling," *TSN*, May 21, 1936, p. 41.
40. www.ballparkwatch.com/ leagues/federal_league.htm.
41. "KC Baseball History," *Kansas City Sports History*, http://kc.rr.com/starrpower/sports/history.hym#baseball.
42. Okkonen, p. 5.
43. "Couldn't Hit Henning," *Kansas City Star*, July 13, 1913, p. 8A.
44. *New York Times*, August 12, 1913, p. 8.
45. "League President is Granted Leave," *Washington Post*, August 3, 1913, p. 6; "Fogel Springs New One," *Boston Daily Globe*, August 3, 1913, p. 13.
46. *Kansas City Star*, July 6, 1913, p. 11.
47. *TSN*, August 7, 1913, p. 1.
48. *TSN*, August 28, 1913, p. 1.
49. *TSN*, August 28, 1913, p. 4.
50. *Indianapolis Star*, August 31, 1913, p. 6.

Chapter 2

1. "They Boss the Federal League," *The Sporting News*, January 22, 1914, p. 3; Harvey Woodruff, "James Gilmore Has Been to the Front Before," *Sporting Life*, February 21, 1914, p. 9.

2. *Washington Post*, March 8, 1914, p. S1.
3. "Baseball War Declared," *New York Times*, November 1, 1913, p. S1.
4. Ibid., p. S1.
5. Lawrence S. Ritter, "Jimmy Austin," in *The Glory of Their Times* (New York: The MacMillan Company, 1966), pp. 76–77.
6. Ibid., p. 76.
7. *Baseball Magazine* 13, no. 3 (July 1914).
8. Ibid.
9. *TSN,* November 13, 1913, p. 4.
10. Bruce Roth, "Larry Schlafly," *The Baseball Biography Project*, bioproj.sabr.org.
11. *TSN*, November 26, 1914, p. 1.
12. Stuart Shea, *Wrigley Field: The Unauthorized Biography* (Washington, D.C.: Brassey's, 2004), p. 25.
13. *TSN,* January 8, 1914, p. 3.
14. *Washington Post*, March 8, 1914, p. S1.
15. Lee Allen, *The American League Story* (New York: Hill & Wang, 1962), p. 77.
16. *Chicago Daily Tribune*, November 5, 1913, p. 17.
17. *TSN,* November 13, 1913, p. 4.

Chapter 3

1. Shea, p. 15.
2. *Washington Post*, March 8, 1914, p. S1.
3. Pete Cava, *Tales from the Cubs Dugout* (Champaign, IL: Sports Publishing, 2000); Peter Golenbock, *Wrigleyville* (New York: St. Martin's Press), pp. 117–18.
4. Lee Allen, "The Cincinnati Reds," in *The National League*, ed. Ed Fitzgerald (New York: Grosset & Dunlap, 1959), p. 214.
5. Frederick Lieb, "Inside of Game's Most Famous Deals," *TSN,* November 25, 1943, p. 11.
6. "A Personal Reason," *Sporting Life*, January 10, 1914, p. 14; *TSN,* January 8, 1914, p. 5.
7. *New York Times*, December 28, 1913, p. S1.
8. Seymour, pp. 35–36.
9. "Ebbets Confers With Joe Tinker," *Chicago Daily Tribune*, January 17, 1914, p. 14.
10. "Death Ends Meteoric Career of Charley Weeghman, *TSN,* November 10, 1938, p. 7.
11. "'Lucky Charley' Weeghman, President Chicago Feds," *Chicago Daily Tribune*, April 26, 1914, p. B4.
12. Ibid., B4; "C.H. Weeghman, 64, Dead in Chicago," *New York Times*, November 3, 1938, p. 23.
13. *Chicago Daily News*, April 8, 1911, p. 23.
14. "Famous Magnates of the Federal League — Messers Weeghman and Walker and How They Gained Success," *Baseball Magazine*, no. 5 (September 1915): p. 56.
15. Ibid., p. 56.
16. Ibid., p 60.
17. *TSN,* October 12, 1939, p. 13.
18. *TSN,* May 21, 1936, p. 20.
19. "Charley Williams, Secretary of Chicago Federal League Club," *Chicago Daily Tribune*, April 19, 1914, p. B3.
20. Shea., p. 61; *Chicago Daily News*, April 23, 1914, p. 18.

Chapter 4

1. *Chicago Daily Tribune*, January 6, 1914, p. 14.
2. *Atlanta Constitution*, January 7, 1914, p. 4.
3. Robert W. Creamer, *Babe: The Legend Comes to Life* (New York: Simon and Schuster, 1992), p. 55.
4. *TSN,* January 8, 1914, p. 1.
5. Ibid.
6. *TSN,* January 8, 1914, p. 3.
7. *TSN,* January 15, 1914, p. 1.
8. *Los Angeles Times*, January 8, 1914, p. III1.
9. *Atlanta Constitution*, January 7, 1914, p. 4.
10. *Los Angeles Times*, January 29, 1914, p. III1; *Chicago Daily Tribune*, May, 9, 1915, p. S1.
11. *TSN,* March 12, 1914.
12. "Hofman Sues Cubs For $3,000," *Chicago Tribune,* July 15, 1913, p. 13; Seymour, p. 181.
13. Ritter, p. 123.
14. "Claude Hendrix, Star Pitcher, Chifeds," *Chicago Daily Tribune,* May 10, 1914, p. B3.
15. Jack Kavanaugh, "King Cole," www.baseballlibrary.com.
16. *TSN,* February 5, 1914, p. 1.
17. *TSN,* June 17, 1937, p. 2.
18. *TSN,* March 5, 1914, p. 2.
19. F.C. Lane, "The Emery Ball, Strangest of Freak Deliveries," *Baseball Magazine* 15, no. 3 (July 1915): pp. 65–66.
20. "Three More Naps to Reds," *Atlanta Constitution*, January 29, 1914, p. 7.
21. "The Emery Ball, Strangest of Freak Deliveries," p. 69.
22. Dellinger, p. 53.
23. *Wichita Daily Times*, March 16, 1914, p. 2.
24. *Wichita Weekly Times*, March 27, 1914, p. 6.
25. "'Whoa Bill' Has Narrow Escape," *Indianapolis Star*, March 28, 1914, p. 12.
26. *Indianapolis Star*, March 28, 1914, p. 12.
27. *Wichita Daily Times*, April 9, 1914, p. 1.

Chapter 5

1. "Baseball's Reserve Clause," speech given by Dennis Archer at the annual luncheon of the Michigan Supreme Court Historical Society on April 12, 2000.
2. David Quentin Voight, *American Sport: From Gentleman's Sport to the Commissioner System* (Norman, OK: University of Oklahoma Press, 1966), p. 168.
3. *New York Times,* November 1, 1913, p. S1.
4. *TSN,* January 15, 1914, p. 2.
5. Ibid., p. 2.
6. John I. Taylor, "Few Clubs Have Made Money," *Boston Daily Globe*, October 11, 1914, p. 3.
7. Seymour, p. 204.
8. "Killefer Comes Back," *TSN,* January 29, 1914, p. 1.
9. Seymour, p. 204.
10. Archer.
11. *Chicago Daily Tribune*, April 11, 1914, p. 17.
12. *Los Angeles Times*, December 19, 1913, p. III4.
13. *TSN,* October 1, 1914, p. 6.

Chapter 6

1. *TSN,* January 22, 1914, pp. 1, 3.
2. "Baseball Storm Fails to Kill off Federal League," *Chicago Daily Tribune*, January 18, 1914, p. B1.
3. *Sporting Life*, March, 4, 1914; Shea, p. 31.
4. *TSN,* January 29, 1914, p. 1.
5. "Owners of the St. Louis Feds," *Baseball Magazine,* October 1915, pp. 68–69.
6. "Caustic Words Save Federal League," *Washington Post*, May 3, 1914, p. S2.
7. Ibid., p. S2.
8. *Washington Post*, March 8, 1914, p. S1.
9. F.C. Lane, "Famous Magnates of the Federal League — R.B. Ward, the Master Baker," *Baseball Magazine* 15, no. 3 (July 1915): pp. 24–32.
10. Ibid., pp. 108, 110.
11. *Washington Post*, March 8, 1914, p. S1.
12. "Famous Magnates of the Federal League — R.B. Ward, the Master Baker," p. 112.
13. Ibid., pp. 112, 114.
14. *New York Times*, March 11, 1914, p. 12.
15. Trey Strecker, "Solly Hofman," *The Baseball Biography Project*, bioproj.sabr.org.
16. Ibid.
17. Jack Kavanaugh, "Claude Cooper," www.baseballlibrary.com.
18. *Sporting Life*, March 21, 1914, p. 8.
19. *Chicago Daily Tribune*, February 19, 1914, p. 14.
20. "Famous Magnates of the Federal League — R.B. Ward, the Master Baker," pp. 28–29.

Chapter 7

1. Joe Overfield, "Return of the Miracle Man," *The 100 Seasons of Buffalo Baseball*, www.bisons.com/history.php3.
2. "Brennan Death Recalls Kayo over McGraw," *TSN*, January 17, 1962, p. 28; Charles Alexander, *John McGraw* (Lincoln, NE: University of Nebraska Press, 1988), pp. 169, 174.
3. *Boston Daily Globe*, May 19, 1915, p. 3.
4. Gene DeLisio, "Tom Seaton," *The Baseball Biography Project*, bioproj.sabr.org.
5. "Tom Seaton," *The Baseball Biography Project*; *Chicago Daily Tribune*, April 2, 1914, p. 13.
6. "Tinker's Faculty Teaches Blokes," *Chicago Daily News*, March 17, 1914, p. 13.
7. "Phils Secretary Invades Fed Camp," *Chicago Daily Tribune*, April 2, 1914, p. 13.
8. "The Wisdom of Realizing the Value of Silence," *Chicago Daily News*, April 9, 1914, p. 15.
9. *Chicago Daily Tribune*, April 11, 1914, p. 11.
10. *Chicago Daily Tribune*, April 10, 1914, p. 15.
11. *TSN*, September 10, 1914, p. 6.

Chapter 8

1. Paul Mittermeyer, "Mickey Doolan," in *Deadball Stars of the National League*, ed. Tom Simon (Washington, D.C.: Brassey's, 2004), p. 197.
2. James E. Elfers, *The Tour to End All Tours: The Story of Major League Baseball's 1913–1914 World Tour* (Lincoln, NE: University of Nebraska Press, 2003).
3. Paul and Eric Sallee, "Steve Evans," in *Deadball Stars of the National League*, p. 352.
4. *Washington Post*, March 5, 1914.
5. *New York Times*, March 2, 1914.
6. "Battle of the Docks," *TSN*, March 14, 1914, p. 1.
7. "Speaker Stays with Red Sox," *Boston Daily Globe*, March 7, 1914, p. 1.
8. Timothy Gay, *Tris Speaker: The Rough-and-Tumble Life of a Baseball Legend* (Lincoln, NE: University of Nebraska Press, 2005), p. 144.
9. *Boston Daily Globe*, March 7, 1914, p. 1.
10. *New York Times*, March 8, 1914, p. S1.
11. *TSN*, March 12, 1914, p. 2.
12. *New York Times*, March 8, 1914, p. S1.
13. "Battle of the Docks," *TSN*, March 14, 1914, pp. 1–2.
14. *TSN*, January 22, 1914, p. 2.

Chapter 9

1. *Baltimore News*, April 13, 1914, p. 1.
2. Frederick Lieb, *The Baltimore Orioles* (Carbondale, IL: Southern Illinois Press, 2005), pp. 88–90.
3. Burt Solomon, *Where They Ain't* (New York: Free Press, 1999), p. 200.
4. Lieb, pp. 91–94.
5. Ibid., p. 116.
6. Ibid., p. 122–23.
7. *Baltimore News*, April 13, 1914, p. 1.
8. Ibid., p. 1.
9. www.baseballhalloffame.org/exhibits/online_exhibits/dressed_to_the_nines/lettering.htm
10. *New York Times*, July 1, 1914.
11. Ritter, "Edd Roush," in *The Glory of Their Times*, p. 211.
12. Paul Green, "Edd Roush," in *Forgotten Fields* (Waupaca, WI: Parker Publications, 1984), p. 27.
13. Russell O. Wright. *Dominating the Diamond: The 19 Baseball Teams with the Most Dominant Single Season, 1901–2000* (Jefferson, NC: McFarland, 2002).
14. *Washington Post*, December 7, 1914.

Chapter 10

1. "Hamilton's Jump Big News of Week," *TSN*, April 16, 1914, p. 1.
2. *Boston Daily Globe*, April 10, 1914, p. 14.
3. *TSN*, April 16, 1914, p. 4.
4. *Chicago Daily Tribune*, April 17, 1914, p. 11.
5. "Pitcher Hamilton Sued for $25,000," *New York Times*, April 17, 1914, p. 9.
6. *TSN*, April 23, p. 7.
7. *TSN*, August 27, 1914, p. 8.
8. Jeffery Powers-Beck and Joseph B. Oxendine, *The American Indian Integration of Baseball* (Lincoln, NE: University of Nebraska Press, 2004), pp. 121–24.
9. Ibid., pp. 135–36.
10. "Indian Johnson Jumps the Reds," *TSN*, April 23, 1914, p. 1.
11. Peter T. Toot, *Armando Marsans: A Cuban Pioneer in the Major Leagues* (Jefferson, NC: McFarland, 2004), pp. 87–88.
12. "Cheney May Join Fed Team," *Chicago Daily News*, April 22, 1914, p. 19; April 23, 1914, p. 18.
13. *TSN*, April 30, 1914, p. 3.
14. Ibid., p. 3.
15. *TSN*, May 14, 1914, p. 5.
16. *Washington Post*, July 16, 1914.
17. "Who's Who in the Federal League," *Baseball Magazine*, June 1915, p. 64.
18. *Chicago Daily Tribune*, April 26, 1915, p. 9.
19. A black man named Ed Gillespie was hauled in by police and was charged with the murder of Chief Johnson. A jury found Gillespie not guilty of killing and robbing the baseball player.
20. "The Federal League," http://synapticflatulence.blogspot.com/2004/08/federal-league.
21. *Chicago Daily Tribune*, July 5, 1914, p. B1.
22. *Boston Globe*, July 6, 1914, p. 9.
23. "Gilmore Kept on Jump Making Peace," *TSN*, July 9, 1914, p. 1.

Chapter 11

1. Dick Farrington, "Famed Mordecai Brown," *TSN*, November 27, 1941, p. 3.
2. Brian Marshall, "Mordecai Brown," in *Deadball Stars of the National League*, pp. 103–06; Farrington, p. 3.
3. Farrington, p. 3.
4. Joan M. Thomas, "Federal League Park—St. Louis," in *Major League Baseball in St. Louis*, pt. 3 of 6 from *Senior Circuit*, www.seniorcircuit.net/memories/baseball3.shtml.
5. R.J. Lesch, "J.O. 'Doc' Crandall," in *Deadball Stars of the National League*, p. 67.
6. Ibid., p. 67.
7. Ibid., p. 68.
8. "'Old Doc' Crandall Jumps to Federals," *New York Times*, February 21, 1914, p. 9.
9. "Federal League Park, St. Louis"; *Indianapolis Star*, April 17, 1914, p. 6.
10. *Sporting Life*, April 25, 1914, p. 12.
11. "'Biddy' Dolan's Batting Gives Hoosiers Victory in Opening Game of Fed Season," *Indianapolis Star*, April 17, 1914, p. 6.
12. *Sporting Life*, June 18, 1914, p. 13.
13. *Sporting Life*, May 30, 1914, p. 13.
14. "Boost Appeases Player," *Washington Post*, July 19, 1914. p. SP1.
15. *New York Times*, May 7, 1915, p. 6.

Chapter 12

1. Shea, p. 6.
2. Ibid., p. 8.
3. *Chicago Daily Tribune*, December 30, p. 6.
4. "Park of Federals Object of Attack," *Chicago Daily News*, January 19, 1914, p. 12.
5. Shea, p. 27.
6. Ibid., p. 34.
7. *Chicago Daily Tribune*, April 13, 1914, p. 8.
8. *Chicago Daily News*, March 29, p. B1.
9. *Chicago Sun-Times*, July 9, 1973, p. 86.
10. *Chicago Daily Tribune*, April 30, 1914, p. 19.
11. *Chicago Daily Tribune*, June 14, 1914, p. B2.
12. Shea, pp. 48–50; *Chicago Daily Tribune*, April 24, 1914, pp. 15, 16.
13. *Chicago Daily Tribune*, April 26, 1914, p. B1.
14. Shea, p. 58; *Chicago Daily Tribune*, April 28, 1915, p. 15.

15. *Chicago Daily Tribune*, April 28, 1915, p. 15.
16. Ibid., p. 15.
17. *TSN*, July 16, 1914, p. 4.
18. *Chicago Daily Tribune*, July 8, 1914, p. 14.
19. *Chicago Daily Tribune*, May 11, 1914, p. 13.
20. Ibid., p. 13.
21. Shea, pp. 54–55.
22. *TSN*, July 2, 1914.
23. Shea, p. 67.
24. *TSN*, May 20, 1915, p. 1.
25. *TSN*, August 13, 1914, p. 1.
26. Editorials, *Baseball Magazine*, no. 3 (July 1915): pp. 13–14.
27. "Famous Magnates of the Federal League — Messers Weeghman and Walker," p. 58.

Chapter 13

1. *New York Times*, August 14, 1914.
2. "The Emery Ball: Strangest of Freak Deliveries," pp. 59–60.
3. Ibid., p. 61.
4. Ibid., p. 62.
5. Ibid., pp. 63–64.
6. "Ford Discovered Emery Ball," *Atlanta Constitution*, November 8, 1914, p. A4.
7. "The Emery Ball: Strangest of Freak Deliveries," pp. 67–68.
8. Ibid., p. 68.
9. *Sporting Life*, April 11, 1914, p. 11.
10. "The Emery Ball: Strangest of Freak Deliveries," p. 70.
11. Dean A. Sullivan, ed., *Middle Innings: A Documentary History of Baseball, 1900–1948* (Lincoln, NE: University of Nebraska Press, 2001), p. 2.
12. Joe Overfield, "New Kid in Town," in *The 100 Seasons of Buffalo Baseball*, www.bisons.com/history.
13. Okkonen, p. 11.
14. *TSN*, May 14, 1914, p. 4.
15. *TSN*, March 19, 1914, p. 1.
16. "Big Crowd at Buffalo Game," *Chicago Tribune*, May 12, 1914, p. A4.
17. Dick Thompson, "Bob Smith," in *The Baseball Biography Project*, www.bioproj.sabr.org.
18. "Ford Blanks Hoosiers in Great Battle," *Indianapolis Star*, May 4, 1914, p. 10.
19. David Anderson, "Bonesetter Reese," in *The Baseball Biography Project*, bioproj.sabr.org.
20. *Los Angeles Times*, September 25, 1914, p. III2; *Sporting Life*, August 29, 1914, pp. 12–13.
21. "The Emery Ball: Strangest of Freak Deliveries," p. 66.

Chapter 14

1. "George Franklin Suggs," *TSN*, April 13, 1949, p. 22.
2. *TSN*, April 24, 1946, p. 20.
3. *Boston Globe*, May 29, 1914, p. 4.
4. "The Oldest veteran in the Major Leagues," *Baseball Magazine*, September 1930.
5. Ibid.
6. *Chicago Daily Tribune*, May 24, 1914, p. D1.
7. "Federal Player Kicks Umpire," *New York Times*, May 28, 1914, p. 14.
8. David Larson, "Fielder Jones," in *The Baseball Biography Project*, bioproj.sabr.org.
9. *Washington Post*, July 13, 1914.
10. *Boston Daily Globe*, July 7, 1914, p. 7.
11. Seymour, p. 218.
12. Fred Lieb, *Baseball as I Have Known It* (New York: Coward, McCann & Georghegan, 1977), p. 136.
13. Creamer, p. 72.
14. *TSN*, July 2, 1914, p. 1.
15. *TSN*, July 23, 1914, p. 7.
16. W. Harrison Daniel and Scott P. Mayer, *Baseball and Richmond* (Jefferson, NC: McFarland, 2003), p. 67.
17. Creamer, pp. 78–79.
18. Ibid., p. 81.

Chapter 15

1. *TSN*, January 22, 1914, p. 1.
2. *New York Times*, June 28, 1934.
3. *Chicago Daily Tribune*, May 15, 1914, p. 15.
4. *Chicago Daily Tribune*, June 15, 1914, p. 15.
5. *TSN*, June 25, 1914, p. 7.
6. *TSN*, July 27, 1914, p. 4.
7. *New York Times*, September 1, 1914
8. *Chicago Daily Tribune*, December 1, 1912, p. C1.
9. *New York Times*, December 12, 1912, p. 14.
10. *TSN*, December 24, 1914, p. 5; October 8, 1914, p. 8.
11. *New York Times*, June 17, 1927, p. 19.
12. "Diamond Flashes," *Atlanta Constitution*, October 15, 1916, p. A4.
13. "Umpire Brennan Passes," *Los Angeles Times*, September 14, 1933, p. A13.

Chapter 16

1. *New York Times*, February 15, 1914, p. S1.
2. *Boston Daily Globe*, March 11, 1914, p. 1.
3. *New York Times*, May 12, 1914, p. 9.
4. *TSN*, March 19, 1914, p. 1.
5. *New York Times*, May 25, 1914.
6. *New York Times*, July 12, 1914, p. S2.
7. *New York Times*, June 30, 1914, p. 9.
8. *New York Times*, July 5, 1914, p. S2.
9. Ibid., p. S2.
10. *New York Times*, July 26, 1914, p. S2.
11. *New York Times*, September 13, 1914.
12. *New York Times*, September 9, 1914, p. 10.
13. "Georgia Tech Baseball Records," www.geocities.com/beesball/recordbook.html.
14. "No-Hit Game for Lafitte," *New York Times*, September 20, 1914, p. S2.
15. Powers-Beck and Oxendine, p. 22.
16. "Pitcher Bluejacket is a Genuine Indian," *Washington Post*, August 16, 1914, p. S4.
17. "Indian Bluejacket Wins," *New York Times*, August 7, 1914, p. 9.
18. *New York Times*, September 8, 1914, p. 8.
19. *TSN*, April 9, 1947, p. 18.

Chapter 17

1. *TSN*, May 14, 1914, p. 1.
2. "Federals After Phillies," *Washington Post*, November 5, 1913, p. 4.
3. *Chicago Daily Tribune*, January 11, 1914, p. 8.
4. *New York Times*, January 14, 1914, p. 12; *Sporting Life*, February 7, 1914.
5. "Defection in Federal," *New York Times*, January 25, 1914, p. 31.
6. *Boston Globe*, March 6, 1914, p. 7; "Here Are Men Who Take a Chance on Success of Federals," *TSN*, January 15, 1914, p. 5.
7. "Pittsburgh Feds Reorganized," *New York Times*, March 11, 1914, p. 12.
8. *New York Times*, March 11, 1914, p. 12.
9. "Who's Who in the Federal League," *Baseball Magazine*, July 1915, pp. 79–80.
10. "How Manager Stallings Routed Doc Gessler," *Sporting Life*, March 28, 1914, p. 7.
11. "Davy Jones," in *Glory of their Times*, p. 40.
12. *TSN*, April 4, 1914, pp. 1, 2.
13. *Los Angeles Times*, April 15, 1915, p. 4.
14. "Who's Who in the Federal League," *Baseball Magazine* 15, no. 3 (July 1915): p. 79.
15. "Pittsburgh Leads All in Stogie Making," *Pittsburgh Gazette Times*, July 12, 1915, p. 15. The term "stogie" dated back to days when tobacco leaves were transported from tobacco farms by Conestoga wagons. In order to distinguish Pittsburgh's unique product from other cigars, theirs were called stogies, taking the last half of the word "Conestoga."
16. *TSN*, April 9, 1914, p. 4.
17. *TSN*, September 17, 1914, p. 6.
18. *Chicago Daily Tribune*, August 14, 1914, p. 10.
19. *Sporting Life*, August 22, 1914, p. 13.

Chapter 18

1. Stanley T. Milliken, "Tinker after Johnson is Latest of 'Yarns,'" *Washington Post*, May 24, 1914, p. S1.
2. *Washington Post,* May 25, 1914.
3. *TSN*, July 9, 1914, p. 3; Seymour, pp. 207–08.
4. Henry W. Thomas, *Walter Johnson: Baseball's Big Train* (Washington, D.C.: Phenom Press, 1995), pp. 130–31.
5. Keene Gardiner, "Largest Salary Ever Paid Ball Player Offered Eddie Collins by Brookfeds," *Chicago Daily Tribune,* June 15, 1914, p. 15.
6. "Chase May Jump to Buffalo Federals," *New York Times,* June 16, 1914, p. 10.
7. "Yankees Have Star Pitcher in Schulz," *New York Times,* February 3, 1913, p. 9.
8. "Al Schulz," www.baseballlibrary.com.
9. *New York Times*, June 21, 1914, p. S1.
10. "Who's Who in the Federal League," *Baseball Magazine*, July 1915, p. 80.
11. Ibid., p. 80.
12. Seymour, p. 208.
13. Eric Enders, "Armando Marsans," in *Deadball Stars of the National League*, p. 255.
14. F. Lennox Campello, "Before El Duque There was Luque," http://campello.tripod.com/firstblackinbaseball.html, 2000–2003; *Cincinnati Tribune*, June 23, 1911.
15. "Marsans, Sore At Reds, Wants to Join Federals," *Los Angeles Times*, April 7, 1914, p. III1.
16. "The War of the Leagues," *Baseball Magazine*, no. 4 (August 1914): p. 34.
17. "A Red Rebellion Makes Diversion" *TSN*, June 11, 1914, p. 2.
18. Hugh C. Weir, "The Famous Marsans Case," *Baseball Magazine*, no. 5 (September 1914): p. 55.
19. Toot, p. 104.

Chapter 19

1. "Graham's Corner," *TSN* May 28, 1947, p. 15.
2. Martin Kohout, *Hal Chase: The Defiant Life and Turbulent Times of Baseball's Biggest Crook* (Jefferson, NC: McFarland, 2001), p. 31.
3. *TSN*, April 15, 1905, p. 1.
4. Kohout, p. 73.
5. Seymour, p. 289.
6. Green, p. 31.
7. Kohout, p. 113.
8. Ibid., p. 130.
9. *Chicago Daily Tribune*, March 1, 1914, p. B1.
10. Kohout, p. 132.
11. Joe Overfield, *Buffalo Bisons History*, http://web.minorleaguebaseball.com/index.
12. "Buffalo's Experience," *Sporting Life*, July 4, 1914, p. 3.
13. "Barnumizing Buffalo," *TSN*, July 2, 1914, p. 4.
14. Kohout, pp. 134–35; *Buffalo Express*, June 26, 1914.
15. *Sporting Life*, July 4, 1914, p. 3; *Los Angeles Times*, June 26, 1914, p. III4.
16. Kohout, pp. 135–37; *Buffalo Express*, June 26, 1914.
17. "Chase to Play with Feds," *Chicago Daily Tribune*, July 22, 1914, p. 15.
18. Steve Steinberg, "Ray Caldwell," in *The Baseball Biography Project*, www.bioproj.sabr.org.
19. Ibid..
20. Kohout, p. 143.
21. *TSN*, January 14, 1915, p. 1.
22. Steinberg, "Caldwell."
23. *Indianapolis Star*, September 25, 1914, p. 6.

Chapter 20

1. Box scores from the *Los Angeles Times*, May 13–June 9, 1914. A game report from the *Indianapolis Star* (June 10, 1914) read, "Kauff, who until yesterday hit safely in no less than 32 consecutive games, beginning with the second contest of the season at St. Louis and continuing until Monday's game with Baltimore." The number of games played by the Hoosiers up to June 9 and contemporary box scores do not support a 32-game hitting streak. The writer may have included non-league games in the streak.
2. Jack Kavanaugh, "Charlie Carr," www.baseballlibrary.com.
3. Box scores from the *Los Angeles Times*, June 11–June 24, 1914.
4. *Chicago Daily Tribune*, July 3–13, 1914.
5. *Washington Post*, July 17, 1914, p. 8.
6. "Kauff Ranks with Best Fed Hitters," *Clearfield Progress*, August 1, 1914, p. 3.
7. "Ty Cobb of the Federal League," *Baseball Magazine* 14, no. 1 (November 1914): p. 48.
8. "Benny Kauff," in *Deadball Stars of the National League*, p. 84.
9. *TSN*, February 3, 1916, p. 4.
10. "Kauff, Fed Star, A Brainy Player," *Washington Post,* February 28, 1915, p. 52.
11. Clarence F. Loyd, "Chapter on Kauff," article from player file, National Baseball Library, June 19, 1915.
12. *Indianapolis Star*, July 8, 1914, p. 8.
13. Dellinger, p. 53.
14. "Big Hands Aids Ball Players," *Washington Post*, February 9, 1913, p. S5.
15. *Chicago Daily Tribune*, April 7, 1908, p. 8.
16. Frederick G. Lieb, *The Pittsburgh Pirates* (Carbondale, IL: Southern Illinois University Press, 2003), p. 158.
17. *New York Times*, February 19, 1911, p. C5.
18. "Campbell to Wed and Quit Baseball," *Boston Daily Globe*, October 14, 1912, p. 6.

Chapter 21

The main source for this chapter was game reports from the *Chicago Daily Tribune*, August 3–September 8, 1914.
1. *TSN*, August 13, 1914, p. 2.
2. *TSN*, September 10, 1914, p. 6.

Chapter 22

1. *New York Times*, June 17, 1914, p. 9.
2. *TSN,* June 23, 1914, p. 7.
3. *Washington Post*, July 19, 1914, p. SP1.
4. *TSN*, August 27, 1914, p. 8.
5. "Owners of the St. Louis Feds," p. 70.
6. *Chicago Daily Tribune,* August 23, 1914, p. B3.
7. *TSN,* March 22, 1934, p. 4.
8. "Brown Declares He's Badly Treated," *TSN*, August 20, 1914, p. 1.
9. "Fielder Jones: Ex-Sox Manager to Lead St. Louis," *Chicago Daily Tribune*, August 17, 1914, p. 13.
10. *Chicago Daily Tribune*, September 1, 1914, p. 15.

Chapter 23

1. "Seaton's Talk Loses Game," *New York Times*, September 15, 1914, p. 9; "Brooklyn Feds are Annihilated by Hoosiers," *Indianapolis Star*, September 15, 1914, p. 10.
2. *TSN*, October 1, 1914.
3. *Chicago Daily Tribune*, September 27, 1914, p. B2.
4. Dellinger, p. 56; *Indianapolis Star Magazine*, 1978.
5. *Chicago Daily Tribune*, October 6, 1914, p. 13.
6. "Kansas City is Flooded," *Los Angeles Times*, September 8, 1914, p. I1.
7. *Chicago Daily Tribune*, September 28, 1912, p. 13.
8. *Chicago Daily Tribune*, October 7, 1914, p. 13.
9. "Hoofeds Play Brilliant Ball and Clinch 1914 Pennant," *Indianapolis Star*, October 10, 1914, p. 6.
10. *Indianapolis Star*, October 10, 1914, p. 7.
11. *TSN*, January 7, 1915, p. 5.
12. "Indianapolis Challenges," *New York Times*, October 10, 1914, p. 8.
13. *TSN*, February 18, 1915, p. 4.

Chapter 24

1. Bill James, *Bill James Historic Baseball Abstract* (New York: Villard Books, 1988), p. 101; Rossi, p. 81.

2. Seymour, p. 219.
3. Ibid., p. 234.
4. James, p. 101.
5. *New York Times*, June 30, 1914, p. 9.
6. J. B. Sheridan, "Dawn of a New Era in (the) National Game," in *Major League Baseball in St. Louis*, pt. 3 of 6 by Joan M. Thomas, *Senior Circuit*, www.seniorcircuit.net/baseball3.shtml.
7. Seymour, p. 219.
8. John I. Taylor, "Few Clubs Have Made Money," *Boston Daily Globe*, October 11, 1914, p. 3.
9. *Washington Post*, October 20, 1914, p. 8.
10. "Feds to Discuss Offer of Peace," *Chicago Daily Tribune*, October 19, 1914, p. 14; "Gary Herrmann Talks," *Chicago Daily Tribune*, October 20, 1914, p. 8.
11. *TSN*, October 22, 1914, p. 1.
12. *Washington Post*, October 21, 1914, p. 10.
13. *TSN*, November 26, 1914, p. 5.
14. "Federal Leaguers Meet and Talk," *New York Times*, October 24, 1914, p. 14.
15. *TSN*, November 24, 1914, p. 1; *TSN*, March 2, 1916, p. 4. A year and a half later, a Chifeds stockholder, C.L. Sherlock, sued the Chicago Federal League club for his "profits" from the 1914 season or a statement of the club's losses. Federal League Secretary Tom Gilmore admitted under oath that the Chicago Federals lost $27,000 (in round figures) in 1914.
16. Joe Overfield, *The 100 Seasons of Buffalo Baseball*, www.bisons.com/history.php3.
17. "Feds Talk Peace," *New York Times*, October 21, 1914, p. 9.
18. *Sporting Life*, April 17, 1915, p. 8.
19. "Federal Leaguers Meet and Talk," *New York Times*, October 24, 1914, p. 14.
20. 1914 Federal League home attendance as computed by Organized Baseball's "clockers": Chicago, 200,729; Indianapolis, 136,186; Baltimore, 124,672; Buffalo, 71,101; Brooklyn, 77,101; Kansas City, 65,346; Pittsburgh, 63,482; St. Louis, 47,586; "Feds' Heavy Deficit May Mean Downfall," *Washington Post*, November 24, 1914, p. 10.
21. "The Man Who Made La Crosse Famous," *La Crosse Tribune*, February 1, 1913, p. 9. Phonetic spelling of Konetchy came from the column by Lee Dunbar in the *Oakland Tribune*, May 30, 1947.
22. F.C. Lane, "The Star of the Cardinals," *Baseball Magazine* 9, no. 6 (October 1912), p. 59.
23. Paul and Eric Sallee, "Edward J. Konetchy," in *Deadball Stars of the National League*, p. 339.
24. *TSN*, November 26, 1914, p. 2.
25. *TSN*, December 10, 1914, p. 2.
26. *TSN*, October 22, 1914, p. 2.
27. National Baseball Hall of Fame, letter, January 1916, Edward Gwinner to August Herrmann; Sallee, p. 341.
28. *TSN*, December 24, 1914, p. 3.
29. "Case of Sour Grapes," *Atlanta Constitution*, December 18, 1914, p. 5.
30. "Pittfeds Land Two Cardinals and One Redleg," *Chicago Daily Tribune*, October 14, 1914, p. 14.
31. *TSN*, October 22, 1914, p. 2.
32. *TSN*, October 29, 1914; *TSN*, January 1, 1958.
33. *TSN*, December 15, 1914.
34. *TSN*, December 24, 1914, p. 2.
35. Ibid., p. 2.
36. *TSN*, November 26, 1914, p. 1.
37. *Chicago Daily Tribune*, December 15, 1914, p. 16.

Chapter 25

1. Shirley Povich, *The Washington Senators: An Informal History* (New York: Putnam's, 1954).
2. "Feds Sign Johnson," *Washington Post*, December 4, 1914, p. 1.
3. Thomas, *Walter Johnson*, p. 132.
4. "Feds Sign Johnson," *Washington Post*, December 4, 1914, p. 1.
5. *TSN*, October 6, 1948.
6. *New York Times*, December 6, 1914.
7. *Los Angeles Times*, December 4, 1914, p. III1.
8. *TSN*, December 10, 1914, p. 1.
9. Seymour, p. 208.
10. *TSN*, March 4, 1915, p. 6.
11. "Feds Sign Johnson," *Washington Post*, December 4, 1914, p. 1.
12. "Griffith Will Fight, He Says," *Boston Daily Globe*, December 4, 1914, p. 7.
13. Thomas, p. 136.
14. Povich.
15. Walter Johnson, "Why I Signed With the Federal League," *Baseball Magazine*, no. 6 (April 1915): pp. 54, 62.
16. *Boston Daily Globe*, April 21, 1914, p. 7.
17. "May Enjoin McConnell," *New York Times*, April 6, 1915, p. 11.
18. "Thomas and Weeghman break up Friendship," *Chicago Daily Tribune*, April 9, 1915, p. 14.
19. www.redwingsbaseball.com/history.
20. *TSN*, March 4, 1915, p. 6.
21. *TSN*, March 11, 1915, p. 4.

Chapter 26

1. "The Prayers of the Feds," *TSN*, January 14, 1915, p. 3.
2. Ibid., p. 3.
3. *Chicago Daily Tribune*, January 6, 1915, p. 9.
4. "Feds Pull Greatest Boner in all their Erratic Career," *TSN*, January 14, 1915, p. 1.
5. Seymour, p. 196.
6. *TSN*, January 14, 1915, p. 1.
7. "Magnates Welcome Court Test," *TSN*, January 14, 1915, p. 3.
8. *TSN*, January 21, 1915, p. 5.
9. "Federal League Opens Court Battle Against O.B.," *Chicago Daily Tribune*, January 21, 1915, p. 9.
10. *TSN*, January 21, 1915, p. 5.
11. Ibid., p. 5.
12. *TSN* January 28, 1915, p. 3.
13. Ibid., p. 3.
14. "Temporary Injunction is Asked by Federals," *Washington Post*, January 24, 1915, p. S1.
15. *TSN*, July 1, 1915; *Chicago Daily Tribune*, January 24, 1915, p. B1.
16. Spink, p. 43.

Chapter 27

1. Bryan Di Salvatore, *A Clever Base-Ballist: The Life and Times of John Montgomery Ward* (New York: Pantheon Books, 1999), pp. 383–84; *Washington Post*, January 25, 1915, p. 8.
2. J.C. Kofoed, "A Rival To Cravath," *Baseball Magazine*, no. 3 (July 1915): p. 75.
3. Ibid., p. 76.
4. *TSN*, January 14, 1915, p. 8.
5. Ibid., p. 8.
6. *Atlanta Constitution*, January 6, 1915, p. 7.
7. *Chicago Daily Tribune*, January 4, 1915, p. 9.
8. "Les Mann," Nebraska High School Hall of Fame, www.nebhalloffame.org/2002/mann.htm.
9. "1914 Miracle Braves: 50 Years Later," *Baseball Digest*, October–November 1964.
10. Ibid.
11. Shea, p. 62.
12. "Pol Perritt, Pitcher," *Baseball Magazine*, June 1915, p. 32.
13. *Sporting Life*, May 8, 1915, p. 12.
14. *New York Times*, March 3, 1915.
15. *Los Angeles Times*, October 21, 1914, p. III3.
16. *TSN*, April 8,1915.
17. Seymour, p. 230.
18. "Sportsman," *TSN*, April 29, 1915.
19. Harry T. Brundidge, "Phil Ball, an 18-Karat Sportsman, Has Lost Money on Browns All but One Year of Ownership Since 1916," *The Sporting News*, October 20, 1932, p. 3.
20. Roger A. Godin, *The 1922 St. Louis Browns* (Jefferson, NC: McFarland, 1991), p. 6.
21. Brundidge, p. 3.
22. Ibid., p. 3.
23. *Los Angeles Times*, September 11, 1914, p. III3.
24. *Los Angeles Times*, January 19, 1915, p. III1.
25. *Los Angeles Times*, January 29, 1915, p. III1.
26. "1972 J. G. Taylor Spink Award Winner—J. Roy Stockton," The National Baseball Hall of Fame web site, baseballhalloffame.org.
27. *St. Louis Globe-Democrat*, March 7, 1915.

28. *St. Louis Globe-Democrat*, March 9, 1915.
29. "Terriers are Rounding into Shape," *St. Louis Globe-Democrat*, March 7, 1915.
30. Toot, p. 115.
31. *St. Louis Globe-Democrat*, March 9, 1915.
32. Ibid.
33. *St. Louis Post Dispatch*, April 5, 1915, p. 5.
34. *St. Louis Globe-Democrat*, March 10, 1915, p. 10.
35. "Terriers Suffer First Defeat at Hands of Cubans," *St. Louis Globe-Democrat*, March 19, 1915.
36. Toot, p. 118.
37. "Winning Form Is Shown by Jones' Pitching Staff," *St. Louis Globe-Democrat*, March 26, 1915, p. 11.
38. *Kansas City Star*, March 8, 1915, p. 10.
39. Walter Eckersall, "Players Call Big Fight Fake," *Chicago Daily Tribune*, April 11, 1915, p. B4.
40. *St. Louis Post Dispatch*, April 5, 1915, p. 5.
41. www.cubanball.com/spring.html; Jorge S. Figueredo, *Cuban Baseball: A Statistical History, 1878–1961* (Jefferson, NC: McFarland, 2003). The *St. Louis Globe-Democrat* reported on April 5, 1915, that "of eleven games the Terriers captured nine."

Chapter 28

1. *New York Times*, February 9, 1915, pg 10.
2. Ibid., p. 10.
3. *TSN*, November 21, 1956, p. 22.
4. *Baseball Magazine*, August 1915, p. 112.
5. "Famous Magnates of the Federal League — Harry Sinclair, Oil Wizard," *Baseball Magazine*, August 1915, p. 112.
6. Frank G. Menke, "Observation," *TSN*, November 9, 1933, p. 4.
7. Janice Lee, "Biography of Conrad Mann, 1871–1943, Civic Leader," 1999, biography collection of the Kansas City Public Library, item i.d.: 35072.
8. *TSN*, March 4, 1915, p. 3.
9. "The Most Sensational Pitcher of the Year," *Baseball Magazine*, no. 6 (October, 1916): p. 54.
10. "Cullop, Bought by Cleveland," *Washington Post*, January 9, 1913, p. S2.
11. "The Case of Cullop," *Sporting Life*, May 9, 1914, p. 10.
12. *TSN*, April 1, 1915, p. 2.
13. *TSN*, March 18, 1915, p. 2.
14. *Chicago Daily Tribune*, March 16, 1915, p. 8.
15. *TSN*, August 6, 1914, p. 6.
16. "Feds New Angels Prove Stubborn," *TSN*, April 1, 1915, p. 5.
17. "Indianapolis Won't Give Up Club," *New York Times*, March 20, 1915, p. 11.
18. "Hoofed Directors Reject Transfer Order," *Indianapolis Star*, March 20, 1915, p. 10.
19. "Fed Champs Seem Lost to the City," *Indianapolis Star*, March 23, 1915, p. 11.
20. Ibid., p. 10.
21. *TSN*, April 1, 1015, p. 2.
22. *Chicago Daily Tribune*, March 24, 1915, p. 11.
23. "Stockholders Agree to Sell the Hoofeds to the League," *Indianapolis Star*, March 24, 1915, p. 18.
24. Ibid, p. 8.
25. "Feds New Angels Prove Stubborn," p. 5.
26. *TSN*, February 25, 1915, p. 4.
27. *TSN*, March 20, 1915, p. 7.
28. "Threw Bottles at Umpire," *Kansas City Times*, September 20, 1915, p. 8.
29. *Amarillo Daily News*, September 13, 1915.

Chapter 29

1. *New York Times*, April 11, 1915, p. S1.
2. Ibid.
3. Shea, p. 61; *TSN*, February 11, 1915.
4. "Local FL Club Adopts Nickname of Whales," *Chicago Daily Tribune*, February 5, 1915, p. 12.
5. Shea, p. 61.
6. Shea, pp. 60, 62.
7. *Kansas City Star*, April 11, 1915, p. S1.
8. *TSN*, April 1, 1915.
9. "Baseball Fever Hits Newark Hard," *New York Times*, April 17, 1915, p. 12.
10. *New York Times*, April 16, 1915, p. 12.
11. Ibid., p. 12.
12. "Patrick Powers Gave Credibility to Start of NAPBL," www.minorleaguebaseball.com/app/milb/history/presidents.
13. Bob Golon, "Federal League Nicknames," *The Society for Baseball Research: Casey Stengel Chapter* 4, no. 2 (August 2003), p. 9.
14. Dellinger, pp. 69–70.
15. *Washington Post*, May 23, 1915, p. 56.
16. Green, "Edd Roush," in *Forgotten Fields*, pp. 26–27.
17. Dellinger, pp. 45–47.
18. Ibid., p. 67.
19. Ibid., pp. 64–65.
20. Jim Sandoval, "Edd Roush," in *Deadball Stars of the National League*, p. 264.
21. "Edd Roush," www.baseballhalloffame.org/hofers.
22. *Indianapolis Star*, October 9, 1914, p. 7.
23. *TSN*, October 14, 1915, p. 4.

Chapter 30

1. "Benny Kauff, Federal League Jumper to Giants Starts New Baseball War," *New York Times*, April 30, 1915, p. 10.
2. *New York Times*, April 11, 1915, p. S1.
3. *New York Times*, April 16, 1915, p. 11.
4. Damon Runyon, "Th' Mornin's Mornin'," August 1915, unidentified newspaper, player file, National Baseball Library.
5. *TSN*, May 6, 1915, p. 2.
6. "Boston Wins After Fight Over Kauff," *New York Times*, April 30, 1915, p. 10.
7. *TSN*, May 6, 1915, p. 1.
8. *New York Times*, May 2, 1915, p. S1.
9. Benny Kauff, "The Inside Story of Bennie Kauff's Holdout," *Baseball Magazine*, no. 1 (May 1916): p. 20.
10. *TSN*, July 8, 1915, page 1.
11. *Chicago Daily Tribune*, July 8, 1915, p. 11.
12. Kauff, p. 20.
13. "Nothing Slow about Kauff," *New York Times*, December 13, 1915, p. 10.
14. Harry A. Williams, "Benny Kauff Quite Windy," *Los Angeles Times*, February 9, 1916, p. III3.
15. "Looking Them Over With Billy Evans," *Atlanta Constitution*, January 5, 1916, p. 12.
16. "Ward Blackmailed Over a Girl," *New York Times*, May 30 , 1922, p. 1.
17. *New York Times*, June 2, 1922, p. 2.
18. "Ward is in Havana," *New York Times*, January 17, 1927, p. 19. Two years earlier, George S. Ward formed the Companie de Productos de las Granjas Americas to promote the dairy industry in Havana. George S. Ward died at age 73 on September 3, 1940, in Havana.

Chapter 31

1. "Fed Fans See No Merit in Allen's No Hit Conquest," *St. Louis Post-Dispatch*, April 5, 1915, p. 5.
2. Column by Thomas S. Rich, *TSN*, October 15, 1914, p. 2.
3. *Chicago Daily Tribune*, May 15, 1915, p. 13.
4. *New York Times*, May 17, 1915, p. 7.
5. "The League Leaders," *Sporting Life*, June 12, 1915, p. 13.
6. *Sporting Life*, May 29, 1915, p. 13.
7. *TSN*, May 27, 1915, p. 2.
8. "Howard Camnitz," in *Deadball Stars of the National League*, p. 164.
9. Obituary, *The Sporting News*, October 21, 1959, p. 26.
10. *TSN*, August 27, 1914, p. 2.
11. "Stars of the Federal League," *Baseball Magazine*, no. 6 (April 1916): p. 27.

12. Peter Gordon, "Mike Mowery," in *Deadball Stars of the National League*, p. 353.
13. *Sporting Life*, June 5, 1915, p. 12.

Chapter 32

1. *Chicago Daily Tribune*, May 8, 1915, p. 17.
2. "Tinker Ruptures Side," *New York Times*, May 9, 1915, p. S2.
3. "Chifeds Blanked on Tinker Day," *New York Times*, May 9, 1915, p. S1.
4. *Chicago Daily Tribune*, May 16, 1915, p. B3.
5. *TSN*, July 15, 1915, p. 7.
6. *Chicago Daily Tribune*, August 28, 1915, p. B1.
7. *Chicago Daily Tribune*, June 27, 1915, p. B1.
8. *New York Times*, August 6, 1915, p. 10.

Chapter 33

1. "Pitcher Wiffs 42 Batters," *Chicago Daily Tribune*, July 26, 1908, p. B2; *TSN*, August 7, 1965, p. 38.
2. Bruce Roth, "Larry Schlafly," in *The Baseball Biography Project*, bioproj.sabr.org.
3. "Hal Chase Assaulted," *Sporting Life*, May 1, 1915, p. 12.
4. Kohout, p. 147.
5. "Harry Lord Quits," *Chicago Daily Tribune*, May 14, 1914, p. 15.
6. Kohout, p. 147.
7. *Amarillo Daily News*, May 22, 1915.
8. Overfield.
9. Roth, "Larry Schlafly."
10. Ibid.
11. Ibid.
12. *Sporting Life*, July 3, 1915, p. 10.
13. *New York Times*, July 14, 1915, p. 10.

Chapter 34

1. *TSN*, July 22, 1915.
2. *TSN*, November 25, 1915, p. 4.
3. Howard B. Tyler, "The Federal League Race," *Baseball Magazine*, no. 6 (October 1915): p. 112.
4. F.C. Lane, "George Stovall: The Hero of 1911," *Baseball Magazine*, no. 5 (September 1912): pp. 58, 61.
5. Ibid., pp. 61–62.
6. Ibid., p. 62.
7. Ibid., pp. 58, 61.
8. "1911 Denver Grizzlies," by Bill Weiss and Marshall Wright, www.minorleaguebaseball.com; "Who's Who in the Federal League," *Baseball Magazine*, no. 2 (June 1915): p. 64.
9. "Million for a Player," *Sporting Life*, September 4, 1915, p. 9.
10. "Two Wins in One Day," *Kansas City Star*, June 14, 1914, p. 12.

11. *TSN*, July 30, 1914, p. 30; August 6, 1914, p. 4.
12. *TSN*, September 24, 1914, p. 8; "Rawlings Makes a Hit with Stovall," *Los Angeles Times*, October 12, 1914, p. III3.
13. "A Great Packer Victory," *Kansas City Times*, July 14, 1915, p. 8.
14. *New York Times*, July 23, 1916, p. 10.
15. Billy Evans, "Cullop Fooled Many By Motion," unidentified newspaper, player file, National Baseball Library.
16. Ibid.
17. "But They're Still on Top," *Kansas City Times*, July 21, 1915, p. 8.
18. "A No-Hit Game for Main," *Kansas City Times*, August 17, 1915, p. 8.
19. Ibid., p. 8.
20. "'Stovall Day' Postponed," *Kansas City Star*, July 29, 1915, p. 1.
21. "Tribute to Stovall," *Sporting Life*, June 5, 1915, p. 12.

Chapter 35

1. *TSN*, August 27, 1914, p. 2.
2. "The Colonial League" by David Pietrusza, www.davidpietrusza.com/Colonial-League.html. Excerpt from David Pietrusza, *Major League: 18 Professional Baseball Organizations, 1871 to Present* (Jefferson, NC: McFarland, 2005).
3. *TSN*, August 27, 1914, p. 2.
4. *Boston Daily Globe*, April 3, 1917, p. 6.
5. "Bannwart Behind Colonial League," *Boston Daily Globe*, June 3, 1914, p. 10.
6. Pietrusza, op. cit.
7. "Feds to Furnish Players," *Kansas City Star*, January 31, 1915, p. 15.
8. *Boston Daily Globe*, June 15, 1915, p. 7.
9. *TSN*, June 10, 1915, p. 8.
10. *Boston Daily Globe*, July 7, 1915, p. 6.
11. "Pennant Goes to Hartford," *Boston Daily Globe*, September 8, 1915, p. 7.
12. *TSN*, October 21, 1915, p. 7.
13. Robert Obojski, *Bush League* (New York: Macmillan, 1975), pp. 323–400.
14. *Boston Daily Globe*, April 3, 1917, p. 1, 6.
15. *Boston Daily Globe*, April 3, 1917, p. 1.

Chapter 36

1. *New York Times*, August 18, 1915.
2. *TSN*, December 3, 1914, p. 1.
3. Ibid., p. 1.
4. *TSN*, December 10, 1914, p. 6.
5. I.E. Sanborn, "Magee to Lead Brooklyn Feds," *Chicago Daily Tribune*, December 19, 1915, p. 8.
6. *TSN*, January 7, 1915, p. 1.

7. *TSN*, March 11, 1915, p. 1.
8. *TSN*, March 25, 1915, p. 6.
9. "Hofman Quits Brookfeds," *New York Times*, April 6, 1915, p. 9.
10. "Magee Grills Hofman," *New York Times*, April 7, 1915, p. 11.
11. *New York Times*, April 13, 1915, p. 9.
12. "Kauff Again Quits Federal League," *New York Times*, July 2, 1915, p. 8.
13. *Sporting Life*, May 8, 1915; June 12, 1915; June 19, 1915.
14. *New York Times*, July 1, 1915, p. 8.
15. "A Fussy Double Header," *Kansas City Times*, June 29, 1915, p. 7.
16. Ibid., p. 6.
17. "Lee Magee Strikes Umpire Corcoran," *New York Times*, July 29, 1915, p. 7.
18. "Lee Magee Arrested," *New York Times*, August 5, 1915, p. 9.
19. *TSN*, July 8, 1915, p. 1.
20. *Chicago Daily Tribune*, June 29, 1915, p. 11.
21. "Ten Cent Baseball and What It Really Means," *Baseball Magazine*, no. 6 (October 1915): p. 81.
22. *TSN*, August 19, 1915, p. 8.
23. "Cheap Ball Attracts 2,500," *New York Times*, August 13, 1915, p. 30.
24. *TSN*, August 19, 1915, p. 1.
25. *Rochester Democrat and Chronicle*, August 6, 2002.
26. *TSN*, January 6, 1916, p. 4.
27. *TSN*, September 9, 1915, p. 8.
28. *TSN*, August 26, 1915, p. 7.
29. Ibid., p. 7.
30. *New York Times*, September 7, 1915, p. 10.
31. *TSN*, January 21, 1959, p. 22.

Chapter 37

1. "Sloufeds 'Take' St. Louis," *Kansas City Times*, July 3, 1915, p. 10.
2. "Terriers' Leader Sends His Resignation to Ball," *St. Louis Globe-Democrat*, July 6, 1915.
3. Ibid.
4. Ibid.
5. "Fielder Jones Quits as Fed Manager after Row With Ump," *Chicago Daily Tribune*, July 6, 1915, p. 12.
6. "Magee Assaults Umpire," *New York Times*, July 11, 1911, p. 5.
7. Tom Simon, "Sherry Magee," in *Deadball Stars of the National League*, p. 195.
8. "Fielder Jones Suspended," *New York Times*, July 7, 1915, p. 12.
9. *TSN*, July 8, 1915, p. 1
10. "Why Fielder Jones Resigned," *Sporting Life*, July 24, 1915, pp. 1, 3.
11. "Jones Returns; Goes East with S'Loufed Team," *Chicago Daily Tribune*, July 8, 1915, p. 11.
12. *Sporting Life*, August 28, 1915, p. 9.
13. "Baker Rejects Federal Offer," *New York Times*, July 20, 1915, p. 9.

14. "F. Jones Ire Up," *Chicago Daily Tribune*, October 1, 1915, p. 13.
15. Eric Enders, "Armando Marsans," in *Deadball Stars of the National League*, p. 257.
16. Toot, p. 121.
17. "Reds Lose Case: Marsans to go with S'Loufeds," *Chicago Daily Tribune*, August 20, 1915, p. 9.
18. Ibid., p. 9.
19. "Marsans to Feds is Court Decree," *Washington Post*, August 20, 1915, p. 8.
20. *Chicago Daily Tribune*, August 26, 1915, p. 11.

Chapter 38

1. Di Salvatore, p. 384.
2. Seymour, p. 28.
3. *TSN*, March 17, 1914, p. 1.
4. Seymour, p. 219.
5. *Washington Post*, October 20, 1914, p. 8.
6. *TSN*, January 28, 1915, p. 4.
7. *TSN*, July 29, 1915, p. 2.
8. Ibid., p. 1.
9. "Burk Jumps to Feds," *New York Times*, July 27, 1915, p. 7.
10. *TSN*, August 12, 1915, p. 4.
11. *TSN*, September 24, 1915, p. 4.
12. *TSN*, September 16, 1915, p. 8.
13. *TSN*, August 12, 1915, p. 4.
14. *TSN*, October 14, 1915, p. 2.

Chapter 39

1. "Famous Magnates of the Federal League—Harry Sinclair, Oil Wizard," p. 112.
2. "McKechnie, Flag-Winner in 3 Cities, Dead," *TSN*, November 13, 1965, p. 25.
3. "Daguerreotypes: Edward Marvin Reulbach," *TSN*, October 12, 1939, p. 13.
4. Cappy Gagnon, "Ed Reulbach," in *Deadball Stars of the National League*, p. 111.
5. Ibid., 111.
6. Ibid., 112.
7. *TSN*, February 18, 1915, p. 4.
8. Ibid., p. 4.
9. *TSN*, August 19, 1915, p. 8.
10. Dellinger, p. 71.
11. *New York Times*, August 11, 1915, p. 7.
12. *Chicago Daily Tribune*, August 6, 1915, p. 9.
13. "Newark's Shock," *Sporting Life*, September 18, 1915, p. 9.

Chapter 40

1. *Chicago Daily Tribune*, August 3, p. 10.
2. "Eastland Fund Gets $955.14 at Feds Park," *Chicago Daily Tribune*, July 30, 1915, p. 9.
3. *Chicago Daily Tribune*, August 1–31, 1915.
4. "Ras Gets Rowdy; Ump Fines Him for Talkin' Back," *Chicago Daily Tribune*, August 18, 1915, p. 9.
5. *Sporting Life*, September 4, 1915, p. 9.
6. "Plot That Failed," *Sporting Life*, August 28, 1915, p. 9.
7. Ibid., p. 9.
8. Donald Gropman, *Say It Ain't So, Joe!* (New York: Little, Brown, 1979), pp. 134–35.
9. *Chicago Daily Tribune*, August 10, 1915, p. 11.
10. "Play or No Pay Rule for Federals," *Sporting Life*, August 7, 1915, p. 2.
11. *TSN*, November 5, 1915, p. 1.
12. Steinberg, p. 44.
13. "Many Odd Superstitions Practiced By Ball Players," *Washington Post*, September 13, 1914, p. S2.
14. "Broken Arm Helped Doolan's Great Whip," undated newspaper article in player's file, National Baseball Hall of Fame Library.
15. Paul Mittermeyer, "M.J. Doolan," in *Stars of the National League* (Washington, D.C.: Brassey's, 2004), p. 197.
16. *New York Times*, September 12, p. S3.
17. *Chicago Daily Tribune*, September 15, 1915, p. 9.
18. *Chicago Daily Tribune*, September 22, 1915, p. 11.

Chapter 41

1. *St. Louis Globe-Democrat*, August 1, 1915, p. 10.
2. Ibid., p. 10.
3. "Who's Who in the Federal League," *Baseball Magazine*, no. 3 (July 1915): p. 80.
4. *TSN*, October 27, 1954, p. 24.
5. "Who's Who in the Federal League," *Baseball Magazine*, no. 3 (July 1915): p. 80.
6. "Davenport Unhittable," *St. Louis Globe-Democrat*, September 11, 1915, p. 6.
7. "29 Batters Face Plank, Who Beats Chief Bender, 2–0," *St. Louis Post-Dispatch*, June 27, 1915, p. 18.
8. "The Federal League Race," *Baseball Magazine*, September 1915, p. 108.
9. *Chicago Daily Tribune*, July 14, 1915, p. 11.
10. *Baseball Magazine*, July 1915, p. 55.
11. "Terriers Made a Finish," *Kansas City Times*, October 1, 1915, p. 10.

Chapter 42

1. "Whales on Heels of Rebels when Errors Net 6–3 Victory," *Chicago Daily Tribune*, September 30, 1915, p. 11.
2. *Chicago Daily Tribune*, October 3, 1915, p. B1.
3. "Cullop Furled the Flag," *Kansas City Star*, October 3, 1915, p. 3.
4. "Stovall is Honest Man," *Los Angeles Times*, February 8, 1916, p. III2.
5. "Whales Win Pennant," *Chicago Daily Tribune*, October 4, 1915, p. 13.
6. "Whales Take Fed Pennant," *Los Angeles Times*, October 4, 1915, p. III1.
7. Ibid., p. III1.
8. Shea, pp. 70–71.
9. *Chicago Daily Tribune*, October 7, 1915, p. 11.

Chapter 43

1. James, p. 101; Seymour, p. 234.
2. Seymour, p. 206.
3. Joe Villa, "Feds Again Seek A Peace Settlement," *TSN*, October 14, 1915, p. 1.
4. *TSN*, October 21, 1915, p. 1.
5. *TSN*, November 18, 1915.
6. *TSN*, October 21, 1915, p. 1.
7. *TSN*, October 14, 1915, p. 1.
8. "Robert Boyd Ward Laid to Final Rest," *Sporting Life*, October 30, 1915, p. 12.
9. "Ward's Death Hard Blow to Federals," *New York Times*, October 20, 1915, p. 13.
10. "Ward Lost Million in Federal League," *New York Times*, May 6, 1917, p. 17.
11. *TSN*, November 11, 1915, p. 1.
12. *TSN*, November 18, 1915, p. 1.
13. *TSN*, November 11, 1915, p. 1.
14. "Feds to Invade New York City," *Chicago Daily Tribune*, November 10, 1915, p. 13.
15. *TSN*, December 9, 1915, p. 6.
16. "Kansas City Club to be Transferred," *Washington Post*, November 10, 1915, p. 8; *Kansas City Star*, October 26, 1915, p. 10.
17. *New York Times*, November 12, 1915, p. 9.
18. Ibid., p. 9.
19. Frank G. Menke, "Observation," *TSN*, November 9, 1933, p. 4.
20. *TSN*, April 4, 1946, p. 5; *TSN*, November 21, 1956; Fred Lieb, "Federal's Fate Haunts 'Third Major' Prospects," *TSN*, November 23, 1944, p. 5.
21. F.C. Lane, "Famous Magnates of the Federal League—Harry Sinclair, Oil Wizard, The Live Wire of the Feds," *Baseball Magazine* 15, no. 4 (August 1915): p. 30.
22. "Sinclair: A Great Name in Oil," www.sinclairoil.com, 2005, p. 1.
23. Ibid., p. 2.
24. Kenny Franks, Paul Lambert, and Carl Tyson, *Early Oklahoma Oil* (College Station, TX: Texas A&M Press, 1981), p. 108.
25. *TSN*, August 22, 1915, p. 8.
26. *TSN*, August 19, 1915, p. 1.
27. *New York Times*, September 24, 1915, p. 9.
28. *New York Times*, November 30, 1915, p. 20.

29. *TSN*, September 17, 1915, p. 8.
30. *New York Times*, November 30, 1915, p. 20.
31. *TSN*, November 25, 1915, p. 5.
32. *TSN*, September 17, 1915, p. 8.
33. "Play baseball at Night," *New York Times*, October 27, 1915, p. 12.
34. *TSN*, October 14, 1915, p. 2.
35. *TSN*, December 2, 1915.
36. *TSN*, October 28, 1915, p. 7.
37. *TSN*, November 11, 1915, p. 1.
38. Rick Swaine, "Joe Gedeon," in *The Baseball Biography Project*, bioproj.sabr.org.
39. *Boston Daily Globe*, November 19, 1915, p. 6.
40. *Chicago Daily Tribune*, December 12, 1915, p. B1.
41. *TSN*, November 25, 1915, p. 1; *TSN*, December 9, 1915, p. 6.
42. *TSN*, January 20, 1916, pp. 4, 25; *Chicago Daily Tribune*, December 11, 1915, p. 14.
43. *Chicago Daily Tribune*, December 11, 1915, p. 14.
44. *Chicago Daily Tribune*, December 16, 1915, p. 16.

Chapter 44

1. George S. Robbins, "Still Dubious as to success of Peace," *TSN*, December 23, 1915, p. 1.
2. *TSN*, December 30, 1915, p. 4.
3. Ibid., p. 4.
4. "Baseball Peace is in Sight," *New York Times*, December 15, 1915, p. 12.
5. Ibid., p. 4.
6. Seymour, p. 243.
7. Joan Thomas, "H.R. Britton," in *Deadball Stars of the National League*, p. 361.
8. *TSN*, January 7, 1916, p. 6. Mrs. Britton finally sold the St. Louis Cardinals and their ballpark in 1918 for $350,000.
9. *TSN*, October 20, 1932, p. 5.
10. *TSN*, December 30, 1915, p. 3.
11. *TSN*, October 20, 1932, p. 5.
12. Arthur Clarke, "Ban Johnson Proves Savior of Feds at Crucial Moment," *TSN*, December 23, 1915, p. 1.
13. *TSN*, December 23, 1915, p. 3.
14. Seymour, p. 243.
15. Bill Weiss and Marshall Wright, "100 Greatest Minor League Teams — Baltimore 1919," www.minorleaguebaseball.com.
16. James Crusinberry, "Weeghman Admits He Has Secured the Cubs," *Chicago Daily Tribune*, December 21, 1915, p. 1.
17. "Long Baseball War is Settled," *New York Times*, December 23, 1915, p. 10.
18. W.A. Phelon, "Merry To Some, But XMAS for Others," *TSN*, December 30, 1915, p. 3.
19. *New York Times*, September 4, 1940, p. 32. George S. Ward remained a prominent figure in the baking industry and never returned to the business of baseball. Government reports during the World War that described the poor condition of men deemed unfit for military service led Ward to increase the vitamin content of bread. In 1918, Ward was elected president of the American Bakers Association and he was instrumental in establishing the American Institute of Baking in Chicago. In 1924 Ward established the first modern bakery and dairy in Cuba. George Ward died in Havana, Cuba, at age 73 on September 3, 1940.
20. "Provisions of the Peace Pact," *TSN*, December 30, 1915, p. 3.
21. "Gwinner Pans Mates of Federal League," *Chicago Daily Tribune*, December 23, 1915, p. 8.
22. Joe Overfield, "The 100 Seasons of Buffalo Baseball."
23. *TSN*, January 20, 1916, p. 4.
24. "Costs $550,000 for Majors to Settle for Death of Feds," *Chicago Daily Tribune*, February 24, 1918, p. a2.
25. "Mrs. Gilmore Names Dancer," *Chicago Daily Tribune*, September 1, 1916, p. 15.
26. "Judge May Reopen Secret Divorce of Mrs. James Gilmore," *Chicago Daily Tribune*, December 14, 1916, p. 1.
27. "J.A. Gilmore, Federal League Figure is Dead," *Chicago Daily Tribune*, March 20, 1947, p. 31.

Chapter 45

1. "Sinclair Controls Many of the Federal Players," *Washington Post*, December 24, 1915, p. 8.
2. *TSN*, January 20, 1916.
3. *TSN*, January 13, 1916, p. 1.
4. *TSN*, January 7, 1916, p. 3.
5. "Kauff, Anderson and Rariden for Giants," *New York Times*, January 18, 1916, p. 8.
6. Though married with a daughter, Anderson's draft status was changed to class 1 in 1918 and he left the Giants on July 17 to report to the Army. The Giants expected Anderson to come to spring training in March 1919, but the Carolina dentist decided not to rejoin the New York club.
7. *TSN*, January 20, 1916, p. 1.
8. Ibid., p. 1.
9. *TSN*, March 9, 1916, p. 1.
10. *TSN*, February 3, 1916, p. 1.
11. *Atlanta Constitution*, May 1916–April 1919; *TSN*, February 17, 1962, p. 28. As a manager with the Ban Johnson League in Kansas City from 1931 to 1949, Brennan developed many baseball players, including Mort Cooper, pitcher of the St. Louis Cardinals.
12. *TSN*, February 10, 1916, pp. 3, 7. Gwinner never returned to the baseball business and became involved in varied business interests in Pittsburgh. He died at age 84 on August 31, 1939. (*TSN*, September 14, 1939)
13. National Baseball Hall of Fame, letter, January 1916, Edward Gwinner to August Herrmann.
14. *TSN*, February 10, 1916, pp. 3, 7.
15. *Boston Daily Globe*, February 15, 1916, p. 7.
16. "Players Released by the Fed Clubs," *Boston Daily Globe*, January 20, 1916, p. 7.
17. *TSN*, February 10, 1916, p. 2.
18. Obituary, *The Sporting News*, January 1, 1958.
19. *New York Times*, February 29, 1916, p. 8.
20. *Boston Daily Globe*, February 3, 1916, p. 7.
21. Unidentified clipping, National Baseball Hall of Fame.
22. Frank Graham, *New York Giants: An Informal History of a Great Ball Club* (Carbondale, IL: Southern Illinois University Press, 2002).
23. "Stovall, Former Manager of Indians, Browns, Dies," *TSN*, November 14, 1951, p. 15.
24. *Washington Post*, August 10, 1919, p. 9.
25. *Atlanta Constitution*, February 22, 1920, p. 2B.
26. *Boston Daily Globe*, October 17, 1917, p. 9.
27. "Necrology — Harry Sinclair," *TSN*, November 21, 1956, p. 22.
28. "Sinclair: A Great Name in Oil," p. 28.
29. Ibid., p. 39.

Chapter 46

1. *Chicago Daily Tribune*, February 5, 1916, p. 10.
2. *TSN*, February 10, 1916, p. 1.
3. Ibid., p. 1.
4. *TSN*, February 10, 1916, p. 2.
5. Seymour, p. 244.
6. "Baltimore Fed Clubs Files $900,000 Suit, Calling O.B. Trust," *Chicago Daily Tribune*, March 30, 1916, p. 11.
7. "Jury's Verdict Gives $240,000 to Federal League Club," *Chicago Daily Tribune*, April 13, 1919, p. A1.
8. "240,000 Verdict for Feds may Revolutionize Baseball," *Chicago Daily Tribune*, April 14, 1919, p. 15.
9. Glenn Stout, *Yankees Century: 100 Years of New York Yankees Baseball* (New York: Houghton Mifflin, 2002), p. 76; Glenn Stout, "When the Yankees Nearly Moved to Boston," http://espn.go.com/mlb/s/2002/0718/1407265.html.
10. "Court of Appeal Court Reverses Antitrust Suits Decision," *Washington Post*, December 7, 1920, p. 10; *National League of Professional Baseball Clubs v. Federal Baseball Club of Baltimore, Inc.*, 269 F. 681 (1920).
11. "34 Years in Baseball," *Chicago*

Daily Tribune, March 3, 1929, p. A3. In part, Judge Holmes's decision read:

The business is giving exhibitions of base ball, which are purely state affairs. It is true that in order to attain for these exhibitions the great popularity that they have achieved competitions must be arranged between clubs from different cities and States. But the fact that in order to give the exhibitions the Leagues must induce free persons to cross state lines and must arrange and pay for their doing so is not enough to change the character of the business. According to the distinction insisted upon in Hooper vs. California (155 U.S. 648, 655, 15 S. Sup. Ct. 207), the transport is a mere incident, not the essential thing. That to which it is incident, the exhibition, although made for money would not be called trade of commerce in the commonly accepted use of those words. As it is put by defendant, personal effort, not related to production, is not a subject of commerce. That which in its consummation is not commerce does not become commerce among the States because the transportation that we have mentioned takes place. To repeat the illustrations given by the Court below, a firm of lawyers sending out a member to argue a case, or the Chautauqua lecture bureau sending out lectures, does not engage in such commerce because the lawyer or lecturer goes to another State.

12. Doug Pappas, comp., "Document of the Month," reprinted in the Fall 1999 issue of *Outside the Lines*, the SABR Business of Baseball Committee newsletter.
13. Seymour, p. 236.
14. "Johnston Will Not Join Superbas," *New York Times*, February 16, 1916, p. 12; Seymour, p. 234.
15. Seymour, p. 235.
16. Pappas, op. cit.
17. David Fleitz, "The Honor Rolls of Baseball," *The Baseball Research Journal*, Society for American Baseball Research, 2005, p. 58.
18. Seymour, p. 253.
19. *Washington Post*, January 9, 1924, p. S3.
20. Seymour, p. 261.
21. Ibid., pp. 262–63.
22. Ibid., p. 24.
23. Seymour, pp. 264–67.
24. Doug Pappas, "75th Anniversary of the Commissioner's Office," *Outside the Lines*, SABR Business of Baseball Committee Newsletter, Fall 1995.
25. *TSN*, October 21, 1920.
26. Pappas, "75th Anniversary of the Commissioner's Office."
27. Ibid.
28. Spink, p. 135.

Chapter 47

1. "St. Louis Feds Lost $182,000, Ball Asserts," *Chicago Daily Tribune*, February 18, 1916, p. 16.
2. *TSN*, October 20, 1932, p. 5.
3. *TSN*, January 14, 1916, p. 2; "Stock Increase Shows St. Louis Browns' Owners," *Boston Daily Globe*, February 12, 1916, p. 7.
4. David Larson, "Fielder Jones," *The Baseball Biography Project*, bioproj.sabr.org.
5. *Chicago Daily Tribune*, February 8, 1916, p. 13.
6. *TSN*, March 2, 1916, p. 5.
7. "Doc Crandall," *Pacific Coast League Hall of Fame*, www.cybcity.com/solons/hof/crandall.html
8. *Washington Post*, July 31, 1916, p. S1.
9. Larson, "Fielder Jones."
10. Ibid.
11. "'Browns Quitting' is Charge as Big Series Draws Near," *Los Angeles Times*, September 6, 1917, p. 16.
12. *Washington Post*, April 10, 1918, p. 10.
13. Larson, "Fielder Jones."
14. Ibid.
15. *TSN*, September 11, 1919, p. 2.
16. *Washington Post*, July 15, 1922, p. 22; *New York Times*, July 5, 1921, p. 24.
17. *TSN*, November 17, 1921, p. 2.
18. Godin, p. 210.
19. Brian Monaco, "St. Louis Brewing History: Falstaff Part 3," falstaff4ever@msn.com; Donald Roussin and Kevin Kious, "The Dutch Act," www.beerhistory.com.
20. "Phil Ball, Whose Ambition Was Pennant, Dies," *TSN*, October 26, 1933, p. 6.
21. Spink, pp. 167–70.

Chapter 48

1. "Half a Million in Cash on Deadline! And Cubs Are His," *Chicago Daily Tribune*, January 4, 1936, p. 19.
2. Ibid., p. 21.
3. "Rivals in Loop Now Partners in New Club," *Chicago Daily Tribune*, January 23, 1916, p. B1.
4. Ibid., p. B1; *Chicago Daily Tribune*, January 4, 1936, pp. 19, 21.
5. *Chicago Daily Tribune*, January 21, 1916, p. 11.
6. *TSN*, February 3, 1916, p. 1.
7. "C.G. Williams, Ex-Cub Official, Dies on Train," *Chicago Daily Tribune*, January 13, 1938, p. 17.
8. Shea, p. 77.
9. *Chicago Daily Tribune*, June 8, 1916, p. 19.
10. "Dutch Zwilling," at *Oakland Oaks Baseball*, http://oaklandoaks.tripod.com/zwilling.html.
11. *TSN*, April 14, 1932, p. 3.
12. Ibid., p. 3.
13. Daniel, p. 71.
14. Shaun Payne, "Hugh Fullerton and the Press's Revealing Coverage of the Black Sox Scandal, 1919–1921," www.historicbaseball.com/scplayers/jackson media.html.
15. *TSN*, February 17, 1921, p. 1.
16. Jim Hamilton, "Time to set story straight on Claude Hendrix," June 1, 2002, *Oneotna Daily Star*, www.thedailystar.com/sports/.
17. *TSN*, November 10, 1938, p. 7.
18. *Chicago Daily Tribune*, January 4, 1936, p. 20.
19. *New York Times*, November 3, 1938, p. 23.
20. *TSN*, November 10, 1938, p. 7.

Chapter 49

1. "The Hal Chase Place," www.chaseplace.iwarp.com/ScandalsX.html by Ray Istorico.
2. "Chase is Cleared of Betting Charge," *New York Times*, February 6, 1919, p. 12.
3. "McGraw Tells How He Chased Crooks," *TSN*, November 11, 1920, p. 8.
4. Ibid., p. 8.
5. "Lee Magee, Cast Out of N.L., Threatens to Bare Scandal," *Washington Post*, March 24, 1920, p. 14.
6. *Chicago Daily Tribune*, April 15, 1920, p. 8; June 10, 1920, p. 17.
7. Kohout, p. 240.
8. Ibid., p. 246.
9. Seymour, p. 292; "Babe Borton is Released," *Los Angeles Times*, August 11, 1920, p. III1; *Los Angeles Times*, December 25, 1920.
10. *Los Angeles Times*, May 8, 1920, p. 16.
11. Ibid., p. 16.
12. *Atlanta Constitution*, June 19, 1920, p. 10; June 22, 1920, p. 10; December 11, 1920. p. 10.
13. Gene DeLisio, "Tom Seaton," in *The Baseball Biography Project*, bioproj.sabr.org.
14. Lynn F. Bevill, "Outlaw Baseball Players in the Copper League: 1925–1927" (master's thesis, Western New Mexico University, 1988), www.bevillsadvocate.org/histweb/bbindex.html.
15. Ibid.
16. Kohout, pp. 270, 277.

Chapter 50

1. "Nothing Slow about Kauff," *New York Times*, December 13, 1915, p. 10.
2. *TSN*, May 16, 1916, p. 1.
3. Frank Graham, "There was only One Benny Kauff," *Baseball Digest*, February 1962.
4. "Nothing Slow about Kauff," p. 10.
5. "Kauff Likable, Matty Says," *Boston Daily Globe*, March 27, 1916, p. 6.
6. *Boston Daily Globe*, April 3, 1916, p. 7.
7. *Washington Post*, September 24, 1916, p. A15.
8. Max Blue, "The Streak," http://

baseballguru.com/maxblue/analyssmaxblue01.html.
9. *New York Times*, September 19, 1916, p. 12.
10. "Dauntless Giants Win Another Pair," *New York Times,* September 20, 1916, p. 10.
11. *New York Times*, September 29, 1916, p. 10.
12. "Benny Kauff Bids Farwell to Fans," *New York Times*, June 23, 1918, p. 27.
13. "Benny Kauff is Married," *New York Times*, March 20, 1919, p. 10.
14. *TSN*, November 11, 1920, p. 8.
15. David Jones, "Benny Kauff," in *Deadball Stars of the National League*, p. 85–86.
16. Bill Weiss and Marshall Wright, "Team #21: 1920 Toronto Maple Leafs," www.minorleague baseball.com/app/milb/history/top100.
17. Craig Burley, "Free Benny Kauff (Part Two)," *The Hardball Times,* April 19, 2004, www.hardballtimes.com/main/article/free-benny-kauff-part-two/.
18. "Benny Kauff Involved in Bribe Mess," *Los Angeles Times*, September 30, 1920, p. 11.
19. Ibid., p. 11.
20. *Boston Daily Globe*, October 6, 1920, p. 11.
21. *Chicago Daily Tribune*, October 6, 1920, p. 17.
22. *TSN*, December 30, 1920, p. 2.
23. *New York Times*, March 9, 1921, p. 21.
24. Burley, op. cit.
25. "Landis Declares Kauff Ineligible," *New York Times*, April 8, 1921, p. 21.
26. Ibid., p. 21.
27. "Partners Accuse Kauff," *New York Times*, May 11, 1921, p. 22.
28. *Washington Post*, May 13, 1921, p. 10.
29. Burley, op. cit.
30. "Injunction Issued on Kauff's Behalf," *New York Times*, September 13, 1921, p. 24.
31. Ibid., p. 24.
32. "Kauff Loses in Supreme Court," *New York Times*, January 18, 1922, p. 23.
33. Spinks, p. 89.

Chapter 51

1. William A. Phelon, "The Greatest Race in Baseball History," *Baseball Magazine* 18, no. 1 (November 1916): p. 51.
2. David S. Neff and Richard M. Cohen, *The Sports Encyclopedia*, 9th edition (New York: St. Martin's Press), pp. 76–81.
3. Dellinger, pp. 30–31.
4. Frank Graham, *McGraw of the Giants* (New York: Putnam's, 1944).
5. Dellinger, pp. 80–82.
6. Ritter, p. 208.
7. Green, p. 36.
8. "Les Mann," Nebraska High School Hall of Fame.
9. Paul MacFarlane, *Daguerrotypes of Great Stars of Baseball* (St. Louis: C.C. Spink and Son, 1961), p. 144.
10. "McKechnie, Flag-Winner in 3 Cities, Dead," *TSN*, November 13, 1965, pp. 25–26.
11. *TSN*, December 31, 1941, p. 6.
12. Bill Weiss and Marshall Wright, "1916 New England Planters," www.minorleaguebaseball.com.
13. "William Jennings (Duke) Kenworthy," obituary, *TSN*, October 4, 1950, p. 54.
14. *New York Times*, April 15, 1916, p. 14.
15. David Sturm, "Jack Dalton walked out of his life one day in 1948," December 27, 2004, www.marylandmissing.com. Ralph Harris, editor of the church newspaper, asked Dalton's two sisters what happened to their brother. The sisters told him they had no clue as to why he disappeared. "I don't think there was anything suspicious about it in terms of something criminal happening to him," Harris told Sturm, who was doing an article on Dalton for a missing persons web site. "He [Dalton] had absconded with subscription funds for the church paper."

Epilogue

1. Okkonen, p. 25.
2. "Pittsburgh Hears Lineup of New League," *Chicago Daily Tribune*, December 28, 1926, p. 17.
3. "Legionnaire, Former Ball Player, Disrupts Plans to Laud Lenin," *New York Times*, February 4, 1924, p. 21.
4. *Chicago Daily Tribune*, February 9, 1927, p. 17.
5. Michael Gershman, *Diamonds: The Evolution of the Ballparks* (New York: Houghton Mifflin, 1993), pp. 178–79.
6. David Quentin Voigt, "Danny Gardella," www.baseballlibrary.com.
7. "Critics of the Federal League," *Baseball Magazine* 15, no. 3 (July 1915): p. 56.
8. Joseph Reichler, ed., *The Baseball Encyclopedia*, 4th edition (New York: Macmillan, 1979), p. 2233; John Thorn, Pete Palmer, Michael Gershman and David Pietrusza, *Total Baseball: The Official Encyclopedia of Major League Baseball*, 6th edition (New York: Total Sports, 1999), p. 620.
9. Gershman, p. 131; "Rediscovering Washington II," SABR-ZINE, www.sabr.org.
10. Denis Rapp, "Locating Exposition Park," *Black and Gold* (the Pittsburgh Pirates' Alumni newsletter).

Bibliography

Newspapers & Periodicals

Atlanta Constitution
Baltimore News
Baseball Digest
Baseball Magazine
Boston Daily Globe
Chicago Daily News
Chicago Daily Tribune
Indianapolis Star
Kansas City Star
Kansas City Times
La Crosse Tribune
Los Angeles Times
Mansfield News
New York Times
Outside the Lines
St. Louis Globe-Democrat
St. Louis Post-Dispatch
Sporting Life
The Sporting News
Washington Post
Wichita Daily Times

Books

Alexander, Charles. *John McGraw*. Lincoln: University of Nebraska Press, 1995.
Allen, Lee. *The American League Story*. New York: Hill & Wang, 1962.
Cava, Pete. *Tales from the Cubs Dugout*. Champaign, IL: Sports Publishing, 2000.
Creamer, Robert W. *Babe: The Legend Comes to Life*. New York: Simon and Schuster, 1974.
Daniel, W. Harrison, and Scott P. Mayer. *Baseball and Richmond*. Jefferson, NC: McFarland, 2003.
Dellinger, Susan. *Red Legs and Black Sox*. Cincinnati: Emmis Books, 2006.
Di Salvatore, Bryan. *A Clever Base-Ballist: The Life and Times of John Montgomery Ward*. New York: Pantheon Books, 1999.
Elfers, James E. *The Tour to End All Tours: The Story of Major League Baseball's 1913–1914 World Tour*. Lincoln: University of Nebraska Press, 2003.
Figueredo, Jorge S. *Cuban Baseball: A Statistical History, 1878–1961*. Jefferson, NC: McFarland, 2003.
Fitzgerald, Ed, ed. *The National League*. New York: Grosset & Dunlap, 1959.
Franks, Kenny, Paul Lambert, and Carl Tyson. *Early Oklahoma Oil*. College Station: Texas A&M Press, 1981.
Gay, Timothy. *Tris Speaker: The Rough-and-Tumble Life of a Baseball Legend*. Lincoln: University of Nebraska Press, 2005.
Gershman, Michael. *Diamonds: The Evolution of the Ballpark*. Boston: Houghton Mifflin, 1993.
Godin, Roger A. *The 1922 St. Louis Browns*. Jefferson, NC: McFarland, 1991.
Golenbock, Peter. *Wrigleyville*. New York: St. Martin's Press, 1996.
Graham, Frank. *McGraw of the Giants*. New York: Putnam's, 1944.
_____. *New York Giants: An Informal History of a Great Ball Club*. Carbondale: Southern Illinois University Press, 2002.
Green, Paul. *Forgotten Fields*. Waupaca, WI: Parker Publications, 1984.
Gropman, Donald. *Say It Ain't So, Joe!* New York: Little, Brown, 1979.
James, Bill. *Bill James Historic Baseball Abstract*. New York: Villard Books, 1988.
Kohout, Martin. *Hal Chase: The Defiant Life and Turbulent Times of Baseball's Biggest Crook*. Jefferson, NC: McFarland, 2001.
Lieb, Frederick. *The Baltimore Orioles*. Carbondale: Southern Illinois Press, 2005.
_____. *Baseball as I Have Known It*. New York: Coward, McCann & Geoghegan, 1996.
_____. *The Pittsburgh Pirates*. Carbondale: Southern Illinois University Press, 2003.
MacFarlane, Paul. *Daguerrotypes of Great Stars of Baseball*. St. Louis: C.C. Spink and Son, 1961.
Mittermeyer, Paul. "M.J. Doolan." In *Stars of the National League*. Washington, D.C.: Brassey's, 2004.
Neff, Davis S., and Richard M. Cohen. *The Sports Encyclopedia*. 9th edition. New York: St. Martin's Press, 1989.
Obojski, Robert. *Bush League*. New York: Macmillan, 1975.
Okkonen, Marc. *The Federal League of 1914–1915: Baseball's Third Major League*. Garrett Park, MD: Society for American Baseball Research, 1989.

Pietrusza, David. *Major League: 18 Professional Baseball Organizations, 1871 to Present*. Jefferson, NC: McFarland, 2005.

Povich, Shirley. *The Washington Senators: An Informal History*. New York: Putnam's, 1954.

Powers-Beck, Jeffery, and Joseph B. Oxendine. *The American Indian Integration of Baseball*. Lincoln: University of Nebraska Press, 2004.

Reicher, Joseph, ed. *The Baseball Encyclopedia*. 4th edition. New York: Macmillan, 1979.

Ritter, Lawrence S. *The Glory of Their Times*. New York: Macmillan, 1966.

Rossi, John P. *The National Game: Baseball and American Culture*. Chicago: Ivan R. Dee, 2000.

Seymour, Harold. *Baseball: The Golden Age*. New York: Oxford University Press, 1971.

Shea, Stuart. *Wrigley Field: The Unauthorized Biography*. Washington, D.C.: Brassey's, 2004.

Simon, Tom, ed. *Deadball Stars of the National League*. Washington, D.C.: Brassey's, 2004.

Solomon, Burt. *Where They Ain't*. New York: Free Press, 1999.

Spink, J.G. Taylor. *Judge Landis and 25 Years of Baseball*. St. Louis: Sporting News, 1974.

Steinberg, Steve. *Baseball in St. Louis, 1900–1925*. Charleston, SC: Arcadia, 2004.

Stout, Glenn. *Yankees Century: 100 Years of New York Yankees Baseball*. New York: Houghton Mifflin, 2002.

Sullivan, Dean A., ed. *Middle Innings: A Documentary History of Baseball, 1900–1948*. Lincoln: University of Nebraska Press, 2001.

Thomas, Henry W. *Walter Johnson: Baseball's Big Train*. Washington, D.C.: Phenom Press, 1995.

Thorn, John, Pete Palmer, Michael Gershman and David Pietrisza. *Total Baseball: The Official Encyclopedia of Major League Baseball*. 6th edition. New York: Total Sports, 1999.

Toot, Peter T. *Armando Marsans: A Cuban Pioneer in the Major Leagues*. Jefferson, NC: McFarland, 2004.

Voight, David Quentin. *American Baseball: From the Commissioners to Continental Expansion*. State College: Penn State University Press, 1983.

_____. *American Sport: From Gentleman's Sport to the Commissioner System*. Norman: University of Oklahoma Press, 1966.

Wright, Russell O. *Dominating the Diamond: The 19 Baseball Teams with the Most Dominant Single Season, 1901–2000*. Jefferson, NC: McFarland, 2002.

Web Sites

www.ballparkwatch.com/leagues/federal_league.htm
baseballguru.com/maxblue/analyssmaxblueO1.html
www.baseballhalloffame.org
www.baseball-reference.com
www.baseballlibrary.com
www.beerhistory.com
www.bevillsadvocate.org/histweb/bbindex.html
bioproj.sabr.org. (*The Baseball Biography Project*)
www.bisons.com/history.php3 ("The 100 Seasons of Buffalo Baseball" by Joe Overfield)
campello.tripod.com/firstblackin baseball.html
www.chaseplace.iwarp.com
www.cincysports.net/BlueSox.htm.
www.cubanball.com/spring.html
www.cybcity.com (*Pacific Coast League Hall of Fame*)
www.davidpietrusza.com/Colonial-League.html
espn.go.com/mlb/s/2002/0718/1407265.html
falstaff4ever@msn.com
www.geocities.com/beesball/recordbook.html
www.hardballtimes.com/main/article/ (*The Hardball Times*, "Free Benny Kauff" by Craig Burley)
www.historicbaseball.com/scplayers/jacksonmedia.html
kc.rr.com/starrpower/sports/history.hym#baseball
www.marylandmissing.com
www.minorleaguebaseball.com
www.nebhalloffame.org/2002/mann.htm
www.newspaperarchive.com/
oaklandoaks.tripod.com/ (*Oakland Oaks Baseball*)
www.retrosheet.org/
www.redwingsbaseball.com/history
www.sabr.org. (SABR-ZINE)
www.seniorcircuit.net/memories/baseball3.shtml (*Major League Baseball in St. Louis*, from *Senior Circuit*)
www.sinclairoil.com
synapticflatulence.blogspot.com/2004/08/federal-league
www.thedailystar.com/sports/
www.zazzle.com/collections/products/gallery/

Index

Ackerland, Harry 312
Adams, Franklin 28
Addington, Keene 175
Agler, Joseph A. 96
Alcock, J.J. 77, 254, 263
Alexander, Grover Cleveland 280, 315
Allen, Frank "Lefty" 166, 173, 195, 207–208, 209, 213, 226, 259, 260, 262, 269, 274, 293, 294
Allen, John M. 101, 102
Allen, Lee 28, 338
Allen, Nick 97, 291, 332, 334
Almeida, Rafael 126, 188
Altrock, Nick 197
American Association (major league) 17, 46, 66, 67, 84, 338
American Association (minor league) 6, 13, 18, 41, 73, 85, 202, 224–225, 246–248, 294
American League 5, 13, 23, 26, 46, 95, 119, 174, 175, 284, 303, 304
Ames, Leon "Red" 124
Anderson, Fred "Spitball" 105, 106, 209, 221, 291, 292, 330, 351n
Anderson, George 112, 143, 153, 235, 239, 262
Anderson, Oliver "Ollie" 70, 105, 107, 137, 152, 227
Armour, J. Ogden 311, 312
Ash, Eddie 139
Ashenfelter, Ray 12, 13, 16
Auspurger, Owen 131
Austin, Jimmy 23, 24, 166–167, 173, 179, 181, 212

Bailey, William "Bill" 144, 262, 269, 272, 273, 274
Baird, Charles 187, 192
Baker, Frank "Home Run" 203, 241, 267
Baker, William F. 48, 49, 59, 64
Baldwin, Jesse 188, 189, 190
Ball, Philip D.C. 52 53, 79, 90, 167, 181–182, 240–242, 244, 276, 285–286, 288, 296, 301, 305, 307, 308, 310, 329
Baltimore Federal League club 23, 40, 64, 66, 68–71, 92, 96, 99–103, 105–106, 108, 139–140, 143, 144, 153, 156, 162, 164, 169, 196, 216, 230, 234, 237, 251, 260–262, 266, 278, 285, 287, 298–299, 333
Baltimore Federal League Club vs. Organized Baseball 3, 298–300, 337, 352n
Baltimore Orioles 23, 39, 40, 66–68, 69, 103–104, 106, 246, 287
Bancker, C.E. 23
Bancroft, Frank 126
Bannwart, Alexander (Al Winn) 228–231
Barbour, John 38, 117, 118
Barger, Eros "Cy" 120, 121, 211, 262, 269, 270
Barnes, Jesse 325, 327
Barrow, Ed 9, 104, 128, 186, 197, 286, 287
Bartholomew, P.W. 190
Baseball Players' Fraternity 3, 6, 23, 45, 48, 49, 71, 75, 165, 173, 174, 176, 251, 300, 301–302, 306
Bates, John 92, 144
Baum, Spider 319
Baumgardner, George 63, 72, 73
Beck, Frederick 47, 86, 106, 108, 137, 145, 146, 153, 215, 216, 258
Becker, Sheriff Fredric 131
Beckley, Jake 11, 165
Bedient, Hugh 173, 201, 211, 218, 221, 264, 267, 291, 294
Bender, Charles "Chief" 7, 77, 80, 169, 173, 196, 198, 251, 260, 266, 294, 333–334, 339
Benton, Rube 124, 319
Berghammer, Martin "Marty" 166, 173, 207, 209, 212, 213, 258, 269, 270, 273, 293, 294, 295
Berry, Claude 119, 121, 154, 208, 211, 213
Billiard, Harry 19, 139, 145, 159, 230, 231
Bissell, Judge Herbert 132
Black, David 262
Black Sox Scandal 303, 318, 325, 332

Blair, Walter "Heavy" 96, 98, 105, 106, 134, 219, 220, 227, 258
Blake, John 228
Blanding, Fred 43, 49, 63, 73
Block, James 59, 142, 144, 146
Blue laws (Sunday baseball ban) 61, 102, 112, 142, 200, 209, 230, 269
Bluejacket, Jim (James Smith) 114–116, 234–235, 262
Bodie, Ping 323
Bonin, Ernest "Luther" 96
Booe, Everett 130
Borton, William "Babe" 83, 129, 182, 183–185, 207, 240, 266, 267, 268, 319
Boston American League club 63, 112, 122, 143, 149, 164, 211, 218, 248, 292, 299–300, 310, 332
Boston National League club 50, 164, 179, 180, 247, 249, 280, 282, 294, 302, 323, 331, 333, 334
Boudreau, Lou 333
Brace, John E. 47
Bradley, Hugh 111, 154, 230
Bradley, William "Bill" 10, 47, 53, 55, 56, 60, 106, 112–114, 124, 135, 152, 154, 188, 191, 222, 223, 225, 226, 238
Brady, King 257
Bramley, M.F. "Fred" 9, 25, 53, 167
Breadon, Sam 333
Brennen, Addison "Ad" 36, 48–49, 58–60, 86, 89, 142, 145, 148, 152, 154, 171, 216, 230, 252, 254, 260, 293
Brennan, Bill 82, 89, 105–109, 111, 114, 156, 227, 235, 243, 259, 273, 274
Brennan, Portia Durnell 58, 60, 66
Bresnahan, Roger 23, 147, 175, 232, 263, 296, 299
Bridwell, Al 39, 80, 83, 207, 242, 267, 268, 293
Britton, Helen 10, 32, 285–286
Britton, Schuyler 24, 25, 65, 79, 166
Brooklyn Federal League club 54–57, 60–61, 100, 106–107, 110–116,

355

120, 124, 147, 152–154, 167, 193, 200–205, 208, 215, 216, 219, 223, 224, 229, 232, 247, 262, 265, 267, 282, 191
Brooklyn National League club 30–32, 67, 149, 164, 178, 179, 207–208, 211, 250–251, 301, 331, 336
Brown, Bob (Robert A. Smith) 97
Brown, Drummond 227
Brown, John A. 34
Brown, Mordecai "Three-Finger" 7, 31, 36, 50, 63, 78–82, 90, 98, 103, 120, 147–148, 150, 153, 156, 169, 172, 175, 184, 215, 257, 258, 259, 263, 269, 270, 272, 312, 339
Brundidge, Harry 182, 286, 310
Brush, John T. 68, 278
Buffalo Federal League club 23, 25, 69, 93, 95–98, 125, 130–134, 143, 163, 178, 179, 193, 209, 218–221, 227, 235, 256, 258, 263, 264–265, 278, 291, 291
Burk, Charles Sanford "Sandy" 247, 248, 294, 296
Burke, Jimmy 308
Burns, Bill 107, 325
Burns, George 327
Bush, Garnet 102, 105–106
Byrne, Bobby 264

Cabana, Oliver 95
Caldwell, Ray 96, 132–133, 143, 172–173, 306
Callahan, James 14, 63
Camnitz, Samuel "Howie" 37, 111, 119–120, 153, 208, 209–210, 294
Campbell, Arthur V. "Vin" 39, 44, 140–141, 145, 157–158, 198, 265, 296
Campbell, Katherine (Munhall) 141
Cantillon, Joe 25, 84, 175
Cantillon, Mike 84–85, 161
Carey, Max 141, 165, 323
Carr, Charles 112, 135–136, 157, 294, 322
Carroll, Richard "Dick" 23, 25, 42, 52, 95, 97, 130, 133, 143, 178, 202, 203, 218, 233, 235, 236, 281
Carter, Paul 315
Chadbourne, Chester "Pop" 38, 158, 225, 242, 254, 334
Chance, Frank 13, 29, 34, 40, 50, 96, 125, 129, 133, 172, 241, 250, 312
Chandler, Senator Happy 337
Chapin, Charles T. 238, 247
Chaplin, Charlie 197
Chapman, Harry 158, 185, 264, 265, 268
Chappelle, Bill 113, 229
Chase, Harold "Prince Hal" 7, 96, 103, 124, 128–134, 138, 142, 143, 154, 165, 172, 173, 199, 218–221, 264, 265, 291, 295, 318–321, 324, 325
Cheney, Larry 75, 171, 183

Chesbro, Jack 13
Chicago American League club 62, 64, 101, 129–130, 149, 152, 171, 178, 183, 198, 219, 303, 332
Chicago Daily Tribune amateurs 256–257, 259
Chicago Federal League club 12, 14–15, 30–34, 84–91, 100, 102, 105–106, 108, 121, 123, 130, 137, 142–146, 150, 152–159, 164, 166, 171–172, 179, 193–195, 208, 212, 214–217, 221, 226, 244, 252, 250–263, 265, 266–267, 269–275, 330
Chicago National League club 28–29, 34, 39, 40, 50, 79, 117, 119, 140, 152, 161–162, 171–172, 183, 250, 257, 262, 263, 287–288, 292, 293, 295, 314, 318, 329, 330, 332, 333, 334
Chivington, Tom 13, 107
Chouinard, Felix 110, 233
Cincinnati National League club 29–30, 39, 68, 73–75, 99, 118, 123–124, 126–127, 157, 164, 166, 179, 183, 225, 244–245, 265, 291, 293, 295, 314, 318, 329, 330, 332, 333, 334
Clark, James 118
Clark, Tom 124
Clark, Win 296
Clarke, Fred 40, 166, 170
Clements, Clement 72, 142
Cleveland American League club 42–43, 164, 188, 223, 225, 257–258, 283, 289, 301, 333
Cleveland Federal League club 9–11, 15, 19–20, 25, 53, 167
Cobb, Ty 6, 13, 46, 56, 65, 73, 118, 138, 142, 159, 204, 276, 304, 323, 331
Cochrane, F.W. 222
Cole, Leonard "King" 36, 40
Collins, Eddie 3, 8, 38, 124, 280
Collins, Jimmy 55, 238
Collins, Ray 47
Colonial League 108, 216, 228–231
Columbian League 6
Comiskey, Charles 5, 12, 14, 26, 62–64, 101, 129, 130, 149, 170–171, 175, 219, 220, 258, 285–287, 303, 329
Comiskey Park, Chicago 84, 85
Compton, Albert "Pete" 246–248
Comstock, C.B. 52, 118, 280
Comstock, Ralph 248, 260, 265, 269, 293
Continental League 337
Cooper, Claude 56, 111, 112, 113, 230, 235
Copper League 320–321
Coppin, Charles 229
Corcoran, Tom 108, 227, 235, 236, 243
Corriden, Red 13
Coumbe, Frederick 143
Covington, Kentucky, Federal League club 7, 10, 11, 15, 17, 20
Cracker Jack Baseball Cards 179

Crandall, James Otis "Doc" 80–83, 138, 156, 184, 185, 207, 225, 243, 264, 267, 268, 306
Cravath, Gavvy 38
Crawford, Sam 62, 64, 65, 73, 118
Cree, Birdie 92, 104
Cross, Monte 105, 106, 107, 144, 215
Crusinberry, James 106, 311, 315
Cullop, Norman "Nick" 137, 157, 187, 188, 222, 223, 225, 226, 235, 242, 270–271, 292, 331
Cusack, Stephen 105, 107, 158
Cutshaw, George 148

Dahlen, Bill 15
Dalton, Jack 178–179, 209, 212, 334–335, 353n
Daubert, Jake 38, 46, 47, 56, 118, 165, 251
Davenport, David 124, 125, 127, 151, 158, 184, 213, 222, 226, 242, 264–266, 268–271, 306–307, 308–309
Davis, Harry 164, 223
Davis, Ralph 120, 165, 210
Davis, Robert 291, 292
Davis, Zachary Taylor 85
Deal, Charles 179, 180, 182, 207, 216, 242, 243, 247, 268, 306, 314
Delahanty, Frank 97, 131, 154
Delahanty, James 116, 124, 156, 230, 233
Detroit American League club 115, 119, 197, 260, 294, 332, 334
Dickson, Walter 114, 143, 245, 262, 269, 294
Doby, Larry 333
Doerr, Bobby 332
Dolan, Cozy 40
Dolan, Leon "Biddy" 20, 82, 135, 136
Donlin, Mike 62
Donovan, Bill 133, 333
Dooin, Charles, 36, 58, 59, 167, 241
Doolan, Michael 28, 35, 47, 58, 62, 64, 69, 102, 103, 106, 153, 175, 260, 261–263, 269, 270, 273, 274, 312, 333
Douglas, Phil 331
Downey, Thomas 96, 97, 113
Doyle, Larry 80, 313, 322, 326
Drake, Delos "Del" 83, 148, 207, 246, 266, 268
Dreyfuss, Barney 9, 91, 117, 140, 141, 165, 249, 277, 284–287, 293, 296, 302, 333
Dugdale, Daniel 123, 124
Duncan, Vernon "Duke" 100, 299
Dunn, Jack 39, 68, 69, 92, 103–104, 195, 231, 246, 287, 299, 314
Dyer, Judge David 243–244

Eason, Malcolm 202
Easterly, Theodore "Ted" 38, 73, 183, 223, 224, 225, 227, 242, 254

Index

Eastern League 58, 68, 95, 103, 138, 172, 197, 211, 238
Eastland Disaster 256–257
Ebbetts, Charles 15, 29, 30, 31–32, 67, 68, 179, 208, 251, 286, 287, 289, 301
Egan, Ben 62, 65, 92, 104, 143
Ehmke, Howard 181, 218, 219, 331, 332
Eichoff, D.J. 194
Ellis, Rube 181
Engle, Arthur "Clyde" 134, 211, 218, 265
Enos, Laurens 95
Erickson, Eric 282, 294
Esmond, James "Jimmy" 140, 145, 152, 155, 157, 198, 199, 252, 254, 263, 294
Evans, Bill 205, 226
Evans, Louis "Steve" 56, 62, 64–65, 83, 114, 115, 143, 152, 159, 233, 234, 236, 294, 299
Evers, Johnny 28–29, 50, 63, 233, 241, 281
Exposition Park, Pittsburgh 10, 118, 120, 121, 142, 270–271, 338–339

Falkenberg, Frederick "Cy" 41–43, 47, 82, 91, 94, 95, 97, 98, 134, 135, 137, 140, 144, 145, 146, 152–155, 157–159, 191, 195, 197, 238, 239, 252, 262, 265, 266, 296
Farrell, Frank 68, 94, 111, 129, 133, 167
Farrell, John "Jack" 15, 88, 112, 137, 144, 145, 153, 158, 216
Farrell, John H. 286, 294
Federal League of Base Ball Clubs: affect on minor leagues 38, 161, 245–248; annual meeting of, 9, 22, 23, 163, 278–279; attendance figures for 121, 160, 163–164, 237, 270, 272, 279, 346n; auction of players 291–295; Colonial League and 229; declares war on Organized Baseball 22–23; drives up salaries 6, 50, 63, 161, 276; financial losses of 163–164, 278–279; impact on the major leagues 3, 48, 160–162; legacy of 3, 336–340; major league status of 21–23, 338; as a minor league 10–20, 86; 1914 season of 66–159; 1915 season of 193–227, 232–244, 249–277; origins of 6, 7, 9–10; owner revolts 51, 53; peace overtones by 161–162, 176–177, 284; player limit for 113, 228; player's contract of 47; players reinstated 288; press on 4–5; promotions by 91–92, 236–237; and recruits from the major leagues 7, 30, 35–43, 63, 65, 72–74, 118, 120, 124–127, 164, 166, 168–170, 178–181, 257–258; reduced ticket prices by 113, 237, 258; reorganization of 23; reserve clause of 50; ridiculed in the press 16, 26, 27, 91–92, 174, 238; and settlement with Organized Baseball 285–289; sued by Kansas City club 186–189; suits against Organized Baseball 17, 173–177, 298–300; umpires of 105–109; World Series challenge by 159, 274–275; *see also* Blue laws; Cleveland Federal League club; New York Federal League club; reserve clause; ten day rule; Toronto Federal League club
Federal League Park, Buffalo 97, 131, 338
Federal League Park, Indianapolis 41, 135, 192
Federal League vs. the National League, the American League... 173–177
Ferguson, Charlie 23–24, 223
Finneran, Joseph "Happy" 113, 114, 116, 154, 230, 294
Finneran, William 107, 241, 243
Fischer, William "Bill" 164, 173, 216, 226, 259, 269, 312, 313
Fiske, Maximillan 86–87, 91, 100, 105–106, 137, 143, 148, 154, 157, 158, 171
Flack, Max 142, 144, 145, 212, 226, 252, 259, 274, 312, 314, 330
Fleishmann, Julius 29, 30
Fletcher, Art 319
Flood, Curt 75
Foell, Judge Charles 76, 125, 127, 289
Fogel, Horace 23
Ford, Russell 37, 93–98, 130, 132, 134, 138, 172, 211, 219, 221, 227
Foster, John B. 292
Foster, Rube 275
Fournier, Jake 60
Frank, Sydney 68
Franklin, Jim 95
Frazee, Harry 299, 300, 303, 316
Freedman, Andrew 68
Fritz, Harry 90, 144, 215, 216, 226, 261
Fuchs, Emil 326, 327, 333
Fuhrman, Mayor Louis P. 69, 97
Fultz, Dave 45–48, 165, 174, 251, 301, 302
Fyfe, Louis 107, 193, 203, 242

Gaffney, James 92, 179, 202, 280, 286, 287, 291, 292
Gallagher Resolution 17
Gandil, Chick 320
Ganzel, John 172, 211, 238, 239, 244, 245, 262, 282, 294
Gardella, Danny 337
Gardiner, Keene 124
Gardner, Ed 94
Garneau, James W. 305
Gates, Edward 9, 17, 36, 52, 76, 161, 174, 176, 188, 190
Gedeon, Joe 282, 292
Gehrig, Lou 128
George IV 62, 211
George, John 9, 25, 52, 189, 192
Gessler, Harry "Doc" 37, 117–121

Gill, Mayor Joseph 41
Gilmore, Ernest "Grover" 214, 224, 226, 294, 334
Gilmore, Genevieve 289
Gilmore, James A. 37, 40, 52, 60, 68, 76, 127, 154, 159, 168, 208, 234, 248, 257, 271, 292; accused by King Cole 23; Charles Weeghman and 28, 32, 33, 51, 84; and Cleveland Federal League franchise 167; Colonial League and 229; dealings with his owners 51, 53, 54, 77, 117–118, 120, 167, 172, 216, 271; death of 290; early life 21–22; elected president of Federal League 17, 21, 25–26, 163, 279; Fielder Jones and 148–149, 242–243; and game's protested 106, 108, 144; and George Stovall, 77, 108, 227; Indianapolis club and 172, 189–192; Kansas City club and 186–189; 164, 279; and Kauff defection 202–204; Killefer case and 49; life after baseball and death, 289; opening day games attended by 69, 75, 110, 193, 195; peace overtones and 161; and phantom New York franchise 279, 281–283; pitches banned by 98, 254; president of Chicago Federal League club 18, 22, 32; quoted 22, 72–73, 148, 163, 169, 186, 190, 202, 204, 247, 260, 280; quotes about 26, 33, 110; on realization Federal League is doomed; 276, 279; on recruitment of minor league players 247; recruits Organized Baseball players 38, 143, 149, 164, 166, 179, 251; Robert Ward and 54–55, 59; on rules and appeals 98, 108, 120, 254; settlement with Organized Baseball and 276, 284–288; and suit against Organized Baseball, 173, 174; suits named in 71, 187, 248, 299; suspensions and fines accessed 70, 101, 102, 114, 202, 227, 233; on ten cent baseball 237, 258; and Toronto franchise 53–54; umpires and 70, 105, 106, 107; world tourists and 63
Gilmore, Marie 290
Gilmore, Tom 346n
Glasgow, William 299
Gleason, Kid 42, 219
Goeckel, Eddie 106, 158
Goldman, Harry 23, 40, 52, 67–68, 169
Goldman, L. Edwin 52
Goodwin, Claire "Pep" 38, 73, 116, 222, 225, 235, 254, 271
Gordon and Koppel Field, Kansas City 17–18, 73, 157, 195, 222
Goss, Ralston 159, 190
Gowdy, Hank 324
Graham, Charles 320
Graham, Frank 128

Index

Gregg, Vean 143
Griffith, Clark 42, 123–124, 128, 133, 168, 170–171, 174, 181, 197, 282, 292, 303, 304, 308
Griggs, Art 116, 147, 205
Groehl, District Attorney Frederick 326
Groom, Robert "Bob" 80, 82, 100, 107, 184, 207, 225, 240, 264, 268, 306, 307
Guerra, Juan 184
Gwinner, Edward 117–118, 120, 195, 210, 230, 276, 288, 289, 293, 351n

Haff, D.J. 186
Halt, Al (Holt) 83, 156, 215, 237
Hamilton, Earl 49, 72–74, 77
Hanford, Charles 70, 95, 97, 134, 144, 195, 208, 226, 252, 254
Hanlon, Edward "Ned" 23, 35, 40, 46, 52, 63, 66–68, 71, 103, 149, 285, 300, 339
Harris, Ben 136, 224
Harrison Federal League Park, 196, 199, 237, 253, 338
Harter, Edward 281
Hartley, Grover 81, 83, 207, 239, 240, 264, 265, 267, 268, 306, 332
Haughton, Percy 282
Hauser, Arnold "Peewee" 254, 260–261
Havana, Cuba, (spring training site) 183–185
Havenor, Charles 84
Hearn, Bunn "Bunny" 209, 210, 334
Hedges, Robert 17, 24, 51, 65, 72–73, 166, 167, 286
Heishman, John 115
Helfrich, Ty 235
Hempstead, Harry 91, 202, 204, 292, 322
Henderson, Marshall 6, 9
Hendricks, Jack 21, 202, 203, 224, 247, 257
Hendrix, Claude 36, 39–40, 61, 73, 86, 122, 130, 137, 143, 145–146, 150, 153–154, 156–158, 171, 193, 195, 209, 215, 251, 258, 259, 267, 269, 272, 312, 314–315
Henning, Ernest "Pete" 18, 20, 237
Hepburn, Bernard 53
Herrmann, Gerry 29, 30, 36, 47, 51, 75, 79, 126–127, 161, 162, 174, 175, 188, 225, 244, 275, 276, 277, 284, 286, 288, 289, 291, 293, 295, 298, 300, 302, 303, 314, 329
Hertz, John 311, 316
Herzog, Buck 74, 124, 126–127, 179, 315, 330
Heydler, John 315, 318, 325
Hickman, Dave 260, 299
Hindman, James 189
Hofman, Arthur "Circus Solly" 39, 56, 65, 111, 114, 116, 120, 152–153, 220, 232, 233, 236, 265, 313

Hogg, Bill 55
Holke, Walter 282, 318
Holland, John 292–293
Holly, Edward 111
Holmes, Justice Oliver Wendell, Jr. 300, 352n
Hornsby, Rogers 309
Houck, Byron "Duke" 147, 229, 233
Howell, Harry 107, 240, 241, 242, 243
Huggins, Miller 118, 232
Huhn, Emil 199, 213, 226, 252, 294
Huston, Tillinghast 133, 167, 292, 300, 303

Indianapolis American Association club 18–19, 41, 135, 202, 247, 248, 296
Indianapolis Federal League club 11–12, 18–20, 41–44, 82, 97, 134, 135–140, 144–146, 152–159, 162, 189–198, 202, 296, 322
International League 40–41, 103, 161, 186, 197, 218, 221, 238, 245–247, 282, 294
Irvin, Arthur 138
Isaminger, James 133

Jacklitsch, Frederick 70, 245, 260, 294, 334
Jackson, Bill 216, 267, 293
Jackson, Joseph "Shoeless Joe" 257–258, 292
Jacobson, Merwin 231
James, Bill 180
Jennings, Hugh 68, 106, 115, 169, 295
Johnson, Adam "Rankin" 143–145, 152, 155–156, 171, 216, 299
Johnson, Ban 5, 13, 22, 24–26, 31, 47, 51, 67–68, 72, 95, 98, 129–130, 149, 162, 167, 170, 174, 175, 181, 183, 245, 248, 276–277, 283, 284–286, 292, 295, 302, 303, 304, 325
Johnson, Don 332
Johnson, Ernest 83, 182, 183, 191, 195, 240, 241, 242, 265, 267, 268, 301, 306, 332
Johnson, George "Chief" 74–78, 88, 116, 120, 127, 142, 150, 158, 173, 223, 268, 289, 334, 343n
Johnson, Hiram 303
Johnson, Jack 185
Johnson, Walter 38, 42, 94, 123, 133, 143, 168, 170–171, 172, 173, 181, 197, 307, 309
Johnson, Willis 17, 34, 83, 124, 183
Johnston, Jimmy 282, 301
Johnstone, James 105, 107, 108, 201, 233, 254, 274
Jones, David "Davy" 47, 111, 118–120, 143, 197, 294
Jones, Fielder 55, 63–64, 91, 101, 125, 148–151, 168, 172, 178, 180, 183–185, 195, 207, 216, 238, 240–243, 251, 264, 265, 267–269, 271, 305–309

Joss, Addie 225
Jost, Mayor Henry 18, 195
Justus, Walter 11

Kahler, George 43
Kaiser, Al 12, 20, 198
Kaiserling, George 18, 19, 20, 146, 153, 154, 159, 199, 213, 294
Kane, Steve 105, 106
Kansas City American Association club 39, 171, 246, 247, 248, 313, 314
Kansas City Federal League club 17–18, 43–44, 72–77, 86, 88, 89, 115, 151, 156–158, 162, 163, 164, 186–189, 191–192, 195, 203, 208, 222–227, 235–237, 240–242, 252, 254, 268–271, 278, 279, 291
Kauff, Benjamin "Benny" 41, 43, 82, 108, 135–140, 145, 152, 153, 155–159, 191, 198, 201–204, 219, 230, 233–236, 237, 239, 248, 262, 267, 292, 322–328, 330
Kauff, Hazel (Cassley) 324, 325–327
Kavanagh, Leo 14, 20
Keeley, Burt 10
Keil, Mayor Henry 82
Kelley, Joe 68, 106
Kelly, George 330
Kelly, James 207, 209, 211, 212, 226, 247, 259, 269, 270, 273, 293
Kelly, John L. 95
Kendall, Martha 205
Kenworthy, William "Duke" 73, 89, 115–116, 150, 224, 226, 227, 268, 334
Kerr, Robert J. 118
Kerr, William W. 117–118
Keupper, Hencry 16, 107, 135
Killefer, Bill 36, 48–50, 60, 63, 330
Kinney, Michael 13
Kirby, Larue 147–148
Kirkpatrick, Enos 36, 40, 102, 153, 156, 299
Kleinow, John 11
Kling, Johnny 223
Knabe, Otto 29, 35–36, 38, 40, 42, 66, 69, 71, 91–92, 101–103, 106, 108, 114, 117, 144, 153, 175, 299, 313, 314
Knetzer, Elmer "Baron" 15–16, 20, 98, 119–121, 136, 143, 153–155, 208, 259, 270, 273, 274, 293, 294
Kommers, Fred "Bugs" 82, 101–102
Konetchy, Aubrey 166
Konetchy, Edward 30, 118, 164–166, 173, 195, 207, 208, 209, 212–213, 232, 259, 269, 270, 274, 293, 294, 331, 346n
Koob, Ernie 308
Kores, Arthur "Dutch" 247
Kraft, Clarence 282
Kramer, Harry 122, 236
Krapp, Eugene 97, 219, 221, 243, 257

Index

Krause, J. Ed 9, 20, 23, 52, 189, 190
Krueger, Arthur 37, 38, 73, 157, 183

Lafitte, Edward 113, 115, 153–154, 208, 234, 235, 236, 264, 293
Lajoie, Napoleon "Nap" 13, 38, 48, 128, 215, 223
Lalouge, Mickey 294
Land, F.C. 164, 223
Land, Grover 111, 112, 152
Landis, Judge Kenesaw Mountain 173–177, 243, 286, 288, 296, 298, 299, 301, 303–304, 310, 315, 326, 327, 331, 337
Lane, F.L. 92
Lange, Erwin "Irv" 86, 130, 137, 145, 158, 171
Lange, Jack 338
Lannin, Joseph 63, 211, 218, 245, 248, 285, 299, 300
LaPorte, Frank 97, 136, 137, 140, 152, 156, 158, 196, 198, 252, 254, 263, 282
Lardner, Ring 40, 56, 85, 87
Lasker, Albert 303, 304
Lavin, Doc 307
Leach, Tommy 13, 117
Leever, Sam 10, 15
Leib, Fred 29, 129, 133
Lennox, James "Eggie" 111, 121, 153, 154, 212, 224, 259, 293
Leverenz, Walter 62, 65
Lewis, John "Jack" 15, 19, 209, 212, 258, 259, 273
Link, Fred 13
Lloyd, N. Ashley 278
Lobert, Hans 167, 295
Lodge, Senator Henry Cabot 231
Lord, Harry 219, 220, 221
Louden, William "Baldy" 96, 97, 132, 209, 263, 313
Lucas, Henry 45
Luke, Fred 228
Lundsford, Carl 77
Luque, Dolph 125, 294
Lynch, Thomas 58, 107

Mack, Connie 26, 38, 46, 103, 105, 124, 164, 169, 215, 227, 230, 266, 296, 308
Mackall, J.L. 326
Madison, Charles C. 17, 23, 72, 73, 74–75, 77, 187, 188, 243, 246
Magee, Lee (Leo Hoernschmeyer) 62, 65, 107, 167, 173, 174–175, 191, 193, 215, 216, 230, 232–236, 238, 244, 262, 265, 267, 291, 292, 319, 325
Magee, Sherry 167, 241
Maggart, Karl 319
Maharg, Billy 325
Mahon, John 68
Main, Miles "Alex" 191, 195, 223, 225, 226–227, 240, 294
Major, Governor Elliott 82
Manassau, Al 100, 101, 105, 107
Mann, Conrad 187, 192, 195, 279
Mann, Leslie 179–180, 195, 208, 212, 215, 254, 259, 260, 267, 270, 273, 274, 312, 314, 330–331
Maranville, Rabbit 29
Marquard, Rube 169–170, 173, 179
Marsans, Armando 74, 75, 83, 124, 125–127, 132, 173, 176, 183, 184, 243–244, 265, 271, 289, 306
Martin, John 320
Mathes, Joseph 83
Mathewson, Christy 38, 46, 75, 178, 218, 318, 319, 322, 323, 324, 330
Mattis, Ralph, 229
Maxwell, James "Bert" 107, 113–114, 172, 188, 191, 223, 229, 230, 231
Mayer, Erskine 247
Mayer, Sammy 247, 248, 293
Mays, Carl 303
McAleer, Jimmy 184
McCandless, Jack 299
McCarthy, Joe 282, 294
McCarthy, William H. 319, 320
McCloskey, John 123–124
McConnell, George "Slats" 171–172, 208, 215, 216, 221, 254, 259, 263, 269, 272, 273, 312
McCormick, William "Barry" 105, 107, 109, 154, 157–158, 208, 214, 243, 257, 264
McCulloch, Charles A. 311, 316
McCullough, William T. 9, 18, 23, 117–118, 209, 248, 336
McDonald, Charles "Tex" 120, 140, 264, 265, 293, 293
McGill, James C. 41, 202, 248, 296
McGraw, John (Roy Elmer Hoar) 114
McGraw, John J. 13, 33, 50, 56, 58, 62, 67–69, 80, 106–107, 115, 165, 166, 170, 180, 204, 243, 291, 292, 295, 300, 308, 318, 319, 322, 324, 325, 326, 327, 329, 330, 331
McGuigan, Paddy 219
McGuire, Thomas 11, 14, 86, 100, 143, 148, 171
McInnis, Stuffy 280
McKechnie, William "Bill" 43, 97, 111, 134, 137, 140, 155, 198, 199, 249–250, 252, 254, 255, 295, 330, 332–333, 335, 339
McKeever, Edward 179
McNally, Dave 176, 337
McNulty, Jack 13
McQuillan, George 120
McRoy, Robert B. 132
Mendez, Jose 184, 185
Menke, Frank 26, 187, 279
Menosky, Mike 12, 15, 121–122, 154, 210, 229, 230, 259, 294, 332
Merkle, Fred 174, 315
Messersmith, Andy 176, 337
Meyer, Bernard "Benny" 70, 156, 227
Meyers, Chief 77
Meyers, Judge Quincy 176
Milan, Clyde 219
Miller, George 174
Miller, Henry 15, 19
Miller, Jack 47, 121
Miller, Marvin 176
Miller, Ward 80, 82, 90, 156, 185, 240, 264, 265, 267, 268, 306
Milliken, Stanley 245
Minor, Benjamin 169, 285
Misse, John 156
Mitchell, Fred 314, 315
Moore, Earl 69, 96, 142, 130, 169, 204, 294
Moran, Harry 199, 214, 252
Moran, Pat 184
Moseley, Earl 145, 153, 155, 159, 213, 214, 226, 252, 254, 263, 291
Mowrey, Harry "Mike" 30, 40, 165, 208, 212, 213, 226, 247, 259, 269, 270, 273
Mullen, Walter 52, 95, 130
Mullin, George 7, 41–42, 108, 137, 169, 196, 250, 294
Mullin, John 108
Murphy, Charles 28–30, 50, 79, 92, 117, 140, 289, 312
Murphy, Danny 7, 39, 56, 111, 203, 230, 233, 235, 236, 294
Murphy, William 9
Murray, F.L. 189, 190
Murray, Red 202
Myers, Ralph "Hap" 29, 56, 83, 111, 216, 233, 245, 262, 265

Nash, Ken 294
National Agreement 3, 5, 14, 15, 16, 36, 46, 132 173, 175, 197, 288, 300, 303
National Baseball Hall of Fame 28, 29, 185, 199, 330, 333, 338, 339
National Brotherhood of Professional Players 45–46
National Commission 5, 14–15, 38, 133, 202, 243, 276–277, 300, 301, 302–303, 312
National League 5, 46, 95, 162, 174, 175, 284, 303, 304
Navin, Frank 51
Neily, Harry 32, 44, 77, 190, 316
New York American League club 68, 94–95, 100, 125, 128–129, 132–133, 138, 161, 172, 244, 292, 300, 303, 306, 331, 332
New York Federal League club 164, 279, 280, 282
New York National League club 58, 62, 68, 69, 80, 107, 115, 169, 170, 181, 202–204, 210, 225, 247, 257, 278, 291, 292, 295, 318–319, 322–325, 329, 330, 336, 337
Newark Federal League club 187–189, 191, 196–200, 213, 214, 219, 226, 233, 237, 239, 249–255, 263, 266, 267, 291, 296, 301, 332
Noyes, Wynn 309

Oakes, Ennis "Rebel" 111, 117–118, 120–122, 143, 155, 166, 181, 207,

208, 210–213, 232, 247, 259, 269, 273, 274, 293, 296
O'Brien, Joseph 192, 243, 271
O'Connor, John "Jack" 13–14, 18
O'Connor, Patrick 166, 173, 221, 247, 259
O'Farrell, Val 325
Okkonen, Marc 336
Olmsted, Fred 12
O'Rourke, Tim 123
O'Toole, Marty 165
Owens, Frank "Yip" 108, 299

Pacific Coast League 37–38, 166, 173, 181, 183, 221, 225, 247, 259, 282, 296, 306, 319, 320, 334
Packard, Eugene 36, 73, 136, 157–158, 222, 223, 225, 226, 237, 242, 254, 269, 293, 294, 312
Paskert, Dode 315
Pechous, Charles 256, 257, 262, 263, 269, 270, 274
Pepper, Senator George 49, 174, 175, 176, 300, 301
Perring, George 115, 158, 225, 268, 271
Perritt, W.D. "Pol" 121, 164, 166, 173, 180–181
Perry, Scott 302
Pershing, John J. 303
Pesky, Johnny 332
Peters, Clarence 205–206
Peters, Oscar "Rube" 114, 229
Phelon, William 75, 126, 286, 288, 312, 329
Philadelphia American League club 39, 112, 124, 169, 180, 215, 242, 296, 302, 303
Philadelphia National League club 36, 38, 48–49, 58, 59, 60, 62, 64, 119–120, 140–141, 164, 167, 184, 241, 261, 315, 333, 334
Phillippe, Charles "Deacon" 9–11, 15–16, 117, 120
Phillips, William "Bill" 14–15, 19–20, 41, 44, 135–137, 145, 152, 154, 157–158, 172, 191, 196, 197, 198, 249, 250, 251
Pick, Charles 282, 294
Pittsburgh Federal League club 12, 15–16, 111–112, 114, 116, 117–122, 136, 140, 142–143, 147–148, 153–155, 163, 166, 180, 195, 205, 207–213, 215, 221, 230, 247, 248, 254, 258–260, 262, 269–274, 289, 293, 334
Pittsburgh National League club 40, 164, 165, 212, 249–250, 293, 296, 302, 314, 332, 333
Plank, Edward "Eddie" 7, 164, 169, 171, 173, 180, 182, 184, 185, 193, 195, 222, 225, 238, 264, 266–268, 270, 306, 307, 338, 339
Players League 5, 10, 46, 338
Povich, Shirley 170
Powers, John T. 6–7, 9, 13, 17, 18, 22, 26
Powers, P.T. "Pat" 95, 186, 187, 188,
189, 190, 191, 196, 197, 199–200, 277, 291, 292, 294, 295
Pratt, Del 307
Pratt, Lester 235
Prendergast, Michael 121, 143, 156–157, 171, 259, 270, 272, 273, 294, 312
Professional Protective Association 46

Quigley, Ernest 202
Quinn, Billy 219
Quinn, Bob 304, 308
Quinn (Picus) John "Jack" 69–71, 96, 99–100, 140, 143, 156, 196, 299, 303, 331–332
Quirt, Joe 111

Racey, Edward 9, 18
Ragan, Pat 323–324
Rariden, William "Bill" 39, 134, 136, 140, 153, 157, 198, 199, 252, 253, 255, 292, 318, 323, 330, 332
Rasin, Carroll 285, 286, 287
Rassmussen, Harry "Heinie" 257, 262, 263
Rath, Morrie 282
Rawlings, Johnny 115, 225, 226, 227, 240, 268, 271, 294, 332
Reach, A.J. 36
Reed, Ted 255
Reese, John "Bonesetter" 61, 93, 98, 152, 216, 255, 258, 260, 273
Reichler, Joe 338
Reiden, William 10
reserve clause 15, 22, 26, 45, 49, 50, 175–176, 244, 337
Reulbach, Edward 47, 191, 250–252, 254, 255, 267
Reymer 12
Reynolds, George 311
Rheam, Flint "Cy" 143, 270, 273
Rice, Thomas 176, 179, 208
Richlow, Oscar 315
Richter, Francis 4, 302
Rickart, Lloyd 10, 17, 18, 25, 52, 163, 181, 265
Rickey, Branch 166, 167, 305, 306, 307, 331, 337
Rigler, Cy 241, 324
Ring, Jimmy 318
Risberg, Swede 332
Ritter, Lawrence 330
Roach, Wilbur "Roxey" 218, 221, 247, 263
Robbins, George 162, 176, 182, 284
Roberts, Clarence "Skipper" 76, 119, 120, 142
Robertson, Dave 329
Robertson, William E. 95, 130, 167, 189, 221, 278
Robinson, M. Stanley 285
Robinson, Wilbert 30, 40, 67–68, 300
Rogers, Jon T. 36
Rogge, Frances "Clint" 209, 213, 259, 269, 272–273, 294
Rooney, Frank 136

Ross, James A. 9, 159
Roth, Mark 129
Rothstein, Arnold 325
Roush, Edward "Edd" 3, 70, 129, 140, 152–153, 155, 198–199, 250, 252, 254, 263, 329–330, 331, 332, 335, 338, 339
Roush, Essie (Mrs. Edward Roush) 253
Roush, Will 198
Rumler, Bill 319, 320
Runyon, Damon 80, 201
Ruppert, Col Jacob 133, 167, 276, 285, 300, 303, 316
Russell, Allan 307
Ruth, George Herman "Babe" 92, 103–104, 128, 299, 300
Ryan, Jimmy 256

St. Louis American League club 23–24, 51, 65, 72–74, 166, 184, 244, 286, 287, 294, 295, 302, 305–310, 312, 329, 332
St. Louis Federal League club 12–14, 78–83, 111–112, 114, 116, 117–122, 136, 140, 142–143, 147–148, 153–155, 163, 166, 180, 195, 205, 207–213, 215, 221, 230, 247, 248, 254, 258–260, 262, 269–274, 289, 293, 334
St. Louis National League club 32, 62–64, 67, 118, 155, 165, 166, 167, 179–181, 212, 232, 285–287, 306, 330, 333, 337
Sallee, Harry "Slim" 121
Sanborn, Irv 84–85
Sanborn, Judge W.H. 132
Savage, James "Jimmy" 114, 121, 215, 229
Schaefer, Herman "Germany" 62, 191, 197, 199, 255, 292, 329
Schanberger, C.L. 103, 195, 245
Scheer, Allan "Jap" 82, 153, 198, 233, 252, 254, 263
Schlafly, Harry L. "Larry" 25, 42, 63, 95–97, 134, 171, 178, 179, 220–221
Schleunes, George 52
Schneider, Pete 123–124, 312
Schorling, J.M. 85
Schreckel, Johnny 74–75
Schulte, Wildfire 313
Schulz, Albert "Heinie" 124–125, 134, 199, 221, 264, 291, 294
Seaton, Rene (Fournier) 59, 61
Seaton, Thomas 58–61, 80, 100, 106, 111–113, 120, 138, 143, 147, 152, 154, 215, 224, 234, 236, 238, 239, 263, 292, 312, 313, 320, 321
Sessions, Judge Clarence W. 49
Seymour, Harold 6–7, 160, 285, 302
Shannon, William "Spike" 107, 235
Shaw, Albert 188, 222, 223, 225, 254
Shea, Bill 337
Sheckard, Jimmy 36, 117
Sheridan, J.B. 161

Index

Sherlock, Charles 9, 18, 346n
Shettsline, William 48–49, 59–60
Shocker, Uban "Red" 308
Shore, Ernie 92, 104
Simmons, George "Hack" 41, 70, 106, 144, 156, 172, 245, 294
Simon, Michael 50
Sinclair, Harry 186, 187, 189, 190, 191, 196, 237, 249, 277, 278–280, 283, 284, 286, 288, 291–293, 295, 296–297, 301, 305, 311, 316, 322, 329
Sisler, George 128, 302, 306, 307, 309
Smith, Frank "Piano Mover" 40, 101–103, 169, 196, 234, 236
Smith, Frederick 96, 134, 262
Smith, James F. "Jimmy" 214, 215, 216, 244, 252, 259, 260, 261, 332
Smith, Luther "Casey" 320
Smith, Red 148, 180
Smith, Robert 229
Snodgrass, Fred 323
Society for American Baseball Research (SABR) 338, 339
Somers, Charles 25–26, 42–43, 53, 129, 188, 227, 258, 283, 289
Sommers, Rudy 113, 116, 147, 152, 229
Speaker, Tris 56, 62–65, 138, 276, 301, 304
Spencer, Vern 325
Spink, Alfred 57, 308
Spink, Charles 4
Spink, J.G. Taylor 5, 177, 181, 185, 280, 315
Sporting Life 4, 302
Sporting News 4–5, 40, 65, 77, 91–92, 162–163, 174, 302, 338
Stafford, Justice Wendell 299, 300
Stahl, Jake 55, 62–63, 238
Stallings, George 25, 118, 129, 172, 180, 294
Stanley, Jimmy 143, 145
Steininger, Lloyd H. 10, 18, 23, 52, 79, 81, 147, 149, 181, 182
Steininger Field (Handlan's Park), St. Louis 79–80, 82, 338
Stengel, Casey 314
Stewart, R.C. 10
Stifel, Otto 6, 9, 10, 18, 28, 51–53, 63, 79, 90, 148, 149, 182, 305, 309–310
Stockton, J. Roy 183–185
Stone, Dwight 88
Stoneman, Charles 326
Stovall, Charles 326
Stovall, George 23–25, 26, 37, 38, 44, 63, 72, 73, 74, 76, 77, 108, 115, 155, 157, 183, 188, 191–192, 195, 222–227, 235–236, 242, 243, 246, 268, 271, 282, 294, 295, 296, 301, 308
Strands, Johnny 255
Strauss, Arthur 110
Suggs, George 39, 99, 108, 140, 143, 299
Swacina, Harry 41, 69, 100, 103, 156, 260, 294

Swartling, Hugo 181
Swartz, Stuard 298
Sweeney, Ed 37, 93, 94, 95, 129

Taft, Charles 50, 162, 287, 288, 311, 312
Taft, President William Howard 50, 52, 303
Taylor, Charles 300
Taylor, John I. 48, 63, 161
Teapot Dome Scandal 297
Tebeau, George 17, 26
Tebeau, Pat 46, 246, 247
Ten Day Clause 75, 127, 129–130, 132, 133, 302
Tener, John 15, 35, 38, 50, 104, 174, 202, 203, 276, 277, 279, 284–286, 288, 303
Terrapin Park, Baltimore 66, 69, 70, 196, 338
Terry, Bill 128
Thomas, Charles H. 171–172, 312
Thompson, Mayor Bill 150, 195, 275
Thompson, H.A. "Frock" 315
Thorpe, Jim 62
Tillman, John 230, 231
Timmerman, Whitey 16
Tinker, Joe 7, 17, 28–32, 35, 36, 38, 40, 49, 50, 59, 60, 73, 74, 78, 79, 85–91, 103, 105–106, 117, 123, 124, 126, 130, 142–146, 153, 154, 156, 158, 170, 172, 175, 179, 180, 193, 195, 208, 214–216, 221, 223, 226, 254, 256, 257–259, 260–262, 287, 292–293, 307, 312–314, 330, 339
Tobin, John "Jack" 14, 20, 83, 147, 156, 158, 184, 195, 207, 265, 268, 306, 309, 310, 330
Toney, Fred 324, 325, 326
Toole, John C. 189
Toronto Federal League club 53–54
Trautman, Fred 230
Twombly, George 92, 104

Union Association 5, 17, 45, 338
United States League 6–7, 9, 10, 12

Van Sycle, C.F. 144
Vaughn, Hippo 294, 309
Vaughn, Robert "Bobby" 242, 266, 268, 271
Veeck, William Sr. 315, 316
Victor Sporting Goods 89
Villa, Joe 5, 91–92, 128, 133, 204, 236, 238, 278, 291, 302
Viox, Jimmy 120, 165
Von Der Horst, Harry 66, 67, 68

Wagner, Honus 28, 38, 118, 126, 128, 249, 261, 292
Walker, William M. 32, 33, 37, 84, 85, 144, 278, 311, 312, 316
Wallace, Bobby 223
Walsh, Austin 142
Walsh, Ed 20, 61, 87
Walsh, John "Jimmy" 34, 103, 56, 260, 266

Walsh, Michael "Runt" 36, 40, 102, 103, 106, 271
Ward, Beryl 206
Ward, George S. 52, 54, 63, 110, 167, 205, 206, 238, 281, 286, 288, 348n, 351n
Ward, John Montgomery 45, 46, 55, 56, 63, 178, 228, 245, 282, 322, 339
Ward, Robert B. 26, 52, 54–57, 92, 110, 112–113, 124, 230, 154, 161, 169–170, 174, 189, 190, 202–205, 232, 233, 237, 238, 277–278, 280, 287
Ward, Walter 52, 60, 61, 113, 124, 164, 205–206, 230
Ward, William S. 229
Washington American League club 122, 168, 170–172, 181, 224, 248, 282, 292, 308
Washington Park, Brooklyn 89, 110–115, 236–237, 338
Wasservogel, Justice Isadore 327
Watkins, William H. 41, 156, 175, 192, 198
Watson, Charles "Doc" 83, 86, 143, 150, 156, 267
Weart, William 36
Weaver, Buck 62, 183, 320
Weeghman, August 282
Weeghman, Bessie (Webb) 32, 316
Weeghman, Charles 26, 28, 30, 32–34, 37, 39, 40, 49–53, 60, 75, 84–92, 137, 144, 161–163, 167, 168, 170–172, 180, 181, 189, 193–194, 199, 204, 221, 225, 246, 256–258, 263, 272, 275, 277, 278, 282, 285–289, 292, 293, 296, 301, 305, 311–313, 316
Weeghman Park, Chicago 75, 84–85, 87–91, 142, 194–195, 272, 274, 317, 340
Weeghman vs. Killefer 49
Weiss, Joseph 259, 263, 269
Weller, Sam 38, 51, 60, 61, 73, 87, 89, 90, 150, 267
Western Telegraph 36
Westervelt, Fred 107, 109, 264
Westerzil, George "Tex" 40, 111, 114, 115, 120, 216–217, 233, 234, 242, 259, 265, 292–293
Wheat, Zack 30, 330
Whitaker, Judge Edward 327
Whitehouse, Gilbert 231
Whiteman, George 281, 294
Wichita Falls, Texas, (spring training site) 43–44
Wickland, Albert 86, 90, 112, 146, 155, 199, 212, 213, 259, 269, 273, 293, 294
Wilhelm, Irvin "Kaiser" 108, 230, 245, 333
Wilkinson, Bill 116
Willard, Jess 185
Willett, Robert E. "Ed" 80, 184, 185
Williams, Charles Green 33–34, 152, 312
Williams, Claude "Lefty" 321

Williams, Gus 63, 72
Williams, Harry 181
Williams, Ted 332
Wilson, Arthur "Dutch" 38, 50, 73, 88, 89, 137, 142, 143, 144, 156, 157, 195, 208, 216, 258, 274, 313, 332
Wilson, Finis 154, 183, 293
Wilson, Luke 43, 44
Wilson, President Woodrow 91, 172, 231, 336
Wiltse, George "Hooks" 235
Wingo, Ivy 62, 65, 121, 164, 166, 173, 179, 180, 218
Winters, Jesse 325
Wise, Arthur 282

Wittman, William 6, 12
Wood, Smoky Joe 38
Woodman, Courtney 229
Wright, Dick 235
Wright, Russell 70-71
Wrigley, Philip K. 316
Wrigley, William 311, 316
Wrigley Field, Chicago 317, 340

Yerkes, Stephen 116, 154, 155, 209, 211-212, 213, 247, 259, 292, 293, 312, 313
Young, Cy 10, 11, 15, 19, 53
Young, Delmer "Del" 229, 230
Young, Harry 138
Youngs, Ross 324

Zeider, Rollie 39, 106, 129, 142, 143, 144, 145, 156, 158, 195, 215, 216, 226, 263, 267, 274, 312, 314
Zev 297
Zimmerman, C.X. 23
Zimmerman, Heinie 241, 312, 313, 318, 319, 324, 325, 326
Zinn, Guy 40, 100, 102, 106, 172, 260
Zwilling, Edward "Dutch" 40, 88, 90, 137, 142-144, 146, 154, 155, 208, 212, 224, 226, 263, 269, 273, 274, 292, 312, 313-314